W9-ANN-080

ANCIENT ROME

ANCIENT ROME

THE DEFINITIVE VISUAL HISTORY

DK London

Senior Editors Stephanie Farrow, Christine Stroyan
Senior Art Editor Gadi Farfour
Senior US Editor Megan Douglass
Project Art Editor Katie Cavanagh
Editors Daniel Byrne, Ian Fitzgerald, Andrea Page, Alison Sturgeon
Designer Daksheeta Pattni
CGI Coordinator Phil Gamble
New CGI Artworks Peter Bull Art Studio
Senior Managing Art Editor Lee Griffiths
Managing Editor Gareth Jones
Production Editor Andy Hilliard
Senior Production Controller Rachel Ng
Picture Researcher Sarah Smithies
Jacket Design Development Manager Sophia M.T.T.
Publishing Director Jonathan Metcalf
Associate Publishing Director Liz Wheeler
Art Director Karen Self

DK Delhi

Senior Art Editors Ira Sharma, Kanika Kalra
Project Art Editor Shipra Jain
Art Editor Aanchal Singal
Senior Editor Janashree Singha
Project Editor Hina Jain
Managing Editor Soma B. Chowdhury
Senior Managing Art Editor Arunesh Talapatra
Senior Cartographer Mohammad Hassan
Cartography Manager Suresh Kumar
Senior Jacket Designer Suhita Dharamjit
Senior Jackets Coordinator Priyanka Sharma Saddi
Senior DTP Designer Jagtar Singh
DTP Designers Rakesh Kumar, Bimlesh Tiwary
Pre-production Manager Balwant Singh
Production Manager Pankaj Sharma
Editorial Head Glenda Fernandes
Design Head Malavika Talukder

First American Edition, 2023
Published in the United States by DK Publishing
1745 Broadway, 20th Floor, New York, NY 10019

23 24 25 26 27 10 9 8 7 6 5 4 3 2 1

001-331853-Apr/2023

Published in Great Britain by Dorling Kindersley Limited

A catalog record for this book is available from the Library of Congress.
ISBN 978-0-7440-6982-2

Printed in the UAE

For the curious
www.dk.com

contents

1 The Roman Kingdom
753–509 BCE

2 The Roman Republic
509–133 BCE

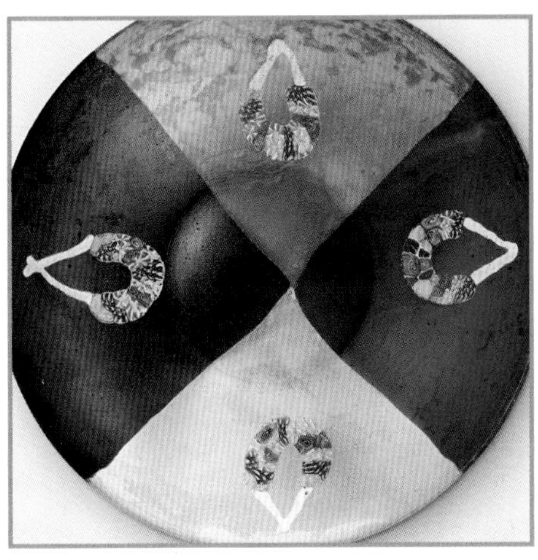

3 The Republic in Crisis
133–27 BCE

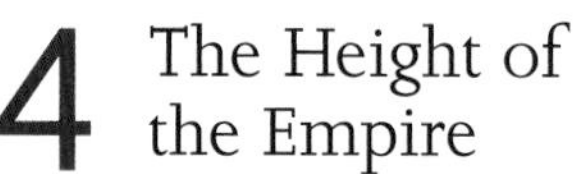

4 The Height of the Empire

27 BCE–192 CE

5 An Empire in Transition

192–395 CE

6 The Fall of the Western Roman Empire

395–476 CE

contributors

CONSULTANTS

Dr. Andrew James Sillett
Dr. Sillett is a Departmental Lecturer in Latin Literature and Roman History at the University of Oxford, where he teaches at Brasenose and St. Hilda's College. He wrote his doctorate on the reception of Marcus Tullius Cicero in the early Roman Empire. His research primarily focuses on the life and works of Cicero, taking in the literature, history, politics, and philosophy of the Late Roman Republic.

Professor Matthew Nicholls
Matthew Nicholls is Senior Tutor at St. John's College, Oxford, and Visiting Professor of Classics at the University of Reading. Professor Nicholls has published widely on books, intellectual culture, and public libraries in the Roman world. He has also developed a 3D digital model of ancient Rome, used for this book and for a popular online course at Reading University, and for which he has won several teaching awards.

WRITERS AND SPECIALIST CONSULTANTS

Laura Aitken-Burt
After studying Classical Archaeology and Ancient History at the University of Oxford, Laura Aitken-Burt teaches Classics, History, and Politics in London. An archaeologist and author of history textbooks, she also acts as a historical consultant for broadcast and print media. Outside the classroom, she seeks to bring overlooked narratives to the wider public sphere through her research, writing, interviews, and documentaries.

Dr. Alex Antoniou
After completing an MPhil in Ancient History at the University of Adelaide, Australia, and a DPhil in Ancient History at University College, Oxford, Dr. Antoniou became an Associate Researcher at the Faculty of Classics in Oxford. His research focuses on Roman priesthoods, the evidence of emperor worship in the Italian peninsula, and the role of prodigies (or strange natural events) in religion in Rome and the empire.

Dr. Jeremy Armstrong
Associate Professor in Classics and Ancient History at the University of Auckland, Dr. Armstrong specializes in archaic Italy and early Rome. His research interests include the wider history and archaeology of the Republic, ancient warfare, state formation, economy, and historiography. His research also explores aspects of early Roman society, including industry, the economy, and state cults.

Dr. Kevin Feeney
Faculty Fellow in Roman History at New York University, Dr. Feeney earned his BA and MA from Trinity College, Oxford, before completing a PhD at Yale University and then becoming Visiting Assistant Professor of Classical Studies at Fairfield University, Connecticut. His research focuses on the political, legal, and administrative history of the Later Roman Empire, as well as the religious and social history of Late Antiquity.

Dr. Liz Gloyn
Dr. Gloyn is Reader in Latin Language and Literature at Royal Holloway, University of London. Her research focuses on the intersections between Latin literature, philosophy, and gender studies, focusing on innovative approaches to familiar texts, particularly from a feminist perspective. She also specializes in representations of the ancient world in modern media.

Dr. Kieren Johns
Dr. Johns completed a PhD at the Department of Classics and Ancient History at the University of Warwick, and works for the British Academy. His thesis examined the epigraphic representation of the Severan emperors. His other interests include the study of collective memory in antiquity, the political use of art and architecture in ancient cities, and the representation of ancient leaders in modern culture.

Olivia Thompson
Olivia Thompson read Classics at Corpus Christi College, Oxford, before completing a MSt in Greek and Roman History at Balliol College, Oxford, where she is pursuing a DPhil in Ancient History on the rhetoric of household management in Roman political debate. Her research interests encompass the political, social, and cultural history of the Republican and Early Imperial periods, as well as the history of scholarship.

▷ **Fig tree fresco**
This fresco, from the House of the Orchard in Pompeii, dates from the 1st century CE. It shows a snake winding around a thriving fig tree and possibly symbolizes prosperity and regeneration.

△ Found in 1937 in the ruins of a villa at Daphne-Harbiye, near Antioch (in modern Türkiye), this mosaic floor had at its center the bust of a woman traditionally identified as Spring, wearing a wreath of flowers around her head and a floral garland over her left shoulder.

Introductions

Dr. Andrew James Sillett

At the height of the Roman Empire, an intrepid voyager could walk on exclusively Roman territory while traveling from England to Iraq, from the Black Sea to the Straits of Gibraltar, from Vienna by the Danube to Aswan by the Nile.

To travel across the Roman Empire was to move through a network; a system of relationships in which every citizen—from a formerly enslaved laborer to the emperor himself—was bound together in a complex system of favor, obligation, and reciprocity. The formation of these relationships, the resulting transformation of the people and landscape of the Roman world, and the voices and experiences of those who inhabited that world are the subjects of this book.

We are used to hearing tales of Roman conquest and cultural "Romanization," but the story we have to tell is one of negotiation and adaptation. What it meant to look, dress, act, and build like a Roman changed constantly from period to period, and from region to region. The gleaming marble of the emperor Augustus's Forum would have seemed unthinkably alien to the founders of the Republic; while the clay figurines of Jupiter, Juno, and Minerva in the temples frequented by the citizens of early Rome would have looked primitive and heretical to the empress Theodora, accustomed as she was to the city of Constantinople and its Christian icons. And none has any greater claim to being Roman than another.

"Roman" culture was a series of hybrids, forged through armed conflict and negotiated resolution. Rather than conceptualizing Rome as a destroyer and crusher of local cultures, this book aims to show how the Romans' unique identity developed through their interactions with other peoples, and was shaped by the religious and social traditions of those they encountered. We hope that the Rome you find in this book reflects that vibrant cultural force of talents and ingenuity.

Professor Matthew Nicholls

Ancient Rome had an intensely visual culture. Magnificent public buildings characterized its cities and towns; private dwellings—whether townhouses, apartments, or country villas—were furnished with frescoes and mosaics in recognizably Roman styles. In the Imperial era, coins and statues carried the portrait of the emperor into every corner of the vast empire.

The Romans took a naturalistic style of portrait art and the principles of Classical architecture from the Greeks. They also shared the Greek view of art as an expression of human potential and its relationship to the divine. As the empire grew in size and prosperity, the Romans absorbed many other influences and developed engineering and architectural techniques of their own, using economical concrete construction to build aqueducts, bathhouses, harbors, and other buildings of unprecedented scale and sophistication. Rome itself grew to a city of approximately one million people, with infrastructure to house, feed, and entertain them, bring in fresh water, and take away waste.

In my research and teaching work, I create and use 3D digital reconstructions, based on research into written and visual sources that include ancient literature and maps, archaeology, inscriptions, and the imagery on coins. For this book, I have worked with professional artists and designers to bring some of these reconstructions to life, presenting a new and vivid way to see how the Romans lived, worked, and built, and how their capital city—and some of its most impressive buildings—may have appeared to them. I hope that the CGI artwork in this book, along with the rich selection of other images, offers you new insights into the architecture, engineering, artistic achievements, and day-to-day life of the ancient Roman world and its inhabitants.

Chronology of Rulers

Kings, consuls, and emperors led Rome throughout its history. They were usually drawn from the same pool of powerful clans, but by the 2nd century CE military might was often more important than family connections for would-be emperors.

The Kings of Rome

753–509 BCE

By tradition, Rome was ruled by seven kings during its early years. The city grew under their regimes, but ultimately rejected monarchical control.

Romulus (753–715 BCE)
The city was named after Rome's legendary founder.

Numa Pompilius
(715–672 BCE)

Tullus Hostilius
(672–640 BCE)

Ancus Marcius
(640–616 BCE)

Lucius Tarquinius Priscus
(616–578 BCE)
Lucius was the first of Rome's three Etruscan kings.

Servius Tullius (578–534 BCE)
Builder of Rome's Servian Walls, he also introduced the city's first coinage.

Lucius Tarquinius Superbus
(534–509 BCE)
The unpopular "Tarquin the Proud" lost power in a coup and was Rome's last king.

The Roman Republic

509–27 BCE

With the monarchy abolished, two consuls were elected each year to oversee the city. There were more than 1,000 consuls in the Republican era. These are some of the most notable.

Lucius Junius Brutus
(509 BCE)
One of the founders of the Republic, Brutus died in battle that same year fighting to protect the state he had helped establish.

Spurius Cassius Vecellinus
(503, 495, 486 BCE)
Cassius was a successful and popular general. This led to his execution in 485 BCE, allegedly for plotting a coup.

Appius Claudius Sabinus Regillensis (495 BCE)
A conservative opponent of plebeian rights, his descendants included the Julio-Claudian emperors Tiberius, Caligula, and Claudius.

Lucius Quinctius Cincinnatus (460 BCE)
The model of Republican virtue, Cincinnatus was given supreme power to command Rome's armies at a time of crisis. After defeating the enemy he voluntarily gave up power to return to his farm.

Marcus Furius Camillus
(401, 398, 394, 386, 384, 381 BCE)
Consul six times, dictator on four occasions, and winner of four Triumphs, Camillus was called Rome's "Second Romulus" for his military victories and for his political reforms that allowed plebeians to be elected as consuls.

Appius Claudius Caecus
(307, 296 BCE)
The builder of Rome's first aqueduct and paved road also introduced the law allowing the sons of formerly enslaved people to become senators.

Publius Cornelius Scipio Africanus (205, 194 BCE)
Scipio would defeat Rome's great enemy Hannibal in the Second Punic War.

Gaius Marius
(107, 104–100, 86 BCE)
A great military leader, he was consul seven times. His later career was marked by a bitter rivalry with the Roman general Sulla.

Marcus Tullius Cicero
(63 BCE)
"Saved" Rome as consul when he uncovered a plot to seize power by the renegade noble Catiline. Later, in the civil wars following Julius Caesar's murder, he was assassinated on the orders of Mark Antony.

Gaius Julius Caesar
(59, 48, 46–45, 44 BCE)
Successful general and the first Roman to be appointed dictator for life.

ROMAN **NAMING CONVENTIONS**

Roman men had at least two names: the *praenomen* (first name) and the *nomen* (family, or *gens*, name). Many men also had a third name, or *cognomen*, which could be a nickname or indicate a sub-branch of a family. For example, the statesman Publius Cornelius Scipio was Publius of the Cornelius clan and "Scipio," from the Latin word for a staff carried by a triumphing general. When in 202 BCE Scipio defeated Hannibal at the Battle of Zama, in modern Tunisia, he was awarded a second *cognomen*, also called an *agnomen*: Africanus, celebrating him as the "conqueror" of Africa.

The Roman Empire

27–476 CE

The Imperial era saw men of every kind rule vast territories. In the process, power shifted from Rome to the east.

Augustus (27 BCE–14 CE)
Rome's first emperor reigned for four decades and founded the Julio-Claudian dynasty.

Tiberius (14–37)
Unpopular with the Roman citizens, he ran the empire from the island of Capri in 26.

Caligula (37–41)
His cruelty and excesses led a group of army officers, senators, and courtiers to arrange his assassination.

Claudius (41–54)
He expanded the empire by conquering parts of Britannia.

Nero (54–68)
His early promise as emperor gave way to dissolution and, when facing rebellion, suicide.

The "Year of the Four Emperors"
(68–69)
Legions in different parts of the empire proclaim Galba, Otho, Vitellius, and Vespasian in quick succession.

Vespasian (69–79)
The Flavian dynasty he founded—which included his sons Titus (79–81) and Domitian (81–96)—conquered Jerusalem and built the Colosseum.

Nerva (96–98)

Trajan (98–117)
The empire reached its greatest extent under his rule.

Hadrian (117–138)
Builder of Hadrian's Wall and rebuilder of the Pantheon.

Antoninus Pius (138–161)

Marcus Aurelius (161–180)
Wrote *Meditations*, a classic of Stoic philosophy. Shared parts of his reign with adoptive brother, Lucius Verus (161–169), and son, Commodus (177–192).

The "Year of the Five Emperors" (193)
Five men claimed the title emperor: Pertinax,

◁ Vespasian, the first emperor to be directly succeeded by his natural-born son.

△ The emperor Julian, known as "the Apostate" (seated, on right), failed to restore traditional beliefs to an increasingly Christianized empire.

Didius Julianus; Pescennius Niger, Clodius Albinus, and Septimius Severus.

Septimius Severus (193–211)
The first emperor of African origin and founder of the Severan dynasty. Shared part of his reign with his sons, Caracalla and Geta.

Caracalla (198–217)
Granted citizenship to all free men of the empire. He killed his coruler, Geta (209–211).

Macrinus (217–218)

Elagabalus (218–222)

Severus Alexander (222–235)
The last Severan ruler.

The "Third Century Crisis" (235–284)
The death of Severus Alexander initiated a period of instability, in which the empire split into three rival states: the Gallic Empire, the Palmyrene Empire, and the Roman Empire. The latter saw more than 20 emperors during this period and almost collapsed.

Aurelian (270–275)
The most notable emperor from this period reunited the empire by conquering the Palmyrene and Gallic Empires. He also built Rome's Aurelian Walls—which still stand—to protect the city against Germanic invaders.

Diocletian (284–305)
Ended the Third Century Crisis. He divided the empire in two in 286, giving the Western Empire to Maximian; and established the Tetrarchy ("rule of four") in 293.

Maximian (286–305; W)

Constantius I (305–306; W)

Galerius (305–311; E)

Severus (306–307; W)

Maxentius (306–312; W)
Recognized as emperor in Italy and North Africa by the Senate, but considered illegitimate by the Tetrarchy.

Constantine I (306–337)
He defeated rival emperors Maxentius and (later) Licinius to become sole emperor in 324. He founded the city of Constantinople and converted to Christianity, establishing a new Christian empire in the east, which would evolve into the Byzantine Empire.

The Fall of the Western Roman Empire (337–476)
Following Constantine I's reign in 337, the Western Empire declined in power, overwhelmed by Germanic invasions and a fractured political system. The following are some of the most notable or ineffective emperors from this period.

Constans I (337–350; W)
Constantine's sons split the empire between themselves after his death, with Constans I and Constantine II (337–340; W) sharing the west, and Constantius II taking the east. In 340 Constans defeated Constantine II to become sole Western emperor, but was killed by his Germanic general, Magnentius.

Constantius II (337–361)
He briefly reunited the empire in 353 when he crushed the usurper Magnentius.

Julian (361–363)
He attempted to revive the traditional Roman religion, but his successor, Jovian (363–364), immediately reinstated Christianity as the state religion.

Valentinian I (364–375; W)
The administration of the empire divided again under his rule. He gave his brother, Valens, the eastern provinces, and retained the west.

Valens (364–378; E)
His death at the Battle of Adrianople began the so-called "age of invasions."

Theodosius I (379–395)
The last emperor to rule both the east and the west, he won two civil wars and oversaw Christian religious reforms.

Honorius (393–423; W)
His rule saw the Visigoths sack Rome in 410.

Valentinian III (425–455; W)
He became emperor at six years old; his mother, Galla Placidia, ruled as regent for 12 years.

Leo I (457–474; E)
The first emperor to legislate in Greek, rather than Latin.

Romulus Augustus (475–476; W)
The last Western emperor was deposed by a Germanic general, who ruled as a king.

The Byzantine Empire (330–1453)
The Roman Empire survived for 1,000 years in the east as the Byzantine Empire, while Western Europe was controlled by new powers.

KEY

Dates shown are for when the holder was in power.
For the emperors:
W = Western Empire
E = Eastern Empire

◁ **Votive head of woman**
Votive heads, such as this Etruscan example from the 6th century BCE, were placed in temples to accompany offerings to the gods. Earrings once hung from its ears and pigment traces indicate that its hair was painted bright red.

1

The Roman Kingdom

753–509 BCE

A City Born in Legend

Founded by the son of Mars, with its people descended from a hero of Greek legend, Rome was special. At least that is the story the city's earliest chroniclers wanted to tell. Writing up to a thousand years after the events described, Rome's first historians (by their own admission) blended history and myth in a way that makes them hard to separate. What does emerge, however, is the idea of Rome as a place of continuity and *mos maiorum* ("the ways of the ancestors"). Equally strong was their description of Rome as embodying its institutions and its public offices, many of which were created under the city's first seven rulers, the *reges* ("kings").

Separating myth and reality

Much of the knowledge of how Rome's religious, political, and social structures worked was told orally from generation to generation, and in the telling was most probably adapted to fit contemporary needs. When this knowledge began to be written down from the 2nd century BCE, it was done by those who sought to make sense of the city's past in a way that resonated with their present. In the Republican era, this could mean denigrating monarchical power in favor of government by the people; in the Imperial age, Rome's historians were perhaps less disapproving of one-man rule.

Similarly, each of Rome's seven kings was ascribed a personality—Numa was philosophical, Tullus Hostilius warlike—that explained aspects of an ideal Roman character it was expedient to promote. Roman writers seem to have treated this era differently from other periods. In general, their accounts are dramatic, often improbable, and full of details that it would have been impossible for later Romans to know with any certainty. Was Rome's founder really Romulus, for example? And was he as an infant suckled, with his brother Remus, by a she-wolf?

Modern evaluations and understandings

Today's interpretations of Rome's Regal period are shaped by study of the archaeological evidence combined with a critical view of the literary sources. Some of the broader trends these sources refer to are plausible, such as the growing tensions between the city's elite families in the 6th century BCE, as well as Rome's increasing social and political complexity.

The archaeology supports the idea that Rome began to emerge as a major urban center in the 6th century BCE. It is also clear that Roman history must be understood within the context of a wider central Italian narrative during this period. While the literature focuses on Rome's origins and the growth of its identity through the tales of Aeneas, Romulus, Tarquinius, and Brutus, this may reflect later perspectives that sought to assign to Rome a "noble" provenance. It could also have been an attempt to link the story of the Roman people to ancestors—genuine or invented—from the wider Mediterranean world, appropriating a share of their heritage and prestige. In reality, in its era of Regal rule, Rome was one of many communities in a region of shifting local populations. When Rome emerged as the leading power among neighbors that included Praeneste and the city-states of Etruria such as Caere, later generations perhaps sought to explain this through stories that blended myth and metaphor once the state had transitioned from kingdom to republic.

◁ **The she-wolf suckling Romulus and Remus**

c. 1150 BCE According to legend, the Trojan warrior Aeneas arrives in Italy and founds Lavinium

1100 BCE Approximate date of the founding of Alba Longa by Aeneas's son Ascanius

775 BCE Rhea Silvia, a princess of Alba Longa, gives birth to Romulus and Remus, fathered by the god Mars

753 BCE Traditional foundation date of Rome by Romulus, the first king

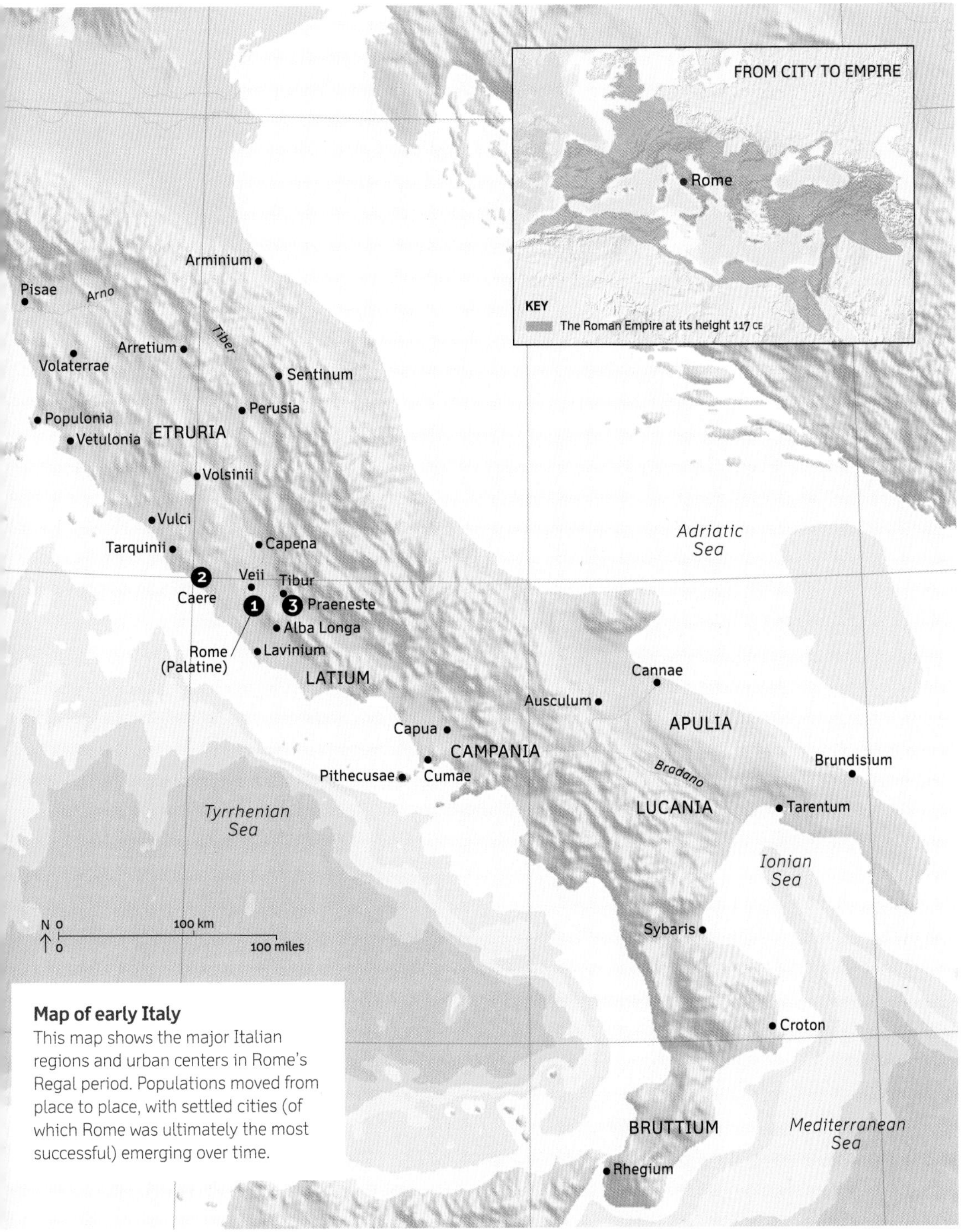

Map of early Italy
This map shows the major Italian regions and urban centers in Rome's Regal period. Populations moved from place to place, with settled cities (of which Rome was ultimately the most successful) emerging over time.

1 The Palatine Hill, Rome's first settlement

2 Necropolis of Caere (modern Cerveteri)

3 Praeneste's Sanctuary of Fortuna

715 BCE Numa Pompilius becomes Rome's second king

672 BCE Tullus Hostilius becomes the city's third king

640 BCE Ancus Marcius takes power as Rome's fourth king

616 BCE Lucius Tarquinius Priscus becomes the fifth king

578 BCE Servius Tullius assumes power after his predecessor's murder

534 BCE Lucius Tarquinius Superbus usurps Servius Tullius

509 BCE Brutus and Collatinus remove Tarquinius; the Republic is founded

495 BCE Death in exile of Lucius Tarquinius Superbus, Rome's last king

The Italian Iron Age

Rome's origins, from humble settlement to urban center

Early Rome was not home to a stable population or culture but emerged gradually as an important urban center for communication and interaction in the late Italian Iron Age.

△ **Fibula**
This bronze fibula from the 7th century BCE was typically used to fasten clothing; it was often worn on the right shoulder and is a common grave find.

Before the creation of its empire, Rome was just one community among many in central Italy and had a relatively fluid and mobile population. While some families and individuals may have lived permanently on the site where the city grew, most people in the community probably came and went. It was a hub of interaction rather than a self-contained, stable settlement, particularly in the earliest periods. In light of this, it is important to view early Rome in the context of the wider region that surrounded it.

The Italian Iron Age

Around 900 BCE, at the start of the Italian Iron Age, archaeological records show the emergence of a "Villanovan society" (see box). The society emerged from a previous Bronze Age culture and would go on to develop into the peoples known as the Etruscans and Latins (including the Romans). What the Villanovans called themselves, or whether they identified as a single or discrete culture, is unknown. They left behind distinctive material remains, however—most notably the characteristic burial of their cremated dead in small, hut-shaped urns.

While most of our evidence for the Villanovans comes from burials, over time the slow development of urban centers can be discerned, particularly in Etruria (see pp. 20–21). Early communities consisted of loose collections of huts, which seem to have acted as focal points for local industry and agriculture, and as stable locations for burial grounds. Based on slightly later evidence, when temple-building begins, these settlements also served as religious centers and marketplaces. However, they always existed within a much larger and shifting human environment that saw much movement and activity outside of the urban zones—a dynamic comparable to that of a shopping center or economic district, which relies on attracting visitors from a wide area.

Greeks and the wider Mediterranean

By the 8th century BCE, urban centers were changing across the Mediterranean. Although still evolving, they were increasingly substantial and stable, and began to gain a permanence and identity of their own. In Italy, more distinctive regional cultures began to develop around settlements, and these are associated with the rise of cultures such as the Etruscans and Latins.

▷ **Hut urn**
Dating from the 8th century BCE, this elaborate bronze hut urn is from Vulci. Urns provide clues about the huts Villanovans actually lived in.

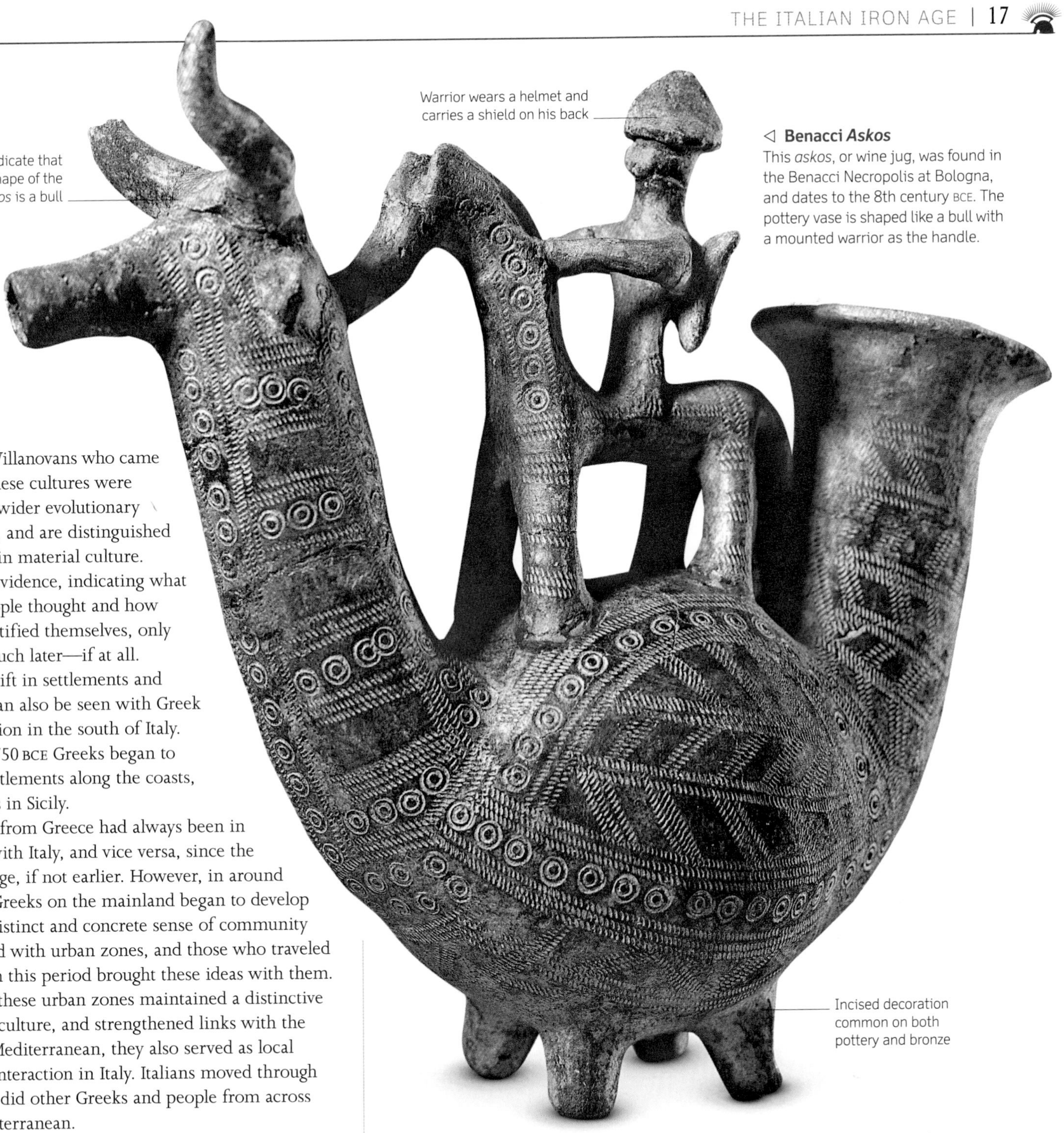

Horns indicate that the shape of the *askos* is a bull

Warrior wears a helmet and carries a shield on his back

◁ **Benacci *Askos***
This *askos*, or wine jug, was found in the Benacci Necropolis at Bologna, and dates to the 8th century BCE. The pottery vase is shaped like a bull with a mounted warrior as the handle.

Incised decoration common on both pottery and bronze

Like the Villanovans who came before, these cultures were part of a wider evolutionary sequence, and are distinguished by shifts in material culture. Written evidence, indicating what these people thought and how they identified themselves, only comes much later—if at all.

This shift in settlements and culture can also be seen with Greek colonization in the south of Italy. Around 750 BCE Greeks began to found settlements along the coasts, as well as in Sicily.

People from Greece had always been in contact with Italy, and vice versa, since the Bronze Age, if not earlier. However, in around 750 BCE Greeks on the mainland began to develop a more distinct and concrete sense of community associated with urban zones, and those who traveled to Italy in this period brought these ideas with them.

While these urban zones maintained a distinctive material culture, and strengthened links with the eastern Mediterranean, they also served as local hubs of interaction in Italy. Italians moved through them, as did other Greeks and people from across the Mediterranean.

A geographical hub

For much of the Iron Age, Rome seems to have been a relatively small and unimportant community. As connective networks evolved, however, the community grew in size and prominence, due largely to its location on a key crossing of the Tiber River, which controlled movement between Etruria in the north and Latium in the south. Regionally, all roads did indeed lead to Rome, allowing it to emerge as a natural base for powerful social, political, and economic networks within central Italy.

DISCOVERY OF THE "VILLANOVANS"

In 1853, Count Giovanni Gozzadini began excavations on his land near the Italian city of Bologna. Over the next two years he unearthed a cemetery with over 190 tombs dating to the early Iron Age (c. 900–c. 700 BCE). The graves contained cremations, with the physical remains put into urns shaped like huts and buried in pits along with various grave goods. This became the "type site," defining the culture that became known as Villanovan, after the nearby village Villanova (now Castenaso). Grave goods could include military equipment, such as this crested helmet (right).

The Tomb of the Leopards
Dating from c. 470–450 BCE, this burial chamber is named after the animals confronting each other at the top of the fresco. It was discovered in 1875 in the necropolis of Monterozzi, close to the ancient Etruscan city of Tarquinii, and depicts what could be a funeral feast for the tomb's inhabitant, with musicians and processional figures. The men and women at the banquet wear laurel wreath crowns and one of the male figures holds an egg—a common symbol of regeneration. Equally symbolic are the leopards themselves, which in the ancient world often appeared in art and sculpture to represent immortality.

The Etruscan Civilization

Rome's neighbors to the north

The Etruscans lived in the area now known as Tuscany. With a distinctive language, rich tombs, interesting origins, and impressive cities, their culture had a strong influence on early Roman society.

△ **Jewels from the east**
The amber used in this 7th-century BCE Etruscan necklace found at Caere (modern Cerveteri), comes from the Black Sea region. It shows the extent of Etruria's trade links across the Mediterranean world.

The north-central Italian region of Etruria, bounded to the south by the Tiber River and to the north and east by the great arc of the Apennine mountains, was home to the people known to history as "the Etruscans." This name was given to them by the Romans, from the Latin *Tuscī* or *Etruscī*, which was probably derived from the Greek *Tyrrhēnoi*, a reference to the Tyrrhenian Sea which bounded Etruria along the Italian peninsula's west coast. The Etruscans called themselves the Rasna.

The origin of the Etruscan people has been a subject of debate since antiquity. Some ancient authors, such as the historian Herodotus, suggested they came from Greece or modern-day Türkiye—an argument which has been taken up in modern times by those who point to their distinctive language and their similarities with eastern Mediterranean cultures in areas such as the arts. Other ancient writers, however, suggested they were native to the Italian peninsula, and modern archaeology and developments in DNA sequencing have been able to support this. It appears that the Etruscans developed from the central Italian "Villanovan" culture of c. 900–700 BCE (see pp. 16–17). Whether they were native-born or of overseas origin, the Etruscans, throughout the period that their civilization flourished, did not exist in isolation. They were always connected to, and influenced by, the wider Mediterranean world beyond Italy.

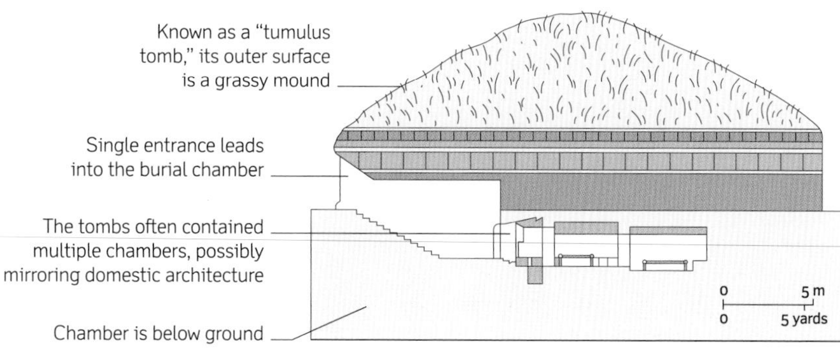

◁ **A house for the dead**
Tomb styles varied across the region, and over time. This circular tomb type emerged in the 7th century BCE in southern Etruria and would have been created for a family.

Life and death in Etruria

Etruscan society was largely based around urban centers that began to emerge in the region some time after 900 BCE in settlements such as Vetulonia, Tarquinia, Veii, Volsinii, and Caere. The civilization's early cities served as hubs for local populations to come together for economic, military, political, religious, and other reasons, although it is unclear how many people lived in these cities on a permanent basis. Excavations of early Etruscan cities show houses or huts clustered together in what has been called a "leopard spot" pattern.

Over time, the cities in Etruria grew and became more sophisticated. For example, by the 6th century BCE there was an increase in monumental architecture—especially temples. The Etruscans were noted by the Romans for their religious devotion and practices, especially as soothsayers in later times. However, Etruscan temple-building was not just about religion. Temples were also centers of political power and commerce; the presence of one in an Etruscan city indicated that the settlement was a place of importance.

Outside their cities, the Etruscans built necropolises (literally, "cities of the dead"). Usually cut into the soft volcanic stone that was common in the region (known as tufo, or tuff), these great graveyards often grew to be larger than the living cities next to them. Necropolises are today the main source of information for archaeologists and historians about the Etruscans. They are typically better preserved than the city sites and were filled with rich art and a variety of fascinating grave goods, including bronze and silver mirrors, drinking vessels, pots, vases, and ornaments.

A prime location

There was contact between Etruria and Rome, though it is not clear how much. Etruria was not yet a unified state. It was more a confederation of city-states and the Etruscans may not even have seen themselves as a single people. Populations were fluid during the Italian Iron Age, with people freely moving from place to place. A "Roman," by relocating to a new settlement a day's ride away, could become an "Etruscan" (if they thought in those terms). These shifting affiliations happened across central Italy: Rome's last three *reges*, or kings, came from Etruria (see pp. 10–11). This is one reason why it was thought that Etruria dominated Rome early on.

In this era of population movement, Rome benefited from its position on the Tiber River between the peoples of Etruria to the north and Latium to the south and east. Political, religious, cultural, and commercial influences flowed in all directions, and the story of Rome's rise is not one of isolated growth and expansion. The Romans did eventually become the dominant power in Italy by the 3rd century BCE, but only as part of a wider social and cultural network that included their neighbors to the north.

COLLECTORS' ITEMS

One of the reasons the Etruscans were long thought to have descended from the Greeks is the large number of Greek vases found in Etruscan tombs. It is now believed that this is because the Etruscans were enthusiastic purchasers of Greek pottery. This black-figured Greek amphora (right), made in Athens c. 530 BCE, was found in a tomb at Chiusi, a town midway between Florence and Rome. It is not known exactly why the Etruscans liked to use Greek items in particular in their funerary rites and in their places of burial, although many of them have been discovered there. This is something to be thankful for—most of the painted Greek pottery held in the world's museums and private collections today comes from Italian, often Etruscan, tombs.

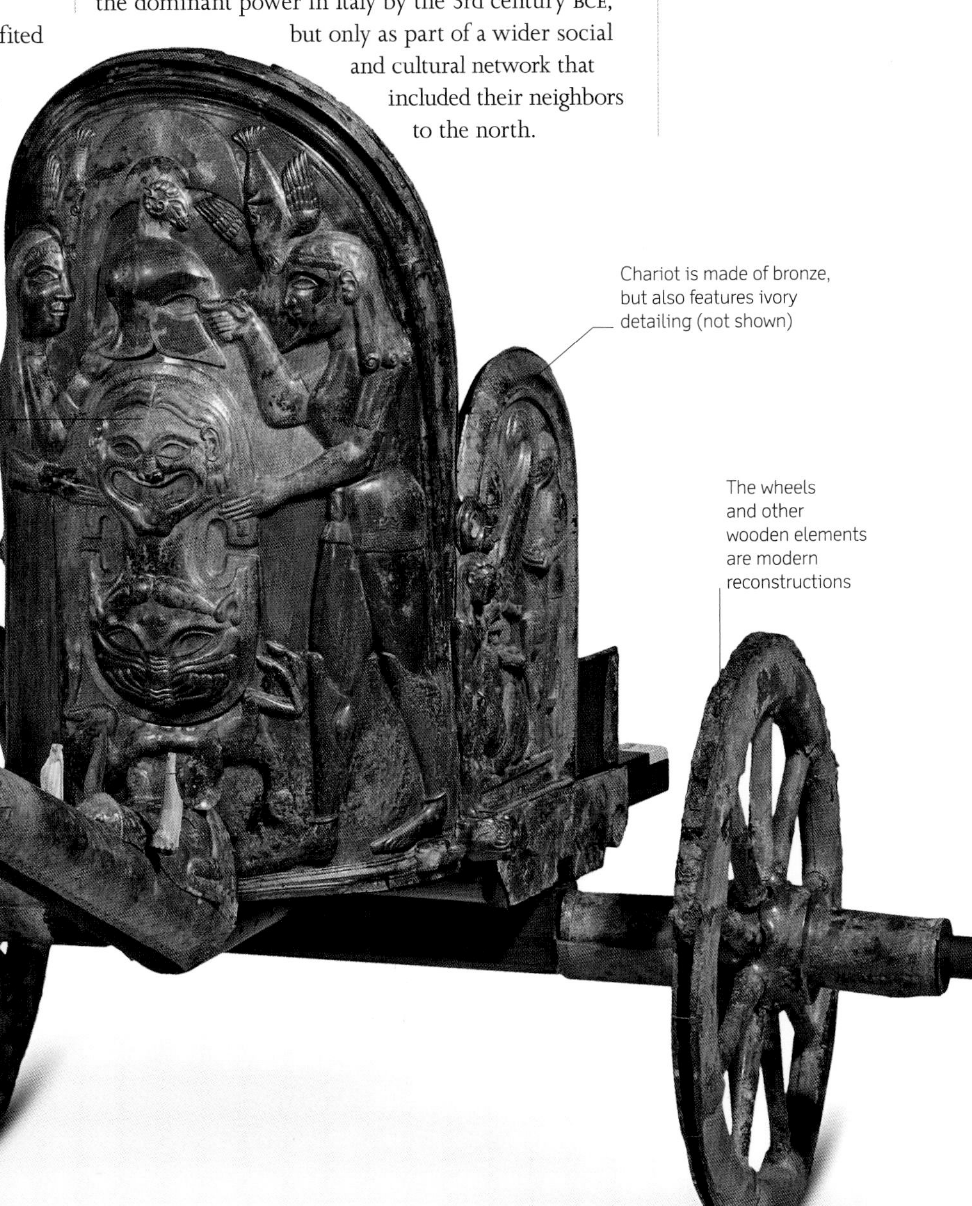

Front panel features a scene from Homer in which Achilles receives armor from his mother, the sea nymph Thetis

Chariot is made of bronze, but also features ivory detailing (not shown)

The wheels and other wooden elements are modern reconstructions

Known as a *biga*, this type of chariot was designed to be pulled by two horses

▷ **Traveling in style**
The Monteleone Chariot dates from c. 530 BCE and was discovered in Monteleone di Spoleto, Umbria, in 1902. It was probably created as a burial item and is one of the largest and best-preserved Etruscan artifacts.

Rome's Founding Myths

From Aeneas to Romulus

While Rome's foundation stories are unlikely to be based on real figures or events, they reveal how Romans thought about themselves and their relationship to other Italians and the wider Mediterranean.

△ **The dutiful son**
This gold *aureus* of Emperor Antoninus Pius from the 2nd century CE shows Aeneas, carrying his father Anchises and leading his son Ascanius, as he flees the city of Troy.

Rome traditionally had two mythical founders, Aeneas and Romulus, who each served an important role in the Romans' conception of their origins and identity.

Aeneas can be found in the epic poems of the Greek poet Homer from around the 8th century BCE, and features in Italic art from the 6th–5th centuries BCE. However, the earliest solid evidence of his association with the city of Rome is relatively late (3rd–2nd centuries BCE) and comes from histories written by early Roman authors, such as Ennius and Cato.

Aeneas was a pan-Mediterranean hero, who was revered across the region. According to myth, the Trojan prince escaped the destruction of his city after a war with the Greeks, carrying his father Anchises on his back as he fled. Aeneas supposedly traveled widely before arriving in Italy (see box). Although he is often described as a founder of Rome, Aeneas only had a passing connection to the city in most stories.
In the Roman poet Virgil's *Aeneid*, he is the founder of a precursor settlement on the Italian coastline and pays a single visit to the site of Rome, which is already inhabited by Greek settlers. It was his descendants, the twins Romulus and Remus, who founded the city of Rome. Despite this seemingly loose connection,

△ ***The Intervention of the Sabine Women*** **(1799)**
Romulus and his men abducted the Sabine women, sparking a war that was only resolved by the intervention of the women themselves, as shown in this painting by Jacques-Louis David.

Aeneas was a vitally important figure for the Romans as he linked Rome to the wider Mediterranean world. Many ancient cities and elite families, and especially those in Italy, claimed descent from various Greek heroes as a way to both increase their prestige and connect their community with others. Aeneas's Trojan descent allowed the Romans to relate to as well as rival the Greeks, while his wide popularity gave the Romans a shared hero with other groups.

The myth of Romulus

Romulus seems to have been a more local hero, despite being a descendant of Aeneas. According to Livy's version of his story from c. 1st century BCE, Romulus and his twin Remus were the sons of the Vestal Virgin (see pp. 32–33) Rhea Silvia. She was the daughter of Numitor, king of Alba Longa (a town south of the later site of Rome). Rhea Silvia had been forced to become a Vestal Virgin after her uncle Amulius ousted her father. Nevertheless, Rhea Silvia was supposedly impregnated by the god of war, Mars, and gave birth to Romulus and Remus. Fearing a rival

THE ORIGINS OF THE PUNIC WARS

Aeneas famously traveled around the Mediterranean after leaving Troy and before landing in Italy, and there are many local myths that connect him with Sicily and North Africa in particular. By the Late Republic, the Romans began to use these myths to explain the origins of their great conflict with Carthage—the Punic Wars (see pp. 82–85). In Virgil's retelling, Aeneas visited Carthage and fell in love with the Carthaginian queen Dido, before leaving her to pursue his destiny in Italy (as depicted in this painting by Guido Reni, c. 1630). Devastated by this betrayal, Dido cursed Aeneas and laid the foundation for the later conflict.

to his throne, Amulius ordered his servants to drown the babies in the Tiber River. The twins were placed in a basket on the river's banks. Before they were harmed, a she-wolf saved them and nurtured them until the shepherd Faustulus discovered and raised them. As adults, the twins founded Rome on the site where the she-wolf had saved them. However, they soon quarreled and Romulus killed Remus, assuming full authority over the community.

As a ruler, Romulus shaped Rome's social and political systems, supposedly laying the foundation of later Roman society through a combination of warfare and integration. While the myth of Aeneas helped the Romans declare their place within the wider Mediterranean, Romulus helped shape Roman identity in their local region. Although his myth may have circulated earlier, it seems to have come to particular prominence as Rome began to construct its Italic empire in the 4th century BCE.

> "**Romulus** and Remus were **seized by a desire** to **found a city** ..."
>
> LIVY'S HISTORY OF ROME, *AB URBE CONDITA*

Two shepherds, probably Faustulus and his brother Faustinus

Jupiter's eagle watches over the scene

The she-wolf, suckling the twins Romulus and Remus

Personification of the Tiber River

◁ **Altar of Mars**
This altar to the god Mars was unearthed in Rome's port of Ostia and dates to the early 2nd century CE. The front depicts Mars alongside Venus, while the back shows Romulus and Remus being discovered by Faustulus.

The Kings of Rome

Philosopher kings and tyrants

The histories of early Rome, which were written hundreds of years after the events they describe, suggest that Rome had seven *reges* ("kings") who ruled during what we now call the Roman Kingdom, or "Regal period," from 753 BCE to 509 BCE.

Although *rex* is usually translated as "king" in English, this oversimplifies a more complex institution. The Roman system did not involve hereditary rule, and the power of the *rex* was not absolute. The fact that Romans supposedly hated kingship yet venerated the *reges* (with the exception of the tyrannical leader Lucius Tarquinius Superbus) hints that they recognized such a difference themselves. *Reges* seem to have been a combination of chief priest, high judge, and war leader. They were thought to have been chosen by the Senate and confirmed by a vote of the Curiate Assembly, the legislative body, although they then governed for life.

Early kings

The history of the Roman Kingdom is usually regarded as being composed of two parts. The first set of kings are generally considered mythic figures. These are Romulus (see pp. 22–23), Numa, and Tullus Hostilius. Romulus (traditionally regarded as ruling 753–715 BCE) is the archetype of Roman leadership, and Numa Pompilius is remembered as being a philosopher king who created many of Rome's religious institutions. Tullus Hostilius is the epitome of a warrior king, while Ancus Marcius, the fourth *rex*,

△ **Numa Pompilius**
Said to have ruled 715–672 BCE, Numa oversaw a relatively peaceful period and is associated with many religious reforms, including the introduction of the calendar, various cults (see pp. 32–33), and the office of chief priest (*pontifex maximus*).

△ **Tullus Hostilius**
Tullus Hostilius's reign (672–640 BCE) was defined by warfare. He oversaw the conquest of Alba Longa, a city near Rome that was the old center of power in the region and regarded as the original home of Romulus and Remus.

△ **Ancus Marcius**
An unusual figure with aspects of both previous *reges*, his reign (640–616 BCE) was largely uneventful. He is best remembered as the ancestor of the Marcii, one of Rome's oldest and grandest families.

> "The **ancient Romans** [...] all wished for a **king**, not having yet tasted the **sweetness of liberty**."
>
> LIVY'S HISTORY OF ROME, *AB URBE CONDITA*

is a sort of hybrid figure—part mythic and part historical—a leader who bridged the two halves but is accorded few defining features in the histories.

Later kings

Rome's final three *reges*, Lucius Tarquinius Priscus, Servius Tullius, and Lucius Tarquinius Superbus, are considered more historical figures. Although their stories are still heavily embellished, these later rulers are more complete characters in the narrative and were associated with Rome's historic rise in the 6th century BCE. Lucius Tarquinius Priscus and Lucius Tarquinius Superbus were great builders, and were associated with Etruria (see pp. 20–21), while Servius Tullius was a lawgiver. The final *rex*, Lucius Tarquinius Superbus, was also remembered as a tyrant whose excesses ultimately prompted the elite families to rise up and replace the monarchy with a republic.

It is difficult to differentiate myth and history in this period. The existence of the Regia (traditional home of the *rex*) in the Forum and inscriptions from the 6th century BCE that contain the word "*rex*" hint that the office did exist in some form. Beyond that, it is unclear. However, Romans always liked to look back to tradition and the *mos maiorum* ("the ways of the ancestors"), so the laws and systems supposedly laid down by the *reges* were held to be essential to the Romans' conception of themselves. Whether these figures were real or not, they were vitally important to Roman identity and society.

△ **Lucius Tarquinius Priscus**
The first of the "Etruscan *reges*," his reign (616–578 BCE) saw the major expansion of Rome through construction (including the Circus Maximus and the Cloaca Maxima sewer), war, and politics. He was murdered by the sons of Ancus Marcius.

△ **Servius Tullius**
The rule of Servius Tullius (578–535 BCE) began brutally, following the murder of Tarquinius Priscus, which marked a period of increased violence in Rome. Remembered as a reformer and unifier (see pp. 28–29), Servius was killed by his son-in-law, Lucius Tarquinius Superbus.

△ **Lucius Tarquinius Superbus**
The final king of Rome's reign (534–509 BCE) was defined by tyranny and the oppression of the aristocracy. Following his son's rape of the noblewoman Lucretia and her subsequent suicide, Lucius Tarquinius Superbus was forced from the city, ending the monarchy.

The Peoples of Early Italy

The movement and mingling of central Italy's varied people

Archaic central Italy was a diverse and dynamic region home to a number of different cultural groups alongside the Romans and Etruscans. These often mobile populations interacted in both peaceful and hostile ways.

The area around Rome, which included both Latium and southern Etruria, has a distinctive geography. To the east are the Apennine mountains, which run down the center of the Italian peninsula, and to the west is the Tyrrhenian Sea. The broad coastal plains lie in between, divided up by a series of rivers—most notably the Tiber. By the 8th century BCE, the flat coastal areas had started to fill with small urban hubs that acted as centers of agricultural production. The mountains, however, were home to more mobile populations who seem to have focused on pastoralism (animal herding).

◁ **Bucchero *kantharos***
This 7th-century BCE drinking vessel is an example of a bucchero ceramic, found in central Italy. Bucchero wares have a black shade, produced by firing without oxygen.

Divided peoples

Ancient sources and modern scholars usually divide the peoples of central Italy into two groups: coastal farmers/city-dwellers and mountain tribes. On the coastal plains there were the Etruscans and Latins, and further south, the Greek communities of Magna Graecia. The Romans were part of this group. In the mountains were the Aequi, Volsci, and Umbrians, as well as the Samnites and Lucanians further south. The Sabines and Hernici were tribal groups who seemed to operate in between, alongside many others, such as the Marsi and Sidicini.

These two broad populations seem to have been separated by a number of important features. They often had distinctive languages, with Oscan and Umbrian being the dominant language groups of the mountains, while Latin, Etruscan, and Greek were common in the plains and coastal areas.

Literature suggests that the people of the coasts were constantly defending their territory from raids by the "barbarian" groups of the highlands. Early Roman history is full of battles against the Hernici, Aequi, Volsci, and—later—the Samnites. However, even in these battles, the identity of the groups is often far from clear: these were not stable states or alliances.

▽ **Parade of horses**
A temple frieze from c. 500 BCE, found at the site of Praeneste, depicts a military procession with chariots. The presence of the winged horses suggests a divine element.

Dynamic relationships

Despite their differences, it is likely that the peoples of early Italy were quite closely connected. Labels and divisions were fairly fluid, and people could, and did, move easily between these groups. One such example is that of the Roman noble Coriolanus, who was exiled from Rome in the 5th century BCE and joined the Volsci—a shift in identity that seems to have been quite a common occurrence.

One reason that not all movement and interaction was violent was because populations of the mountains and coastal plains were probably interdependent, and possibly even related. It is likely that the pastoralists of the highlands migrated seasonally, along regular routes, coming down to the plains during the winter before returning to the mountains in the summer. Members of families or groups may have stayed in communities in the coastal areas, while others herded

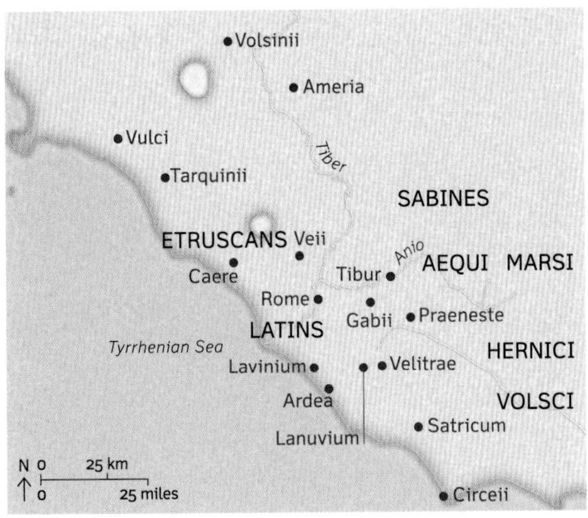

△ **Early peoples of central Italy**
Etruscans and Latins were found in the urban centers on the Tyrrhenian coast of central Italy, while other groups, such as the Volsci and Aequi, were associated with the mountains.

animals in the hills. The groups probably traded with each other regularly, with the mountain-dwellers acquiring pottery and other materials to trade, while the people of the cities obtained animals, needed for sacrifices and food.

The story of early Roman history is largely defined by conflicts against "other people." Later Roman authors contrasted the Romans with the various groups, both on the coastal plains (including Etruscans and Latins) and in the highlands (such as the Volsci and Samnites). By doing this, the writers defined (in often mythic terms) who "the Romans" were in these early years.

Loosely defined differences

In reality, the divisions seem to have been far less absolute: while local cultures and practices were significant and varied, similarities and connections would have been more obvious and important. While groups may have emphasized their particular cultural traits in their inscriptions and burials, they often did so in a mutually comprehensible way that highlighted their uniqueness within an accepted set of cultural norms.

The peoples of early central Italy lived in close proximity, interacting regularly, both peacefully and through war and raiding. They often intermarried, as hinted at by the story of the Sabine women in early Roman myth (see pp. 22–23), and were not isolated cultures but parts of a broader Italic whole.

"The **Volsci** and **Aequi** ... crossed the border and **raided** the lands of the **Latins** and **Hernici**."

LIVY'S HISTORY OF ROME, *AB URBE CONDITA*

Satyr, a male nature spirit

Maenad and satyr clasp hands in a dance

▷ **Temple antefix (roof ornament)**
A terra-cotta decoration dating from c. 490 BCE shows a satyr and maenad (female follower of Dionysus) from the temple of the Latin goddess Mater Matuta at Satricum, south of Rome. Greek figures like these were common on early Italian temples.

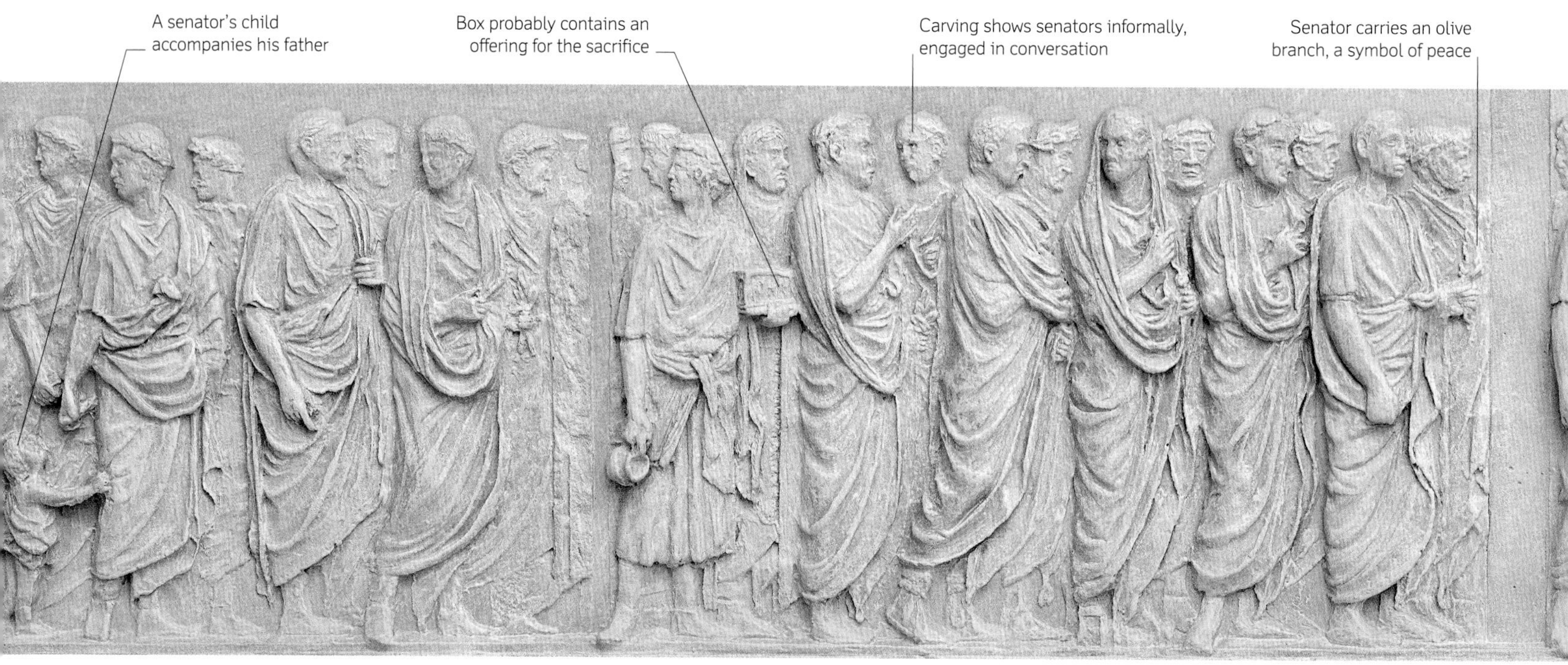

Governing Rome

Sovereignty, power, and influence

Rome was led by kings, consuls, or emperors over the centuries. For much of its history, however, the day-to-day running of the city was the work of the people's assemblies and elected magistrates, watched over by the Senate.

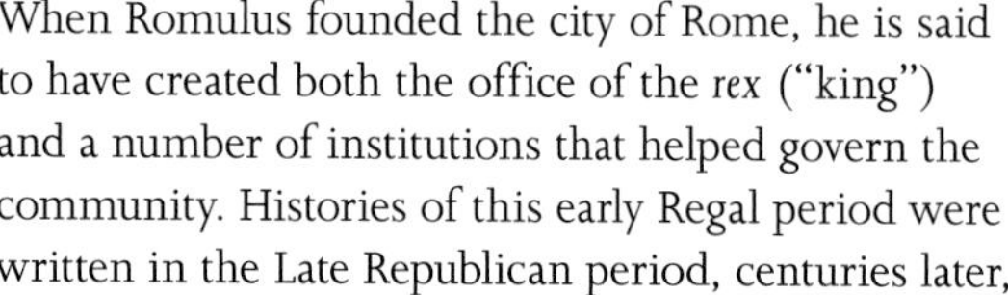

When Romulus founded the city of Rome, he is said to have created both the office of the *rex* ("king") and a number of institutions that helped govern the community. Histories of this early Regal period were written in the Late Republican period, centuries later, and are almost certainly inaccurate. While a few points are known with some certainty about governance during this age, more is understood about the later Republican and Imperial eras.

The Senate

In popular legend, the Senate was set up by Romulus as an advisory council and used as such by the kings who followed him in the Regal period. The Senate's composition may have been fluid in Rome's early years, as the elites who comprised it moved around the region when Rome was just one of several settlements competing for power in central Italy (see pp. 54–57). Membership of the Senate may have changed annually, up until 318 BCE when the *lex Ovinia* was passed, a law paving the way for a more stable institution. However, senators almost certainly represented the collective authority of the great families and clans of Rome.

With the founding of the Republic (see pp. 36–37), the Senate worked with the two consuls selected annually by people's assemblies. Consuls occupied the most

◁ **Portals of power**
The doors of the Senate House, dating from the 1st century CE, are now in use in Rome's church of St. John Lateran.

△ **The great and the good**
This relief from the north side of the Ara Pacis in Rome depicts a procession of senators, wearing togas, going to a sacrifice. During the Imperial era, the Senate ceded much of its importance to the emperor, but continued to meet and debate.

powerful and sought-after elected positions (see pp. 62–63), and the Senate offered them guidance. Until the end of the Republic, the Senate was also the chief advisory body to Rome's elected magistrates, who carried out official tasks. In general, the Senate approved laws and actions favoring the interests of Rome's elites.

In the Imperial era, the Senate was discouraged (with varying degrees of force) from acting in opposition to the emperor. In return for this loyalty, the Senate's corporate power and prestige was allowed to grow.

The role of the assemblies

Power in Rome was wielded by its elected magistrates, but the *populus Romanus* ("the Roman people") played a role, too. This did not include women as they could not vote or hold office. In the Regal period, the "people's" influence seems to have been exerted through the Curiate Assembly, but little is known of its workings or responsibilities. With the advent of the Republic, the people are thought to have played a more prominent role. Rome's citizens, convened into assemblies by their elected magistrates, formed the body that elected the next year's magistrates and passed legislation. The Curiate Assembly of the Regal period was replaced by the wealth-based Centuriate Assembly, supplemented by the more egalitarian Tribal Assembly (see pp. 50–51). The Centuriate Assembly's key responsibility was the annual election of Rome's two consuls. It also assigned other important civic and military posts. The Tribal Assembly voted for the lower magistracies, election to which was crucial for admission to the Senate.

> "**Romulus** created a **hundred senators** ... called the **'Patres'** in virtue of **their rank**."
>
> LIVY'S HISTORY OF ROME, *AB URBE CONDITA*

These assemblies were the means by which Roman laws were made. Magistrates brought their proposals before the people, who would either ratify or reject them. This placed much power in the hands of the people, but Rome's elite still exercised a great deal of control. Magistrates or other officials could veto decisions or invalidate the assembly by declaring the omens were bad if decisions were not going their way. Most importantly, the Senate ensured that magistrates were aware of the negative consequences of proposing legislation that the Senate, although technically only an advisory body, had not scrutinized and rewritten first.

◁ **Roman democracy at work**
This silver *denarius* from 113–112 BCE shows citizens at election time. The figure on the right casts his vote as the man on the left receives his ballot from an attendant (center).

THE KING WHO **HELPED MAKE REPUBLICAN ROME**

Servius Tullius became Rome's sixth king in c. 578 BCE. He is traditionally associated with the introduction of the wide-ranging set of reforms known as the Servian Constitution. He kept the political bodies established by Romulus, particularly the Senate, and is said to have created the Centuriate Assembly and the Tribal system. These would play critical roles in how Rome was run and the way its officials were appointed throughout the Republican era that followed. Although he was one of Rome's kings, the social and political innovations he is said to have put in place paved the way for the Republic.

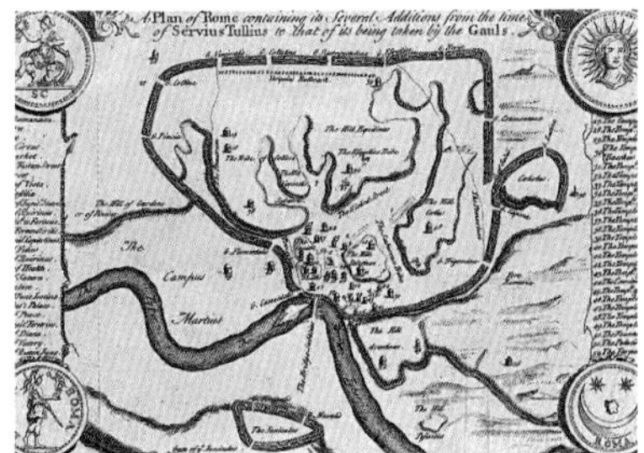

18TH-CENTURY MAP OF ROME WITH SITES FROM SERVIUS TULLIUS'S REIGN

The Potter's Art

Using ceramics in the Roman world

The Romans used pottery to eat from, to decorate their buildings, to ornament their homes, to transport commodities, and more. It was cheap to produce, easy to work with, versatile, and practical. Pottery finds have been invaluable in helping to date and piece together our knowledge of Roman history.

▷ **Clay oil lamp**
This is a 1st-century CE clay oil lamp. Olive oil was poured into the hole in the top and a wick was inserted into the spout. Many lamps were decorated with symbolic scenes.

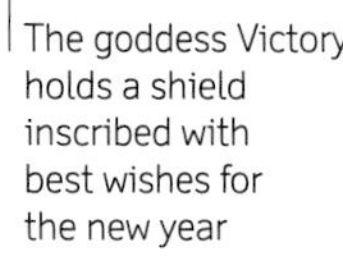

△ **Lotus and palm plaque**
This early terra-cotta piece from the 4th century BCE covered a wooden temple exterior. Made in a mold, it was originally brightly painted, and traces of red and blue paint can still be seen.

△ **Theatrical mask**
This tragedy mask from the 1st or 2nd century CE would have been worn by actors for stage performances. Using soft terra-cotta meant that details such as expressive eyebrows could be rendered.

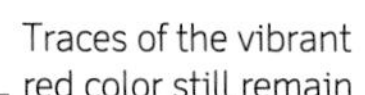

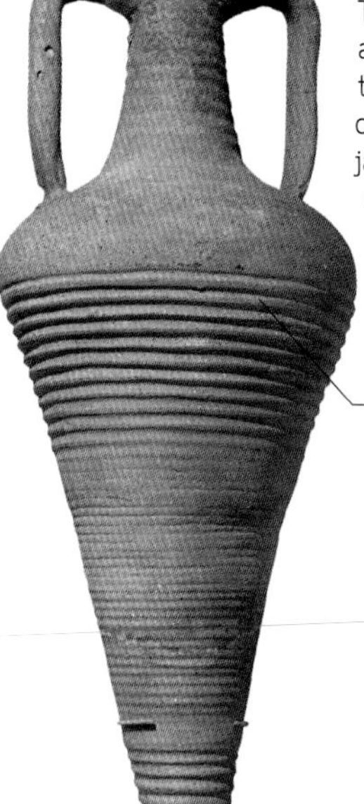

◁ **Red clay amphora**
This 3rd-century CE amphora was used to transport wine or olive oil by ship. The pointed jars were stacked on top of each other in transit.

▽ **Decorative terra-cotta head**
This sculpture of a panther head from the 1st century CE is in fact a waterspout and probably adorned a fountain in Rome. Panthers were associated with the god of wine, Bacchus, appearing with him in art.

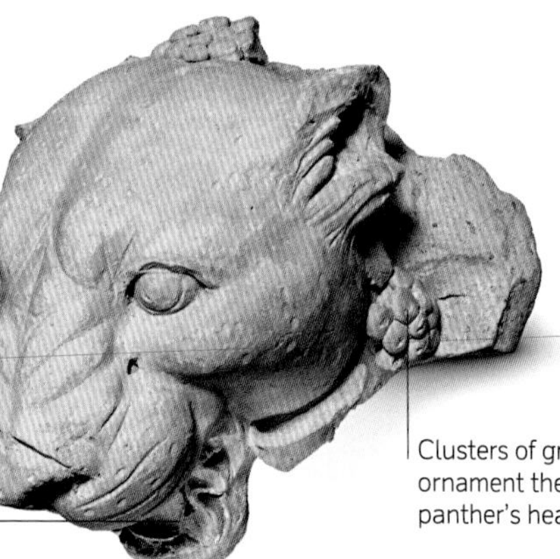

△ **Terra-cotta antefix**
Antefixes are ornamental pieces that anchor and protect a row of roof tiles. This painted Etruscan antefix from the 6th century BCE probably decorated a temple.

The figure wears earrings shaped like flower heads and a painted diadem headpiece

Terra sigillata was the most iconic pottery style used in the empire

◁ **Ceramic drinking cup**
Roman cups like this example from the 1st century CE were modeled on two-handled Greek vessels, or *skyphoi*. It is decorated with rosettes and leaves and finished in a green glaze.

△ **Glazed terra-cotta dish**
This dish from the 2nd century CE is a pottery type known as *terra sigillata*, or "sealed earth." It may be from Gaul and features figures affixed onto the sides that were molded in soft, watery clay known as barbotine.

◁ **Rooster flask**
Romans were fond of unusually shaped vessels, especially in the form of animals. This ceramic rooster from the Late Republic wears an ivy collar and has a spout and handle molded into its back. It was made in Campania, in southern Italy, and was found in central Greece.

Oenomaus was an ancestor of Agamemnon and Menelaus, leaders of the Greeks in the Trojan War

△ **Plaque of King Oenomaus**
Romans decorated their homes, temples, and public buildings with terra-cotta plaques depicting mythological scenes, like this one from the Late Republic.

Blue-green glaze achieved using lead and copper compounds

Lines, details, and patterns were scored into the wet clay

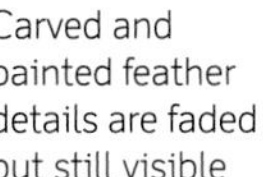

Carved and painted feather details are faded but still visible

△ **Ornamental amphora**
Unlike transportation amphorae, those made for home use had flat bottoms. They were often glazed and decorated, like this example from Roman Syria from the 2nd century CE.

△ **Figurine of a woman**
It is not known what this statuette from the 1st century CE was used for. It could be from a temple, or even be a simple copy of a more expensive bronze or marble figure.

Bacchus wears a cap surrounded by wreaths of ivy

△ **Terra-cotta herm of Bacchus**
Herms are square pillars topped with a head carving. This 1st-century CE example may have had some cultic function, but definite information about its use has not survived.

Early Religion

Rome's first religious institutions

Rome's earliest religious beliefs and institutions are shrouded in mystery: the first descriptions of them were written 700 years after the city was founded. But it is known that religion played a key role in Roman life from the city's foundation.

Roman historians believed that Romulus was an augur, a priest who divined the will of the gods by examining the flight paths of birds. In legend, it was this ability that led him to the site where he founded Rome. He was also believed to have instituted most of the city's important religious institutions. Numa Pompilius, the city's second king (see pp. 24–25), was credited with establishing most of the rest. While several different Roman religious institutions developed across the city's history, two of the earliest and most important were its temples and the Vestal Virgins.

The role of temples

Most temple buildings were the focus of worship for a divinity and contained cult statues of that particular god. However, all of that worship, including sacrifices and ceremonial offerings, took place outside the temple. Aside from their cult statues, temple interiors were generally used to store artworks, trophies, and treasures won in battle.

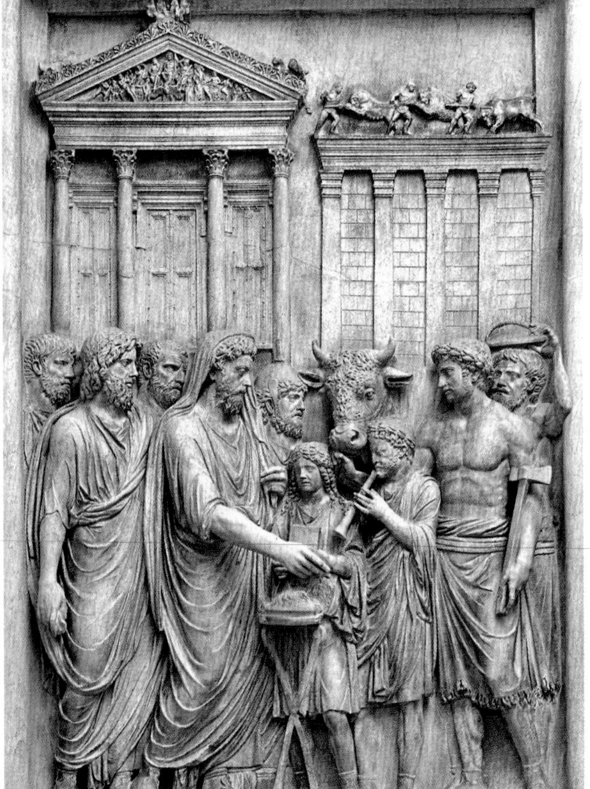

◁ **Temple of Jupiter**
This relief (2nd century CE) shows the emperor Marcus Aurelius making a sacrifice. The Temple of Jupiter Optimus Maximus is behind him.

The largest and most ancient building of worship in Rome was the Temple of Jupiter Optimus Maximus on the Capitoline Hill. Allegedly begun by the fifth legendary king of Rome, Lucius Tarquinius Priscus (see pp. 24–25), the temple was dedicated to the worship of three deities: Jupiter, Juno, and Minerva. It was destroyed by fire in 83 BCE, 69 CE, and 80 CE (it was rebuilt each time). The Temple of Jupiter was the first of thousands of temples built in Rome and across the empire. Unlike Greek temples, which could be approached from any side, Roman temples were front-facing, with stairs leading up to the temple doors flanked by a porch of many columns. While the remains of all standing temples in Rome are stone structures, in the city's earliest period they would probably have been made of wood, clay, and thatch.

Vestal Virgins

There was a legend that the institution of the Vestal Virgins was older than Rome itself: Rhea Silvia, the mother of Romulus and Remus, was said to have been a Vestal impregnated by the god Mars. Other sources suggest Numa Pompilius established their office.

Six priestesses devoted to the goddess of the hearth, Vesta, the Vestal Virgins were charged with keeping the eternal flame of Rome burning in the Temple of Vesta in the center of the Forum. It was believed that if the fire was extinguished, Rome would fall. Negligent Vestals who let the fire go out were punished harshly, but not as harshly as those who

> "Now **roofed in bronze**, in that **long distant time** they would have been **thatch roofed**."
>
> OVID, ON THE EVOLUTION OF ROME'S TEMPLES

◁ **Chief of the Vestals**
This statue of Flavia Publicia, chief of the Vestals, from the 3rd century CE, depicts the Vestal in her distinctive costume. A touching epitaph to Flavia accompanies this statue, honoring her for being "most sacred, and most holy."

The Vestals' elaborate headdress was made up of long loops of woolen material

△ **Temples in the Forum**
The Roman Forum was the site of many temples. These still-standing columns once belonged to the temples of Saturn (left) and Castor and Pollux (right).

broke their vows of chastity. Selected for service between the ages of six and ten, Vestals were required to uphold their chastity for a minimum of 30 years, after which they were free to leave the order. Most, however, stayed on and served Vesta until they died.

Vestals risked accusations of unchastity at any moment, and some were accused of breaking this vow when things were going badly for Rome. If found guilty, unchaste Vestals were buried alive, but proving their innocence was difficult. In the 3rd century BCE, the Vestal Tuccia was accused of unchastity and appealed to Vesta for help in miraculously carrying water in a sieve from the Tiber to her temple without spilling any, to prove her innocence. When she successfully did this, the allegations against her were withdrawn.

Despite their precarious status, Vestals were among the most important and privileged women in Roman society. They were given special seats in the theater; could own property; wrote their own wills; and were preceded in public by officials known as lictors, who forced crowds to part before them. In the early empire, some of the most important women of the imperial family, such as Livia and Octavia (Augustus's wife and sister, respectively), were honored by being allowed to share the privileges of Vestals. The order lasted until 394 CE, when it was ended by Theodosius I.

The Latin Language

The evolution of the language of the empire

Latin was the main language used by the Roman state, and that has left a tremendous legacy. As well as being the foundation of other languages, Latin is still directly used in the lexicons of law, medicine, religion, and science.

Latin is an Italian language that seems to have originated in the region of Latium—a flat coastal plain (Latium means "flat land") between the Tiber River to the north, the Apennines to the east, and the Pontine marshes and Monti Lepini to the south. Latin was originally one of many languages used in Italy but became the dominant language through its association with the Roman state. It was exported across both the Mediterranean region and northern Europe as part of Rome's imperial structures. Latin also helped shape many modern European languages, including Italian, Spanish, and French.

The development of Latin

Although we know very little about the language until the 3rd century BCE, Latin was likely to have been used from at least the 8th century BCE. All of our evidence for the early period comes from short inscriptions, written using an alphabetic script that was probably acquired through interactions with Greeks, Phoenicians, and Etruscans as part of trade. We know that longer inscriptions existed in the early periods, particularly laws and treaties, although these no longer survive. Roman authors often commented

◁ **Diploma**
This fragment of a bronze military diploma, c. 113–114 CE, documents in Latin the discharge of sailors from a warship at Misenum by Trajan.

that early Latin was sometimes difficult for them to read and understand. During the 3rd and 2nd centuries BCE, there was a sudden boom in Latin, linked to Rome's rise to power, since Latin was the language associated with Rome's emerging empire. Although the evidence is still fragmentary, it shows that longer texts were being produced in this period.

By the Late Republic, Latin had become the official language of the Italian peninsula. Its skillful use could bring fame and fortune even to those born far from Rome's walls, whether they were orators like Cicero (see pp. 118–119) or poets like Virgil.

In the Imperial era, Latin became increasingly widespread as the language of state, although in the east it continued to share space with Greek among the elite. The style of Latin continued to evolve, but in this period, Romans still regarded the Late Republic as the "Golden Age" of the language.

Over time, Latin slowly evolved into regional dialects. As the various regions of the empire started to become less connected, these regional dialects grew more pronounced and eventually became the Romance languages. Latin later developed into the more academic forms of medieval Latin and Renaissance Latin, which became a shared language of the educated elite across Europe.

◁ **Tombstone**
The Latin inscription on this tombstone from c. 80 BCE is written in verse and describes the relationship of Lucius Aurelius Hermia and his wife Aurelia Philematium, who were freed from slavery and stayed together more than 30 years.

The letter is written on papyrus, made from the woven pith of the papyrus plant

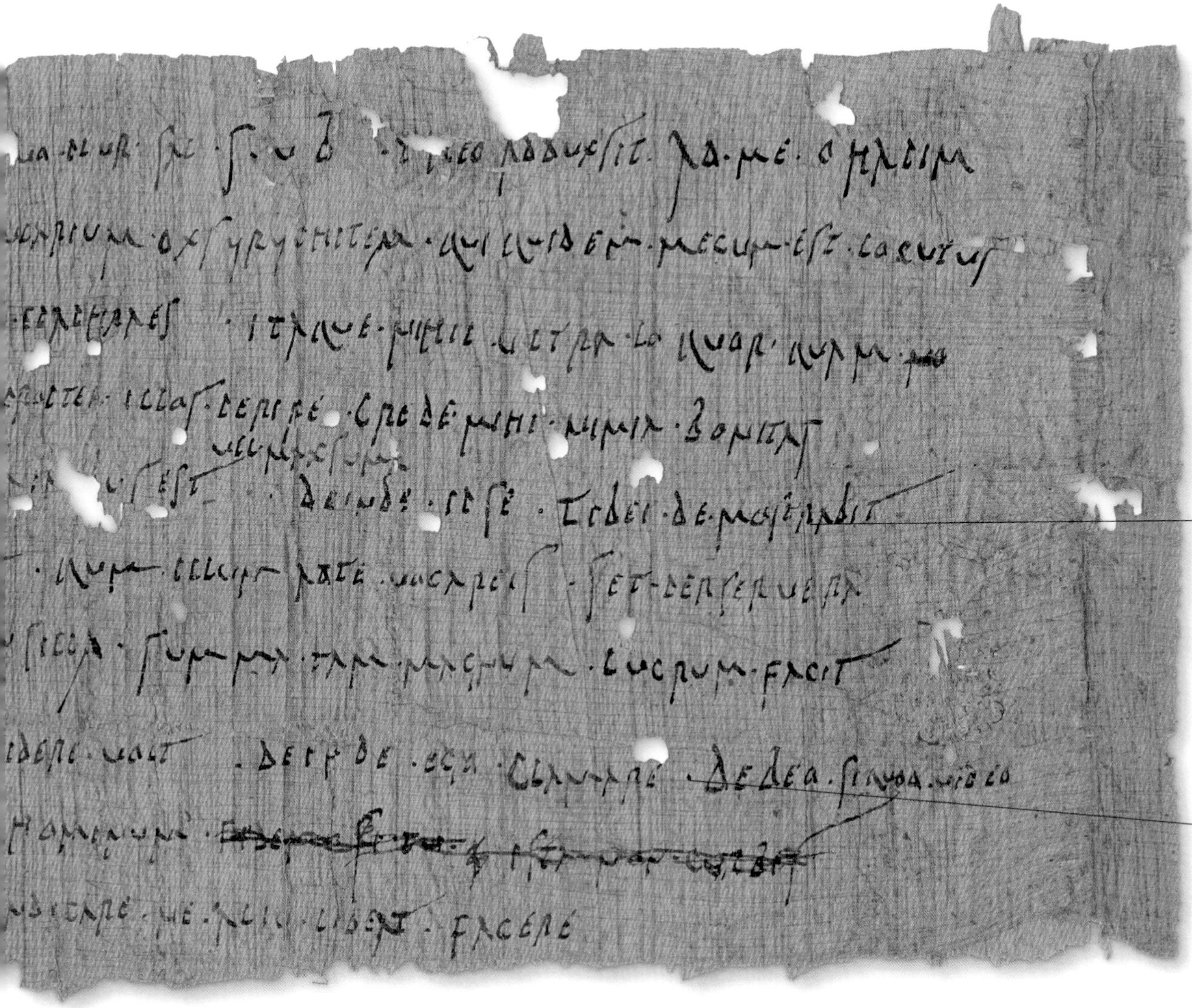

◁ **Oxyrhynchus Papyri**
This letter is from a man called Syneros to "Chius (slave) of Caesar," written during the reign of Augustus. It is one of the few Latin letters to have survived in the "capitalis cursive" script, used for informal purposes in the 1st–3rd centuries BCE.

Text probably written by a scribe

Words separated by dots instead of spaces

Multilingualism

The Latin of ancient Italy was part of a rich linguistic landscape, where other languages (especially Greek, but also Oscan and other Italic dialects) were vitally important. It is likely that most people in the ancient world spoke more than one language—perhaps three, four, or more. The choice to write in Latin was probably a social and cultural one. Interestingly, the most important early Latin authors were not from Rome itself—most notably the poet Ennius (c. 239–169 BCE), who was of Greek descent and spoke Greek, Latin, and Oscan. Publication and dissemination of works by these writers helped standardize the language.

EARLIEST INSCRIPTION IN ITALY

The "Duenos inscription" is one of the earliest examples of the Latin language, although the exact date of the inscription is uncertain. The remarkably long inscription is on a *kernos*, or triple vase, and is written right to left (retrograde) in three parts. The artifact was found in the 19th century in Rome while workmen were digging foundations. The letters seem to be an Italian version of the Greek alphabet, but there is no separation between the words, making translation difficult. One of the words that has been identified is *duenos*, which is an archaic version of the Latin *bonus*, meaning "good." Some interpretations suggest that the text on the vase may refer to marriage.

INSCRIPTION ON *KERNOS* VASE

The Birth of the Republic

From tyranny to oligarchy

Rome's transition from regal rule to Republic was a defining event in the state's history. The "official" story of how it happened may or may not be true, but it reveals much about the Romans' attitude to power—and who should wield it.

Looking back from his vantage point in the early 2nd century CE, the Roman historian Tacitus identified 509 BCE as the moment Rome won its *libertas*, or freedom, and embarked on its journey to greatness. This was the year when Tarquinius Superbus, the city's final *rex*, or king, was removed and the republican system instituted.

The freedom and greatness Tacitus described did not apply to all Romans. For most of the city's inhabitants, the replacement of one king with several republican leaders meant very little, and their lives continued much as they had before. For those at the top of Roman society, however, the new system offered tremendous opportunities.

◁ **Silver *Libertas* coin**
Marcus Junius Brutus issued this *denarius* in 54 BCE to honor his namesake and founder of the Republic. Ten years later, Brutus killed Julius Caesar while trying to "save" the Republic.

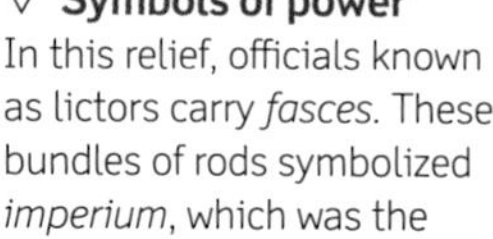

▽ **Symbols of power**
In this relief, officials known as lictors carry *fasces*. These bundles of rods symbolized *imperium*, which was the power exercised by kings and, later, consuls.

The official version of events

The traditional narrative of the fall of the monarchy is that of a righteous uprising against a tyrannical ruler. As king, Tarquinius was portrayed by writers such as Livy in his history of Rome—*Ab Urbe Condita*, written more than 450 years later—as a classic villain. He came to power by murdering the king, Servius Tullius (who was also his father-in-law), and held onto it by oppressing Rome's elites. Matters came to a head when his son, Sextus Tarquinius, raped Lucretia, the wife of a prominent Roman named Lucius Collatinus. Lucretia asked her husband and a group of his friends to avenge her and then took her own life. In response, Collatinus's kinsman Lucius Junius Brutus led a coup that seized control of Rome while the king was away. Brutus called the new form of government he established the *res publica* (literally, "the public thing") and was installed as its joint leader with Collatinus. With the notable exception of Lucretia, Rome's republican revolution had been virtually bloodless. Despite attempts by Tarquinius over the years to retake power, the Republic endured.

While this narrative is at best highly mythologized, it is significant that it presents Lucretia as among the first in a long line of influential women in Roman history who shaped events through both their life and their death. Although Roman society was deeply patriarchal and male-dominated, women were often described—albeit by male writers and for a male audience—as active participants in key events. The portrayal of Lucretia's role in the fall of the monarchy not only played on Roman conceptions of honor, but also highlighted the importance of family and kinship networks in the city's political life.

Different but similar

Apart from the king's authority being divided between two new leaders, traditionally called consuls (although they were possibly called praetors at first), there seems to have been very little difference in the governmental systems of the early Republic and the Regal period. All of Rome's main political institutions, such as the Senate and the assemblies (see pp. 28–29), appear to have carried on working as they did before. As a result, the people who benefited most from the change in leadership were Rome's elites, who now had more opportunities to gain high office through the

△ **Avenging Lucretia**
Casto Plasencia's *Origin of the Roman Republic* (1877) depicts the legendary moment described in Livy's *Ab Urbe Condita* where, after Lucretia's death, Brutus holds her knife aloft and swears to free Rome of the tyrannical king, Tarquinius Superbus.

annual elections that took place. As the city grew, new elites joined Roman society, creating competition for positions of power that fostered a more dynamic system than under the kings and slowly increased the power of the assemblies.

Separating myth from reality

While the creation of the Republic might have been the result of the rule of a tyrannical king, an act of violation by his son, and an uprising of the elites, this was more likely a tale the Romans told themselves that dramatized a far more mundane origin story. During the final century of the monarchy, Rome underwent a marked transformation—one that is visible in the archaeological record, which shows how the settlement in the 6th century BCE grew to such a size that it became too large and too important for a single family to control. This may have led to a conflict between the king and the city's leading families that ended in the abolition of the monarchy. Regal rule was replaced by a power-sharing arrangement among the elite, working with the assemblies and the Senate and utilizing the new, annually elected consulships. This regular rotation of power among the elite families became the basis of republican rule.

The story of Lucretia, Tarquinius, Collatinus, and Brutus formed a key part of Roman identity, especially for the elites; it took on a new importance in the last decades of the Republic, when another Brutus took up arms to help remove another "tyrant," Julius Caesar (see pp. 128–129).

> "Junius Brutus ... was **most resolute** in **dethroning the Tarquins**."
>
> PLUTARCH, *LIFE OF BRUTUS*

◁ **Bronze musician**
From the 4th century BCE, this ornament shows a musician holding a lyre, an instrument often associated with Greece. Its use here perhaps reflects Rome's growing contacts with the wider Mediterranean world during that period.

2

The Roman Republic

509–133 BCE

From City-State to Superpower

With the monarchy overthrown, the Romans now had to decide who they were. Rome was at this point a relatively modest city-state, one of several in central Italy. It was not as sophisticated or as powerful as the established Greek colonies of southern Italy and Sicily, such as Syracuse or Capua. Its future success was not a foregone conclusion. Yet during the Republic, from 509 BCE to 27 BCE, Rome built an empire that spread across the Italian peninsula and dominated the entire western Mediterranean. The question is: how?

Conflict resolution

From the outset, the main occupation for Roman men was soldiering. Hard-won victories against Etruscans, Samnites, and the Latin League saw Rome gain preeminence in Italy. The city then extended treaties, rights, and citizenship to neighboring communities in exchange for their support in wars which ranged farther afield. The most significant of these were the long-running Punic Wars against Carthage. Rome's decisive victory in this conflict at Zama in 202 BCE established its hegemony in the Mediterranean.

Although written records play an important role in how the Republic is understood, the sources of Roman literature date from 240 BCE, more than 250 years after the Republic was founded. Accounts by later authors of how the Republic was established were colored by the events and concerns of their own age. A consistent theme was the clash between the patricians (the dynastic elite families) and the plebeians, who protested against their ill-treatment and demanded a greater role in government. Linked to this was the issue of how to balance the increasing monopolization of land by a small elite with the Republic's ongoing need for soldiers, who at that time had to be property-owners.

An empire built to order

Culturally, the Republic borrowed from other civilizations even as it conquered them. Roman authors wrote in dialogue with Greek literature, and the earliest surviving Latin literature consists of translated Greek comedies performed at religious festivals alongside games and music. Greek models also influenced Roman law, religion, and architecture. Like Greece and its other Mediterranean neighbors, Rome was by any measure a slave society, in the number of enslaved people, their contribution to the economy, and the proportion of the population who owned them. No consideration of the innovations of the Roman Republic nor of the speed of its growth, particularly in public building and infrastructure, can afford to ignore that this was only made possible by enslaved labor.

Life for the Roman elite in the Mid- and Late Republican periods reached heights of luxury that were unimaginable at the Republic's inception. That magnificence, along with the need to reward Roman citizens for their contributions to the state's growth, came at a high cost to subject peoples in the provinces. As the Roman Republic subsidized corn for its citizens and reduced or removed their taxes, the inhabitants of territories conquered by the armies of Rome and its allies saw the better portion of their resources confiscated to pay for their new masters' civilization.

◁ **Roman statue of the Greek hero Hercules**

494 BCE Struggle of the Orders begins; the plebs leave Rome in protest at patrician privilege

450 BCE The Twelve Tables are issued, codifying Roman law, rights, and responsibilities

390 BCE The Gauls sack Rome after defeating the Romans at the Battle of the Allia

316 BCE A Roman army is forced to surrender at the Battle of the Caudine Forks

312 BCE The Appian Way and the Appian aqueduct are initiated

287 BCE Struggle of the Orders ends with plebeians and patricians agreeing a settlement

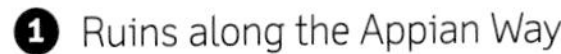

❶ Ruins along the Appian Way

❷ Carthage, destroyed then rebuilt by Rome

❸ Roman amphitheater in Syracuse, Sicily

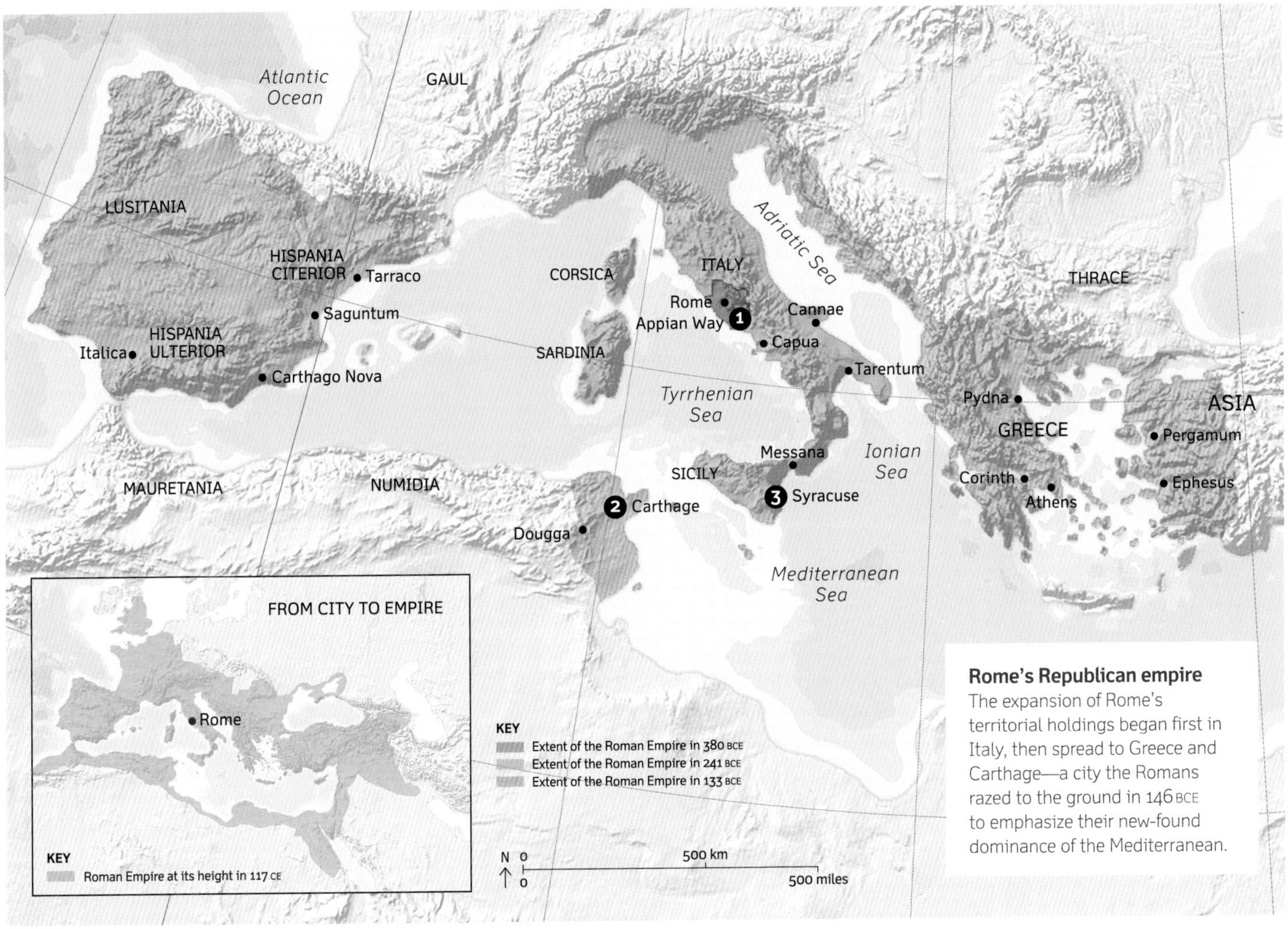

Atlantic Ocean
GAUL
LUSITANIA
HISPANIA CITERIOR
Tarraco
Saguntum
HISPANIA ULTERIOR
Italica
Carthago Nova
CORSICA
SARDINIA
ITALY
Adriatic Sea
Rome
Appian Way ❶
Cannae
Capua
Tarentum
Tyrrhenian Sea
THRACE
Pydna
GREECE
ASIA
Pergamum
Ephesus
Corinth
Athens
Ionian Sea
Messana
SICILY
❸ Syracuse
MAURETANIA
NUMIDIA
❷ Carthage
Dougga
Mediterranean Sea

FROM CITY TO EMPIRE
Rome
KEY
Roman Empire at its height in 117 CE

KEY
Extent of the Roman Empire in 380 BCE
Extent of the Roman Empire in 241 BCE
Extent of the Roman Empire in 133 BCE

N
0 500 km
0 500 miles

Rome's Republican empire
The expansion of Rome's territorial holdings began first in Italy, then spread to Greece and Carthage—a city the Romans razed to the ground in 146 BCE to emphasize their new-found dominance of the Mediterranean.

275 BCE After several costly victories, Pyrrhus of Epirus abandons his Italian allies to Roman rule

241 BCE First Punic War ends with Rome's naval victory at the Battle of the Aegates Islands

240 BCE Livius Andronicus stages the first play in Latin, rather than Greek, in Rome

216 BCE Hannibal crushes the Romans at the Battle of Cannae

206 BCE Italica, the first Roman settlement outside Italy, is founded in Spain

202 BCE Hannibal's defeat by Scipio at the Battle of Zama ends the Second Punic war

168 BCE Victory over Perseus of Macedonia at the Battle of Pydna leaves Rome supreme in Greece

146 BCE Rome sacks Carthage and Corinth. Its mastery of the Mediterranean is complete

Patricians and Plebeians

The caste system in ancient Rome

Everybody knew their place in Republican Rome. The aristocratic elites justified their position as ordained by Romulus, while the common people embarked on a long, slow fight to secure their rights—and their share of the spoils of conquest.

△ **A giving goddess**
Ceres, shown with Bacchus in this 1st-century CE fresco, was (with Liber and Libera) one of the "Aventine Triad," a trio of deities popular with Rome's plebeians. From the triad's temple on the Aventine Hill, officials known as aediles oversaw tasks including the distribution of food among the plebeians.

For much of the Republican Era, social and political life was characterized by tension and occasional open rivalries between the state's two "classes": the aristocratic patricians and the plebeians comprising the lower orders.

The original patricians were by legend the 100 men Romulus appointed as Rome's first senators. They were the heads of Rome's leading families, each one a *paterfamilias*, or *pater* ("father"), from which the word patrician derived. The group grew as Rome expanded, but membership was always exclusive, selective, and hereditary.

The plebeians, or plebs, were Rome's commoners. That is not to say they were "the poor." Many were, but some were relatively wealthy. The distinction between patrician and plebeian was always about more than money.

The fight for plebeian rights

As Rome's territories increased, tensions sharpened between patricians and plebeians. War and conquest enriched the patricians, but the plebeian farmers who made up most of the Roman army fared less well. Soldiers from the lower orders took time away from their homesteads to fight in the wars with Rome's neighbors and bore the brunt of the combat. Unscrupulous patrician generals failed to reward them with their fair share of war booty and conquered territory. Plebeians who took out loans to see them through resulting times of economic hardship could easily find themselves joining the ranks of the enslaved if they failed to pay back their creditors, a situation known as debt bondage.

In 494 BCE, Rome's plebs protested at their plight by leaving the city and decamping to the Sacred Mount, an hour's walk away. They returned only after a new magistracy was established to protect their interests: the Tribune of the Plebs. Although the ten annually elected tribunes often clashed with the patrician-controlled Senate—in later years sometimes violently (see pp. 104–105)—the office provided a legitimate channel for plebeian grievances. Patrician and plebeian rights and duties were further clarified in the Twelve Tables of 450 BCE, the first great codification of Roman law (see pp. 50–51). While in no way threatening the patricians' dominance, the new laws abolished debt bondage and established property rights and judicial procedures that addressed some of the plebs' most pressing concerns. This whole period was later known as "The Conflict of the Orders."

Political organizations

The road to greater equality remained bumpy, however. As late as 81 BCE the patrician dictator Sulla briefly succeeded in removing the most basic powers of the tribunes, and in 64 BCE the lower orders were further degraded as a ban was placed on the *collegia*, the tradesmen's guilds that operated within plebeian communities. These guilds were restored in 58 BCE by Clodius, a renegade patrician who had renounced his status to be elected a tribune of the plebs. Like many of the people's champions, Clodius met a violent death—murdered by his rival Milo, with his body dumped on the side of the Appian Way, a road built for Rome's foot soldiers by his ancestor Appius Claudius Caecus.

◁ **The *subsellium*, or tribunes' bench**
This coin from 55 BCE was struck in honor of Palicanus, a tribune of the plebs. It shows the bench in the Forum where tribunes sat during the day to arbitrate in disputes.

▽ **Grain measurers at work**
This mosaic from Ostia, from the 2nd century CE, shows men from the *collegium*, or guild, controlling the port's grain supply. One figure is smaller than the others to indicate he is an enslaved worker.

The *mensor* ("grain measurer") holds a leveling stick

A single measure of grain weighed about 14½lb (7kg)

"It was owing to [the patricians'] **artful canvassing** that the plebeians found the **road to office** blocked."

LIVY, *AB URBE CONDITA*

APPIUS CLAUDIUS CAECUS THE CENSOR

In 312 BCE Appius Claudius Caecus was elected to the important office of censor (see pp. 86–87). He angered most of his fellow patricians by giving urban plebs more voting power in Rome; he also levied taxes on the newly enfranchised plebs, which upset some of them, too. The debate continues about whether his reforms were driven by a democratic impulse, to win support among the plebs, or to raise income—or a combination of all three. Appius famously built Rome's first aqueduct and first main road, the Appian Way. His surname Caecus meant "blind," and to later Romans the sightless Appius personified the ideal of a just and impartial moralist. This painting from 1888, by Cesare Maccari, shows Appius as a respected elder statesman being led into the Senate by his sons.

The head of Medusa, a popular Greek and Roman motif, sits prominently on Alexander's breastplate

Alexander is shown without a helmet, to emphasize his bravery

Alexander's horse, Bucephalus, was considered untamable—until Alexander tamed him

Alexander wields the traditional Macedonian sarissa, a 20-ft (6-m) spear

△ The Alexander Mosaic
Livy began his great history of Rome by asking: what if Alexander the Great had led his armies west into Italy rather than east against Persia? Italy's fascination with the Macedonian Greek Alexander is evident in this magnificent Pompeiian mosaic from c. 100 BCE. Made from around 1.5 million tiny colored tiles, or tesserae, it depicts Alexander fighting against the Persians at the Battle of Issus (333 BCE).

"**Captive Greece** took captive her **fierce conqueror** and introduced her **arts** into **rude Latium**."

HORACE, POET AND COURTIER TO AUGUSTUS

A Conqueror Conquered

Rome's love-hate relationship with the Greek world

The art and culture of the Mediterranean, including that of Rome, was shaped by the city-states of the ancient Greeks. The spread of Rome's empire went hand-in-hand with its emulation of (and competition with) Greece's cultural ascendancy.

When Roman authors from the Late Republican period onward tried to explain the perceived degeneracy of the times in which they lived, they often blamed it on their state's conquest of Greece (see pp. 76–77) and the subsequent importation of Greek art into the city of Rome. In reality, Rome had been closely engaged with Greek culture from its earliest days. At some times this was celebrated as beating the Greeks at their own game; at others it was reviled as a dilution of Rome's cultural essence.

◁ **Unique style**
This *rhyton*, or cup, shows a style of vase painting developed by Greeks living in Apulia, in southern Italy, that differed to the Greek pottery imported into Italy.

Cultural spread

By the time Rome emerged as a major power in Italy it was already well acquainted with Greek life and culture. There had been Greek colonies in the south of Italy and Sicily since the 8th century BCE, resulting in a long-standing cultural exchange between the two civilizations. This ongoing contact is one reason why the Romans largely avoided being labeled by the Greeks with the derogatory appellation they used for non-Greek-speaking peoples: *barbaroi*, or "barbarians." Several of Rome's foundation myths, notably the story of Aeneas's arrival in Latium from Troy (see pp. 22–23), were embedded in Greek mythology, and the two cultures worshipped most of the same deities—albeit under different names. Rome's imperial expansion in the 3rd century BCE saw its temples, already indebted to Greek architecture, fill with art plundered from Greek cities across the Mediterranean. This happened alongside another form of cultural competition unique to Rome: the translation and adaptation of Greek literature into Latin. The actors who performed in Italy's theaters wore masks originally crafted for Greek plays, but now they declaimed the verses in Latin to their audiences. No other Mediterranean culture so boldly claimed to have supplanted the Greeks within their own former sphere of influence.

Power and prestige

The increasingly "Greek" appearance of Roman public life was not universally endorsed. The moralist Cato the Elder rarely missed an opportunity to upbraid his fellow Romans in public for their descent into "soft" Greek ways. The author Lucullus, in the 1st century BCE, followed the Roman tradition of writing his history in Greek, but dotted it with deliberate grammatical errors to signal his Roman identity. Some Roman generals, though schooled in Greek from an early age, insisted on addressing conquered Greeks in Latin and would receive their replies only through an interpreter. These actions, and the Roman stereotyping of Greeks as servile, deceptive, effeminate flatterers, arose in part from the conquerors' discomfort in acknowledging the cultural debt they owed to the conquered.

△ **Greek influence**
In legend, the Greek demigod Hercules made the site of Rome habitable by killing the monster Cacus. This temple in Rome from around the 2nd century BCE was dedicated and built in the Classical Greek style—a round structure, with Corinthian columns—and made from Greek marble.

HADRIAN AND ANTINOUS

Emperor Hadrian's great love of all things Hellenic (relating to Greece) found its most literal expression in his relationship with his Greek lover, Antinous. In Antinous's lifetime, and even more so after his drowning in the Nile in 130 CE, Hadrian used Greek cultural modes to celebrate their relationship. In literature, art, and religion, Hadrian analogized their love to that between the historical Alexander the Great and his general Hephaestion, and the mythical Achilles and Patroclus. In imitation of Greek hero cults (alien to Roman traditions), Hadrian set up sites of worship to his dead lover, and founded a city in Egypt in his name.

MARBLE PORTRAITS OF HADRIAN (LEFT) AND ANTINOUS (RIGHT)

Theater, Music, Dance

Performing in public and private

A sophisticated understanding of the beauty of music and dance was at the heart of Roman theater, but also pervaded religious festivals, processions, and home lives. In all of these areas, contact with the Greek-speaking world influenced the performances, although the result remained distinctively Roman.

Music and dance

Dancers and musicians performed at religious festivals and rites, funerals, or as part of private entertainments. Musicians played a variety of instruments, including a harp-like lyre and its larger cousin, the kithara; the tibia (a V-shaped double flute); percussion instruments; and brass instruments such as the long-necked Roman tuba and the spiral-shaped cornu.

Although much is known about the instruments, it is unclear what Roman music sounded like, as it was largely an aural tradition. No musical notation system has survived, but the words of a type of hymnic chant, called a *carmen*, have been found in ancient Latin texts. These verses had many purposes, such as prayer, poetry, and spells for good fortune, and were often synchronized with a dance. For example, the "leaping" priests of Mars, known as the Salii, walked through the streets of Rome in suits of armor, stopping at certain points to repeat hymns and perform sacred dances. While the Salii belonged to the elite and their choreography was highly formal, most dance in Rome was for entertainment and was undertaken by enslaved or lower order performers.

△ **Backstage at the theater**
In this mosaic from Pompeii, a *choregos* (an Athenian patron) addresses actors. Pompeii had two stone theaters, built decades before Rome's first permanent theaters. It is likely that Pompeii's theater-goers saw themselves as successors to the Athenians.

△ **Face to face with the audience**
So audiences in large theaters could see characters more easily, and to allow actors to take on more than one role in a play, performers wore large masks with exaggerated features made of painted linen, wax, wood, clay, and leather. The masks' hollow design also amplified the actors' voices.

△ **A dance for the departed**
Chain dances performed by groups of women were a feature of Etruscan funerals in particular. This 4th-century BCE fresco from Ruvo, in southern Italy, indicates that the tradition was known about, and perhaps practiced, in other parts of the peninsula.

> "No one **dances sober**, unless he happens to be **insane**."
>
> CICERO, *PRO MURENA*

Roman theater

The first recorded theatrical performance in Rome was in 364 BCE. It was a set of speeches and dances set to music, and was part of the *Ludi Romani*, or Roman Games—a religious festival of athletics and hunting. The earliest recognizable dramas—plays performed on stage—originated in Athens in the 5th century BCE as part of festivals honoring the god Dionysus. Drama was introduced to Italy via Greek colonists. Livius Andronicus, a native of Tarentum (a Greek colony city in southern Italy), translated Homer's *Odyssey* into Latin and premiered an adaption of a Greek play at the *Ludi Romani* in 240 BCE. His plays were staged on temporary wooden structures, which were modeled on Greek semicircular stone theaters found in Sicily. Only a few fragments of Roman tragedies still exist. What they show is that playwrights such as Ennius in the 2nd century BCE used Greek writers including Aeschylus, Sophocles, and Euripides as their models. By creating a tradition of theater, the Romans separated themselves from other Italic peoples, believing that their own language was worthy of great literary works—a sign of a culture growing in confidence.

Theaters were largely male spaces. Plays were written and performed almost exclusively by men, while seating at the theater was segregated by sex to give male viewers the best seats. Consequences of this were the troublingly frequent references to sexual assault and violence against female and enslaved characters, which were often presented for comic effect.

△ **Bacchic dancers**
The Bacchanalia was a riotous Roman festival that honored the god of wine. Such was its reputation for drunken dancing and revelry that it was banned in 186 BCE. This 2nd-century CE mosaic shows how its popularity persisted nevertheless.

△ **Entertainers for hire**
Wearing a mask and holding a tambourine-like drum, this man was probably part of a traveling troupe that sold its skills to theaters and worked as street performers. Music and theater were popular across the empire, but actors, musicians, and dancers were not held in high esteem and usually came from the lower orders.

△ **Inspirational goddess**
Drama, music, dance, and poetry were popular subjects for mosaics. In this one from Augusta Treverorum (Trier in modern Germany), Erato, the Greek Muse of lyric poetry, holds a lyre. Erato was one of the nine Muses representing different aspects of the arts.

Gods and Goddesses

The deities of Rome's pantheon

Roman society was polytheistic, worshipping a variety of deities of different types. Many had Greek counterparts, for example Mercury. Sometimes they personified virtues and qualities (Honor, Liberty, etc.), or were deified mortals, particularly emperors. Across the empire, people were also allowed to worship their own divinities.

This hand once held a scepter that is now missing

▷ Juno
Worshipped mainly by women, Juno protected Rome and its empire. Her sacred geese reputedly honked when the Gauls attempted a surprise attack on the city in the 4th century BCE (see p. 50).

This hand would have originally held a spear

Exotic symbols of conquest adorn Mars's helmet, breastplate, and sandals

This figure is shown as *Mars Ultor*, or Mars the Avenger, in full military uniform

◁ Mars
As a society founded on conquest, the Romans particularly venerated Mars, the god of war, who according to legend was also the father of Romulus.

Figures of Minerva often show her wearing an animal-skin *aegis*, or breastplate, with a gorgon's head

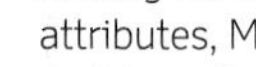

◁ Minerva
Among her many attributes, Minerva was goddess of wisdom, law, victory, arts, crafts, and war. She is often depicted helmeted, holding a spear and with her iconic owl.

Bronze statuette dating from the 2nd century CE

A winged cap signifies his other role as messenger of the gods

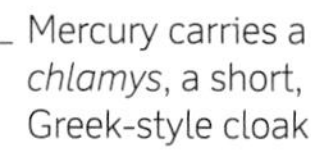

Mercury carries a *chlamys*, a short, Greek-style cloak

▷ Mercury
The trickster Mercury was the god of commerce and shopkeepers and was often shown holding a bag of money. Mercury was also believed to guide souls of the dead to the underworld.

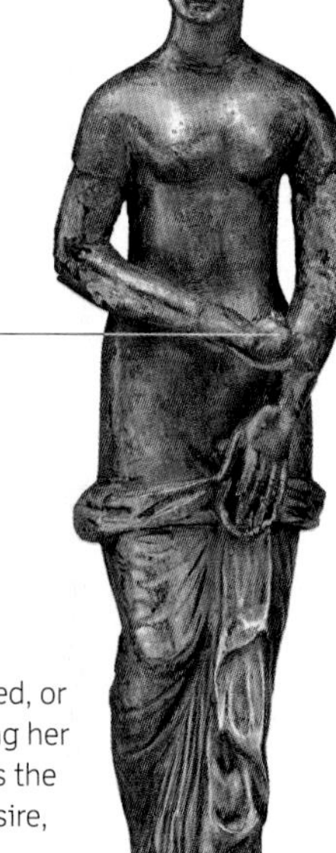

The apple is the prize Venus was awarded by the Trojan prince Paris for being the most beautiful of all goddesses

▷ Venus
Often depicted naked, or half-heartedly hiding her modesty, Venus was the goddess of love, desire, and fertility. Julius Caesar claimed Venus as his ancestor.

◁ **Jupiter**
Often seen with an eagle and holding a thunderbolt or scepter, Jupiter was Rome's principal god. Major decisions were made only with Jupiter's "approval," oaths were sworn in his name, and military victories were attributed to him.

◁ **Neptune**
The dolphin at his feet symbolizes Neptune's role as protector of water and the sea. His temple near Rome's racetrack also showed his devotion to horses.

▷ **Hercules**
Counterpart of the Greek hero Heracles, this demigod was the bringer of civilization in many Italic foundation myths. He is shown here holding his knobbed club.

◁ **Bacchus**
The god of wine includes elements of the Greek deity Dionysus and *Liber Pater* ("the Free Father"), a divinity worshipped by the people of Latium.

▽ **Roma**
As the personification of the city of Rome, depictions of Roma shared features with Minerva and Victory. She was most often shown as a powerful, militaristic deity.

◁ **Epona**
A Celtic deity, Epona was the protectress of horses. She became popular among the Roman cavalry, who brought her worship back to Rome from Gaul.

◁ **Magna Mater**
Originating from Phrygia in Anatolia, the *Magna Mater* ("Great Mother") is enthroned on a cart drawn by lions. Her self-castrated priests led wild, ecstatic forms of worship.

People and Power

Early Rome's laws and institutions

Although Rome had no written constitution, it did have a system of offices, laws, and practices that were strictly adhered to. Most of these favored wealthy landowners and patricians; plebeian rights were harder won.

△ **Capitoline Brutus**
This bronze bust is thought to represent Brutus, one of Rome's first two consuls. It was found on the Capitoline Hill and was made between the 4th and 1st centuries BCE.

After Rome's monarchy was ended (see pp. 36–37), the powers formerly held by the king were shared between two consuls, while his council of ministers became the Senate, which debated policy and drew up laws. Its legislation had to be approved by a vote of Rome's sovereign body, the *populus Romanus* ("the people of Rome"). All citizens could vote, but not everybody did. Each voting assembly was announced with just three days' notice and this was often not long enough for those who lived far away and who traveled on foot—overwhelmingly Rome's poorer citizens—to arrive on time. Women and Rome's enslaved population could not vote at all.

Republican Rome had two main assemblies. Major decisions and the annual elections of higher officials on the *cursus honorum* (see pp. 86–87) were made in the Centuriate Assembly. It was controlled by Rome's wealthier citizens, who formed the majority in more than half of its 193 voting groups, or "centuries." Less important laws and decisions were passed by the Tribal Assembly, which also elected lower-ranking public officials. This body was composed of Rome's 35 districts, or "tribes." Thirty of those districts were rural areas, where more-affluent Romans had their luxury villas. Unsurprisingly, the decisions of both assemblies were heavily weighted in favor of the city's patricians and monied elite.

MANLIUS AND THE SACRED GEESE

In 390 BCE Rome was sacked by Gaulish raiders. The only part of the city that held out was an armed garrison on the Capitoline Hill commanded by the patrician Marcus Manlius (in legend, he was alerted to a surprise attack by the honking of sacred geese kept in the Temple of Juno Moneta). After the city's sacking, Rome's plebs had to borrow money at high rates of interest from the patricians. When he intervened on behalf of the plebs, Manlius was accused of kingly ambition and put to death. Rome's patricians did not hesitate to sacrifice one of their own—even a hero—if they felt their profits and power were threatened.

In addition, patricians controlled most of the priestly offices in the city. Among other things, this gave them the power to veto legislation they did not like if they decided that the omens for it were bad.

The Twelve Tables

Although Rome's lower orders enjoyed political representation through the tribunes of the plebs (see pp. 42–43), sometimes they needed to take direct action to resolve their disputes. In 451 BCE, Rome's plebeian soldiers revolted and demanded written laws to protect them from what they claimed was the patricians' arbitrary use of power. In response, the Senate appointed ten patricians, the *decemvirs*, to codify Rome's legal system. Having drawn up

The paint shows a high level of craftsmanship for the period

◁ **Terra-cotta torso**
This fragment is from a 5th-century BCE sculpture of a wounded soldier in fine armour, who was probably from a non-plebeian class.

▷ **Rome's earliest history painting**
This fresco from a tomb on the Esquiline Hill dates from c. 300 BCE. It is thought to show one of Rome's early enemies, the Samnites, surrendering to patrician representatives of the Senate.

a set of laws called the Ten Tables, the legislators were replaced by a second set of *decemvirs* who, after drafting a further Two Tables, unsuccessfully tried to seize power. Despite their troubled genesis, the Twelve Tables were enacted in 450 BCE and became the basis of Roman law for centuries. They were far from perfect, but they at least established written legislation covering, for example, property rights, debt bondage, marriage, and inheritance that, in theory at least, applied to all.

Rome and its boundary

Underpinning Rome's institutions and laws was the concept of what—and where—the city was. After the sacking of Rome by the Gaulish chieftain Brennus in 390 BCE, some argued that the nearby hilltop settlement of Veii would be a safer place to live. The city's leaders held firm. Rome, they argued, was a sacred space defined by the *pomerium*, the area marked out by Romulus when he founded the city in 753 BCE. Moving to Veii would mean not just leaving a physical area but abandoning the idea of Rome itself. As Rome expanded, so did its *pomerium*, sometimes with the raising of high, defensive walls or, later, in the form of stone markers known as *cippi*. In either case, they symbolized where Rome began and ended, and where its laws and its institutions held sway.

> "Taking our **political freedom** does not grant you a **tyrant's license** over our wives and children."

ICILIUS, A ROMAN CITIZEN, DENOUNCING THE *DECEMVIRS* IN LIVY'S *AB URBA CONDITA*

The Roman Army

From local gangs to imperial force

Rome's army is arguably its most famous institution. It existed in some form for at least 1,000 years and its operations spanned three continents. There was, as a result, no single "Roman army"—its composition, tactics, and equipment were adapted to meet new terrains, tasks, and enemies.

The army in the Republic

Warfare during the Regal and Early Republican periods was dominated by militias of wealthy citizens. They fought with and against each other in and around Rome and across the surrounding territories. In the 5th and 4th centuries BCE, power in central Italy coalesced around Rome as it outmaneuvered its opponents and local clan leaders agreed—or were forced—to unify within the expanding city. Rome's early successes were owed, in part, to its ability to enlist large numbers of well-equipped recruits from its clans.

The next three centuries witnessed Rome's imperial expansion across the Mediterranean. The sheer breadth of the empire forced Rome to adapt its military system, as its army of part-time citizens was ill-suited to long campaigns abroad. However, how the Roman army changed is hotly debated due to the unreliable nature of literary sources: the "professionalization" of the army and the effects of the so-called Marian reforms of the late 2nd century BCE (see pp. 106–107) have been reevaluated. What is clear, however, is that all areas of Roman life were affected during this time, including army recruitment and organization. For example,

△ **Regal period**
This fresco from the François tomb in Vulci in central Italy, depicts Macstarna (center), who in at least one version of Rome's origin story became Rome's sixth king, Servius Tullius. If he did exist, it is more probable that Macstarna was a local Etruscan warlord.

△ **Early–Middle Republic**
The image on this *krater* (a large wine vessel) is of a battle between warriors from central Italy. Dating from the 4th century BCE, it shows a mounted Italic soldier wearing a triple-disk cuirass (see p. 80) and a feathered helmet. Its fairly realistic depiction differs from the idealized images of the military often associated with this period.

△ **Late Republic**
The 2nd-century CE Altar of Domitius Ahenobarbus in Rome depicts soldiers wearing Montefortino helmets and carrying *scuta* (shields)—equipment of Celtic origin. This is probably how soldiers would have looked in the Punic Wars (see pp. 82–85).

"**Victory** in war does not depend entirely **upon numbers** or **mere courage**."

VEGETIUS, *DE RE MILITARI (MILITARY INSTITUTIONS OF THE ROMANS)*

△ **More than money**
Romans used their coinage to convey information. This *denarius* from 55 BCE celebrates the state's military victories in Gaul.

Rome's military manpower expanded to integrate poorer soldiers and more auxiliary units, who were recruited from subordinate allies across the empire.

Military developments in the Imperial age

After a period of civil war between Rome's powerful families (see pp. 134–135), Emperor Augustus reformed the army to ensure that his family had ultimate control. He reduced the number of legions, paid their salaries directly, and rewarded auxiliaries with Roman citizenship—soldiers now swore allegiance to the emperor rather than a variety of generals. However, controlling such a diverse force, spread across the Mediterranean, proved difficult. The "Year of the Four Emperors" in 69 CE, for example, saw Rome's legions proclaim Galba, Otho, Vitellius, and Vespasian as emperor in quick succession. In the 2nd and 3rd centuries, rulers tried to harness the power of the army with varying degrees of success. The widespread wars and rebellions in the empire, known collectively as the "Crisis of the Third Century" (see pp. 248–249), led to the emperor Diocletian's partition of the empire and the division of Rome's military forces among the four-man Tetrarchy he established (see pp. 254–255).

The military system further fragmented in the 4th and 5th centuries, largely because the emperors began to wield less power than their (often non-Roman) commanders. Ultimately, Rome's military downfall was not a decline in manpower, but a breakdown in the networks of power that harnessed it.

△ **Early Empire**
Portraying the army in idealized form on monuments such as Trajan's Column (above) was a way for emperors to publicize their power and control. Real army life was not as well-organized as the propaganda images suggest.

△ **2nd and 3rd centuries**
This scene from the Column of Marcus Aurelius in Rome displays not only the brutality of ancient combat but also a shift in how the army was depicted in art. Earlier portrayals, such as Trajan's Column, show the army as a structured, machinelike force. Here, the individualized figures are dramatized in a more grittily realistic fashion.

△ **4th and 5th centuries**
The Roman army had always comprised a range of peoples and equipment, but Rome's rulers often wanted to present a homogeneous force to imply order. In contrast, the Arch of Constantine (erected in 312) shows diversity, displaying the extent of his controlled territories and peoples.

The Conquest of Italy

Rome's rise to regional dominance

Throughout its earliest centuries, Rome was just one of several settlements struggling to survive and assert itself in central Italy. By 275 BCE, however, the city had gained control of the peninsula through conquest and diplomacy.

△ **Temple decoration**
This terra-cotta antefix (roof ornament) dates from c. 510 BCE. It is thought to be from the roof of the Portonaccio Temple at Veii, Rome's great regional rival in its early period.

The nature of the rise of Rome and the Roman conquest of Italy are hotly debated. There are no contemporary Roman literary sources to draw from—the first accounts were written centuries later, in the Late Republic and in the Early Imperial era. Modern interpretations that drew on these works were produced in, and influenced by, very different social and political environments. Today, archaeological evidence in particular is leading historians to question some of these older ideas about Rome's development.

Early Roman expansion

Most people in central Italy in Rome's earliest years did not live in urban communities. They also tended to move from place to place, and membership of a community could be temporary and fluid, with a person not tied to any one settlement. In its earliest period, Rome's relationship with its neighbors was possibly similar to that between businesses competing to attract customers and investors. Land ownership was flexible (if it existed at all), and warfare was focused on raiding for portable wealth.

This changed during the 6th and 5th centuries BCE. Communities in and around Rome, and the elites who dominated them, began to claim control of nearby land in a permanent way, and thus cement their relationship with the people who wanted to use that land. Early conquests included the immediate area around Rome and the nearby land of a people known as the Hernici (see p. 27). In the past, Roman raiders would have invaded this land, taken what they wanted, and left. Now they stayed. This reflected a change in focus from the end of the 5th century BCE to capturing, holding, and settling land. Archaeological evidence bears this out, revealing a gradual rise in the number of permanent farms and villas in central Italy.

The conquest of Veii in 396 BCE marked a turning point for Rome. Veii was Rome's closest rival community, 10 miles (16 km) away. Its capture after a prolonged siege left Rome as the only large hub for communication and interaction in the region. During the conquest of Veii, the Romans created the *tributum*, a "war tax" on the citizenry to fund a new measure called the *stipendium*, a payment given to soldiers. This was further proof that war was moving away from individual raiding toward being a more community-based endeavor.

A group identity is created

One key event in the city's development was the sack of Rome by Gauls in 390 BCE (see box, and pp. 50–51). This event changed the Romans' outlook, forging the community into a more cohesive group. Rome quickly recovered but, rather than continue to seize land, it focused instead on political reform in order to strengthen itself. This included upgrading the role of the consuls by giving them greater military authority and, in 367 BCE, creating the new political post of praetor. The two praetors stood one rung below the consuls on the *cursus honorum* (see pp. 86–87) and controlled the judiciary and were also allowed to command armies.

▷ **Etruscan battle frieze**
The battle depicted on this terra-cotta cinerary urn from the 3rd century BCE is not known, but its inclusion on a family memorial object reflects the importance of warfare in this period. It comes from Chiusi in Etruria, north of Rome.

Rome and the Latins

The growing importance and unity of the community of Rome created tensions in the surrounding region known as Latium, leading to the Great Latin War c. 340 BCE. It took place between Rome and an alliance of local peoples known as the Latins, who were worried by the regional power shift taking place. After Rome won the war, the populations of some communities were made Roman citizens. Meanwhile, other localities, such as the city-states of Praeneste and Tibur, were allowed to keep a degree of independence and were affiliated with Rome as allies (*socii*). It is not known why or on what basis Rome divided its defeated enemies in Latium into citizens and allies—no records were kept and in time the distinctions were lost as the Republic expanded. What is known is that the Romans tried to integrate conquered communities where possible (while also seizing land and wealth and crushing those who resisted). For Rome's elites, the aim was to expand aggressively—and keep control of—the political system they had created. This approach appears to have worked. Despite being outnumbered by the peoples their city had conquered, the Roman elites thrived and Rome continued to grow. »

△ **Italian armor**
Discovered at a warrior burial site at Todi in Etruria, this bronze helmet with silver accents dates from the end of the 5th century BCE.

Traces of pigments show that this frieze would have originally been polychrome (see p. 125)

LESSONS FROM DEFEAT

Rome did not gain control of Italy without experiencing setbacks. In 390 BCE, the Romans were beaten at the Battle of the Allia River by a force of Gauls which then occupied and sacked Rome. The Romans agreed to pay a ransom in gold to the Gallic leader, Brennus, to make him leave the city. But when they accused Brennus of using rigged scales to weigh the gold, the Gaul threw his sword onto the scales and proclaimed "*vae victis*" ("woe to the conquered"), meaning that the Romans now had to add the extra weight of his sword to their payment. Rome never forgot this defeat; in some ways it helped drive the city on toward its future successes.

▷ Dressed to kill
This 4th-century BCE tomb painting from Paestum on Italy's southwestern coast features a line of warriors wearing the elaborate bronze armor that was typical of the period.

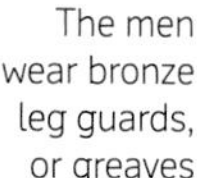

The men wear bronze leg guards, or greaves

This warrior carries a Greek-style circular shield (*aspis*); rectangular shields became common a century later

The Samnite Wars

Rome's conquest of nearby Latium, and the growth of the Roman network of citizens and allies, brought the city into conflict with a wider range of peoples, most notably the Samnites. It is difficult to know who exactly "the Samnites" were. The name was used by the Romans to refer to the Oscan-speaking people living in the south-central Apennines, around the present-day Italian region of Campania. However, people across Italy, and especially in this area, were mobile and fluid in their affiliations. The Samnites came together in broad tribal federations, based on *touta* (extended clan structures), but did not seem to have a clear ethnic or political association. The Samnite designation was probably contextual, given to them by the Romans, although it originally may have related to a local label (*safinus*) used by some families in the region as early as the 5th century BCE.

The First Samnite War (343–341 BCE) was a relatively minor set of skirmishes. The Second Samnite War (326–304 BCE), by contrast, was a major test for Rome. It brought the emerging empire into direct engagement with Campania and the Greek cities of southern Italy, especially Capua, which had drawn Rome into the conflict by asking for its help against Samnite attacks. Rome's fortunes ebbed and flowed in the Second Samnite War, and it suffered a major defeat at the Battle of the Caudine Forks in 321 BCE, but the city eventually emerged victorious in

◁ Early Roman money
From the 3rd century BCE, this is one of the first-ever Roman coins. It bears the Greek legend *ΡΩΜΑΙΩΝ*

("Roman"), and was probably made in southern Italy.

304 BCE. The conflict had seen the Samnites ally with both Etruscans and Gauls from central and northern Italy, reflecting the connected nature of Italic society by this time.

As was Rome's practice, after winning the Second Samnite War it granted citizenship to the people of conquered areas and made new alliances. Rome also created new communities (*coloniae*) in Samnite territory in order to establish outposts and loyalist "pockets" in non-conquered territory.

The Third Samnite War (298–290 BCE) was short but spanned the entire peninsula, with significant hostilities in Etruria and Gauls once more fighting alongside the Samnites. It is not entirely clear what motivated the conflict—perhaps the Romans' need or desire for new lands (and their riches), their obligation to protect their allies from rival states, or a combination of both—but the end of the war left Rome in control of most of Italy. Rome's victory fifteen years later in the Pyrrhic War (see pp. 76–77) saw it achieve dominance over the rest of the peninsula. By 275 BCE, Rome was the master of all Italy, from the southern tip of its "boot" to the Po River in the north at the foot of the Alps.

SUBMISSIVE **BEHAVIOR**

One of Rome's most humiliating defeats, the Battle of the Caudine Forks in 321 BCE was an engagement barely worthy of the name: the Romans were ambushed by the Samnites in a narrow valley and forced to surrender without a fight. The Romans were then made to "march under the yoke" as a sign of their submission. This was a form of ritual punishment where defeated soldiers had to bow their heads before their captors, probably by marching under an arch of crossed spears or, as in this 19th-century imagining by the Swiss artist Charles Gleyre, actual wooden yokes like those used to attach horses, oxen, or other working animals to a plow or cart.

The birth of Roman Italy

During the conquest of Italy, the Roman state and Roman society were constantly evolving. In fact, the idea that a distinctive Roman culture even existed during this period has been challenged. The city of Rome was not home to a stable population, and its citizen body was always expanding. The establishment of its early empire was more like a business setting up branches or franchises than the coordinated actions of an expansionist nation state. But Rome's wars and political reforms in the 4th and 3rd centuries BCE did result in the creation of a distinctive "Roman" system where power remained largely in the hands of a small group of elite families dominated by those who had been there the longest. Newcomers from allies or conquered communities could join this system—but, it seems, as members of the plebeian class rather than as part of Rome's traditional patrician cadre. As Rome conquered more and more of Italy, so the plebeians' ranks were swelled by new powerful and influential members. One outcome of this was the conclusion of the "Conflict of the Orders" of the 5th and 4th centuries BCE (see pp. 42–43), when the plebeians fought for greater rights and more parity with patricians. As it entered the 3rd century BCE, "Rome" was no longer simply a city; it was the center of a network of elites, citizens, and allies controlling the length and breadth of Italy. While some chafed under Roman rule, which could be oppressive and was certainly backed by violence, others grasped the new opportunities that being part of Rome offered—especially as these included the protection of Roman military might and the possibility of a share, however small, in the wealth of the growing and successful empire.

The armor is made from hammered bronze backed with leather

▷ **4th-century BCE Italian armor**
Samnite warriors often wore triple-disk cuirasses, or breastplates. The armor was common throughout Italy, and could be used by infantry and cavalry.

> "But the **Romans have subjected** to their rule not portions, but nearly the **whole of the world**"
>
> POLYBIUS, *HISTORIES*

Being a Roman Citizen

Security, opportunity, and a recognized status

In Rome's early history, citizenship was a birthright, although this changed as the state grew. Free citizens (*cives Romani*), especially men, enjoyed specific social, legal, and political privileges denied to non-citizens and the enslaved.

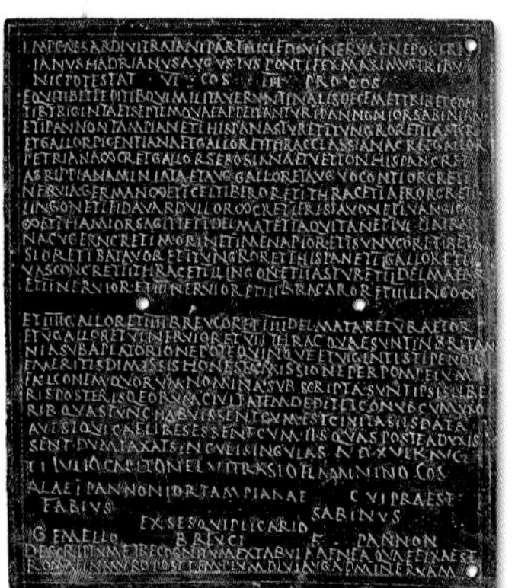

△ **Status symbol**
This bronze plate records the grant of citizenship to Gemellus, an army auxiliary (foreign-born soldier). He gained Roman citizen status on July 17, 122 CE.

The fundamental right of the Roman citizen was the *ius suffragium*—the right to vote. His fundamental responsibility was participation in civic life. Even poor Romans could vote at their assigned Tribal and Centuriate Assemblies (see pp. 50–51). In reality, though, wealthier citizens could prioritize their interests by manipulating how votes were distributed in assemblies, and by controlling the Senate. With citizenship also came the right to run for office—*ius honorum*—and the opportunity to amass influence and wealth by climbing the *cursus honorum*: the ladder of public offices (see pp. 86–87). Roman women, while considered citizens, could not vote or hold public office.

Other rights and responsibilities

Another essential tenet of citizenship was the security and legal protection it afforded to citizens located anywhere within the boundaries of Rome's territory. They could not be enslaved, subjected to certain corporal punishments, or executed without a trial in Rome, and could appeal local judicial decisions there. Citizens could also use Roman law to settle their disputes, and had defined property rights. (While women's legal rights varied over time, in general those without a *paterfamilias*, or male head of household, could own and inherit property: see pp. 70–71). All citizens had the right to marry lawfully, guaranteeing their children citizenship, too (see pp. 182–183).

Economic benefits of citizenship included the right to make contracts and farm on public land, freedom from direct taxation (abolished from 167 BCE until the 3rd century CE and collected primarily from provinces), and an entitlement to free or subsidized grain, or later bread, from the public supply. Roman citizens were obliged to take part in a regular census that evaluated their family, possessions, and assigned tribe within society, for taxation, voting, and military purposes. Only citizens could volunteer for Rome's legions or, at certain points during the state's history, be conscripted. Non-citizens served as auxiliaries.

▷ **Keeping up appearances**
A Roman husband and wife are portrayed as model citizens on this funerary stele from the 1st century BCE. For men, the toga was the visual marker of citizenship; different styles denoted social status (see pp. 68–69).

Text is in Greek; it was translated for each territory in which it was issued

▷ **Revolutionary document**
This is the only surviving contemporary copy of Caracalla's *Constitutio Antoniniana* edict, which extended citizenship rights around the empire.

The fragile papyrus edict has survived only as fragments

"Once our **native-born citizens** sufficed for people of **our own kin.**"

TACITUS, *ANNALS*

The expansion of citizenship

For centuries, citizenship was restricted to those born free in Rome (and later, Italy) of free parents. Manumitted (freed) enslaved people automatically became citizens and their children were considered freeborn (see pp. 88–89). Their *libertus* status afforded some, but not all, the rights of a freeborn Roman; they had to declare it to the censor and their former enslaver became their patron. The system of patronage—whereby citizens at different levels of society exchanged financial, legal, political, or social favors—was ingrained in Rome, and helped drive the spread of citizenship. The army was also a route to citizenship, which was granted to non-Roman soldiers after 25 years of service.

As Rome's territory expanded across Italy in the 4th and 3rd centuries BCE, people in some communities that had fallen under Roman control were given citizenship (although not all with the right to vote in Rome). Others became allies (*socii*), with no right of citizenship, but a duty to supply soldiers to serve alongside the legions.

Tensions caused by these unequal relationships led, in the 1st century BCE, to the Social War, when a number of Italian territories denied equal voting and citizenship rights rebelled against Roman control (see pp. 104–105). To pacify the rebels, Rome passed the *lex Iulia de civitate* in 90 BCE, granting citizenship to eligible members of all communities across Italy.

The scope changed again in 212 CE; the emperor Caracalla's *Constitutio Antoniniana* edict gave citizenship to all freeborn men in the empire (and to women the same status as Roman women). This increased the number of citizens liable to pay his new taxes; it may also have won the loyalty of conquered peoples. However, by then, many citizenship privileges—notably the right to vote—had less meaning in a state ruled by an emperor.

THE RIGHTS OF CITIZENSHIP

The Bible is not the first place most people would look for evidence of the importance of Roman citizenship. But *Acts* 22.22–29 contains just that. In 57 CE, Saul of Tarsus, now remembered as Saint Paul, was facing trial in Jerusalem, accused of defiling the Temple of Solomon by preaching the teachings of Jesus. (Paul had angered many of his fellow Jews in the city with his apostolic work, and knew his life was in danger.) Invoking his right to be tried in Rome before the emperor, Paul was able to declare "*civis Romanus sum*" ("I am a Roman citizen") to his captors. Paul then spent two years imprisoned in Rome before he disappeared from history, probably martyred during the reign of Nero.

MOSAIC OF SAINT PAUL IN ROME FROM 1220

Priests and Religion

How the Romans worshipped their gods

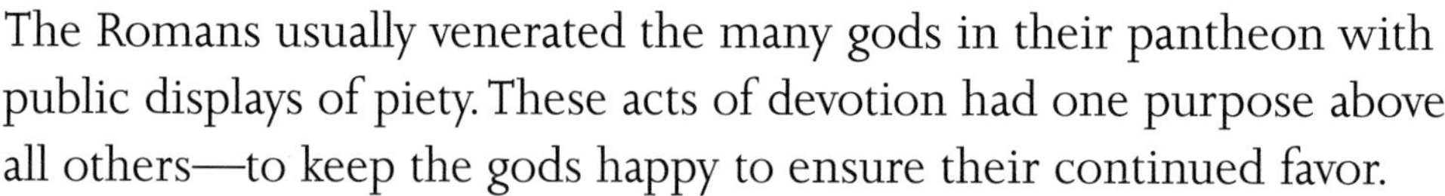

The Romans usually venerated the many gods in their pantheon with public displays of piety. These acts of devotion had one purpose above all others—to keep the gods happy to ensure their continued favor.

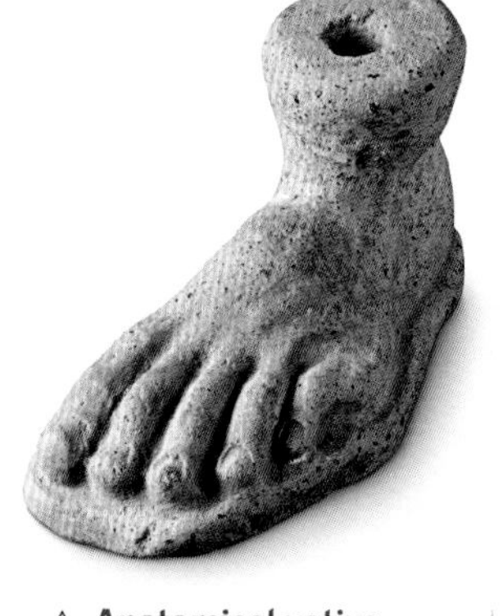

△ **Anatomical votive**
Sick or wounded people left terra-cotta models of afflicted body parts in the temples of healing gods such as Asclepius. They hoped the deity would accept these so-called votive offerings and cure the afflicted part.

Romans believed that if they performed acts of piety the gods would be pleased and would treat them and the state with favor. They also believed that every detail of a ritual had to be strictly performed in the way that it had always been done. In the 3rd century BCE, when Quintus Sulpicius (a *flamen*, or priest, of Jupiter) was making a sacrifice to the god and the ceremonial hat he was wearing fell off, he was forced to resign in case Jupiter took offense at the mistake.

Observing rituals

The worship of the gods largely occurred during public festivals (see pp. 120–121), when sacrifices were made on altars outside temples—the "houses" of each god within the city. These sacrifices might involve incense, offerings of wine, or the slaughter of live animals (cows, sheep, or pigs). In addition to public expressions of worship and the veneration of one's family gods (see pp. 122–123), individuals could also ask the gods for help. Men and women of all social standings, even the enslaved and freed people, often petitioned for aid by writing prayers, or penned curses against those who had wronged them, on thin sheets of lead. These were rolled up and left at

◁ **Interpretive aid**
Haruspices used the map of the universe inscribed on this bronze model of a sheep's liver to read the gods' will in animal entrails.

temples and sacred spaces for their chosen god to read. One, written by a Romano-British woman called Basilia, hoped that the gods would curse "the blood, eyes, and limbs" of whoever had stolen her ring, or else "have all their intestines completely eaten away."

Priests and preferment

Public expressions of worship were nominally the responsibility of the Senate, but in practice priests were primarily in charge of ensuring that the gods were appeased. The key priestly offices, such as pontiffs, augurs, *flamines*, and the "king of sacrifices," were filled by elite senatorial men. A handful of priesthoods were reserved for women, however. These positions, which included the Vestal Virgins (see pp. 32–33), the *flaminicae*, and the "queen of sacrifices," were fundamental to maintaining the relationship between mortals and the gods.

Omens and superstitions

Interpreting what the gods thought of their mortal subjects was a task performed by trained diviners. During important public meetings, priests known as augurs scanned the skies for bad omens sent by the gods, such as birds flying strangely overhead or the sudden onset of thunderstorms. They even watched how Rome's sacred chickens ate their food for signs of divine displeasure.

To interpret especially important or complex signs of divine favor or disfavor, the Senate would send for haruspices, holy men from what is now Tuscany, trained in the ancient Etruscan art of reading animal entrails. If they found anything indicating the gods' disfavor, a new animal was sacrificed. Strange events or prodigies, such as rains of blood, crying statues, or talking animals, were explained as evidence that the gods were unhappy and needed to be placated.

△ **A sacrifice to Mars**
Roman rituals often included sacrifices. This frieze shows the *suovetaurilia*: the sacrifice of a pig (*sus*), sheep (*ovis*), and bull (*taurus*) to the god Mars. This sacrifice was intended to ritually cleanse the land, perhaps for the establishing of a colony or a temple.

> "Cows, with their horns **bound with gold**, were **sacrificed** to the Bright Goddess."
>
> *RECORDS OF THE RITUALS OF THE ARVAL BRETHREN (ANCIENT COLLEGE OF 12 PRIESTS)*

AUGUSTUS **AS PRIEST**

Roman men could usually hold just one religious office at a time. As emperor, Augustus broke all the rules and held seven. Most notable among these was the position of *pontifex maximus*, or "chief priest," which gave him control over all religious matters in the empire. All subsequent emperors took up this position until the late 4th century CE; the emperor Gratian was the last to use the title. With the rise of Christianity, the role—and the name—was adopted by the bishop of Rome, who became known as the pontiff, or pope. In this 1st-century BCE marble statue of Augustus (right), he is most probably depicted as the *pontifex maximus*: the fold of toga covering his head indicates that he may be performing a priestly sacrifice.

The Role of the Consuls

Rome's joint supreme command

The consulship was Rome's highest elected political position. In legend, the office was established along with the Republic in 509 BCE, with the overthrow of Rome's last king, Lucius Tarquinius Superbus. This was the moment Rome's leading families decided that no one person should ever rule the state again. From that date, two consuls were elected each year, the first of whom were Lucius Junius Brutus and Lucius Collatinus (see pp. 36–37).

Shared responsibility

The consuls' powers were extensive in the Republican era. They presided over the Senate, summoned the assemblies, and put legislation to a vote. They also commanded the army in war and, later in the Republican period, went on to govern a province after their term in office. It was possible to be consul more than once, and many men held the office multiple times. The two consuls entered office on the first day of January and alternated leadership of the Senate each month. Such was the office's prestige that, instead of being numbered, Roman years in the Republican era were named after the consuls for each 12-month period. The presiding consul was accompanied in public by lictors, attendants who carried the *fasces*, a bundle of rods surrounding an ax—a symbol of the violent roots of the consuls' authority (and a piece of imagery adopted by Italy's Fascists in the early 20th century). The consuls presided over the elections of their successors, to ensure the stability of government.

△ **Lucius Quinctius Cincinnatus**
A very capable military leader, the consul for 460 BCE was venerated by later generations of Romans for supposedly resigning twice as the city's dictator. This position, usually bestowed in times of crisis, gave its holder absolute power.

△ **Titus Manlius Torquatus**
Three times consul and three times dictator, Titus Manlius was given the name "Torquatus" after he defeated a Gaul in single combat and claimed his torque (a metal neck-ring) as a trophy. He became a model of devotion to duty when, in around 340 BCE, he publicly executed his own son for defying his orders in battle.

△ **Marcus Atilius Regulus**
Elected consul in 256 BCE, Regulus was captured in battle the following year by the Carthaginians. When they sent him to Rome with peace terms, he urged the Senate to refuse. He was executed on his return to Carthage, and so became a Roman hero.

> "My **whole hopes** rest upon **myself**, which I must sustain by **good conduct** and **integrity**."
>
> MARIUS, QUOTED IN SALLUST'S *THE JUGURTHINE WAR*

Each consul could veto the other's decisions. When the electoral system produced a noble with a reforming agenda, the Senate usually supported a candidate who would keep his colleague in check. This did not quite work in 59 BCE, in the consulship of the populist Julius Caesar and the conservative Calpurnius Bibulus. When Bibulus attempted to veto all of his co-consul's reforms, Caesar had him physically attacked. Fearing for his safety, Bibulus retreated to his home, effectively leaving Caesar as sole consul for the year. The consulship's greatest strength could thus also be its biggest weakness.

Great consuls were lauded as heroes. Noble families displayed in the atriums of their houses wax masks, or *imagines*, bearing the faces of ancestors who had achieved high office, and the most exalted consuls served as role models for a young Roman's moral education.

A changing position

During the Imperial era, Rome still had two consuls, and they still presided over the Senate, but the emperor now held true power (see pp. 86–87). When Augustus built his new forum in Rome, he included in it 108 statues of selected consuls and other notables from the city's history. As many of these men also had ties to the emperor's family, their inclusion was perhaps intended as much to emphasize Augustus's links to Rome's heritage as it was a celebration of the city's greatest leaders.

△ **Lucius Opimius**
In 121 BCE the consul Lucius Opimius, who minted this coin depicting Victory in a chariot, executed 3,000 supporters of the reforming tribune Gaius Gracchus (see pp. 104–105).

△ **Lucius Mummius Achaicus**
Mummius was the Roman commander during the sack of Corinth in 146 BCE. The historian Polybius, who witnessed the destruction, praised Mummius for his self-restraint when he could have taken the opportunity for personal enrichment.

△ **Marcus Claudius Marcellus**
Marcellus won Rome's highest military award, the *spolia opima* ("the rich spoils"), for defeating a Gallic enemy in hand-to-hand combat. In 212 BCE he conquered Syracuse during the Second Punic War. He died in battle four years later and was personally honored by Hannibal, who sent his ashes back to Rome in a silver urn.

△ **Gaius Marius**
As consul in 107 BCE, Marius helped end the Jugurthine War (see pp. 106–107). He was reelected consul six more times and enjoyed military success against the Gauls. His rivalry with the Roman general Sulla led to years of civil war and turmoil (see pp. 108–109).

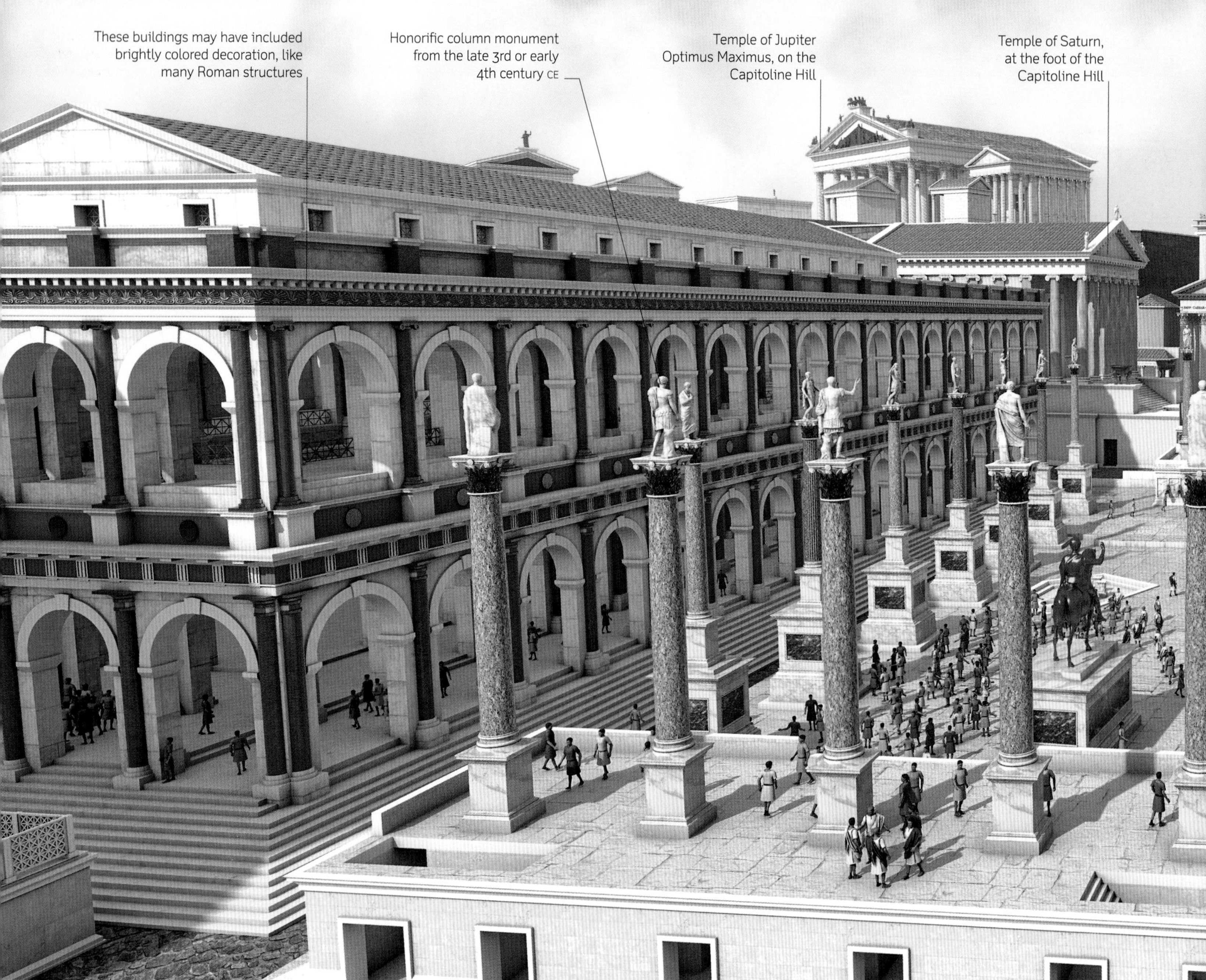

The Roman Forum

The heart of ancient Rome

The Roman Forum (shown here c. 4th century CE) sits in a marshy valley between the Capitoline and Palatine hills. It was drained and developed in the 7th century BCE under Rome's kings, and by the Early Republic it was the center of the growing city-state. At first, stores and aristocratic houses ringed a lively, open central space, full of civic and legal activity, religious rituals, commercial life, and festivals. Roman politics also centered on the Forum, with Senate meetings in the Curia (Senate House) and popular assemblies outside in the Comitium area (built over during Caesar's reign). After conquering the wealthy cities of the Greek east (see pp. 76–77), Rome's rulers took inspiration from Greek royal architecture, replacing houses and stores with grand public buildings, such as basilicas and theaters. Some of the new structures were more distinctively Roman, including triumphal arches and impressive vaults. By the Imperial era, the Forum had a primarily ceremonial purpose. Under Julius Caesar and Augustus, it became a monumental precinct, commemorating dynastic achievements.

Temples to Fausta Felicitas, Venus Victrix, and the Genius Publicus

The *umbilicus urbis*, symbolic center of Rome and the empire

Temple of Juno Moneta, site of Rome's ancient mint

Shrine of Venus Cloacina, directly above the Cloaca Maxima (Great Sewer), marks its route

Curia, or Senate House

Basilica Aemilia had spaces for civic and commercial activity

Lapis Niger

◁ **Forum remains**
The Forum was deserted in the 8th–9th centuries CE, and robbed for building materials. Gradually, it filled up with earth and debris. Excavations began in the 19th century.

▷ **Lapis Niger**
The "Black Stone" marks an ancient sacred site underneath the Forum where this 6th-century BCE tufa block was buried; its inscription may set rules for a religious ritual.

Visual Tour

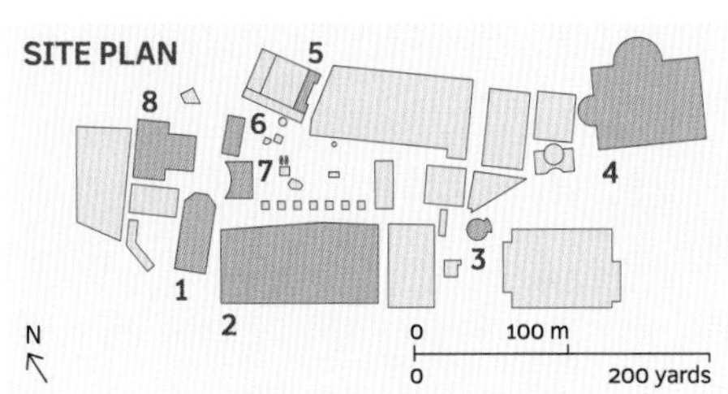

▷ **Basilica Julia**
Julius Caesar's grand marble basilica was dedicated in 46 BCE. Augustus finished it then rebuilt it after a fire, completing it in 12 CE. The three-story aisled hall was used for law courts and banking. The final version, rebuilt in 283 after yet another fire, became an important focal point in the later years of the Forum.

▷ **Temple of Saturn**
The worship of Saturn at the Forum dates back to the earliest years of the Republic, but this temple is one of the latest on this site. It was rebuilt after a fire c. 380 CE (very late for a temple to a traditional god), using existing granite columns from other structures.

1

2

▷ **Curia**
The surviving version of the Senate House dates from 283 CE, and was preserved intact by being converted into a church. It replaced a previous Curia planned by Julius Caesar and finished in 29 BCE by Augustus.

▽ **The evolution of the Forum**
The Forum developed over the course of a millennium. It began as a royal space, developed as a Republican civic and social hub, and became an imperial precinct. Many of its buildings also had several phases of development.

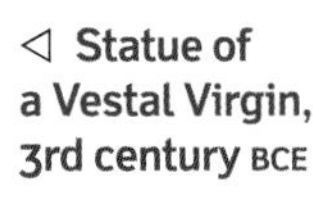

◁ **Statue of a Vestal Virgin, 3rd century BCE**

5

6

△ **Arch of Septimius Severus**
This triumphal arch (see pp. 264–265) was erected in 203 CE to celebrate victories won in Parthia by the Severan dynasty. That eastern campaign had been connected to a civil conflict, which brought Septimius Severus to power. Standing just outside the Senate House, the arch was a reminder of the family's dominance.

7

753 BCE Legendary foundation date of Rome

8TH–7TH CENTURIES BCE Vestal Virgins established in Rome under Numa Pompilius, Rome's second king

7TH CENTURY BCE Regia (the house for Rome's kings and high priests) built

c. 570 BCE Inscription on tufa pillar later buried under the Lapis Niger

509 BCE Rome becomes a republic. Political spaces—Comitium and Curia—take on new importance

497 BCE Earliest Temple of Saturn

484 BCE Earliest Temple of Castor and Pollux

338 BCE First Rostra built after the naval battle of Antium during the Latin War

216 BCE Early version of the Temple of Concord

179 BCE First basilica (Fulvia) built along the Forum's north side

169 BCE Basilica Sempronia (later site of Basilica Julia) built along the south side

▽ Temple of Vesta

Vesta was the goddess of home and hearth, and her round temple—which protected her eternal sacred flame—may echo the shape of Iron Age round houses. This marble version, from the late 2nd to early 3rd centuries CE, was rebuilt from fragments in 1930. It stands next to the House of the Vestal Virgins (see pp. 32–33).

▽ Basilica of Maxentius and Constantine

The last great building in the Forum was the early 4th-century CE Basilica of Maxentius and Constantine. The enormous concrete vaults show the prowess of Roman engineering and the influence of Roman architectural styles developed in, for example, bathhouse buildings (see pp. 236–237).

◁ Temple of Concord

This temple honored the personified virtue of harmony within the state. Naturally, this dedication, in the heart of the Forum, was highly political. The first temple (121 BCE) commemorated the defeat of populist reforms by the aristocracy. The later version, completed in 10 CE by Tiberius, was a reminder of the "harmony" enforced by imperial power.

◁ Rostra

The speakers' platform was named after the battering rams (*rostra*, in Latin) of captured enemy ships, which were nailed to it. Originally standing on the edge of the Comitium (an older area for popular assembly), it was relocated by Julius Caesar in 46 BCE, and extended by Augustus.

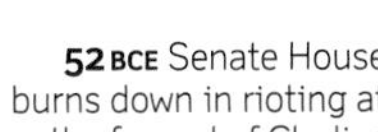

52 BCE Senate House burns down in rioting at the funeral of Clodius

121 BCE New version of the Temple of Concord dedicated

46 BCE Basilica Julia dedicated under Julius Caesar, on the site of the Basilica Sempronia

29 BCE Temple of the Deified Julius Caesar dedicated by Augustus on the site of his cremation

14–9 BCE Major fires create opportunities for Augustus to continue redeveloping the Forum

10 BCE Temple of Concord dedicated by Tiberius

141 CE Temple of Faustina built by her widower Antoninus Pius

203 Arch of Septimius Severus dedicated

303 Honorific columns erected on the Rostra under Diocletian

c. 313 Emperor Constantine completes the Basilica of Maxentius and Constantine

△ **Head of Constantine, 4th century CE**

The Toga

Rome's national dress

The toga, the distinctive garment worn by Roman men, became a status symbol among Roman citizens and distinguished them from non-citizens. The presentation of their first toga was the rite of manhood for Roman boys.

△ **Togate figures**
This *denarius* from 135 BCE depicts togate figures—on the left holding loaves of bread, and on the right holding a *lituus* (a ritual trumpet used by augurs).

The toga was a semicircular piece of cloth made of wool, worn by men over a short-sleeved tunic. One half was draped down over the left shoulder, and the other half brought under the right shoulder, around the body, and up over the left shoulder. The toga was made from up to 16 sq ft (1.5 sq m) of material, and was not held in place by any pins or fastenings. It was cumbersome to put on, and a man often needed up to four attendants to help drape it properly. This lengthy routine contributed to the toga being a symbol of the wearer's high status. Togas were originally worn by both men and women, but over time became an exclusively male garment.

Social distinctions

Personal appearance, gait, and gestures all indicated and enforced social roles in Rome, and a person's dress was no exception. The "togate" statue—depicting a man dressed in a toga—was considered the most distinguished representation of a citizen. During rituals and sacrifices, the toga was draped over the head.

There were several different types of toga, some of which were dyed or decorated with colorful stripes (*clavi*) to denote status. The *toga pura*, undyed and unadorned, could be worn by any Roman citizen, and a dark toga (*pulla*) could be worn in mourning.

Candidates for office wore the *toga candida*, brightened with white chalk, while the *toga praetexta*, with its reddish border, was worn by young boys and magistrates. The *toga trabea*, worn by various elites, had a purple or saffron border (*latus clavus*), while a triumphant general's *toga picta* was dyed a solid color, with decorations in gold thread. Some people deliberately sullied their toga in protest or to evoke pity, for example if they or a relative were on trial.

Cultural significance

The toga's semicircular shape distinguished it from Greek clothing: the Greek himation, worn similarly, was rectangular. The toga was white, and longer than the colorful Greek tunics that only reached the knee.

The toga carried emotional weight: when boys came of age, their father presented them with their first *toga virilis*, the plain white toga of manhood, in a special ceremony. Exiles could not wear the toga. While toga wearing had declined by the reign of Augustus, he played a key role in reviving it, decreeing that no citizen could enter the Forum without one.

▽ **Aeneas makes a sacrifce to the *Penates***
The mythical hero Aeneas (right) wears a toga draped over his head and without a tunic underneath as he makes a sacrifice to the household gods he rescued from Troy.

Wart possibly added in the 17th century due to identification with Cicero

Left shoulder more covered, leaving right arm free to gesture

> "The Romans, **masters of the world**, and the people who wear the **toga**."
>
> JUPITER, KING OF THE GODS, IN VIRGIL'S *AENEID*

◁ **Togate statesman**
This marble togate statue is thought to depict Cicero, who famously gave a speech called *Oratio in Toga Candida* (alluding to the brightened white togas the candidates were wearing) while campaigning for the Consulship in 64 BCE. The statue is part of a collection of Greek marble sculptures, held by the Ashmolean Museum in Oxford.

Inclusion of a scroll presents Cicero as a learned figure

WOMEN'S CLOTHING

The toga developed from the Etruscan *tebenna*, a unisex cloak, but became exclusively men's dress. Women's equivalent of the toga was the *stola*, which was worn after marriage (unmarried girls wore lighter tunics). The *stola* was a woolen dress in one of a variety of colors, tied at the shoulders with clasps, and worn with ribbons tied under the bust and around the waist to exaggerate the folds of cloth. It was usually worn over a tunic (as shown below). Designs varied depending on social status. More folds denoted wealth, as did stripes and other embellishments. Courtesans and women convicted of adultery were forbidden to wear the *stola* and some wore the toga as a mark of their failure—or refusal—to meet patriarchal standards.

Roman togas were floor-length, unlike their shorter Greek counterparts

Women of Ancient Rome

Private lives and public influence

In contrast to classical Athens, where elite women were kept secluded, women in ancient Rome were not meant to be publicly invisible and had many rights under Roman law. But they were still part of an intrinsically patriarchal system.

Unlike their Greek counterparts, Roman women were not confined to the home. However, they still lived in a strictly enforced patriarchal society where the *paterfamilias* (usually the father) had the power of life and death over the women in his household, and made decisions for them.

On the birth of a girl, he decided if the baby would be kept, enslaved, or left exposed to die. He chose whether to educate her, and selected her husband—often a considerably older man she was forced to marry in her early teens. At this point, the *paterfamilias* could transfer guardianship to her husband, or retain it. If the latter, he could trigger divorce at any time and marry her to other suitors to further his own social standing.

On the death of their *paterfamilias*, women were free to own property in their own right, as well as buy, sell, and inherit. They could also free the enslaved and make a will. In the 1st century CE, new laws released women from a guardian's "care," but only if they had produced at least three children.

"Female" virtues

Male authors described an idealized image of how a Roman woman "should" behave, which may not have correlated with the social reality. In contrast with men, who were expected to take part in military, political, and public life, women were expected to be devoted to their husbands, bear children, look beautiful, take care of the home, and weave. *Pudicitia* ("modesty" or "chastity") was held as a key virtue for Roman women, because of the questions female promiscuity raised over a child's paternity. Any accusations of adultery led to severe punishment for women. The chastity of women was also used as a metaphor for Rome's security, and was even woven into the city's early foundation myths, such as the rapes of the virtuous noblewoman Lucretia and the Sabine women (see pp. 36–37 and 22–23). The harsh reality was that without any reliable ways to prevent pregnancy, most women faced decades of childbirth, or dangerous methods of abortion.

◁ Clay uterus
As childbirth was a serious danger to life, Romans often left clay votive offerings at shrines to ask for support from the gods. The wavy lines on this Roman votive may represent contractions.

Women in politics

Men controlled the legal and political systems, and created rules to entrench their privileges; nevertheless, some Roman women found ways to resist these

▽ Eumachia
The largest building in the forum at Pompeii was financed by a woman named Eumachia, who also set up a laundry workers' guild with the wealth from her family's brick-making business.

▷ Women playing games
This terra-cotta statuette shows two women playing the game *tali*; players threw knucklebones from a sheep or goat and tried to balance them on the back of the hand or throw them at a target.

◁ **Fresco of women dressing**
In this fresco (3rd or 2nd century BCE) found at baths in Herculaneum, a servant dresses the hair of a young girl wearing a fine tunic, while an older woman and young girl look on.

Golden buttons

Matrona, or married woman, not yet fully dressed, holds her *palla* (shawl) in her hand

controls. For example, when the *lex Oppia* aimed to restrict women's wealth and possessions by law in 215 BCE, Roman women blocked the streets in protest, forcing the law's repeal. While all women were forbidden from voting and running for office, some were able to gain influence through their ties with male relatives (see box). Women in the imperial family could gain proximity to, and influence with, the emperor. Those who exercised power indirectly, such as Augustus's wife Livia (see pp. 142–143), were often disparaged by later, male, Roman historians. In contrast with elite women, who could derive reflected power via family connections, lower-class and enslaved women endured lives of hard work. These women could be seen in many roles across Roman society, from waitresses to construction workers, shopkeepers to midwives, and laundry workers to sex workers. Whatever their role, Roman women were essentially seen by men as either requiring strict control to preserve their chastity, or as sexual objects.

FULVIA

Fulvia, an aristocratic Roman, was known for her strong public voice during the political turmoil of the Late Republic. She was married in turn to three powerful populists in Rome: Publius Clodius Pulcher, Gaius Scribonius Curio, and Mark Antony. Fulvia gave testimony at the trial of Clodius's murderer and retained the loyalty of his strong political following. In 40 BCE, she raised eight legions in Italy to fight for Mark Antony's claim to power. Octavian (later Augustus) made a cautious peace with his rival Antony for the next decade, and Fulvia died in exile; she was later blamed for much of the political turmoil.

Fresco from Pompeii's Villa of the Mysteries
Against a striking red background, a group of women and girls prepare themselves for an unidentified ceremony in Pompeii's aptly named Villa of the Mysteries. The most common interpretation of the fresco, which covers all four walls in what was probably the villa's dining room and dates from around 60–80 BCE, is that it shows the young woman seated on the right being initiated into the cult of Bacchus, the Roman god of wine and fertility; in another reading, she is preparing for her wedding ceremony.

City and Country

Contrasting experiences of urban and rural life

Throughout Roman history there was an ongoing debate about the best place to live: the city or the countryside? During Rome's expansion—both as a state and an empire—that debate sharpened into a question of how to live.

△ **Hut-shaped urn**
This funerary urn was designed to resemble the simple huts lived in by Rome's earliest settlers, including Romulus himself.

There was a clear distinction between city and country life in the Roman mind. The former—whether Rome or any other city—was usually imagined as sophisticated, corrupt, crime-ridden, and exciting, while the latter was simple, honest, safe, and sedate. In reality, the experiences for those who lived in either place were more mixed.

◁ **A Roman villa at Stabiae**
Some Romans flaunted their wealth by building opulent ("unnatural," in the words of the poet Horace) country houses and villas such as the one in this fresco from the 1st century CE.

The ups and downs of city life

Rome's Palatine Hill was the city's most desirable address. It was close to the Forum but its elevated position allowed Rome's elite to place their town houses and villas above their fellow citizens'. By contrast, the Suburra, at the foot of the Palatine Hill, was widely seen as Rome's seediest, most dangerous district. Most ordinary Romans lived between these two extremes, usually in *insulae*: fire-prone apartment buildings with wealthier residents taking the lower levels and poorer families confined to the more crowded floors higher up (see pp. 78–79).

To all its inhabitants—rich or poor, native-born or immigrant—Rome was above all the *urbs*, the city at the center of everything, which offered both opportunity and danger to those who lived there, whether by choice or circumstance.

Changed fortunes in the countryside

Roman poets such as Virgil and Horace celebrated the countryside as a refuge from city life (see pp. 144–145), with its self-sufficient smallholders embodying strength, economy, and virtue. But not everyone who lived in the countryside was a landowner. Many were paid farmhands; others were enslaved labor. Their experiences of life were different from those of wealthy landowners—most of whose hands never touched a plow. As Rome's empire grew, small farmers lost their land while they were away fighting in the state's wars of expansion. This led to social tension, the influx of poor, landless workers into the cities, and eventually the consolidation of small farmholdings into the large estates known as *latifundia* owned by a handful of very wealthy men (see pp. 246–247).

Toward the end of the Republic, the countryside became an even more contested space, as rival generals vying for control of the state promised their legions land that was not always available in return for their support.

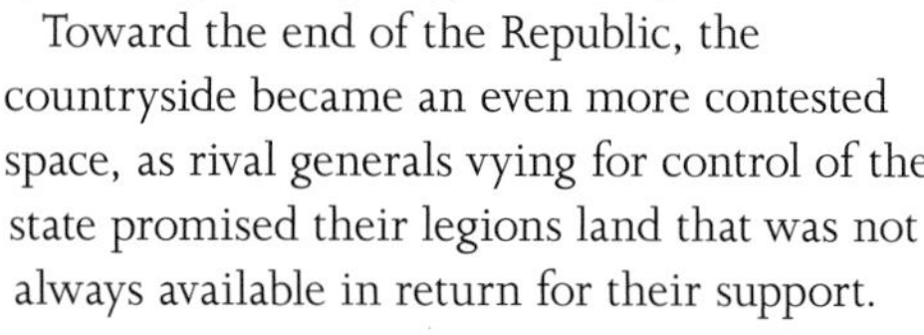

◁ **Roman town planning**
This undated relief from Avezzano in central Italy shows a walled Roman town with dwellings stacked closely together in a grid pattern, suggesting it was originally a military encampment.

CATO THE ELDER (234–149 BCE)

From relatively humble origins, Cato rose to become a soldier, senator, historian, and, most notably, censor. Famed for his strict conservatism, ruthless practicality, and stern moralism, he was a living example of what he regarded as the traditional Roman values of frugality and moderation. As censor, he relentlessly pursued those accused of the misuse of public funds for private gain. His *Origines* from c. 168 BCE was the first history book written in Latin, while his thoughts on farming, *De agri cultura*, was used as a practical guide by landowners. Cato had a farm in the Sabine country, the hilly and fertile area north of Rome, and his advice to his fellow farmers was typically uncompromising: if an enslaved worker fell sick they were to be put on half rations; when they became too old or infirm to work they were to be sold.

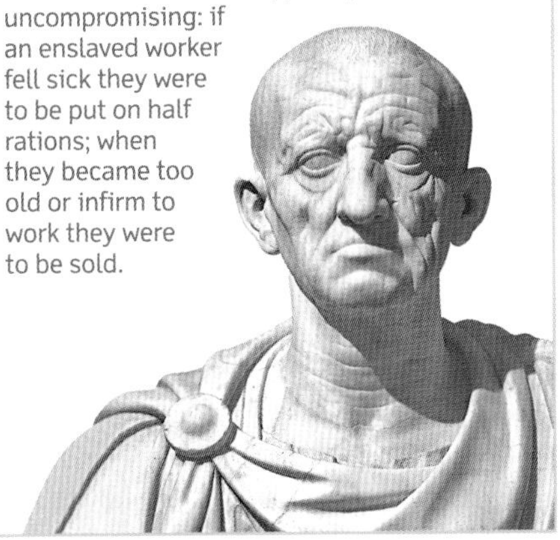

This grueling activity would have been carried out by enslaved workers or hired hands

"**Oh farmers**, only too fortunate, if they are **aware of their blessings**!"

VIRGIL, *THE GEORGICS*

△ **Grape harvesting**
This mosaic from Hispania (Spain and Portugal) shows an idealized view of country life. By the time it was created in the 3rd century CE, less "romantic" but more efficient wine-making methods had been developed, such as lever-operated presses.

The grapes are pressed by foot, in the traditional method

After pressing, grape juice was fermented in clay pots to make wine

The Conquest of Greece

Rome's expansion into the Hellenistic world

Rome's success in taking over most of the Greek-speaking Mediterranean was called by the Greek historian Polybius "an achievement without parallel in human history." It was a conquest that began in Italy and ended in Egypt, 250 years later.

Rome's growing power within Italy by the 4th century BCE (see pp. 54–57) brought it into direct contact with Greek powers in the south of the peninsula, and from there with Greeks in their own home territory. Among them were the Macedonians of the northern Greek mainland, who, until the death of their king Alexander the Great in 323 BCE, had dominated the region. Alexander's demise saw Greece revert for the most part to a patchwork of autonomous city-states, whose lack of unity Rome would exploit.

Defeating the Greeks in Italy

The Greek colonies in southern Italy had, by the early 3rd century BCE, established cautiously friendly relations with Rome. In 282 BCE, however, Roman ships (by accident or as provocation) broke an assurance that they would not sail into the Gulf of Tarentum. When the Greek colony city of Tarentum responded by sinking Roman ships, Rome declared war. Tarentum summoned its ally, King Pyrrhus, from nearby Epirus (modern northwestern Greece), who won a series of personally costly "Pyrrhic" victories against the Romans. After defeat at the Battle of Beneventum in 275 BCE, Pyrrhus returned to Epirus and left Rome in control of the whole of Italy.

▽ **Role model**
This carving from Tarentum, in southern Italy, is thought to show Pyrrhus in battle. His Macedonian sandals and the gorgon's head on his cuirass suggest his depiction was modeled on Alexander the Great.

◁ **"Greek hero"**
Following his Greek victories, Quinctius Flamininus became the first living person to be represented on local Greek coinage, as on this gold *stater*.

The end of Macedonian power

In 217 BCE Philip V of Macedonia received news of the catastrophic defeat Hannibal had meted out to the Romans at Lake Trasimene in the Second Punic War (see pp. 84–85). This, and the Carthaginians' victory at Cannae the following year, prompted Philip to enter into an alliance with Carthage that he hoped would end Rome's increasing influence in the Greek-speaking world. Rome retaliated by allying with the Aetolian League, a Greek federation opposed to Macedonia's regional dominance.

The First Macedonian War (214–205 BCE) between Philip and the Aetolians deprived Hannibal of his ally's forces, and aided Rome's victory over Carthage. Once it was free of its Carthaginian entanglements, Rome embarked on the Second Macedonian War in 200 BCE. When the conflict ended in Rome's favor four years later, the commanding general of the Roman forces, Quinctius Flamininus, declared that, with Philip V vanquished, the city-states of Greece were once more free and autonomous. But having proclaimed "the freedom of the Greeks," Quinctius Flamininus left behind a sizable garrison of Roman soldiers to show who really controlled the territory.

Greece falls to Rome

Philip V's son Perseus attempted to restore Macedonian hegemony by allying and rebuilding relations with other Greek powers. This raised tensions with Rome's regional allies, leading finally to war with Rome itself. Macedonia's forces were routed by the Roman general Aemilius Paullus at the Battle of Pydna in 168 BCE, and Perseus was led through Rome in a Triumph.

Macedonia's defeat left another confederation of Greek cities—the Achaean League, in southern Greece—as the main regional power. The league was allied to Rome, although not always harmoniously. In 146 BCE tensions between Rome and the Achaeans boiled over. In the war that followed, the city of Corinth was razed to the ground (as was Carthage that same year, during the Third Punic War) and mainland Greece was brought under direct Roman control for the first time.

A last stand in the east

Away from the mainland, a few Greek states and kingdoms held out for a while. Pergamum (in modern Türkiye) was allowed to retain its independence until 133 BCE, when its king, Attalus III, bequeathed the country to Rome in his will. In 88 BCE King Mithridates VI of Pontus, on the southern shores of the Black Sea, organized and coordinated a massacre of an estimated 80,000 Roman troops and citizens across Anatolia (in Türkiye) on a single night that was designed to drive the occupiers out of Asia Minor for good. In the resulting war, Mithridates resisted until 63 BCE, when he was defeated by Pompey the Great. In the south, the Macedonian descendants of Alexander the Great's general Ptolemy continued to rule in Egypt. But as Rome expanded ever eastward, Ptolemaic territories fell one by one. In 30 BCE the last of the Ptolemies, Cleopatra VII, died by her own hand rather than surrender to Roman forces led by Octavian, the future emperor Augustus (see pp. 134–135).

△ **Total Triumph**
Carle Vernet's *The Triumph of Aemilius Paulus* (1789) depicts the general's victory procession in Rome after Macedonia's final defeat in 168 BCE. Macedonia's king, Perseus, and his family walk behind the general's golden cart. His fate is unknown.

▷ **Roman cavalry charge**
This frieze adorned a monument in Delphi, Greece, commemorating Rome's victory at Pydna. Different phases of the battle are depicted across several panels.

Atrium Villa

A typical Roman home

In ancient Rome, housing varied depending on the location and period, and also on the owners' wealth, social status, and aspirations. The most common types of dwellings resembled the examples shown here. The layout of the atrium villa was described by the Roman writer Vitruvius in the 1st century BCE, and well-preserved examples survive in Pompeii. In this design, rooms for working, sleeping, and eating were arranged around a central atrium that was open to the sky. Roman homeowners appreciated lavish decoration, and some added the luxury of a "peristyle" colonnaded garden (see pp. 117–118). In larger cities, those of lesser means lived in multistory apartment buildings known as *insulae* (see opposite).

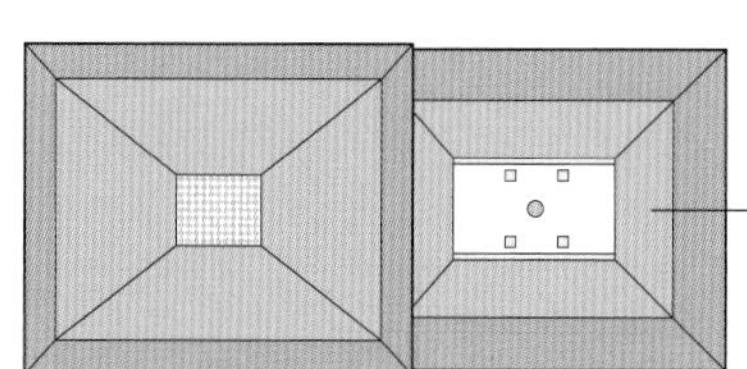

△ **Overhead view**
The roof was open over both the garden and atrium. Rainwater was gathered in a cistern beneath the atrium, for use in the home.

▽ **House of Menander atrium**
The central hall, or atrium, was designed to impress visitors. In this magnificent home in Pompeii, elaborate columns like those in public buildings flank the *tablinum*, where the master received them.

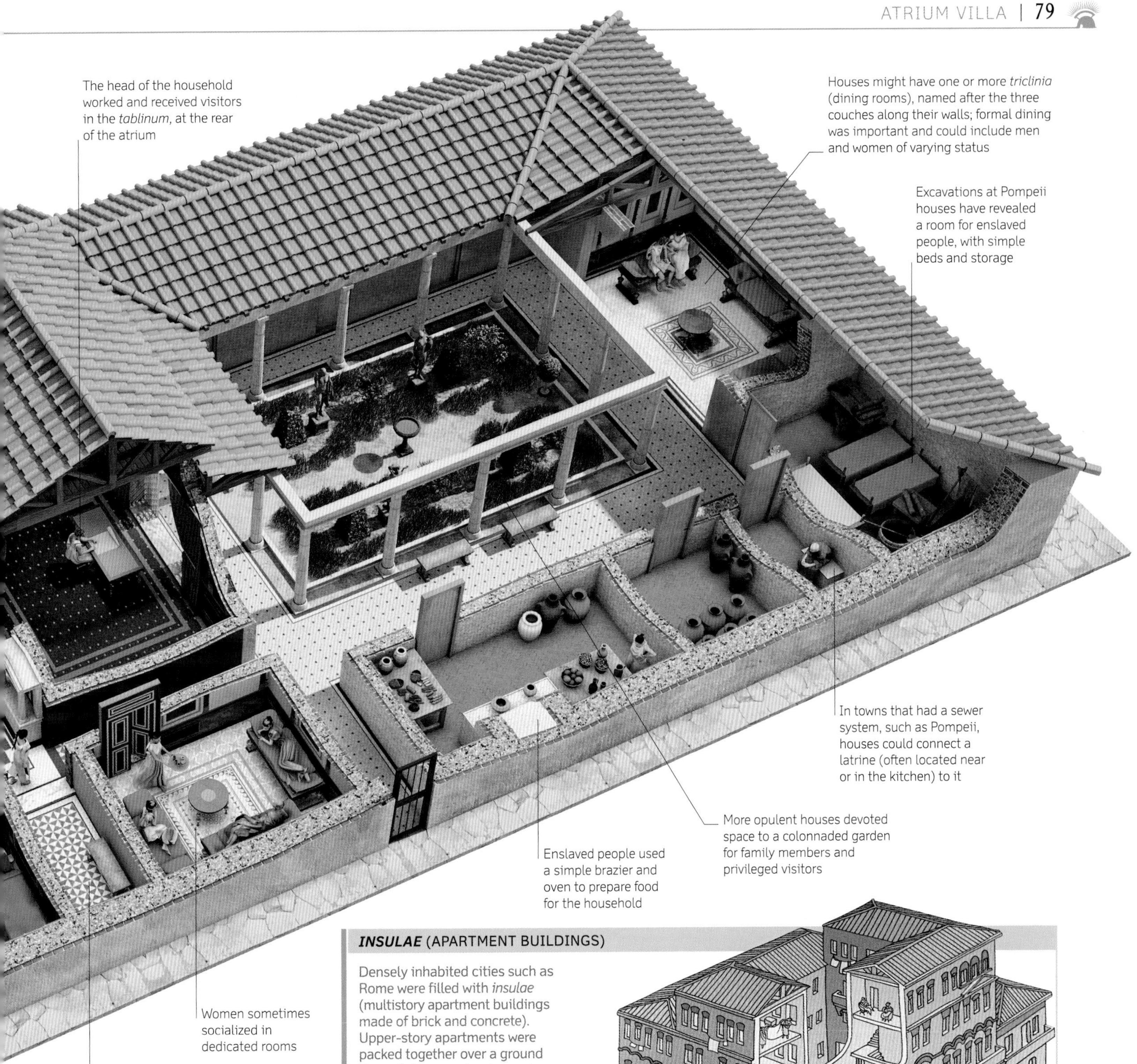

The head of the household worked and received visitors in the *tablinum*, at the rear of the atrium

Houses might have one or more *triclinia* (dining rooms), named after the three couches along their walls; formal dining was important and could include men and women of varying status

Excavations at Pompeii houses have revealed a room for enslaved people, with simple beds and storage

In towns that had a sewer system, such as Pompeii, houses could connect a latrine (often located near or in the kitchen) to it

More opulent houses devoted space to a colonnaded garden for family members and privileged visitors

Enslaved people used a simple brazier and oven to prepare food for the household

Women sometimes socialized in dedicated rooms

Durable, decorated mosaic floors were made of thousands of tiny stone cubes (tesserae)

△ **Roman house (reconstruction)** Rooms and spaces were adapted to different purposes, while frescoes and mosaics gave an impression of wealth. As in the example shown, homeowners liked to set up vistas and strong axes of symmetry throughout the house.

INSULAE (APARTMENT BUILDINGS)

Densely inhabited cities such as Rome were filled with *insulae* (multistory apartment buildings made of brick and concrete). Upper-story apartments were packed together over a ground floor of stores and restaurants, with a central courtyard housing a communal water fountain and latrine (aqueducts and sewers were essential to urban living at this density). In general, the higher up in the building, the cheaper the accommodation: the top floors were notorious for squalor, drafts, and the difficulty of escape in the event of a fire. By contrast, life in the frescoed multiroom apartments on lower floors could be very comfortable.

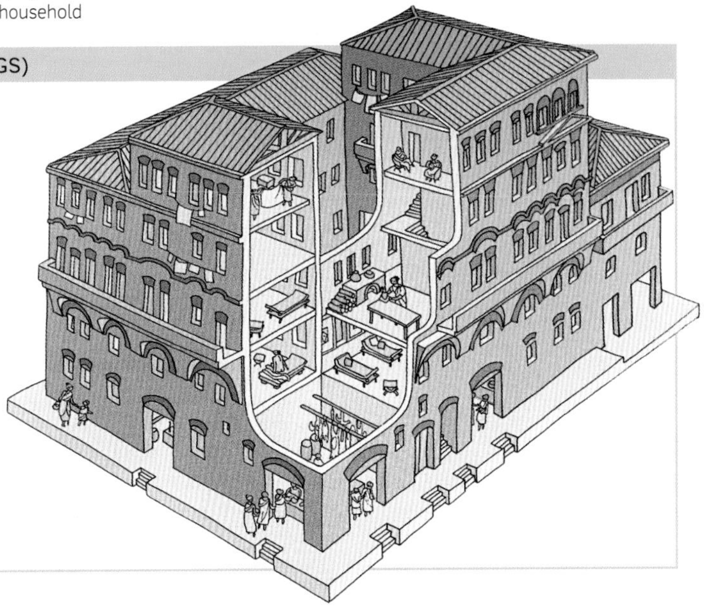

Weapons and Armor

Tools of war

Roman military equipment was extraordinarily diverse. Over a thousand years of history, the Roman army frequently changed its weaponry by integrating soldiers from across a vast territorial area, assimilating technologies of other societies into its arsenal. While equipment was more standardized during the Imperial era than in other periods, variety was still expected and often encouraged.

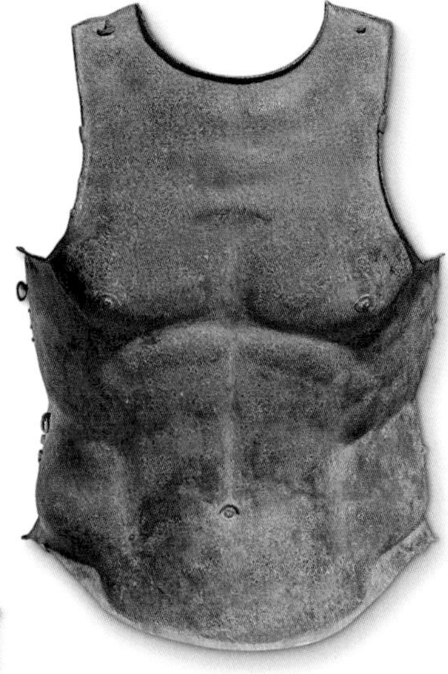

△ **Bronze cuirass**
The muscled bronze cuirass was popular for a long time throughout the ancient Mediterranean. Although often associated with the Greeks, most excavated examples are actually from Italy.

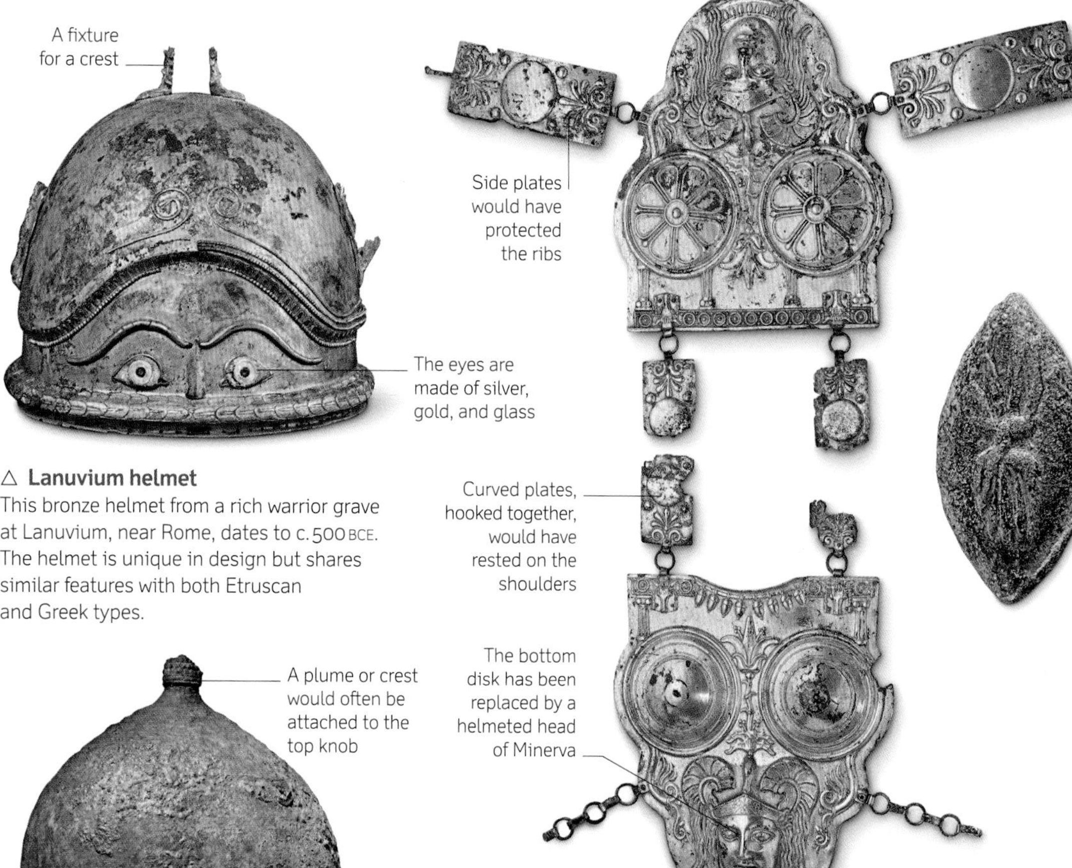

△ **Lanuvium helmet**
This bronze helmet from a rich warrior grave at Lanuvium, near Rome, dates to c. 500 BCE. The helmet is unique in design but shares similar features with both Etruscan and Greek types.

◁ **Lead bullet for a sling**
The Roman arsenal contained a wide range of missile weapons, including slings. Slingers used both rocks and manufactured bullets. A well-placed bullet could even bring down a heavily armored warrior.

△ **Ksour Essef cuirass**
This is an exceptional example of the triple-disk cuirass worn by soldiers in Italy during the 4th and 3rd centuries BCE. It was found in North Africa, possibly carried there by an Italian mercenary.

△ **Montefortino helmet**
The Montefortino-style helmet, brought to Italy by Celtic warriors, became a popular Roman helmet during the 4th century BCE. It was the archetypal Roman helmet by the Middle Republic.

△ ***Pilum***
Probably introduced by Celtic warriors, the *pilum* was a heavy javelin used across Italy during the 4th and 3rd centuries BCE. Designed to pierce shields, it was often used alongside and against the oblong *scutum*.

△ **Greaves**
Lower leg armor of one type or another was worn throughout the Roman period. These bronze greaves are from a 5th-century BCE warrior burial.

△ ***Scutum***
The rectangular *scutum* replaced the circular *aspis* as the Roman shield by the Middle Republic. This example, from the city of Dura-Europos (in present-day Syria) and dating from the 3rd century CE, is one of the best preserved.

△ ***Pugio***
Often richly decorated, the *pugio* was a dagger used during the Imperial era. Its full significance is not known, although it probably served as a backup weapon.

△ **Spear points**
Spears were the most common weapons used in ancient warfare, and points like these could be found on spear shafts throughout the Roman period.

△ ***Gladius***
By the Late Republic, the Roman *gladius*, or short sword, was the main infantry weapon. This example is a "Pompeii type" (the most common) and dates to the 1st century CE.

The tang of the blade would have been covered by a wooden handle

△ ***Spatha***
The *spatha* was a longer version of the infantry sword, or *gladius*, and was originally used by cavalry and auxiliary troops. With its longer reach, it gradually replaced the *gladius* and was the basis for early medieval swords.

△ **Iron legionary helmet**
This legionary helmet, found in Brigetio (in modern Hungary), dates to the 1st century CE. A descendant of the bronze Montefortino helmets of the Republic, this thick iron helmet offered significant protection.

△ **Iron ridge helmet**
This exceptional Roman ridge helmet from the 4th century CE was excavated in the village of Berkasovo in Serbia. Its name derives from the raised band that unites the sheets of iron. This example is decorated with glass and silver.

△ **Hot-headed god**
This unusual object is an incense burner in the shape of Baal-Hammon, the chief god of Carthage. It is from the mid-2nd century BCE, between the Second and Third Punic Wars.

The Punic Wars

A titanic battle for supremacy in the west

The three Punic Wars spanned a century and fundamentally changed Roman and Carthaginian society. Rome began the wars an emerging power and ended them the master of the western Mediterranean. Carthage, meanwhile, was destroyed.

The people of Rome and Carthage had been in contact since at least the 6th century BCE. Inscriptions dating from c. 500 BCE suggest that Carthaginian traders were common in Italy from that time. Sources also record a treaty between the states supposedly dated to 509 BCE. While parts of the treaty, which was renewed in 349 BCE and 306 BCE, may hint at potential tensions, there is little to suggest that the relationship would develop into one of the great conflicts of the ancient world. At one time, during the Pyrrhic War of 280–275 BCE, the two states were even allies. This took place at a time when Rome's territorial expansion into

◁ **Weapons of mass destruction**
Hannibal Crossing the Alps on an Elephant by the French artist Nicolas Poussin (1594–1665) shows the Carthaginian general Hannibal Barca on one of the animals that, initially, terrified Roman soldiers during the Second Punic War. Of all the Punic leaders, Hannibal came the closest to defeating Rome.

◁ **A Mediterranean war**
The Punic Wars were fought across the entire western half of the Mediterranean. The epicenter of the first war was Sicily, but the conflict widened to encompass much of the territory controlled by Rome.

southern Italy (see pp. 56–57) was bringing it into contact—and conflict—with local power-brokers, chief among them Pyrrhus, king of Epirus (modern-day northwestern Greece). Carthage chose to ally with Rome in the war, as it was vying with Pyrrhus at the time for control of the island of Sicily.

Rome's costly but successful confrontation with Pyrrhus was an outcome of its increasing involvement in the complicated network of social and political struggles that had been festering for centuries in southern Italy and the surrounding region. As Roman power and influence spread south toward the Mediterranean, it became ever more likely that there would be a confrontation with the area's other main expansionist state: Carthage.

The First Punic War (264–241 BCE)

The Punic Wars began in Sicily (the word "Punic" derives from "Phoenecia," as the first Carthaginian settlers came from Phoenicia—modern Lebanon—in the Middle East). After Pyrrhus had been defeated in 275 BCE, Carthage became the preeminent power on the island—but not without opposition. Syracuse and other Greek and native Sicilian communities contested the Carthaginians' ascendancy, and the First Punic War began when the city of Messana in northern Sicily asked the Romans for help against Carthaginian "aggression" in 264 BCE. It is not clear why Rome agreed to Messana's request, but its recent expansion across Italy must have played a part. Rome now stood at the head of a federation of states and families whose interests it needed to protect, including those of its new southern citizens and allies.

Fighting in Sicily spread quickly, with Syracuse and other settlements joining the Roman alliance against Carthage. Rome did well on land, but struggled at sea. The Greek historian Polybius, writing in the 2nd century BCE, suggested it was because the Romans were naval beginners. This is unlikely: there is evidence that Rome created a small navy as far back as the 4th century BCE, and the state had maritime links across the Mediterranean. What is clear, however, is that the Romans were not operating nautically at the same scale as Carthage—at least not at first. An important factor in Rome's victory in the First Punic War was its rapid development of an enormous navy, which it used to defeat Carthage in a series of key naval engagements—most notably the Battle of the Aegates Islands in 241 BCE. After the war, Carthage ceded control of Sicily, Corsica, and Sardinia to Rome and shifted its focus west to Spain. Hostilities between the states were over—for now. »

A ROMAN **VICTORY AT SEA**

The Battle of the Aegates Islands was a naval encounter fought on March 10, 241 BCE. Although outnumbered, the Roman fleet defeated the Carthaginians, which led directly to the conclusion of the First Punic War. In the early 2000s the battle site was discovered and since 2005, 19 bronze rams (*rostra*) have been recovered from the sea floor, with other pieces of military equipment, including helmets (the excavations are continuing). The *rostra* were mounted on the front prows of ancient ships, slightly below the waterline, allowing them to ram and sink enemy vessels (see pp. 134–135).

The Romans collected the rams of enemy ships as war trophies

264 BCE First Punic War begins when Romans land in Messana, Sicily

241 BCE Naval Battle of the Aegates Islands ends the First Punic War

218 BCE Hannibal besieges Saguntum; the Second Punic War begins

216 BCE Hannibal defeats the Romans at the Battle of Cannae

205 BCE Scipio Africanus is victorious in Spain

202 BCE Scipio Africanus defeats Hannibal in North Africa at Zama

151 BCE Rome's ally Numidia provokes Carthage to battle, starting the Third Punic War

146 BCE Carthage is sacked and destroyed; the Third Punic War ends

The Second Punic War (218–201 BCE)

Competing interests in Spain led to the Second Punic War. In 226 BCE Rome and Carthage signed a treaty agreeing to recognize the Ebro River as the limit of their respective influences. Soon after, however, Rome allied itself with the town of Saguntum, located in what was considered to be Carthaginian territory south of the Ebro. In 218 BCE Saguntum was attacked by forces led by Hannibal Barca, the Carthaginian commander-in-chief in Spain. The Romans declared war in order to protect their ally and conflict quickly spread across the central and western Mediterranean.

Taking the fight to the Romans, Hannibal famously invaded Italy. He marched across the Alps with 20,000 infantry, 6,000 cavalry, and 37 elephants, while also avoiding a Roman army taking an easier route in the opposite direction. Once in Italy, Hannibal led a successful campaign against Rome and its allies with victories at Ticinus, Trebia, and Lake Trasimene in the north. This campaign culminated in 216 BCE with his destruction of a Roman army of 80,000 men at Cannae, in southeastern Italy.

After these defeats the Romans avoided direct engagements with Hannibal, preferring to adopt guerrilla tactics against him. This allowed Hannibal to range freely across Italy. He even approached Rome itself, although he did not attack the city, owing to its impressive fortifications. Instead, the Carthaginians concentrated on attempting to break up the network of alliances that Rome had established across Italy,

▽ ***Aeneas and Dido* (1675)**
In Virgil's *Aeneid*, the hero Aeneas and Queen Dido of Carthage fall in love. When he leaves her (shown in this painting by Claude Lorrain), Dido takes her own life. In the story, Dido (representing Carthage) is passionate and volatile; Aeneas (as Rome) is dutiful and strong.

but it was something they managed with only limited success. While a few communities, such as Capua and Tarentum, went over to Hannibal, most did not and honored the treaties they had agreed with Rome during its conquest of the Italian peninsula.

While Hannibal was winning in Italy, the Romans were active in Spain. However, their efforts proved inconclusive until the arrival of Publius Cornelius Scipio in 210 BCE as the Romans' new commander. Young and inexperienced (he was not yet 30), his appointment broke with several conventions. But he also came from one of Rome's oldest and most illustrious patrician clans and had family connections in Spain that saw his generalship approved. With Scipio's arrival the war moved in Rome's favor. By 205 BCE Spain had largely been secured for Rome. The following year Scipio invaded the Carthaginians' home soil of North Africa, forcing Hannibal to leave Italy and return to Carthage. Hannibal had not yet arrived when, in 203 BCE, a surprise Roman attack at Utica, near Carthage, caught his compatriots unawares. The next year, Hannibal was decisively defeated at the Battle of Zama by Scipio's legions, aided by local Numidian allies (see pp. 106–107).

Following the war, Carthage lost all of its overseas territories and some of its North African possessions. Its army and navy were reduced to a token force and the state was forced to pay an indemnity of 10,000 talents of silver to Rome, the equivalent in weight of more than 275 tons (250 metric tons). In recognition of his achievements, Publius Scipio was awarded a Triumph and given the honorific title "Africanus."

Hannibal's legacy

Entering the war, Rome had been a powerful federation of elite Italian families and communities. Exiting it, Rome was a cohesive and ambitious state and society. The conflict helped forge a distinct Roman identity and an ideal of citizenship that had been slowly emerging since the late 4th and 3rd centuries BCE. The war forced Italians together, and toward Rome. Some were unwilling but saw, for example, citizens of Carthage's ally Capua deprived of their political rights. The Second Punic War also saw a new type of Roman leader and public servant emerge: men who believed in the direction their state was taking and were enthusiastic about Rome's growing empire. After the Second Punic War, Rome embarked on an era of conquest across the Mediterranean (see pp. 76–77 and pp. 90–91). At the same time, a distinctively "Roman" culture began to flourish.

The Third Punic War (149–146 BCE)

Although Rome had defeated Carthage, it continued to fear its old enemy. The deeply conservative Roman censor and senator Cato the Elder (see pp. 74–75) waged an almost lifelong campaign against Carthage and the threat he believed it posed. He ended every public speech he made with the words "*Carthago delenda est*" ("Carthage must be destroyed") and, ultimately, his wish was granted. In the 150s BCE Carthage came into conflict with Masinissa, the Numidian king, and Roman ally. Forbidden to have its own army, Carthage appealed to Rome for help. When this was not forthcoming, Carthage took up arms to defend itself—leading Rome to launch the Third Punic War against it. Carthage was indeed destroyed at the end of the war. It was rebuilt, however, and by the 3rd century CE was one of the largest cities in the Roman Empire.

THE GREAT **HARBOR OF CARTHAGE**

The Carthaginians were skilled seafarers, and the Great Harbor of Carthage was one of the major civil engineering achievements of the ancient world. It was heavily defended and monumental in scale, with an outer section for civilian ships leading to a circular inner harbor (the *cothon*) that could supposedly berth up to 220 military vessels. It was built either just before or just after the Second Punic War, and therefore can be seen as an imposing symbol of continued military might, or a monument to Carthage's lost glory.

△ **Carthaginian crafts**
Glassmaking was an important industry in Carthage. This colored glass pendant from the 4th or 3rd century BCE showcases the Carthaginian artisan's skill.

▷ **Source of information**
The Greek historian Polybius's *Histories* was written in the mid-2nd century BCE and is one of the earliest sources on the Punic Wars.

> "**Crossing their borders** with a hostile army, Hannibal **laid waste** to their country."
>
> LIVY'S HISTORY OF ROME, *AB URBE CONDITA*

Equestrian statues indicate this is an important public space, possibly a forum

A citizen wears his "best" white toga to receive news of the proclamation

After being read out, the notice may have been posted onto one of the statues

△ The art of politics
This fresco from Pompeii is thought to show citizens gathering together to listen to an official announcement being issued. Civic administration was not usually a subject for Roman artwork, making this is a rare example of the genre.

The Cursus Honorum

Ascending the ladder of political power

A comfortable career in the Senate was not enough for some ambitious politicians in Rome. But those seeking high office knew that the only way to secure the top position of consul was to rise through the ranks, one step at a time.

In Rome, men—and only men—interested in a political career were expected to work their way through the *cursus honorum* ("course of honors"), Rome's hierarchy of public magistracies. Achieving high office guaranteed a man's family distinction and the preservation of their memory. Positions were elected and were held for one year. Candidates exploited family networks and spent huge sums to win office, sponsoring public games, for example. A guide to electioneering, supposedly written for Cicero (see pp. 86–87) by his brother Quintus, states that a candidate had to maintain a high public profile, make as many promises to as many interest groups as possible (even if he could not fulfill them), and attack his political enemies while extolling his own virtues.

This system favored Rome's wealthy and well-connected elites, but talented "new men" such as Cicero, from more humble backgrounds, were able to break in. He, in fact, made a virtue of this, and went on to hold all four of the main *cursus honorum* offices.

◁ **Seat of power**
Despite its modest appearance, the foldable bronze and canvas curule seat symbolized senior magistracy roles, such as chairing the Senate.

Climbing the *cursus honorum*

The lowest rung on the *cursus honorum* was occupied by the 20 *quaestors*, who looked after Rome's treasury and were aged at least 30. From then on, competition intensified. The next office was that of the four aediles, who supervised Rome's festivals, oversaw public order, and maintained the city's buildings. Two aedileships were reserved for plebeians; the minimum age was 35. Above the aediles were the eight praetors, with powers covering administrative and judicial matters, who essentially kept Rome running. In 180 BCE the *lex Villia annalis* specified their age as at least 40.

The highest rung on the *cursus honorum* was the Consulship. The two men who reached this position each year led Rome's armies and presided over the Senate (see pp. 62–63). When both consuls were in Rome they alternated power each month; for much of the Republic at least one was away, either visiting provinces or on military campaign. Consuls had to be at least 42 years old.

There were other magistracies and offices, but the *cursus honorum* was the main route to success in the Republic; it was also a necessary step toward governing a colony (Proconsulship) or province (Propraetorship). While the Consulship remained highly prestigious, in the Imperial age candidates were appointed at the favor of the emperor, who looked to his inner court for advice. This enabled talented men from nontraditional backgrounds, even freedmen, to bypass the *cursus honorum* by taking up administrative roles at the imperial court.

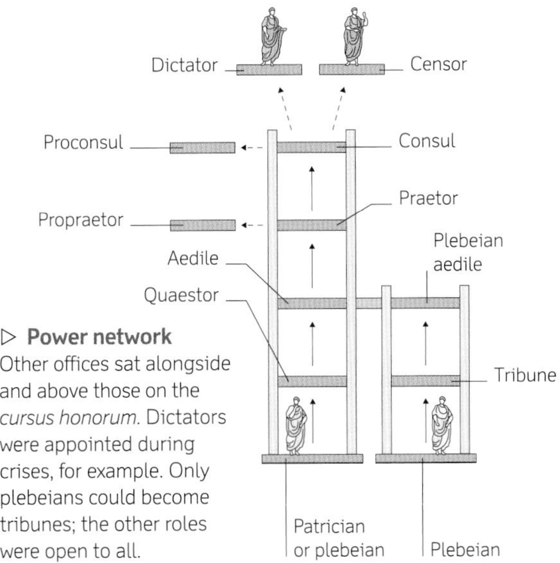

▷ **Power network**
Other offices sat alongside and above those on the *cursus honorum*. Dictators were appointed during crises, for example. Only plebeians could become tribunes; the other roles were open to all.

▽ **Planning permission**
This shrine, the Altar of the Lares Augusti (c. 2 CE) was built by *vico magistri*. Under Augustus, these lower-level officials, often freedmen, were responsible for shrines to guardian deities in each Roman neighborhood.

Slavery

Dependency and abuse in every Roman household

Roman society depended on slavery and gloried in its dehumanizing violence toward enslaved people. Yet throughout their hardships many of the enslaved maintained their dignity, protested, survived, and in some cases even thrived.

△ **Collar**
The message on this neck collar offers a reward in gold for its wearer's return. This suggests the wearer had skills that needed to be protected, or had previously attempted escape—or both.

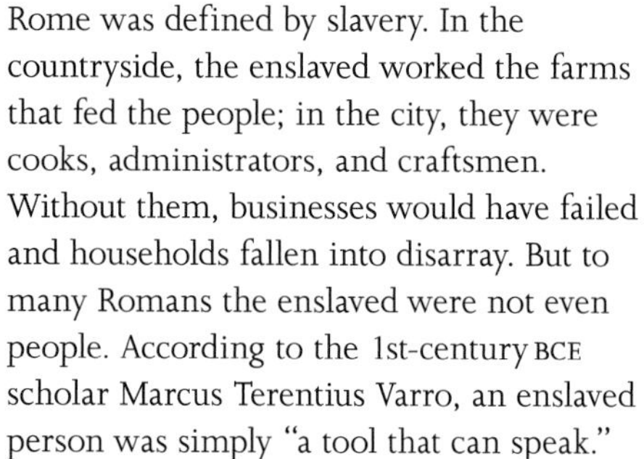

Rome was defined by slavery. In the countryside, the enslaved worked the farms that fed the people; in the city, they were cooks, administrators, and craftsmen. Without them, businesses would have failed and households fallen into disarray. But to many Romans the enslaved were not even people. According to the 1st-century BCE scholar Marcus Terentius Varro, an enslaved person was simply "a tool that can speak."

△ **Supplementing their rations**
Two men prepare an animal for a feast in this fresco from the 1st century CE. Roman kitchens could be hot, crowded places, but for the enslaved people working in them they could also be sources of extra food to add to the daily rations they received.

People as personal property

Roman history's most famous enslaver-and-enslaved relationship was that between Cicero and Tiro. Letters sent to and from Tiro suggest an affectionate (even loving) relationship between the two, which culminated in Tiro's emancipation. Less well-known is Dionysius; like Tiro, he was enslaved and one of Cicero's secretaries. Unlike Tiro, Dionysius found life in Cicero's household so intolerable that he risked torture, mutilation, and death escaping Rome and seeking refuge with a rebellious tribe in the freezing wilds of the Balkans. Cicero's agents pursued Dionysius for years, but his fate is unknown. Of the two enslaved men, Tiro's story is the least representative.

For most enslaved people, the power imbalance between them and their enslavers was clear. They were property and had no autonomy. The threat of sexual assault was ever present and they could be beaten for any reason. If an enslaved person attempted escape, they could be shackled, branded, and crucified.

◁ **Roman rough justice**
This scene from Trajan's Column shows a soldier harshly treating a captured warrior from Dacia (in present-day Romania). Many such prisoners of war were enslaved.

Capture and rebellion

The main source of slavery was conquest, and captured men, women, and children were publicly bought and sold in the Forum and the Saepta, the voting grounds on the Campus Martius.

Yet despite their "servile" and inferior status, the enslaved were aware that Rome's survival depended on their economic input. This gave them a form of power, as did the fact that they outnumbered Rome's citizenry. The three large revolts known as the Servile Wars showed that the enslaved were ready to assert their humanity and their dignity when they were pushed too far. The First Servile War (135–132 BCE) began as an act of resistance in Sicily against a brutal enslaver and was led by the Syrian Eunous and Kleon, from Cilicia (in modern Türkiye) The Second Servile War (104–101 BCE) arose after an order to free a number of plantation workers in Sicily was revoked. The Third Servile War (73–71 BCE) was initially a revolt of enslaved gladiators, led by the Thracian Spartacus (see pp. 110–111). Although suppressed, all three uprisings left deep scars on the Roman psyche.

Aspiration and assimilation

Some owners manumitted (freed) enslaved people, usually in their wills. An enslaved person could also buy their liberty. But even after manumission, a former enslaved person still owed many obligations to their ex-master. Their rights were curtailed, too; they could not hold public office, for example. Their children enjoyed full citizens' rights, but the social stigma associated with freedpeople and their descendants was long-lasting. This had as much to do with envy as snobbery: many freedpeople were better off than most Roman citizens, especially if in their servitude they had mastered a trade or skills such as literacy. In fact, freedmen dominated the emperor's staff in the Imperial age. Pallas, a Greek freedman, was an important imperial secretary in the reigns of Claudius and Nero.

This power shift enraged the aristocratic elite, who saw their own influence decline with the marginalization of the Senate that they controlled. Sidelined and frustrated, nobles began to treat their households as their own miniature empires—all, of course, at the expense of the enslaved.

▷ **Prisoners in chains**
This undated relief is from the gate of the Roman camp at Mogontiacum (modern Mainz, in Germany). Although rudimentary in execution, it graphically depicts the harsh fate that awaited men after their capture in battle. The gate on which this relief was affixed would have been built by enslaved people.

Thick, heavy chains bind both captives at the neck

Germanic warriors fought virtually naked, wearing just a small cloak

"**Iucundus,** slave of Taurus, as long as he lived, he was a man and **stood up for himself and others.**"

FROM THE COLUMBARIUM OF THE STATILII TAURI FAMILY: EPITAPH OF AN ENSLAVED MAN CONTRIBUTED BY FELLOW ENSLAVED MEMBERS OF HIS HOUSEHOLD

Conquering Hispania

From Carthage to the Caesars

When the Romans conquered the Iberian Peninsula—known to them as Hispania—they took over a territory with a rich culture, shaped by centuries of colonization. In time, the Romans, too, would leave their mark on the land.

Centuries before its conquest by Rome, the Iberian Peninsula—what we now call Spain and Portugal—was already of interest to other colonizers from across the Mediterranean world. These included both the Phoenicians and the Greeks, who had explored the southern and eastern coasts of the peninsula, establishing colonies at Gadir (modern Cádiz), Malaca (Málaga), and Eivissa (Ibiza). Around the same time they colonized the Iberian coast, the Phoenicians also established one of the most important cities in the ancient world: Carthage, in modern Tunisia. It was the Carthaginian presence in Iberia that brought the peninsula to the attention of Rome.

△ **Iberian jewelery**
Made of bronze and silver, this belt clasp was probably worn by a Celtiberian soldier. Hispania's silver mines attracted ancient empires.

Hannibal in Hispania

Following its defeat by Rome in the First Punic War (264–241 BCE), the Carthaginian Empire was forced to give up its territory in Sicily (see pp. 82–83). The Carthaginians tried to rebuild their trading empire by expanding their territories on the Iberian Peninsula, which was known to be rich in silver. This campaign was led by Hamilcar Barca, the father of Hannibal. By around 229 BCE the Carthaginians controlled about half of the peninsula (in the south and on its eastern coast), a situation Rome viewed with increasing concern. This led to a treaty in 226 BCE, limiting both powers' expansion there. Hannibal, however, had vowed never to be a friend to Rome; in 219–218 BCE he conquered Saguntum (modern Sagunto, near Valencia), a prosperous city that had allied itself to Rome, which initiated the Second Punic War (see pp. 84–85).

While Hannibal marched his forces overland (including over the Alps) to invade Italy, the Roman forces of Publius Cornelius Scipio were defeating the Carthaginians in Hispania. After victories in key battles in 208–207 BCE, Scipio's army was able to eject Carthage from the region, and Scipio himself returned to Rome in 206 BCE. (He later used his successes in Hispania as a launchpad for an invasion of North Africa, the Carthaginian homeland, leading to Rome's eventual victory in the Second Punic War.)

EARLIER **COLONIZATION OF HISPANIA**

The cultures of the major Mediterranean seafaring powers that arrived on the Iberian Peninsula before the Romans—notably those of the Phoenicians and Greeks—all left an impression. This Iberian statue, known as the Lady of Elche (near Valencia in southeastern Spain), dates from the 4th century BCE. The figure is believed to be Tanit, the main goddess of Carthage. Although the subject is Phoenician, as are the headdress and jewelery, the style of the statue also shows clear evidence of Greek artistic influences, demonstrating the cultural interactions that took place across the ancient world. Once, it would have been brightly colored and perhaps part of a seated statue rather than merely a bust.

THE LADY OF ELCHE

▷ **La Olmeda Roman Villa mosaic**
Hispania was home to some exceptional Roman mosaics. This *venatio*, or beast-hunting, scene was found in a Roman villa from the 4th century CE, in Palencia, Spain. It shows trained hunters fighting various animals for sport—a popular public spectacle.

In the following centuries, Rome extended its control over the peninsula, but not without cost. The empire encountered fierce resistance from the local Celtiberian tribes, against whom it fought (and won) several long and costly wars. The conflicts between Romans and Iberians would continue well into the late 1st century BCE.

Roman provinces

The Cantabrian Wars (29–19 BCE), the final stage of the Roman conquest of the Iberian Peninsula, were waged in northern Hispania. Emperor Augustus's defeat of the Cantabri Celtiberians ended Iberian resistance to the Romans, and three provinces were added to the empire: Hispania Citerior (literally "nearer Spain"); Hispania Ulterior ("further Spain"); and Lusitania. In time, Hispania would become one of the most secure and important regions of the empire. The emperors Trajan and Hadrian were both from Hispania; they were born in Italica (near modern-day Seville) in the 2nd century CE. Revered poets and philosophers would also come from Roman Hispania, including Martial, Lucan, and Seneca (see pp. 272–273).

Just as it had been before the Roman conquest, Hispania under the Romans was a rich melting pot of different cultures: archaeological finds there show the influences of both Roman and older cultures. Many features of a recognizably Roman way of life were adopted. New cities, including Tarraco (Tarragona), Emerita Augusta (Mérida), and Zaragoza (Caesaraugusta), were built with grand Roman civic structures, such as theaters and aqueducts.

△ **Grand theater**
This Roman theater was built in Emerita Augusta (Mérida) around 15 BCE on the orders of Marcus Agrippa, the close associate of Augustus. It was restored by later emperors.

Exotic animals were brought from distant corners of the empire

Despite this natural setting, these events took place in Roman theaters

A *bestiarius* ("beast hunter") felled by his prey

Ruling the Provinces

Controlling and connecting an empire

The fundamental building blocks of the empire were the provinces—regions ruled by Republican governors and, later, emperors themselves. Over time, intricate networks of communication and exchange were established between them.

Outside Italy, the Roman Empire was divided into administrative units called *provinciae* (provinces). These were introduced as Rome expanded its power during the Republican period and remained—with ongoing reform and revision—throughout the Imperial period. The provinces provided the administrative framework for controlling the vast territory of the Roman Empire. Over time they became increasingly connected, enabling the movement of goods, people, and ideas.

◁ **Empire-building**
The labor of building an empire, including road construction, was a celebrated virtue and was depicted on Trajan's Column (see pp. 214–215).

Administration and authority

The province defined a territory that was controlled by Roman authorities. Provinces were introduced to coincide with the expansion of Roman power outside Italy during the Republican period; this began after Rome's victory over the Carthaginian Empire in the First Punic War in 241 BCE. (see pp. 82–85). Sicily became the first province as a result of this, followed shortly after by Sardinia and Corsica in 237 BCE.

Each province was controlled by a governor to whom the Senate had awarded *imperium*: authority to command troops and oversee the area. This magistrate was appointed by the Senate, and was supported by a quaestor and a *legatus*, high-ranking legal and military delegates. Distance from Rome and the Senate's authority often allowed governors free rein; consequently, the decades of Rome's rapid expansion in the 2nd and 1st centuries BCE were marked by accounts of exploitation, with governors often using their power to extort riches from their provinces. In fact, Cicero (see pp. 118–119) first came to prominence in 70 BCE for prosecuting a corrupt provincial governor; his speeches excoriating Gaius Verres, the former governor of Sicily, appear in a text known as *In Verrem*.

▽ **Roman rule**
This map shows the empire's provinces and major roads at its greatest geographic expanse, at the time of Trajan's death in 117 CE.

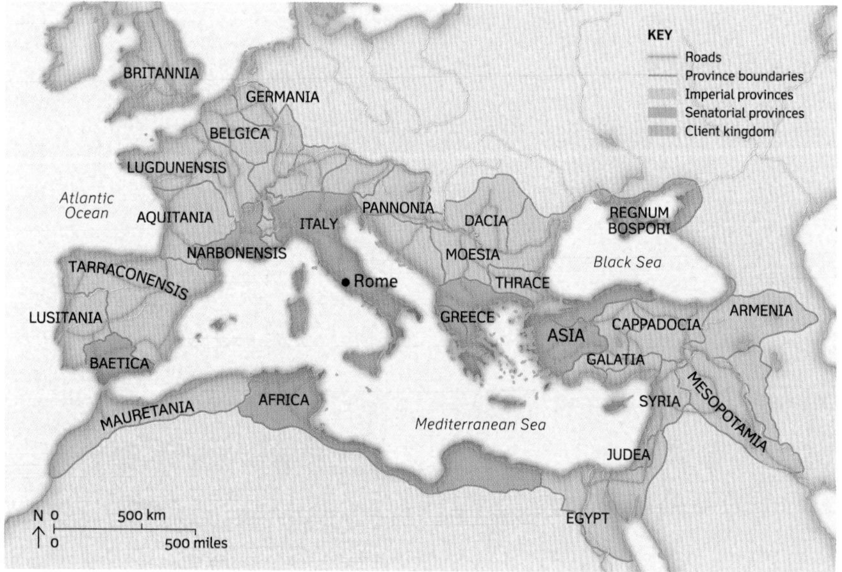

Imperial age

Provinces remained the fundamental unit of imperial administration, but the rise of the emperors changed their organization. A key development was the recognition of two types of province: senatorial provinces that were administered by a Senate-appointed magistrate, and imperial provinces ruled by the emperor through his delegate. In 27 BCE Augustus decreed that several strategically important provinces would remain governed by the emperor himself or by his official delegate. Egypt was a significant imperial

province with special status; it was responsible for much of the grain that fed Rome and was controlled by a *praefectus* (prefect), who was of equestrian rank, a wealthy landowning class below the senatorial class.

During the Imperial period, the number of provinces continued to grow, albeit less rapidly. Britannia (England and Wales) was added by Claudius, while Trajan added the province of Dacia (now Romania). Client kingdoms, such as Regnum Bospori, were also established on the periphery. While these regions were not officially part of the empire, the Romans wielded control over them by influencing their rulers.

By land and sea

The provinces were connected by numerous highly intricate and well-maintained transportation routes. On land, an extensive road network linked cities both within and across provincial boundaries. Road-building was closely linked to empire-building and had begun with the construction of the Appian Way in 312 BCE (see pp. 220–221). Large sections of this road, which connected Rome to Brundisium (modern Brindisi, Italy), can still be seen today. It was highly important that emperors and other provincial administrators were seen to care for the roads that allowed the empire's inhabitants to travel and trade.

The empire was also connected by routes across the water. The city of Rome was served by two main harbors: Ostia and Portus (see pp. 216–217). Around the empire, ships navigated coasts, rivers, and canals to reach provincial ports such as Carthage and Ephesus. Evidence has shown that Roman merchants were able to use both sea and land routes beyond Europe to trade with the ancient civilizations in India and China. These eastern passages help explain why cities such as Palmyra, in the province of Syria, became such important trading centers.

GOLDEN **MILESTONE**

Milestones were common sights on the roads of the Roman Empire. These measured out distances between cities, connecting the urban centers of the empire. They commemorated an emperor's care for the roads (*cura viarum*), an important imperial responsibility. The emperor Augustus notably erected a golden milestone (*milliarium aureum*) in the Forum in 20 BCE. This was a symbolic marker, the starting point of the empire's entire road network, in which all roads famously led to Rome.

MILLIARIUM AUREUM

△ **Loading goods**
This fresco, from Rome's port city of Ostia, dates from the early 3rd century CE. It depicts foodstuffs, labeled as *res* ("things"), being loaded onto a river boat, the *Isis Geminiana*, ready for transporting.

Daily Bread

Baking in ancient Rome

As the most important ingredient in the Roman diet, the humble bread loaf became a symbol of the empire's security—and of the vast inequality between its richest and poorest citizens.

◁ **Baker's tomb**
The frieze on the tomb of Eurysaces, a Roman freedman and baker, depicts the process of baking in a commercial bakery around the 1st century BCE. Here, the bread oven is being operated.

Bread was a staple food across the Roman Empire. Symbolically, it was cooked on the family hearth, but in practice, larger houses had a separate bakery within the enslaved workers' quarters. This was usually near the household shrine, which the enslaved workers tended with devotion (see pp. 122–123). At home, bread was made with a leaven (starter) and millet or barley flour. Because there were no refrigerators, the starter was baked into cakes that could be hydrated later.

In *insulae*, or apartment buildings (see p. 79), ovens were a fire hazard, so residents took their grain to a baker, and the bread made from their grain would be stamped before baking to identify it. Commercial bakeries contracted to supply state institutions would also stamp their dough for accountability.

Bakeries were originally combined with mills. Most baking was done by enslaved people; this work was one of the most brutal forms of labor. Bakery owners treated their enslaved workers poorly and meted out harsh punishments. In state-affiliated commercial bakeries, officials checked the bread produced against the amount of grain delivered to prevent theft.

△ **Stamp of ownership**
This mark ("century Quintinius Aquila") is from a military bread stamp found in Wales. Each "century" of soldiers had its own stamp, to claim bread from shared ovens.

Grains of power

As Rome's empire expanded, a state grain dole was set up to ensure that all citizens received a share in the profits. Poorer Romans relied heavily on grain rations, to the extent that rations were often distributed by politicians canvassing for favor.

The *cura annonae* ("care of the grain supply") became more important as Rome grew increasingly dependent on imported grain from provinces such as Sicily, which Cicero called the "nursemaid of the Roman plebs." The general and politician Pompey the Great (see pp. 126–127) owed much of his success to his defeat of pirates who threatened Rome's import routes. His son, Sextus, learned from this: during his standoff with Octavian (later Augustus), he used Sicily as a base to block Rome's grain supply (see pp. 134–135).

THE *THERMOPOLIUM*

For residents of *insulae*, who tended to eat outside their homes, local street food vendors provided a community hub. A *thermopolium* ("hot food shop") was a precursor to modern-day fast-food outlets; these shops sold ready-to-eat meals, typically served with coarse bread. Many were attached to inns and were run by both men and women. As a society obsessed with cleanliness, richer Romans preferred to eat and entertain at home, so frequenting *thermopolia* was considered a sign of lower status. The *thermopolium* below, excavated in 2019–20 in Pompeii, features a fresco of the shop itself, showing the *dolia*, or masonry jars, that held the dishes on sale.

Figures wear short cloaks associated with travel

Panis quadratus ("segmented loaf") has a distinct shape

Whitened toga shows this man is a candidate for election

▽ **Distribution of bread**
This fresco from the wall of a *tablinum*, or office, in Pompeii depicts bread distribution as part of a political campaign. The loaves shown here match those found in Pompeii (see pp. 136–137).

Symbols

The signs of Roman power and identity

As Roman control spread across the Mediterranean world, the use of symbols allowed the conquerors to communicate their supremacy. Some of these have lasted to this day as powerful icons in modern politics and culture.

△ **Bearing the *fasces***
Fasces, a bundle of wooden rods around an ax, were carried before magistrates by their attendants or lictors. *Fasces* were symbols of Roman political authority.

The Roman Empire was a world of images, with numerous icons and symbols used to express different ideas. These were often about power, culture, and identity. Many symbols originated in Rome but they soon spread across the empire's provinces, and have been found throughout the Mediterranean world and beyond. The widespread presence of these symbols shows how important they were to Romans as a way to both proclaim their dominance and link disparate communities in a shared understanding of the might of Rome.

Icons of identity

Images could cut across the linguistic and cultural differences that existed across the vast empire. In the provinces, they informed conquered people of their place within the wider Roman world. The image of the she-wolf suckling the twins Romulus and Remus was a commonly used symbol of Rome. The goddess Roma was also often used to represent Roman identity, and temples to the goddess were built around the empire. She was depicted in various forms, such as on coins where she was often shown seated atop a pile of weapons—a reminder of the relationship between Roman identity and military strength.

In Roman politics, symbols could denote rank and authority, such as the *fasces*—a bundle of rods surrounding an ax—which represented official power. These were carried by lictors, the bodyguards of Roman magistrates (see pp. 28–29), whose importance was indicated by the number of lictors in attendance. The bundled sticks stood for strength through unity, while the ax symbolized the magistrate's power (*imperium*) and his authority to punish those who disobeyed. Combined, the bundle of rods and ax conveyed Roman power, political order, and justice.

The wreath was another potent symbol of prestige. Different kinds of wreaths, called *coronae* ("crowns"), were awarded depending on the achievement of the individual, and were made from foliage, such as oak or myrtle. Laurel wreaths, in particular, were awarded to Roman generals celebrating a great military triumph, and some emperors portrayed themselves adorned in them. The wreath became an icon of Roman power, used in art around the empire, and its association with honor and victory has endured, with imagery of the laurel wreath still appearing on military medals, as well as sports and academic awards today.

SENATUS POPULUSQUE **ROMANUS**

The four letters "SPQR" are ancient in meaning and stand for "*Senatus Populusque Romanus*," or "the Senate and the People of Rome." The abbreviation signified the authority of the Roman Republic, referring to the sources of power in the ancient state. It appears on ancient coins, inscriptions, and the dedications on monuments, and also features in the works of the statesman Cicero and the historian Livy. The earliest evidence of this abbreviation of Roman civic and political identity dates from 80 BCE, when it first appears in inscriptions. It continued to be used throughout the centuries and can still be seen today in Rome, on buildings and even manhole covers. It has also been adopted by some other communities around the world, substituting their own city's initial for the fourth letter.

◁ **Gemma Augustea**
This cameo gem, cut from Arabian onyx, is rich in symbolism. The top tier shows the emperor Augustus, dressed as the god Jupiter, while the lower tier celebrates the military successes of Tiberius, his successor.

Augustus, to the right of the goddess Roma, is identified by the sign of Capricorn in a roundel by his head

The scepter symbolizes the right to rule

An eagle sits below Augustus, showing his close ties to Jupiter

Roman soldiers erect a *tropaeum*, or trophy, of captured arms and armor above a defeated Dalmatian soldier

Symbols of conquest

Spoils of war were also used as part of Roman iconography. The Rostra was a large speaker's platform in the heart of the Forum (see pp. 66–67) in Rome, named for the six bronze ramming beaks, or *rostra*, that decorated it. These had been seized from the prows of enemy warships after the Roman navy's victory at the Battle of Antium in 338 BCE. The *rostra* were also depicted on coins, emphasizing Rome's glorious past and circulating a message of power far and wide.

Centuries later, in 29 BCE, Augustus built a second Rostra before the Temple of Caesar in the Forum, similarly decorated with *rostra* taken from the ships sunk by his forces at the Battle of Actium (see pp. 134–135), fought against Antony and Cleopatra. Augustus became emperor following this victory, and his use of the *rostra* was proof of his power as well as his respect for Roman tradition.

Around the empire, *tropaea* ("trophies") were common emblems of Roman strength. These were collections of captured arms and armor taken from defeated enemies and displayed on the battlefield. Images of these appeared on coins, and in sculpture and monumental architecture.

Eagles also symbolized Roman military might, with each legion carrying standards topped by an *aquila* ("eagle"), representing the divine support of Jupiter, ruler of the gods. Eagles were also sometimes released from the top of emperors' funeral pyres to suggest the ruler's deification.

Eagles represented Rome's relationship with the gods

▷ **Augustan funerary monument**
The eagle atop the *tropaeum* is part of a marble urn that may once have held the ashes of the general Marcus Valerius Messalla Corvinus.

Roman Wall Paintings

Windows onto other worlds

Ancient Romans painted on various materials, such as wood or ivory, but the paintings that have survived the millennia are those that were painted on wet plaster in the enduring medium of fresco.

Roman painting was an exercise in making the best use of the space available in order to transport the viewer into new landscapes. Citizens decorated their houses with dramatic scenes from Greek mythology or idealized the lush gardens that they created outside.

Romans also painted their temples, tombs, statues, and public buildings, but the colors have largely faded over the centuries. In the houses preserved at Pompeii, however, the frescoes have retained their vibrant pigments, giving us an unrivaled glimpse of the bright interiors of Roman buildings.

◁ **Realistic vegetation**
Many Roman frescoes depicted carefully observed renderings of plants and vegetation (see also pp.116–117). This detail is from the painted garden that decorated the wall of the dining room of the Villa of Livia in Rome.

Painters and pigments

Pliny the Elder's *Natural History* gives us a detailed account of painting in the Roman world. Frescoes were painted on plaster, with paint applied while the plaster was damp, so it absorbed the color of the paint. Most pigments were natural minerals, but blue was notably synthetic—Egyptian blue was made by heating a mixture of sand, sodium bicarbonate, and copper. Paints were mixed from dried balls of pigment that were crushed with a mortar and pestle, then dissolved in water and honey. Prices of pigments varied, with yellow ocher the cheapest and red lead the most coveted. As well as brushes, made from pigs' bristles, the painter required tools to lay out the design, and compasses, weights, string, and pointed implements were used to sketch straight lines.

There were two types of painters—those who did background block colors (*parietarii*) and those who painted figures (*imaginarii*). Similar motifs can be seen across different buildings, suggesting there may have been pattern books for clients to choose from or shared artistic workshops with their own designs.

As with other art forms, Romans often employed artists from the Greek world. Women could also become successful painters, such as Iaia of Cyzicus, who lived in Rome during the 1st century BCE. It was said that Iaia worked faster than her male contemporaries and therefore charged higher prices for her artwork. She remained unmarried, suggesting her work gave her an unusual degree of independence.

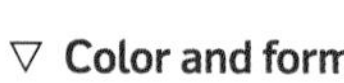

▽ **Color and form**
This iconic wall design, from the Villa Farnesina in Rome, is one of the best examples of an interplay of styles, with blocks of color interspersed with figures and painted panels (see also pp.250–251).

"When these **colors** are laid on, they present a **brilliant** appearance to the **eye**."

VITRUVIUS, *ON ARCHITECTURE*

Silenus, the tutor of Bacchus, with his distinctive pointed ears

Satyrs play pipes and feed young goats

A startled woman looks at the reclining Bacchus on the adjacent wall

The thyrsus, a staff wrapped in vines, was carried by Bacchus

Bacchus reclines across the lap of a goddess

Painting styles

The frescoes found at Pompeii have been roughly grouped into four phases and "styles." The earliest dates to c. 150 BCE and emphasizes masonry, with blocks of color imitating marble. Shaped stucco plaster was added to create a raised texture and shadows.

From c. 90 BCE, the second style uses perspective techniques, enhancing a space by painting architecture. Columns appear to project out or recede, with profiles of overlapping buildings in the distance.

From Augustus's consolidation of power in 31 BCE, the third style of painting mimicked the grand public architecture that was being built in Rome. This was interspersed with vegetal and mythological scenes. The depiction of gods and heroes might have also been intended to offer protection to a house.

The fourth style, from c. 1st century CE, combined all of the previous styles in an extravagant display. Framed by complex architectural elements, brightly colored backgrounds filled with birds, animals, vegetation, and people acted as windows to the outside.

The main subject matter for narrative panels was Greek mythology, showcasing the owner's education and taste. In this way, the rich bought into interior design as a way to demonstrate "the good life" of *otium* (leisure). Many scenes feature dramatic landscapes with a sweeping perspective. Other scenes were more functional, such as an image of a sacrifice at a shrine.

△ **Bacchic rite**
This scene from the main room of the Pompeiian Villa of Mysteries shows a large-scale narrative capturing what is perhaps a Bacchic initiation (see also pp. 72–73). It may have been a metaphor for a woman's coming of age.

◁ **Landscapes and perspective**
This is an example of the third style of painting, from the Villa of Agrippa Postumus. The Roman mastery of perspective is on display in this idyllic landscape of travelers in front of a fountain.

◁ **Glass masterwork** Rome's decorative arts flourished even in turbulent times. This multicolored glass bowl adorned with flower garlands is from the late 1st century BCE, when the Republic was engulfed in civil war and crisis.

3 The Republic in Crisis

133–27 BCE

The Road to One-Man Rule

From 133 BCE onward, the Roman Republic was engulfed in a series of crises that destabilized the political institutions that had governed the state for centuries.

Social discontent

By the late 2nd century BCE, riches from the expanding empire were flowing into Italy, and Rome's citizens, especially the city's elite families, were taking the lion's share. Longstanding discontent at the growing inequalities between rich and poor, and between Romans and Italians, reached breaking point in this period. Populist reforms that sought to improve conditions for Rome's poorest citizens were paid for by those who lived beyond its borders. Meanwhile, the rich used their resources to hold onto their wealth and their privilege, resulting in bloody violence on Rome's streets and rebellion farther afield.

Tiberius and Gaius Gracchus, in 133 BCE and 121 BCE respectively, saw the use of violence as a political tool escalate. Three revolts by the enslaved in as many generations ended in a rebellion led by the gladiator Spartacus that severely shook the state. This followed the Social War, in which Rome's allies in Italy had risen up in protest at their second-class status. Rome emerged from that conflict with the peninsula firmly under its control, but at a great cost.

Republican rivals

In the following years, military victories brought wealth and glory to army generals, who sought to circumvent the Republican constitution and rule in their own right while competing with their rivals for power. Marius and Sulla were the first major figures to clash, their contest plunging Rome into civil war and dictatorship. Later, the Republic fell under the sway of three men—Crassus, Caesar, and Pompey—whose alliance, for a time at least, maintained an uneasy status quo.

The death of Crassus in 53 BCE ended this power-sharing arrangement, leaving Caesar and Pompey to compete for sole control of the empire in what became another brutal civil war. Pompey's assassination in Egypt left Caesar as the sole authority in Rome, eventually appointed dictator for life.

Dawn of the emperors

The assassination of Julius Caesar by a cabal of younger Senators set off a chain of events that resulted in a formalized triumvirate whose two most prominent members—Octavian and Mark Antony, respectively Caesar's great-nephew and trusted lieutenant—ultimately went to war with each other.

Octavian emerged as the sole ruler of the Roman empire after his defeat of Mark Antony and Cleopatra VII at the Battle of Actium in 31 BCE, a victory he celebrated with the foundation of a new city where the naval battle took place: Nicopolis, "the City of Victory." By changing his name to Augustus, and benefiting from a complex state propaganda scheme that reconfigured the brutality of his ascent to power as an act of purification, he transformed himself into Rome's first emperor. Through his marriage to Livia, he initiated the Julio-Claudian dynasty that would remain in power for generations. Rome's transformation under Augustus from republican to imperial rule would define the state's political configuration for the rest of its existence.

◁ **Coin showing Julius Caesar, from 44 BCE**

133 BCE Murder of Tiberius Gracchus, tribune of the plebs who initiated controversial land reforms

112 BCE Jugurthine War begins in Numidia

91 BCE Rome's Italian allies rise up in the Social War

82 BCE Sulla is declared dictator after civil war with Marius

73 BCE Third Servile War begins

62 BCE Mithridatic War ends with Pompey expanding Rome's empire into Syria

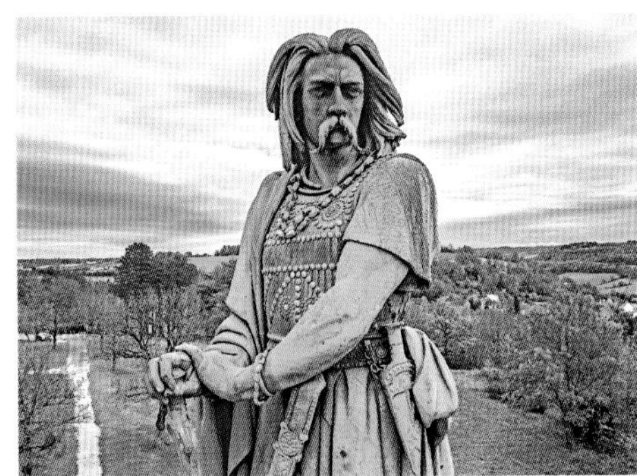

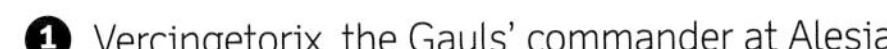

1 Vercingetorix, the Gauls' commander at Alesia

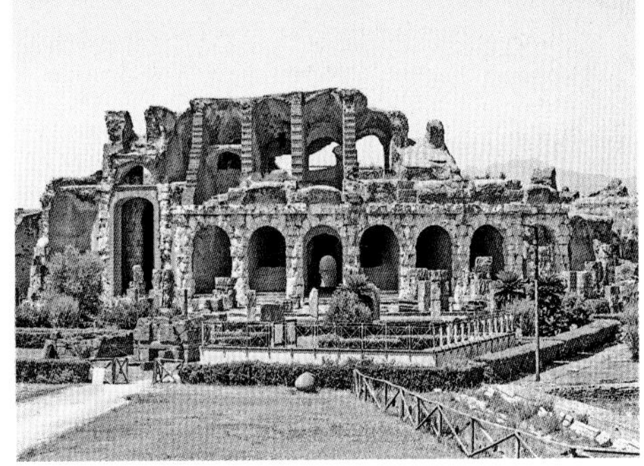

2 Capua, where Spartacus's revolt began

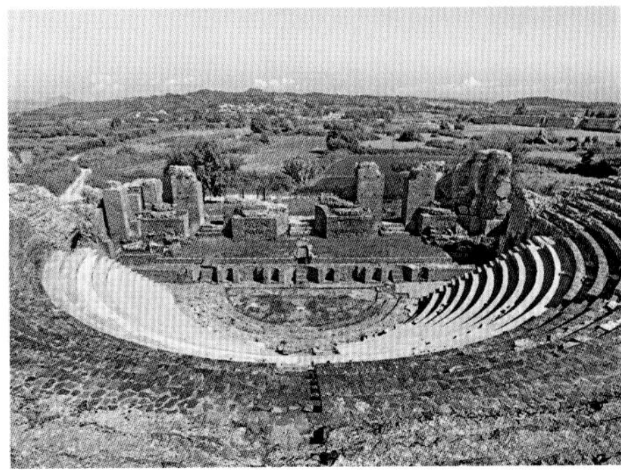

3 The Roman theater at Nicopolis, near Actium

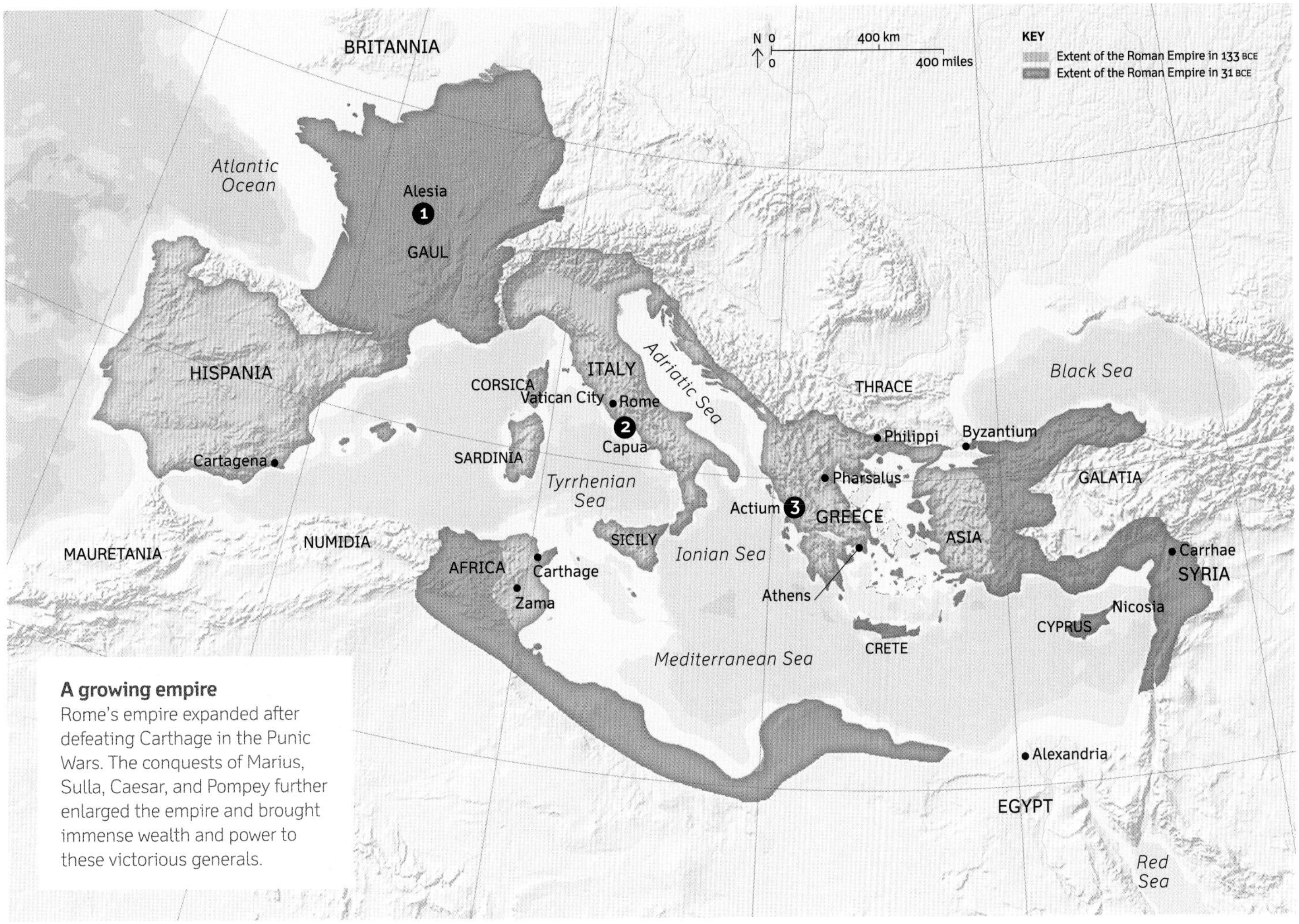

BRITANNIA
N
0
400 km
0
400 miles
KEY
Extent of the Roman Empire in 133 BCE
Extent of the Roman Empire in 31 BCE
Atlantic Ocean
Alesia
1
GAUL
HISPANIA
Cartagena
CORSICA
Vatican City
Rome
ITALY
2
Capua
SARDINIA
Adriatic Sea
Tyrrhenian Sea
THRACE
Black Sea
Philippi
Byzantium
Pharsalus
GALATIA
Actium
3
GREECE
ASIA
Carrhae
SYRIA
MAURETANIA
NUMIDIA
AFRICA
Carthage
Zama
SICILY
Ionian Sea
Athens
Nicosia
CYPRUS
CRETE
Mediterranean Sea
Alexandria
EGYPT
Red Sea

A growing empire

Rome's empire expanded after defeating Carthage in the Punic Wars. The conquests of Marius, Sulla, Caesar, and Pompey further enlarged the empire and brought immense wealth and power to these victorious generals.

59 BCE Formation of the so-called First Triumvirate of Caesar, Crassus, and Pompey

53 BCE Crassus is killed by the Parthians at the Battle of Carrhae

52 BCE Caesar defeats the Gauls at the Battle of Alesia

49 BCE Caesar crosses the Rubicon River in northern Italy; civil war begins

48 BCE Pompey is assassinated after the Battle of Pharsalus

44 BCE Julius Caesar is assassinated by senators led by Brutus and Cassius

31 BCE Octavian wins the Battle of Actium against Mark Antony and Cleopatra VII

27 BCE Octavian is proclaimed Augustus

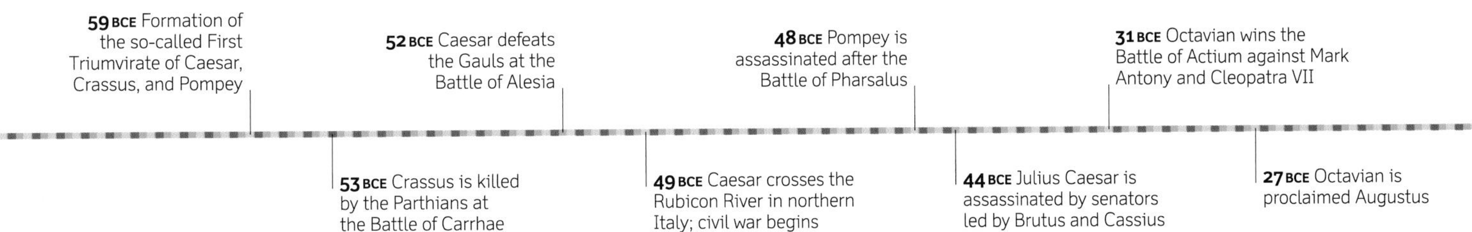

Civil Unrest

Discontent in Rome and its territories

By 146 BCE Rome was established as the Mediterranean's dominant power after significant victories against Carthage and Greece. But these conquests abroad, and the wealth and power they brought, caused trouble at home.

The traditional Roman army was made up of farmers, who worked the land for most of the year and were only called up to fight in battles and campaigns close to home. As Rome began waging wars in distant lands that lasted several years, however, many soldiers had to sell their farms, which made them landless on their return from military service.

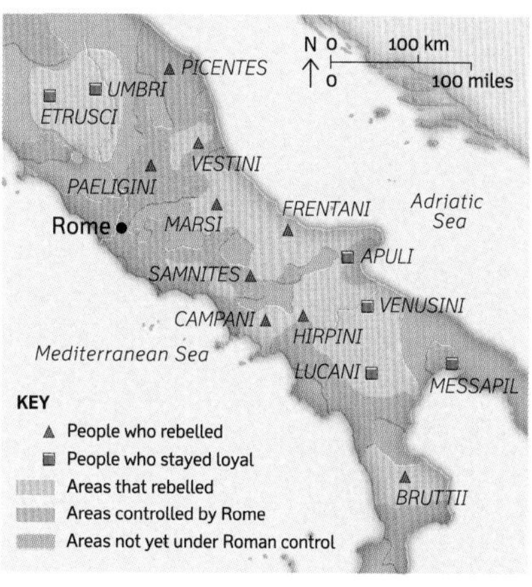

◁ **Rebel areas in the Social War**
This map shows the areas and peoples of the Italian peninsula that rebelled against Rome in the Social War and those that remained loyal.

In the meantime, the *ager publicus*—the fertile land in Italy that had been confiscated by the Roman state, divided up into smallholdings, and made available to rent by all Roman citizens—was also under threat. Rome's conquests had brought huge wealth to the city, in the form of war booty and swingeing taxes imposed upon the new provinces. As their wealth increased, elite landowners forced poorer farmers off their farms and began to dominate the *ager publicus*. The gap between rich and poor was widening.

The Gracchan reforms

In 133 BCE Tiberius Gracchus was elected as one of the ten tribunes of the plebs. The tribunes were meant to act as a check on magistrates and the elite interests of the Senate, either by proposing legislation or by vetoing the actions of magistrates and the decrees of the Senate. Tiberius passed a reform known as the *lex agraria* through a vote in the plebian assembly. This law reaffirmed the *ager publicus* as a common good to be enjoyed by all citizens, not just the elite. He hoped the reform would ease unemployment and poverty, and reduce agriculture's reliance on enslaved labor. To enact the reform, he set up a commission staffed by himself; his father-in-law; and his brother, Gaius.

The wealthiest Roman landowners, whose interests were well represented in the Senate, strongly opposed these reforms. Having failed to prevent Tiberius from passing his bill in the plebeian assembly, the Senate refused to release the funds required to enforce it. Realizing that his policies were being deliberately frustrated and that his term in office was running out, Tiberius used his powers as tribune to appropriate the vast treasury recently bequeathed to Rome by King Attalus III of Pergamum. Breaking with precedent, he then announced that he would stand for reelection. Claiming that Tiberius was aspiring to tyranny, a gang of senators incited public riots that saw the tribune and his supporters beaten to death and their bodies thrown into the Tiber.

For later historians, this first murder of an elected politician in 133 BCE marked the beginning of the Republic's decline. When Gaius Gracchus attempted to

GRACCHI BROTHERS

Tiberius and Gaius Gracchus both fought in the Roman army before embarking on political careers. Despite both being tribunes of the plebs, the Gracchi were aristocrats. Their father, Tiberius Sempronius Gracchus, had been consul in 177 BCE and their mother, Cornelia, was the daughter of Scipio Africanus, the victor over Hannibal in the Second Punic War. Their sister, Sempronia, was married to Scipio Aemilianus, the statesman who may have organized the mobs that killed her brothers. The progressive reforms they initiated, and the establishment's response to them, marked a new period in Roman civic life of increased political violence.

introduce similar and more wide-ranging reforms as a tribune of the plebs a decade later, he met the same fate as his brother. The Gracchi had shown how important the office of tribune of the plebs could be as a source of popular power, as well as how far the elites were willing to go to maintain their hegemony.

Rebellions against Rome

Discontent and violence were not just boiling over in Rome. The Italian peninsula was composed of several regions, each with its own language and culture. Many had been loyal allies to Rome for centuries, but their people were still denied equal standing with Romans, and were locked out of the benefits of citizenship, which granted its holders status, influence, and the right to vote in elections. In 91 BCE the Marsi and Samnite people rebelled, proposing to create a federation known as *Italia* that would be separate from Rome. Although they gathered allies and minted their own coinage, the Marsi and the Samnites failed to unite all the regions of Italy against Rome.

At the outbreak of the four-year conflict—known as the Social War—Rome offered citizenship to all Italic peoples who laid down their arms. This eventually stopped the rebellions in 87 BCE. Over time, Roman and Italian identities fused, with Latin becoming the official language of the whole peninsula.

△ ***Latifundium***
A Roman mosaic showing a large farming estate, or *latifundium*. The Gracchi wanted to break up such holdings so that the rich did not have a monopoly on agriculture at the expense of landless citizens.

▷ **Statue of a Samnite warrior**
The Samnites' enmity with Rome went back to at least 321 BCE, when they defeated Rome at the Battle of the Caudine Forks. Ever after, relations between both powers were uneasy.

"Tiberius **sought to win** the favor **of the multitude** by fresh laws."

PLUTARCH, *THE LIFE OF TIBERIUS GRACCHUS*

The Jugurthine War

Bribery in the Roman Republic

The North African region of Numidia had enjoyed a close relationship with Rome since 203 BCE, when its leader Masinissa allied himself with Scipio Africanus to help defeat Carthage and carve out his own kingdom. Then everything changed.

△ **Jugurtha's Numidia**
Rome's victory in the Punic Wars altered the balance of power in North Africa. This map shows the extent of the allied kingdoms of Numidia and Mauretania in 107 BCE, two years before renewed conflict with Rome began.

Numidia was renowned for its horses, and had provided cavalry detachments crucial to the defeat of Hannibal at the Battle of Zama in 202 BCE, which ended the Second Punic War. The local leader Masinissa ruled over the kingdom he created for 54 years, dying in 148 BCE at the age of 90 while still leading his armies. On his death, Masinissa's kingdom was divided between three of his sons.

Descent into warfare

In 118 BCE a dispute broke out between Masinissa's grandchildren, Hiempsal and Adherbal, and their adopted brother Jugurtha. This royal trio ruled their three kingdoms in collaboration. Jugurtha, however, wanted to unite the territories into a single state, with himself at the head. To this end, he arranged the murder of Hiempsal and then set his sights on Adherbal. Adherbal appealed to Rome for help, but Jugurtha had already bribed enough senators to ensure that no aid would be forthcoming. Given a free hand, in 112 BCE Jugurtha laid siege to the city of Cirta, where Adherbal had sought refuge. When the siege was broken, Jugurtha killed Adherbal and massacred Cirta's inhabitants—many of whom were Roman citizens. This brought Jugurtha into direct conflict with Rome.

As Roman troops marched into Jugurtha's kingdom his famous cavalry proved its worth, keeping the invading forces at bay and avoiding heavy Numidian losses. The peace treaty that resulted from this military impasse was so favorable to Jugurtha that accusations were made that he had once again bought off Rome's senators. Taken to Rome to testify at a hearing, Jugurtha bribed two tribunes to shut down the proceedings. While in the city, he also arranged

▷ **Marius receives a hero's welcome**
The Triumph of Marius over Jugurtha by the 16th-century artist Friedrich Sustris shows the general's procession into Rome in celebration of his victory in Africa. Prisoners of war and exotic animals such as elephants can be seen behind Marius's chariot.

"Only a few [senators] held their **honor dearer than gold.**"

SALLUST, *THE JUGURTHINE WAR*

▷ **Numidia, Africa's cultural crossroads**
This votive stele (1st or 2nd century CE) from Ghorfa, in modern-day Tunisia, fuses elements of Numidian, Berber, Punic, Roman, and Greek religious and cultural symbolism.

A Punic crescent symbol sits above a carving of Tanit, the Carthaginian mother-goddess

Figures symbolize the Roman gods Bacchus (left) and Cupid (right)

the murder of his cousin, Massiva, who had a rival claim to Numidia's throne. Jugurtha was expelled from Rome and the war was restarted.

The conflict ebbed and flowed until 107 BCE, when the general and newly elected Roman consul Gaius Marius decided to bring an end to the fighting once and for all. At the same time, Marius revitalized the Roman army. He enlisted non-property-owning plebeians among his troops, and reorganized the structure of the legions, replacing the small units known as maniples with larger, more effective forces called cohorts. The Jugurthine War gave Marius the chance to see if his reforms worked.

Jugurtha betrayed

Ultimately, however, a combination of battlefield expertise and bribery—this time used against Jugurtha—enabled Marius to triumph over his rival. Faced with Marius's onslaught, Jugurtha allied with the king of neighboring Mauretania, Bocchus I (who was also his father-in-law). But after several military reverses, in 105 BCE Bocchus secretly met with Marius's lieutenant, Lucius Cornelius Sulla, and agreed to hand over Jugurtha in exchange for extending his own kingdom into Numidia. Captured and bound in chains, Jugurtha was brought to Rome, paraded through the streets, and cast into the Tullanium prison on the Capitoline Hill. There his guards ripped off his earlobes in their eagerness for his golden earrings. He was starved for six days and then strangled. Bocchus, meanwhile, was allowed to raise a monument on the Capitoline Hill to memorialize his role in Rome's victory.

From the 1st century CE, through the account of the Jugurthine War by the Roman historian Sallust, it has been held up as an example of the moral decay afflicting Rome in the Late Republic. It also showed men such as Marius and Sulla the importance to Rome—and themselves—of a well-trained and loyal army.

Iron will
This marble bust, commonly associated with Sulla, has been marred—as was Sulla's legacy following his death. His epitaph, supposedly in his own words, claimed that no friend of his went without their due reward, nor enemy without their just deserts.

Sulla

The blood-soaked reformer

The first dictator in Rome in over a century and the first Roman general to march his army against Rome, Sulla seized power at a time of crisis and forced through reform with the sword.

Lucius Cornelius Sulla was born into an undistinguished patrician family. He sought to elevate his status by attaching himself to Rome's greatest living general, Marius, and served under him with distinction in campaigns in North Africa and against the German tribes threatening northern Italy. His greatest triumph was in 105 BCE, when he persuaded the Numidian prince Bocchus to betray his commander Jugurtha, ending a lengthy war. Sulla's reputation brought him an important command in the east, and he played a crucial role in Rome's victory in the Social War.

◁ **Enemy ruler**
Mithridates VI the Great is depicted in this marble bust. In spite of Sulla's victories over him, he resurfaced and was only finally defeated in 63 BCE.

Red in tooth and claw

Marius objected to Sulla's new rank and when Sulla was tasked with stopping the renegade Greek prince Mithridates, Marius had Sulla stripped of his command and himself appointed in his stead. In response, Sulla marched his army on Rome and put Marius and his allies to flight. While Sulla pushed Mithridates back to the Black Sea, the Marians seized control of Rome once more. Sulla's response was swift and brutal: on landing in Italy, he published a list of his enemies' names, decreeing their property forfeit and a reward for their killer. Within a year, he had defeated his Marian enemies and their Italian allies. After his victory at the Colline Gate, Sulla gathered the Senate at the Temple of the war goddess Bellona to announce his supremacy. As he began his address, the signal was given to massacre his surrendered enemies who were assembled nearby. Accompanied by the screams of the vanquished, the Senate acknowledged their new master.

Unlimited power

Sulla was appointed dictator—the first man to hold this emergency office in peacetime—and used these powers to radically alter Rome's constitution, with the aim of preventing a recurrence of the chaos that had enabled his own elevation. He curtailed the powers of the tribunes of the plebs, removing their right to pass legislation and barring them from higher office. He tightened the Senate's grip on the courts and on Rome's generals in the field. To ensure loyalty, Sulla settled his soldiers on confiscated land throughout Italy. His legislation passed, he then voluntarily retired, dying a few years later as a private citizen. His constitution did not long outlast him: he could legislate against many things but not his own example. Successful military men commanding loyal armies dismantled most of his constitution in pursuit of private glory.

▽ **Bloodless victory**
This coin commemorates the end of the Jugurthine War. Bocchus hands the enthroned Sulla an olive branch while the defeated Jugurtha kneels on the right.

138 BCE Born in Rome into an old but undistinguished patrician family

107 BCE Serves with distinction under Marius, fighting in the Jugurthine War

89 BCE Ensures Roman victory in the Social War with his generalship in southern Italy

88 BCE Marches on Rome to restore his command over the Mithridatic campaign

85 BCE Drives Mithridates from Greece and makes peace; returns to Italy

82 BCE Is victorious at the Colline Gate, ending the civil war

81 BCE Appointed dictator; passes far-reaching legislation

78 BCE Dies of natural causes after retiring from public life

The Third Servile War

Italy's enslaved rise up again

Rome's economy depended on enslaving and trafficking vast numbers of people across the Mediterranean. Enslavement was always a potential consequence of defeat in war. As Rome expanded, the number of enslaved people rose.

The First and Second Servile Wars of 135 BCE and 105 BCE left Rome's rulers with an abiding fear of rebellion from enslaved populations, especially as those conflicts had taken years to quell. Despite this, Rome's leaders were slow to respond when a new revolt occurred in southern Italy.

◁ **Metal manacles**
Shackles such as these were tied around the wrists or ankles of enslaved people, with locks to hold them in place.

Spartacus leads an uprising

Spartacus was a warrior captured by Rome during a raid on Thracia (Thrace, southeastern Balkans). Sent to the gladiatorial school in Capua, southern Italy, in 73 BCE he led an escape of 78 of his fellow enslaved gladiators. Fleeing first to the slopes of Mount Vesuvius, Spartacus and his force's coleaders, the Gauls Crixus and Oenomaus, led their men across the Italian countryside, picking up more fugitives as they went until their force reputedly numbered more than 100,000. Rather than overthrow the state, the rebels' aim was to fight their way to freedom in a region outside Roman control.

Crixus and 30,000 of his men were defeated by the Romans in 72 BCE, but Spartacus and the remaining rebels held out for another year. Spartacus was a superb commander and his abilities were probably enhanced by his experiences as a gladiator. It also helped that many of his men were former soldiers who had fought in the Social War of 91–87 BCE (see pp. 104–105) and still held anti-Roman sentiment.

▽ **Gladiatorial arena**
The amphitheatre at Capua, built some time after 31 BCE, was exceeded in size only by the Colosseum. The gladiator school on the site predated the amphitheatre, and was where Spartacus trained.

Quelling the revolt

Alarmed at the success of the revolt and fearing it would spread to Sicily, the crucible of the First and Second Servile Wars, the Senate appointed Marcus Licinius Crassus to crush Spartacus and his forces.

The rebel army was finally defeated at the Battle of the Silarius River in 71 BCE, during which Spartacus himself is thought to have died. When 6,000 of the rebels attempted to flee the battlefield they were captured by Roman legions commanded by Pompey (see pp. 126–127), who had arrived just in time to assist Crassus and to claim some of the credit for the victory. Afterward, to discourage

> "He had a **great spirit** and great **physical strength**."
>
> PLUTARCH, ON SPARTACUS

◁ **Thracian gladiators**
This mosaic from the 4th century CE shows a Roman gladiatorial school with Thracian gladiators. As a Thracian, Spartacus would have worn this type of armor.

A Thracian gladiator, or *thraex*, can be identified by his winged helmet and visor

Trainers used sticks to direct the fighters

Thraex gladiators used a small shield called a *parmula*

Leg guards, or greaves, offered some protection for the shins

further uprisings Crassus had the 6,000 rebel survivors crucified along the Appian Way from Capua to Rome.

To Crassus's fury, he had to share the acclaim for victory in the Third Servile War with Pompey, who was awarded two Triumphs and was allowed to stand for the Consulship even though he was under the qualifying age of 42 and had not yet held any other political offices in the *cursus honorum*. In 70 BCE, both Crassus and Pompey were elected consuls—further proof that the republic was now ruled by men with immense personal power and wealth who were unafraid to manipulate the constitution for their own gain.

A MAN OF **WEALTH AND INFLUENCE**

Marcus Licinius Crassus was the richest man in Rome. His money came from human trafficking, silver mining, and confiscating real estate from those he murdered when commanding Sulla's armies during the First Civil War. His alliance in 60 BCE with Julius Caesar and Pompey saw the three rivals for control of Rome temporarily set aside their differences. This arrangement was ended with Crassus's death at the Battle of Carrhae in 53 BCE, while he was attempting to extend his power base in the eastern provinces. The Parthian general Suren defeated Crassus, killing 20,000 or more of his men and, according to legend, pouring molten gold down the general's throat in mockery of his lust for riches.

△ **Gallic defeat**
Lionel Royer's 1899 painting *Vercingetorix Throws Down His Arms at the Feet of Julius Caesar* imagines the moment the Gallic chieftain ended the debilitating siege of Alesia by surrendering to the Roman general.

The Conquest of Gaul

Vercingetorix's last stand against Caesar

The people of Gaul were split into competing groups that supported and opposed Rome until Vercingetorix formed some of them into a single army determined to hold at bay Rome's—and Julius Caesar's—imperial ambitions.

△ **Golden torc**
Members of the Gallic elite wore torcs around their necks. Golden torcs, like this one, weighed up to 2.2 lb (1 kg).

The Romans had been fearful of the Gauls ever since they first entered and sacked the city as far back as 390 BCE. Almost 200 years later, at the end of the Second Punic War (see pp. 82–83), the Romans gained some revenge when they defeated the peoples of Cisalpine Gaul ("Gaul this side of Alps"), who had allied with the Carthaginian general Hannibal. In 121 BCE the Romans took even more territory in the region, seizing Transalpine Gaul ("Gaul across the Alps") from the Allobroges people.

Caesar's Gallic Wars

The region had been prone to conflicts between rival groups, and when Julius Caesar was appointed proconsul for Transalpine Gaul in 58 BCE he saw an opportunity to build himself a reputation as a conqueror that would surpass that of his sometime ally, Pompey the Great. In 58–57 BCE 300,000 Helvetii men, women, and children migrated into independent Gallic territories. Caesar used this as a pretext to attack and slaughter thousands, claiming

THE FIRST TRIUMVIRATE

In 60 BCE Julius Caesar met with the rich and powerful generals Pompey and Crassus and made them an offer: if they backed his campaign to become consul the next year, he would pass whatever laws they wanted when he was in office. With Pompey and Crassus's money and support, Caesar was elected and, in time, the three men joined together to unofficially share power across the empire. This alliance later became known as the First Triumvirate. The 46-year-old Pompey even married Caesar's 16-year-old daughter Julia, to tie him more closely to his new ally. But the three men did not always see eye to eye. They were jealous of each other's successes, and Caesar's accomplishments in Gaul helped to bring about his final breach with Pompey, leading ultimately to civil war (see pp. 128–129).

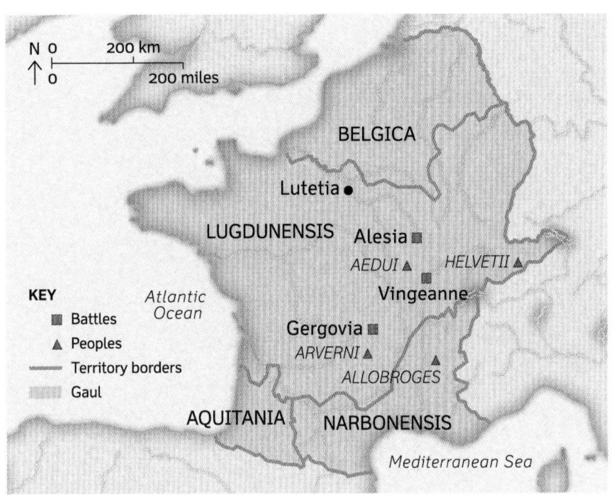

◁ **Expanding empire**
Before Julius Caesar arrived in Gaul, Rome's territory there comprised what is today northern Italy and France's Mediterranean coast. This map shows Roman Gaul by the time Caesar left the territory.

"forward defense" of the border, followed by further incursions northward. Caesar thought these could be promoted as conquests to secure Rome from Gallic invasion rather than as personal glory-hunting.

The Gauls proved formidable opponents. Their long swords were effective in battle and their cavalry units were superior to those of the Romans. Ultimately, however, they succumbed to the Roman army's weaponry, professionalism, and tactical acumen. As he pushed farther north, Caesar sent dispatches to Rome, informing the Senate of the gains he was making for the Republic. At the same time, Caesar's wealth, fame, and power grew—helped in part by his self-serving written account of the campaign, *On the Gallic War*.

In 55 BCE the consuls Pompey and Crassus extended Caesar's proconsulship by another five years, and in August that year he led an expedition across the English Channel to Britain. Caesar sent a larger invasion force the next year, but unrest in Gaul forced him to cancel plans to conquer the island that a century later would become the Roman province of Britannia (see pp. 174–175).

Uniting the Gauls

Vercingetorix was a chieftain of the Arverni people, and in 52 BCE he forged an alliance with at least 15 other Gallic groups to drive out the Romans from Gaul once and for all. The Gauls were successful at first, avoiding pitched battles with the disciplined Roman forces and instead attacking their supply lines. Vercingetorix's victory at the Battle of Gergovia saw more groups rally to his cause, including the Aedui, which until then had been loyal to Rome.

But Gergovia was to be Vercingetorix's last success against the Romans. Defeat at the Battle of Vingeanne in July 52 BCE, where German cavalry mercenaries proved decisive for Caesar, forced Vercingetorix to retreat with 80,000 of his troops to their fortress stronghold of Alesia. After a siege that saw many of his people starve to death, Vercingetorix surrendered to Caesar. All Gallic survivors were enslaved and Vercingetorix himself, in a major propaganda coup, was brought to Rome. After several years in the subterranean Tullianum prison on the Capitoline Hill, Vercingetorix was paraded in Caesar's quadruple Triumph of 46 BCE and then strangled to death.

Caesar had exploited the perennial unrest in Gaul to his own advantage. After the Gallic Wars, the territory would remain firmly under Roman control for the next five centuries, and was in time split into four provinces known as Narbonensis, Lugdunensis, Aquitania, and Belgica.

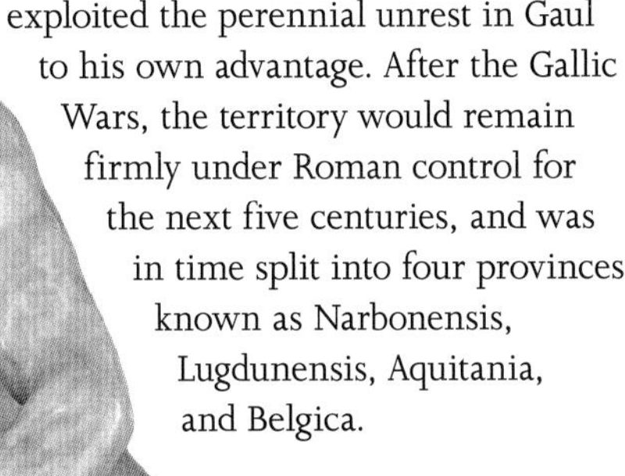

▷ **The *Dying Gaul***
This is a Roman copy of a lost bronze Hellenistic sculpture from Pergamum. The mustache and torc identify the subject as a member of the Celtic people, which included the Gauls. Artwork of vanquished Gauls became popular after Caesar's conquests.

△ **Gallic coin**
This gold coin was minted around 52 BCE by the Arverni. The figure on the front could be Vercingetorix, but is more likely that of a god.

Roman Street Life

Day and night in the ancient city

From the avenues of the upper-class Palatine Hill to the paved walkways of the Forum and the rough cobbles of the lower-class Suburra, the streets of Rome and other cities teemed with life during daylight, and bristled with danger after dark.

△ **Meeting point**
Free, and fresh, aqueduct water fed street fountains in Roman towns and cities (like this one from Pompeii, decorated with a goddess of plenty). Fountains were social hubs, where people exchanged news and gossip.

Roman city-dwellers spent a lot of time outdoors, working, shopping, trading, eating, socializing, or simply loitering in the Forum, hoping to see or be seen.

◁ **Basic but effective**
Customers in bars and taverns drank from simple terra-cotta beakers. They were cheap to produce and easy to replace, unlike much more expensive metal or glass vessels.

Life during the day

Each morning, the single-room stores that lined the streets and occupied the ground floors of Rome's apartment buildings, called *insulae* (see pp. 78–79), would throw open their shutters and set out their wares. Excavations at Pompeii revealed the painted signs and frescoes that decorated storefronts—and the graffiti that covered city walls in a mixture of news, abuse ("Stronnius is an idiot"), political electioneering ("Innkeepers, make Sallustius Capito aedile"), and gossip.

Rome's thoroughfares became so crowded that, in around 44 BCE, Julius Caesar banned wheeled vehicles from the streets during daylight hours, and under Domitian stores were ordered to stop blocking pavements with their wares. Some towns, including Pompeii, introduced one-way systems to regulate road traffic. But Romans continued to grumble about the crush, and the 2nd-century CE poet Juvenal wrote earthily in his *Satires* of "the endless traffic" and the "narrow twisting streets, and the swearing at stranded cattle" as he made his way across the city, complaining how "I'm forever trampled by mighty feet from every side, while a soldier's hobnailed boot pierces my toe." Many of the people Juvenal evoked so convincingly could have been heading to a tavern for a meal after a long day's work. Many Roman homes had no cooking facilities, and cheap meals could be bought at a *thermopolium*: a "fast-food" café identifiable by its stone counter with sunken containers, called *dolia*, to hold food (see pp. 190–191).

◁ **Trying their luck**
This fresco shows men playing a gambling game with dice, a popular tavern pastime. It is just one of 13 similar scenes painted onto the wall of a bar, or *caupona*, in Pompeii.

The city at night

After sunset, the character of the streets changed. There was no public lighting and streets at night were dark and forbidding places. Only occasionally would a public monument be lit up for a special event, or a house celebrating a feast, and illuminated by torches, stand out in the gloom. Stores were shuttered and closed, apart from the bars and brothels in seedier districts, such as the infamous Suburra, close to the Forum. Surviving frescoes and graffiti suggest drinking, fighting, and gambling were common.

Dark streets and shady corners offered opportunities for robbers and ruffians. Rich individuals could venture outside with bodyguards and torches, but most citizens could not afford such protection. Other hazards included unruly drunks and the fallout from chamber pots emptied from a building's upper floors.

Fires were more common at night, often caused by fallen lamps or torches. Augustus set up a paramilitary night watch in 6 CE called the *vigiles* and supplied it with basic firefighting tools. However, some later emperors restricted the *vigiles'* activities, which they saw as a threat to their monopoly of power.

◁ **Tavern scene**
This funerary relief from Roman Gaul dates from the 2nd century CE and shows a tavern scene, with seated drinkers, drinking vessels, shelves, barrels, and geese or ducks. In the lower half, an ox cart makes a delivery, probably to the tavern.

Customers are waited on at their table

Low archways were just one of the city's obstacles that carters faced when making their deliveries

The cart is probably carrying a barrel of wine to supply the bar

Oxen, rather than horses, were used for hauling heavy loads

▽ Idealized illusionary gardens
This remarkable 1st-century CE garden fresco from the House of the Golden Bracelet, Pompeii—depicting birds, lavish planting, busts, and a fountain—would have helped the garden seem bigger than it actually was. It would also have displayed the wealth and taste of its owner.

> "If you have **a library with a garden**, you have **everything you need**."
>
> CICERO, *AD FAMILIARES*

Planting includes oleander, bay, plane, palm, and ivy

As well as this turtledove, pigeons, sparrows, swallows, magpies, thrushes, and other birds inhabit the lush garden

A fountain with flowing water is an indication of wealth

Flowers include violets, roses, chamomile, poppies, and lilies

Earthly Paradise

Practical and pleasure gardens

Gardens were an important feature of life in Rome. From the grand recreational estates of emperors and aristocrats to the more humble domestic gardens in places such as Pompeii, gardens had a diverse range of functions and meanings.

Representations of panel paintings possibly add focal points to the scene

Gardens in the Roman world, much like houses, reflected the lifestyle, aspirations, and personal tastes of their owners. They had a range of purposes: gardens were used for growing food, for leisure, as a display of wealth and social status, and as an extension of the home.

Horticulture—the art of cultivating plants in gardens—was part of the larger enterprise of farming and agriculture. Gardens were an important source of flowers, fresh vegetables and fruit, and herbs, as well as delicacies such as fish and birds. Many urban and countryside houses had a practical *hortus* (garden), and Roman authors gave advice on how to cultivate and use their produce for the benefit of the household or as a source of income.

◁ **Ornamental fountain statue**
Roman gardens often included statues and ornaments, such as this hippopotamus water feature, made from imported red marble in the 1st century CE.

Ornamental peristyle gardens

Greater wealth, concern for display, and contact with the Greek-speaking world led Romans to place more emphasis on ornamental gardens. In Rome itself, aristocrats, and then emperors, built luxurious garden estates around the city, with statues, groves, pools, and planting. In their country estates and coastal villas, the elite added courtyards, fountains, aviaries, walkways, sculpture collections, exotic planting, and more. The remains of the emperor Hadrian's Villa at Tivoli and descriptions of Nero's imperial Golden House in Rome (see pp. 186–187) offer glimpses of these huge, managed landscapes.

Ordinary Romans aspired to these levels of luxury and sought to recreate them. Many of the larger houses at Pompeii gave considerable space to "peristyle" gardens—rectangular plots bounded by a colonnade for strolling, protected from both sun and rain. These gardens could be used as private spaces behind the more public areas of the "atrium" house (see pp. 78–79), with room for socializing, exercise, and dining. Their planting was often quite formal. Flowing water added to the sense of nature tamed and controlled, and statues (and frescoes in the colonnade and rooms) provided talking points.

The boundary between interior and exterior space was quite fluid; rooms could be decorated with idealized or fantasy garden scenes. Just as architectural frescoes amplify or exaggerate the size and grandeur of a house, these garden frescoes may suggest what their owners would have liked their gardens to be. Certainly, the loving descriptions of their gardens by influential Romans like Cicero and Pliny show how highly valued these spaces were.

▷ **Peristyle townhouse garden**
This reconstruction of the garden of the House of the Vettii in Pompeii includes key features of the ornamental garden, such as a peristyle colonnade, formal planting, fountains, and statues.

◁ **Bust of Cicero**
This sculpture of Cicero, produced a century after his death in 43 BCE and housed in Rome's Capitoline Museum, depicts him as he was at the end of his life: weathered, reflective, and still full of fight.

Marcus Tullius Cicero

Called "most eloquent of the children of Romulus"

Born far from Rome and lacking in senatorial ancestry, Cicero was a skilled orator, lawyer, and statesman whose eloquence took him to the pinnacle of Roman Republican politics, although his ego would take him to its nadir.

Cicero's rhetoric and support of popular causes ensured his election to every office on the *cursus honorum* (see pp. 86–87) at the earliest age permitted by law. He was elected to hold the Consulship (the highest political office of the Republic) in 63 BCE, an extraordinary achievement for a *novus homo*—a man new to Roman politics, lacking a family tree studded with great generals and magistrates.

The Consulship proved a poisoned chalice. Famine and debt were ravaging Italy, and the wealthy elite, who had reluctantly helped vote Cicero to power, feared populist legislation that threatened to empty the treasury by redistributing land to the urban poor. After Cicero successfully argued down such a law, the bankrupt patrician Catiline seized on the populace's desperation, plotting with supporters to overthrow the government. Cicero exposed Catiline's conspiracy in a set of famous speeches, uniting the poor and the elite of Rome. With Senate support, Cicero approved the execution of five aristocratic conspirators without trial.

Fortune's wheel

Cicero's triumph was short-lived, ending with the rise of Julius Caesar. Since the murder of the reforming tribune Tiberius Gracchus (see pp. 104–105), the execution of Roman citizens had been a matter of fierce contention. Caesar allowed the tribune Clodius to drive Cicero into exile for his role in the bloody resolution to the Catiline affair. After 18 months, Cicero was pardoned and returned a diminished figure. He was barely involved in the events leading to the second civil war and Caesar's dictatorship, nor his later assassination (see pp. 128–129).

After Caesar died, Cicero made a verbal assault on Caesar's self-appointed successor, Mark Antony. This made him, briefly, the embodiment of the free Republic fighting autocratic Roman generals. In response, Mark Antony added his name to the list of Caesar's assassins and Cicero was executed. His head and hands were nailed to the speaker's platform, but the works they had produced survived to inspire future generations.

△ **Silver *cistophorus***
Cicero briefly governed the province of Cilicia (in modern Türkiye). This coin bears his name and the title *imperator*, honoring his victory over a group of rebels.

▷ ***Fulvia With the Head of Cicero* (1898)**
After Cicero's murder, Mark Antony's wife, Fulvia, was given his head and stuck pins in the tongue with which he had assailed his enemies, as imagined in this painting by Pavel Svedomsky.

106 BCE Cicero is born in Arpinum, a hill town 75 miles (120 km) southeast of Rome

80 BCE Cicero proves his skills as an orator in his first public trial

70 BCE Cicero secures the conviction of the governor Verres for corrupt practices in his province

66 BCE Cicero supports Pompey to command the war against Mithridates

63 BCE Cicero is elected consul, despite his non-senatorial background

58 BCE Cicero is exiled from Italy for executing citizens without trial

52 BCE Cicero defends his friend Milo, accused of killing Cicero's mortal enemy Clodius

45 BCE Cicero begins translating Greek texts into Latin

43 BCE Cicero is executed as revenge for his speeches against Mark Antony

Being struck by the whips of the *Luperci* was thought to bring fertility

"Throughout the city **was heard pipes**, the **clash of cymbals**, and the **beat of drums**."

ATHENAEUS ON THE PARILIA FESTIVAL IN ROME

△ ***Lupercalia***
This 17th-century depiction of the *Lupercalia* evokes the chaotic nature of the festival. Sacrifices of incense, wine, and goats are made to the gods, while the half-naked *Luperci* whip the assembled onlookers.

Each of the *Luperci* carries a whip made of goat hide

Bloody animal sacrifices are made to the gods

Celebrating the Gods

Roman festivals and processions

The Romans worshipped their gods in great festivals, with hundreds celebrated every year. These celebrations brought together different sections of society in worship, including senators, elite women, the Roman people, and the enslaved.

The *Luperci* are dressed in goatskins, and wear little else

Festivals were huge gatherings, often accompanied by feasting and sacrificing, and centered on the worship of one or more gods on what were often public holidays. Great calendars, often erected on temple walls (see pp. 132–133), listed the festivals, of which there were hundreds. For instance, the Robigalia, on April 25, saw the sacrifice of a dog to protect crops from disease. The Floralia, celebrated a few days later, was a fertility festival in which only plebeians took part. For the Liberalia on March 17, boys marked their transition to manhood by adopting the toga. Three of the most interesting Roman festivals were the Saturnalia, Lupercalia, and Parilia.

Saturnalia

This festival, held between 17 and 23 December, involved sacrifices at the Temple of Saturn in the Forum, public feasting and banqueting, and the exchange of gifts between friends and family, much like more-modern religious festivals. Various social restrictions were relaxed during the Saturnalia, such as prohibitions against public dice games and gambling, and household servants were treated as equals, with the enslaved waited on by their masters at mealtimes.

Lupercalia

Social norms were overturned even further in the Lupercalia. Celebrated on February 15, this festival saw young men, or *Luperci* ("the brothers of the wolf"), sacrificing goats and young dogs in the Lupercal, the sacred place where Romulus and Remus were said to have been nursed by the she-wolf. The goats were butchered, with their skins used primarily to partially clothe the *Luperci*, and also to make whips. The *Luperci* would then run manically through the city, scantily clad, using their goatskin whips on the assembled crowds. Women especially came forward to be whipped, hoping the blows they received would bring fertility both to themselves and to Rome.

◁ **Decorative wall painting**
This painted stucco fragment (1st century CE) comes from a tomb or Roman villa and may have been part of a scene of the Lupercalia.

Parilia

Celebrated on April 21, the Parilia was dedicated to the deity Pales, the protector of flocks and herds. In its unusual rites, Vestal Virgins mixed the ashes of an unborn calf (sacrificed and burnt during the Fordicidia fertility festival of 15 April) with the blood of a horse (sacrificed in the October Horse festival the previous year) and added them to a great bonfire. A shepherd and his sheep would then pass through or jump over the bonfire three times in a ritual act of cleansing. During the Imperial period, the Parilia was adopted as the official date of Rome's "birthday."

△ **Saturn**
The Saturnalia was devoted to the god Saturn, depicted here with a fold of his toga over his head and holding a curved sacrificial knife, indicating his participation in a religious rite.

Household Gods

Ritual worship in the Roman home

Roman society was based first and foremost around the family unit. Placating one's family gods was believed to be vital to ensuring the prosperity of the household and to procuring blessings for important life events.

△ ***Penates* figurine**
Statuettes of the *Penates*, such as this figurine of a household god carrying a cornucopia and a sacrificial dish, would have adorned a *Lararium*.

Alongside public veneration of the gods and goddesses of the pantheon (see pp. 48–49), the household was also a focus for ritual activities that were an essential part of daily life in Rome. Worship was administered by the *paterfamilias* ("father of the family"), the most senior male member of the household. The Roman concept of *familia* ("the family") extended beyond husband, wife, and children, and incorporated the people enslaved by the family, their freedmen, and other dependents within the household. On large farming estates the whole "family" (including enslaved people) might gather together to pray for bountiful crops and the purification of the fields. Many stages in the lives of family members were marked by religious rites, including marriages, childbirth, and funerals.

Household shrines and family gods

A number of deities were worshipped in the Roman household, with prayers and offerings of food and incense intended to protect the safety and prosperity of the home and its members. Worship was performed by the entire family to the *Lares familiares* ("protective spirits of the family"), the *Penates* ("gods of the storeroom"), and the *genius* ("guardian spirit") of the *paterfamilias*. The female counterpart of the *genius* was the *juno*, who watched over the wife of the *paterfamilias*, but little is known of her worship. As the goddess of the hearth, Vesta was also worshipped within the household. While the *paterfamilias* organized and conducted the rites, the women of the household were responsible for maintaining the supplies necessary for the offerings.

The focus of these rituals was the shrine for the *Lares*, which was usually found in the *atrium* ("entrance hall") of a Roman household. These varied in size and could be grand marble structures, smaller wooden cabinets, or even shelves.

> "My wife, **pray that our residence** may become **good**, blessed, **happy**, and successful."
>
> CALLICLES, IN *TRINUMMUS* BY PLAUTUS

▷ **Tomb inscription**
Roman tomb inscriptions often included the dedication *Dis Manibus* or *Diis Manib*, meaning "to the departed spirits," in this case of Cornelia Thalia from c. 50 CE.

Celebrating births and commemorating deaths

Worship in the household often marked significant events and rites of passage. Upon the birth of a child, the family hung garlands around their doors and lit a fire on an altar. A ritual couch and a meal were also placed in the *atrium* to appease the gods. A baby was only accepted into the family when it reached eight or nine days old. The *dies lustricus* ("day of purification") marked the day when the child officially became a person and was given a name. Rituals to purify the baby were performed and the child was cleansed of any "pollution." At the other end of life, funerals and burials also required ceremony and worship. The *Manes* were believed to be the spirits of deceased family members that needed to be placated, especially immediately following a death.

△ ***Lararium* of the House of the Vettii in Pompeii**
The family gods have here been painted onto the surface of the shrine, which is designed to look like a temple, but some shrines contained small bronze statuettes of the household gods.

Carved Creations

Roman decorative and applied sculpture

Roman sculpture was influenced by Etruscan and Greek artistic fashions, but also developed independently over time. Sculpture was everywhere in Rome, filling private villas and gardens, and crowding public spaces such as the Forum. It celebrated wealth and power, commemorated lives, honored the gods, beautified buildings, and formed pleasing objects for people to enjoy.

Precious gems are set into the lions' eyes

Fine contrasting glass inlays have been set in geometric patterns

△ **Carved 1st- or 2nd-century CE couch**
This piece may have come from the villa of the Roman co-emperor Lucius Verus. The elaborate ivory leg carvings show figures from Greek myths.

Leg carvings depict Ganymede, a Trojan youth abducted by the Greek god Zeus

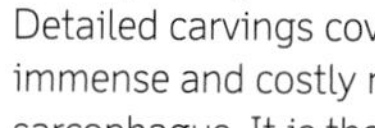

▷ **Imposing tomb**
Detailed carvings cover this immense and costly red porphyry sarcophagus. It is thought to have held the remains of Constantine the Great's mother, Helena, who died c. 330 CE.

The eyes—and possibly the whole head—would once have been painted

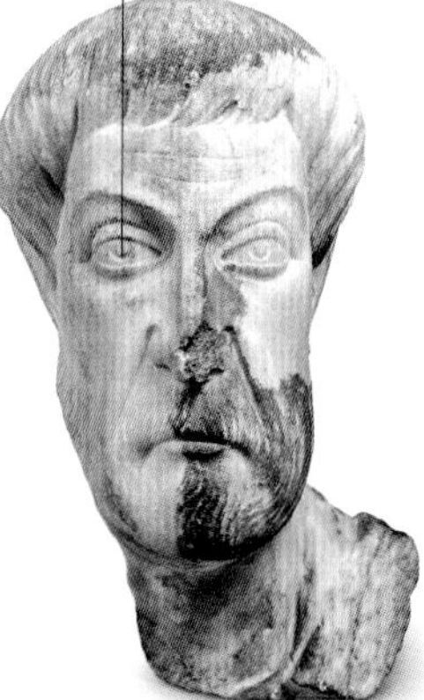

△ **Stylized sculpture**
Naturalistic bust styles gave way to approaches where long and exaggerated features were the norm in late antiquity. This striking figure may be a philosopher.

△ **True-to-life bust**
Favored by prominent men in the Republican era, the "veristic style" displayed the subject's lines, sagging skin, and furrowed brow to emphasize his age and reliability.

Agrippina the Elder, granddaughter of Augustus, wore this hairstyle

◁ **Roman matron**
Casting statues in bronze from wax or terra-cotta molds allowed for finer detailing than carving in stone or marble.

The sculpture stands 9½ in (24.1 cm) tall

Lions and cupids decorate the top of this huge casket

Roman soldiers trample over their captured enemies

Lion sculptures were added at the Vatican's request in the 18th century

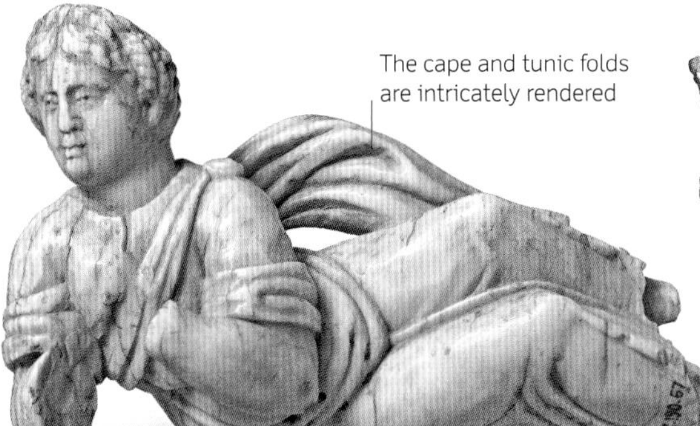

△ **Carved tusks and teeth**
Ivory was a rare luxury item and was carved to make a variety of expensive personal objects, such as this 3rd- or 4th-century CE reclining woman. A garland of leaves adorns her brow.

△ **Carved pilaster capital**
The tops, or capitals, of marble Roman pilasters and columns were often carved in the ornate Corinthian style, especially those used for lavish public buildings.

△ **Molossian Hound**
The Romans liked to copy statues from ancient Greece and the Greek-speaking world. This c. 2nd-century CE statue is a marble replica of a bronze original.

◁ **A small wonder**
Carved from sardonyx, this tiny cameo is just 1¼ in (3.2 cm) across; it shows Triton, a Greek sea god, carrying a Nereid, or sea nymph, on his back. Such fine work was only affordable for the very rich.

▷ **Bronze attachment**
Wealthy Romans liked to decorate most things. This fine bronze sculpture is a satyr (a follower of Bacchus, the god of wine), and was an attachment for a wine bucket's handle.

△ **Sculpted wellhead**
The carved reliefs on this wellhead, or *puteal*, from the 2nd century CE display episodes from the Greco-Roman myths of Jason and the Argonauts, and Narcissus and Echo.

◁ **Funerary carving**
Carved depictions that faithfully represented the deceased were common sights on Roman funerary monuments, as on this one for Cominia Tyche, who died c. 90–100 CE, aged 27.

POLYCHROME SCULPTURES

While the buildings and sculptural remains of the ancient world that exist today are overwhelmingly white, they would have looked very different to the people of the time. Most (if not all) sculptures, and many buildings and edifices, were painted. For sculptures, this included hair, eyes, and skin tones, as well as clothing. In many cases it is only possible to guess at the original colors, but sometimes patches of pigments survive. These suggest that the Romans often used very bright, even gaudy, colors to decorate their works. In other instances, scanning technologies can be used to discern traces of colors and layers that are no longer visible to the naked eye. This statue of Diana, the goddess of the hunt, from Pompeii (right) has been recreated using scientific techniques, giving modern eyes a glimpse of the polychrome world as the Romans saw it.

Marble portrait
This bust of Pompey is in the unadorned "veristic" style popular in the Late Republican era. The general's face is shown worn and lined with experience. He wears his hair in the style of Alexander the Great, from whom he acquired his nickname.

Pompey the Great

Commander and conqueror of the Late Republic

Gnaeus Pompeius, or Pompey, enjoyed military glory and political power. In the tumultuous years of the mid-1st century BCE he both protected and undermined Rome's republican system, paving the way for the Imperial age that followed.

Pompey was born in 106 BCE in Picenum, on Italy's east coast. As an ambitious *novus homo* (a "new man" from a non-senatorial family), his provincial father diligently worked his way up the *cursus honorum* to become consul in 89 BCE. On inheriting control of his father's three legions aged just 20, Pompey took a different route to power. Rome was at that time riven by a civil war (see pp. 108–109) and his bloody support for the side led by the general Sulla earned Pompey the nickname *adulescens carnifex* ("the young butcher"); others called him Pompey *Magnus* ("the Great").

Pompey's suppression of revolts in North Africa, Sicily, Hispania (Spain and Portugal), and Naples saw his self-confidence and influence increase: he demanded Triumphs he was not entitled to (he was not a senator) and in 71 BCE, despite never having stood for election before, he was elected by the people to be consul for the following year.

Power struggles in Rome

In 60 BCE Pompey joined Crassus and Julius Caesar in the so-called First Triumvirate (see p. 113), the three men ruling Rome and its territories between them until Crassus's death in 53 BCE. Political unrest in Rome the following year saw Pompey appointed sole consul by the Senate, so that he could "save" the Republic. Seeing Pompey's elevation as a threat to his own political power, in 49 BCE Caesar initiated a brutal civil war against Pompey and the Senate when he led his armies across the Rubicon (see pp. 128–129). A year later, Pompey was dead, assassinated in Egypt on the orders of its pharaoh, Ptolemy XIII, who sided with Caesar.

Throughout his career, Pompey had several opportunities to make himself Rome's dictator, but despite repeatedly circumventing the constitution, Pompey's respect for the Republic prevented him from taking that final step. Instead, ironically, having done much to unravel the fabric of the Republic, he became one of its staunchest defenders in its final years.

◁ **Assassination of Pompey**
In this early-18th-century painting by Giovanni Antonio Pellegrini, Caesar reacts with disgust when presented with the decapitated head of his former friend Pompey.

△ **Mithridates VI**
This *tetradrachm* coin shows King Mithridates VI of Pontus and Bithynia. His defeat by Pompey in the last of the three Mithridatic Wars in 65 BCE secured Rome's control of the eastern Mediterranean.

- **106 BCE** Born in Picenum, eastern Italy
- **83 BCE** Supports Sulla in the civil war
- **71 BCE** Helps end the Third Servile War
- **70 BCE** Elected consul after threatening Senate with his troops
- **65 BCE** Defeats Mithridates VI of Pontus and Bithynia
- **60 BCE** Alliance between Pompey, Crassus, and Caesar
- **52 BCE** Senate makes Pompey sole consul to end violence between political gangs in Rome
- **49 BCE** As Caesar crosses the Rubicon, Pompey and the Senate flee Rome
- **48 BCE** Defeat at Battle of Pharsalus, followed by assassination in Egypt

Caesar's Civil War

Risking everything to rule supreme

In 54 BCE the so-called First Triumvirate began to unravel when Caesar's daughter Julia died giving birth to Pompey's child. The next year, Crassus was dead. A showdown between Rome's two most powerful men would follow.

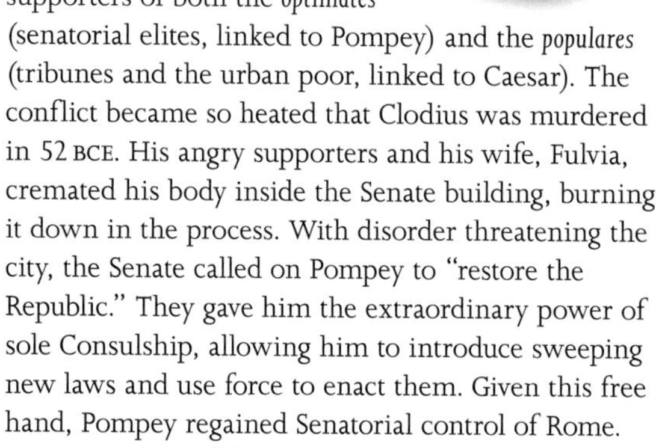

◁ **Silver *denarius***
Julius Caesar was the first living Roman to have their image portrayed on coinage. This was an indication that he perhaps aimed to make himself a monarch.

Violence had been escalating on the streets of Rome since 57 BCE, when political rivals Publius Clodius Pulcher and Titus Annius Milo began to organize riots and street brawls that drew in supporters of both the *optimates* (senatorial elites, linked to Pompey) and the *populares* (tribunes and the urban poor, linked to Caesar). The conflict became so heated that Clodius was murdered in 52 BCE. His angry supporters and his wife, Fulvia, cremated his body inside the Senate building, burning it down in the process. With disorder threatening the city, the Senate called on Pompey to "restore the Republic." They gave him the extraordinary power of sole Consulship, allowing him to introduce sweeping new laws and use force to enact them. Given this free hand, Pompey regained Senatorial control of Rome.

Caesar, who had been campaigning in Gaul since 58 BCE (see pp. 112–113), felt uneasy about these developments in Rome. He now had more wealth and glory to his name than Pompey and, with the First Triumvirate broken, believed there was no need to keep up the pretense of an alliance. He also worried what fate would await him when his proconsulship of Gaul came to an end in 50 BCE.

Crossing the Rubicon

In Roman law, a general was not allowed to enter Italy with his army unless specifically invited to do so by the Senate. If a general did defy the Senate in this way it was viewed as an act of aggression against the state. But this is what Caesar did on January 10, 49 BCE, when he led his men across the Rubicon river in northeast Italy. He was partly motivated by self-preservation, knowing that his enemies in Rome would prosecute him for his unlicensed conquests in Gaul. It is also possible that Caesar truly believed that the Senate's threats against tribunes of the plebs loyal to him represented a tyrannical threat to the sovereignty of the *populus Romanus*, the people of Rome. "Let the die be cast," he supposedly said on entering Italy. The civil war had begun.

As Caesar headed toward Rome, Pompey and most of the magistrates and the senators loyal to the *optimates* withdrew first to southern Italy and then Greece. In the meantime, Pompey raised armies from the provinces and from client kingdoms, widening the conflict into Hispania (Spain and Portugal), North Africa, and Greece.

▽ **Rome's territories in the time of Caesar**
This map shows the Roman Republic's empire and vassal states in the 1st century BCE, including Gaul.

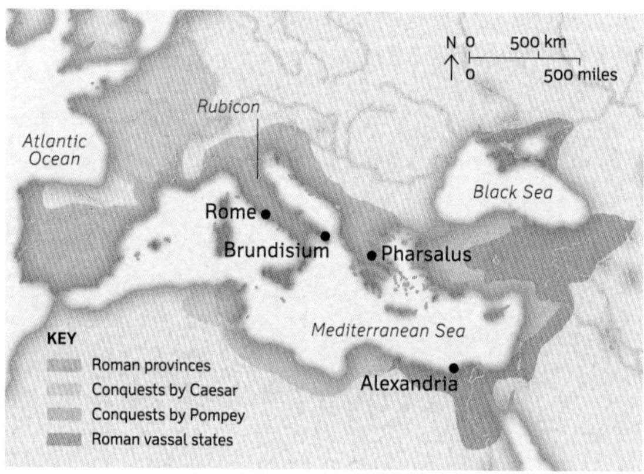

▷ **Julius Caesar's column**
This pillar in Rimini, on Italy's northeastern coast, marks the spot where Caesar addressed his troops after crossing the nearby Rubicon.

All hail Caesar

It was in Greece that the decisive engagement of the civil war took place, when Caesar's forces defeated Pompey's at the Battle of Pharsalus on August 9, 48 BCE. Pompey fled to Alexandria, in Egypt, but was murdered on his arrival on the orders of the pharaoh, Ptolemy XIII, who hoped to gain favor with Caesar. When he arrived in Alexandria in pursuit of Pompey and discovered his rival's fate, an outraged Caesar deposed Ptolemy and installed his sister, Cleopatra VII, as ruler. This led to civil unrest in the city, with Caesar and Cleopatra under siege in the royal palace until Roman reinforcements arrived. During Caesar's time in Alexandria, Cleopatra became pregnant with his child, whom she would name Caesarion.

After subduing *optimate* resistance in North Africa and Spain, Caesar returned to Rome in 46 BCE. In complete control of the empire, he passed laws and oversaw the appointment of senators and magistrates. He built his own forum and created a semi-divine cult around himself, claiming descent from the goddess Venus.

The Senate, wary of his army and his support among the people, showered Caesar with praise and honors. But there were opponents, too, especially among the remaining *optimate* faction and those who saw the Republican ideal under threat when Caesar was declared "dictator for life" in 44 BCE. Refusing to believe Caesar when he denied he was planning to make himself king, a group of senators assassinated him on March 15 (the "Ides of March") that year.

△ **Murder in the Senate**
Vincenzo Camuccini's 1806 painting *The Death of Julius Caesar* dramatizes the moment when a group of up to 60 senators, led by Brutus and Cassius, stabbed their victim more than 23 times at the foot of the statue of Pompey, Caesar's great rival.

> "**Nothing is left** but to **fight it out** in arms."
>
> SUETONIUS, *THE TWELVE CAESARS*

Coinage

Currency, politics, and culture

Since the world's first coins were minted in around the 6th century BCE, they have played an important role in constructing identity and conveying ideology. Through cultural and political symbols, as well as portraiture, governments and rulers have used images on coins to create an iconography of power.

△ **Early Republic coin**
The two faces of the god Janus allude to the growing power of Rome as an empire following the victories of the Punic Wars 225–217 BCE. Its naval battles are symbolized on the reverse by the ship's ram.

△ **Silver Roman *denarius***
This coin is a Gallic imitation of a 1st-century BCE *denarius* from the Republican period. It shows the head of Roma, the female personification of Rome; on the reverse is a *biga,* or two-horse chariot.

△ **Copper alloy coin**
Unlike gold and silver issues, Roman bronze coins contained less than the full nominal value in metal. Their value was fixed by decree of the Senate, noted by the initials "SC" for *senatus consulto*.

△ **Ides of March**
This coin celebrates Julius Caesar's assassination in 44 BCE, showing two daggers and a hat—a metaphor for supposed liberty from a tyrant.

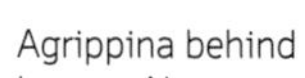

△ **Nero and Agrippina**
Agrippina the Younger was one of the most prominent women in the Julio-Claudian dynasty (Rome's first five emperors) and secured the throne for her son Nero. She appeared on coinage until she fell from his favor.

Commemorates the rebuilding of the temple after it burned down

△ **Rome's greatest temple**
This copper-alloy coin from the reign of Vespasian (69–79 CE) shows the Temple of Jupiter Optimus Maximus on the Capitoline Hill.

▽ **A challenge to Rome**
During the Social War of 91–87 BCE, the Italian peninsula was divided on whether to support Rome's primacy. Here the bull of the Italic peoples attacks the she-wolf of Rome.

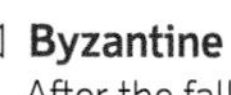

◁ **Byzantine coin**
After the fall of the Western Roman Empire, the Eastern or Byzantine Empire flourished for another thousand years and was well known for its riches and gold coinage.

Empress Irene ruled with her husband, 797–802 CE

△ **Bust of Plautilla**
As the wife of Emperor Caracalla (r. 198–217 CE), Plautilla could have been influential, but the political marriage was unhappy and she was ultimately executed.

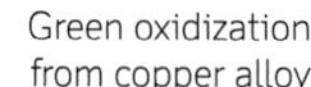

△ **The *Chi Rho***
This coin shows the emperor Magnentius, who reigned during the 4th century CE. The reverse shows the Christian *Chi Rho* symbol—the two Greek letters for "Xristos" or Christ.

Oak wreath is a symbol to mark him "saving" Rome

△ **Caesar Augustus**
Rome's first emperor was adept at promoting his own image. Here his bust and the new name bestowed by the Senate in 27 BCE are shown, erasing old connotations of the civil war under "Octavian" and ushering in a new period of stability, the Pax Romana, under "Augustus."

△ **Client kings of the East**
Rome used client kings as a way to expand the empire and gain tribute with limited direct control. Sauromates II was ruler of the longest-surviving client kingdom, the Bosporus.

Nicknamed Augustulus, he was a teenager when he ascended the throne

△ **Last Western Roman coin**
The last of the imperial coins of the Western Empire shows the final emperor, Romulus Augustus, who was deposed by the Germanic general Odoacer in 476 CE.

Defaced portrait of Nero

△ **Erased from history**
This coin from the reign of Nero has been cut, a part of the campaign to remove images of Nero from the public domain.

The tetrarchs swear loyalty

△ **The Tetrarchy**
When the emperor Diocletian, shown here, ascended the throne in 284 CE, he instituted a new form of government with four rulers. The coin's reverse shows four rulers swearing allegiance to each other.

Inscription reads *Aegypto capta* ("Egypt captured")

△ **Egypt captured**
This coin depicts a crocodile and a clear message that Egypt was now part of the empire after the defeat of Cleopatra VII and Mark Antony at the Battle of Actium in 31 BCE.

△ **Late Imperial coin**
This gold *solidus* shows the emperor Honorius, his foot on a captive. It belies the disasters in his reign as the Western Empire declined, such as the Visigoths' sack of Rome in 410 CE and the need to temporarily move the capital to Ravenna.

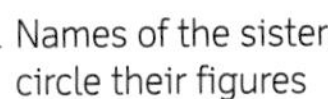

◁ **Caligula's three sisters**
Shown emulating the Roman concepts of Securitas, Concordia, and Fortuna, Caligula's three sisters Livia, Drusilla, and Agrippina were important for the continuation of the Julio-Claudian dynasty.

Names of the sisters circle their figures

△ **Augustus's heirs**
Depicted are Augustus's grandchildren, Gaius and Lucius, who would die in their early teens before they could inherit power.

THE MAKING OF **ROMAN COINS**

Roman coins were all struck by hand. First, small metal disks were made either by cutting cold sheets of metal or by pouring hot metal into circular molds. Afterward, coins were put into a "die," which was stamped with the details to be hammered onto the flat pieces of metal. The most prevalent coin of the empire was the *denarius*, made from silver. Even following the fall of the Western Roman Empire in 476 CE, Roman coinage still remained so widespread that it was used as the model for medieval kingdoms and Islamic caliphates, which even named their currency *dinars*.

TERRA-COTTA COIN MOLDS, 308–320 CE

The Roman Calendar

Reckoning time in ancient Rome

Like the ancient Greeks, Egyptians, and Babylonians, the Romans measured time by the movements of astral bodies, basing their calendars on the cycles of the sun and moon to create a system that is used—almost unchanged—today.

◁ **Portable Roman sundial**
A traveler could find the time with this portable bronze sundial (3rd century CE) marked with latitudes across the Roman Empire.

The Roman calendar developed gradually. The earliest Roman year had 10 months and only 304 days, which meant the months soon fell out of step with the seasons. In the Republican period, the calendar was extended to 12 months, and the *pontifex maximus* priest would occasionally decree an additional month to realign the lunar and solar calendars. To regularize the year and keep the months aligned with the seasons, Julius Caesar reformed the calendar, making the year 365 days and adding an extra day to February every four or five years.

The Roman year was punctuated with great festivals (see pp. 120–121), announced on large calendars that were painted or inscribed on temple walls. These also indicated which days were *nefasti*—those on which political gatherings and law courts were forbidden.

Naming the months

In the earlier, 10-month Roman calendar, the first four months were named after divinities, for instance, *Junius* (June) after the goddess Juno. The final six were named for the month's position in the calendar, such as September after seven and October after eight. When the calendar was lengthened to 12 months, these numbered names were kept, despite no longer reflecting their chronology, which is why the tenth month retained the name December despite being the 12th month. Each month had three important days: the *Kalends* (first day), *Nones* (fifth or seventh day), and *Ides* (13th or 15th day). Every other day of the month was dated backward from one of these dates. Thus, January 3 was three days before the *Nones* of January, and July 25 was six days before the *Kalends* of August.

For most of the Roman period, the week had eight days, each named after a deity. For instance, Monday was the day of Luna, and Friday the day of Venus. The Romans had no weekends, but worked until the next festival day in Rome.

△ **The month of Mars**
Martius (March) was named for the god Mars, portrayed in this Romano-British statue, as this was the month campaign season started.

Year of the politician

Unlike the modern system, which uses numbers to name a year, the Romans called their years after the two consuls (the highest elected political office) of the year (see pp. 62–63). For instance, the year 63 BCE was known to the Romans as the year of the consuls Marcus Tullius Cicero and Gaius Antonius Hybrida. In the Roman Forum, Augustus erected lists of the consuls going back to the distant past so that years could be accurately dated.

ROMAN AND **MODERN CALENDARS**

The Roman month *Sextilis* was renamed after Augustus (now the month of August) and *Quinctilis* was renamed after Julius Caesar, becoming *Julius* (now the month of July). The calendar that Caesar adopted later became the Gregorian calendar that many still use today: 365 days with an extra day every four years. In many European languages, the names of the months still indicate Roman roots. As depicted in this mosaic from North Africa (3rd century CE), the Roman year began in March and ended in February; vignettes illustrate each month, such as a sacrifice to Mercury in the month of May.

◁ **Public calendar**
Calendars such as this one, from Praeneste in central Italy, were common across the empire. Erected publicly, they announced festival days, as well as days on which public business and legal trials were prohibited.

Descending Roman numerals indicate the day of the month

Public calendars often included details explaining how particular days should be observed

Letters from A to H indicate the day of the eight-day week

The Battle of Actium

Octavian's showdown with Egypt

Julius Caesar named his 18-year-old great-nephew Octavian as his heir, but Octavian's lack of military experience or political office made him an unpromising contender to inherit power after Caesar's assassination in 44 BCE.

△ **Mark Antony**
This gold *aureus* bearing the likeness of Mark Antony was made in 38 BCE, two years before the alliance between Antony, Octavian, and Lepidus—commonly known as the Second Triumvirate—began to fail.

In contrast with Octavian, Mark Antony was a seasoned general. He had governed Rome in Caesar's absence during the civil war and been a consul in 44 BCE. His speech at Caesar's funeral turned public opinion against the assassins, framing himself as the provider of justice. Another significant figure was Marcus Aemilius Lepidus, a close ally of Caesar.

After initial hostilities, Octavian, Mark Antony, and Lepidus formed a triumvirate charged with restoring the shattered Republic. Their first task—to eliminate those who had betrayed and murdered Julius Caesar—was achieved in 42 BCE with the deaths of Brutus and Cassius at the Battle of Philippi in Macedonia.

The alliance unravels

By 36 BCE Pompey's son Sextus was still leading a faction in Sicily, a revolt Lepidus failed to subdue. His legions defected to Octavian and he was stripped of his power.

Meanwhile, Mark Antony ruled the east like a Hellenistic monarch, gaining loyalty from the Greek-speaking world. He sought to expand Rome's eastern provinces and conquer Parthia, but needed to strengthen Rome's alliance with its eastern vassal, Egypt, to succeed. When Antony had three children with Cleopatra and sent his wife Octavia (Octavian's sister) back to Rome, however, Cleopatra was vilified in the capital, where Octavian portrayed Antony as opposing Roman ways. He publicized what he claimed was Antony's will, which supposedly gave away Rome's eastern territories as kingdoms for Antony's children with Cleopatra. In 32 BCE the Senate revoked Antony's powers as consul and declared war on Cleopatra in Egypt.

CLEOPATRA VII OF EGYPT

Cleopatra was the last ruler of the Ptolemaic Dynasty. Coming to power as a teenager, she skillfully carried out internal coups against her siblings, and saw off external threats. In 48 BCE, when Julius Caesar landed in Egypt in pursuit of Pompey, she saw a potential ally. By having a son with Caesar, she hoped to secure her kingdom, visiting Rome in 46 BCE for two years to ensure their son Caesarion's recognition as heir. After Caesar's murder, and with Caesarion not named in Caesar's will, she fled to Alexandria. Later, she allied with Mark Antony to crush Octavian, having more children to ensure the continuity of a Ptolemaic–Roman Empire. The defeat at Actium ended her ambitions.

Octavian rules the waves

In September, 31 BCE, Antony assembled 500 warships at Actium on the western coast of Greece, drafting in allies from eastern client kingdoms, such as King Herod of Judea. Instead of advancing into Italy, however, he set up camp in Greece. Octavian sent a naval force with Marcus Vipsanius Agrippa to capture key towns and blockade Antony's base to cut off supplies. After several months of food shortages and disease, Antony resolved to fight through the naval blockade. However, his large ships were difficult to maneuver and a stalemate ensued as both sides feared being encircled. When a gap in the line emerged, Cleopatra fled to Alexandria with her 60 ships, and Antony followed. Octavian's men pursued them toward Egypt. Hearing of his approach and seeing his soldiers defect to his rival, Mark Antony stabbed himself with his sword. Cleopatra supposedly used a poisonous snake to kill herself rather than be executed by Octavian in triumph back in Rome.

Octavian had Caesarion murdered and ordered all Antony's remaining supporters to be killed. With Cleopatra's death, Egypt was annexed by Rome. Octavian was now master of the Mediterranean.

△ **Ruins at Nicopolis**
Octavian founded the city of Nicopolis in 29 BCE with a monument to his patron deity Apollo, decorated with the rams from Mark Antony and Cleopatra's captured ships.

▽ **Battle of Actium**
This marble frieze commemorates the naval battle fought at close quarters, with metal rams used by both forces to smash enemy ships and infantry boarding to fight hand-to-hand on deck.

Eating Like a Roman

Food and drink across the empire

Diet varied hugely around the Roman world, depending on geographical location and disposable wealth. Archaeological evidence shows that luxurious ingredients were widely used in affluent households, often as a display of wealth.

Regional climates around the empire played a significant role in what was eaten locally, but food was traded across the empire, meaning that provinces could import the luxury foodstuffs that were unavailable in their particular climes.

The Romans also introduced new produce to some parts of the empire. They took more than 50 different foods to Britain, for example, including cucumbers, apples, and leeks, and turned Spain, with its plentiful supplies of seafood, into a key supplier of garum, the fish sauce that was one of the Romans' favorite condiments.

Rich Romans could afford more varied diets, and displayed their wealth with lavish feasts of exotic animals. Poorer people were still able to buy delicacies, just less frequently, while enslaved people could eat only what was provided for them.

◁ Daily bread
Carbonized in the extreme heat of the volcanic eruption at Pompeii, this loaf shows the typical form of Roman bread.

▽ Terra-cotta amphora
Food was stored and transported in jars such as this one, which is about 1ft (30cm) high. The largest amphorae could reach up to 5ft (1.5m).

Roman staples

The Roman diet was based primarily on cereals and grains, which could be made into bread (see pp. 94–95), porridge, and cakes. These foodstuffs were considered so fundamental that Rome distributed a monthly grain ration (the *annona*) to urban citizens. Legumes such as chickpeas, beans, and lentils were also important, and literary evidence reports that Romans ate vegetables such as onions, artichokes, beets, and cabbages, although archaeological evidence is slim.

An abundance of fruit grew around the Mediterranean in the Imperial period, including figs, pears, pomegranates, and melons, while North Africa exported dates. Nuts such as walnuts, hazelnuts, and pistachios were eaten, too, and herbs and spices were used to season basic foodstuffs.

Olive oil was essential for cooking, as well as lighting and bathing. Meat was expensive, and came mainly from livestock, such as sheep, goats, pigs, and cows. In the northern provinces, it was common to keep chickens, which were used mainly for eggs. The Romans ate a lot of freshwater and saltwater fish, particularly in coastal settlements, along with shellfish and oysters. In warmer climates, milk was preserved as soft and hard cheeses.

Most Romans drank wine mixed with water—the Mediterranean islands of Kos, Rhodes, and Crete produced valued vintages—while beer was common in the northern provinces. Water was usually safe to drink, especially from aqueducts.

Eating in and out

Larger houses had dedicated kitchens, unlike *insulae* (see pp. 78–79), where food was either cooked on a brazier, prepared and cooked elsewhere, or purchased. Bakeries were numerous, and hot food was sold at *thermopolia*, outlets with cooking facilities (some of which survive at Pompeii and Herculaneum).

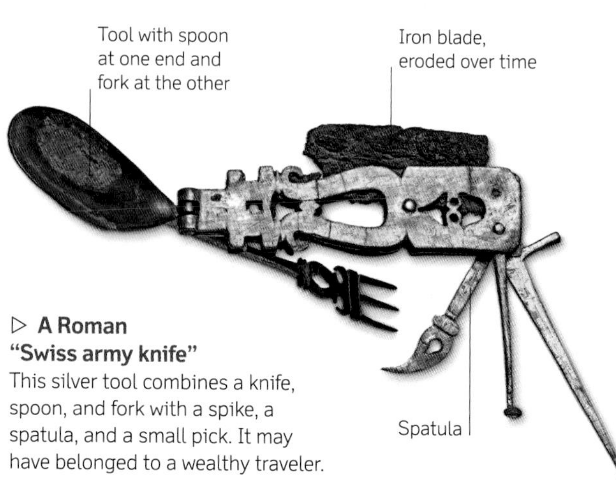

▷ A Roman "Swiss army knife"
This silver tool combines a knife, spoon, and fork with a spike, a spatula, and a small pick. It may have belonged to a wealthy traveler.

△ **Everyday edibles**
Roman interior decoration often included depictions of commonly eaten food. This mosaic captures a still life of fish, poultry, shellfish, dates, and vegetables. It was made in the 2nd century CE for a villa at Tor Marancia in Rome.

GARUM

Garum was a type of fermented fish sauce, widely traded across the empire. It was made by blending whole fish or parts of fish with salt. The mixture was left to ferment in the sun for one to three months, after which the garum (the clear liquid that formed at the top of the production vat) was drained off. It could be made by families, but archaeologists have also found sites of industrial salteries across the empire. Some versions were very expensive luxury items, but lower-grade garum was probably much more affordable. Garum containers are widespread in Pompeii, in both rich and poor households; and papyri from Egypt frequently show garum on shopping lists and inventories.

Pax Romana

Augustus's propaganda campaign

After his victory at Actium in 31 BCE and the brutal proscriptions against his enemies that followed, Octavian launched a propaganda campaign to consolidate and extend his power under the guise of bringing peace and stability.

Remembering that his great-uncle Julius Caesar had been killed for attempting to rule as an autocrat, Octavian saw that he needed to conceal his power behind a very public respect for Rome's Republican traditions and institutions.

He was careful to avoid the trappings of monarchical rule, such as the all-purple toga or the diadem worn by Rome's former kings. He only accepted offices and awards when they were bestowed on him by the Senate, which it did on a regular basis; Octavian was elected consul each year between 31 and 23 BCE, for example. He was also given *imperium maius* by the Senate, a form of absolute military power to be used to suppress uprisings in the provinces and along the empire's borders. Slowly but surely, Octavian tightened his grip on power with the complicity of Rome's political elites. By 27 BCE the Senate had recognized Octavian as Rome's *princeps* ("first citizen"). On coins he was portrayed as *Caesar divi filius* ("Caesar, son of a god").

◁ **Gold *aureus* of Augustus**
This coin shows Augustus "restoring and giving back the laws" to the Senate, cleverly both emphasizing and downplaying his power.

▽ **Augustan arch**
Triumphal arches like this one in Orange, France, were erected across the empire as symbols of the peace that Augustus had brought to the provinces. Their depictions of war and conquest also acted as a reminder to populations of Roman power.

The new world order

Most significantly, he was now officially known as Augustus ("the illustrious one"). By dropping the name associated with the civil war, Octavian was symbolically ushering in a new era of peace and security—the *Pax Romana*—as Augustus.

In 13 BCE Augustus became *pontifex maximus*, making him Rome's religious as well as political leader. He promoted himself as the ultimate moral authority, claiming he was the best role model for others to follow, a position that would later become formalized as a form of worship to the "imperial cult." He emphasized the traditions that he was restoring to veil the fact that he was creating a new autocracy. His power remained unrivaled, as many individuals relied on his patronage and favor—behind which always lay the threat of force, even if disguised.

Shaping the narrative

An early master of public relations and "spin," Augustus ensured that even as he deconstructed the Republican constitution, the official narrative would present him as the defender of the status quo. The large-scale inscription to him in Rome known as the *Res Gestae* ("Things Done") describes how Augustus "placed the whole world under the sovereignty of the Roman people," and details the "amounts expended on the state" for the benefit of all citizens. The portrait the inscription paints is of a humble man

Raised arm is an *adlocutio* ("address") to soldiers, showing his authority

Sphinx decorations on shoulder straps celebrate the victory over Mark Antony and Cleopatra VII at Actium in 31 BCE

Augustus takes back the standards lost in battle by Crassus in 53 BCE

The cornucopia, or "horn of plenty," represents the riches delivered by the *Pax Romana*

Cupid signifies Augustus's claim that his ancestors, via Julius Caesar, were descended from the gods

The dolphin is a symbol of Venus, from whom the emperor's great-uncle Julius Caesar claimed direct descent

His feet are bare, like those of a god or hero

△ **Mausoleum of Augustus**
Augustus's tomb, partially restored in 2019, was once a grand, marble-faced structure topped, some archaeologists believe, by a monumental bronze statue of the emperor.

and a loyal servant of the Republic. It was displayed in front of Augustus's mausoleum after his death.

Just as ironic was the idea of an Augustan *Pax Romana*. While Roman rule did lead to peace and relative stability in the areas it conquered, it also meant taxation, stolen resources, and military occupation. It also led to more imperialism, and the rebellion and war that went with it, as Rome looked for new lands to seize and more wealth to extract from them. Some of this plunder went toward the beautification of Rome. According to the historian Suetonius, Augustus claimed that, "I found Rome a city of bricks, and left it a city of marble." Many of the new buildings, such as the *Ara Pacis* (see pp. 140–141), celebrated Augustus as much as the state.

In keeping with his image as a mere protector of the Republic, Augustus left the naming of his heir to the Senate, which dutifully selected his stepson, Tiberius, in 13 CE. As he lay dying the following year, the 75-year-old Augustus's last words were supposedly, "since the play has been so good, clap your hands."

◁ **Symbolic statue**
The *Augustus of Prima Porta* is the most famous sculpture of Rome's first emperor. It was found in 1863 at the villa of his widow, Livia, and portrays the usually understated Augustus in heroic, godlike mode.

"I was **named Augustus** by **decree of the Senate** …."

INSCRIPTION ON THE *RES GESTAE*

▷ **Processional frieze**
The altar's processional friezes show portraits of Augustus and his family among officials and citizens. Here, his son-in-law, Agrippa (far left, with head covered), stands with a female figure (also with head covered)—maybe Augustus's wife, Livia, or his daughter, Julia.

The Ara Pacis

A monumental celebration of peace

The Ara Pacis ("Altar of Peace") was a marble altar adorned with magnificent sculptural decorations representing Rome's mythical origins and the stability and prosperity of Augustus's rule. It was commissioned in 13 BCE by the Roman Senate to celebrate the emperor's victorious return from campaigns in Hispania (Spain and Portugal) and Gaul.

Dedicated in 9 BCE to Pax, goddess of peace, the altar commemorated an end to warfare, including the civil war that had brought Augustus to power (see pp. 134–135). Although it was nominally erected by the Senate, the Ara Pacis was almost certainly initiated by Augustus, to demonstrate the values and priorities of his regime. It was part of a carefully calculated program of art and architecture that honored traditional gods and mythical heroes, while reinforcing imperial ideology. In practical terms, it was a site for ritual animal sacrifices to the gods.

Significant location

The open-topped altar stood on the outskirts of Rome in the Campus Martius ("Field of Mars"), a floodplain of the Tiber originally used for military elections. Under Augustus, this area was dotted with buildings for entertainment and religious practices. The altar was part of a complex of monuments that included the original Pantheon, Augustus's own vast tomb, and a huge solar meridian marker, similar to a sundial, whose gnomon was a captured Egyptian obelisk. The traditional U-shape of the inner altar recalls older Italian altars, referencing a simpler past. The rich sculpture included an inner frieze that echoed these earlier altars' decoration. On the lower outer frieze, acanthus leaves and fruits and flowers of other plants symbolized the abundance of the new Augustan age.

Complex imagery

Processional friezes on the two longest sides of the altar depicted the emperor and his family among the leaders, priests, and people of Rome. On the two open ends, carved panels showed figures and scenes from Rome's mythological past, along with the city's protective gods and goddesses. The fragmentary state and complex imagery of the panels means that multiple interpretations are possible, but scholars have identified the twins Romulus and Remus (see pp. 22–23) and the wolf that suckled them. Other figures may include Aeneas, the forefather of Rome, and goddesses of fertility and abundance. Again, the visual message was that, in a culmination of myth and history, Augustus had brought the fruits of peace and stability to Rome and her people.

The numerous fragments of the Ara Pacis were gradually excavated, then painstakingly reconstructed, and eventually put on display in the center of Rome in the 20th century.

She-wolf suckling the twins Romulus and Remus in the Lupercal cave

The god Mars, father of Romulus and Remus

"**The Senate** voted **in honor** of my return the consecration of an altar to **Pax Augusta**."

AUGUSTUS, *RES GESTAE*

▽ **Artist's reconstruction of the Ara Pacis**
Marble fragments from the altar began to be uncovered from the 16th century, but it was not until the late 1930s that major reconstruction took place. The marble reliefs, like much Roman sculpture, would originally have been brightly painted, as suggested here.

Figure thought to be Aeneas or Numa Pompilius

Shrine to the household gods (see pp. 122–123)

The U-shaped altar itself sits in the interior of the structure

Inner decoration of garlands and ox skulls

Richly embellished relief panel of leaves and flowers

▷ **Bust of Livia Drusilla as Ceres**
After Claudius overturned Tiberius's ban on the deification of Livia in 42 CE, statues and busts were made portraying her as Ceres, the motherly goddess of grain and fertility. This cemented Livia's official image as a nurturing, steadfast, and maternal figure.

> "I have an **equal share** in whatever happens to you … so **I also take my part** in the **reigning**."
>
> LIVIA, QUOTED IN CASSIUS DIO'S *ROMAN HISTORY*

Livia Drusilla

Matriarch of the Julio-Claudians

As wife to Rome's first emperor, mother to its second, and grandmother of the next generation, Livia Drusilla's proximity to the new sources of ultimate power made her the most influential woman in Early Imperial politics.

As a young girl, Livia saw the collapse of the so-called First Triumvirate (see p. 113), and her Pompey-supporting family was involved in the civil wars that followed the murder of Julius Caesar. After a period of exile in Sicily and then Greece, Livia and her three-year-old son Tiberius returned to Rome when Octavian issued an amnesty for Pompey's former allies.

◁ **Grieving widow**
Livia holds a bust of Augustus in this cameo produced around the time of his death. Her image as a dignified matriarch helped legitimize the Julio-Claudian dynasty her husband had founded.

From enemy to husband

When a heavily pregnant Livia was introduced to Octavian (later Rome's first emperor, Augustus) he was allegedly so struck by her beauty that he forced her husband to divorce her. Octavian divorced his own wife, Scribonia, on the day their daughter Julia was born. He and Livia married on January 17, 38 BCE.

Livia became one of her husband's most trusted confidants. Later writers often portrayed her as overly ambitious, circulating rumors, for example, that she poisoned Augustus when she decided it was time for Tiberius to succeed him. It should be remembered, however, that all of the sources for Livia's life are by male authors, who resented her influence; under the Republic, women had been formally excluded from power, but in the Imperial Age Livia showed, to their discomfort, that a woman could exercise authority.

When Augustus introduced new morality laws in 18 BCE, Livia was presented as an example of the ideal wife and mother. The harsh reality was that this legislation criminalized adultery, allowed men to kill or exile their wives, forced the remarriage of divorced or widowed women, and placed tight social restrictions on the already narrow lives of young girls living under the strict control of their fathers.

Livia publicly honored her husband's memory when he died and, as the mother of his successor Tiberius, helped normalize the idea of imperial rule and dynastic succession. To Tiberius's increasing irritation, she remained a key figure at the imperial court for the rest of her life. Today, she is remembered as one of the originators of Rome's imperial system.

△ **Julia the Elder**
Livia was celebrated by Augustus as the embodiment of female virtue, unlike his daughter from his first marriage, Julia the Elder, who was exiled in 2 BCE for flouting her father's strict morality laws—as was her own daughter, Julia the Younger, ten years later.

▷ **A woman of means**
This relief shows a papyrus farm similar to those owned by Livia in Egypt. These, along with her palm groves in the Near East, made Livia a wealthy woman.

- **59 BCE** Born in Rome
- **42 BCE** Father kills himself when Battle of Philippi is lost; son Tiberius is born
- **40 BCE** Flees to Sicily to avoid arrest and joins Pompey's son, Sextus Pompeius
- **38 BCE** Marries Octavian; second son Drusus is born (dies 9 BCE)
- **27 BCE** Octavian becomes Augustus
- **14 CE** Augustus dies, poisoned by Livia, her detractors say. Tiberius becomes emperor
- **29 CE** Dies aged 86. Tiberius misses her funeral and vetoes the honors awarded to Livia by the Senate
- **42 CE** Deified by her grandson, Claudius; given the title Augusta

Virgil, Horace, and Ovid

Latin literature's finest poets

The Augustan period saw a surge in literary interest, cultivated by the emperor and his inner circle. Poetry was fundamental to this epoch of literary activity and helped the Romans develop their identity and national story.

The rule of Augustus saw the creation of works that are now part of the literary canon—texts that have been read, studied, and cherished for more than two millennia. One of the men who helped this period's literary culture to flourish was Augustus's friend and political adviser Maecenas. Along with the emperor, he was a patron of poets and writers, the most famous of which were Virgil and Horace. Other poets, such as Ovid, wrote from outside this charmed circle.

Virgil: Roman myth-maker

Publius Vergilius Maro, or Virgil (70–19 BCE), is the foremost Latin poet of the Roman period. His books are the bucolic and pastoral *Eclogues* and *Georgics*, and the *Aeneid*. Drawing on Homer's *Iliad* and *Odyssey*, the *Aeneid* is a 12-book epic in which the Trojan hero Aeneas journeys to Italy and establishes the city of Lavinium, which will lead to the foundation of Rome. On his deathbed, Virgil supposedly asked for his unfinished manuscript of the *Aeneid* to be burned, but Augustus insisted that it be published. Virgil's poem celebrated the future glory of Rome under Augustus, while meditating on the costs of the violence and civil wars that brought Augustus to power.

▽ **Apollo and Daphne**
Gian Lorenzo Bernini captured in marble c. 1625 the moment in Ovid's tale when Daphne transforms herself into a laurel tree to escape the unwanted attentions of Apollo.

Horace: poet of the Golden Age

The son of a freedman, Quintus Horatius Flaccus, or Horace (65–8 BCE), died Rome's preeminent poet. His early works, the *Satires* and the *Epodes*, charted the collapse of Roman society during the civil wars, while his mature *Odes* used the meters of Greek lyric poetry to celebrate the joyful, balanced, philosophical life Romans were now able to enjoy under Augustus.

◁ **Horace reciting poetry**
The writer publicly recites his poetry in this late-19th-century oil painting by Adalbert von Rössler. Although stylized, it reflects the fascination with poetry among Rome's elite in the early empire.

The apex of his career came in 17 BCE when he was asked to compose the *Carmen Saeculare* ("the Secular Hymn"), the centerpiece of a festival of theater, sports, and animal sacrifice designed to initiate Augustus's golden age.

Ovid: myth and morality

Publius Ovidius Naso, or Ovid (43 BCE–c. 18 CE), grew up during the long period of peace initiated by Augustus's rule. He excelled at versifying new perspectives on familiar topics, such as mythological heroines and, in the *Ars Amatoria* (*The Art of Love*), the amorous adventures of the young. This is a problematic work that legitimizes sexual assault by framing it as "seduction." His work culminated in the *Metamorphoses*, a 15-book epic retelling Greco-Roman mythology through the theme of transformation, beginning with the famous story of Apollo and Daphne. In 8 CE Ovid was banished by Augustus to Tomis on the Black Sea for an unknown offence. He produced poetry from exile until his dying day, bewailing his fate and blaming his predicament on "a poem and a mistake." He never saw Rome again.

▷ **Virgil with Clio and Melpomene**
This mosaic from Tunisia shows a figure identified as Virgil holding a passage of the *Aeneid*. He is flanked by his two great inspirations when writing the epic: Clio, the Muse of History, and Melpomene, the Muse of Tragedy.

"A **greater series** of events begins, a **greater task** awaits me."

VIRGIL, ON WRITING THE SECOND HALF OF THE *AENEID*

Melpomene carries the theatrical mask of tragedy, while her fellow muse, Clio, holds a scroll, symbolizing history

The Palatine Hill and Circus Maximus

Rome's oldest site and seat of emperors

In Roman legend, the Palatine Hill was where the she-wolf suckled the twins Romulus and Remus. One of the area's natural hills, the Palatine was considered by Roman writers to be the oldest inhabited part of the city, and archaeology suggests that it was settled in the early 1st millennium BCE. Early on it provided a defensive stronghold, and, later, its proximity to the Forum below made it a fashionable address in the Republic. From Augustus onward, Roman emperors lived here, transforming the hill over time into a complex of palace buildings—the word "palace" derives from "Palatine." While Augustus's Palatine house was relatively modest, tyrannical emperors such as Caligula, Nero, and Domitian were much more extravagant. The view shown here contains the additions made by various dynasties over three centuries.

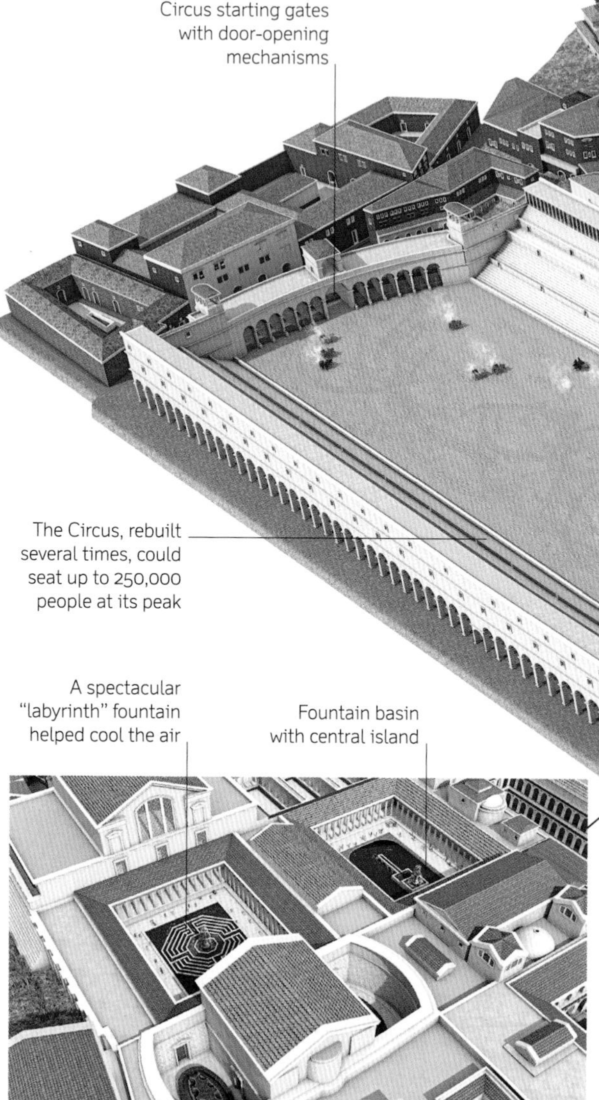

House of Augustus

Library buildings built by Augustus, restored under Domitian

Circus starting gates with door-opening mechanisms

The Circus, rebuilt several times, could seat up to 250,000 people at its peak

▷ The Palatine Hill and Circus Maximus
The valley that separated the Palatine from the plebeian Aventine Hill had been used for horse racing since the earliest days of Rome. Over time this space became the Circus Maximus. Here, the emperors appeared in front of a quarter of a million of their subjects seated in the oval stadium.

EXPANDING **GRANDEUR**

From the reign of Augustus, the site of the Palatine Hill was the exclusive preserve of Rome's emperors. Successive phases of expansion filled the hillside with a series of brick-and-concrete terraces supporting audience halls, courtyards, libraries, temples, and dining pavilions, as well as accommodations for the imperial household and its officers. However, emperors trod a fine line between magnificence and overambitious building, as exemplified by Nero's Domus Aurea, or "Golden House" (see pp. 186–187), a lavish construction on the Palatine that contributed to his downfall.

REMAINS OF THE PALATINE'S VAULTED TERRACING

A spectacular "labyrinth" fountain helped cool the air

Fountain basin with central island

▷ Fountain courtyards
A dedicated aqueduct branch delivered copious running water to the hilltop. The emperors' architects took advantage of this to lay out complex fountain courtyards with geometric basins and cascades, satisfying the Roman love of water also evident in much smaller houses in Pompeii.

▷ Circus Maximus
This reconstruction shows a training day, but during the races, four-horse chariots sprang from starting gates to do seven laps around a central barrier, or *spina*. The course was decorated with lap counters, fountains, statues, and an obelisk brought from Egypt by its conqueror Augustus.

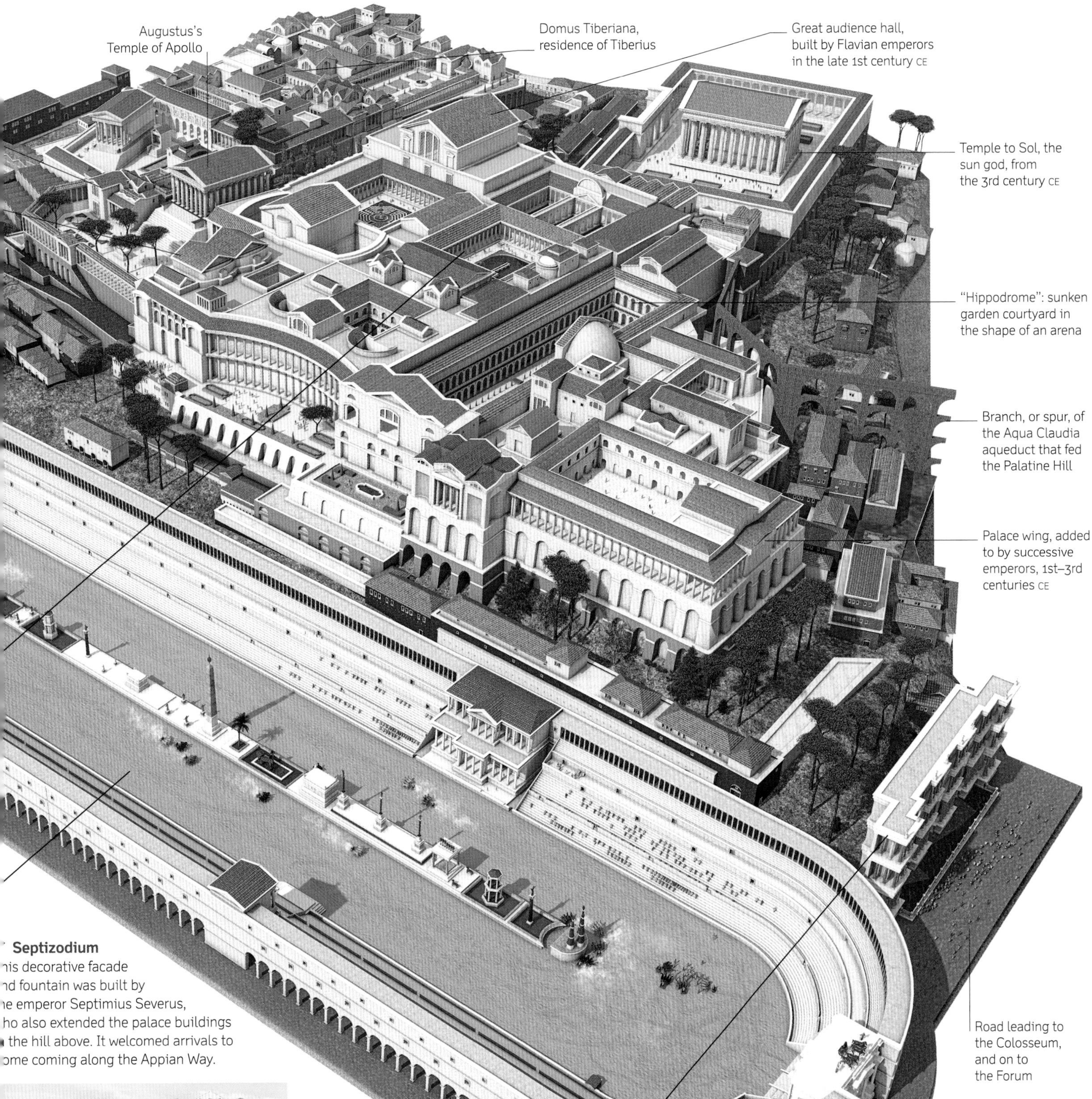

Augustus's Temple of Apollo

Domus Tiberiana, residence of Tiberius

Great audience hall, built by Flavian emperors in the late 1st century CE

Temple to Sol, the sun god, from the 3rd century CE

"Hippodrome": sunken garden courtyard in the shape of an arena

Branch, or spur, of the Aqua Claudia aqueduct that fed the Palatine Hill

Palace wing, added to by successive emperors, 1st–3rd centuries CE

Septizodium
ʼnis decorative facade ɲd fountain was built by ʼne emperor Septimius Severus, ʼho also extended the palace buildings ɴ the hill above. It welcomed arrivals to ɔme coming along the Appian Way.

Road leading to the Colosseum, and on to the Forum

Arcades with rooms for stores and taverns

Triumphal arch of the emperor Titus

Medicine

Roman health and healing

Roman medicine followed in and built upon the Hippocratic and Greek tradition, with practitioners leaving behind many influential texts. Romans also made strides in public health with clean water and sanitation.

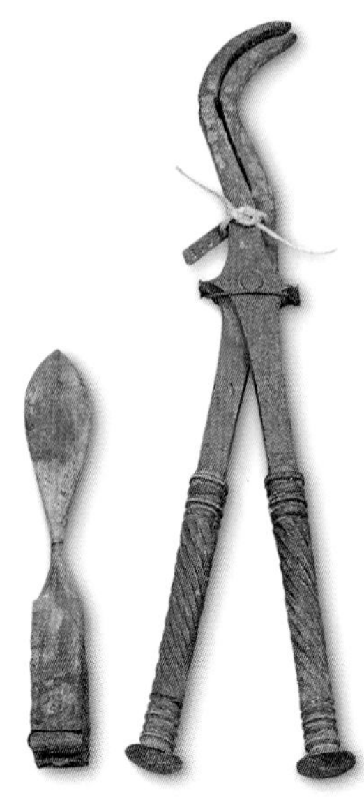

△ **Roman surgical tools**
These surgical instruments from Pompeii (1st century CE) include a scalpel and a bone forceps for removing fragments of skull.

Roman medicine was a combination of traditional practices, such as herbal remedies, and the more scientific approaches that were the legacy of ancient Greece. The Romans were among the first to implement public health measures, such as general hygiene, clean drinking water, and organized sanitation in urban areas. There was also a focus on good diet and exercise. The Romans had various medical deities, and treatments often involved appeals to these gods as well as the receipt of medical care.

Herbal remedies and surgery

The Romans used a wide range of herbal medicines and other remedies in their healing. Roman houses often had herb gardens, which would have contained many herbs in popular use today, such as fennel, mint, thyme, parsley, and garlic. Plants were eaten or applied in poultices, such as aloe, which was used in healing wounds. War was a fact of life in ancient Rome and physicians would have done their best to treat battle wounds, but surgery was only performed when unavoidable, due to the risks it posed. Surgeons performed a range of operations, such as the removal of cataracts from the eye, extraction of gallstones, and removal of the tonsils. Ancient surgical instruments, such as scalpels or spathas (used to mix medicines), have been found across the Roman Empire.

GALEN

Born in Pergamum (Türkiye) in 129 CE, Galen was the foremost medical authority of the Roman Empire. He studied at the Great Library of Alexandria in Egypt and built on the work of Hippocrates and other Greek physicians. His dissections of animals led to numerous accurate discoveries, and his teachings on human anatomy, and the causes, symptoms, and treatments of diseases, endured as core medical practice for over 1,300 years. A prolific writer, Galen wrote hundreds of texts, many of which were lost over time.

FRESCO OF GALEN AND HIPPOCRATES FROM THE 13TH CENTURY

Childbirth and women's health

Roman midwives were treated with great respect in ancient Rome. Records of medical instruments relating to childbirth include a birthing stool, with a crescent-shaped opening for the delivery of the baby, along with various surgical tools, such as forceps and obstetric dilators. Pregnancy-related deaths were a leading cause of mortality, due to the likelihood of infection or complications during birth. Roman women who wished to limit the number of children they had could turn to various remedies, some more effective than others. One of the most well-known herbal remedies of ancient Rome was silphium, a fennel-like plant that grew only in Cyrene (Libya) in North Africa. It both prevented pregnancy and induced abortion. It was exported to Rome and beyond, but was soon harvested to extinction.

▷ **Birthing scene**
This marble plaque from Ostia, Italy, shows a reclining woman who has just given birth, tended by midwives. The midwife on the left holds the newborn while the midwife in the center may be helping to deliver the placenta.

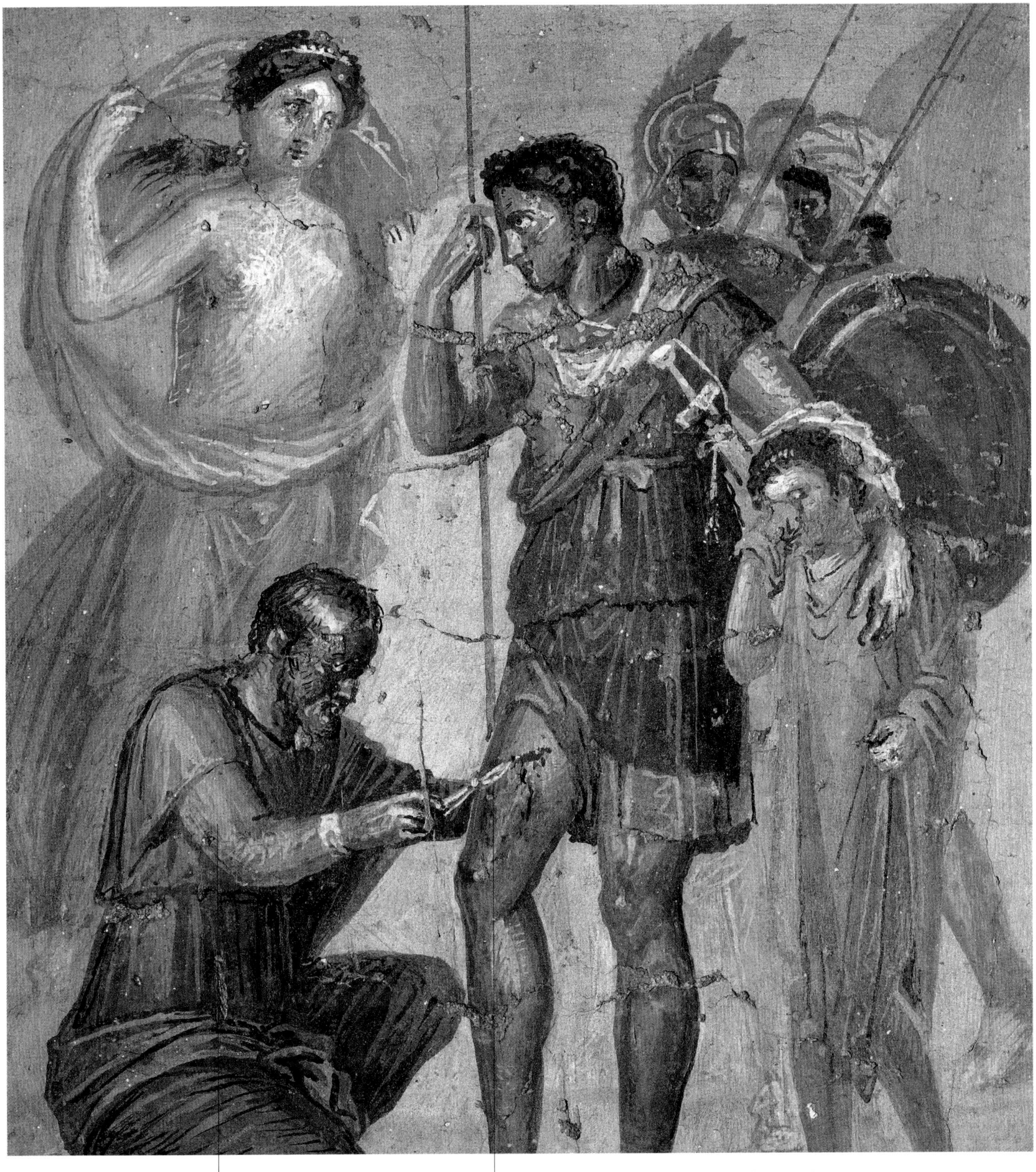

Iapyx, the god of healing, performs the surgery on Aeneas

The extraction is performed with either a scalpel or forceps

△ **Treating battle wounds**
In this Roman fresco from the 1st century CE, an illustration from Virgil's *Aeneid*, a wounded Aeneas leans on his spear as an arrowhead is removed from his thigh; this procedure would have been conducted with little pain relief in ancient Rome.

△ **Roman columbarium**
Located just outside the city walls to the south of Rome, this large columbarium was constructed in the early 1st century CE. It was later upgraded in the same century by Gnaeus Pomponius Hylas for himself and his wife; their urns occupied the central niches.

Side niches held the remains of "lesser" family members

"His son extols the **virtues of the deceased**, and **the great deeds** ... performed by him."

THE GREEK WRITER POLYBIUS, ON A ROMAN SENATORIAL FUNERAL

Death and Burial

Remembering the dead in ancient Rome

Romans practiced elaborate rituals and ceremonies to honor and commemorate the dead. The fundamental aim of all their funerary customs was to make sure that the deeds and virtues of the deceased were always remembered.

The ways in which Romans commemorated and buried their dead differed significantly, depending on the social status of the deceased and the financial means available to their family.

Funerals and public participation

The most lavish funerals were reserved for Rome's emperors, after which some were said to have undergone apotheosis—ascension to heaven as gods. The funerals of Roman senatorial families were similarly grand. In book VI of his *Histories*, the Greek author Polybius (2nd century BCE) marveled at the spectacle of a Roman senator's funeral, at which the deceased was carried through the city to the Forum, where a male relative addressed the crowd (some of whom may have been paid to attend) to speak of his family's achievements and the virtues and great deeds of the deceased. Finally, a wax *imago* ("image") was made of the dead man's face, which was carried in the procession of every subsequent funeral of a family member. In this way, the whole city commemorated the dead person in a combination of public spectacle and private remembrance.

Burial and cremation

Roman burial practices changed over time, with periods when burial or cremation were preferred—for example, from the 2nd century CE Romans began to use catacombs (see pp. 234–235). Some tombs contain sarcophagi, to hold a human body, while others, such as columbaria, have chambers in which to store ash-filled urns. All tombs and funerary monuments were found outside settlements, as it was forbidden to bury the dead within a city's walls. This is why the roads into Rome or Pompeii bristled with burial places known as necropolises (literally, "cities of the dead"), some of which still exist.

Tombs as status symbols

Wealthy Romans competed to create the most elaborate or innovative burial places. The tomb of Gaius Cestius Epulo in Rome, for example, is a large white pyramid. No tombs were grander than those of the emperors, however. In Rome, the circular Mausoleum of Augustus was opulent and adorned with statues. By contrast, poorer people in Rome often joined "funeral clubs," where they paid a subscription so they could be interred with dignity in columbaria when they died.

As a final act of remembrance, most Roman tombs included often heartfelt inscriptions that still have the power to move the reader today.

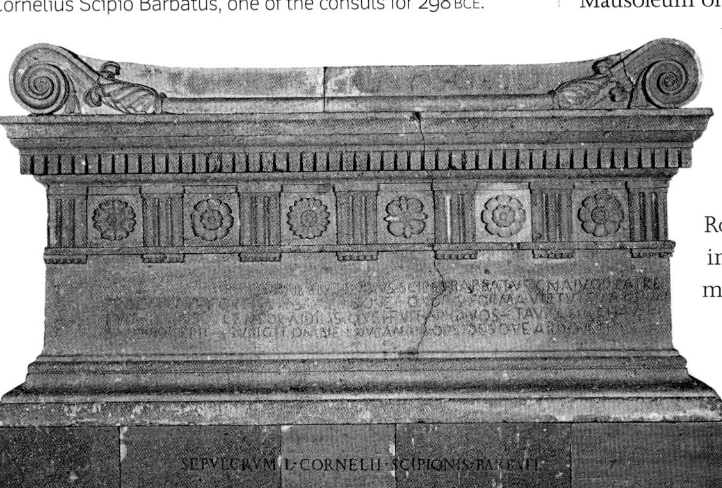

▽ **Sarcophagus for a Scipio on the Appian Way**
The Scipios were one of Rome's most illustrious families. Their tomb held ornate sarcophagi, such as this one for Lucius Cornelius Scipio Barbatus, one of the consuls for 298 BCE.

△ **Proud professional**
The large tomb in Rome of the freedman Marcus Vergilius Eurysaces from the 1st century BCE celebrates his career as a baker, with the circles proably representing dough-kneading devices.

▷ **Roman ancestor worship**
In this 1st-century CE sculpture known as the *Togatus Barberini*, the figure—probably a senator—holds *imagines* (wax death masks) of his deceased ancestors.

The vase was accidentally smashed in 1845; the repair marks are still visible

◁ **The Portland Vase**
This iconic object is technically an amphora: a narrow-necked, two-handled jug. It is named after one of its previous owners, the Duchess of Portland, and has inspired artists for centuries, particularly the great British potter Josiah Wedgwood.

The cobalt color intensifies if light is shone through the vase from within

The intricate detailing was probably carried out by a *diatretarius*, or master gem-cutter

△ **Woman of influence**
This figure may be Octavia, one of Rome's most important women. The emperors Caligula, Claudius, and Nero were all her direct descendants.

◁ **Figures on the vase**
This flat view displays both faces of the vase, separated by bearded, horned faces below the handles. Whether there is a unifying story between these images depends on which interpretation of the vase the viewer accepts.

The winged cupid indicates this is a story of love

The white glass carved reliefs are just ⅛ in (3 mm) thick

The Portland Vase

An enigmatic expression of beauty and desire in glass

The Portland Vase is one of the most remarkable yet enigmatic Roman objects ever discovered. Its first recorded mention in history was not until 1600, and for a long time it was erroneously thought to have been made to hold the ashes of Alexander Severus, emperor in the 3rd-century CE, but it is now believed the piece was made in the 1st century CE. Why it was created, and what it depicts, remain a mystery.

It is made entirely of glass: a thin white cameo layer over a dark but translucent cobalt-blue shell. The carvings were probably created using a dip-overlay method, where the blown-glass blue underlayer was completely coated in molten, opaque white glass, which then dried before being chipped away and carved into reliefs.

The seated trio

Three seated figures feature on one side of the vase. In one interpretation of this scene, the central figure is Octavia, who has just been abandoned by her husband, Mark Antony. She is flanked by her brother, Augustus, and Venus Genetrix, the ancestor of their family, according to legend.

Another interpretation suggests the central figure is Ariadne, the Cretan princess who helped the Greek hero Theseus navigate the labyrinth of Knossos and defeat the Minotaur. A further theory links the scene to the Trojan War, with the woman representing Helen, whose kidnapping by, or elopement with, Paris (the figure on the left) triggered the conflict. In this version, the woman on the right is Aphrodite, the Greek goddess of love, beauty, desire, and sexuality.

More questions of interpretation

The other side of the vase shows what could be the marriage of the sea nymph Thetis to Peleus, presided over by a sea god. Or it could be a representation of the legend that the emperor Augustus was sired by Apollo in the form of a snake. Others believe that the woman is the Egyptian pharaoh Cleopatra, who is stereotypically depicted "seducing" the Roman general Mark Antony in an image that is intended to vilify her.

These are only the most common interpretations of the Portland Vase's disputed iconography. What all observers agree on, however, is that it is one of the finest surviving artworks of Classical antiquity.

> "**I do not believe** that there are any **monuments of antiquity** … executed by so **great an artist** …"
>
> SIR WILLIAM HAMILTON, IN A LETTER TO JOSIAH WEDGWOOD, 1782

The Romans in Germania

Conquest and resistance in the north

Beset with armed invasions and uprisings, the land the Romans called Germania was a volatile but prosperous territory, rich in natural resources. Rome's attempts to subdue it met with mixed results—and, on one occasion, total catastrophe.

◁ **Glass bowl**
Commerce was an important aspect of life on Rome's frontier. This bowl (1st century CE) was found in Nijmegen. It may have been made within Roman territory or traded across the border with Magna Germania.

The territories of Germania encompassed parts of modern Germany, Scandinavia, Switzerland, Belgium, Poland, Slovakia, the Czech Republic, Hungary, and Austria. The people of this land included the Cherusci, Marsi, and Alemanni. What is known of them today is courtesy of mostly Roman sources, where they are often portrayed as uncivilized. Alternatively, writers such as Tacitus described the people of Germania in highly romanticized terms, where their strength and virtuous simplicity stands in contrast to the softness and moral laxity of their fellow Romans.

Imperial expansion

Although Julius Caesar made forays into Germania during his conquest of Gaul, it was Augustus who first attempted to expand Rome's borders across the Rhine. His stepson Drusus and, a little later, Drusus's older brother Tiberius had some limited successes, but any gains they made were overshadowed by the disaster at Teutoburg Forest in 9 CE. In this battle, three Roman legions commanded by Publius Quinctilius Varus were destroyed by an alliance of Germanic peoples. The Romans had been led into an ambush by Arminius, an officer in Varus's army who was also a prince of the Cherusci. Arminius had long been plotting to drive the Romans from his homeland, secretly building a union among a number of peoples. His victory at Teutoburg traumatized the Romans, a distraught Augustus famously crying, "Varus, give me back my legions!" upon hearing of his army's defeat.

After Teutoburg, Augustus abandoned his plans for further conquests in the region. When Tiberius became emperor, he and his adopted son Germanicus focused on consolidating rather than expanding Roman control. Germanicus did, however, recover the captured Roman legionary standards from Teutoburg. He also abducted Arminius's pregnant wife Thusnelda and paraded her as a trophy through Rome during his Triumph of 17 CE.

A turbulent frontier

Despite its troubles in Germania, Rome committed significant resources to keeping hold of the territories it managed to conquer there. The Rhine became the outer limit of Roman territory in the 80s CE, with the provinces of Germania Superior and Germania Inferior (Upper Germania and Lower Germania) created within the empire and another, Magna Germania (Greater Germania), lying outside Roman control along the 340-mile (550-km) *Limes Germanicus* (Germanic frontier). This was a heavily guarded border that comprised at least 60 defensive forts, 900 watchtowers, and thousands of troops.

▽ **The Roman Empire and Magna Germania**
Despite Rome's best efforts, its holdings in Germania remained relatively small, with large swathes of Magna Germania controlled by a number of local peoples.

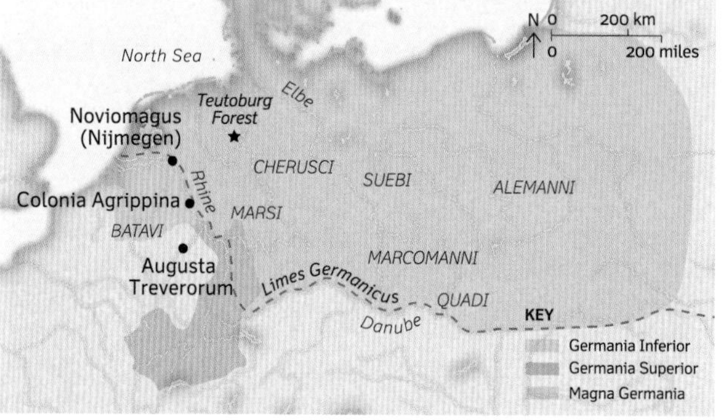

△ **Cavalry helmet**
This cavalryman's parade helmet found in Germany is a reminder of Rome's ties to Germania, with many former legionnaires settling there after retirement.

△ **Birth of a nation**
Completed in 1875, five years after the country was unified, the *Hermannsdenkmal* (Arminius Monument) in northern Germany commemorates both the victory at Teutoburg Forest and the sense of national identity it helped foster.

Rome also created settlements, such as Augusta Treverorum (modern Trier) and Colonia Agrippina (modern Cologne), close to the frontier. These cities were home to Roman citizens, retired military men, and local people who had reconciled themselves to Roman rule. It would be at least another 50 years after the creation of the *Limes Germanicus* before Rome made another major foray across the border, when Marcus Aurelius attempted with mixed results to subdue the Marcomanni tribe.

Germanic resistance

Roman rule in Germania was fraught and contested for four centuries; the Battle of Teutoburg Forest was the most prominent of several major clashes. The revolt of the Batavi in the mid-1st century CE, for example, saw the defeat of several Roman legions before it was crushed, and in the 3rd century the Alemanni and Franks continually raided Roman Germania. Rome finally left the region in the early 5th century, when its legions there were sent away to fight in the Balkans. The power vacuum was filled by the Franks and the Alemanni, the latter of whom in particular would make large areas of Germania their own.

◁ **Porta Nigra**
Built in the 1st century CE, the heavily fortified Porta Nigra (Black Gate) at Augusta Treverorum shows the Romans' need for strong defenses in Germania.

◁ **Building for success**
Featuring scrolls, vines, lotus flowers, and acanthus leaves, this 1st-century CE marble capital (the top portion of a column) is a typical example of the decorative Corinthian architectural style used on Imperial Roman edifices.

4
The Height of the Empire
27 BCE–192 CE

Rome's Imperial Expansion

The final years of the Republic had been marked by extensive disruption and widespread civil unrest. The years from 27 BCE to 192 CE were also far from uneventful, and the transfer of power between emperors was rarely a completely smooth process; nevertheless, it rarely unsettled the operation of the Roman state. Although Augustus began his rule as emperor claiming to be the first among equals, his four decades in power ensured that imperial control by a single person had enough time to embed itself in the Roman political system. When Augustus died, the question was not whether he would be followed by another emperor, but what sort of emperor his successor would be.

Changing power dynamics

This period saw the emergence and evolution of rule by emperor as a formal structure of governance, including the growing use of freedmen to administer political business as part of the emperor's secretariat. The addition of the emperor to the Roman political system had wide-ranging social and cultural consequences, not least of which was the formal concentration of power in a single individual rather than the constantly changing figures of the consuls. This altered the way that power moved through the Roman state, and the Senate in particular found itself less able to institute change. The military, on the other hand, continued to hold significant authority, and the competition for power remained as dangerous as it had been in the Republic. Those who chose or felt compelled to resist or challenge the emperor did so at their own risk.

With the emperor's authority established, a new kind of "soft power" emerged alongside it. The women of the imperial family—especially the empress—were now able to exercise influence on the ruler in ways that had not been possible under the political structures of the Republic.

Conquest and commerce

In the first phase of rule by emperor, the dominance of the Roman Empire in the Mediterranean basin, in most of Western Europe, and in large areas of North Africa was unquestionable. The comparatively stable political conditions in Rome freed the military to expand and consolidate Roman authority. The work of these years was one of network-building—weaving every member of the inhabited world into a web of patronage and clientship, at the center of which sat the emperor and his court. Decrees, judgments, and favors coursed through the arteries of this system from the center to the peripheries. Meanwhile, petitions, taxes, and tributes traveled in the opposite direction. This system gave every denizen of the empire a stake in its stability, and encouraged acceptance of the violence that was meted out against those who were deemed potential threats to its future.

This period is notable for advances and achievements in many spheres of activity, including literature, philosophy, law, medicine, architecture, and art. However, despite the temptation to view this period as a golden age, it should be remembered that institutionalized violence was deeply rooted in the Roman sociopolitical system; the number of emperors killed by assassins is a stark reminder of this.

△ **Cast emerald glass bowl, 1st century CE**

4 CE The emperor Augustus adopts Tiberius as his son

14 CE Augustus dies and Tiberius succeeds him as emperor

37 CE Tiberius dies and is succeeded by Caligula

41 CE Claudius becomes emperor after Caligula's assassination

54 CE Nero succeeds Claudius as emperor

69 CE "Year of the Four Emperors;" Vespasian emerges as the next emperor

79 CE Titus becomes emperor following his father Vespasian's death

❶ Well-preserved Roman remains at Dougga

❷ The Temple of Hadrian at Ephesus

❸ Dendera, at the southern edge of the empire

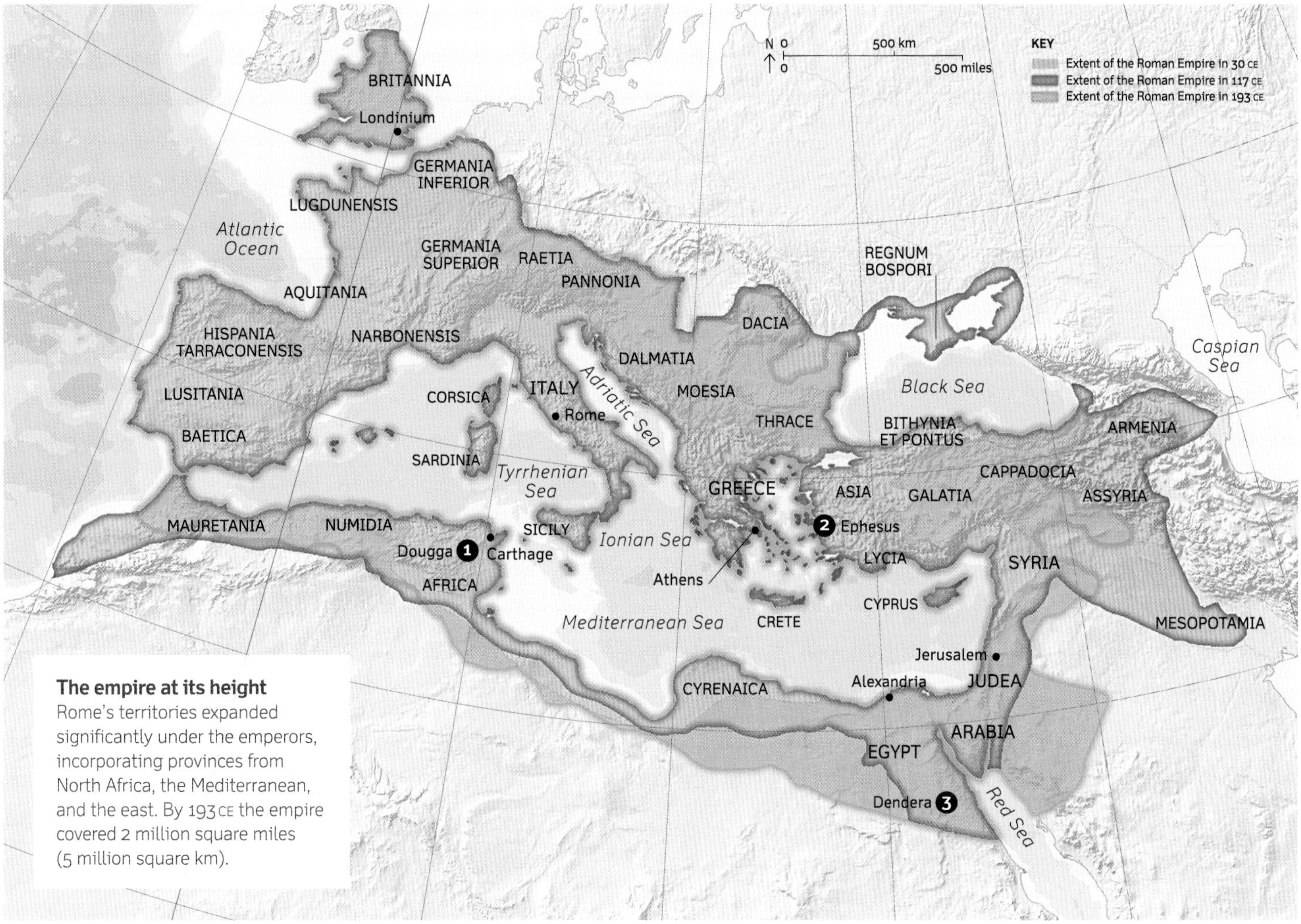

N
0 500 km
0 500 miles

KEY
Extent of the Roman Empire in 30 CE
Extent of the Roman Empire in 117 CE
Extent of the Roman Empire in 193 CE

BRITANNIA
Londinium
GERMANIA INFERIOR
LUGDUNENSIS
Atlantic Ocean
GERMANIA SUPERIOR
RAETIA
PANNONIA
AQUITANIA
HISPANIA TARRACONENSIS
NARBONENSIS
DACIA
REGNUM BOSPORI
Caspian Sea
DALMATIA
LUSITANIA
CORSICA
ITALY
Adriatic Sea
MOESIA
Black Sea
Rome
THRACE
BITHYNIA ET PONTUS
ARMENIA
BAETICA
SARDINIA
Tyrrhenian Sea
CAPPADOCIA
GREECE
ASIA
GALATIA
ASSYRIA
MAURETANIA
NUMIDIA
SICILY
Ionian Sea
❷ Ephesus
Dougga ❶
Carthage
LYCIA
SYRIA
AFRICA
Athens
CYPRUS
Mediterranean Sea
CRETE
MESOPOTAMIA
Jerusalem
CYRENAICA
Alexandria
JUDEA
ARABIA
EGYPT
Dendera ❸
Red Sea

The empire at its height
Rome's territories expanded significantly under the emperors, incorporating provinces from North Africa, the Mediterranean, and the east. By 193 CE the empire covered 2 million square miles (5 million square km).

81 CE Titus dies of fever; his brother Domitian becomes emperor

96 CE Domitian is assassinated; the Senate proclaims Nerva emperor

98 CE Trajan succeeds Nerva, his adopted father, as emperor

117 CE Hadrian becomes emperor after Trajan's death

138 CE Antoninus Pius becomes emperor

161 CE Marcus Aurelius succeeds Antoninus Pius, at first jointly with Lucius Verus

180 CE Marcus Aurelius dies and Commodus is proclaimed emperor

192 CE Murder of the emperor Commodus

A Growing Empire

Consolidating and expanding Rome's control

The expansion of the empire was more dynamic than strategic, a response to specific situations and pressures. Under Augustus, Rome found ways to exercise its influence on other states through a combination of conquest and cooperation.

During the four decades that Augustus headed the empire, its reach grew beyond, primarily, the Mediterranean and areas of northern Europe, into Egypt and parts of Spain, central Europe, the Near East, and Africa. He had to make many decisions about its nature and direction: some planned and strategic, others reactive. Above all, he needed to be flexible on where or whether to expand the empire given the limits of his military capacity and resources. He also had to manage the complex combination of provinces under direct imperial rule and those areas controlled by client kings who had sworn fealty to Rome. Client kingdoms cushioned the empire from other states less inclined to accept Roman influence. Augustus tended to prefer continuity and worked with local rulers where possible, rather than assimilating their kingdoms into the empire. This tactic allowed him to avoid military interventions unless necessary. In this way, he not only made efficient use of his troops, but also limited the future number of veterans (retired soldiers who were promised grants of land that he was obliged to fulfill). In the *Res Gestae*, the long inscription on his mausoleum commemorating his deeds as emperor (see pp. 138–139),

◁ **Sanctified by Roma**
The Temple of Roma and Augustus in Pula, Croatia, was built before Augustus died and was deified, so it was dedicated both to him and to Roma, the goddess who personified the city.

△ **A regal resting place**
Constructed in 3 BCE, the Royal Mausoleum of Mauretania was made for Juba II and his wife, Cleopatra Selene. Juba II helped make his state a Roman client kingdom.

Augustus emphasized how he preferred to pardon rather than destroy foreign adversaries, displaying the virtue of *clementia*. Such a framing also allowed him to present diplomacy as military victory. The wars he did fight, however, would always have involved much physical and sexual violence against civilians, as well as the enslavement of many of the captured. Once territories were subdued, Augustus consolidated Rome's hold on them through procurators—imperial agents who managed local populations and their leaders, and extracted revenues from them.

A tightening grip

In 25 BCE Augustus annexed Galatia (central Türkiye) as a province, with the goal of stabilizing the political situation in Asia Minor more generally. Similar annexations occurred in Syria and Judea in 6 CE (see pp. 188–189). The provinces in Hispania proved a continual challenge; in 26 BCE Augustus himself led a campaign against the rebellious Cantabri Celtiberians, and fighting continued until at least 19 BCE (see pp. 90–91). Although the operation to subdue Spanish uprisings was protracted and required many resources, it did eventually bring the lengthy

△ **Face of conquest** This marble medallion once decorated a portico in Augusta Emerita (modern Mérida, Spain), a *colonia*, or military outpost, founded in 25 BCE following Augustus's incursions into Hispania a year earlier. Augusta Emerita later became the capital of the province of Lusitania.

conflict to a close. The Alps posed a parallel challenge, where the Romans struggled hard, but ultimately successfully, in the difficult mountainous terrain to control the peoples there who might obstruct traffic and trade between Gaul and Italy.

Into Africa and the Near East

As well as strengthening Rome's hold on its existing empire, Augustus also brought new territory into its control. The earliest major addition was Egypt, which became a province under his direct control after Cleopatra VII's death in 30 BCE (see pp. 210–211). Egypt was treated slightly differently to other provinces, because it supplied much of Rome's grain. It had, for example, an equestrian governor under the emperor's direct authority (and from a lower, non-senatorial social class; see pp. 92–93) rather than a governor chosen by the Senate. Senators could not visit Egypt without the emperor's permission. The Romans also, for the most part, maintained Egypt's existing bureaucratic structures, with adaptations to fit with Roman law.

Less successful was Augustus's attempted invasion of Arabia Felix (southern Saudi Arabia and Yemen) in 26–25 BCE, which the *Res Gestae* presents as an exploratory expedition. A subsequent campaign southward from Egypt in 25–24 BCE expanded Roman territory and led to a new treaty with the *kandake* (queen) of the Kushite kingdom (see box). Augustus strengthened the Roman presence in the province of Africa (centered around modern Tunisia), and may even have enlarged its borders, although the details are unclear. He brought fertile Mauretania in North Africa into a client kingdom arrangement with Rome in 25 BCE as part of a strategic plan to protect grain supplies. In Europe, Augustus's grandnephew, Germanicus, and adopted son, Tiberius, led campaigns in 6–9 CE, which created the Balkans provinces of Pannonia and Dalmatia.

BURYING HIS HEAD IN THE SAND

This striking bronze head of Augustus, complete with intact inset eyes, has a strange history. It was discovered at Meroë (in modern Sudan), capital of the ancient kingdom of Kush. Although it clearly comes from a portrait statue, the head was found buried in the sand in a temple dedicated to the local deity, Ammon, under stairs leading to a victory altar. The hot, dry conditions in Sudan contributed to its preservation. The head was most probably detached during a raid on Roman territory by Kushites led by their queen, Amanirenas. Its burial place was symbolic: every time the people of Meroë used the temple stairs they stepped on the head of their enemy, Augustus.

The limits of empire

Germania was a source of conflict in Augustus's later years. His stepson, Drusus, crossed the Rhine and began four years of inconclusive campaigning in 12 BCE. Seven years later, Tiberius advanced to the Elbe. This marked the limit of Augustus's incursions into Germania, especially after the Romans' catastrophic defeat by a coalition of Germanic forces at the Battle of Teutoburg Forest in 9 CE (see pp. 154–155). The rout was so humiliating that the numbers identifying the defeated legions were never used again.

The Augustan expansion of the empire was not only an outward-directed phenomenon. It helped change Rome itself, drawing in people, customs, beliefs, and traditions from across the empire. While Rome had not been a "closed" city before this period, the Imperial age saw it becoming yet more open.

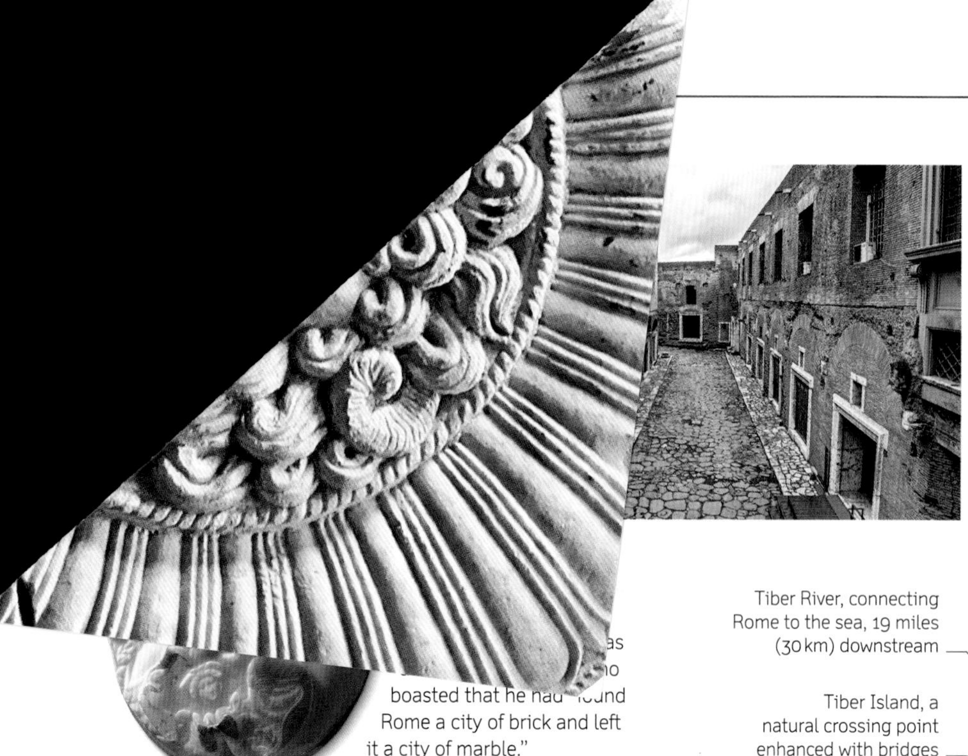

…as …no boasted that he had …und Rome a city of brick and left it a city of marble."

A Grand New City

The monumental city of ancient Rome

The city of Rome held approximately one million people by the 2nd century BCE. Founded on a series of hilltops above the Tiber River, it underwent unplanned growth over the centuries, as well as regular fires and floods, which presented both challenge and opportunity for improvement. Successive emperors attempted to leave their mark with grand public projects and private palaces, along with practical infrastructure such as aqueducts and sewers. Ordinary buildings—stores, warehouses, homes, and apartments—filled the rest of the map. Life in the crowded city could be noisy and hard, but also offered unparalleled opportunities for leisure under the emperors' regime of urban "bread and circuses."

ANCIENT MAP OF THE CITY OF ROME

This fragment of the Forma Urbis Romae, a marble map of Rome, shows public, private, and commercial buildings along a main road, the Vicus Patricius, that ran between two of Rome's hills. The piece was once part of a larger map that measured 60 ft (18 m) by 45 ft (13 m). Made between 203 and 211 CE under Septimius Severus, the map included the names of buildings and streets. It was displayed in the Temple of Peace, but was later broken up for building material.

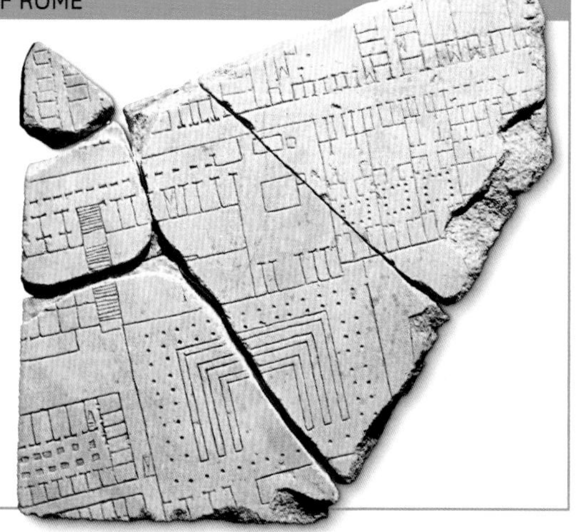

△ **Mausoleum of Augustus**
This tomb was built by the emperor Augustus in 28 BCE. A chamber inside held golden urns containing the imperial family's ashes.

The monumental squares of the Imperial Forum complex (see pp. 212–213)

The Roman Forum, the centre of ancient Rome (see pp. 64–67)

Dense housing filled the city center; farther out, garden estates and suburbs went on for miles

Aqueduct arcades delivered flowing water to the city, even to some of the hills

Large imperial bathhouses ringed the city

The city gained an outer wall circuit, the Aurelian Walls, from the late 3rd century CE

◁ **Sprawling city of Rome**
The original inhabitants of the area built their villages on the hilltops, which offered security and cool summer breezes. As the city grew, many of the hills remained prime land, with busy roads in the valleys below.

Visual Tour

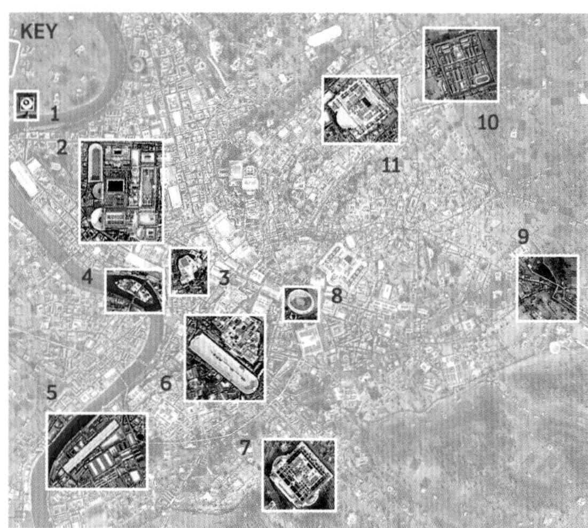

◁ **Mausoleum of Hadrian**
The round mausoleum of the emperor Hadrian echoes the tomb of Augustus on the opposite bank of the Tiber. During the Middle Ages, it was converted into a papal fortress, the Castel Sant'Angelo.

▷ **Campus Martius**
This flat land in the bend of the Tiber River was originally open ground that was used for military assemblies and elections. Under the emperors, its central area took on the character of a parkland with baths, temples, theaters, and an arena.

△ **The Capitoline Hill**
This hill was the site of Rome's greatest temple, the Temple of Jupiter Optimus Maximus, sacred to him and his consort Juno and daughter Minerva. Towering above the Forum, the hill was crowded with many other shrines and temples, and was the destination of the triumphal processions of victorious generals.

△ **Tiber Island**
The island creates a natural crossing point of the Tiber, and is still linked to both banks by bridges. In antiquity, the island housed a temple of the healing god Asclepius (or Aesculapius) and was modified to resemble a ship.

△ **Roman docks**
The Emporium district housed Rome's docks and warehouses from the 2nd century BCE. As the city grew, facilities were added to import staple foodstuffs and luxury goods. The long, barrel-vaulted building here may have been a warehouse or shipshed.

▽ Baths of Diocletian
The largest of the great imperial *thermae*, or bathhouses, was built by the emperor Diocletian between 299 and 306 CE. Part of the building's central block, which was once the *frigidarium*, survives as the exterior of the Basilica of St Mary of the Angels and Martyrs. The structure was converted according to a 16th-century design by Michelangelo and added to later.

▽ Barracks of the Praetorian Guard
The emperor's Praetorian Guard was first gathered into barracks on the edge of Rome by the second emperor, Tiberius. He intended them to provide his personal security, but almost immediately the guards and their commanders began to take an active role in replacing emperors that they disapproved of with more favorable candidates (see pp. 228–229).

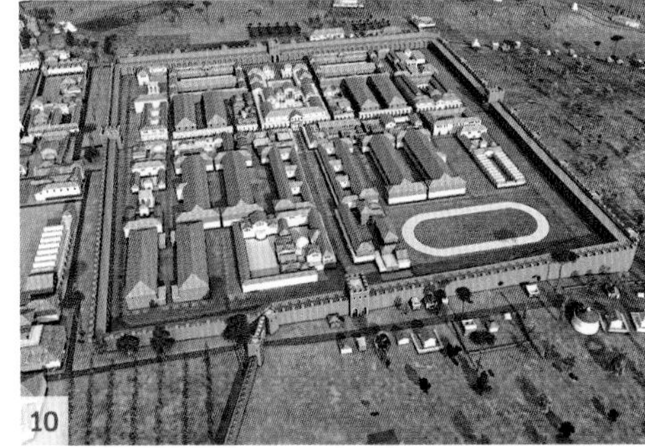

▽ Porta Maggiore
At the eastern edge of the city, two main roads passed through an arched gateway (center), which also carried imperial aqueducts into Rome. Later on these structures were incorporated into the Aurelian Walls, which made use of existing buildings wherever possible.

△ The Palatine Hill and Circus Maximus
The Palatine Hill was the residence of Rome's founder, Romulus, and during the Republic became an aristocratic quarter overlooking the Forum. Successive emperors made their homes here. The valley below was used for horse racing from the earliest days of Rome and was later the location of a great stadium (see pp. 146–147).

◁ The Colosseum
This famous arena for gladiatorial combat (see pp. 194–197) was built by the emperor Vespasian on the site of the vast palace gardens (see pp. 186–187) of his hated predecessor Nero. It became, and remains, a symbol of the city.

◁ Baths of Caracalla
This huge bathhouse was built in only a few years in the early 3rd century. It made extensive use of Roman expertise in concrete vaulted architecture, and incorporated a central bathing block within an outer complex of gardens, halls, and perhaps libraries (see pp. 236–237).

The Power of Words

Literacy in the Roman world

Writing played an important element in all areas of Roman culture. Men and women, enslaved and free, left their words for later generations to read, whether written in books or inscribed on walls.

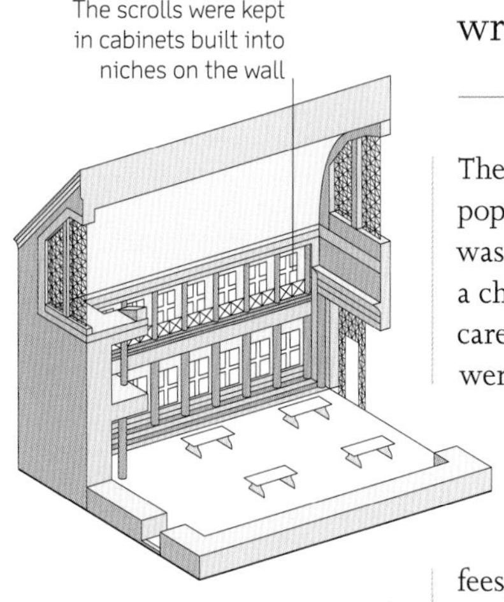

△ **Ulpian Library**
Part of Trajan's Forum in Rome, this library was built in the 2nd century CE. It contained around 10,000 scrolls and had separate rooms for Greek and Roman manuscripts.

The artifacts that survive indicate that the Roman population had many different levels of literacy. There was no formal education system in ancient Rome, so a child's experience would have depended on their carers' preferences and wealth, and which teachers were available locally. Very wealthy families employed private tutors for their children; whether daughters had the same provision as sons depended on the individual family's choices. Schools, accessible to anyone who could pay the fees, provided basic reading, writing, and arithmetic education to children from the age of six or seven. More specialized teachers provided further training in literature and grammar. The wealthy could also train enslaved people to become skilled administrators and secretaries if they decided it was worth the investment, while the illiterate poor could hire a scribe to read and write for them.

Books and public notices

Roman authors wrote in a wide range of genres, including epic, love poetry, historiography, studies of the natural sciences, and drama. In the 1st century BCE, books were shared and copied among elite Romans, but relatively cheap editions began to be sold during the 1st century CE, making them more accessible.

△ **Political graffiti in Pompeii**
Graffiti was often painted onto walls during elections. Here, voters are encouraged to elect one Caius Iulius Polybius (identifiable by the letters "CIP") as *duovir*, or judge.

Martial, a Roman poet, records that a volume of his poetry could be bought for just four *sesterces* (the cost of eight loaves of bread). Writing was also used for official record-keeping, such as accounts, trade agreements, and other business transactions. Wooden tablets excavated from London, England, include the records of a man called Crispus, who documented the beer he either sold or received, reflecting the functional literacy that many Romans running businesses would have had. Political news was shared in Rome through the *Acta Diurna*, daily notices of significant events written on parchment and pasted on boards for public display and consultation.

Inscriptions and graffiti

Inscriptions, many of which survive today, adorned public buildings, recording who had paid for their construction. Other inscriptions noted important senatorial acts and decrees. Uncontrolled writing in the form of graffiti also filled Roman cities. Poor citizens, enslaved people, and even children, used wall space to share what they thought about politics, their lives, and other subjects that interested them. Writing has also endured on objects, such as amphora labels or bricks marked with stamps to identify their makers.

WRITING BY **ENSLAVED PEOPLE**

In the 2nd century BCE, Detfri and Amica, enslaved women, wrote on this roof tile, including their names and marking it with their footprints while the clay was still soft. Amica wrote in Latin and Detfri wrote in Oscan (a now-extinct language spoken in southern Italy): "Detfri, the slave of Herennius Sattius. Signed with a footprint." The prints were made with a shoe common in Samnium. The tile was used to repair a temple roof in Pietrabbondante, Italy. By signing the tile, the women wrote themselves into the history of the building and made their labor visible.

▽ **Pages from the *Vergilius Vaticanus***
This version of Virgil's *Aeneid*, created in the 4th century CE and now held in the Vatican library, is an early example of a codex, or bound manuscript (see pp. 168–69). In this scene, Dido realizes that Aeneas is leaving Carthage and abandoning her.

> "This is a **tale of arms** and of a **man**."
>
> VIRGIL, *THE AENEID*

How Romans Wrote

Instruments for inscription

A culture that relied so heavily on the written word needed readily accessible materials. The Romans used papyrus, parchment, wax, and wood; they wrote, incised, and inscribed their texts, from books of poetry to shopping lists.

The Roman statesman Cicero began a letter to his brother Quintus by telling him that he had his pen, ink, and paper ready. As his statement reflects, every word written by the Romans was produced by hand; the printing press would not be invented for well over another millennium. How long a piece of writing survived depended on the materials on which it was recorded; it was possible to buy high-quality, expensive writing materials, but less affluent Romans could also acquire more affordable versions of these. Despite some changing trends over time, Roman tools and techniques for writing remained fairly consistent.

Writing materials

Initially, books were written on material made from fibers of the Egyptian papyrus plant. Strips of the stem were overlaid to build up a long sheet that was rolled into a scroll, a form particularly popular for literary work. Scrolls could be polished with ivory or pumice (volcanic rock) to create a smoother writing surface, which made them more costly. The Romans also sometimes used scrolls of parchment—animal skin—but papyrus was always their main medium.

Wooden wax tablets, often fastened together into little notebooks, were used for practical writing, such as in businesses. Romans also sometimes wrote directly onto wood; the Vindolanda tablets, found in a Roman fort in Britain (see pp. 204–205 and 258–59), are a famous example of this, and show how thin sheets of wood were folded in half to form tablets.

The major innovation of the 1st century CE was the emergence of the codex. Made of individual parchment sheets joined together, it resembled the modern book and allowed the cheaper production of books as well as more portable notebooks. It went on to replace the scroll as the dominant type of book used in ancient Rome.

Making a mark

When using wax tablets, writers incised their words with a stylus, usually made of iron or sometimes bone. The opposite end of the stylus had a flat end for erasing mistakes, and the entire surface of the wax

▷ **Steady surface**
A wooden tablet frame, found in London, UK, and two styli. The other side of the frame would have been filled with a wax *tabula* ("tablet") for writing on.

◁ **Trusty tools**
This fresco from Pompeii in the 1st century CE shows an ink pot; a wax tablet notebook in the codex form; two papyri rolls (one in a *capsa*, or container); and a stylus.

could be smoothed over to reuse the tablet. The wax sat in a wooden frame, and sometimes writers cut so deeply that their letters marked the wood. Reed pens, used for writing on papyrus, had to be sharpened regularly to keep their points. These pens were dipped in ink, which was made of soot and glue. It was purchased in solid blocks and mixed with water as needed. Achieving the right consistency was not easy: in the 1st century CE, the satirist Persius imagines a student complaining about not being able to mix his ink correctly, finding it either too thin or too thick. The writing of inscriptions on stone required tools such as hammers and chisels, and the people who crafted these required considerable training.

PRESERVATION OF **PAPYRI**

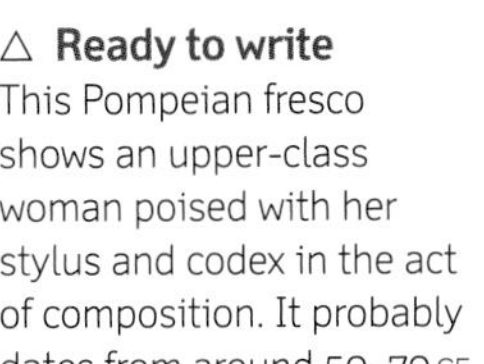

Papyrus fragments, such as this one, survive from antiquity due to their chance preservation in dry or airless environments. In the 19th century, a trove of papyri was discovered during excavations at the Egyptian village of Oxyrhynchus. The low humidity in the deep, ancient garbage pit from which it was unearthed had prevented its decay. A private library was also found in the Villa of the Papyri at Pompeii, protected by a layer of volcanic ash. CT scans and X-ray imaging offer the ability to read these charred scrolls without damaging them.

△ **Ready to write**
This Pompeian fresco shows an upper-class woman poised with her stylus and codex in the act of composition. It probably dates from around 50–79 CE.

> “**Look** behind you; **remember** you are but a **man**.”
>
> WHISPERED TO GENERALS DURING A TRIUMPH, TO REMIND THEM THAT GLORY WAS TRANSIENT, AS REPORTED IN TERTULLIAN’S *APOLOGETICUS*

The Tiberius Cup

Celebrating an emperor-to-be’s victories in war

The Tiberius Cup is a silver *skyphos*, a type of drinking vessel for wine. Ornate cups like this would have been used at fashionable drinking parties and dinners. The two sides of this partially damaged vessel depict the future emperor Tiberius celebrating a Triumph, either the one in 7 BCE held for his victories in Germany or the Triumph of 12 CE honoring his victories in the province of Pannonia (modern Hungary and Austria). The Triumphal procession is shown on one side of the vessel, and sacrifices to the gods on the other.

Procession and sacrifice

Triumphs were great parades through Rome. They celebrated a Roman victor and his army, and were awarded to Roman generals who had been especially successful on the battlefield. The Triumphing general would parade through the city with his army and the spoils of war, which would have included prisoners of war and enslaved civilians. Paintings of battles were carried in the parade so the assembled crowds could vicariously glory in the experience of war. Although victorious generals were carried along the Triumphal route in a chariot drawn by four horses, for the first of the three Triumphs he was awarded, in 81–79 BCE (its exact date is not known), Pompey the Great attempted to use elephants. His plans were thwarted when it was discovered the beasts could not fit through the city gates.

There was no set route for a Triumph, but they usually began at the Campus Martius beyond the city’s limits and passed through the Forum. All Triumphs ended in front of the Temple of Jupiter Optimus Maximus on the Capitoline Hill, where the Triumphing general would make animal sacrifices to the god to thank him for his divine benevolence and for assisting him to victory in war. Some of the sacrifices were followed by public feasting and celebrations, many of which were exceptionally lavish and lasted for several days.

Boscoreale Hoard

The Tiberius Cup was among a cache of 109 silver objects found in the wine cellar of a Roman villa near the modern town of Boscoreale, in the Bay of Naples, Italy. They date from the early 1st century CE and were probably owned by a wealthy woman called Maxima, whose name is stamped on some of the items. The villa belonged to Maxima’s father, a banker from Pompeii, and it is probable that Maxima hid the items there to save them from the eruption of Vesuvius in 79 CE. Other treasures in the collection include silver platters and jugs, an ornate handheld mirror, and a large leather purse containing just over 1,350 coins. Like other pieces in the Boscoreale Hoard, the reliefs on the Tiberius Cup were created using a technique called *repoussé*, where the figures and details are artfully hammered out from the inside of the vessel.

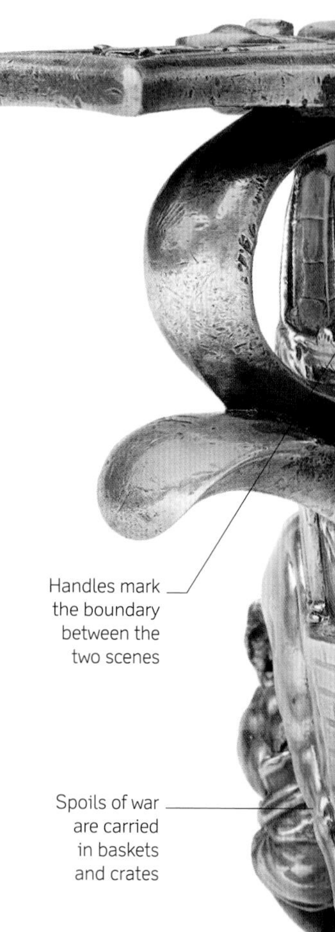

Handles mark the boundary between the two scenes

Spoils of war are carried in baskets and crates

▷ **Triumph of Tiberius**
This side depicts Tiberius in a *quadriga*, or four-horse chariot. In the actual Triumphal procession he would have worn a purple toga embroidered with gold.

▷ **Sacrifices**
This side of the cup depicts the conclusion of the Triumph, with sacrifices in front of the Temple of Jupiter Optimus Maximus.

The Temple of Jupiter is garlanded for the occasion

An attendant readies his ax to deliver a blow to the neck

Attendants hold the bull ready for the sacrifice

Tiberius watches the sacrificial events at an altar in this damaged section

The cup is 4 in (10 cm) high and 4 3/4 in (12 cm) in diameter (not including handles)

REVERSE OF VESSEL

Oak crown symbolizes heroism; according to Tertullian, the enslaved man holding it would whisper reminders of his mortality in the emperor's ear

Tiberius bears an eagle-topped scepter and a laurel branch

Officers of Tiberius's army are wreathed with victory laurels

Cup section showing the four horses pulling Tiberius's chariot suffered later damage

◁ **Claudius**
Claudius wears a *corona civica*, a wreath made of oak leaves. The *corona* was originally awarded to a soldier who saved another man's life in battle; emperors routinely received the honor in the Imperial period.

Claudius

The unexpected emperor

Although he was Tiberius's nephew and Caligula's uncle, Claudius spent most of his adult life on the margins of the imperial court—only to find himself emperor in his fifties. The unlikely ruler turned out to be a capable, efficient administrator.

Claudius was often ill as a child and, seeing his physical ailments as a sign of weakness, his family never considered him for a serious public role. The historian Suetonius reports that Claudius's mother called him "an omen of a man, not finished by nature, but only started off." He spent his time on minor official duties and historical studies until the assassination of Caligula in 41 CE. In the ensuing chaos, the Praetorian Guard ensured his succession as the next emperor.

◁ **Gold *aureus* of Claudius**
Claudius appears on this gold coin issued in both 41 CE and 42 CE, the first two years of his reign.

Political achievements

Despite his limited military experience, Claudius annexed Britannia, Thrace, Lycia, and Judea as provinces of the Roman Empire. He successfully argued that Roman citizens from Gaul should be eligible to join the Senate if they met certain property qualifications. He oversaw building projects in Rome, including completing the Aqua Claudia aqueduct to the city and creating a safe harbor on the Tiber River at Ostia. He was conscientious about hearing legal cases, although Suetonius informs us that Claudius paid more attention to his own ideas of justice than the actual laws, and could be an inconsistent judge.

Constant controversy

Claudius faced plots from the start of his reign. The most notorious of these was led by his third wife, Messalina, who went through a "marriage" ceremony with her lover Silius in 48 CE, while still empress; Claudius executed the pair and their associates. He was also criticized for using imperial freedmen as secretaries to support his work; this reliance was viewed as weakness, although later emperors also used such individuals without critique. Claudius's fourth wife, Agrippina (see pp. 178–179), is alleged to have poisoned him with mushrooms, causing his sudden death in 54 CE. She was also linked to the suspicious death of his son Britannicus in 55 CE.

△ **Messalina**
When Messalina married Claudius in 38 CE, she was in her early twenties; he was 48. They had two children: Britannicus, whom she holds in this statue, and Octavia.

▷ **The Aqua Claudia**
One of the four great aqueducts of Rome, the Aqua Claudia was about 43 miles (69 km) long and was fed by the Caeruleus and Curtius springs east of the city.

10 BCE Claudius is born in Lugdunum, Gaul

41 CE Claudius becomes emperor, following the assassination of Caligula

43 CE Annexation of Britain as a Roman province

46 CE Annexation of Thrace as a Roman province

49 CE Claudius marries Agrippina the Younger, his fourth wife

50 CE Claudius adopts Agrippina's son, the future emperor Nero

54 CE Claudius dies in Rome

△ **Show of wealth**
The Roman villa at Bignor, England, was built close to Noviomagus (Chichester) in the 3rd century CE and was probably home to an affluent Romano-British farming family. The villa's mosaics are among the finest in Britain.

The Edge of Empire

The Roman conquest of Britannia

The province of Britannia lay in the far west of the Roman Empire. The Roman invaders faced much resistance, but they soon created a network of settlements across the province extending as far as the border with present-day Scotland.

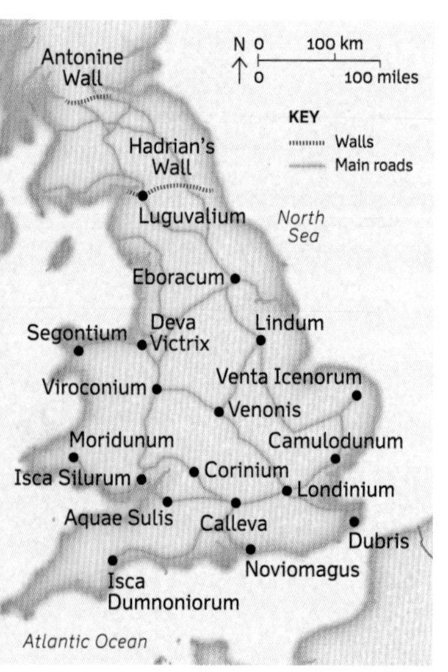

◁ **Settlements and roads**
The Romans built many roads, towns, and forts across Britannia. They were listed in a work known as the *Itinerarium Antonini Augusti* (*The Antonine Itinerary*).

The conquest of Britannia (England and Wales) was a lengthy process. Julius Caesar made two brief expeditions, in 55 and 54 BCE. Claudius mounted an invasion in 43 CE in support of a loyal local chieftain named Verica, who had been usurped—and in the process annexed Britannia as a province. After 69 CE, Vespasian won territory in Wales, and also extended Roman control in the north, taking on the Brigantes, whose towns included Eboracum (York). Other major groups included the Caledones (based in modern Scotland) and the Iceni and the Catuvellauni of what are today eastern and western England respectively.

Resistance to Rome

The Romans were not widely welcomed into Britannia. Caratacus, chieftain of the Catuvellauni people, had been responsible for the exile of Verica and resisted his reinstatement. From the late 40s CE he carried out guerrilla attacks on Claudius's legions until he was captured by Cartimandua, queen of the Brigantes. She handed him over to Claudius's forces and he was taken to Rome, where he died some time after 50 CE.

Roman attempts to seize the territory of the Iceni following the death of their chieftain Prasutagus led to a major rebellion in 60 CE. Prasutagus had left his lands jointly to the empire and his wife, Boudicca, but the Romans ignored Boudicca's claim and annexed the territory. When Boudicca complained, she was flogged and her two daughters raped. Boudicca mobilized the Iceni and other peoples against the

> “Thus the **Britons** display both the **speed of cavalry** and the **firmness of infantry** in battle.”
>
> JULIUS CAESAR, *ON THE GALLIC WAR*

△ **The Staffordshire Moorlands Pan**
This enamelled *trulla*, or bronze pan, from the 2nd century CE is Celtic in design (most of the peoples of Britannia were Celts, including the Brigantes, the Iceni, and the Catuvellauni). The inscription below the rim lists four forts along Hadrian's Wall.

▷ **A trade hub**
Excavated in London, this novelty oil lamp was probably made in the Netherlands. It shows the variety of goods imported into Britannia.

Romans, destroying Camulodunum (modern Colchester)—then the capital city—and Londinium (modern London). According to Roman sources, Boudicca committed atrocities against those she captured, including women and children. She was defeated in 60 or 61 CE, although it is uncertain if she was killed or escaped capture. Once the uprising ended, the Romans were able to establish a relatively stable and strong economic network in the province.

The troublesome north

Construction work on Hadrian's Wall began in 122 in order to protect Britannia's northern border against peoples from areas outside Rome's control (see pp. 204–205). Twenty years later the emperor Antoninus Pius ordered the Antonine Wall to be built farther north, to separate Britannia from Caledonia (modern-day Scotland). This marked the furthest northwestern extent of Rome's imperial expansion. In 164 Antoninus's successor, Marcus Aurelius, withdrew Rome's forces back to Hadrian's Wall.

Resistance to Rome by the people of Caledonia was consistent, if not well documented. One incident was the defeat of the so-called Caledonian Confederacy by Gnaeus Julius Agricola at Mons Graupius in northeast Scotland around 83–84 CE. In his *Agricola*, Tacitus gives Calgacus, one of the Confederacy leaders, a sympathetic pre-battle speech, which decries the Roman occupiers as thieves of the world who “make a desert and call it peace.” In later centuries, emperors would move legions from Britannia when disturbances broke out elsewhere in the empire. This may partly account for Rome's inability to extend its imperial territory beyond Hadrian's Wall.

International links

People from all over the empire came to Britannia for many reasons. Military service was a factor, as was business: the province imported pottery, olive oil, fabric, and jewelery, and exported iron, lead, gold, tin, copper, and grain. The “Spitalfields Woman,” whose tomb was discovered in London in 1999, could well have been a trader from Palmyra in Syria. The grave goods from the tomb in York of the North African “Ivory Bangle Lady” include artifacts that had been bought and sold across the empire—including the (possibly African) bracelets after which she is named. Aside from military service and commerce, religion also drew people to Britannia; the spa town of Aquae Sulis (modern Bath) was an important cult worship site dedicated to the goddess Sulis Minerva.

The Romans left Britannia around 400, but the infrastructure of roads and towns they created still exists today. The new foods, bureaucracy, coinage, plumbing, and countless other innovations they introduced helped shape the territory's future.

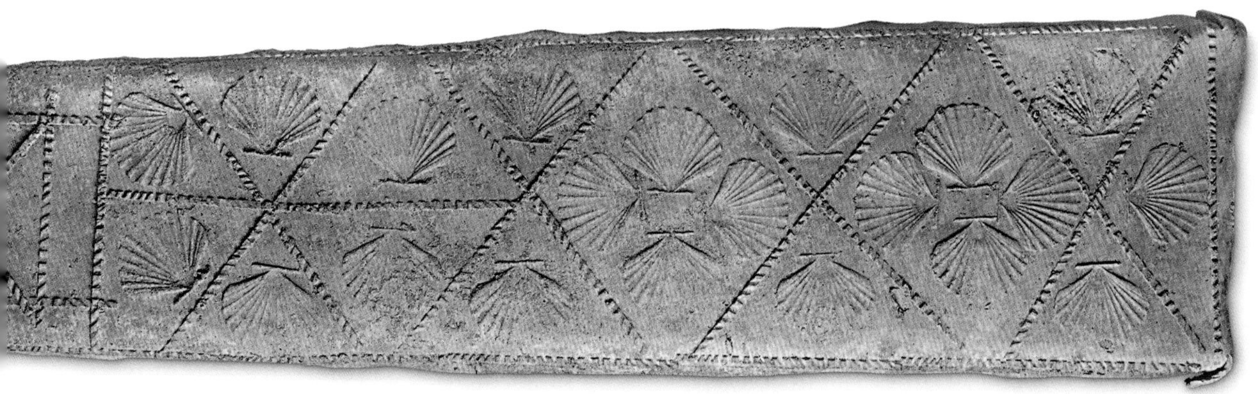

◁ **Coffin of the “Spitalfields Woman”**
The wealthy occupant of this lead coffin from the 3rd or 4th century CE was buried in a silk garment, possibly from Palmyra. The lid is decorated with a scallop-shell design.

Roman Architecture

Building an empire

The many magnificent buildings across the empire—from temples and forts to bathhouses and amphitheaters—reflect the expertise of Roman architects, engineers, and innovators. They also stand as emblems of wealth and power.

△ **Marble decoration** Roman architects imported luxurious colored marbles from across the empire, from huge column shafts to the small pieces laid, as here, in patterned pavements.

From its legendary foundation in the 8th century BCE, the city of Rome was in the shadow of its more sophisticated Etruscan neighbors to the north and Greek communities in the south of Italy. From these it borrowed elements of civic and religious architecture, combining them in various ways, including in temple architecture. As Roman armies expanded beyond Italy from the 3rd century BCE, they encountered the marble temples, theaters, and palaces of the Greek-speaking East, and brought a taste for these back to Rome. From the Greeks, the Romans (and other Italian groups) took architectural elements, such as columns, and also strong theories of design and decoration. Greek ideas, along with materials, examples, and skilled craftsmen, were transported to Rome, adding ambition and sophistication to the city's architectural projects. As the Republican city grew in power and wealth, its politicians competed in largesse, following the kings of the Greek-speaking world in using grand architecture as a political gesture, and when the Roman emperors came to power, they accelerated this trend.

Construction techniques and materials

Although the Romans did not invent the arch, they nevertheless developed and extended its use considerably, both as a structural element and as a decorative feature. Spectacular multiple arches became the trademark of Roman buildings, from theaters and amphitheaters to aqueducts and bridges, with sweeping arches crossing valleys and rivers.

Decorative brick pilaster (flattened rectangular column) between windows

The arch was a hallmark of Roman architecture

A curving street lined with stores ran through this level (see pp. 162–163)

"**All [buildings]** should possess **strength, utility**, and **beauty**."

VITRUVIUS, *DE ARCHITECTURA (ON ARCHITECTURE)*

Similar ingenuity was evident in their adaptation and use of concrete, which allowed them to move away from the post-and-lintel architecture of the Greeks and experiment with curved vaults and domes. Although marble and stone were widely used in Roman buildings, they had to be quarried, worked by skilled masons, and moved at vast expense. By contrast, the components of concrete were inexpensive and easily transported and used, providing an efficient, versatile building material (see pp. 200–201) that could be deployed by an unskilled, often enslaved labor force. This freed architects to imagine ever-more elaborate geometric vaulted spaces: the Domus Aurea (see pp. 186–187) and the Pantheon (pp. 202–203) are striking examples from the 1st and 2nd centuries CE. Concrete also enabled the redesign of entire landscapes, with hills terraced or cut away and retained, as in Trajan's Market (see below).

An enduring legacy

Roman architects developed a highly refined and remarkably consistent set of design principles, combining the formal language of the Greek columnar orders (see box, below) with a tremendous flair for scale and symmetry, elaborate decoration, vaulting, and arcades. Large and grandiose public buildings set these trends, which were then imitated on a far smaller scale in private homes and villas (see pp. 78–79). The Romans' skill in engineering and in the use and adaptation of materials enabled them to build on an unprecedented scale, imposing their architectural style throughout their vast empire. Even today, at historic sites from the Middle East to North Africa and through huge swathes of Europe, the vestiges of Roman architecture make an immediately identifiable impression.

△ **Temple of Portunus**
This small, well-preserved temple in Rome, c. 75 BCE, combines Classical Greek features, including Ionic columns, with Roman elements, such as the high podium and strong frontal emphasis.

◁ **Trajan's Market**
This commercial and residential complex of brick-and-concrete terraces, c. 112 CE, was built adjacent to a hill that was cut away to erect Trajan's Forum (see pp. 212–213). The confident engineering, bold curves, and brick detailing are striking examples of Roman urban architecture.

THE **CLASSICAL ORDERS**

The three main forms of columnar architecture developed by Greek architects and adapted by the Romans are known as the Classical Orders. The sturdy Doric, graceful Ionic, and elaborate Corinthian orders had their own rules of proportion, with distinctive capitals at the tops of columns and associated ornament and detailing throughout the building. The Romans encountered Greek columnar architecture (mainly temples) in the south of Italy and the eastern empire. They soon absorbed these design principles, adding two new orders of their own: Tuscan and Composite. As concrete architecture became more widespread, Roman architects increasingly used decorative elements from these orders in buildings in which columns no longer played a structural role. For example, the engaged pilasters (flattened columns) between the first-floor windows in Trajan's Market (left) are purely decorative, but help determine the rhythm and Classical "feel" of the building.

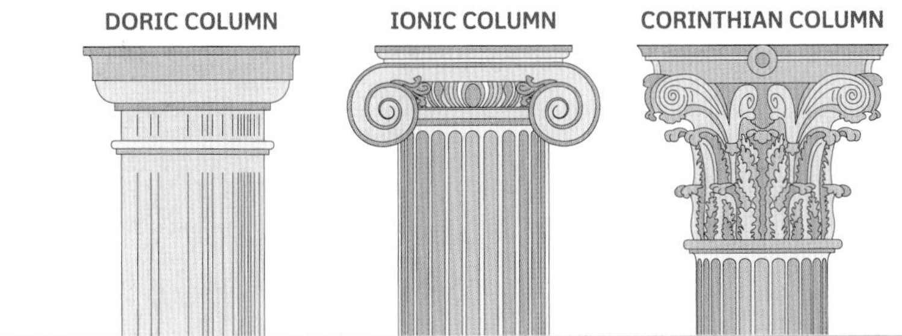

Agrippina the Younger

A powerful woman at the heart of the imperial family

Agrippina held a unique position as sister, wife, and mother of emperors. She used her influence to skillfully navigate imperial power structures despite being excluded, as a woman, from the apparatus of the state.

Julia Agrippina, known as Agrippina the Younger, was born to Agrippina the Elder and Germanicus in Gaul in 15 CE. She had three brothers, including the future emperor Gaius (Caligula), and two sisters. At the age of 13, Agrippina married Gnaeus Domitius Ahenobarbus and in the year 37 CE they had a son, Lucius Domitius Ahenobarbus, who would later become the emperor Nero.

Exile and recall

Agrippina and her sisters had a tempestuous relationship with their brother Caligula when he was emperor. He awarded them many honors, but banished Agrippina and her sister Julia to the Pontian islands in 39 or 40 CE, possibly for conspiring to depose him. Agrippina's first husband died in 40 or 41 CE, widowing her at the age of 25. After Caligula's assassination in 41 CE, Agrippina was recalled from exile by her uncle Claudius, now emperor. She married a second time, but was again widowed.

In 49 CE she married Claudius, despite being his niece; the Senate gave them special dispensation. One justification for the marriage—according to Tacitus—was that it would prevent Agrippina, who was still able to have children, from marrying into another family and removing the line of succession from the Julio-Claudians. As Augustus's great-granddaughter, she embodied the legitimacy of Julio-Claudian rule. Agrippina persuaded Claudius to adopt Nero, and he also founded Colonia Agrippina (now Cologne, Germany) at her birthplace, the first Roman colony to be named after a woman.

▽ **Failed assassination** The ship carrying Agrippina begins to collapse beneath heavy lead weights in this 1874 depiction by Austrian painter Gustav Wertheimer. Agrippina's ship fell apart close enough to land for her to escape unharmed.

Mother of the emperor

After Nero came to the throne, Agrippina played an important role in supporting her young son. She had gathered a group of powerful supporters who became his advisors and her allies. As was common at the time, men who objected to her political authority spread rumours depicting her as a stereotypically ambitious woman who sought to exercise power. She was said to have poisoned Claudius's son Britannicus—and Claudius himself—to secure Nero's path to the throne. Agrippina was similarly accused of incest with both her brother and her son.

As Nero grew older, Agrippina tried to maintain an active role in the management of the empire. This led to conflict and the eventual breakdown of her relationship with her son. Nero ordered her assassination in 59 CE, planning a deliberate shipwreck. When this plan failed, he sent assassins to her villa. She told them to stab her in her womb.

15 CE Julia Agrippina is born to Agrippina the Elder and Germanicus

28 CE Marries the first of her three husbands, Gnaeus Domitius Ahenobarbus

37 CE Gives birth to her only known child—the future emperor Nero

39–40 CE Caligula exiles Agrippina; she is recalled in 41 CE

47 CE Death of Agrippina's second husband, Gaius Sallustius Passienus Crispus

49 CE Marries her uncle, the emperor Claudius; he later adopts Nero

54 CE Nero ascends the throne, making Agrippina mother of the emperor

59 CE After surviving a shipwreck planned by her son, she is assassinated later that year

△ **The Gemma Claudia**
In this onyx cameo from 49 CE, Agrippina and Claudius (left) face her parents—Claudius's brother and sister-in-law. The cameo seeks to justify the unusual imperial marriage.

> "**Stern** and often **proud** in **public**."
>
> TACITUS, *ANNALS*

▷ **Agrippina the Younger**
This Roman marble head of Agrippina reflects her public image after her return from exile. It shows how she might have wanted to be portrayed in her lifetime.

Aeneas, in his native Phrygian cap, supports Augustus and holds a globe signifying Rome's dominion over the Earth

The veiled spirit of Augustus watches over his descendants

A woman cradling a child embodies Rome's control over future generations

A captive sits next to Livia, humbled in the face of Roman majesty

◁ **The Great Cameo of France**
This rare Roman artifact found its way to France in around 1279, most probably via the Byzantine Empire. It was originally known as the *Triumph of Joseph at the Court of the Pharaoh* until it was identified in 1620 as showing figures from the Julio-Claudian dynasty.

> "So that **this work lacks nothing**, gems remain, and the **majesty of nature** forced into small space."
>
> PLINY THE ELDER, *NATURAL HISTORY*

The Great Cameo of France

Power and propaganda as art

Made during the reign of Tiberius or Claudius (the date is contested), the Great Cameo of France is widely seen as a celebration of the Julio-Claudian dynasty. It forms part of a wider visual language—established by Augustus and followed by his successors—of depicting the imperial family as Rome's legitimate, divinely ordained rulers, reinforced by symbolic messaging emphasizing the regime's stability and continuity.

Called to rule

The cameo has three visual zones. The top zone represents the heavens; the middle tier shows members of the imperial family; and the lower section depicts captives from defeated nations under the feet of their conquerors.

In the top tier Aeneas, the mythical forefather of the Roman people, takes centre stage alongside Augustus, transformed by death into a god. They are flanked by Augustus's adopted son Drusus—riding Pegasus—and Marcellus, the emperor's nephew, who was considered an heir until his death in 23 BCE. The lower tier features subjugated Germans and Parthians. They are easily, if stereotypically, identifiable by their shaggy hair and distinctive caps respectively. Their hands are bound as they await their fate.

The middle zone can be read in several ways. In the generally accepted interpretation the seated figures are Tiberius and his mother Livia, Augustus's widow (see pp. 142–143). The standing figure in armor is Germanicus, Tiberius's adopted son, with his wife Agrippina and their son Gaius (later Caligula). Tiberius's son, the younger Drusus, and a woman who may be his mother Vipsania are behind the throne. The scene could be commemorating Germanicus's conquests in the east in 17–18 CE, or perhaps it could show Tiberius's adoption of Caligula and his grandson Tiberius Gemellus in 23 CE. Either reading suggests a stable transition of imperial power from Tiberius to his eventual successor.

Roman cameo technique

A technical and artistic masterpiece, the Great Cameo of France is the largest surviving Roman cameo, at around 12 in (31 cm) high and 10 in (26 cm) wide. It is made from sardonyx, a semiprecious stone comprising, in this instance, five mineral layers, each a different color. By carving into the stone at different depths, the artist has created the cameo's figures in their contrasting colors and textures. Only a small proportion of the cameo is engraved rather than carved, mainly the finer details. Stones for cameos were chosen for their color, durability, transparency, and gloss, as well as how easy they were to work with. Several two-layer sardonyx cameos exist but, with five layers, the Great Cameo of France is easily the finest example of this art form.

▽ **Cameo of Augustus, Nero, and Livia**
This cameo was created in the reign of Nero, to show his link to the founder of the Julio-Claudian dynasty (left) and his wife (right)—both of whom died before Nero (center) was born.

Love, Sex, and Marriage

Ambition, partnership, and even affection

Marriage performed a critical role in Roman society, ensuring legitimate children and mechanisms for inheritance. Love and lust found ways to exist outside formal legal relationships, particularly for people who were not citizens.

△ **Faithful in death**
The couple on this Italian gravestone hold hands to show they are still committed to each other after they have died.

The Romans viewed marriage as fundamentally about continuing family lines: marriage was for procreation, consolidating power, and transferring property. Women were often partnered with much older men. Elite women in particular married early to ensure they could have as many children as possible, and remarried quickly if they were widowed. However, the Romans also valued the ideal of a companionate marriage, in which husband and wife worked together for shared goals.

A stereotypical Roman *matrona* ("married woman") was expected to look after her family and household; her guiding virtues were modesty, fidelity, and obedience. The ultimate model was the *univira*, a woman who married only once, although the realities of Roman marriage meant this was very rare.

◁ **Ring of harmony**
This Greek word *omonoia* (in Latin, *concordia*) inscribed on this gold ring means "harmony", a key virtue associated with marriage for the Romans.

Types of relationship

Roman society recognized a wide range of formal and informal relationships. The most formal was *cum manu* marriage, contracted either by a religious ceremony (*confarreatio*), a mock contract between father and husband (*coemptio*), or living together for a year (*usus*). The year was interrupted if a wife spent three consecutive nights away from her husband's home. In a marriage *cum manu*, the wife became a full member of her husband's family, under control of him or his *paterfamilias* ("head of the family"). Marriage *sine manu* was less formal, and was based simply on a couple's desire to live as husband and wife. Here, the wife continued to be under her own father's control, so could return home if she was mistreated. Marriage *cum manu* gave the husband power over the wife's dowry, but in a marriage *sine manu* the property still belonged to the wife's family. Enslaved people could enter into a union called *contubernium*; however, their enslavers did not have to respect it, could separate families at will, and would automatically assume any children as their property.

Informal relationships

Another kind of union was *concubinatus* ("concubinage"), a quasi-marriage often arising when one partner was not a Roman citizen. Its children were not seen as illegitimate, but could not inherit from the father. Outside of marriage, Roman men might engage in same-gender sexual relations, usually between a younger and older man, with strict conventions of behavior based on age. While there is little evidence of relations between Roman women, this does not mean they did not exist. Rome also had an active sex work economy, although many sex workers were enslaved.

THE EPITAPH OF **ALLIA POTESTAS**

Allia Potestas was a freedwoman who lived in Perugia during the late 3rd to 4th century CE. In her funerary inscription, she is praised for her courage, honesty, modesty, and excellent housekeeping. Although many women were commemorated in these terms, Allia Potestas is unusual—her epitaph was offered by not one, but two men, who were themselves lovers (although unnamed). The men mourn Allia Potestas, who guided and brought them together like Pylades and Orestes (inseparable friends from Greek mythology). They also attest that all three of them lived together in one house; but now she is dead, they will separate and grow old alone.

The satyr shape of the bronze stand signals an erotic moment

The woman is attended by two servants—this one holds an amphora

The lover approaches the woman's couch, his torso bared

△ **Lover's approach**
A moment between lovers in a garden is depicted in this 2nd-century CE mosaic from a villa in Centocelle, Italy. A similar scene was found in a fresco at Rome's Villa Farnesina.

Image control
Nero's hair is fashionably styled in this bust, which suggests he wished to be seen in a more contemporary way than his predecessors.

Nero

A committed performer

Nero became emperor as a teenager, benefiting from a formidable team of advisors. Despite a positive start to his reign, he alienated the Roman elite and ultimately was removed from power.

Nero was born into the imperial family and adopted formally by the emperor Claudius after Claudius's marriage to Nero's mother, Agrippina the Younger (see pp. 178–179). He became emperor in 54 CE aged 16, supported by advisors including his mother, the Praetorian prefect Burrus, and the philosopher-politician Seneca the Younger. The early years of his reign were considered a golden period, but it became increasingly chaotic, characterized by cruelty and ego. He removed his earlier counselors—even ordering his mother's murder—and undermined his support from the senatorial class. His personal life was also turbulent. His relationship with Acte, a freedwoman, caused a scandal. He divorced his first wife, Octavia, and had her executed on a false charge of adultery. He allegedly killed his second wife, Poppaea, by kicking her in the stomach when she was pregnant. (However, many claims about Nero's actions, by later sources such as Suetonius, are debated.)

In the public eye

Nero's love of public performance included theatrical "marriages" to the freedmen Pythagoras (with Nero playing the bride) and Sporus (whom he had castrated first). He went to Greece (66–68 CE) to perform in numerous musical events that he arranged, including during the games at Olympia, and "won" a horse race there, despite falling from his chariot. The trip further lowered his status with Rome's nobility, who viewed his participation in such events as demeaning.

◁ **Cultural legacy**
Nero plays the lyre dressed as Apollo, the god of music, in this gemstone intaglio, or engraving. As emperor, he studied music intensively and saw himself as an artist.

Turmoil and rebellion

Nero oversaw military successes in Armenia and Britannia (England and Wales). But his ambitious building programs after the Great Fire of Rome put financial stress on the state, affecting soldiers' pay and free grain distribution to the poor, and stoked conflict with senators over land. Multiple plots against Nero led to many executions among the Roman elite. Following military revolts, the Senate declared Nero an enemy of the Roman people. He took his own life in 68 CE, the last of the Julio-Claudian rulers.

△ **Poppaea Sabina**
Poppaea (30–65 CE) divorced her second husband, Otho, to marry Nero in 62 CE. Nero had Poppaea's son from her first marriage drowned while he was on a fishing trip.

▷ **The Great Fire of Rome**
In July 64 CE, a fire that started in shops near the Circus Maximus destroyed large parts of Rome. The Domus Aurea (see pp. 186–187) was one of the new building projects that followed.

37 CE Nero is born to Gnaeus Domitius Ahenobarbus and Agrippina the Younger

49 CE Agrippina marries Claudius; he later adopts Nero

54 CE Nero becomes emperor following the death of Claudius

59 CE Agrippina is assassinated on Nero's orders

60 CE In Britannia, Boudica's rebellion against Rome is quelled

64 CE Parts of Rome are destroyed in the Great Fire

65 CE Nero accuses Seneca of conspiring against him and orders Seneca to kill himself

68 CE Nero dies by suicide, after fleeing Rome

▷ Nero's Rome
Nero had ambitions to reshape Rome. A devastating fire in 64 CE gave him the opportunity to build, but this also led to rumors that the emperor had started the blaze to acquire more land for the spectacular palace complexes shown in this reconstruction.

Atrium connecting to the Roman Forum

Giant statue of Nero, later repurposed into a statue of the sun god Sol

Huge boating lake

△ Inspiring frescoes
Nero's palaces were filled with luxurious decorations, including sculptures, stucco, mosaics, and wall paintings. The fantastical "grotesques" amazed and inspired artists such as Raphael and Pinturicchio when the surviving frescoes of the Domus Aurea, by then buried underground, were rediscovered during the Renaissance.

Temple of the Deified Emperor Claudius, converted into a fountain

Aqueduct branch leading to the Palatine Hill (see pp. 146–147)

Famous surviving octagonal room of the Domus Aurea

Wing of the Domus Aurea, surviving today under a later bathhouse on the Esquiline Hill

Extensive gardens and groves

The gardens were filled with pavilions, fountains, and sculptures

△ **Lake**
The Domus Aurea was not just one building but a complex, including extensive gardens and a lake, which the biographer Suetonius described as "like the sea." After Nero's death, the lake was drained and its site used for the Colosseum.

The Domus Aurea

The architecture of excess

The emperor Nero, who reigned 54–68 CE, became notorious for self-aggrandizing excess. His palaces, the Domus Transitoria and Domus Aurea ("Golden House"), took up huge swathes of land in the city's center, as well as costing enormous amounts of money with their pavilions, gardens, groves, large lake, and fountains. Displaying innovative use of interior spaces, such as concrete vaults, the palace buildings contributed to the development of Roman architecture. However, these lavish projects also added to Nero's infamy: satiric graffiti appeared in Rome warning that his palace would consume the whole city. After Nero's downfall and suicide, his successors—the Flavian dynasty—demolished these structures and used the land for new public projects, including the Colosseum (see pp. 194–197).

◁ **Portrayal of strength**
Nero's official coin portraits show him as stockier over the years. As with his palaces, he must have hoped to project an image of wealth and power.

The Jewish Wars

Rage and resistance in the Middle East

△ **Raiders of the Temple**
This reconstruction of a frieze on the Arch of Titus in Rome shows soldiers with the spoils of war from the Temple in Jerusalem, including its large menorah.

While many provinces enjoyed relative stability under Roman control, Judea never did. Unresolvable religious and cultural differences between occupier and occupied meant there could never be peace while the Romans remained.

Judea became a Roman province in 6 CE, when its Senate-approved king, Herod Achelaus, was dismissed by the emperor Augustus for ineptitude. But with the arrival of the Roman governor and his legions came unrest. Roman taxation was one source of anger, as were the religious disputes between groups following the many different traditions of Judaism in the region. Each group was critical of the others' interpretations of the complex regulations of the Jewish faith, sometimes violently so. The Romans' attempts to intervene only made matters worse.

Destruction of the Second Temple

In 66 CE the people of Judea rebelled against Roman rule, establishing an independent (if short-lived) Jewish state. The catalyst was a religious dispute between Greeks and Jews in the Judean capital of Caesarea Maritima. The failure of the Roman governor Gessius Florus to intervene led to Greeks murdering Jews, who retaliated in kind. Soon, cities across Judea erupted in violence, too, with anger directed primarily at the Roman occupiers. Rome's efforts to regain control were thwarted by strong resistance and by the

△ **Jewish freedom coin**
This coin was issued during the Bar Kokhba revolt. It shows the destroyed Second Temple, which became a symbol of hope for Jews.

political chaos and civil wars in Rome that followed Nero's death in 68 CE. It was not until August 70 CE that Rome was able to reassert its control, when the new emperor Vespasian's son Titus sacked Jerusalem after a long siege, looting its treasures and destroying its most sacred building, the Second Temple.

The Romans enslaved or killed the city's inhabitants and acts of brutality and violent sexual assault were widespread. Cultural and religious treasures were destroyed or looted. Pockets of resistance survived but were swiftly quashed. The Romans further punished the Jewish people that same year by imposing the *fiscus Iudaicus* ("Jewish tax"). This financial burden was imposed on all Jews throughout the empire—men, women, and even children. Its aim in part was to discourage further rebellions, not just in Judea but across all Roman-held territories.

Unrest spreads across the region

Yet Rome's draconian response to the rebellion only led to more conflict in Judea and beyond. The Kitos War of 115–117 consisted mainly of revolts by Jewish populations in cities and regions outside Judea. These rebellions were widespread, and included uprisings by Jews in northern Africa, Crete, Cyprus, and Egypt that left many Romans and non-Romans dead and provoked an equally violent response. The revolts were primarily caused by the burden of the *fiscus Iudaicus* and by tensions with local populations. The uprising in Cyprus, for example, allegedly saw thousands of Greeks massacred by Jewish rebels.

The Bar Kokhba revolt that began in 132 was supposedly provoked when the emperor Hadrian outlawed circumcision, an important Jewish ritual. Different sources say it was caused by Hadrian's plan to establish a new colony known as Aelia Capitolina on the site of Jerusalem and build a temple of Jupiter over the ruins of the Second Temple. The Jewish response to this act of desecration was led by Simon bar Kokhba, who was proclaimed a messiah by his followers. The rebels successfully adopted guerrilla warfare tactics against the Romans, forcing Hadrian to redeploy troops from Syria, Egypt, and Arabia. Bar Kokhba and his supporters were finally defeated when their stronghold of Betar fell in 136 after a long siege and all the town's inhabitants were killed. Despite the severity of this war, few sources survive that describe it. This may reflect a reluctance on Hadrian's part to draw attention to the terrible events that had taken place. For the rest of the century the volatile province was occupied by troops and governed by senior generals.

◁ **The Second Temple**
This reconstruction shows the Second Temple in Jerusalem as it would have been before its destruction in 70 CE.

THE SIEGE OF **MASADA**

Josephus was a Jewish rebel who changed sides and joined the Romans. His history of the Jewish Wars contains the only account of a key event in the conflict. Jewish radicals called *sicarii* ("dagger men") occupied the hilltop fort at Masada (below) and held the Romans at bay for months until the invaders finally breached the citadel in 73 CE. Inside, they found its 967 men, women, and children dead. They had killed each other by drawing lots, so that only the last of them would have to die by suicide. Josephus's account has been questioned, but Masada is seen as a defining event in Jewish history.

"**Long ago** we determined that we would **not be slaves** to the Romans ..."

ELEAZAR BEN-YAIR, QUOTED IN *THE JEWISH WAR*

△ **Door keys**
These keys were among artifacts from the Bar Kokhba revolt, found at the Cave of Letters at Nahal Hever in the Judean desert.

The Eruption of Vesuvius

Pompeii and Herculaneum are burned and buried

The inhabitants of Italy's Campania region were completely unprepared for the sudden eruption of the volcano Vesuvius, and hundreds of citizens lost their lives. Ash and debris buried towns and cities, preserving them for hundreds of years.

△ **A lost treasure**
In their haste to flee the eruption, many people left behind valuables, such as this snake motif golden bracelet found in Pompeii. Jewelery was also found with those who died in the disaster.

The Bay of Naples, in Campania in the south of Italy, was a popular place for the rich to relax and avoid the summer heat of Rome. Many members of the Roman elite had extensive villas and estates there, as the land lent itself as much to cultivation as it did to leisure. The slopes of Mount Vesuvius were a popular site for vineyards—the volcano's mineral-rich soil produced grapes that yielded some of the empire's best wines.

Pompeii and Herculaneum were two of the thriving cities around the bay, lying at the southern and western foot of Mount Vesuvius respectively. The volcano had been dormant for centuries, so there had been no sense that the region faced any threat. However, warning signs came in the form of major earthquakes, which hit in 62–63 CE and 64 CE, causing so much damage that the effects were still visible at the site of Pompeii 15 years later.

In 79 CE, Vesuvius finally erupted, causing a natural disaster that completely reshaped the geography of the area and devastated the local populations.

The progress of the eruption

As a teenager, the politician Pliny the Younger witnessed the eruption (which killed his uncle, Pliny the Elder) and his account gives us a framework to which we can apply contemporary scientific understanding of how volcanic eruptions occur.

▽ **The *Macellum* of Pompeii**
The remains of the city's provision market survive at the northeast corner of the forum. Grains, fruit, fish scales, and bones were found in the ruins.

△ **A *thermopolium* (hot food shop)**
A counter with holes for food jars can still be seen in this well-preserved establishment that served drinks and hot food on the Via dell'Abbondanza in Pompeii.

A MOMENT CAPTURED IN TIME

The phenomenon of carbonization has allowed evidence of everyday objects at Pompeii to survive, while also giving us a snapshot of the day of the eruption. The process of carbonization turns organic matter, such as plants or wooden objects, into carbon. At Herculaneum and Pompeii, the extreme heat of the pyroclastic flows and the speed with which they arrived meant that many items, such as furniture—including the child's wooden cradle shown here—and even food, were rapidly transformed into carbon. These artifacts serve as poignant reminders of the human cost of the eruption, and of the many men, women, children, and animals that lost their lives in what must have been for them a traumatic and terrifyingly sudden and incomprehensible event.

The eruption lasted for two days. On the first day, Vesuvius produced a huge cloud of ash and debris, which began to fall on the settlements below. Roman historian Cassius Dio recounted that the cloud was so great it darkened the sun above Rome, and that debris reached as far as Egypt and Syria. Pompeii was directly beneath the cloud, and was soon submerged by ash and pumice. Although Herculaneum was struck by earthquakes, it was not affected by ash because the wind was blowing away from the settlement. Either overnight or early the next morning, the cloud of ash collapsed under its own weight, causing pyroclastic flows—a superheated and fast-moving mixture of ash and gas—to pour down the slopes of the volcano. Pompeii and Herculaneum were in the direct path of these pyroclastic flows, and the extreme temperatures would have killed anyone who had been unable to escape or tried to wait out the eruption.

Both cities were buried under deep volcanic debris that would preserve them for centuries. The eruption also engulfed the smaller towns of Oplontis and Stabiae, as well as many farms and villages on the sides and around the foot of Vesuvius.

Escaping the disaster

When the ash began to rain down, people in the vicinity tried to escape. At Herculaneum, some boarded boats at the beach while the sea remained comparatively calm, but those fleeing later found themselves trapped on the shore as the water became rougher. The preserved skeletons of those who took refuge in the shipsheds, killed by the pyroclastic flow, show a cross-section of society in terms of gender, age, and status; wealth was no guarantee of escape.

At Pompeii, people may have remained in their homes during the initial volcanic storm to protect themselves from falling debris. Those who waited too long to begin their journey out of the city took shelter inside, where they died of suffocation or thermal shock from the scorching temperatures. It is likely, however, that many people were able to flee the affected area, by land or boat, during the first day of the eruption. These people lost everything, and the emperor Titus provided financial aid to those affected, sending two ex-consuls to oversee regeneration work.

▷ **Neptune Mosaic, Herculaneum**
As devastating as the eruption was, the ash and debris it deposited acted as a protective layer that kept many frescos and mosaics in excellent states of preservation.

Extravagant Games

Public games and spectacles

The Romans enjoyed a wide range of public events. They could attend races, historical enactments, staged animal hunts, and gruesome executions. However, these attractions relied upon the labor and lives of enslaved people and prisoners.

Spectacular games for the masses were at the center of Roman social and political culture. For politicians, organizing and paying for games allowed them to show their generosity to the citizens. The satirist Juvenal, writing in the 2nd century CE, complained that the Roman people were only interested in bread and circuses, and would sell their vote accordingly.

Rome's rulers usually held games during religious festivals to honor the gods (see pp. 120–21). The entertainment started with an opening procession and sacrifice, and then a series of events that could be spread over several days. Everyone could attend regardless of gender or social status, and free tickets were available for the very poor. In arenas, seats were reserved for senators and *equites* (cavalrymen), and perhaps their families. Women, enslaved people, and the poor tended to sit or stand toward the back.

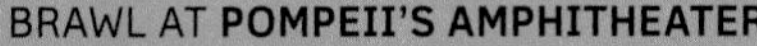

BRAWL AT **POMPEII'S AMPHITHEATER**

Crowd control was also a challenge in the ancient world. The historian Tacitus records a brawl at a gladiatorial show held at the Pompeii amphitheater in 59 CE. Tensions between locals from Pompeii and visitors from the nearby town of Nuceria led to a fight breaking out with stones and swords. Many people were wounded or killed. Some Nucerians went to Rome to complain, and the emperor Nero ordered an investigation. As a result of this, the Senate barred Pompeii from holding another show for ten years. A painter captured the riot in a fresco decorating a house in Pompeii (below).

△ ***A naumachia***
The Temple of Isis at Pompeii is decorated with murals representing a *naumachia*. The goddess Isis was associated with the sea and sailors asked her for protection.

The races

Horse-racing in amphitheaters was a popular spectacle. The most prestigious races, however, were held at the Circus Maximus (see pp. 146–147), where chariots were grouped in teams: the reds, the whites, the greens, and the blues. Support for these teams eventually became a proxy for a person's political affiliation. Charioteers were usually enslaved men, who took great risks to win despite the danger they faced—they could become tangled in their reins and dragged behind their chariots.

Blood sports

Wild beast hunts, or *venationes*, in amphitheaters showed off the wealth and power of Rome, as well as its rulers. They featured exotic animals from across the empire, such as hippopotamuses, crocodiles, and elephants for trained hunters (*bestiarii*) or other wild beasts to fight. These hunts could also take the form of executions, where lions or other big cats would be let loose on convicted criminals or Christians to kill them.

The most expensive public performances were mock naval battles called *naumachiae*. These took place in specially converted spaces, such as the artificial lake that Augustus excavated for a display in 2 BCE. The *naumachiae* often reenacted past military encounters, such as the Battle of Actium (see pp. 134–135), but the outcomes of these battles were allowed to differ from reality. Most of the fighters in these events were prisoners, but gladiators also participated.

△ **Roman chariot racing**
This mosaic depicts the winners of a chariot race. The chariot is a *quadriga*, drawn by four horses. The charioteer is dressed in blue, showing he is a member of the blue team.

A member of the blue team brings water for the horses

An official raises his arm to signal the winner

The charioteer holds a palm branch, signifying his victory

The Colosseum

Rome's great stadium of slaughter

The Colosseum in Rome was the greatest amphitheater in the Roman Empire. Commissioned by Vespasian in 72 CE, it opened eight years later under his son, Titus. It was built on the site of Nero's hated private palace, the Domus Aurea (see pp. 186–187), as a public venue for arena sports such as gladiatorial combat and beast hunts. The structure was a masterpiece of Roman engineering. Behind its impressive arcaded facade was an intricate system of corridors and staircases. These led to an oval *cavea* ("enclosure") of seats for up to 50,000 spectators, who sat at different levels according to their social class, status, or gender. The Colosseum became a partial ruin after the fall of Rome, but it remains a symbol of the city.

△ **Home entertainment**
Arena games often featured in the decor of private homes, a sign of their popularity. This lavish mosaic found at Zliten in modern Libya is from the 2nd century CE and shows gladiators in combat overseen by a referee (in white).

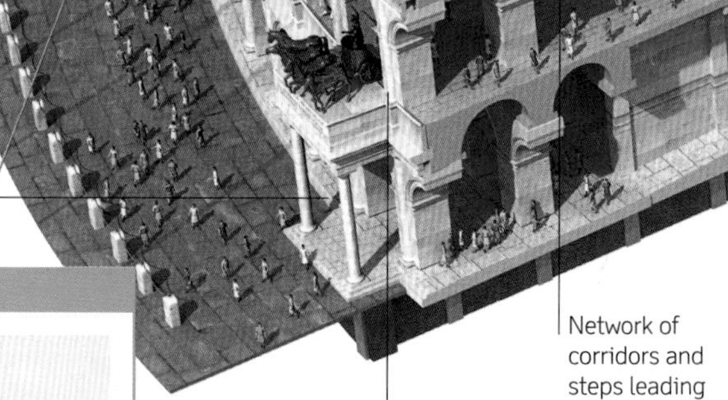

△ **Inside the Colosseum**
Beyond its impressive facade, the Colosseum's warren of corridors, walkways, and staircases led to the *cavea*, or seating area. The *cavea* looked down over the arena (the word "arena" comes from the Latin for sand, which was spread across the wooden floor to soak up blood). Below the arena was the hypogeum.

FLOODED ARENA

Some literary sources suggest that the Colosseum arena could have been flooded for naval battles called *naumachiae* (see pp. 192–193), as pictured in this 1810 engraving. It is unclear how this would have worked; the hypogeum below the arena would have made flooding impractical. But, as the hypogeum was added to the building later, it is possible that the arena could have been filled with water at an earlier stage. The Colosseum was near aqueducts, so water was easily accessed. It was also well served with drains and sewers to take water away.

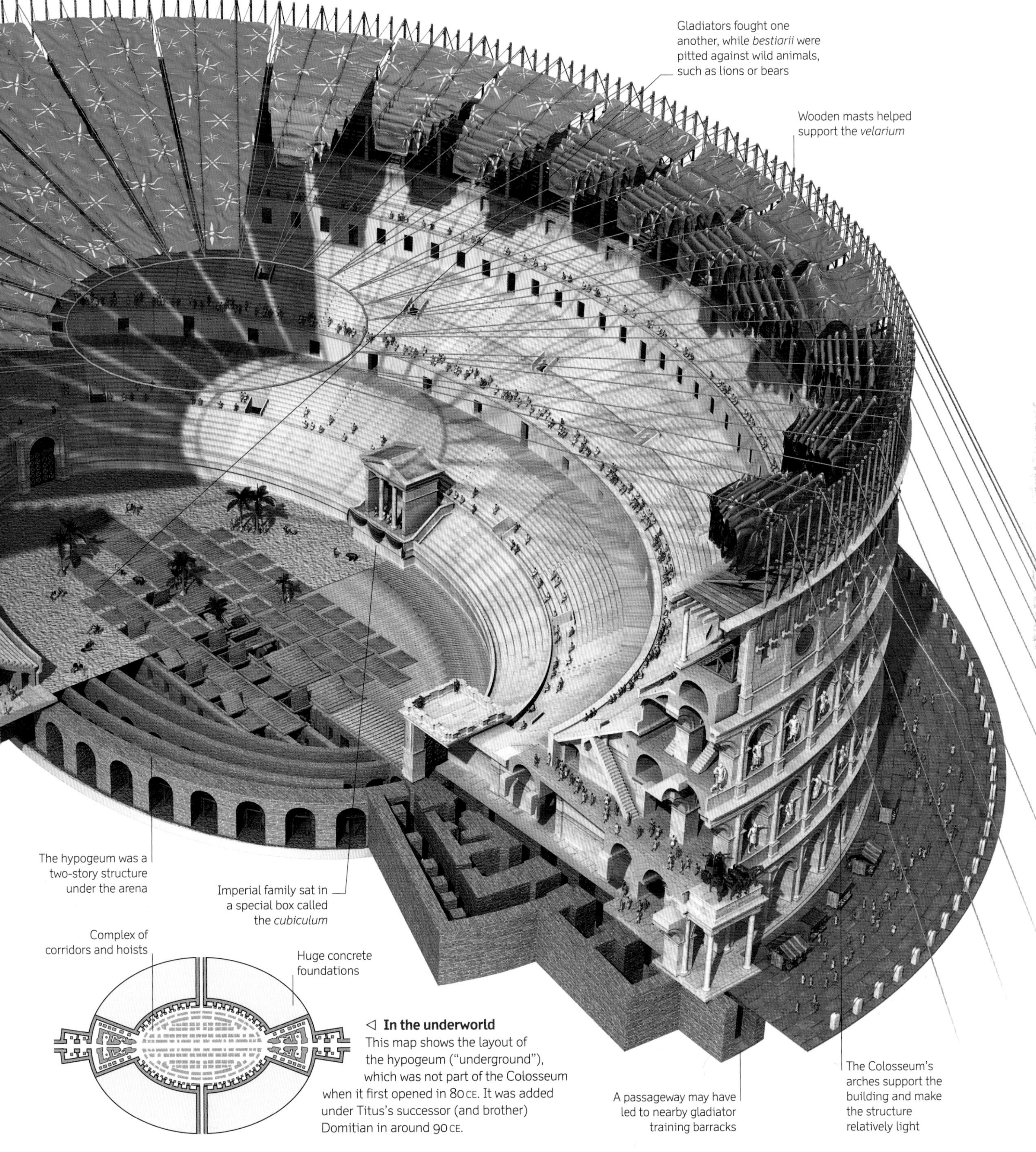

◁ **In the underworld**
This map shows the layout of the hypogeum ("underground"), which was not part of the Colosseum when it first opened in 80 CE. It was added under Titus's successor (and brother) Domitian in around 90 CE.

Visual Tour

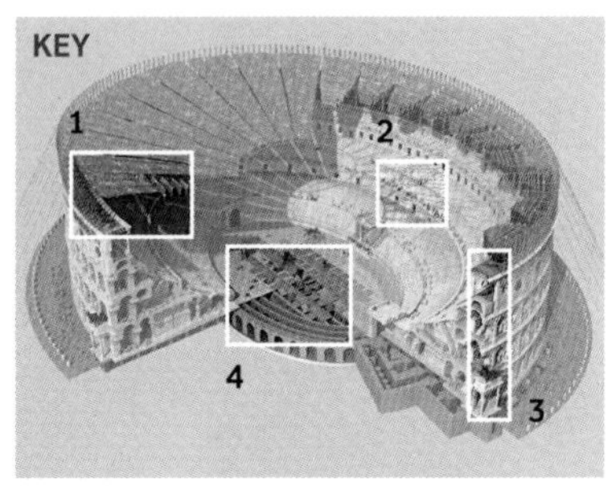

▷ **Under cover**
Roman arenas were sometimes covered by a canvas awning, the *velarium*, to protect spectators from sun. The one shown here is based on a blue star-spangled design that Nero was known to have used at the Theater of Pompey.

△ **A decorative exterior**
The three arcaded tiers are adorned with columns in the Tuscan, Ionic, and Corinthian styles (see pp. 176–177), with a smaller attic story above. The upper arches once contained statues. A main porch stood at each of the four axes (north, south, east, and west).

△ **Under the arena**
While part of the wooden arena floor has been rebuilt today (seen at rear), most of the hypogeum is still exposed. There were different layouts over the centuries, but up to 80 hoists and ramps once raised men, animals, and scenery to the arena.

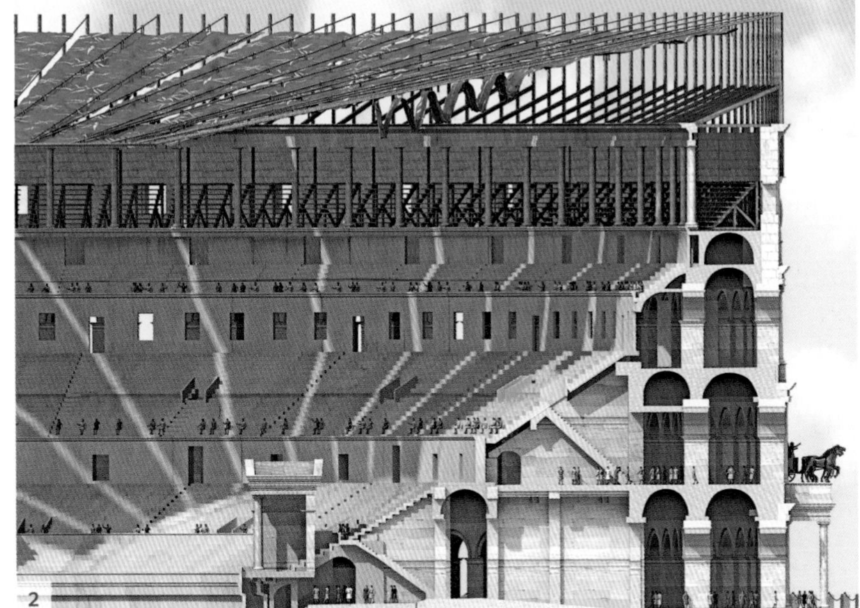

◁ **A view to die for**
Spectators entered the Colosseum through 76 numbered arches. Corridors and staircases directed spectators to their seats. The lowest rows of seats were for senators and high-ranking people; the poor, enslaved, and women sat higher up. The imperial family had a "royal box" at the lowest level.

△ **After the empire**
Following the fall of Rome in the 6th century, the building was used, among other things, as a fort and a graveyard. Over time, its stones were reused for other buildings and it was damaged by earthquakes. In 1749, it was consecrated to the memory of Christian martyrs.

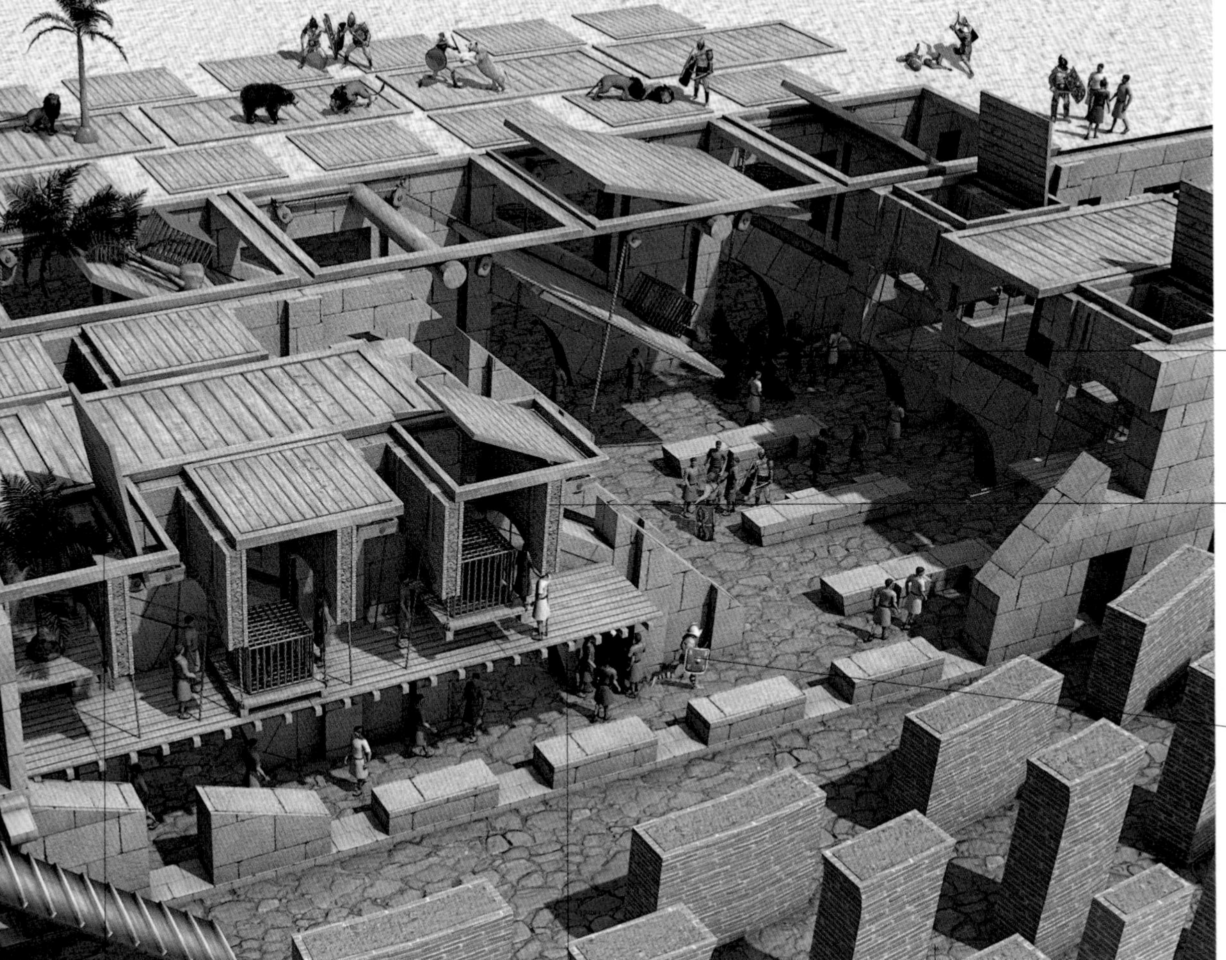

Large ramps, or *pegmata*, raised larger or heavier scenery or animals to the surface

The hypogeum at one point had 60 hoists. Lead counterweights ensured they stayed in position when raised

Gladiators accessed the hypogeum via tunnels from the nearby training barracks

Ancient accounts describe the sudden appearance of scenery and animals from the arena floor's many trapdoors

Corridors would have been crowded, dark, noisy, and smelly

The hypogeum gradually filled up with earth, which was cleared out in the 1930s

◁ **Colosseum hypogeum**
The hypogeum consisted of two levels of corridors and cells. These would have been crowded with combatants, trainers, stagehands, enslaved workers, animal handlers, and wild animals ranging from lions to elephants.

Fighting for Their Lives

Gladiators in the Roman world

Gladiatorial contests were originally practiced as a form of ritualized combat that honored the dead. In time, they evolved into an important and popular type of civic entertainment, with injury and even death a constant possibility.

△ ***Murmillo* helmet**
The grille at the front of this bronze helmet would have protected the gladiator's face but also made it difficult to see his opponent clearly.

The first recorded gladiatorial show was organized in Rome by Decimus Junius Brutus Pera and his brother in 264 BCE as part of their father's funeral. Three pairs of gladiators took part. From this time on, aristocrats staged similar events as part of their family funeral events. Shows were free and were so popular that public figures hoping to win office began to arrange gladiator fights during elections. When Rome's Colosseum opened in 80 CE, it became the model for gladiatorial arenas around the empire.

A history of violence

The figure of the gladiator both attracted and repelled the Romans. In the *Tusculan Disputations* from 45 BCE, Cicero eulogized the gladiators' strength, discipline, and stoicism—all good Roman virtues. But gladiators were regarded with fear and suspicion: Cicero had earlier denounced them as the dregs of society when a number of gladiators supported Catiline, the political rabble-rouser who tried to seize power violently in 63 BCE; the Third Servile War had been a rebellion of enslaved gladiators led by Spartacus (see pp. 110–111).

From the end of the 1st century CE only the emperor could stage gladiatorial shows in Rome, and contests outside the city required special permission. This rule was intended to prevent wealthy men from buying public support and setting themselves up in competition with the emperor. These restrictions contributed to the decline of gladiatorial contests, as did the relative peacefulness of the empire in its later years; with Rome not at war, there was less demand for bloody spectacles in the arena, such as gladiatorial fights and executions, whether of criminals or outlawed and unfavored groups such as Christians and Jews. In 325, the emperor Constantine banned gladiatorial bouts completely.

◁ **Glass cup showing gladiators**
A *retiarius* with net and trident faces a *secutor* on this bowl made in the 3rd century CE. The fighters' names are inscribed under each figure.

Trained to kill

Gladiators were recruited either coercively from the enslaved population or willingly from those prepared to renounce their liberty for a price. They lived in barrack-style "schools" and were trained by a *lanista*, usually a retired gladiator. It took time and money to prepare gladiators to face each other in the arena, so

they were rarely allowed to fight to the death (it is unclear whether a "thumbs up" or "thumbs down" gesture was used to decide on a gladiator's fate). The spilling of blood was fine, so long as fighters were not badly maimed. Conversely, criminals and prisoners of war were viewed as expendable and given less care and training. Successful gladiators lived in comfort and, it was rumored, enjoyed the sexual favors of well-born Roman women. A few fighters won fame, like the Syrian-born Flamma in the 2nd century CE. He fought 34 bouts, won 21, and died at the "old" age of 30. Gladiators were also employed as bodyguards and were hired by, among others, the populist politicians Clodius and Milo in the 50s BCE.

WOMEN IN COMBAT

This marble relief found in Türkiye from the 1st or 2nd century CE commemorates the freeing of two women gladiators, Amazon and Achilia. They may have won their freedom after performing well in the arena. They have the same weapons as men, but no helmets. Their names reference the myth of Achilles and Penthesilea, the queen of the Amazons, who fought each other at Troy; this pair could have specialized in mythic reenactment. Women gladiators were probably a novelty act in the empire. Domitian, for example, had women and men fight at night by torchlight.

Types of gladiator

Gladiators fought in a number of styles, each with its own distinctive uniform and equipment. Fights took place between gladiators of different types in order to create variety in combat. The *Samnite* is the oldest recorded type of gladiator. He was heavily armed with a short sword or a lance and a large shield; his helmet had a visor and a crest and his legs were protected by greaves (shin guards). The *murmillo* was named after the fish motif on his helmet, which had a finlike crest; he fought with a short sword and had a curved, rectangular shield. The *retiarius* wielded a net, a trident, and a short sword; he tried to entangle his opponent in the net and then to disarm or injure him. He was usually paired against a *secutor*, who used a short *gladius* sword and a dagger. The Thracian, or *Thraex*, was identified by a helmet with a griffin-head crest, and a curved sword called a *sica*. He also carried a small shield. There was also a type of gladiator trained to fight wild animals, known as a *bestiarius*.

▽ **Gladiatorial combat**
This mosaic, from 320 CE, shows gladiators in combat, with each person's name written above him. The Ø symbol next to some of the men is called the *theta infelix* ("unhappy theta") and indicates they are dead.

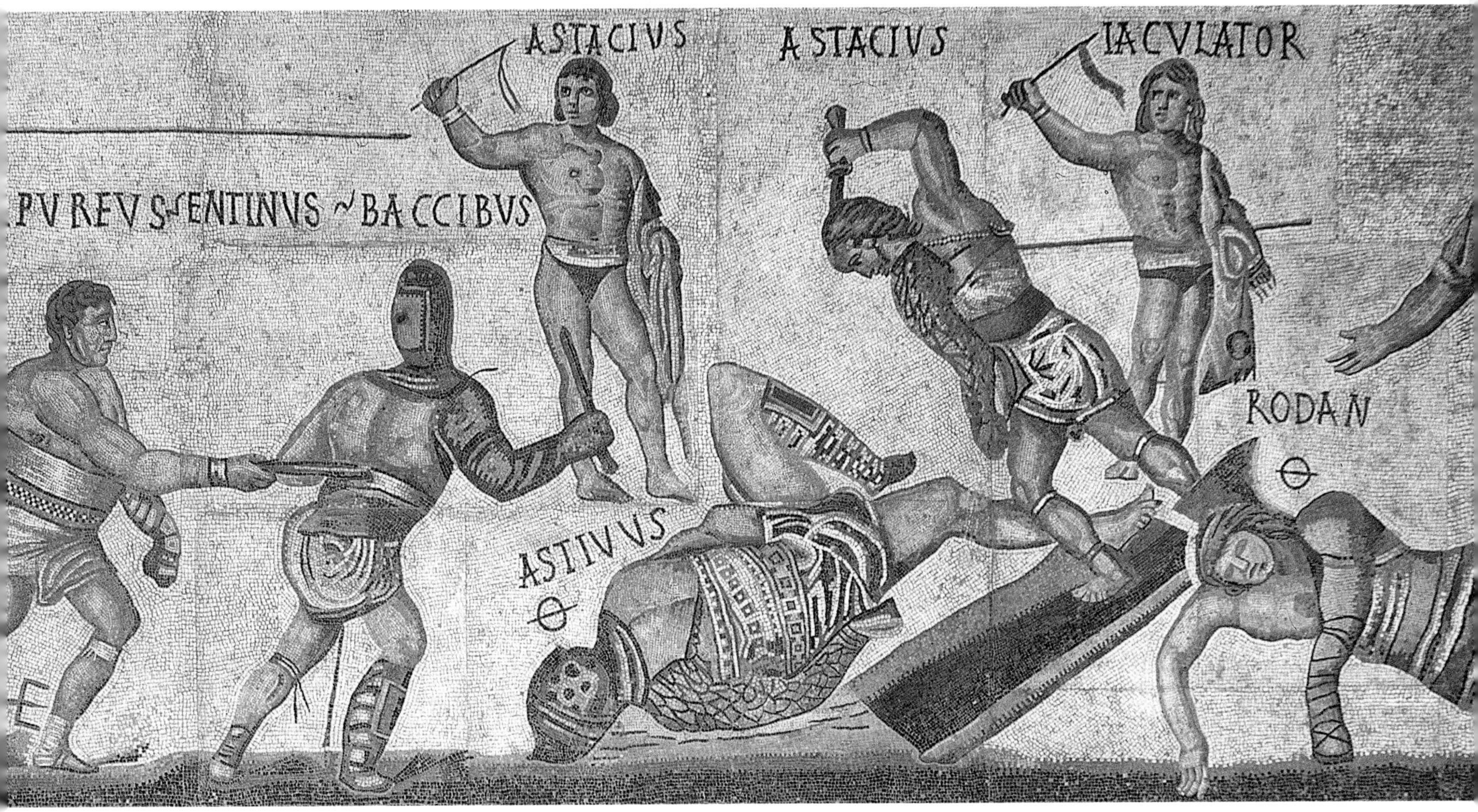

Men guide ropes through a set of pulleys

Known as a *polyspaston*, the treadmill crane was modeled on a similar device used by the Greeks

Laborers, probably enslaved people, work inside the foot-powered treadmill crane

This tomb represents an ideal of aristocratic, Imperial-era funerary architecture

△ **A monument built on success**
The Tomb of the Haterii was made for a family of wealthy builders. Its main relief (above) shows their building crew at work. The Haterii flourished in the 1st century CE and may have helped build the Colosseum.

Engineering an Empire

Laying the foundations for strength and success

Roman architecture was famously influenced by the Greeks, but the engineering the Romans developed for their construction projects was distinctively their own. In typical fashion, it was elegant, straightforward, and brilliantly effective.

Engineering excellence laid the foundations of Rome's empire. Generations of practical knowledge was built up in the army, civilian industries, private workshops, and in the texts of experts such as the 1st-century BCE architect Vitruvius and the 1st-century CE engineer Frontinus. One of the earliest Roman roads—the Appian Way—and the first aqueduct were both completed around 312 BCE. Road- and aqueduct-building would come to define the Romans' engineering achievements.

But there were many more. Roman engineers dug mines; created canals; and, from the 3rd century BCE, covered and channeled the *cloaca maxima*, Rome's massive and extensive sewage network, parts of which are still in use today. They built harbors (see pp. 216–217); harnessed the power of water to operate mills and drive giant saws; and erected vast, innovative buildings such as public baths, or *thermae* (see pp. 236–237), and the Colosseum (see pp. 194–195).

A hard-working, durable material

From the 2nd century BCE, Roman buildings became more ambitious with the development of concrete. It was stronger than stone, but lighter. Created from crushed rock and quicklime or gypsum, concrete could be mixed and laid on site, making it easy to transport. It was versatile and long-lasting, too. This brought huge gains in efficiency and construction times. Adding volcanic ash (*pozzolana*) allowed Roman concrete to set, and be used, under water.

With concrete, buildings could be made cheaply and quickly and then faced with another material for a more attractive finish. Initially, concrete walls were faced using a technique called *opus incertum* ("irregular work"), where chunks of stone were individually placed into the concrete. From the Imperial era, *opus latericium* was developed; for this, brickyards made standardized bricks in their millions that were used to face concrete walls. Brick batches were stamped with the makers' details for quality control, and this now helps archaeologists date Roman buildings. Marble was also used to face some grander buildings.

◁ **Tools of the trade**
With little more than a bronze set square, a plumb line, and compasses, the Romans could survey sites and construct buildings with amazing accuracy.

Surveying tools and techniques

Roman engineering expertise required excellent surveying skills and reliable tools. An aqueduct's angle of incline, for example, had to be measured precisely, so its water did not flow too fast (and flood), or too slowly (and silt up). The *groma* was a pole with plumb lines suspended from cross-pieces mounted on its top and was used for finding straight lines and angles. The *chorobates* was a type of spirit level that measured horizontal planes. With simple instruments like these, Rome's engineers helped build an empire.

△ **Life-giving waterway**
Aqueducts were used to support urban growth across the empire, and could provide fresh, flowing water even in hot and dusty cities, such as Segovia (above) in central Spain.

◁ **Men at work**
In this tomb fresco from the 4th century CE, two workers lay bricks with trowels while the other men clear rubble (bottom left), carry freshly mixed mortar in a halved amphora (center), and mix mortar (bottom right).

The Pantheon

A domed temple fit for the gods

Among the world's finest ancient buildings and surviving in an almost perfect state of preservation, the Pantheon is crowned by a magnificent concrete dome that represents Roman ingenuity and engineering at its best.

One of the most recognizable symbols of Rome, the Pantheon combines a standard columned porch with a revolutionary circular, vaulted interior. Constructed during the reign of Rome's first emperor, Augustus, it burned down—and was rebuilt—twice, first in the reign of Domitian and then under Hadrian.

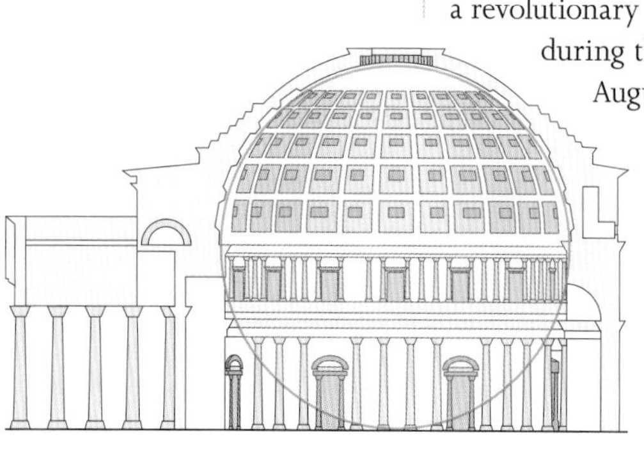

◁ **Precision engineering**
A sphere with the dome's diameter would fit perfectly inside the building's height and width, giving the design harmony despite its huge scale.

The Pantheon's size, architectural and engineering ambition, and interior of colored marble from across the empire, embody the achievements of imperial rule and the emperors' proximity to the gods.

Augustan origins

The Pantheon as it survives today was built by the emperor Hadrian between 118 and 125 CE, although it modestly preserves the name of its original builder, Marcus Vipsanius Agrippa, in the bronze inscription on the front porch. Agrippa was the son-in-law of Augustus, and built the first Pantheon in his honor between 27 and 25 BCE. The Pantheon's exact function

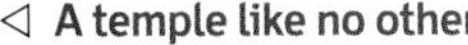

◁ **A temple like no other**
The Pantheon's porch, with 16 giant columns made from Egyptian and Greek granite, blocks the view of the dome. There were also originally colonnades on either side of the temple, so a Roman citizen approaching the front would not expect the circular and domed interior.

is unknown, although its name (from the Green *pan*, meaning "all," and *theōn*, meaning "of the gods") indicates a temple dedicated to all of Rome's deities. Agrippa reportedly offered to place a statue of Augustus inside the building alongside the effigies of the gods; the emperor, with typically conspicuous modesty, insisted that his statue should stand outside.

A great dome that defies gravity

Not much is known about the first two temples, but the surviving Hadrianic structure is an extremely impressive and original piece of architecture. Its dome marks the apogee of Roman concrete engineering, and the fusing of the conventional exterior porch with the vaulted interior space is a landmark in the history of architecture. The huge dome, with its receding rows of coffers, is cast in concrete that grows thinner the higher it reaches: it is 21 ft (6.4 m) at its base and 3 3/4 ft (1.2 m) at the top. This makes the dome both stable and relatively lightweight. In its engineering and execution, the dome owes more to bath house and palace architecture (see pp. 186–187) than to temple design. Until 1958, it was the largest concrete span in the world, measuring 145 3/4 ft (44.4 m) in diameter. As the dome is based on a perfect sphere, this is also the height of the building.

Unusually for a Roman temple, the interior of the Pantheon seems to have been intended to host large numbers of people (in Roman religious ceremonies worshippers usually gathered outside temples). Its marble floor is patterned with alternating squares and circles, and the walls at ground level are recessed with seven large, column-flanked alcoves that may have once held statues of the gods. Apart from through the doors, the only source of light is the circular hole, or oculus, cut into the dome. It allows sunshine (and rainfall) to flood in, the shafts of light moving atmospherically around the temple as the sun crosses the sky throughout the day.

Yet despite its apparent perfection, the Pantheon has its flaws. On the transitional block between the porch and the rotunda is a "false" pediment (triangular gable), aligned with a molding course around the outside of the building (see illustration below). This indicates the original planned height of the porch, which would have needed columns 50 ft (15.2 m) in height, rather than the 40 ft (12.2 m) columns that were actually used. This change forced the porch roof to sit lower down than intended, and has created several other small errors in the building's proportions—but nothing to spoil its beauty and overall symmetry.

The Pantheon underwent restoration work in the 3rd century CE under the Severan emperors, and in 609 it was turned into a church. This undoubtedly helped preserve the building, although the Eastern emperor Constans II removed its bronze roof tiles in 663, and Pope Urban VIII stripped out the porch's bronze roof trusses in 1626, melting down the metal to make cannon. The core of the building, however, is perfectly preserved and stands as one of the greatest expressions of Roman architectural prowess.

△ **Time capsule**
The Pantheon's patterned floor is original, as are the columns of Numidian yellow and Phrygian purple marble; the other interior decoration is mostly from later periods.

▽ **A slice of history**
This illustration shows how the porch, the transitional block, and the drum-like main building, or rotunda, are connected. It is also possible to see how the thick base of the dome bears the weight of the thinner vaulted ceiling that it supports.

The oculus is 27 ft (8.2 m) in diameter

Ornamental moulding course

"False" pediment indicating the intended height of the porch roof

Porch roof may have originally been covered in white marble tiles

> "... because of its **vaulted roof,** it resembles the **heavens.**"
>
> CASSIUS DIO, *ROMAN HISTORY*

Hadrian's Wall

Holding the boundaries of the empire

Hadrian's Wall is an impressive achievement both as a military fortification and as a work of engineering. It divided the Roman province of Britannia (England and Wales) from the peoples to the north, who resisted imperial occupation.

△ **A child's shoes**
This rare pair of shoes formed part of a hoard of 400 shoes found at Vindolanda. They would have fitted a child aged five or six.

The construction of Hadrian's Wall began in 122 CE on the orders of the emperor after whom it is named. It ran for 80 Roman miles (73 miles or 117 km), from Maia (modern Bowness-on-Solway) in the west to Segedunum (Wallsend) in the east. It featured a ditch 10 ft (3 m) deep, an open stretch of land, or berm, a stone-built wall that was 15 ft (4.6 m) high, and a protective earthwork called the *vallum*. There was also a service road, known as the Military Way.

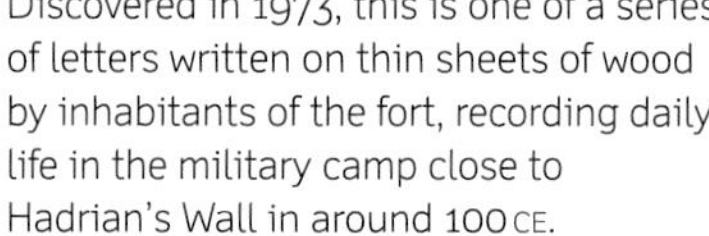

◁ **A Vindolanda Fort letter**
Discovered in 1973, this is one of a series of letters written on thin sheets of wood by inhabitants of the fort, recording daily life in the military camp close to Hadrian's Wall in around 100 CE.

As their name suggests, 80 small forts known as milecastles were built a mile apart along the wall, with two watchtowers between each. There were 17 large forts, too. Additional support forts along the wall included Arbeia, which guarded the port where men and supplies landed in Britannia, and Vindolanda (see pp. 258–259), whose construction actually predated Hadrian's Wall. The forts and milecastles had gates that allowed people to pass through the wall. Towns, or *vici*, grew up around the forts and were home to retired army men, traders, soldiers' families, food vendors, innkeepers, and sex workers, among others.

Life on the wall

Although small groups of soldiers staffed the milecastles, the majority of troops were based in the forts. Each of these complexes contained barracks, a grain store, a hospital, the commander's quarters, and a military headquarters. Forts were generally laid out in a roughly standardized pattern, but the precise configuration depended on each one's location and surrounding terrain. Most if not all of the soldiers at Hadrian's Wall were auxiliaries (non-Romans), such as Batavians from Germania, Dalmatians from the Adriatic coast region and Mauri from North Africa. In the 170s, the Iazyges people of Samartia, in modern Iran, sent 5,000 of their cavalrymen to serve at Hadrian's Wall after signing an agreement with the emperor Marcus Aurelius. Horse-mounted troops were an important element in the wall's defenses. Of the 1,500 or so men based at each of the forts, around two-thirds were cavalrymen; the rest were infantry.

The presence of so many auxiliary troops guarding the wall made the local area uniquely culturally diverse, and this was augmented by the families and dependents, including the enslaved people brought by senior Roman officers and officials. It appears that there was much social interaction between soldiers and the people who lived nearby. Lower-ranking officers could have relationships with locals and perhaps begin families; ordinary legionnaires did not

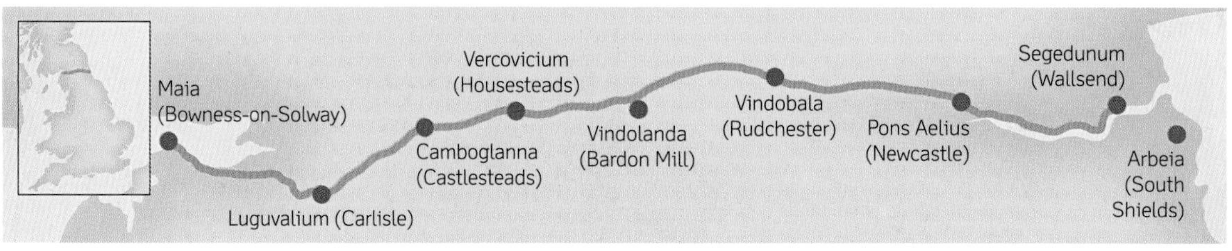

▷ **Defensive forts**
This map shows some of the main fortresses on or close to Hadrian's Wall, with the Roman name of each and the modern name of the site or the nearest settlement.

have the legal right to marry, but that did not stop them from forming more informal attachments. Archaeological finds of shoes, children's toys, jewelery, and other domestic artifacts attest to the depth and diversity of a place that was much more than a military encampment.

A fluid frontier

While the wall is an impressive structure, its precise purpose is not known. For all its watchtowers and forts, the many gates that pierced Hadrian's Wall made it a less-than-secure barrier. Its ultimate importance may have been more symbolic than strategic, as a highly visible monument to Roman power. Twenty years after Hadrian's Wall was built, work began on the Antonine Wall, 60 miles (100 km) further north, which was probably designed to hold back the Maetae and Caldones people who were raiding Roman territory. In the 160s, however, the emperor Marcus Aurelius moved his forces back to Hadrian's Wall, which became Britannia's official northern frontier. At this stage, the wall may have become more of a border control site, regulating human movement and trade. It did suffer periodic attacks, in 197 and 207, for example, but not on any major scale. The wall was seriously breached in 296, when a confederation of peoples called the Picts broke through and reached Deva (Chester), 150 miles (240 km) further south. The Romans' hold on Britannia was relaxing by then, and in the early 5th century Rome withdrew its legions for good. The wall was largely recycled to make local buildings, but enough of it remains today to stand as a lasting emblem of Rome's imperial reach.

▷ Horse and rider bronze brooch
This brooch from the 2nd century was found at the wall. It was probably once enameled in bright colors and worn as jewelery rather than used to fasten clothes.

△ A Roman milecastle
The remains of Milecastle 39 show the typical footprint of one of the wall's small forts. It is known today as Castle Nick, as it sits in a small gully, or "nick," in the hillside. It was occupied until the late 4th century.

The Art of Mosaics

Painting pictures with stone

Mosaics are patterns or pictures produced by setting tesserae (small pieces of stone, marble, tile, glass, or other material) into a mortar base. The technique was invented well before the Romans (in its earliest form, as simple patterns using pebbles found in the Near East in the 8th century BCE) but reached its height under the empire. The Romans innovated by extending the use of mosaic from floors to walls and ceiling vaults in both public buildings and residences. Skilled artisans executed ever more colorful and ambitious layouts that formed part of the overall decoration of a room; enslaved laborers would have cut the stones.

Roman mosaics were assembled in different ways. For example, *opus tessellatum* ("checkered work"), in common use by the 1st century BCE, involved setting small cubes of stone or marble in a bed of mortar to form patterns. *Opus vermiculatum* ("wormlike work") created more realistic pictures by fitting tiny stones so closely together that the results resembled paintings. Large set-pieces featuring a motif or picture panel, called *emblemata* ("emblems"), were created in a studio, then inserted as the centerpiece into a floor; a simpler, tessellated mosaic was then typically used to fill in the gaps around the main panel.

Traditions within Italy

Different areas of the empire favored different styles of mosaic. In Roman Italy, colorful floral designs and black-and-white geometric patterns were especially popular; the black-figure style—in which

△ **Geometric pattern**
This outstanding example of a geometric, *opus tessellatum* mosaic is from Conímbriga in Portugal, where many Roman floor mosaics in this style have been preserved. The centers of the diamonds are fully colored; squares surround a C-shape.

△ **Floral pattern**
Limestone and vitreous paste have been used to make up this intricate design from 1st-century CE Italy. The mosaic is an example of *opus vermiculatum* and features a variety of colored flowers, fruits, and foliage, including a group of acorns. The flowers are shown both in bud and in bloom.

△ **Head of Medusa**
Figures from mythology often featured in mosaics, such as in this 2nd-century CE bust of the Gorgon Medusa from Italy. The *emblematum* floor panel is surrounded by an elaborate circular geometric pattern, possibly suggesting a shield.

"How delightfully his **words fit together**, like all the **little tesserae** ..."

LUCILIUS, *SATIRES* FRAGMENT

black figures are represented against a plain white background—was also developed there. The simplicity of these designs meant that, even with a figurative mosaic, the main focus in a room could remain on the colored wall paintings.

The Roman provinces

In Rome's northern and western provinces, mosaics seem to have mainly consisted of black-and-white geometric patterns similar to those in Italy. When figures and detailed panels appear, they are balanced within the overall design scheme, rather than it having one dominant element. The eastern provinces appear to have favored scenes of figures surrounded by a border; over time, the figural scene became more important and the border thinner. These mosaics were often allegorical, with figures labeled to explain them. They might depict the seasons, months of the year, or even abstract philosophical ideas. Artists in the east also developed the rainbow style, with tesserae laid point to point rather than in rows, which created graded tones of color with a textile-like effect.

In Roman Africa, multicolored patterns seem to have been particularly popular, perhaps because colorful stones were easy to quarry locally. Mosaics from this region are also known for their figure scenes, often depicting episodes from daily life rather than mythology, including events in the amphitheater, such as gladiatorial shows and animal hunts.

△ **Tesserae**
The materials used in mosaics were called "tesserae" after the Latin word for "dice" or "cubes." They came in many shapes and sizes—the smallest were just millimeters wide.

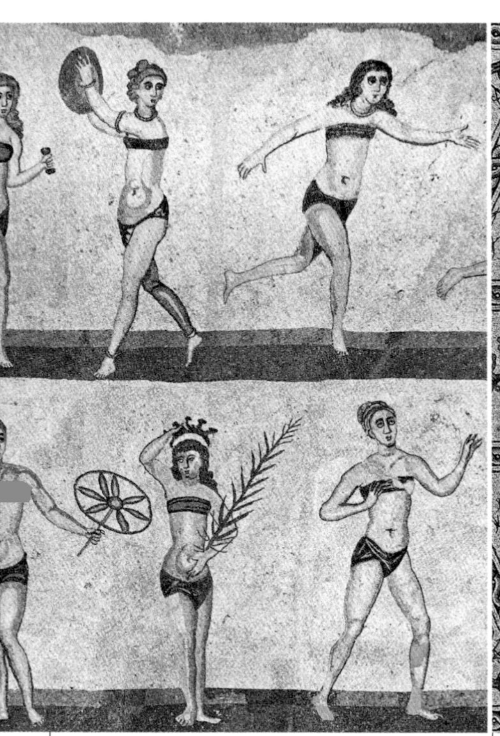

△ **Daily life**
Women engage in sports and exercise in this notable scene, capturing a different aspect of their lives. The 4th-century CE *opus vermiculatum* mosaic decorates the floor of a small room in the Villa Romana del Casale in Piazza Armerina, Sicily.

△ **Wildlife**
This well-preserved *opus vermiculatum* floor mosaic was laid around 300 CE in Lod, modern-day Israel. It features a range of animals, including, in the central panel, lions, an elephant, and a giraffe; surrounding them are birds, fish, a rabbit, and a deer, among others. The absence of humans in the design is unusual.

△ **Religious imagery**
As Christianity became the Roman state religion, mosaics began to depict religious imagery. This 5th-century example from a wall in the mausoleum of Galla Placidia in Ravenna, Italy, shows Jesus as the Good Shepherd among his flock.

Eastern Mediterranean banquet scene
This mosaic from the 3rd–4th centuries CE depicts a *convivium*, a grand but informal gathering where guests ate, drank, and enjoyed music and dancing displays. In this scene, the well-fed and suitably refreshed guests recline on a large, horseshoe-shaped couch, known as a *stibadium*, while servants attend to their needs. The relaxed format of the Roman *convivium* (literally, "living together") borrowed heavily from its Greek equivalent, the *symposium* ("drinking together"), but with one important difference: women were allowed to attend Roman *convivia*—even though this one is an all-male affair.

The Romans in Egypt

Interacting with an ancient culture

Egypt was an already ancient civilization when Roman rule was imposed upon the state in the last years of the 1st century BCE. For the next half century Rome's rulers worked hard to incorporate themselves into its ancient culture.

The last pharaoh of Egypt, Cleopatra VII, sided with Mark Antony in his civil war against Octavian. She died by suicide after the defeat at Actium in 31 BCE (see pp. 134–135), leaving Egypt under the personal control of Octavian. Four years later, he would become Augustus, Rome's first emperor, and Egypt would be one of his and his successors' most valuable possessions.

To ensure his position, Octavian murdered Caesarion, Cleopatra's teenage son fathered by Julius Caesar in 46 BCE. This ended the dynasty that had ruled Egypt since the 4th century BCE, when Alexander the Great captured Egypt and placed it under the command of his general, Ptolemy.

Egypt proved to be a productive province for Rome's emperors. The abundance of grain grown on the fertile land along the Nile solved the food crises created in the Early Imperial era by Rome's expanding population of hungry urban poor. Egypt was also the shortest trade route between the Mediterranean and India. Taxes on goods moving through the country raised huge sums.

◁ **Respecting local beliefs**
Carved reliefs inside this Egyptian temple in Philae, close to Aswan, portray the emperor Trajan as a pharaoh making offerings to the Egyptian gods Osiris, Isis, and Horus.

THE KANDAKES OF MEROË

The Kushite kingdom of Nubia, on Egypt's southern border, was a matrilineal society. Its queen mothers, or Kandakes, were powerful figures, especially when they acted as regents to a boy-king. In the late 1st century BCE the Kandake Amanirenas fought against Roman forces in Egypt with some success, albeit short-lived. Her war trophies included the famous bronze "Meroë Head" of Augustus, which was buried at a temple in celebration. This relief (right) shows a later Kandake named Amanitore.

Life in Roman Egypt

For millennia, Egypt had been a powerful empire—the Pyramids of Giza had been built almost 2,000 years before Rome was founded. The arrival of Alexander the Great changed the country's power dynamic. Alexander and Ptolemy were Macedonian Greeks, and for 300 years settlers from Greece, Asia Minor, and the islands of the Aegean came to Egypt, creating a cultural exchange that saw the two civilizations influence each other's way of life. This continued under Roman rule. In contrast to their ancestral practice of cremation, prominent Romans in Egypt followed the millennia-old Egyptian custom of mummification. However, they created a Romano-Egyptian fusion by including painted representations of themselves on their wooden funeral caskets, in line with Roman traditions of funerary portraiture. In religious practice, Romans across the empire, especially women and enslaved people, became adherents to the cult of Isis (see pp. 232–233), with its distinctively Egyptian rites and rituals.

The conquest of the territory fascinated Rome's elite, who for a time became captivated with all things Egyptian. Obelisks were imported to Rome's public spaces and Egyptian-style architecture and decoration were incorporated into new villas built for Rome's wealthier citizens. Egyptian and Egyptian-influenced jewelery also became popular.

▷ **Mummified man**
This casket shows a young man called Artemidorus, whose name is inscribed on the lid in Greek. Wealthy Romans and other settlers in Egypt took up the practice of mummification, personalizing the burial casket with a portrait of the deceased.

In Egypt, Rome's emperors positioned themselves as pharaohs, claiming that they were the inheritors of the country's ancient traditions. They adopted pharaonic titles and depicted themselves in the guise of god-kings on monuments throughout the territory. However, only a few Roman emperors ever visited the country, among them Augustus, Vespasian, and Hadrian. Instead, most emperors allowed Egypt's long-existing orders of important and influential priests to retain their roles, their temples, and their privileges in Egyptian life and society.

Roman rule and its challenges

In fact, Roman rule in Egypt was not challenged until the late 3rd century CE, and only then by an outsider, Queen Zenobia of Palmyra (see pp. 244–45). Her invasion of Egypt and much of the Middle East saw Palmyra annex great swathes of Roman territory. Egypt's new ruler did not last long, though. When Zenobia cut off Rome's grain supply, the emperor Aurelian acted swiftly. Within a year, the Palmyrenes had been defeated and Egypt and the other lost territories were back under Roman control. In 395 Egypt was incorporated into the Eastern Empire, and in the early 7th century it was conquered by the Sasanians in Persia.

Today, much is known about life in Roman Egypt thanks to the many papyri that were perfectly preserved under the sands of the Egyptian desert. They record everything from home cures for hangovers and eye cataracts to shopping lists and tax records.

▷ **Egyptian music-maker**
Used in rituals particular to female deities of the Egyptian pantheon such as Hathor and Isis, the *sistrum* was a handheld, rattle-like musical instrument of the percussion family.

> "On **piles of masonry Egyptian letters** still remained, embracing the tale of **old magnificence**."
>
> TACITUS ON EGYPTIAN THEBES

△ **Celebrating victory**
Augustus's Temple to Mars Ultor was one-and-a-half times bigger than the Temple of Venus Genetrix in Caesar's Forum. It was paved with yellow, black, and purple marble, and had a white marble exterior.

Shaping Rome's Heart

Rome's Imperial Forums

The Imperial Forums fundamentally defined how Roman citizens of the Imperial era went about their daily business. They created a lavish public space at the center of the city for urban communities and visitors to meet, work, and shop.

A forum was an open space or square for transacting public business in Roman towns. Forums were the focal point for political, legal, and commercial activity; they contained temples, a Senate house, colonnades, statues, and monuments. They also held basilicas containing law courts and public offices for civic and commercial business. The Roman Forum was the central model for forums throughout the empire.

◁ **Squares of the city**
Septimius Severus's *Forma Urbis*, a huge marble map of Rome from the 3rd century CE, was kept in the Forum of Vespasian. About a tenth of it survives, in small fragments.

Civic centers

The emperors Julius Caesar, Augustus, Vespasian, Nerva, and Trajan each constructed a forum to demonstrate their patronage of the city and make their mark on Rome's civic life. Known as the Imperial Forums, these squares were not built to follow a single plan, but together would form an impressive architectural complex. Altogether, the Imperial Forums are more than 656 ft (200 m) wide and more than 1,969 ft (600 m) long.

The Roman Forum was the first forum of Rome. In 54 BCE Julius Caesar began work on enlarging the original space into what would become known as the Forum of Caesar. This new forum, dedicated in 46 BCE, featured long colonnades with stores on the west side, and a new Curia Julia (a Senate House). A temple to Venus Genetrix formed the complex's central point, indicating Caesar's own alleged descent from the goddess. All later Imperial Forums would be built in alignment with Caesar's space. These new forums redirected political and commercial activity away from the original Forum, which became increasingly ceremonial in function throughout the Imperial era.

Constructing the complex

Subsequent emperors dedicated their forums to different themes. Augustus declared the building of his Forum after his victory at Philippi and it was dedicated in 2 CE. As it celebrated a military success, it featured a temple of Mars Ultor (the Avenger) adorned with many statues of Roman heroes and the Julian family, including Augustus himself in the center.

The Forum of Vespasian, dedicated in 75 CE, was also called the Forum of Peace for the temple to Peace along one side of the square, where spoils from the conquest of Jerusalem were kept. Nerva later built his forum, a monumental space featuring a temple to Minerva, along the Argiletum, the road that ran between the Forums of Augustus and Vespasian. The forum was dedicated in 97 CE.

The largest of the Imperial Forums, the Forum of Trajan, was completed in 113 CE, funded by the spoils of the emperor's successful Dacian campaign. Its notable features included a bronze equestrian statue of Trajan, the Basilica Ulpia on the north side, a six-level shopping complex (see pp. 176–177), a market hall, libraries, and Trajan's Column (see pp. 214–215). Hadrian later added a temple there to the Deified Trajan.

△ **Imperial monument**
The column towered over the other buildings in Trajan's Forum, a striking presence in white Italian marble topped by a bronze statue of Trajan. Trajan's ashes were interred in the column's base in 117.

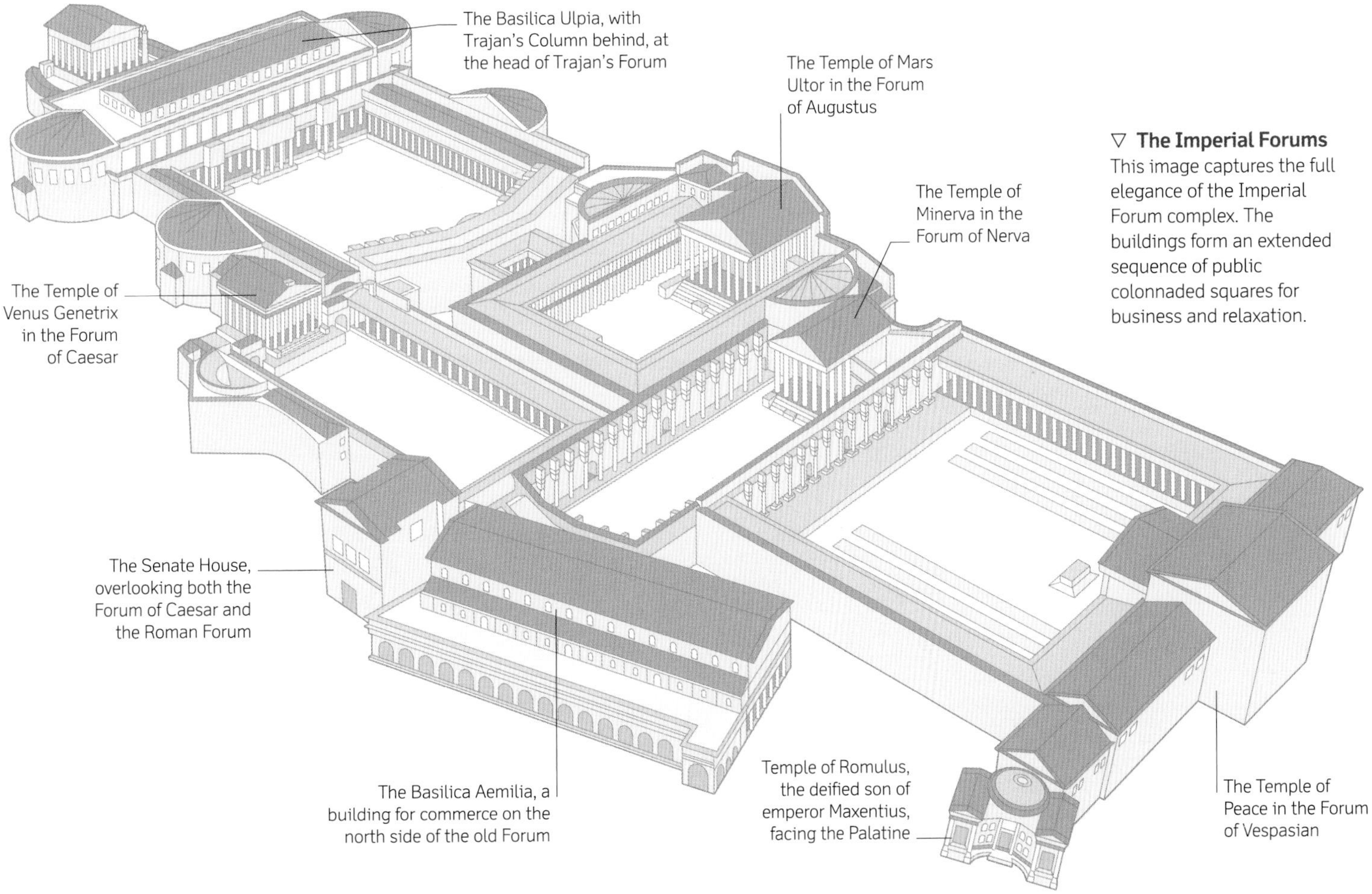

The Basilica Ulpia, with Trajan's Column behind, at the head of Trajan's Forum

The Temple of Mars Ultor in the Forum of Augustus

The Temple of Minerva in the Forum of Nerva

The Temple of Venus Genetrix in the Forum of Caesar

The Senate House, overlooking both the Forum of Caesar and the Roman Forum

The Basilica Aemilia, a building for commerce on the north side of the old Forum

Temple of Romulus, the deified son of emperor Maxentius, facing the Palatine

The Temple of Peace in the Forum of Vespasian

▽ **The Imperial Forums**
This image captures the full elegance of the Imperial Forum complex. The buildings form an extended sequence of public colonnaded squares for business and relaxation.

Warships depicted are biremes with two tiers of oars

△ **The hero**
Trajan himself appears 59 times on the column, in scenes of military leadership, religious sacrifice, and speech-making. Here he symbolically steers a troopship.

Roman soldiers in the *testudo* ("tortoise") formation

Construction and engineering work being done by Roman soldiers

Dacians carry their "dragon" ensign, while retreating from Romans

Roman soldier sets fire to Dacian building

Trajan and his officers greet troops

▷ **Architectural feat**
Trajan's Column is formed by a stack of huge marble blocks. A spiral staircase runs up the inside, lit by slit windows that punctuate the carving on the outer face.

"And he set up in the **Forum** an **enormous column** to serve at once as a **monument to himself** and as a **memorial** of the **work** in the Forum."

CASSIUS DIO, *ROMAN HISTORY*

Trajan's Column

A tribute to the emperor and his soldiers

Trajan's Column was erected in 113 CE to celebrate the emperor Trajan's victories in Dacia (in modern-day Romania) and still stands in Rome today. It was built from 29 huge, skillfully carved blocks of white Italian marble and reaches a height of 124 ft (38 m).

Scenes of triumph

Trajan's Column is most famous for its spiral frieze showing scenes from the emperor's campaigns in Dacia in 102–103 and 105–106. While freestanding victory columns were traditional monuments in Rome, and painted scenes of battles were familiar in triumphal victory processions, this large-scale, continuous spiral narrative of around 656 ft (200 m) in length seems to have been something new. The column's base is covered with fine carvings of captured arms, and a bronze statue of the emperor once stood on top of it, above the viewing platform.

The column was part of a much larger victory complex, Trajan's Forum, which included a great open colonnaded square, a basilica, libraries, and a temple (see pp. 212–213). At the base of the column is an inscription—one of the finest examples of Roman letter-cutting. This dedication explains that the column was built to show the height of the hill that was cut away to make space for the Forum: "... to demonstrate of what great height the hill was ... that was removed for such great works."

The Roman Empire reached its largest extent under Trajan, who behaved courteously toward the Senate, undertook several magnificent building projects, and earned the title "Best of Emperors." He was also a great general, whose early career was spent with the army. As well as conquering Dacia, he expanded the empire in the east, annexing Nabataea (in Arabia) as a province, and campaigned against the Parthians in Mesopotamia. The profits of his Dacian campaigns, which brought the region's gold mines into the Roman Empire, paid for his huge Forum, which was decorated with statues of Dacian captives. Trajan's ashes were buried at the foot of the column, and the complex took on a commemorative aspect.

Historical record

The column's frieze, which was once colorfully painted, has become an important source for military historians: it shows details of Roman arms, equipment, fortifications, construction, ships, siege tactics, and maneuvers. Scenes of actual fighting take up relatively little space—the artist focused instead on constructing a narrative of the campaigns in their entirety, including engineering and logistical activity, speech-making, religious sacrifice, and transportation. Trajan himself appears frequently throughout, making clear his personal role in the empire's triumphs.

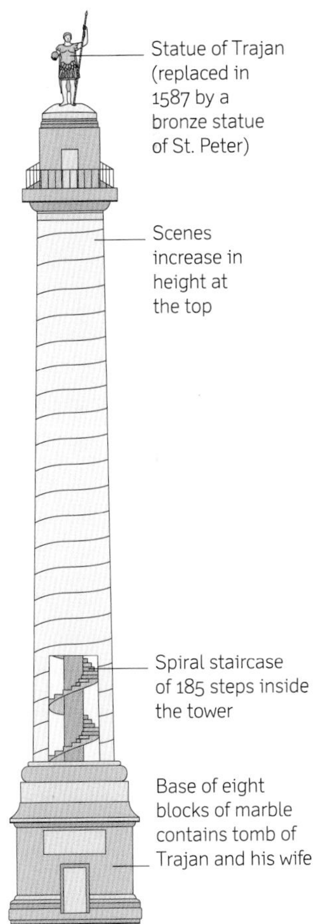

△ **A monument to victory** Trajan's Column stood at one end of a huge forum. Its internal staircase led to a platform offering views over the entire complex.

▷ **Plan of Portus and Ostia**
Portus offered a sheltered anchorage and dedicated facilities for unloading, storage, and customs. It was connected to Ostia by canals and the Tiber River, about 18 miles (30 km) downstream from Rome. The river and excavated land formed an artificial island known as Isola Sacra (Holy Isle).

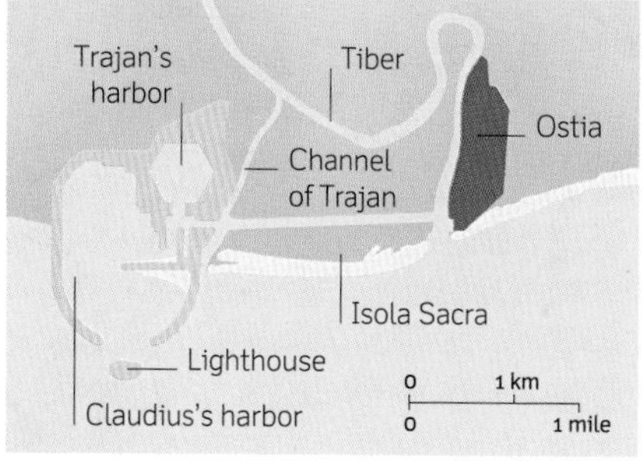

◁ **Bronze coin**
This *sestertius* commemorates the completion of Trajan's addition to Portus in 113 CE. One side shows an aerial view of the harbor with three anchored ships and colonnaded buildings.

Possibly the imperial palace complex

Ships in the Claudian outer basin

Portus

A port fit for an empire

Portus was Rome's great imperial port, connecting the city to its Mediterranean provinces and the wider empire. Emperor Claudius built the first artificial harbor at Portus in 64 CE, placing an enormous lighthouse at the entrance. Trajan added to the port with a large hexagonal basin, which still exists today as an artificial lake.

The port was the primary hub for importing huge quantities of staple foods and luxury goods for Rome's burgeoning population, which had reached one million people by the 2nd century. Grain from Egypt and Sicily, olive oil from Spain and North Africa, and supplies of every sort arrived by sea.

Portus replaced Rome's first sea harbor, the nearby Ostia. Rome's growth had left Ostia's shallow waters unable to cope with the larger grain ships that were now required. Some of these had begun to dock at Puteoli near Naples, before commencing a long, second journey over land and river to the capital. The construction of Portus enabled the grain fleet to anchor safely close to Rome, securing its vital food supply.

A WORKING **HARBOR**

At its height, Portus was a place of bustle, arrival, and departure. This relief from the late 2nd century CE shows a ship arriving after a trading voyage. The multistory lighthouse with its beacon of flame, a symbol of safe arrival, welcomes the ship into harbor. The scene is crowded with the gods who oversaw a safe voyage, statues, people, and a triumphal arch. On the right, the ship (or a sister vessel) is being unloaded by dock porters.

TORLONIA RELIEF DEPICTING PORTUS

◁ **Trajan's harbor**
The hexagonal inner basin of Trajan's harbor was surrounded by wharves, warehouses, and customs buildings. It could hold approximately 200 ships at one time.

The Channel of Trajan, connecting Portus to the Tiber River

Warehouses, ship sheds, and customs buildings

Trajanic inner hexagonal basin

Lighthouse, leading from the outer to inner basin

△ **Original columns**
These deliberately rough-surfaced stone columns from Portus are typical of the architectural style of the emperor Claudius. Part of a portico, the columns were later built into a warehouse.

The *darsena* ("inner harbor"), possibly for cargo or military ships

Adorning the Empire

Craft, elegance, and ostentation

Jewelery allowed Romans to display their wealth and express their personal identities. Skilled artisans produced jewelery in a range of different materials, from the luxurious to the everyday, so men and women from every social class could afford to adorn themselves.

◁ Gold snake ring
The snake form of this 1st-century CE ring was a popular one that was also used for bracelets. Snakes symbolized fertility and possibly also protection from evil.

Wheel-shaped links for the clasp symbolize the sun

△ Gold necklace with pendant
The style of this necklace with crescent pendant, 1st–3rd century CE, was fashionable across the empire: similar designs were found in Britain and appear in Roman burial portraits (see p. 269) from Egypt.

Crescent pendant symbolizes the moon

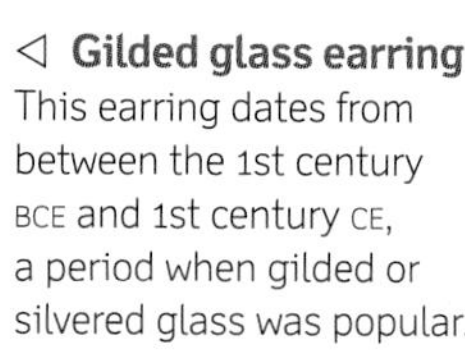

◁ Gilded glass earring
This earring dates from between the 1st century BCE and 1st century CE, a period when gilded or silvered glass was popular.

△ Disc brooch
This brooch, c. 100–300 CE, is decorated with millefiori (flower-patterned) enamel; glass rods of various colors have been fused together, cut into cross-sections, and then attached to a metal base.

△ Bronze bracelet
This 1st–3rd-century CE bracelet would have been a more affordable adornment; the bronze has been twisted into a tight spiral.

△ Gold bracelet with gemstones
Large emeralds alternate with sapphires on this late 4th-century BCE bracelet, while filigree scrollwork and vine leaves cover the band. The empty settings would have once been filled with pearls.

Curled crescent motif

▷ Gold and chalcedony earrings
These 3rd-century CE earrings feature a double pendant and chalcedony, a semiprecious stone that was often used for beadwork.

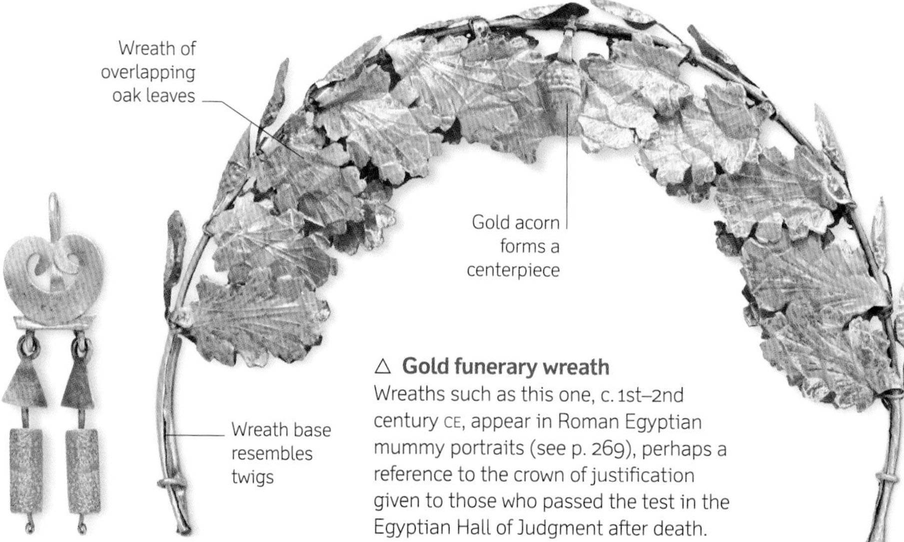

△ Gold funerary wreath
Wreaths such as this one, c. 1st–2nd century CE, appear in Roman Egyptian mummy portraits (see p. 269), perhaps a reference to the crown of justification given to those who passed the test in the Egyptian Hall of Judgment after death.

◁ Gold pin with dove
This pin may have fixed hairstyles in place or held clothes together at the shoulder. The dove's head and back are dotted with tiny granules of gold.

△ Gold triple-finger ring
This extravagant statement piece from the 3rd or 4th century CE features pearls and glass imitation gems. The green bead is a modern replacement. This style was popular in the eastern part of the Roman Empire.

▷ Gold and emerald necklace
Emerald beads alternate with gold links in this necklace from the 2nd or 3rd century CE. This style was fashionable throughout the empire between the 1st and 4th centuries CE.

△ Gold bracelet
The band of this bracelet, late 4th century CE, is covered with a fine scrollwork of spirals, inside of which are vine and ivy leaves, fruit, and animals.

◁ Gold ring with intaglio
This intaglio dates from the 2nd or 3rd century CE and shows a woman's head and shoulders. It may be carved from glass or carnelian, a semiprecious stone.

△ Gold body chain
This chain from the 3rd or 4th century CE looped around the wearer's shoulders and chest, linking to feature plaques at the front and back of the body to form an X-shape.

▷ Gold, amethyst, and emerald necklace
Egg-shape amethysts alternate with box settings containing tiny emeralds on this 3rd-century CE necklace. Other similar necklaces survive from this period.

△ Gold crescent earrings
These 1st-century CE gold earrings measure just $\frac{3}{4}$in (2cm) across and feature detailing of small balls running along their edges.

◁ Intaglio of Julia Domna
This intricate portrait, c. 200–210 CE, was carved onto a beryl gem. Julia Domna came from Syria and was the wife of the emperor Septimius Severus.

Traversing the Empire

Travel, transportation, and trade

Roman leaders understood that the ability to move troops quickly was necessary to conquer and control territory. As the empire expanded, its network of road and sea routes also offered more opportunity for civilian travel.

△ **Camel transportation**
Camels were frequently used for transporting people and baggage; this ancient sculptural relief shows a camel with its driver.

Roman engineers pushed the boundaries of road-building technology, using lime mortar and cambered, compacted stone surfaces to resist wear and promote drainage, allowing for more traffic, year round. Most notably, they constructed highways directly through the landscape between key settlements. Begun in 312 BCE, the Appian Way was the first major road, built from Rome to Capua in Campania for military purposes (see pp. 42–43), then extended as Rome conquered more of southern Italy. By 200 CE, around 50,000 miles (80,000 km) of highways crossed the empire.

Travel opportunities

These roads facilitated travel for state officials, as well as communication between them—the emperor Augustus established the *cursus publicus*, an official system of couriers using fresh horses stationed at regular intervals along key routes. Travel for other reasons also became more common, especially among the wealthy; for example, the 1st-century CE senator and philosopher Seneca moved frequently between Rome and his estate in Córdoba, in modern Spain, and many elite young men visited centers of learning, such as Athens, to further their education.

Wealthy travelers brought an entourage of enslaved attendants; women, in particular, used a *carpentum*, a comfortable, four-wheeled, covered wooden carriage drawn by several horses. (Married women and widows had more leeway for travel than unmarried women.)

△ **Roman coach**
Traveling carriages, like this one from a 1st- or 2nd-century CE relief in Virunum, in modern Austria, made long journeys more comfortable for those who could afford them.

For speedier journeys, *cisia* were light, two-wheeled carriages for two, pulled by mules; Cicero noted that one such vehicle covered 56 miles in ten hours. One form of public transit was the *raeda*, a carriage with benches, while heavy loads were often transported on a slow-moving *plaustrum*, a wooden wagon dragged by oxen—or, in the east, camels. The Imperial era also saw the development of roadside stables and hostels.

Moving heavy goods, such as marble, was easier by sea, and port cities became transportation hubs with wharves, warehouses, and trading districts (see pp. 216–217). A regular grain supply was critical for feeding Rome's populace, and much of this came by sail from Egypt, North Africa, and Sicily. However, seaways were often closed in winter due to the dangers from bad weather. Rivers such as the Nile, Rhine, and Tiber were often used to transport cargo inland, with river craft being rowed, paddled, sailed, or towed by men or animals. Most passengers would have boarded a merchant vessel and slept on deck.

▽ **Lively ancient port**
This glorious mosaic shows Kenchreai, the eastern harbor of Corinth (in Greece) flourishing during the Roman period. It is made of vitreous paste, an opaque colored glass.

"I came in a **closed carriage,** shut up on all sides, as if in **my bedroom.**"

PLINY, *LETTERS*

△ **Rome's main road**
The Appian Way ultimately linked Rome to sea ports in the south of Italy, most notably Brundisium (modern-day Brindisi), which served as the main gateway for travel to Greece and the eastern Mediterranean.

Marcus Aurelius

The philosopher general

Marcus Aurelius provided wise leadership to an empire ravaged by plague and invasions. He is also the only emperor whose words survive in a book rather than an inscription.

△ **Joint rulers**
To commemorate their shared reign, Marcus Aurelius and Lucius Verus are shown clasping hands on this gold *aureus*. Marcus, on the right, wears a laurel wreath.

Marcus Aurelius was born Marcus Annius Verus. His father, Marcus Annius Verus III, died when Marcus was three. In 138 CE, the emperor Hadrian appointed Antoninus Pius, Marcus's uncle, as his heir, specifying that Antoninus adopt Marcus and Lucius Commodus, Hadrian's adopted grandson. Marcus became quaestor when he was named Antoninus's heir in 139 and was consul in 140 and 145. He married his uncle's daughter, Faustina the Younger, in 145. To mark the birth of their first child in 147, Antoninus gave Marcus the powers of an emperor and awarded Faustina the title *augusta*. When Antoninus died in 161, Marcus refused to become emperor unless Lucius was given identical powers. The Senate agreed to his demand and for the first time Rome had co-emperors. Lucius changed his name to Lucius Verus, and Marcus took the name Marcus Aurelius.

Protecting the empire

The new emperors faced war against the Parthians in Mesopotamia in 162. Lucius went to the front line, while Marcus stayed in Rome. The Romans retook Armenia and extended the empire to Dura (in Syria). When this campaign weakened the German border, the Langobardi and Obii peoples invaded the Roman province of Pannonia (in Hungary and Austria) in 166–167, starting the Marcomannic Wars, which would last until 180. The conflict was made worse by the Antonine Plague, which took Lucius's life and spread across the empire, killing as much as one-quarter of its population.

The Roman governor of Syria, Avidius Cassius, revolted against Marcus in 175, but was soon killed. Having toured the eastern provinces to reinforce his position, Marcus returned to Rome in 176 and proclaimed his son Commodus co-ruler. Unrest on the Danube River took Marcus back to the front line in 178. He fell ill just before a campaign in 180, and died in Pannonia.

In his own words

Unusually, some of Marcus's own writing survives. He is best known for his *Meditations*, a series of reflections on his life and experiences from the perspective of Stoic philosophy (see pp. 272–273). They capture Marcus's inner dialogue with himself and his attempts to transform his own moral position. We do not know how this set of private notes survived, but they give a rare insight into the mind of the most powerful man in the empire.

◁ **Bust of Faustina**
Faustina the Younger (c. 130–175) traveled with Marcus Aurelius on his campaigns and was highly respected by the Roman army. He gave her the title of "Mother of the Camps."

- **121** Marcus born to Marcus Annius Verus and Domitia Calvilla
- **145** Marcus marries his cousin, Faustina
- **161** Marcus becomes joint emperor with Lucius Verus on death of Antoninus Pius
- **162–166** The Parthian war leads to expansion of Roman borders to Dura
- **166** The Antonine Plague breaks out in Rome, lasting until 180
- **166–167** The first invasions of the Marcomannic Wars
- **176** Commodus, Marcus's son, is proclaimed joint emperor
- **180** Marcus Aurelius dies on campaign at Sirmium in Pannonia

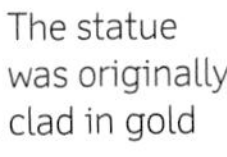

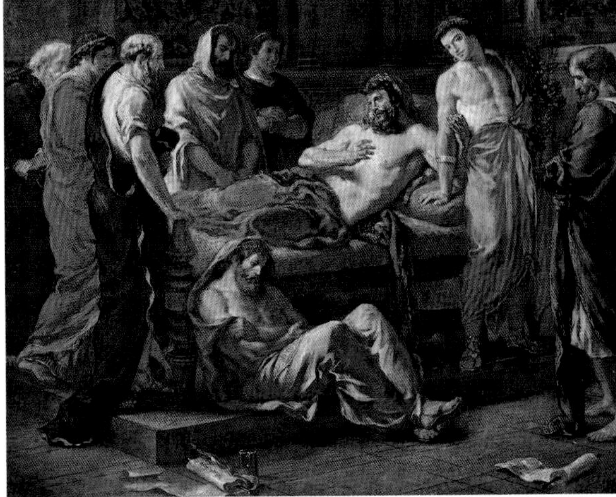

△ **Marcus Aurelius's final moments**
In Eugène Delacroix's *Last Words of the Emperor Marcus Aurelius* (1844), Marcus holds on to his son Commodus. According to the historian Cassius Dio, his last words were, "Go to the rising sun; I am already setting."

◁ **Equestrian statue of Marcus Aurelius**
This bronze statue was probably erected in 176 to mark Marcus's triumph over the Germanic tribes in the Marcomannic Wars, along with other monuments including a column covered with sculpture. It could also have been put up after his death as a civic commemoration.

"In a little while **you will be nothing** and **nowhere,** like Hadrian and Augustus."

MARCUS AURELIUS, *MEDITATIONS*

◁ **Ornamental vessel**
Resembling a soldier's water canteen, this bronze flask dates from the 2nd century CE and is embellished with blue, red, and orange enamel. It was found among grave goods in a Roman cavalry officer's tomb in present-day Croatia.

5

An Empire in Transition

192–395 CE

Crisis and Christianity

According to the senator and historian Cassius Dio, the Roman Empire changed after the death of Marcus Aurelius in 180 CE. At that moment, he wrote, it was transformed from a kingdom of gold to one of iron and rust. Although the philosopher-emperor's reign had been beset by difficulties, including war, uprisings, plague, and economic crises, things grew more unsettled after his death. Only sweeping changes would restore a semblance of order to the empire.

Emperors in times of crisis

What caused the change from gold to rust? According to Dio, it was because Marcus's son could not live up to his father's illustrious reputation. The reign of Commodus was marked by megalomania, cruelty, and erratic behavior—the emperor even fought in the arena as a gladiator.

After Commodus was murdered, there were four years of bloody civil war. The eventual winner, Septimius Severus, attempted to establish a dynasty and presented himself as an emperor in the style of Augustus and Marcus Aurelius. He came from the wealthy port city of Lepcis Magna (see pp. 242–243), in present-day Libya, making him Rome's first African emperor.

There would be many more non-Italian emperors throughout this period. Philip the Arab, for example, was from Syria, while several came from Illyria, including Aurelian, Diocletian, and Constantine. A good number of these men only became emperor because of the difficulties in which the empire found itself throughout most of this period. As enemies massed on the northern frontiers and the Sasanian Empire challenged Roman power in the east, the state looked increasingly to strong men who would save it. These "soldier-emperors," the first of whom was Maximinus Thrax in 235, often came from lowly backgrounds but were popular because of their military prowess. Few of them survived for very long, as the many crises of the 3rd century claimed emperor after emperor in quick succession.

A new world

More lasting change was needed. After he came to power in 284, Diocletian instituted wide-ranging reforms to strengthen the state. The Tetrarchy divided the empire between four rulers, each of them able to mobilize against Rome's enemies. It was a short-lived measure, but one that would be used again. In 395, the emperor Theodosius permanently divided the empire between the West, governed from Rome, and the East, ruled by the new city of Constantinople.

By this time, another profound development was transforming the empire. Roman religion had always been fluid, and new gods from the east, such as Sol, Serapis, and Mithras, had long since found a home in the empire's diverse pantheon. Christianity, however, had been less welcome. Its popularity with women and the enslaved in particular, and its followers' belief in only one true God, meant it was for a long time viewed as a destabilizing force, and its adherents persecuted. This changed in 312, with Constantine's vision of a fiery cross at the Battle of the Milvian Bridge. From this point, a Christian empire would emerge, and everything—art, culture, politics, and society—would change forever.

◁ **Fragment of a sarcophagus with a seated figure**

192 Commodus is assassinated. The Praetorian Guard auction the imperial throne to the highest bidder, Pertinax

212 The *Constitutio Antoniniana* grants citizenship to all free males in the empire

218 Death of Macrinus, the first emperor never to visit Rome during their reign

235 Maximinus Thrax becomes the first "soldier-emperor"

247 The *Ludi Saeculares* games are held to celebrate Rome's 1,000th anniversary

286 Diocletian divides responsibility for the empire between himself in the east and Maximian in the west

1 Remains of the Roman fort at Eboracum (York)

2 Sirmium, birthplace of ten emperors

3 The Roman citadel in Edessa

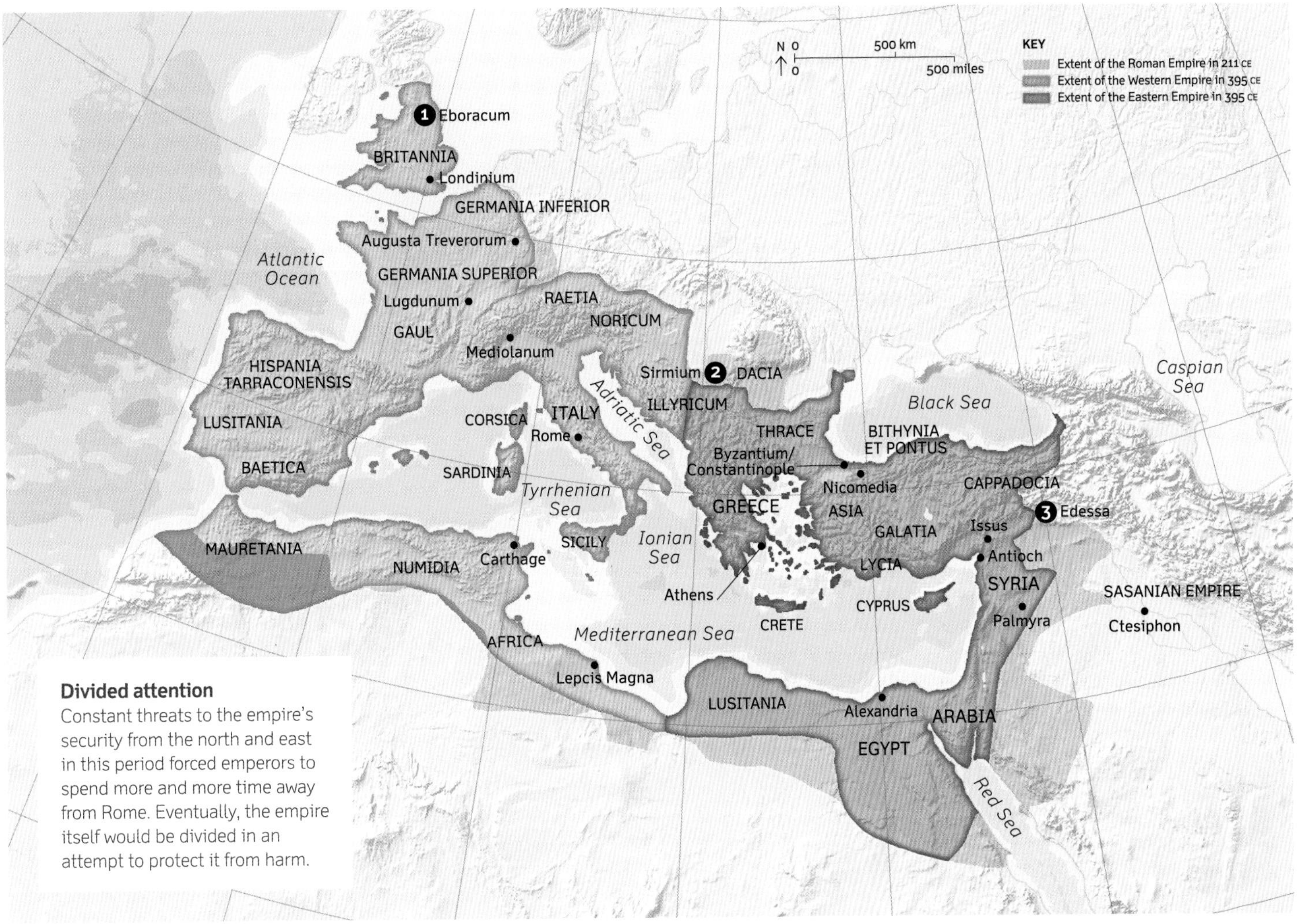

Divided attention
Constant threats to the empire's security from the north and east in this period forced emperors to spend more and more time away from Rome. Eventually, the empire itself would be divided in an attempt to protect it from harm.

306 Constantine's troops proclaim him emperor at Eboracum (York), in Britannia

313 Constantine and Licinius issue the Edict of Milan, giving Christians freedom of worship

330 Constantine refounds the city of Byzantium as Constantinople. The empire has a new capital

361 New emperor Julian the Apostate promotes traditional beliefs over Christianity

376 Goths fleeing the Huns cross the Danube into the empire

378 Emperor Valens is killed by Goths at the Battle of Adrianople

380 Christianity becomes the state religion after Theodosius issues the Edict of Thessalonica

395 The empire is permanently divided between east and west

The Praetorian Guard

Imperial bodyguards and political power brokers

This elite unit acted as the emperor's personal bodyguard for almost 300 years. Over time, the Praetorians became key figures in imperial politics. Winning their support could make—or break—a man's ambition to be emperor.

In the Republican era, the Praetorians had been a small escort of soldiers whose job was to protect military commanders on campaign. They were known as the *cohors praetoria*, after the commander's tent they guarded (the *praetorium*).

In 27 BCE Augustus reorganized the Praetorians into nine cohorts, around 4,500 men, whose role was to protect the emperor and his family (a cohort was usually 500 men, with 10 cohorts comprising a legion). Praetorians were awarded higher pay and enjoyed better conditions of service than regular soldiers. They were led by two Praetorian prefects, answerable only to the emperor.

Prefects and emperors

The Praetorians became highly influential because of their proximity to the emperor. They helped to make new emperors and assassinated several of those who lost their support. One of the most notorious Praetorian prefects was Lucius Aelius Seianus, known as Sejanus. As prefect under Tiberius, he effectively ruled Rome once the emperor had left the city after 26 CE to live on the island of Capri. Sejanus used his position to murder opponents, grow rich, and ultimately try to seize the imperial throne. His plot was thwarted and Sejanus was executed in 31 CE, but this was a sign of things to come; the balance of power between the Praetorian Guard and the emperor had shifted.

In 41 CE, the emperor Caligula was assassinated in a Praetorian-led conspiracy and his uncle, Claudius, was only able to succeed him after offering the supposedly trustworthy imperial cohort of bodyguards a large cash bonus, known as a donative. From then on, the Praetorians expected to be richly rewarded for their loyalty.

▽ **Praetorian *phalera***
Phalerae were sculpted bronze disks awarded as military honors. They were worn on uniforms or affixed to a legion's standard. This one, from c. 215 showing the emperor Caracalla, is from the Castra Praetoria.

◁ **Career opportunities**
Being a Praetorian offered lower-status men the chance to become influential. When the Praetorian prefect Macrinus seized power in 215, he became the first emperor from the non-senatorial equestrian class.

An auction for the empire

In 193 the Praetorians murdered the emperor Pertinax, who had proved to be less generous with his cash handouts than his predecessor, Commodus. According to the historian Cassius Dio, two senators (Titus Sulpicianus and Didius Julianus) became involved in what was essentially a bidding war with the Praetorian Guard in order to buy imperial power, with Didius Julianus emerging victorious. His reign was short-lived, however, and he was killed later in 193 and succeeded by the general Septimius Severus.

CASTRA **PRAETORIA**

According to the Roman historian Tacitus, it was Sejanus who built the first permanent barracks for the Praetorian Guard, in 23 CE. As the force's power base, it was where they proclaimed Claudius emperor in 41 CE, and it was also the site of Didius Julianus's imperial "auction" in 193. In 222, the teenage emperor Elagabalus was murdered there by disaffected Praetorian troops.

The camp (below) was later incorporated into the defensive walls around Rome erected by the emperor Aurelian, and the ruins of the Castra Praetoria still exist at its site to the northeast of Rome's city center.

The new ruler quickly replaced the Praetorians with loyalists from his Pannonian legions, ensuring he was able to reign for another 18 years.

But the Praetorians remained a significant force and, on at least one occasion, a prefect used his position to make himself emperor. The force's end came in 312, when the emperor Constantine disbanded the Praetorian Guard for good.

"There was **more courage** in **bearing trouble** than in **escaping** from it."

PLOTIUS FIRMUS, A PRAETORIAN, QUOTED BY TACITUS IN *THE HISTORIES*

An *aquila* standard was the symbol of a Roman legion and depicted an eagle grasping Jupiter's thunderbolt

Praetorians wore Greek-style, or Attic, helmets. Ceremonial helmets were decorated with carvings and designs, as here

The oval shields suggest these are guards in ceremonial armor; their shields were usually rectangular

◁ **Praetorian Guards**
This relief may come from a lost Arch of Claudius, built around 51 CE. Claudius owed his position as emperor to the Praetorians, which could explain why he included them on one of his public monuments.

▷ **Family gathering**
The Severan Tondo is one of the few surviving examples of wooden panel painting from antiquity. Measuring 12 in (30.5 cm) in diameter, the small artifact surfaced in mysterious circumstances in the early 20th century and is now kept in Berlin's Altes Museum.

> "**Mother** that didst bear me, **help!** I am being **murdered**."
>
> GETA TO JULIA DOMNA, IN CASSIUS DIO'S *ROMAN HISTORY*

The ivory shaft of the *sceptrum augusti*

The Severan Tondo

The changing face of imperial portraiture

A family portrait executed onto a wooden panel, the Severan Tondo is the only surviving painting of an imperial family. Most historians agree it shows the emperor Septimius Severus with his wife, Julia Domna, and their sons, the future emperors Caracalla and his younger brother Geta. It was painted around 200 CE, probably in Egypt to celebrate an imperial visit to the province, and is similar in style and execution to the burial casket portraits produced in the oasis town of Fayum (see pp. 210–211). It was rendered in tempera—a form of paint blended with egg yolk to produce a glossy and long-lasting finish.

The Severan Tondo is a work of striking naturalism. The emperor is shown with tousled hair and a graying, unkempt beard—unlike the heroic, godlike approach of earlier imperial sculpture and friezes, such as the *Augustus of Prima Porta* (see pp. 138–139). Notably, his skin is darker than that of the other figures. Some scholars interpret this as representing his North African heritage, as Septimius was born in Lepcis Magna, in modern-day Libya (see pp. 242–243). It was also usual to portray men as darker skinned than women and children, to emphasize their proficiency in outdoor activities like farming and soldiering. Julia Domna, from the province of Syria, wears pearl earrings and a matching necklace, and her hair is styled in the crimped "eastern" fashion that she helped make popular in Rome. Only the face of one boy, probably Caracalla, is visible.

The three male figures are crowned with gold wreaths studded with precious stones and wear white robes edged in the *alba triumphalis*, the imperial border of purple and gold. Julia Domna also wears a purple and gold garment. Each male carries a *sceptrum augusti*, the ivory scepter surmounted by a golden eagle that represented imperial power and—in this instance—dynastic continuity. The eagles are not visible: the painting was originally square and these details were lost when the tondo (from the Italian *rotondo*, meaning "round") was at some point reshaped into a circle.

Sibling rivalry

The tondo is not perfectly preserved and the most noticeable area of damage is to the face of the figure identified as Geta. This is not ordinary wear and tear. When Septimius Severus died in early 211, his feuding sons succeeded him as joint emperors. In the power struggle that ensued, Caracalla had Geta murdered in December of that year—and then set about erasing him from history. In a practice known as *damnatio memoriae* ("condemnation of memory"), Geta's name and image were removed from every public statue, monument, document, and coin in the empire. He was not the first nor last Roman, nor indeed emperor, to suffer this fate: Caligula, Nero, Commodus, Elagabalus, and Diocletian were similarly condemned, among many others.

Roman Cults

Foreign gods and alternative forms of worship

A variety of cult practices existed alongside traditional Roman religious beliefs (see pp. 32–33). These included the veneration of Bacchus, Isis, Jupiter Dolichenus, Serapis, and Mithras—all deities "imported" from abroad. The worship of these gods and goddesses in Rome oscillated between being permitted, tolerated, and banned. Judaism and Christianity were long perceived as cultic by the Romans, until the latter was adopted as the official state religion in 380 (see pp. 262–263).

The promise of a new life

Cults were often popular among women, enslaved people, and soldiers, because they offered something that Roman religion did not: the hope of salvation after death. The cults tended to be elective, too, with members choosing whether or not to join—and to undergo their sometimes bizarre initiation rituals. While some of these cults existed under the Republic, they proliferated under the empire. Many had foreign origins, and soldiers in particular helped spread belief in gods of eastern origin, such as Mithras and Jupiter Dolichenus, across the breadth of the empire.

"Dangerous" cults

Many cults were viewed with suspicion because they espoused monotheism, the worship of only one god, in opposition to Rome's polytheistic worship of many gods. Those who refused to worship the pantheon of Roman gods were often ostracized and even punished.

△ **Bacchus**
Garlanded with ivy, Bacchus sits astride a panther on this sarcophagus carving. To the left is Pan, the half-goat god. Bacchus was the Roman counterpart of the Greek deity Dionysus. In Roman art, Bacchus is usually shown as a youthful, often cherubic, figure.

△ **Isis**
Communal sacrifices to Isis are being performed in this fresco from Herculaneum. The Isis cult embraced Egyptian symbolism, such as sphinxes, ibises, and the sistrum (a rattle-like instrument). Worship of the goddess, known as Aset in her native Egypt (Isis is the Greek version of her name) reached as far as Britain.

△ **Jupiter Dolichenus**
Little is known of this mystery cult, imported from Doliche in Türkiye. Long-haired and bearded, Jupiter Dolichenus is here seen in full armor, reflecting his popularity among Rome's legionnaires as a martial, conquering god.

> "He **set me** before the goddess's feet and gave me **secret instructions**."
>
> APULEIUS, DESCRIBING AN INITIATION INTO THE RITES OF ISIS

Cults were also considered dangerous because they were secretive, or thought to promote loose morals. In 186 BCE, the worship of Bacchus, the god of wine and intoxication, was banned, with many adherents put to death when they continued to partake in worship. Due to the cult of Isis's popularity with women and enslaved people (and for allowing the inappropriate mixing of free and enslaved people), shrines dedicated to the goddess were destroyed with state approval at least five times, in 59, 58, 53, 50, and 48 BCE.

Secret meeting places

While some cults had officially recognized and visible places of worship, such as the Temple of Isis and Serapis in Rome, others were sequestered in hidden or secluded sites. Some were concealed in order to keep secret the fact that forbidden forms of worship were taking place, whereas others were underground, often literally, because the nature of their rites meant that only the initiated were allowed to know of their existence and participate in worship. The ceremonies of Mithras, for instance, took place in dark "caves" of limited size, often located underneath homes or military camps. While around 35 have been discovered in Rome, scholars hypothesize that possibly up to 700 Mithraic "caves" existed in Rome, with hundreds more across the empire. We know little of what occurred in these subterranean chambers, apart from the initiation rituals which brought new adherents into the worship of Mithras.

△ ***Chi Rho* symbol**
The symbols for *Chi* (X) and *Rho* (P) form the first two letters of the Greek word for Christ, and, when laid across each other, were used by early Christians to represent their religious faith.

△ **Serapis**
Created under the rule of the Ptolemies in Egypt some time after 300 BCE, Serapis was a fusion of the Greek god Zeus and the king-like Egyptian deity Osiris. Here, golden leaves and ivy are woven into his headdress to signify his majesty.

△ **Mithras**
First encountered by Roman troops in Persia, Mithras was a warlike god whose all-male cult spread rapidly among the army. In this relief, Mithras plunges his dagger into a sacrificial bull's neck as a snake slithers up to drink the gushing blood. For a while, Mithraism rivaled the popularity of Christianity in Rome.

△ **Judaism**
A menorah, the seven-armed candelabrum symbolizing God, creation, and knowledge, implies this sarcophagus was made for a follower of Judaism. Jews and Judaism suffered increased persecution after the Jewish revolt against Roman rule began in 66 CE.

Early Christian Art

A new way of looking at the world

In an atmosphere of increasing religious tolerance, early Christian communities in the Roman Empire used art to celebrate their faith and their group identity, drawing inspiration from the Classical symbols and styles around them.

Until the late 2nd century CE, it seems that Christians in the Roman Empire left few visual traces of their faith for historians to find in the form of art. Later generations now argue that this is not because early Christians believed that the creation of such images was immoral; such practices were not considered idolatrous. It may be that Christians still feared persecution, or they may simply have lacked the resources to create enduring art.

◁ **Brescia casket**
Made in the 4th century in northern Italy, this ivory casket depicts 36 scenes from the Old and New Testaments, including one of Christ teaching in Nazareth.

Christian symbolism

One challenge for historians has been distinguishing between early Christian and other ancient art. Often, early Christian art made use of Classical subjects and iconography, but gave these symbols new meaning. This allowed Christian art to remain ambiguous and so protect those connected to it from persecution.

By the end of the 3rd century, a number of Classical motifs had become common, such as the shepherd tending his flock, an image used to represent Jesus the Good Shepherd, as described in John's parable. Likewise, depictions of Orpheus came to be identified with Jesus, while a figure beseeching the heavens, known as the *orant*, came to symbolize Christian piety.

In 313 Constantine the Great (see pp. 260–261) issued the Edict of Milan, legally ending the oppression of Christians. This new tolerance allowed artists more freedom to create Christian art, although for some time they still relied on Classical motifs. Nevertheless, around the empire—and in Rome—frescoes, mosaics, and sculptures were used to tell Christian stories and celebrate Christian identity.

▽ **Catacombs of St. Callixtus**
These Christian catacombs contain several vibrant frescoes, providing evidence of the development of Christian art and symbolism.

Underground art

The best evidence for early Christian art comes from funerary contexts. On the outskirts of Rome, subterranean catacombs were burial places for Christians from around 200 until the 5th century. One of the most famous of these is the catacomb of St. Callixtus (San Callisto) on the Appian Way near Rome. The catacombs contain images drawn from both the Old and New Testaments, such as Jonah and the Whale, and tales of Jesus from the gospels. Many of the scenes seem to have been chosen because they illustrate episodes in which God saved the devout from death. Their use in these burial chambers was probably meant to provide comfort to the families of the deceased.

A *pallium* is a woolen cloak associated with early Christianity

The *Chi Rho* (the letters "XP") is an abbreviation of Jesus Christ's name in Greek

"... in part **openly**, in part **secretly**, **practices prevail** among you."

TERTULLIAN, *APOLOGETICUS*

△ **Depiction of Jesus**
The central detail of the Hinton St. Mary mosaic, from a Romano-British villa in England, is believed to show Jesus Christ. The entire mosaic covered the floors of two rooms, and depicted traditional Roman mythology alongside this Christian imagery.

Baths of Caracalla

Roman public baths

At its height, Rome had more than 800 bathhouses, ranging from small local establishments to the grand imperial *thermae*. Here, the emperors offered ordinary citizens access to the luxury and indulgence associated with wealth—warm-water bathing in heated halls; magnificent gardens, decorations, and sculpture; and space for socializing and exercising. One of the largest and best-preserved of the imperial bathhouses is the Baths of Caracalla. This huge complex, built in less than a decade and dedicated in 216, is a testament to Roman design and engineering. Thousands of bathers could use its sequence of warm, hot, and cold rooms and pools.

▽ Wall and underfloor heating
Hot air from wood-fired furnaces circulated between stacks of bricks under the floors. It then passed through *tubuli* (hollow, box-shape tiles) behind the walls, heating them as well.

▽ Hot-water system
Bathing in warm water, and sweating in steamy hot rooms, was an important part of the bathhouse experience. Underground furnaces heated water in large metal boilers to feed the baths above.

Large, underground passages provided access for enslaved workers and fuel

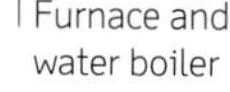

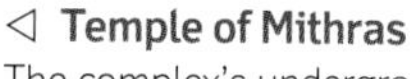

◁ Temple of Mithras
The complex's underground passages housed a shrine to Mithras, a deity of eastern origin who was popular with soldiers, officials, enslaved people, and freedmen. Workers from the baths may have worshipped here.

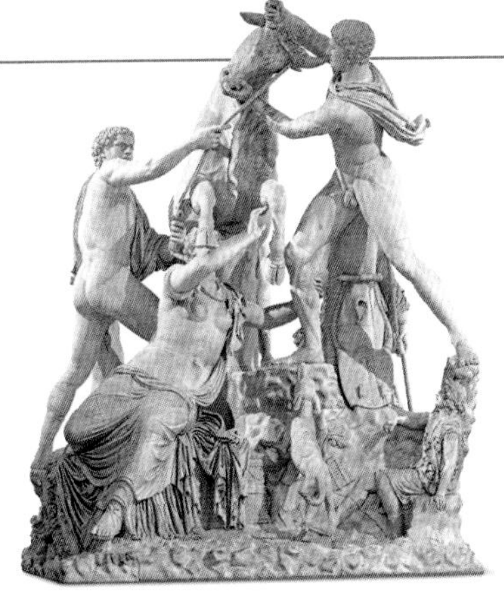

△ **Farnese Bull**
This huge statue group, hewn from a single block of marble, was displayed in the baths. It illustrates the Greek myth of Dirce.

A DEDICATED **AQUEDUCT**

Bathhouses required huge volumes of water. The Baths of Caracalla were served by a dedicated aqueduct branch, the Aqua Antoniniana, which drew from springs that were around 56 miles (90 km) from Rome. The aqueduct fed a series of huge cisterns behind the rear wall of the baths complex. From here, the water was piped to the fountains, boilers, and pools, and then flowed into huge underground drains. The profligate use of water from distant sources was part of the Roman emperors' ostentatious display of wealth to the people of Rome.

Inspection shafts
Aqueduct
Tepidarium
Frigidarium
Caldarium
Drain
Water pipe
Water source
Settling tank to sift dirt
Castellum (distribution tower)
Natatio

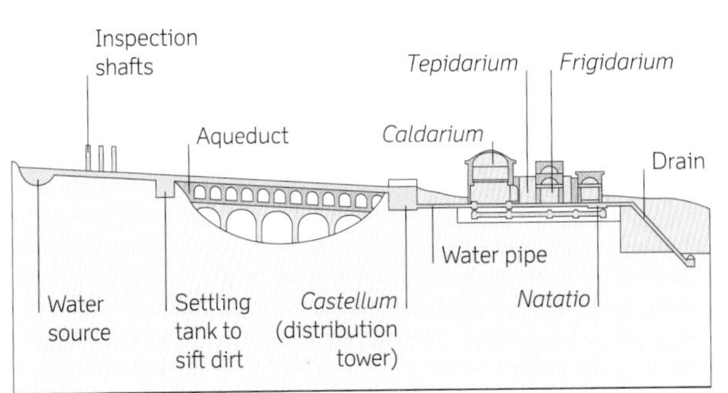

THE BATHHOUSE WATER SUPPLY

▽ ▷ **Bathing complex**
The main bathing block (below and in the plan, right), was only part of the baths. It sat in large gardens, within an outer precinct that contained halls, sculptures, spaces for exercise and athletics, and possibly libraries, offering visitors a range of leisure activities.

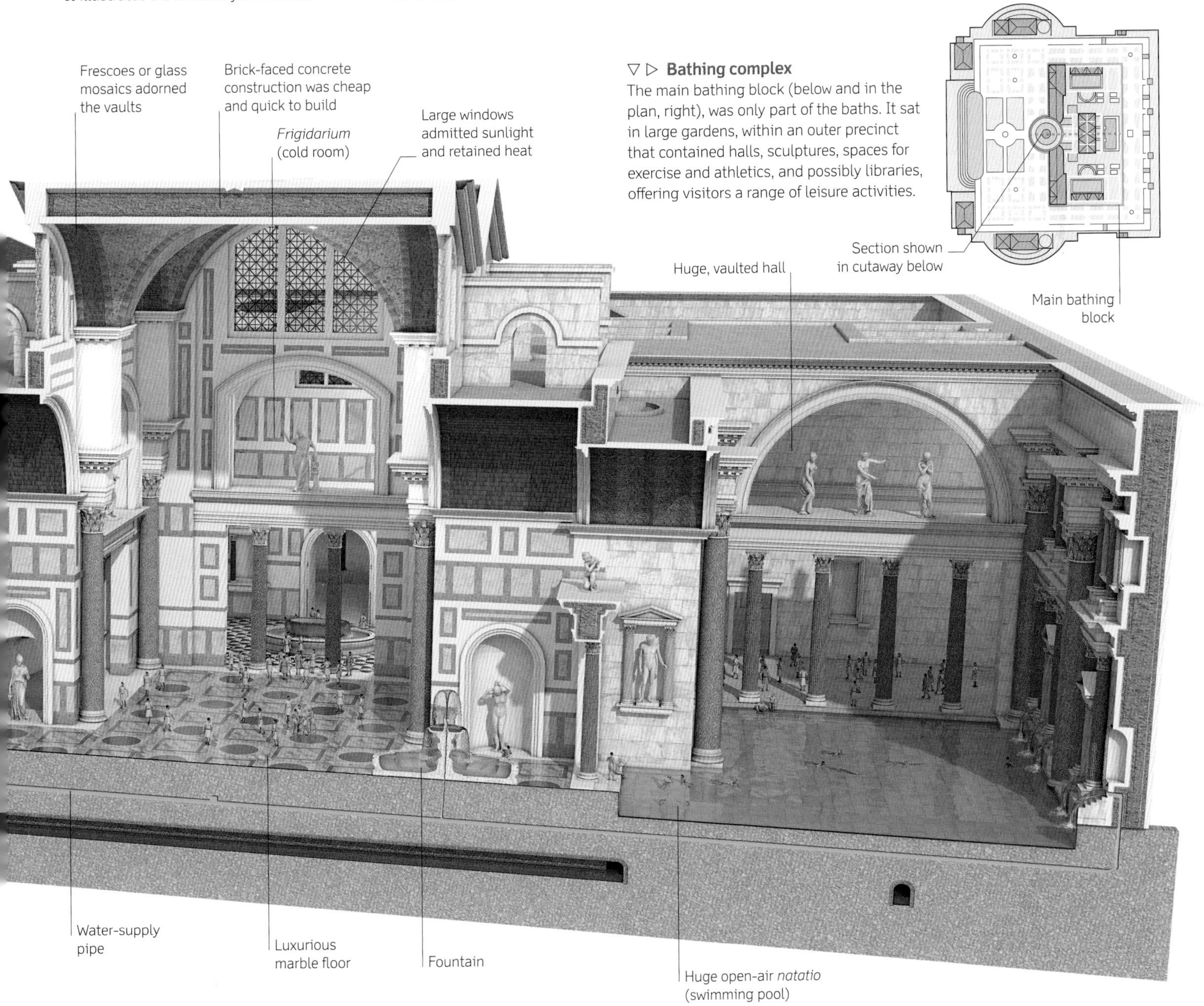

Frescoes or glass mosaics adorned the vaults
Brick-faced concrete construction was cheap and quick to build
Frigidarium (cold room)
Large windows admitted sunlight and retained heat
Section shown in cutaway below
Huge, vaulted hall
Main bathing block
Water-supply pipe
Luxurious marble floor
Fountain
Huge open-air natatio (swimming pool)

Childhood in Rome

Growing up in the empire

Young people in the Roman world grew up fast. Most of a child's early years were spent in preparation for life as an adult, with work, marriage, and responsibility coming at a young age. But there was time for fun and learning, too.

◁ **Girl playing knucklebones**
Knucklebones is still played, and is usually known as Jacks. This statue from the 2nd century CE was perhaps made to decorate the tomb of a young girl.

As children in the Roman world grew, their daily life was determined by their place in society and their gender. Elite and non-elite girls were "trained" from an early age for their future role as a *matrona*, the Roman ideal of a wife and mother. They were schooled in domestic management and, if their family had the means, learned how to weave and sew.

Boys were miniature versions of their fathers and would in most cases follow them into the same trade, whether advocate, baker, or laborer. In poorer rural families, boys would help their fathers work the land.

There is plenty of evidence to show that Roman children of both genders and at all levels of society were loved and valued, but the lives of young people in the Roman world were nevertheless subject to high levels of control. At home, children were subject to the complete authority of the *paterfamilias*, the male head of the household, whose decisions governed every aspect of their lives. A child's daily care,

Marcus's father looks on; he is dressed in a toga over a tunic and wears lightweight boots known as *calcei*

Marcus is nursed by his mother, who is covered in a *stola*, the toga-like garment worn by Roman women

Marcus plays in a child-size chariot drawn by a goat

▷ **Childhood memorial**
This marble sarcophagus from around 150 CE was made for a young boy, Marcus Cornelius Statius, and shows a number of important scenes from his short life, from his birth onward. The male and female figures may be actual likenesses of his parents.

however, was usually the responsibility of his or her mother and, in better-off families, domestic servants, whether free or enslaved.

Roman rites of passage

Children were classed as infants until the age of seven. A girl (*puella*) became an adult—and could be married—at 12. A boy (*puer*) was considered a man at 14, from which time he was able to wear the *toga virilis*, symbolizing adulthood (see pp. 68–69).

In 18 BCE the emperor Augustus passed the *lex Iulia*, followed in 9 CE by the *lex Papia Poppaea*. These laws contained a provision known as the *ius trium liberorum* ("law of three children"), which rewarded parents financially for having three or more offspring. Bearing children meant continuity and stability for a family, especially if at least one of those children was male. For childless couples, adoption was an option—especially in order to secure a male heir.

Children at play

Between school, domestic chores, and work, children in the Roman world did not have a lot of time to themselves, but they were able to play games and enjoy pastimes. Many fabric and wooden dolls and figures have been found across the Roman Empire.

EDUCATION IN THE ROMAN WORLD

Formal education in the Roman world was limited to families who could afford it. Wealthier families used private tutors for both their boys and girls (education was necessary for boys and desirable, but not essential, for girls). Families of more modest means sent their children to a *ludus litterarius*, a primary school where they would learn reading and writing. Teaching methods were based on Greek models. Children from the lower orders received what education they could from their parents, but most of what they learned tended to be the practical skills they would need for a life of domestic or agricultural work.

FRESCO (1ST CENTURY CE) OF A GIRL READING

Trochus involved driving a metal hoop with a stick, while *pilae* were ball-based activities that included *trigon*, a catching game, and *harpastum*, a form of soccer or handball. Children (and adults) played a version of tic-tac-toe known as *terni lapilli* ("three stones in a row"), and *latrunculi* was a board game similar to modern-day checkers. Children who enjoyed more physical activity could play a form of badminton, using wooden paddles for rackets and pine cones for shuttlecocks.

Marcus recites a lesson to his father; both figures hold a *volumen*, a papyrus or parchment scroll

Roman Historians

Making sense of Roman power

Many of the histories that the Romans themselves wrote have survived to the present day. These texts reveal a great deal about Roman thought, with regard to both Roman society and its relationships with the wider world. War is, unsurprisingly, a common theme of Roman history. Over the course of the centuries, Roman historians examined the past to help them understand how Romans had become a dominant force and how to rule most effectively.

The manner in which the Romans wrote their histories owes a strong debt to the techniques and styles developed in ancient Greece, centuries earlier. Famous Greek historians, such as Herodotus and Thucydides, inspired Roman historians. Many "Roman" historians were Greek in origin, including Cassius Dio – the author of *Roman History*. Although the earliest Roman histories began to be recorded in the 3rd century BCE, these were initially written in Greek and only transcribed in Latin almost a century later. Polybius, a Greek hostage in Rome during the 2nd century BCE, is one well-known historian of Rome who had Greek origins. His writings in Greek were intended to explain to his fellow countrymen the events that had led to the rapid rise of Rome, from great city to powerful empire.

There were two main styles of history writing in ancient Rome. Following in the annalistic tradition were writers such as Livy, who recorded history year by year. Later, the monograph tradition, followed by writers like Sallust, was concerned with specific periods or subjects.

△ **Julius Caesar**
Julius Caesar wrote several accounts of historical interest. His *De Bello Gallic* (*On the Gallic War*) narrated his conquest of Gaul. It was a response to criticisms by his enemies in Rome and presented him in a favorable light.

△ **Sallust**
The author of one of the earliest surviving histories to be written in Latin, Sallust focused on events in the late 2nd and early 1st centuries BCE. His *Bellum Jugurthinum* (*Jugurthine War*) describes the conflict between Rome and King Jugurtha in Numidia, a large territory in North Africa.

△ **Titus Livius (Livy)**
Livy's *Ab Urbe Condita* (*From the Founding of the City*) presents a history of Rome from its foundation in 753 BCE to the reign of Augustus in the 1st century BCE (Livy's own time). It includes many *exempla* from the Early Republic.

"The **special benefit** of the study of history is to **behold evidence** of every sort of behavior ...."

LIVY'S HISTORY OF ROME, *AB URBE CONDITA*

Representations of women

Roman society was very patriarchal, which is why no female historians appear among the historians discussed here. In the absence of any female voices in historic accounts, any representations of women are representations by men, reflecting their ideas and beliefs. Often, historians used female characters to illustrate particular points, such as the supposed dangers of powerful women—Boudicca of the Iceni in Britannia, for instance, or Zenobia of Palmyra (in Syria), both of whom threatened Roman order.

There were also differences between what Roman historians and modern readers might expect to find in a "historical" account. For example, there was a fine line between myth and history. If a past event could not readily be explained, then it was not uncommon for it to be described in terms of the influence of the gods and other supernatural elements.

History as morality lesson

Other famous episodes recorded by Roman historians were intended to be educational, telling readers how best to live their lives. The people in these stories were *exempla*, such as the figure of Marcus Curtius, who appears in an account about a chasm that threatened the Forum—it could be closed only if Romans offered what they held most valuable. Marcus charged with his horse into the breach, sacrificing his life to preserve the city, having realized that nothing was as important to Rome as its courageous young men.

△ **Pliny the Elder**
In c. 77 CE this scholar, author, and naturalist wrote the largest single work to survive from ancient Rome to the present day: the *Naturalis Historia* (*Natural History*). Consisting of 37 books, it became a model for later encyclopedias (see pp. 294–295).

△ **Josephus**
Flavius Josephus was a Jewish historian and military leader. He fought against the Romans but was captured in 67 CE by the future emperor Vespasian. He is best known for the *Bellum Judaicum* (*The Jewish War*), and his history of the Jewish people, *Antiquitates Judaicae* (*Jewish Antiquities*).

△ **Tacitus**
Tacitus wrote the *Annals* and the *Histories*, which cover the period of Roman history from the death of Augustus (14 CE) until the death of Domitian (96 CE). Tacitus's accounts offer moralistic portraits of the failure of Roman rule, often focusing on the emperors' vices.

Lepcis Magna

Birthplace of an emperor

A prosperous city on the coast of North Africa, Lepcis Magna already had a long history of commerce and conflict with its Mediterranean neighbors, before it was transformed by its most famous son: the emperor Septimius Severus.

△ **Unusual arch**
The Arch of Septimius Severus in Lepcis Magna is a rare four-sided example of the type of structure, with a striking "broken pediment" on each of its four faces.

Located in modern-day Libya, Lepcis Magna was founded on a natural harbor at the mouth of the Wadi Lebda river in the 7th century BCE by Phoenician colonists from Tyre, in the eastern Mediterranean. To the east of Lepcis (also known as Leptis), was Cinyps, a Greek colony that had been taken over by the Carthaginians. The Phoenicians had been attracted to the area by its climate and fertile soil, and Lepcis Magna became renowned—and very wealthy—for the olives it cultivated and the olive oil it exported around the Mediterranean.

Having seen how Carthage had conquered nearby Cinyps, Lepcis Magna sided with Rome in the Third Punic War of 149–146 BCE (see pp. 82–85). Unfortunately, the city later backed the wrong side in the civil war between Julius Caesar and Pompey in 46 BCE (see pp. 128–129). Following Pompey's defeat, a huge fine of 3 million lb (1.3 million kg) of olive oil was imposed on the city, to be paid each year. In this way, Lepcis became a type of Roman client state. It retained its semi-independence until officially becoming part of the Roman Empire during the reign of Tiberius. Trade and commerce flourished, and the city began to acquire the trappings of Roman rule, including an amphitheater, a theater, and baths.

▷ **Head of Medusa**
This sculpture of Medusa in Lepcis Magna's forum is a reminder of the cultural influence of Greece and the eastern Mediterranean in North Africa at the time.

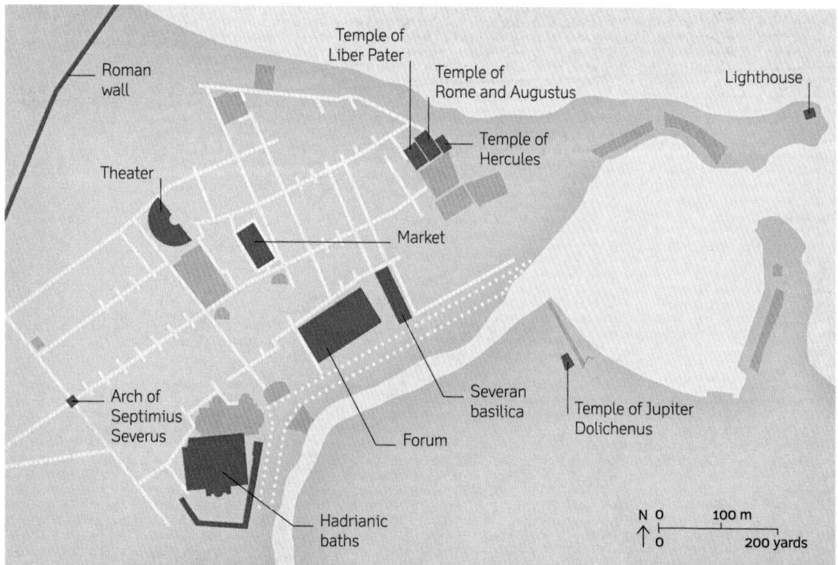

◁ **Lepcis Magna in the Imperial era**
The grid-like layout of streets shows clear evidence of Roman town planning. This map also shows some of the buildings added in the reign of Septimius Severus.

Septimius Severus and after

The city enjoyed its greatest moment in the early 3rd century CE. In 192, the emperor Commodus was murdered, leading to a vicious civil war between five claimants to the imperial throne. The victor, in 193, was Septimius Severus, who had been born in Lepcis Magna around 145. Surviving inscriptions in the city indicate that his father and grandfather had both been important local dignitaries—a magistrate, or *sufes*, in the latter case. Septimius Severus was Rome's first African emperor.

During his reign, which lasted until 211, Severus did not forget his home town. He invested heavily in architecture, creating several impressive structures and monuments across the city. These included a new forum and basilica, both made with expensive marble sourced from across the empire—a visible reminder to the people of Lepcis that one of their own now held absolute power in Rome. The basilica in particular was richly decorated, featuring statues of Lepcis Magna's patron gods, Bacchus and Hercules. Severus also expanded the harbor and built a lighthouse to protect ships traveling to the city. Most impressive of all was the construction of an enormous *quadrifons*, or four-sided monumental arch, that celebrated the emperor, his family, and his relationship with Lepcis Magna (see pp. 176–177).

Although Lepcis Magna was made the capital of the new province of Tripolitania by the emperor Diocletian around 296, its story thereafter was one of decline. The city was inundated by a tsunami in 365 and, though partially rebuilt, it suffered ongoing raids by local Berber peoples and migrating Vandals over the next century or so. To add insult to injury, Lepcis Magna's harbor, the means by which the city was able to trade so profitably across the Mediterranean, began to silt up, making it inaccessible to ships. By the beginning of the 5th century Lepcis Magna had ceased to be an important commercial trading center.

△ **Severan basilica**
The basilica of Lepcis Magna was a huge space, at least 246 ft (75 m) long and 62 ft (19 m) wide. Its exact usage is not clear, though legal hearings and public meetings probably took place there.

"Severus, **a native of Africa**, took possession of **the empire**. His native city was Lepcis …."

HISTORIA AUGUSTA, "SEPTIMIUS SEVERUS"

SEPTIMIUS **SEVERUS**

Born into a well-to-do provincial family, Septimius Severus (right) was of Italic and Punic descent. As his Punic heritage came from his father's side, Severus is recognized as the first emperor of non-Italic origin. (Although his predecessors Trajan and Hadrian had both been born in Spain, their ancestral lineages were "purely" Italic.) He held several important posts in Rome in his early career, and became a senator in 169, later serving as a tribune of the plebs. As emperor, he was a successful general and a good administrator. But there were also downsides to his rule. Severus's reliance on the army to keep him in power greatly increased the influence of the military in public life, while his currency reforms led to inflation and the long-running political unrest of the 3rd century.

Graffiti carved by visitors to the city eager to see its ruins

Roman-style uniforms indicate the mixing of different cultures

△ **Syrian gods**
This relief from the 1st century CE shows the Palmyrene triad, three of the most important gods worshipped in Palmyra. In the center is Baalshamin, the lord of the sky. The moon god Aglibol is to his left and the sun god Malakbel is to his right.

The Roman-Syrian War

Queen Zenobia challenges Rome

Among the most serious of the crises facing the Roman Empire during the 3rd century CE was the breakaway Palmyrene Empire. Led by Queen Zenobia, the prosperous Syrian city of Palmyra challenged the might of Rome.

For long periods of the 3rd century, the Roman Empire was in a state of crisis (see pp. 248–249). Roman control became so weak in some regions that entire swathes of territory began to try to break away from the empire, first in the northwest and then, on the eastern frontier, in the wealthy trading city of Palmyra, in modern-day Syria.

Palmyra had long been important because of its position along the Silk Road. Even after the Romans arrived in 64 BCE, Palmyra retained a high degree of political and administrative autonomy. This openness and independence is reflected in the unique character of Palmyrene art, which combines the styles of Semitic, Greek, Roman, and Parthian cultures.

Breakaway

Palmyra remained loyal to Rome for 200 years. When, in 260 CE, the Roman emperor Valerian was defeated and captured at the Battle of Edessa by Sasanian forces, Palmyra helped lead the retaliation. Its king Odaenathus commanded Palmyra to several victories over the Sasanians. Palmyra's relationship with Rome changed, however, after Odaenathus was assassinated in 267. His son Vaballathus became king, but as he was only ten years old real power passed to his mother and regent, Queen Zenobia.

Initially, the Palmyrenes under Zenobia remained loyal to Rome. They fought military campaigns in support of the empire and minted coinage that, although it depicted Vaballathus as Palmyra's king, was issued in the name of the Roman emperor, Aurelian. Then, in 270, Zenobia directly challenged Roman rule when she conquered Egypt at the head of a 70,000-strong army. This was almost a declaration of war: Egypt was a Roman province and, importantly, supplied Rome with much of its grain. The following year, the Palmyrenes took over large swathes of territory in Asia Minor and, in an open challenge to Roman authority, Vaballathus took the title *augustus* (see pp. 254–55). Zenobia had set up her son as a rival to the emperor; Rome had to respond.

Aurelian and the restoration of empire

Before becoming Roman emperor, Aurelian had been a successful general and he wasted little time putting his military skill to use again. Crossing into Asia Minor in 272, he besieged and took the city of Tyana in Cappadocia, which had sided with Palmyra. As the Romans marched on, other cities surrendered rather than face lengthy and bloody sieges. Aurelian then defeated Zenobia's forces at the Battle of Immae, close to Antioch, and again at the Battle of Emesa, forcing Zenobia and her army to retreat to Palmyra.

Unable to breach the city walls, the Romans laid siege to Palmyra. According to the 6th-century historian Zosimus, when food supplies began to run low, a city council decided that Zenobia should escape toward the Euphrates River, to seek aid from the Sasanian Empire. However, Zenobia was captured by the Romans as she tried to flee and the city was taken. The Romans spared Palmyra at first, but after a second uprising in 273, Aurelian destroyed the city in punishment. Its treasures were looted and taken to Aurelian's Temple of Sol Invictus in Rome.

Although many Palmyrene leaders were executed after the rebellion, the fate of the queen and her son is unknown. One account tells of Zenobia being brought to Rome and paraded in chains as part of Aurelian's Triumph, and this seems likely. Zosimus disputes this, though, writing that she died on the journey to Rome. Another ancient source, the *Historia Augusta*, describes a more unlikely end to her story, claiming that Aurelian gave Zenobia a villa outside Rome, where she lived out the rest of her days in peace.

> "She was the **wife of Odaenathus** but had **the courage** of a man."
>
> ZOSIMUS, ON ZENOBIA

PALMYRA, A CITY AT THE CROSSROADS

A wealthy trading center on the Silk Road between Asia and the Mediterranean, Palmyra stood at a cultural as well as commercial crossroads. Although local Semitic and Arab deities were worshipped in the city, the artwork and temples that venerated them show clear Greco-Roman influence. They include the Temple of Bel and the Great Colonnade (right). The remains were well preserved for centuries, but were badly damaged by terrorist attacks in 2015.

REMAINS OF THE GREAT COLONNADE

▽ **Warrior queen**
Tiepolo's *Queen Zenobia Addressing Her Soldiers* (c. 1725) is a rare example in art of a woman portrayed as a powerful figure. She is dressed in battle armor to emphasize her authority.

Working the Land

Feeding an empire and fueling unrest

Agriculture was central to all aspects of Roman life. Its produce fed millions across the empire, and was the source of the landed elite's wealth—and the cause of social and political upheaval in both the Republican and Imperial eras.

△ **Son of the soil**
This copper figure from 1st–3rd-century CE Britannia shows a farmer driving a cow and a bull. This odd livestock combination indicates he may have been performing a ceremonial rite rather than simply plowing a field.

The vast majority of people in the Roman Empire lived in the countryside. Most of them would have been engaged in some form of farming and agriculture, either on their own smallholdings or working—paid and unpaid—on large estates. The food and resources they grew fed an empire that extended from Britannia in the northwest to Syria in the east, with North Africa and Egypt particularly important as providers of olives and grains such as barley and wheat. As Rome's "breadbasket", Egypt was a strategically important territory throughout the Imperial era.

Roman farming and agriculture was influenced by techniques used by peoples the Romans encountered, including the Greeks and the Carthaginians. Over time, the Romans devised ways of improving agricultural yields through technology: aqueducts were built to deliver water for irrigation, and complex mill systems were developed, as at Barbegal in southern Gaul, to grind wheat, barley, and other crops in large quantities quickly and efficiently.

An idealized way of life?

Several written accounts of Roman farming have survived. One of the most important is *De agri cultura* (*On Farming*), written by the politician and writer Cato the Elder around the mid-2nd century BCE.

Although the book provides valuable insights into rural life in Republican Rome, it also presents a somewhat idealized view of farming. Alongside his practical descriptions of vineyard and farm management, Cato praises agricultural practice as more noble than other occupations. He exalts farming as a source of moral value, its honest toil creating men who are self-sufficient and strong, their "Romanness" rooted in the soil itself.

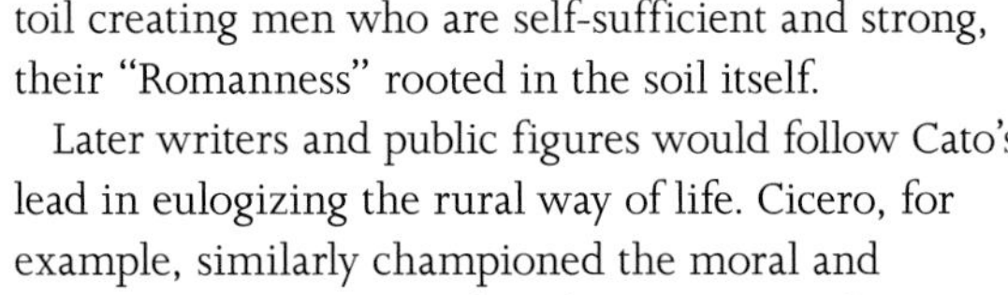

Later writers and public figures would follow Cato's lead in eulogizing the rural way of life. Cicero, for example, similarly championed the moral and character-building benefits of agricultural life, as did the poet Virgil in his didactic work the *Georgics*, written at the end of the 1st century BCE.

Agriculture and aristocrats

Rural life could be contentious and confrontational, too. Over time, wealthy landowners increasingly took possession of smallholdings and *ager publicus* ("public land") belonging to poorer farmers. In some areas these were consolidated into vast estates, or *latifundia*, worked by enslaved people. The shrinking amount of available land drove some farmers to move to the city to seek a living there. Tensions rose, and attempts by the reform-minded Gracchi brothers to redistribute land from wealthier landowners to poorer citizens in the 2nd century BCE ended in violence (see pp. 104–105). Rome's wars of conquest, however, brought in new land to be cultivated. Retired soldiers were re-homed across the empire in new settlements known as *coloniae*, where they were given farmland as reward for their years of service to Rome. Camulodunum (modern Colchester in Britain) was one such newly created town.

◁ **The farmers' friend**
This replica shows how a Roman public calendar, under each of its 12 entries, listed the name of the month, number of days, its protecting divinity, upcoming festivals, and agricultural work to be completed.

This figure is hacking away weeds from the farm's grapevines

Wealthier farmers used teams of oxen to till the soil; poorer smallholders worked by hand only

Farm worker scatters seeds in front of the plow that will turn the soil behind him

△ **Country pursuits**
Made in the 2nd or 3rd century CE, this mosaic from present-day Algeria uses terra-cotta, marble, and limestone to depict different aspects of agricultural life. The piece would probably have decorated an affluent landowner's villa to display the source of his wealth.

ROME'S **IDEAL REPUBLICAN**

In 458 BCE the Republic was faring badly in its war with the Aequi people. As panic began to spread in Rome, the Senate turned to a conservative patrician, Lucius Quinctius Cincinnatus, who years earlier had retired to a quiet life on his farm (right). He reluctantly agreed to the Senate's pleas that he assume dictatorial power and led the Roman army to victory at the Battle of Mount Algidus (near Rome). Fifteen days later, he returned to his farm to plow his fields. In Roman legend, he refused the honors and further dictatorial powers offered to him by the Senate, becoming the model of selfless virtue that political leaders were expected to emulate. The US city of Cincinnati is named after him.

The Aurelian Empire

The empire's difficult third century

In the mid-3rd century CE, the Roman Empire faced several serious threats, known as the "Third Century Crisis." The emperor Aurelian restored some order, preserving both Rome and the empire.

▽ Ludovisi Battle Sarcophagus
The Ludovisi sarcophagus (c.250–260) shows a battle between Roman and Gothic warriors, the writhing figures typical of the way battle scenes were presented during this period of turmoil.

Many historians refer to the period between 235 and 284 CE in the Roman Empire as the Third Century Crisis. The empire faced a series of challenges to its power, as well as extreme political instability internally: 27 emperors reigned during this period, their economic mismanagement leading to the devaluation of Roman coinage. Externally, the empire faced serious military pressures. To the east, the Sasanian dynasty achieved several crushing victories over the Romans. Meanwhile, the empire's northern borders had weakened, with Germanic and Gothic peoples destabilizing the Roman frontier.

Imperial breakup

The crises deepened in the mid-3rd century. The emperor Gallienus spent much of his reign (260–268) dealing with unrest in the northern territories. As frontiers failed in Europe, subjects and soldiers in

Gothic warriors appear with untamed hair and beards

The central figure is a young military commander on horseback

Romans are depicted as having the power to show mercy

△ **Aurelian Walls**
Built between 271 and 275, the Aurelian Walls were designed to defend the imperial capital. The circuit of the walls runs for 11.8 miles (19 km), and measures 26 ft (8 m) in height.

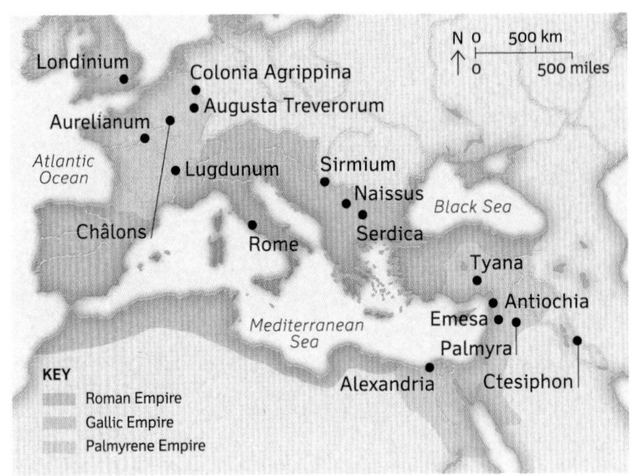

△ **The Roman Empire during the 3rd century**
During the mid-3rd century, the Roman Empire fractured from within. In western Europe, the Gallic Empire emerged, and the Palmyrene Empire challenged in the east.

these regions sought strong leadership. In 260, the governor of Germania—Marcus Cassianius Latinius Postumus—was proclaimed emperor by the troops under his command. Instead of marching on Rome, he set himself up as ruler of the rival Gallic Empire, which encompassed Gaul, Germania, and southern Britannia (England and Wales).

In the east, the city of Palmyra emerged as a powerful rival. The Palmyrenes, originally allies of Rome against the Sasanians, began to seize territory that threatened Roman interests (see pp. 252–253).

"Restorer of the World"

Although he was emperor for only five years (270–275), Aurelian emerges from the 3rd century as one of Rome's most effective rulers. Both practical and a highly successful military leader, he recognized the empire's weaknesses and put in place plans to rectify them. He built new defenses around the city of Rome, the Aurelian Walls, to defend against the Vandal, Juthungi, and Sarmatian tribes that were ravaging Italy in 270 and 271. These walls still stand today. Aurelian then marched against the Palmyrene Empire in a rapid and successful campaign. In 274 he marched northwest against the Gallic Empire and routed its forces at the Battle of Châlons, thus restoring the empire's unity.

Aurelian was celebrated as *restitutor orbis*, "Restorer of the World." In Rome, he promoted the cult of the sun god Sol Invictus. A vast temple honoring the deity was built in the city, and Aurelian's spoils of war were dedicated to the god.

Unfortunately, not even Aurelian was safe from the turbulent politics of the time. On his journey eastward to wage another campaign against the Sasanians in 275, he was killed by his soldiers, who believed they were to be executed on his orders.

"RENEGADE" EMPEROR

Marcus Cassianius Latinius Postumus was a Roman general who became a rival of Rome. After his soldiers proclaimed him emperor in 260 CE, Postumus established the Gallic Empire in northwest Europe. His rule, conducted mainly from Germania (an area in north-central Europe), lasted for about a decade, and he was initially popular for his military successes against the Germanic tribes threatening Gaul. Although Postumus's empire was a rival of Rome, its culture and politics were recognizably Roman. His coinage (above) suggests a wish to be associated with the hero Hercules.

> "**Aurelian** was **not unlike Alexander the Great** or **Caesar**, for in the space of three years **he retook the Roman world from invaders**."
>
> AURELIUS VICTOR, *EPITOME DE CAESARIBUS*

Bedroom wall fresco from southern Italy
In this artwork from the Villa of P. Fannius Synistor in Boscoreale, which was buried following the eruption of Vesuvius in 79 CE, sophisticated three-dimensional effects have been used to create a fresco displaying an imagined cityscape viewed through a colonnaded arcade. The section on the left depicts what could be a shrine to Diana Hecate, a deity fusing elements of the goddess of the hunt and the goddess of the underworld. The work dates from c. 50–40 BCE and was found in a bedroom, or *cubiculum*.

The Roman-Persian Wars

Rome's imperial rivals

Over several centuries, the Roman Empire waged a number of long and costly wars against its main rivals, the great empires of Persia: first the Parthians, and then the Sasanians.

◁ **King Peroz hunting**
This plate, from the 5th–6th centuries, depicts a Sasanian king of kings, who may be King Peroz (r. 459–484). He is shown hunting rams, symbolizing his skill and power.

Although the Roman Empire dominated the Mediterranean after defeating its rival, Carthage, in 146 BCE, it was not the only vast empire in the ancient world. In the east, swathes of territory were dominated by the Persian empires: the Parthians and, later, the Sasanians. There were frequent wars between the two empires as they vied for control and territory. These wars often involved various client kingdoms, such as Armenia, which passed back and forth from the influence of one empire to another over the centuries.

▽ **Lucius Verus**
Joint emperor with Marcus Aurelius from 161 to 169 CE (see pp. 222–23), Lucius Verus led a Roman invasion of the Parthian Empire, an action that ended with Vologases IV, the king of Parthia, suing for peace.

Rome's Parthian problems

Antagonism between the Roman and Persian empires began during the Republican period. Rome launched several abortive campaigns against Parthia in the 1st century BCE, often with disastrous results. Sulla and later Pompey the Great, among others, had at first tried to engage through diplomacy. In 53 BCE, Marcus Licinius Crassus, a member of the so-called First Triumvirate (see pp. 112–113), attempted to invade the Parthian Empire. His army was destroyed by the Parthian mounted archers and cataphracts (heavily armored cavalry), and the Roman embarrassment was compounded by the loss of several legionary standards. Reputedly, Caesar planned a retaliatory campaign against the Parthians but was assassinated before it could get underway. Mark Antony mounted a subsequent campaign that also failed. Roman pride was not restored until the reign of Augustus. The first emperor's diplomatic successes with the Parthians led to the return of the lost standards, and they were deposited in the new Temple of Mars Ultor ("Mars the Avenger").

Several more Roman campaigns were waged during the 1st century CE. However, these were fairly minor compared to events in the 2nd century. First, the emperor Trajan launched a large invasion of the Parthian Empire in 114, taking Mesopotamia as a Roman province and capturing the Parthian capital, Ctesiphon. Although his successor, Hadrian, reestablished the Euphrates River as the empire's eastern boundary, there was another war in 161

> "After easily **subduing the neighboring barbarian nations**, Ardashir began to **plot against the Roman Empire**."
>
> HERODIAN, *HISTORY OF THE ROMAN EMPIRE*

when Vologases IV, the Parthian king, invaded Armenia and defeated the Romans. A Roman counterattack successfully drove the Parthians back, but at huge cost to the Roman Empire. A deadly plague—possibly smallpox—was ravaging the Parthians at this time; it soon spread to the Roman army, and from there around the empire. This so-called "Antonine plague" may have been responsible for as many as 10 million deaths.

The Sasanian threat

By the end of the 2nd century, the Parthians had been defeated by the Romans again. The Arch of Septimius Severus in the Roman Forum commemorates that emperor's victories over his eastern rivals. Within several decades the Parthian Empire had fallen. It was replaced, in 226, by the Sasanians, led by Ardashir I. The Sasanians would prove to be worthy successors to the Parthians as Rome's main imperial enemy.

The patterns of the previous centuries remained similar, with back-and-forth campaigns of Sasanian advances followed by Roman counterattacks. Buoyed by recent successes in capturing Carrhae and Nisibis in 243, the Roman emperor Gordian III advanced deep into Sasanian territory, only to be defeated and killed near Ctesiphon in 244.

At this time, the Sasanians were being led by the formidable Shapur I. In the mid-3rd century, while the Roman Empire was wracked by problems (see pp. 248–249), Shapur launched punishing attacks on the Romans. Armenia was taken and the Romans were defeated in several battles.

The most infamous of these losses occurred at Edessa (in modern Türkiye) in 260. Roman forces were defeated and captured, including the emperor Valerian. An enormous relief was carved into a rock face at Naqsh-e Rostam (in modern Iran), which shows Valerian kneeling in submission before Shapur, the Sasanian king of kings. The historian Lactantius even claimed that Shapur used Valerian as a mounting block, a platform from which to climb onto his horse.

Conflicts between the Romans and the Sasanians would continue into the 4th century. Galerius, one of the tetrarchs, won a series of crushing victories at the end of the century, managing to recover lost Roman territory and prestige.

△ **Emperor Valerian yields**
The Sasanian king Shapur I immortalized his triumph with this relief at Naqsh-e Rostam, showing him on horseback and Emperor Valerian kneeling before him.

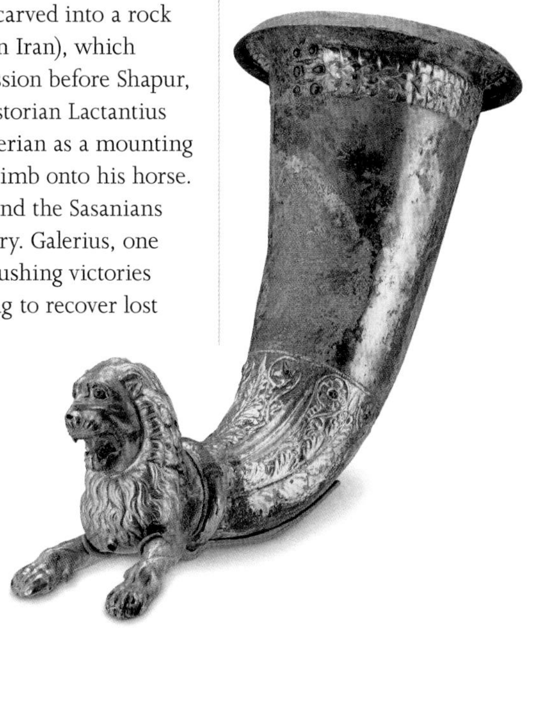

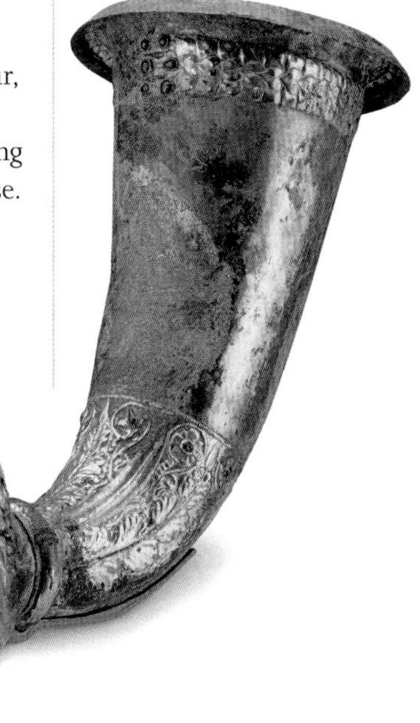

▷ **Lion rhyton**
The roaring lion on this silver vessel from the eastern Parthian Empire, 1st century BCE, had royal connotations and was a symbol of nobility and courage in Parthia.

Diocletian's Tetrarchy

An empire divided by four rulers

The emperor Diocletian reinvented the Roman Empire, with the aim of restoring imperial control. The new system—the Tetrarchy—consisted of four rulers who each managed a part of the empire.

△ **Maximian**
Nicknamed "Herculius," Maximian was *augustus* from 286 to 305 CE, when he abdicated in favour of Constantius.

In 284 CE the emperor Carus died under mysterious circumstances. According to the historian Aurelius Victor, he was struck by lightning while campaigning in Persia, providing Carus's cavalry commander, Diocletian, with the opportunity to seize power.

Diocletian is most famous for ending the turbulence of the Third Century Crisis (see pp. 248–249) by introducing a sweeping political transformation. He turned the empire into a Tetrarchy (meaning "rule by four"). None of the rulers were—at least at first—connected by marriage. Instead, it was a practical solution, whereby each ruler would be able to engage rapidly with problems arising around the empire.

First, in 286, Diocletian appointed Maximian, who had served with him in the army. Diocletian was the senior emperor, the *augustus*, and Maximian the lower-ranking *caesar*. The pair became associated with two gods to indicate seniority: Diocletian with Jupiter, the king of gods, and Maximian with the demigod Hercules. Each took responsibility for one half of the empire. While Diocletian worked to secure the east, Maximian ruled over the western provinces.

Seven years later, in 293, the empire was divided again to provide additional support following new military pressures, particularly in Persia, Gaul, and Britannia. The empire was split between four emperors. Maximian was promoted to the same status as Diocletian: now, there were two *augusti*.

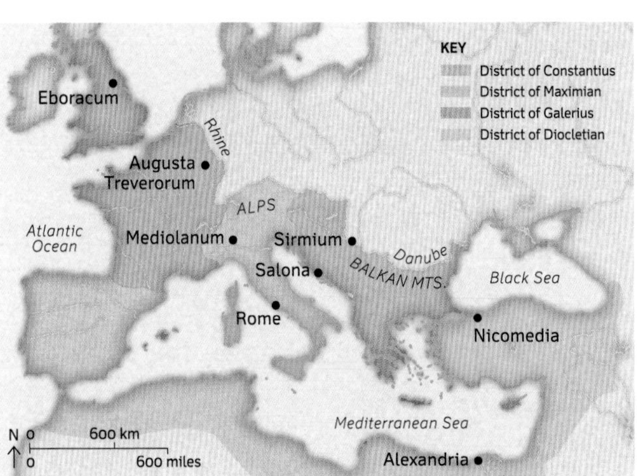

◁ **The tetrarchs' areas of control**
Under the tetrarchs, the empire had four regions of control, with one senior *augustus* and one junior *caesar* in both the east and the west.

△ **Saint Damian and Saint Cosmas**
Damian and Cosmas were doctors and early Christians from ancient Syria who were tortured and executed with their young brothers during Diocletian's persecutions.

Two new junior partners were selected as *caesares*. In the east, Diocletian was assisted by Galerius, and in the west, Maximian was supported by Constantius.

New imperial capitals

Four emperors needed four capitals from which to rule. During the Tetrarchy, the importance of Rome as the imperial capital began to wane. Instead, new cities around the empire became capitals for the tetrarchs, often chosen because they provided the four rulers with quicker access to the frontiers, where they could confront enemies.

Diocletian's capital was Nicomedia, in northwestern Asia Minor, which provided a base for action against the Sasanians in Persia. Maximian took Mediolanum (modern Milan) as his base. Galerius, Diocletian's caesar, was based at Sirmium (in modern Serbia), offering protection on the Danube frontier. Constantius's capital was Augusta Treverorum (Trier, Germany), which offered a headquarters for campaigns in Germania, Gaul, and Britannia (England and Wales). Despite this, the site of Rome remained symbolically important, and Diocletian invested heavily in the vast Baths of Diocletian in the city.

"While **disorder thus prevailed** throughout the world ... **Diocletian promoted Maximian** ... and created **Constantius** and **Galerius caesars**."

THE HISTORIAN EUTROPIUS, *BREVIARIUM HISTORIAE ROMANAE*

Persecutions and political tensions

The Tetrarchy attempted to reassert control over the empire in many ways, such as reorganizing the provinces, while Diocletian aimed to control inflation by setting the prices of goods and services. Diocletian and the other tetrarchs also introduced severe persecutions of Christians around the empire in 303 to bring about religious order, but this had little effect on the religion's growing popularity.

On May 1, 305, Diocletian abdicated, the only Roman emperor ever to give up power willingly, and retired to Salona (modern Split). Reluctantly, Maximian also retired. Galerius and Constantius were promoted to *augusti*, each appointing new *caesares*. Diocletian's ordered system was disrupted as the sons of Constantius and Maximian warred for control. By the time Diocletian died in 311, the Tetrarchy he had established was dying, too.

◁ **Portrait of the four tetrarchs**
This statue group—originally two separate groups—depicts the Tetrarchy: Diocletian and Galerius, and Maximian and Constantius. They are shown clasping each other, a sign of their cooperation and collegiality.

EMPEROR **CONSTANTIUS I**

Constantius became *augustus* in 305 CE after Maximian retired. From his capital (modern-day Trier), Constantius ruled the northwest provinces of the empire, including Gaul and Britannia. A successful soldier, he helped to defeat the rebel Allectus in Britannia. The medal below, found in Arras, France, shows Constantius liberating Londinium (London). He also worked to restore Hadrian's Wall in northern Britannia, and was awarded the title *Britannicus Maximus*. He died in Eboracum (York, England) in 306. Constantius had reportedly not been very active in Diocletian's persecutions, and Constantine, his son who succeeded him as emperor (see pp. 260–261), would become a Christian.

▷ **Trophy armor**
The armor of defeated peoples was hung up on wooden poles, known as a *trophaeum* (trophy)—victory monuments on the battlefield that were dedicated to the gods in thanks.

The Portonaccio Sarcophagus

A battle captured in stone

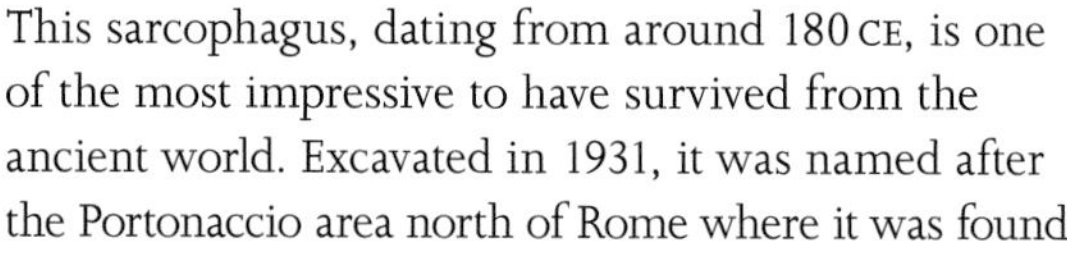

This sarcophagus, dating from around 180 CE, is one of the most impressive to have survived from the ancient world. Excavated in 1931, it was named after the Portonaccio area north of Rome where it was found.

The Portonaccio Sarcophagus is a fine example of the chiaroscuro technique in stone—the art of creating vivid contrasts of light and dark from the shadows created by the deep relief. The entire sarcophagus is sculpted from one piece of marble, making the wide variety of overlapping figures even more impressive. The style mirrors Greek monuments from the 2nd century BCE, such as the Altar of Pergamon.

Military might and Roman mercy

The main battle scene shows a triumphant Roman cavalryman in the center, intended to represent whoever was interred in the sarcophagus as a victorious and successful general. On the left and right are pairs of male and female figures who are recognizable from their hairstyles as belonging to the Suebi and the Sarmatic Iazyges peoples on the northern frontier of the Danube River. The ends of the sarcophagus (not visible here) are sculpted in a shallower relief than the main panel and show prisoners being led over a boat bridge and chieftains submitting to Roman officials. The lid emphasizes Roman citizenship with a birth and a wedding, as well as a scene of clemency toward a prisoner. It was a common to depict themes of the *Pax Romana* (see pp. 138–139) and "just rule" that the Romans believed they practiced. This also artistically conveyed the idea that those who opposed the Roman Empire would be subdued or destroyed.

Marcus Aurelius's frontier wars

The themes on the sarcophagus are similar to those on the Columns of Trajan (see pp. 214–215) and of Marcus Aurelius in Rome. These victory monuments were intended to emphasize Roman superiority and victory. In reality, the Romans were never able to fully quell uprisings and rebellions in their provinces, particularly on the northern frontier. In 117 CE, under Trajan, the empire reached its greatest extent, after which it was consolidated rather than expanded.

The owner of the sarcophagus may have been Aulus Iulius Pompilius, a high-ranking general of Marcus Aurelius—two details of an eagle and boar insignia may allude to legions he commanded—or it may have been made speculatively for the death of an important general in the ongoing and problematic Marcomannic Wars that were fought on the northern frontiers.

▷ **The Portonaccio Sarcophagus**
The main panel of the marble sarcophagus, now held in the Palazzo Massimo Museo Nazionale Romano, depicts Roman soldiers victorious over their foes.

◁ **Cavalryman**
The face of the general is left unfinished, perhaps because a portrait was not obtained in time before the burial or because the sarcophagus was sculpted for potential buyers rather than commissioned for a specific individual.

"**Woe** to the **vanquished**."

LIVY'S HISTORY OF ROME, *AB URBE CONDITA*

Enemies of Rome are all shown in positions of despair and defeat

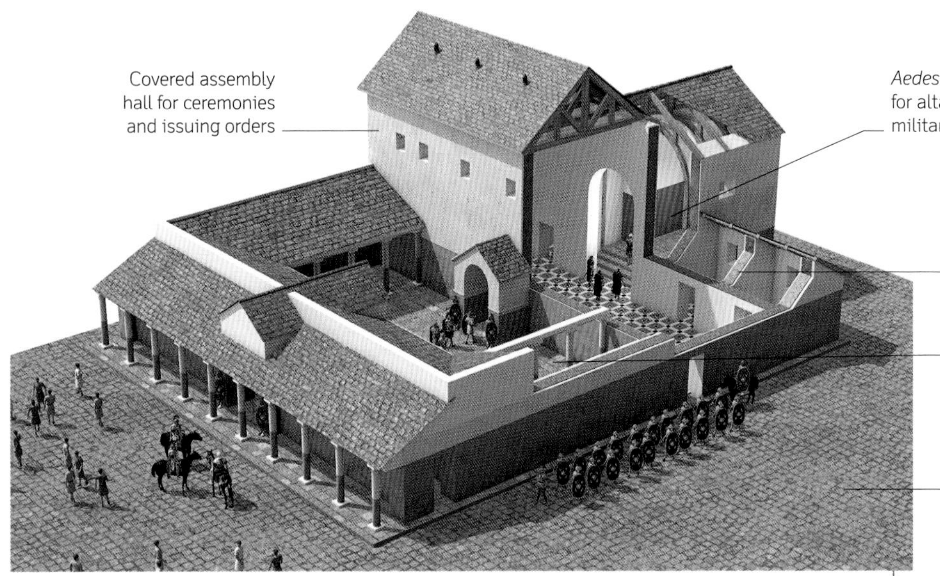

◁ ***Principia***
The typical headquarters building in each fort was a place to meet and review troops, issue orders, and conduct ceremonies, including religious sacrifice. It housed the fort's financial and archival spaces, while its imposing architecture reflected Roman order and discipline.

Barrack blocks

Vindolanda Fort

Guarding the frontier

Vindolanda was a distant outpost of the Roman Empire in the north of Britannia (England and Wales). Soldiers stationed here guarded the empire's border with the unconquered Caledonia (Scotland) in the north. Although the first wooden fort was built at Vindolanda in 85 CE, before the construction of Hadrian's Wall (see pp. 204–205), Vindolanda became a crucial garrison base for the nearby wall.

Various units stationed at Vindolanda demolished and rebuilt the fort nine times during its occupation from the late 1st century to 370. The stone fort shown here was built by an auxiliary unit (the 4th cohort of Gauls) in the 3rd century. These troops provided a reserve force in case of rebellion or attack, and could be sent out on trading and military missions. The archive of more than 1,000 wooden tablets found at Vindolanda illustrates this busy world of travel, transportation, and communication (see p. 204). Outside the fort gates there was a *vicus* ("settlement"), where the soldiers could spend their wages and perhaps keep a family.

VINDOLANDA **MEDAL**

This silver-gilt *phalera*, an award for military valor, was found at Vindolanda in 2006 and dates to the early 2nd century CE. It is a good illustration of the movement of troops around the Roman Empire as its owner, Quintus Sollonius, may well have earned it fighting in Dacia (modern Romania) in Trajan's campaigns. Decorations and awards such as this were an important way to boost morale and loyalty among the troops. The worship of Roman deities such as Mars, god of war, who is depicted on the medal between two legionary standards, also helped develop a shared Roman identity among troops from across the empire.

Built-in hearths provided heat in winter months

Barracks contained rooms for soldiers and their equipment

Shared bunk room for a squad of soldiers

△ **Barracks**
Roman barracks buildings provided robust accommodation for soldiers and their gear. Ordinary soldiers shared bunk rooms, while officers had their own space. There were separate rooms for armor, equipment, and cavalry horses. The consistent design and layout helped operational efficiency and discipline.

▷ **Vindolanda ruins**
Only a small fraction of the fort has been excavated so far. Here, the remains of a heating system, or hypocaust, can be seen.

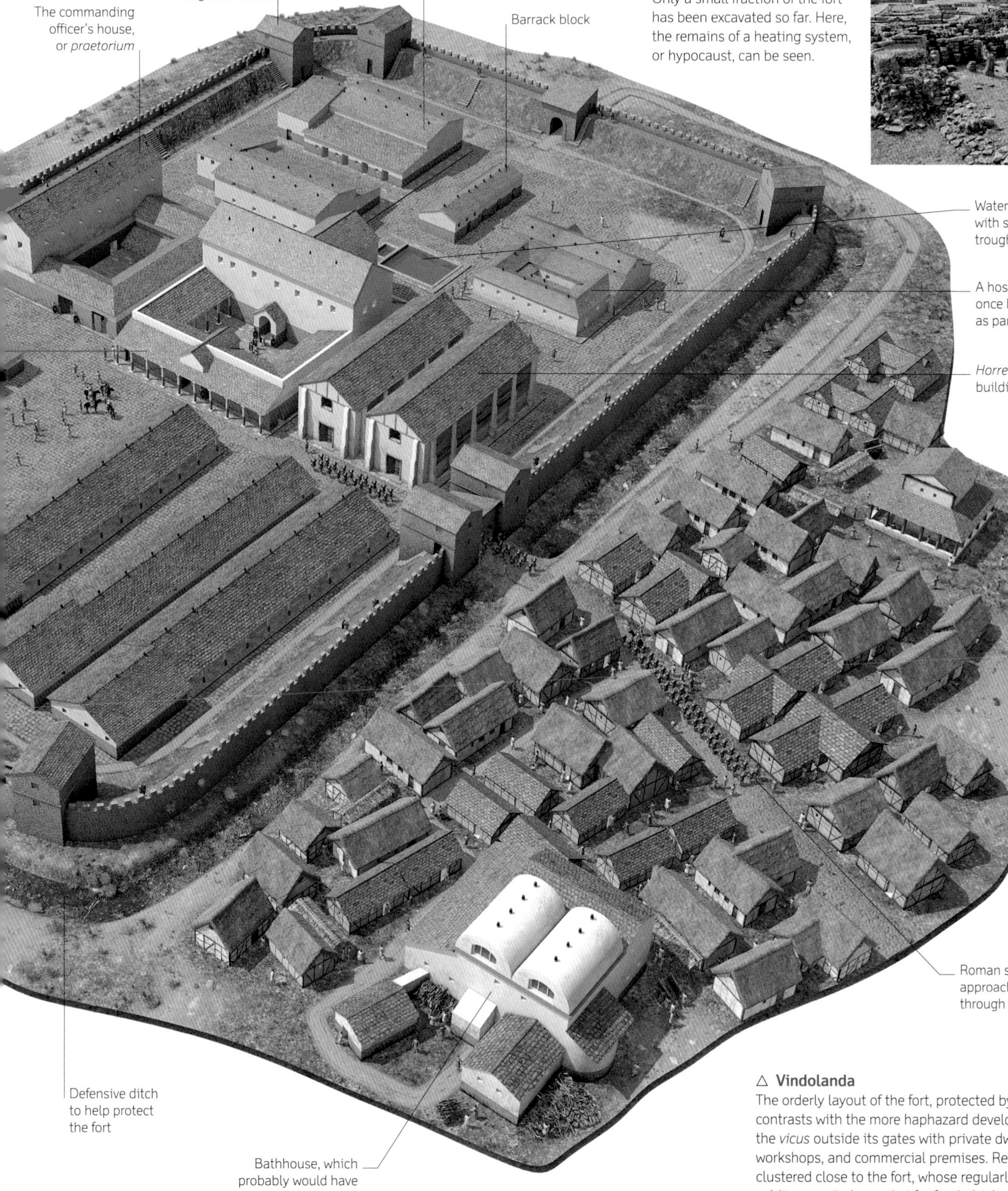

△ **Vindolanda**
The orderly layout of the fort, protected by its walls, contrasts with the more haphazard development of the *vicus* outside its gates with private dwellings, workshops, and commercial premises. Residents clustered close to the fort, whose regularly paid soldiers created a market for food, drinks, and other services. A bathhouse offered a space for relaxation.

Constantine the Great

The first Christian emperor

Constantine was the first Roman emperor to convert to Christianity. Whether driven by faith or political ambition, his support did much to move Christianity into mainstream Roman culture. He also founded the great city of Constantinople.

Constantine was not born in Rome but in Naissus (modern Serbia) around 272 CE. His father, Constantius, was a tetrarch (see pp. 254–255), responsible for restoring order in the empire's northwest. When Constantius died in 306 at Eboracum (York, England), his soldiers saluted Constantine as their new emperor. The other tetrarchs were angered and war soon broke out. Constantine allied with Licinius, the *augustus* (senior emperor) in the east. Maxentius held Rome and Italy.

Miracle at the Milvian Bridge

In 312, Constantine and Maxentius faced each other at the Milvian Bridge, which spanned the Tiber just north of Rome. On the eve of battle, Constantine reputedly had a vision: if his soldiers displayed on their shields *Chi* (X) and *Rho* (P), Greek letters which symbolized the name of Jesus Christ, they would be victorious.

Constantine's forces routed Maxentius's army in the battle, and his epiphany represented a crucial moment in the history of Christianity: an end to the persecution of Christians, whose religion would become the empire's dominant faith. Constantine sponsored the building of churches, especially in Rome, and in 313 he issued the Edict of Milan, officially protecting Christians from persecution.

◁ **Commemorative medallion**
This German copy of a coin shows Constantine in military dress, holding a trophy while addressing an army.

▽ **Battle of the Milvian Bridge**
In this detail from a 1520 fresco, Constantine's soldiers battle Maxentius's forces. Their victory put Constantine in control of Rome and the Western Empire.

Constantine's Christian capital

Although Constantine had secured the site of Rome, he did not much care for the city or its inhabitants. He wanted a new center of power for a new, Constantinian empire. After defeating his former ally, Licinius, in 324, Constantine founded Constantinople (modern Istanbul). Named after the emperor, it was built on the Greek city of Byzantium in 330. Although the city had many Roman features, including baths and a hippodrome for chariot racing, it was a new capital for a new kind of Christian emperor (see pp. 278–279).

272 Constantine is born in Naissus (Serbia)

306 Constantius dies in Eboracum (York); Constantine is saluted by his soldiers

308 Constantine is recognized as *caesar* of the west in the Tetrarchy

312 Defeat of Maxentius at the Milvian Bridge, Rome

313 He enacts the Edict of Milan; Christianity is officially tolerated

324 Defeat of Licinius at Chrysopolis; Constantine is undisputed emperor

330 Foundation of Constantinople (formerly Byzantium) as a "new Rome"

337 Baptized by Eusebius of Nicomedia, the emperor dies on May 22

Constantine the Great
A Christian Constantine is depicted cradling his new imperial capital in this Byzantine mosaic from c. 1000. By founding Constantinople, Constantine could portray his power through politics, religion, and architecture, away from the legacies of Rome.

The Rise of Christianity

A new faith in the empire

From the early 1st century CE, a small religious sect from the eastern Mediterranean began to grow in popularity and spread across the empire. It faced periods of violent persecution until an emperor's conversion changed everything.

◁ **Ewer with biblical engraving**
This 5th-century ewer shows Christ healing a blind person. By this time, mythological scenes in art and ornament had largely been replaced by Christian iconography.

Some decades after the death of Jesus Christ in Jerusalem in around 30 CE, Christianity began to attract converts from different communities and social classes throughout the Roman world. However, most people continued to worship the traditional deities of Roman religion—Jupiter, Juno, Mars, Minerva, and others—and there was a strong consensus that it was this faith that guaranteed the *pax deorum* ("the peace of the gods") across the empire.

Persecuting a minority

Roman religion had always been diverse and adaptable, and when new cults and beliefs were encountered in conquered lands they were often incorporated into the sacred landscape.

◁ **Constantine's conversion**
This painting by Peter Paul Rubens (1622) imagines Constantine before the Battle of the Milvian Bridge in 312. The emperor's relationship with the faith was important, but not clear-cut: for example, he did not receive baptism and become a "full" Christian until he was on his deathbed in 337.

They could be exported, too. At the end of the 2nd century, for example, a soldier named Claudius Hieronymianus was allowed to erect a temple to the Egyptian god Serapis in Eboracum (York, England). But not all non-Roman deities were accepted; when the emperor Elagabalus tried to introduce worship of the Syrian sun god Elagabal to Rome in the early 3rd century he was unsuccessful.

The early Christians also had difficulties gaining recognition for their faith. This was primarily due to their uncompromising monotheism, which rejected the existence of deities other than the one, true God. This led to Christians and other monotheists such as Jews serving as scapegoats whenever disaster struck the empire, as their refusal to offer sacrifices to the traditional gods was said to have upset the *pax deorum*.

Persecutions began in the 1st century, under Nero, who blamed the Christians for the great fire that devastated Rome in 64 CE, and continued off and on until the rule of Diocletian in the early 4th century. Many Christians who died, often horribly, in state-sponsored executions were later venerated as martyrs and saints.

Imperial conversion

A change was coming, however. Before the Battle of the Milvian Bridge in 312, Constantine claimed to have had a miraculous vision of a flaming cross in the sky. According to the Christian writer Lactantius, he ordered his soldiers to draw the cross of Christ on their shields in order to guarantee their victory. Constantine defeated his rival Maxentius and became sole ruler of the empire (see pp. 260–261).

The extent to which Constantine was a true believer in Christ is still debated, but his reign marked the moment from which Christianity would grow into the empire's dominant religion. When Constantine issued the Edict of Milan in 313, which guaranteed freedom of Christian worship, the age of persecutions ended. The rise of Christianity was complete in 380, when the emperor Theodosius I declared it the official state religion of the Roman Empire.

◁ **Early Christian stele**
This 3rd-century funerary monument to Licinia Amias is one of the earliest surviving Christian artifacts. The fish icons represent the Apostles, whom Jesus called "fishers of men."

△ **Death as spectacle**
Condemnation to the beasts (*damnatio ad bestias*) in the arena was a common punishment for criminals in the empire – and for Christians during periods of persecution. It is graphically represented in this 3rd century CE mosaic from El Djem, in modern Tunisia.

> "It was **proper** that **Christians** should have the **liberty** to follow that **mode of religion**."
>
> LACTANTIUS, DESCRIBING THE EDICT OF MILAN IN *ON THE DEATHS OF THE PERSECUTORS*

THE PASSION OF SAINT PERPETUA

Perpetua, shown in this unattributed painting from c. 1520, was a noblewoman from North Africa who in 203 was put to death in the arena in Carthage for her faith. She is one of the earliest named Christian martyrs, and this is partly due to her status; many early Christians were enslaved and poor people, and women of humble birth, their identities unknown. The main reason she is remembered, however, is the text known as *The Passion of St. Perpetua and Felicity*, which tells the story of her arrest and persecution, along with her enslaved companion, Felicity. Although its authorship is disputed, *The Passion* is seen as one of the most important early Christian works. It is all the more remarkable in that it could be both a firsthand account and one written by a woman.

Roman Triumphs

Celebrations of imperial victory

Originating in the Republic to celebrate a general's military success, Triumphs in the Imperial age became the exclusive preserve of the emperors—who celebrated the event by erecting triumphal arches to themselves and their achievements.

△ **Missing monument**
This *denarius* from 18 BCE shows a triple-bayed Arch of Augustus. Now lost, this arch celebrated the recovery of captured military standards from the Parthians.

In Rome's Republican era, generals were sometimes rewarded for important victories with the state's highest military honor: a Triumph. Supposedly initiated by Romulus himself, a Triumph was a great procession where the general would ride a chariot through Rome to the mass acclaim of the entire city. He would wear a magisterial purple-and-gold toga (*toga picta*) and, in some accounts, his face was painted red (possibly in imitation of Jupiter or Mars). The general would be accompanied by his troops and he would put on display the booty and treasure he had won, which often included captured soldiers and civilians. Triumphs were so special that the general and his men were allowed to enter the *pomerium*, the sacred city boundary across which armed soldiers were not usually permitted to pass. After processing through Rome, Triumphs ended in front of the Temple of Jupiter Optimus Maximus on the Capitoline Hill with animal sacrifices and offerings to the gods.

Celebrating Triumphs in stone and marble

In the Republic, triumphing generals would often build temples as lasting symbols of the honor they had received. By the Imperial age, only emperors were allowed to celebrate Triumphs, and the way they chose to memorialize these events in stone and marble was through the construction of triumphal arches. These were designed as huge ornamental gateways that spanned the route of the triumphal procession, along which the emperor in his chariot would pass on his day of acclamation. Each arch was richly decorated with inscriptions, friezes, carvings, and sculptures detailing the events it was built to celebrate.

The first imperial arch was erected by Augustus in the 20s BCE. It no longer exists, but it set a precedent his successors would follow. Indeed, for subsequent emperors, erecting their own triumphal arch became a way not just to show their victories over foreign enemies but to demonstrate that they were worthy heirs to Augustus. The 4th-century emperor Constantine took this idea of imperial continuity and legitimacy even further by reusing carved decorations from earlier emperors' triumphal monuments on his own arch (see pp. 298–299), which was completed in 315.

Today, almost 40 similar arches survive from across the Roman Empire. There are three extant triumphal arches in Rome, dedicated to the emperors Titus, Septimius Severus, and Constantine.

△ **Showing off the spoils of war**
This frieze on the Arch of Titus in Rome shows the emperor celebrating a Triumph. It faces a frieze showing the capture of Jerusalem in 70 CE, the event for which Titus won his Triumph.

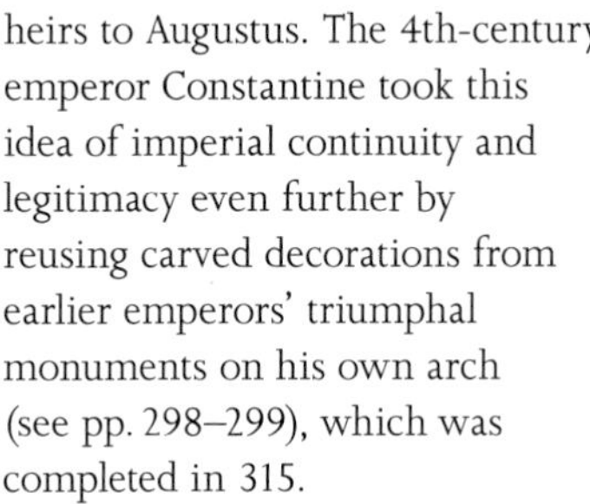

"The **Senate** and **People of Rome dedicated this Arch** to the Emperor **Constantine** ... as a sign of his triumphs."

INSCRIPTION ON THE ARCH OF CONSTANTINE, ROME

▽ Rewriting history
The Arch of Septimius Severus in Rome was built in 203 CE to celebrate his victories in the Parthian War of the 190s. The arch was also dedicated to his sons, Caracalla and Geta. After Septimius's death in 211, Caracalla murdered Geta and erased his name from the arch.

The keystone at the apex of the central arch features a statue of Mars

Geta's name was once on this line, but was chiseled out on Caracalla's orders

This relief shows Roman siege engines attacking the Parthians' ally, Edessa

Inscription listing the victories of Septimius Severus and his sons was originally gilded in bronze

Glassware

Practical and ornamental beauty

The Romans produced many different types of glass, ranging from decorative to more domestic, practical pieces. The industry developed rapidly during the 1st century CE, thanks to the discovery of glass-blowing techniques in the Hellenistic East. As glass became more common, artists grew more creative.

▷ **Lycurgus cup**
This 4th century CE drinking glass is decorated with scenes showing the capture of King Lycurgus of Thrace. Silver ornamentation surrounds "dichroic" glass, which can display multiple colors depending on lighting conditions.

Opaque white glass is overlaid on translucent blue glass

△ **Morgan cup**
The Morgan Cup is decorated with a frieze showing a fertility ritual that was intended to help women conceive. Made in the 1st century CE, it was found in Heraclea Pontica (Türkiye).

△ ***Pyxis***
A *pyxis* was a cylindrical box used to hold cosmetics or jewelery. This example from the late 1st century BCE shows the skill of Roman artisans in creating colorful ornaments.

Glass mimics the rich blue of expensive lapis lazuli, a stone used to make dyes

△ **Glass portrait**
This highly detailed glass portrait from the 2nd century CE may represent the goddess Juno. It was created by pressing molten glass into a mold.

Young man identified as "Gennadios"

◁ **Gold glass medallion**
From the Egyptian city of Alexandria, this 3rd-century CE medallion, designed to be worn as a pendant, shows an educated youth from the city. It is thought to celebrate a victory in a musical contest.

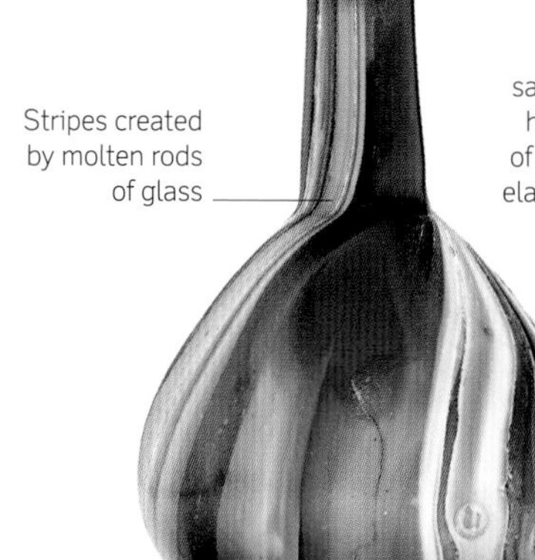

Stripes created by molten rods of glass

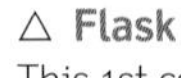

△ **Flask**
This 1st century CE flask was made using glass-blowing techniques, combining three canes of colored glass to create swirling ribbons of blue, white, yellow, and green.

Section of a satyr's face may have been part of a larger, more elaborate design

△ **Satyr inlay**
This image of a theater mask shows the wide range of subjects that Roman glassworkers depicted. The piece comes from Europe, and was made in the 1st century CE.

◁ **Sarcophagus of Trees**
On this early Christian sarcophagus, the *Chi Rho* (XP) monograph of Christ is central, flanked by vignettes of biblical scenes, such as Cain and Abel, and the arrest of Peter.

and all temples to the traditional gods were closed, never to reopen for official forms of worship. Nonetheless, there were still some leading senators who followed traditional forms of worship. The most prominent of these were the Symmachi and Nicomachi families, but their "pagan" practices petered out over the next few decades.

Although *paganus* (pagan) is a term that has commonly been used to describe non-Christian forms of worship, it was not an official descriptive term. Because it translates as "rural" or "rustic", it was used pejoratively by Christians to describe people following a different religious system. Romans such as the Symmachi and Nicomachi families would not have regarded themselves as "pagan", and there is little or no evidence that the term was ever employed throughout the existence of the Roman Empire.

Traditional and Christian imagery

Early Christians did not immediately abandon the mythologies of traditional Roman worship. Some used traditional imagery to disguise their Christian beliefs, while others appear to have used it to both interpret and display their faith, on personal treasures and on their sarcophagi. For instance, the mythical figure Orpheus was often used to depict Christ; this remained popular after Christianity became the official state religion.

Venus, in a shell, is held up by mythical beasts

Flanked by her attendants, a seated Projecta regards herself in a mirror

◁ **The Projecta Casket**
This casket (c. 380) for toiletries was probably a wedding gift for a couple called Secundus and Projecta. The casket is adorned with traditional mythologies, but its inscription reads "Secundus and Projecta, live in Christ."

▽ **Traditional imagery**
This Late Roman ivory panel depicts the apotheosis ("divinization") of a Roman, possibly of the Symmachi family, carried to heaven by personified winds, watched by the sun god—an image of traditional Roman religion.

Roman Philosophy

Roman thinkers build on the ideas of Greek philosophers

Philosophy is the study of fundamental questions about life, knowledge, and the values that guide us. For the Romans, the answers to these questions were shaped by their experience of empire.

Philosophy is a Greek term that translates as "the love of wisdom". Some of the questions it addresses, such as "How do I live a good life?", or "What is the best way of governing a city?", were investigated by thinkers and teachers in the Greek world of the 5th and 4th centuries BCE including Socrates, Plato, and Aristotle. As interactions with the Greek world increased, aspects of Hellenistic culture were incorporated into the empire, including philosophy.

Thinking like a Greek

For a long time, the idea of "Roman" philosophy would have seemed odd. If a Roman wanted to study philosophy, then he—and it was almost exclusively a male pursuit—had to travel east, to the great centers of Greek culture. In cities such as Athens, different schools of philosophy competed with one another.

In fact, when Greek philosophers had first begun to arrive in Rome in the mid-2nd century BCE, they were initially met with resistance and skepticism. In 155 BCE Cato the Elder persuaded the Senate to send away some philosophers, lest they corrupt the city's youth with their ideas. He was particularly concerned that Carneades—a Greek whose persuasive public lectures in Rome, first supporting the virtue of justice, then refuting this concept—could threaten the authority of Rome's courts.

▽ Plato's Academy
From a villa in Pompeii, this mosaic imagines a view of Plato's Academy in Athens, showing the broad interest in philosophy. Plato himself is the central figure.

Over time, this attitude changed. By the 1st century BCE, prominent Romans visited Athens to study philosophy, Cicero among them. He saw argument for and against a proposition as a valuable tool for establishing its truth—and recognized the value of reasoning and debating skills to a political and judicial career. By writing in Latin, Cicero helped to spread Greek philosophical ideas and principles in the Roman world.

In the empire, two philosophical schools were especially prominent: Stoicism and Epicureanism. Both offered their adherents principles to follow in order to enjoy a "good" life, although their views of how to achieve this differed quite significantly. Devised in the early 3rd century BCE by Zeno of Citium, Stoicism argued that only by living a virtuous life—and not giving in to passions—could someone achieve *eudaimonia* (a good and happy life).

Emperors and philosophy

A sure sign of the changing attitudes toward philosophy was its growing prominence in the imperial court. Philosophers found employment with some emperors. Famously, the Stoic philosopher Seneca was a tutor of the emperor Nero. His attempts to instruct the emperor in a virtuous life were unsuccessful, however. He was ordered to take his own life when a plot against Nero was uncovered

EPICUREANISM'S GOOD LIFE

Epicurus (341–270 BCE) was a Greek philosopher. His beliefs, known as Epicureanism, argued that pleasure is the only good. He defined pleasure as an absence of pain, therefore the goal of life is to be constantly free from physical and mental distress; this state of *ataraxia* can be reached by curbing desires and seeking contentment in living simply. Epicurean schools opened around the Roman Empire, although the ethos died out in the 3rd century. Few of Epicurus's writings survive, but his ideas are perhaps preserved in the poet and philosopher Lucretius's epic poem *De rerum natura* (*On the Nature of Things*).

> "You are teaching **philosophy in Latin**, and, so to speak, making it a **Roman citizen**."
>
> CICERO, *DE FINIBUS*

in 65 CE. When Vespasian became emperor in 69 CE, however, he began his ten-year reign by banishing philosophers from Rome, purging them from the court and Senate.

Later emperors would continue to show an interest in philosophy. During his tour of Greece, Hadrian is known to have attended philosophical lectures. The emperor Marcus Aurelius (see pp. 222–223) is today considered by many people to have been a philosopher in his own right. While waging war, he wrote his *Meditations*. Almost in diary form, they record his ideas about Stoic philosophy, and how to judge one's actions and their place in the universe.

Marcus Aurelius's reputation as a philosopher endured. In the 4th century, the emperor Julian, who promoted philosophy, admired Marcus Aurelius and Hadrian. Julian promoted Neoplatonism, an ethos that built on the ideas of Plato and won some popularity. In 4th-century Alexandria, both philosophy and mathematics were taught by Hypatia, a great female astronomer and mathematician (see pp. 294–295).

Although Seneca cut his wrists and took poison, his death was slow

The belt and basin were Renaissance additions to tell Seneca's story

To speed up blood loss, Seneca immersed himself in a warm bath

◁ **Seneca's death**
This statue may depict a fisherman from a folk tale, but has also been interpreted as showing Seneca at the moment of his suicide. Stoics saw suicide as a choice to be made rationally.

◁ **Marcus Aurelius**
A gold bust of the emperor Marcus Aurelius, whose *Meditations*, written in Greek, showed the emperor's personal interest in Stoic philosophy.

Ornate breastplate

◁ Holy pendant After Christianity became the official religion of the Roman Empire, its symbols were used in jewelery design. This gold cross was made using the *opus interrasile* method, where the metal is skillfully pierced to pick out a pattern. It was a style popular in the Eastern Empire in particular.

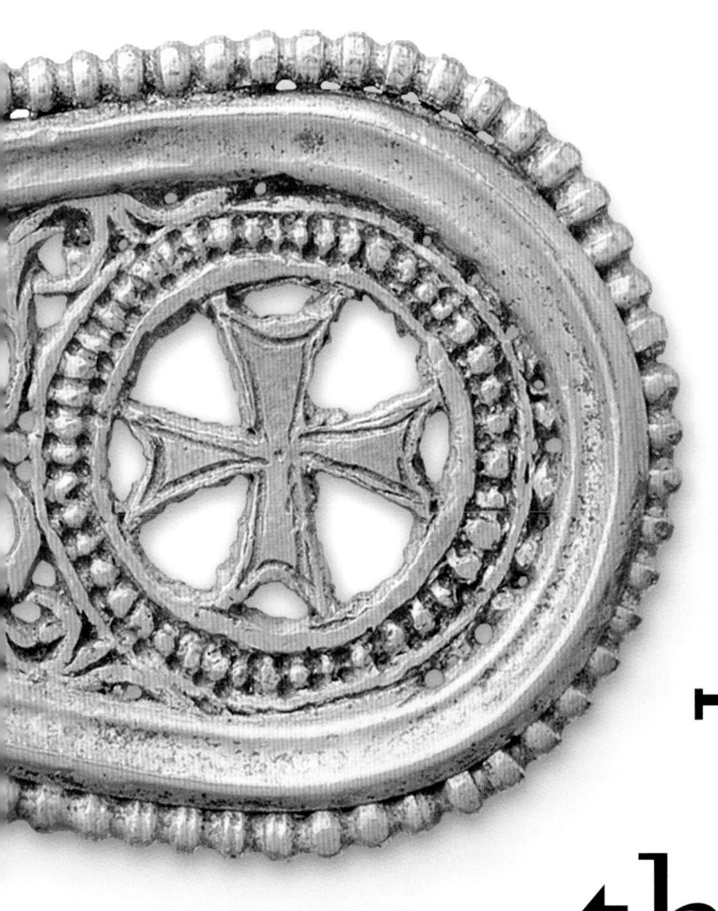

6

The Fall of the Western Roman Empire

395–476 CE

Decline and Fall

Although the Roman Empire had been divided into eastern and western halves in 286 CE, imperial power had not. Constantine the Great, for example, ruled both the Eastern and Western Empires for a time, as did his son, Constantius II. So, too, did Theodosius I who, on his death in 395, became the last emperor to have achieved that feat. From that moment on, the two halves of the Roman Empire would never again be under the control of a single leader.

A parting of the ways

No one at the time knew that the empires were parting ways forever, and power passed in an orderly fashion to Theodosius's two sons. Arcadius, the eldest, became the Eastern Emperor in Constantinople, while his younger brother Honorius was appointed Western Emperor—based not in Rome, however, but in Milan (and later Ravenna). Officially, the Roman Empire remained a single, indivisible state with two emperors, coequal in power. In practice, though, it was developing into a pair of parallel entities. The post-Theodosian Eastern and Western Empires did share a common approach in some areas, such as law and citizenship, but took their own paths in areas such as culture, religion, and foreign policy.

The endurance of this split shows that its origins went deeper than one emperor's succession. Theodosius's descendants controlled both empires for more than 60 years after his death, during which time there had been opportunities to unite east and west.

The societal differences between the peoples of both empires ensured that reunification would be a difficult proposition that only became more unlikely over time. Latin, for example, was the dominant tongue in the west, while Greek was widely spoken in the east. Latin remained in use for all official imperial business, but most people across the empires thought, spoke, wrote, and prayed in different languages.

On the edges of the empire

This cultural gap was widened by the changing political situation within the empires and the military situation outside them. Even with emperors no longer going into battle personally after 395, the threats from the Sasanian Empire and Huns in the east and the increasingly organized Germanic confederations in the west made it important for power to be located near the frontiers of each empire, to enable a rapid response to the pressures created by sudden shifts in the strategic situation. At the same time, emperors faced another kind of pressure from citizens—especially those of high rank and social status—competing for the patronage their rulers offered in wealth and position at court.

In some respects, the death of Theodosius in 395 marked the moment when the Roman Empire's political organization finally aligned with the social, cultural, and strategic developments that had led to the division between east and west a century earlier. Rather than two halves of a whole, east and west became increasingly separate entities with different concerns and priorities. This division would have huge implications in the chaotic century to come, leading ultimately to the fall of the Western Roman Empire itself.

◁ **Carving of the late 4th-century consul Anicius Petronius Probus**

395 Death of Theodosius I; final division of Roman Empire into east and west

402 Western Empire capital moves from Milan to Ravenna

406 Massed Germanic peoples cross the Rhine into the Western Empire

410 Visigoths sack Rome. Britannia separates from the Roman Empire

418 Visigoths take control of southwestern Gaul from the Western Empire

425 Valentinian III is installed as emperor in the west by the Eastern Empire

1 Ravenna, capital of the Western Empire from 402

2 Hagia Irene, Roman-era church in Constantinople

3 Alexandria, in the Eastern Empire

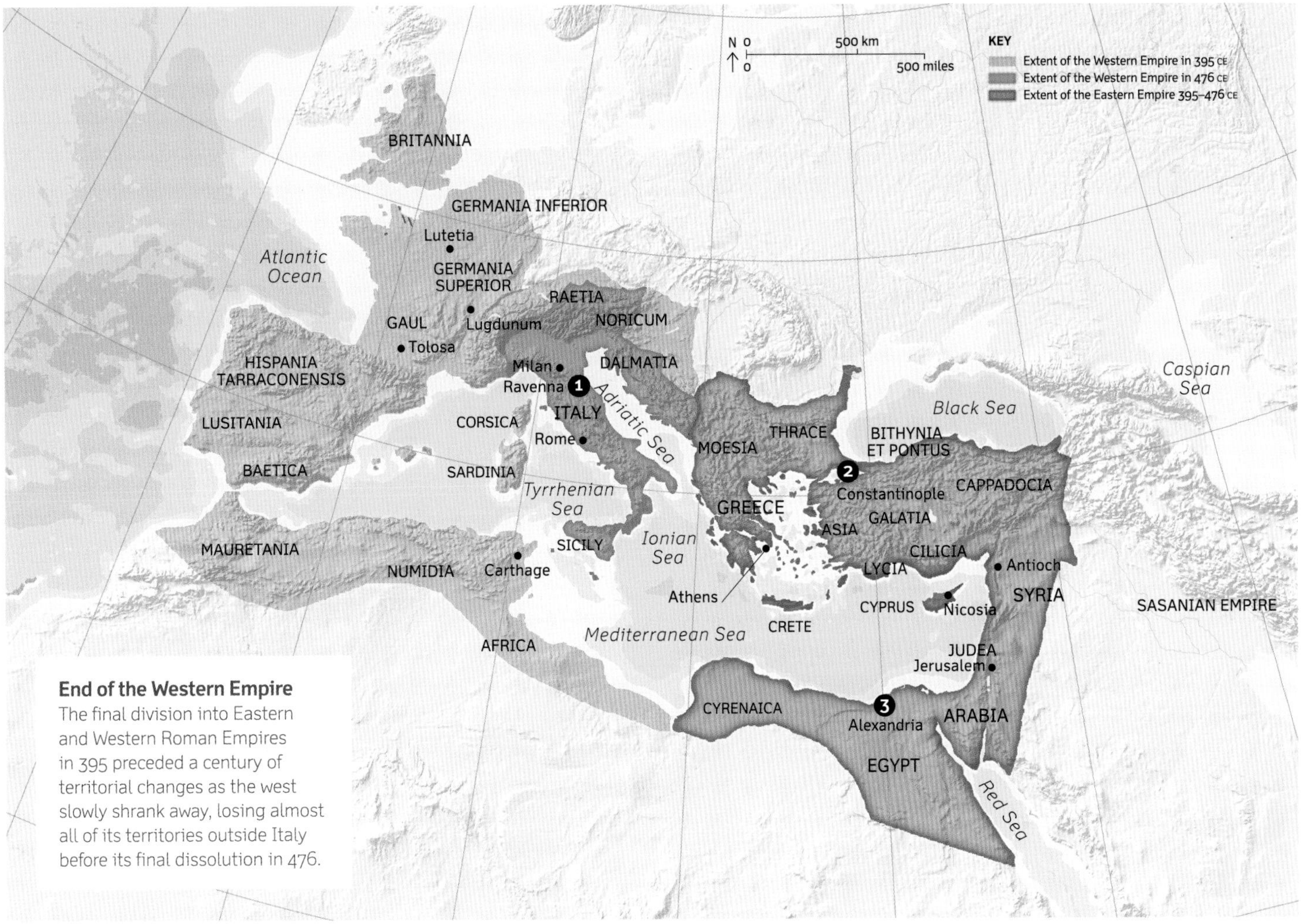

KEY
Extent of the Western Empire in 395 CE
Extent of the Western Empire in 476 CE
Extent of the Eastern Empire 395–476 CE

End of the Western Empire
The final division into Eastern and Western Roman Empires in 395 preceded a century of territorial changes as the west slowly shrank away, losing almost all of its territories outside Italy before its final dissolution in 476.

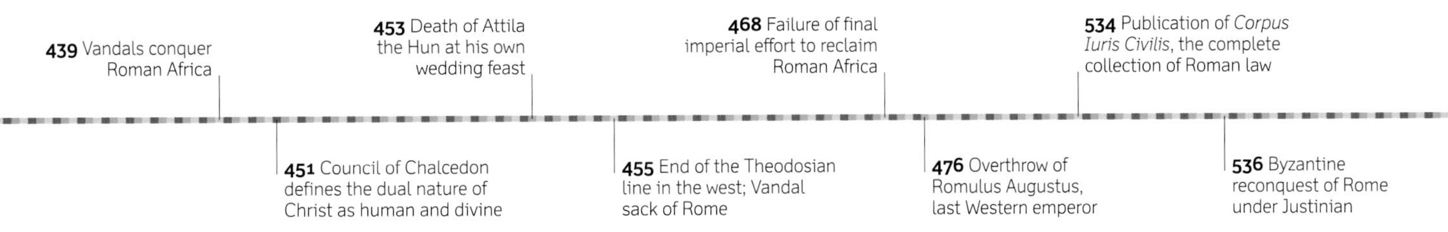

△ **Giving thanks**
This mosaic from the Hagia Sophia shows the 12th-century Byzantine emperor John II Komnenos and the empress Irene with gifts for Mary and Jesus.

Constantinople

The Christian capital of the Eastern Roman world

The emperor Constantine's founding of the city that took his name marked a permanent and seismic shift in the political, geographic, and religious emphasis of the Roman Empire, whose capital it became on May 11, 330 CE.

In 657 BCE a prince named Byzas, from the Greek city of Megara, is said to have established a colony on a peninsula guarding the straits between the Black Sea and the Mediterranean. This new settlement was called *Byzantion* in Greek—in Latin, Byzantium.

As well as its strategic position, Byzantium boasted a natural harbor, known as the Golden Horn, that saw the city become a busy port over the next century. Byzantium's commercial success brought it to the attention of Persia, the main regional power. Persian occupation was followed by Athenian, Spartan, and Macedonian rule in the centuries that followed.

Early encounters with Rome

The city's interactions with Rome were relatively minor until the end of the 2nd century CE, when it became embroiled in the civil war that engulfed Rome after the assassination of the emperor Commodus in 191. Byzantium backed an imperial claimant called Pescennius Niger, who lost out to the war's eventual victor, Septimius Severus. As emperor, Septimius punished Byzantium by razing it to the ground in 196. He partially rebuilt the city afterward, giving it the short-lived name of Augusta Antonina, but it would become something of a backwater for the next

"Oh City, City, **head of all Cities**! Oh City, City, head of the **four corners** of the **world**!"

DOUKAS, 15TH-CENTURY BYZANTINE HISTORIAN

century or so, until the ascent to imperial power of Constantine and structural changes across the Roman empire combined to put Byzantium back on the map.

From the late 2nd century, power in the empire had shifted from the center to the periphery. Invasions, rebellions, and migrations along the imperial borders had forced Rome's emperors to spend more and more time away from the capital, directing operations at the empire's most vulnerable flash points. By the early 3rd century, few sites were more sensitive than the Bosporus, the strait at the entrance to the Black Sea where Europe and Asia face each other across a channel of water just 2,450 ft (750 m) wide. Whoever controlled this area oversaw access to Rome's troubled territories in the Near East, the volatile Balkans, and the frontier formed by the Danube River between the Roman Empire and unconquered Northern Europe. And there, looking out over the Bosporus, was Byzantium. When Constantine became sole Roman emperor in 324 (see pp. 260–261) he saw the need for a permanent new capital and chose what was, at that point, a lowly eastern outpost.

WALLS OF **CONSTANTINOPLE**

The walls Constantine built for Constantinople soon proved too narrow to contain his growing city, and by the 5th century the emperor Theodosius had to construct new fortifications across a much wider area. The improved defenses centered on a set of massive double walls, the inner of which were almost 20 ft (6 m) thick, studded with towers 39 ft (12 m) high, and defended by a moat. So imposing were Theodosius's walls that they remained unbreached for 1,000 years until the advent of gunpowder and cannon that enabled the fall of the city, and the Byzantine Empire, in 1453 (see pp. 302–303).

△ **House of worship**
The Hagia Sophia, with its famous domes, was founded in the 6th century by the emperor Justinian I on the site of an earlier church built by Constantine's son, Constantius II. It is now a mosque.

The grand new capital

Constantine's "New Rome" represented a decisive break with the past. Unlike Rome, it was a distinctly Christian municipality. One of its earliest buildings was the Hagia Irene, the first of many Christian churches. A central square—the Augustaeum—was laid out, and two separate Senate houses were built. Bisecting the city and crossing several new forums was a colonnaded main street, the Mese. The whole city would eventually be enclosed in walls that were virtually impregnable (see box, left). In a symbolic act, Constantine erected the Milion, a domed structure resting on four triumphal arches that acted as the marker from which all distances in the empire were measured. It signified that Constantinople was now the center of the Roman Empire.

It was his predecessor, Diocletian, who divided the empire between west and east (see pp. 254–255), but it was Constantine who ensured that as the Western half declined, the other half endured, first as the Eastern Empire and later as the Byzantine Empire—and always with Constantinople as its capital. Today, as Istanbul in modern Türkiye, the city remains a thriving and important metropolis. Its name, however, derives from the Greek for "toward the city": namely, the ancient city of Constantinople.

▷ **Woman of substance**
This lead-filled weight from c. 400–450, which may depict an empress of the Eastern Empire's Theodosian dynasty, was used as a measuring counterbalance.

The Germanic Migrations

The transformation of the Western Mediterranean

At the turn of the 5th century CE, a series of major migrations from Eastern and Central Europe would remake the Roman world, with consequences for both the east and west.

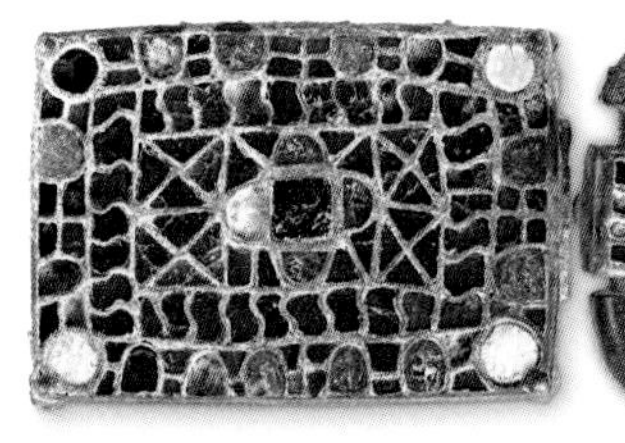

△ **Belt buckle**
This eye-catching Visigothic buckle is particularly lavishly decorated with inset rare stones and glass, almost in imitation of Roman style.

From the later 4th century, the Roman Empire was rocked by a series of political, demographic, and military changes, set in motion by the arrival of the nomadic Huns in Europe. Originally from Central Asia and the Caucasus, the Huns may have been driven westward by changes in the climate, reducing the availability of grazing land. The Romans did not directly encounter the Huns for some time, but their arrival set off a domino effect, displacing many of the peoples already settled north of the Danube River, in the region of Germania. These Germanic peoples probably originated from southern Scandinavia, and shared cultural and linguistic roots.

Warriors and civilians

In the following decades, many of these Germanic peoples formed confederations and migrated west and south toward the Mediterranean. Although most of these groups included armed men, they were largely made up of civilians, including women and children, fleeing worsening conditions. Rome reacted with a mixture of acceptance of this influx, exploitation, and, finally, aggression. The emperor Valens tried to have the leaders of one confederation (the Visigoths) assassinated. This failed, and the resulting escalation of violence led to Valens's death, and a catastrophic Roman defeat, at the Battle of Adrianople in 378.

Mass movement

Later waves of mass migration would follow, notably the crossing of the Rhine by the Vandals (from modern southern Poland), Suebi (from modern Germany and the Czech Republic), and the Alans (from the north Caucasus) late in 406. These corresponded with a series of dramatic internal political crises in the west, and a collapse in relations with the east, leaving the empire highly vulnerable. Within only a few years, much of the Western Empire began to drift outside of imperial control, including Britannia, northern Gaul, and much of Hispania. Rome itself would face a historic disaster (see pp. 282–283), and Vandals and Alans managed to cross the sea from Hispania to settle in Roman Africa.

Shifting identities

This process of migration was considerably more nuanced than the "barbarian invasions" of popular imagination. "Barbarian" was a derogatory term that the Romans had adopted from the Greeks to refer to people of foreign origins who were believed to lack the sophistication of Classical culture. Yet, by the 5th century, the line between "Roman" and "barbarian" was no longer straightforward.

Stilicho, leader of the Western response during the early crisis, had a Vandal father and a Roman mother. Theodosius II, emperor of the Eastern Empire for 42

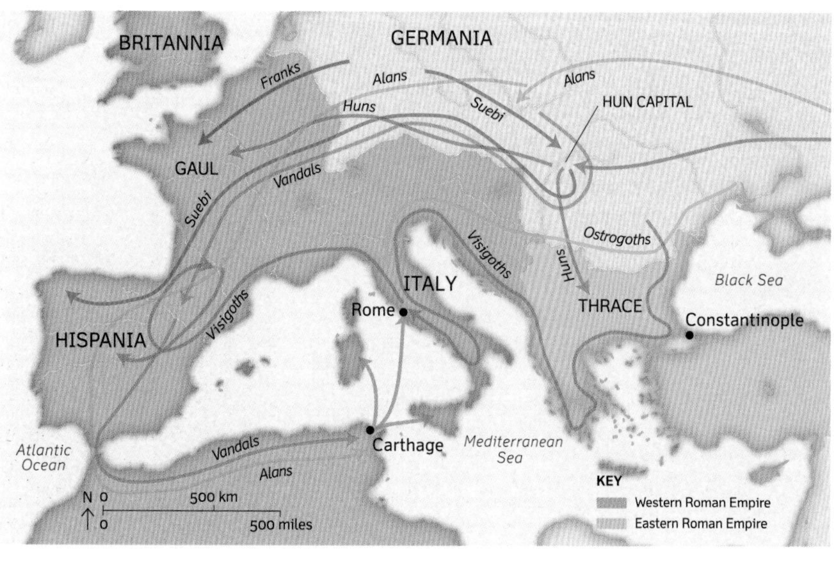

◁ **Migration routes**
Over the 5th century, many peoples of various origins migrated to settle down across the Mediterranean world, both inside and outside the Roman Empire.

◁ **Stilicho Diptych**
The man in this ivory diptych is traditionally identified as Stilicho, a Roman general of mixed ethnic heritage who effectively ran the Western Empire for many years in the early 5th century.

An aristocratic woman, who is traditionally identified as Serena, the wife of Stilicho

The shield's medallion depicts small figures with disputed identities

The diptych's two panels were originally connected by a hinge

years, was the grandson of a Frank. The majority of the Roman army was in fact made up of soldiers of "Germanic" origins, whether as allied troops or mercenaries, or by descent. Similarly, although militarized invasions were a part of the story of this period, they did not account for all of it. As Rome descended into civil wars, usurpers and emperors alike were happy to strike deals with various Germanic groups, offering them land in exchange for military support. The result was a complex series of developments in which the power of the central Roman state dwindled away and flowed increasingly to local communities of mixed Roman citizens and new migrants.

THE BATTLE OF **ADRIANOPLE**

Rome's crushing defeat at Adrianople (Edirne, in modern Türkiye) in August 378 CE was a sure sign that its previously unchallenged dominance was nearing an end. Following the mishandling of the arrival of a sizable group of Visigothic refugees, provoking a destructive war, the Eastern emperor Valens refused to wait for aid from his nephew, the Western emperor Gratian. Believing his force to be more than sufficient, and reluctant to share credit, Valens rushed to attack a Visigothic camp but was surprised by the sudden appearance of the Gothic cavalry. Two-thirds of the Roman army were wiped out and Valens was killed, making it Rome's worst military disaster since the Battle of Cannae in 216 BCE.

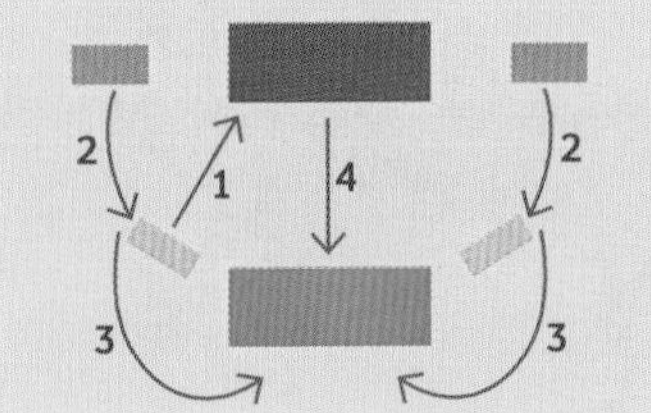

1 Left flank of Roman cavalry attacks early.
2 Gothic cavalry attacks the Roman cavalry on both flanks.
3 Gothic cavalry attacks the Roman infantry from behind.
4 Gothic infantry advances.

The Visigoths Sack Rome

The Western Empire's former capital is pillaged

The fall of the ancient capital of Rome in August 410 CE was a vivid demonstration of the extent to which Roman power had declined in the western Mediterranean.

The Sack of Rome was neither the culmination of a grand plan, nor the inevitable result of a hostile invasion. This infamous event, which has echoed through the centuries, was originally just the last resort of a frustrated commander whose plans had gone awry.

Germanic allies

As the Western Empire spiraled deeper into political and military turmoil in the early 400s, its preeminent general (and effective regent) Stilicho sought help from the Visigoths, a Germanic confederation already settled within the empire's borders. Some Visigoths had fought as mercenaries for Rome (for instance, against the Persians in the 3rd century), but their increasing discontent with Roman rule led to revolt, and victory at Adrianople in 378 (see pp. 280–281). To contain them, the emperor Theodosius let the Visigoths settle on land in the province of Moesia (in modern Bulgaria) in return for their help in defending imperial borders. Later, the Visigothic leader Alaric hoped to receive official status in the Roman hierarchy, and money for his soldiers. This arrangement with Stilicho fell victim to the unstable court politics of the 5th century. As confidence in his government decreased, Stilicho was deposed and murdered by rivals who hoped to control the weak emperor, Honorius.

▽ **Rome is overrun**
Centuries later, the Sack of Rome was viewed as a pivotal moment in the fall of the Western Empire and commemorated in engravings such as this one.

Alaric betrayed

In order to legitimize their coup, Stilicho's assassins deliberately emphasized his mixed ethnic heritage to stir up anti-Germanic prejudices.

◁ **Visigoth sword**
The Visigoths who sacked Rome had access to high-quality armor and weapons, due to their frequent work as Roman allies and mercenaries.

As well as provoking waves of popular violence, this strategy provided justification for reneging on Stilicho's arrangement with the Visigoths.

Furious at the betrayal, Alaric invaded Italy to force the emperor to pay, targeting the city of Rome in 408. By then, Rome had not been the imperial capital for over a century: Honorius's government was instead based securely in Ravenna, much less accessible due to surrounding swamps. Yet the ancient capital of Rome remained the ideological linchpin of the Roman Empire. It was by far the most populated city in the Mediterranean and perhaps the world, its monuments continued to enjoy imperial sponsorship, and the Senate based there remained the beating heart of the Western aristocracy.

A last resort

Even at this point, however, Alaric did not want to sack Rome, hoping that the threat would force Honorius to surrender. He withdrew after Rome's residents agreed to pay a sizable ransom, and tried to restart talks with Ravenna. Although the only realistic option was negotiation, given the Roman army was occupied with internal struggles and mass Germanic migrations throughout Gaul and Spain, Honorius's regime dug in and refused all talk of peace.

Therefore, when Alaric ultimately unleashed his Visigoths on Rome in August 410, it was more the result of frustration arising from diplomatic failure than strategic military aggression on the part of the Visigoths. Regardless of Alaric's motivations, the city of Rome was ransacked by a foreign foe for the first time since the Gauls had taken it, exactly 800 years before.

◁ **Eagle fibula**
The eagle was originally a Roman icon. It was widely adopted by Germanic peoples, including the Visigoths, as on this gilded brooch, one of a pair that was found in Spain.

Sheet gold is laid over bronze

Garnets, amethysts, and colored glass insets

Pendants once dangled from loops at the bottom of the brooch

> "In **one city**, the **whole world** perished."
>
> JEROME, *COMMENTARY ON EZEKIEL*, PROLOGUE

Contrary to the popular idea of the fall of Rome as uncontrolled "barbarian" pillaging of the cradle of civilization, the sack was restrained by contemporary standards. Relatively few major buildings were destroyed, the general population was not massacred, and there were even designated refuge sites, in particular churches, owing to the Visigoths' Christian faith. Nevertheless, as with the sack of any city, it was an inherently destructive event which saw countless civilians killed, enslaved, and subjected to torture and rape. There is no question that the event was horrific for all those who endured it.

A legend shaken

The sack of Rome also sent shock waves throughout the Mediterranean. Writers as far away as Syria and Africa found the news almost impossible to believe, and many began to question all that they had held true about the invincibility of the Roman Empire. The great African theologian Augustine of Hippo responded to the calamity by beginning work on his magnum opus *The City of God*, which would argue that Christians had to focus on the immortal realm of Heaven rather than any mortal state. Although military conquest was not the intention of Alaric, and Rome was no longer the capital of the empire that bore its name, its fate was the sign that an era of history was drawing to a close.

EMPEROR HONORIUS

In contrast to his father, Theodosius I (known as Theodosius the Great), the feeble young emperor Honorius (r. 393–423) embodied the weakness of the Western Empire during this period of decline. Honorius (right) became emperor aged 10, and was one of the empire's least successful rulers. According to the Greek author Procopius, Honorius was initially horrified to hear (while in Ravenna) that Rome had fallen—but only because he believed that this meant his pet chicken, named Rome, had died. Upon learning the truth, he was delighted that his pet was alive, even if the heart of his empire was not.

Gold and Silverware

The wealth of a far-reaching empire

As rulers of a vast empire spanning the Mediterranean, the Romans had access to both spoils of war and raw materials. They crafted luxury goods in precious metals such as gold and silver to display their wealth, ranging from ornate ceremonial artifacts for ostentatious display to everyday practical objects for use within wealthy households.

◁ **Votive plaque**
Both polytheistic and Christian Romans dedicated fine offerings to their chosen deities. This plaque is marked with the Christian *Chi Rho*, the sign of Christ.

△ **"Empress" pepper pot**
Practical objects could be both playful and ornate, such as this silver pepper pot, or *piperatorium*, shaped in the form of a wealthy Roman noblewoman.

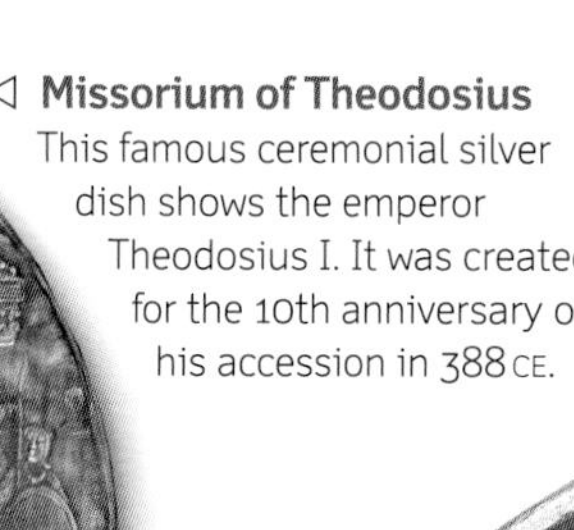

◁ **Missorium of Theodosius**
This famous ceremonial silver dish shows the emperor Theodosius I. It was created for the 10th anniversary of his accession in 388 CE.

Silver cast to form the shape of a leaping tigress

△ **Handle**
This silver handle for a vase or amphora (5th century CE) was found in 1992 in England's largest-ever Roman hoard, at Hoxne.

Achilles drags the body of Hector before the gates of Troy

△ **Ewer**
Part of Normandy's Berthouville treasure, this Early Imperial silver wine jug shows scenes from Homer's *Iliad*. Greek mythology remained a popular theme for decoration.

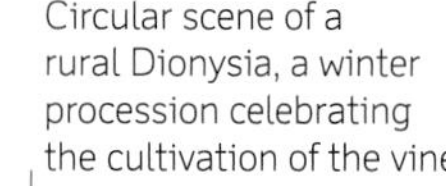

Circular scene of a rural Dionysia, a winter procession celebrating the cultivation of the vine

Inset medallions depict Roman emperors

▷ ***Patera* of Rennes**
Used for offering drinks to the gods, this golden *patera* or libation dish shows mythological scenes. In the center, Hercules and Bacchus engage in a drinking contest.

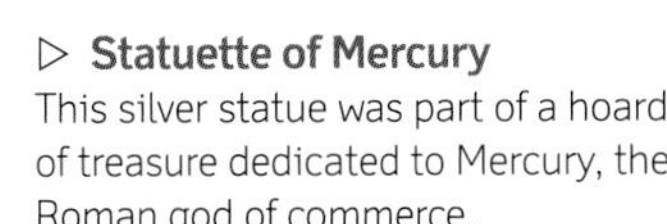

▷ Statuette of Mercury
This silver statue was part of a hoard of treasure dedicated to Mercury, the Roman god of commerce.

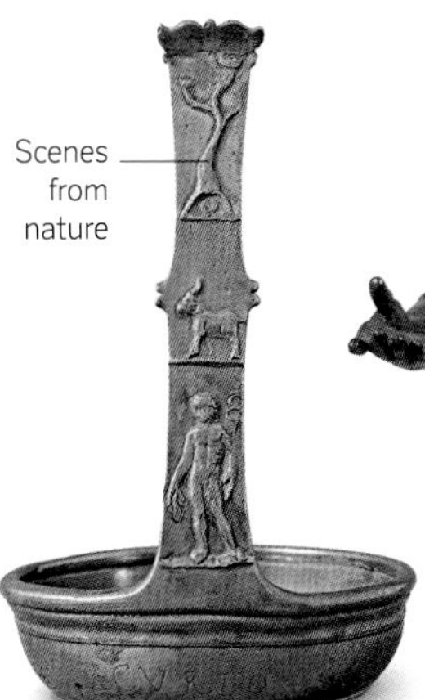

△ Ladle
A dedication to the god Mercury can be seen engraved at the bottom of this elaborate ladle.

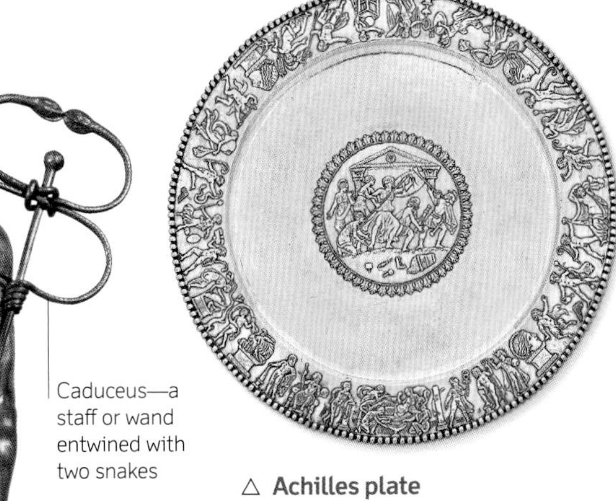

△ Achilles plate
The rim of this silver display plate is decorated with scenes from the life of the Greek hero Achilles. The centerpiece shows the moment when the hero, disguised as a girl, has his true identity revealed.

△ Goblet
This ornate silver drinking vessel commemorates the Isthmian Games, one of the four great Panhellenic Games that were held in Greece throughout antiquity.

△ Bowl
Decorated with finely rendered silver foliage, this bowl was used for dining as well as for displaying wealth. It is similar in design to other bowls found in hoards buried during raids in the mid-3rd century CE.

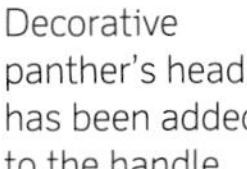

△ Fork and spoon
Unusually, this silver-and-gold piece of cutlery from the 3rd century CE could be used as both fork and spoon. Forks were rarely used by the Romans, and were for adding food to the plate rather than eating from directly.

▷ Furniture pin
The enthroned Tyche of Alexandria, a protective goddess, is depicted in this Roman furniture decoration. It was cast in silver, then gilded.

▷ Muse casket
This silver cosmetic box was probably made for Projecta, a wealthy Roman woman, in the 4th century CE. It was designed to hang from chains and is decorated with images of the Muses, the goddesses of artistic inspiration.

Late Roman Empresses

The women who helped rule the Roman Empire

Unlike societies such as that of Ancient Egypt, Roman men never accepted the idea of independent female rule. The title of empress, or *augusta*, the female version of *augustus*, was bestowed on the wife of the emperor, or on other female members of his family such as mothers and sisters, but it was an honorific only and gave its holder no political power. It was only rarely that women such as Livia, wife of Rome's first emperor, Augustus, could forge a distinctive public profile for themselves (see pp. 142–143).

By the Late Imperial era, however, cultural and political changes in Roman society caused both the power and the prominence of empresses to rise significantly. One factor was the increasing number of child emperors. These young rulers needed a regent and the position was often filled by the child-ruler's mother, seeking to preserve her son's inheritance against possible male rivals.

The role of religion

The other development that allowed Roman women a more prominent role was the empire's embrace of Christianity. Mary, the mother of Jesus, became a role model of female leadership whose example was followed by empresses, particularly in the Roman east. The 5th century CE *augusta* Pulcheria promoted herself as a latter-day Mary to legitimize her dominant position in the court of Theodosius II, her younger brother. Although only two years older than Theodosius, Pulcheria was stronger-willed and more

△ **Livia Drusilla (59 BCE–29 CE)**
The wife of Augustus was not a Late Imperial empress, but she set the template for those that followed. She ensured her son from her first marriage, Tiberius, would succeed Augustus, although Tiberius's resentment of her influence soon led to their estrangement.

△ **Helena (c. 246–c. 330)**
The mother of Constantine the Great and a devout Christian, Helena came from a humble background; some sources describe her as a "stable-maid." In later life she toured the Holy Land, founding churches and collecting Christian relics, including, it was claimed, parts of the True Cross on which Jesus was crucified.

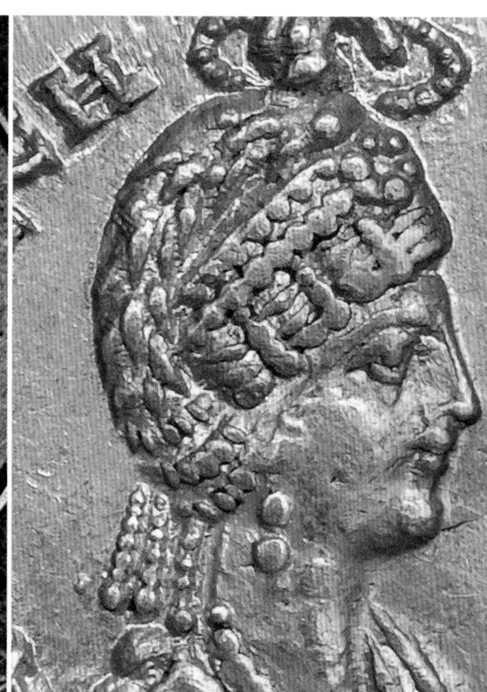

△ **Pulcheria (c. 398–453)**
The older sister of Theodosius II was a dominant figure in his court. Pulcheria's vow of religious chastity stopped her rivals from forcing her to marry and reducing her influence. She did finally marry, in 450; her husband was the emperor Marcian.

> **"Rule of the Roman Empire belonged not to women but to men."**
>
> THE HISTORIAN PRISCUS, FRAGMENT 20.1

assertive than her sibling. Other Late Imperial Roman empresses used their proximity to power to help direct state policy. Theodora, in the early to mid-6th century, played a role in the law codes issued by her husband, the emperor Justinian. A former sex worker from a poor background, Theodora influenced the social legislation he introduced that prevented women being forced into such work against their will.

A change in status

Their increased public profile also gave Late Imperial empresses a changed role in the succession. On at least one occasion in the 5th century, a vacancy on the throne was filled with the help of the existing empress, when she chose the deceased emperor's successor and then married him in order to legitimize his position. Although it is unclear how much say she had in these decisions, the fact that the endorsement of these empresses mattered reflected the shift in their status in Roman society.

None of this altered the fact that imperial society remained deeply patriarchal. The *augustae* who succeeded in obtaining and wielding some power did so through their connection to men, whether fathers, sons, brothers, or husbands. Even the most powerful empress commanded less formal institutional power than the feeblest emperor. Yet the new circumstances of Late Antiquity did increase the scant opportunities available, and several women took advantage of this to become remarkable and important historical figures.

△ **Galla Placidia (c.388–450)**
In her youth, Galla Placidia (above, right, with her daughter, Honoria) was made to marry the Visigoth king Ataulf and then the emperor Constantius III. Later in life, she became a powerful figure as the guardian of her son, Valentinian III.

△ **Ariadne (c.450–515)**
Daughter, wife, and mother of Eastern Empire rulers, Ariadne was at the heart of Constantinople's court politics for 40 years. When her first emperor-husband Zeno died in 491, she is said to have personally hand-picked his successor, Anastasius I, as both her new spouse and the new imperial leader.

△ **Theodora (c.500–548)**
The remarkable Theodora rose from desperate childhood poverty and teenage sex work to marry the future Eastern emperor Justinian. As empress, Theodora exercised tremendous legal and political influence, and has been called the most powerful woman in Byzantine history.

Ravenna's Byzantine Basilica of San Vitale
Ravenna, in northeast Italy, became the capital of the Western Roman Empire in 402 CE. Construction of the city's Basilica of San Vitale began in 526, with Ravenna by now under the control of the Eastern Roman emperor Justinian I, the Western Roman Empire having collapsed in 476. San Vitale's interior shows the influence of Ravenna's new Byzantine rulers, with rich, golden mosaics covering its walls, ceiling, and domes. In this image of the apse, Christ and angels are flanked by Ecclesius (far right), Ravenna's bishop who built the basilica, and the 1st-century CE Christian martyr Saint Vitalis (far left), after whom the church is named.

MOSE

The Feast of Attila
In the 19th century, Attila was reclaimed as a national hero by Hungary. In this c. 1870 painting by the Hungarian artist Mór Than, he is shown as a stern and authoritative ruler rather than the murderous despot of legend.

Attila the Hun

The warlord known as *flagellum Dei*, "the scourge of God"

This powerful steppe chieftain forged a Central European empire that challenged the might of Rome and helped bring down the Western Empire. His name remains a byword for ruthless military success.

△ **Hunnic jewelery**
Usually portrayed simply as violently destructive "barbarians," the Huns produced creative works, too, such as this gilded bronze belt buckle inlaid with gems.

A major reason for the Germanic migrations of the 5th century CE that so disrupted the Roman Empire (see pp. 280–281) was the arrival in Europe of a people from the east, possibly Russia. Under their leader Attila, the Huns briefly but devastatingly threatened the existence of the empire.

◁ **Attila's would-be empress**
This gold *solidus* celebrating Honoria was issued around 450, before she invited Attila to become her husband. Her fate after 451 is unknown.

Brothers in arms

Attila and his brother Bleda were originally corulers of a confederation of tribal groups, but when Bleda died in 445, probably on his sibling's orders, Attila assumed sole control. By this time the Huns had established a successful *modus operandi*, invading and looting the territories they came across and then extorting even more plunder from the areas they subjugated by demanding payment to leave.

This tactic served Attila and Bleda well in lands held by Germanic tribes and, from the early 440s, in the Eastern Empire. In 443 they sacked Naissus (in modern Serbia), one of several major victories. In each instance they demanded huge tributes from the Eastern Empire in return for their withdrawal.

Following Bleda's death, Attila targeted the Western Empire, which had been weakened by repeated civil and foreign conflicts. In one version of the story, Honoria, the sister of Valentinian II, wrote to Attila and offered to become his wife if he could prevent her marriage to a senator to whom she had been forcibly betrothed. Attila agreed, in return for a dowry of half of her brother's empire. After laying waste to much of Roman Gaul, Attila was halted in 451 when he suffered his only military defeat, at the hands of a Roman and Visigothic army at the Battle of the Catalaunian Fields (close to modern Reims). This meant he could take neither Honoria's hand nor his half share of the empire. Thwarted, he invaded Italy instead. He suddenly withdrew from the country in 452 after he was visited by Pope Leo I. The details of their meeting are unknown, but the pope's intervention was hailed as a miracle.

An ignominious end

Attila died in early 453 at the feast celebrating his wedding to a woman called Ildico. He developed a nosebleed while drunk and incapacitated, and choked to death on his own blood.

The Hunnic empire collapsed without its leader, but Attila left a deep wound on the Roman psyche. As the Huns left no written records, everything we know about Attila comes from Roman sources, which treat him with a mixture of fear and fascination.

▽ **Leo I and Attila**
In Raphael's 1513–1514 fresco, Pope Leo I convinces Attila not to sack Rome. It may actually have been his troops' war-weariness that influenced Attila's decision.

c. 434 Attila and Bleda become rulers of the Huns

443 Major Hun invasion of the Eastern Empire; sack of Naissus

c. 445 Death of Bleda, possibly on Attila's orders

447 More Hun invasions of the east

450 Alleged betrothal to Honoria; decision to invade the west

451 Invasion of Gaul; Battle of the Catalaunian Fields

452 Invasion of Italy; negotiation with Pope Leo I

453 Marriage and death at wedding feast

The End of Roman Europe

The slow disintegration of the Western Empire

During the 5th century CE, the Western Empire slowly drifted apart due to spiraling political, military, and economic crises, accelerated by the invasions of Attila's Huns, and incursions by Goths, Vandals, Franks, and other peoples.

The Western Empire did not collapse at once, but in stages. Decades of civil and foreign war resulted in a weak executive and an empty treasury that could no longer afford the upkeep of so many provinces. Regions became increasingly independent as they learned to survive without a central governing authority. This process of becoming post-Roman happened against a backdrop of continued Germanic migrations and the forging of new local identities.

An empire fraying at the edges

Different regions experienced different fates as the empire disintegrated, each preserving or discarding elements of their Roman past while embracing cultural aspects from recent migrants to create a unique synthesis.

Britannia, on the fringes of the Roman world, had been dropped from centralized control by around 410 CE. Its experience of post-Roman life was extreme, marked by the near-total end of urban living. The population shrank, cities were abandoned, and living standards fell drastically. Education and literacy virtually disappeared, along with Christianity. Its practices were only kept alive by rare figures such as the Romano-British missionary and writer Patricius, better known today as Saint Patrick (c. 385–461).

Incomers from Scandinavia and the Low Countries, such as Angles, Saxons, and Jutes, gave both their name and their language to part of the region, which became Angle-land or "England," speaking the Germanic dialect that would later become English.

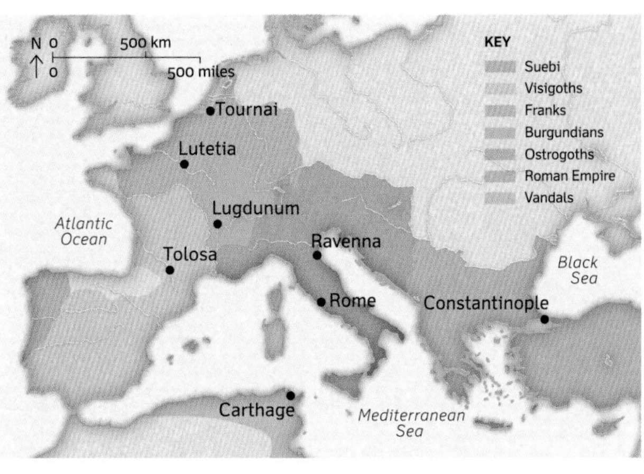

△ **Europe in 500**
A generation after the fall of Rome, the outlines of the modern states of France, Spain, Portugal, Britain, Germany, and Italy were already taking shape.

Changes and continuities

Regions such as Hispania (Spain and Portugal) and Gaul charted courses that kept even more of their Roman inheritance. After the Romans left Gaul in the late 400s, it became Francia (and later France), after its new rulers, the Franks. They preserved many Roman institutions and customs. Under their king, Clovis, who died in 511, they converted to Catholicism and gradually adopted Latin as their mother tongue. A similar process occurred with the Visigoth kings of Spain, such as Euric, who issued a series of Latin law codes in the late 470s modeled on Roman precedents. The Latin of these regions would ultimately merge with other dialects and evolve into modern Romance languages such as French, Spanish, and Portuguese.

△ **Childeric's ring**
The father of Clovis, Childeric based his Frankish kingdom at Tournai (in modern Belgium), on land given to him by Rome in return for his military support.

KING ARTHUR IN FACT AND FICTION

The end of Roman rule in Europe led to the Dark Ages, so-called because very little history was recorded in this period. What has survived are myths and legends—such as that of King Arthur. By the Middle Ages, poets and bards had embellished the stories passed down to them into tales of a heroic, quasi-supernatural ruler. There could have been a warlord who led opposition to the Saxon invasions that followed Roman rule in Britain, but if such a man existed he was not named Arthur, had no Round Table at Camelot, was not married to Guinevere, and never quested for the Holy Grail with Lancelot.

TAPESTRY OF KING ARTHUR FROM C. 1385

◁ **King Euric**
On taking power in 466, Euric, the Visigothic ruler of Gaul, exploited the Western Empire's fragility to extend his territory into most of Hispania.

Compared to Europe, the end of Roman rule in North Africa was far more turbulent. The Vandals conquered Roman Africa after invading from Spain in 429, claiming the capital of Carthage in 439. Practitioners of a proscribed variant of Christianity known as Arianism, they clashed with and persecuted their Catholic subjects. Their violence and desecrations of sacred buildings made their name a byword for wanton destruction.

Unlike areas such as Britain, for example, North Africa remained Christian, and many Roman cities, buildings, and institutions there survived until the Byzantines reconquered the province in the 6th century and were able to take over and better preserve their usage.

There was, then, no single process of becoming "post-Roman" in the 5th century. Dramatic changes in culture, language, religion, and society played out very differently in each corner of the former empire. Some regions saw sharp declines, which they viewed as near-apocalyptic, while others enjoyed much easier transitions.

"What **hatred inspired** them all to **take arms against** each other?"

BYZANTINE HISTORIAN JORDANES, *ON THE ORIGINS AND DEEDS OF THE GOTHS*

Copper and silver eyebrows form the "wings" of a soaring bird or dragon

Nose and mustache form the body and tail of the flying beast

Cheek guards were decorated with carved metal panels, now worn away

▷ **Sutton Hoo Helmet**
In 1939, the largest-ever hoard of Anglo-Saxon treasure in Northern Europe was found at Sutton Hoo in Suffolk, England. Dating from the 6th–7th centuries, the artifacts show clear Roman influences, as well as displaying local designs and styles.

Science and Knowledge

Following the Greek tradition

While less innovative than their Ancient Greek predecessors, the Romans nonetheless maintained a lively interest in science and in developing their knowledge of the world around them.

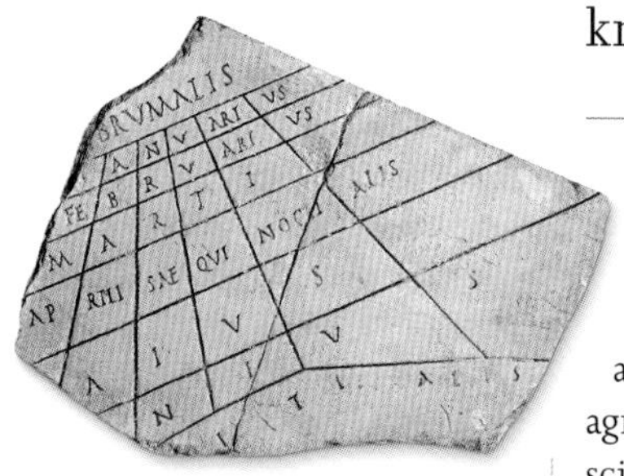

△ **Roman numerals**
The Roman decimal counting system, as shown on this fragment of an ancient sundial, is still in use today.

The Romans saw themselves—and were viewed by others—as practical people rather than deep thinkers. Many of their contributions to knowledge are in the fields of architecture, engineering, and agriculture. Yet they were also active in the field of science, and in areas such as medicine, astronomy, and natural history the Romans profited from and built on the achievements of their Greek forebears.

Well-educated Romans in the Early Imperial era became interested in the collection of knowledge from diverse sources and began to assemble them into larger comprehensive works. The most important of these compilers was Pliny the Elder, who wrote his multivolume *Natural History* in the later 1st century CE. This wide-ranging work of 37 books has been called the world's first encyclopedia, covering a vast array of subjects, from astronomy and geography to agriculture and mathematics. Pliny drew on the knowledge of the Greeks, particularly Aristotle, as well as on his own experiences. He died in 79 CE while attempting to investigate the eruption of Mount Vesuvius from a ship in the Bay of Naples.

Other Romans compiled encyclopedic works that have survived in less complete form than Pliny's masterpiece. One such volume, traditionally known as *On Medicine*, by Aulus Cornelius Celsus, reveals a great deal about the Roman understanding of diet and health care, although it constitutes only one part of what was once a far larger work that is now lost.

△ **Ancient aqueduct**
The Los Milagros aqueduct in Mérida, Spain, is one of more than 200 the Romans built around the empire, demonstrating their skill at large engineering projects.

Non-Roman contributions

As well as "Roman" individuals, science was advanced by peoples who lived within the empire and its orbit, particularly Greeks and Egyptians. Many of these men focused on areas in which they enjoyed professional expertise, such as the Greek medical writer Galen. One of the ancient world's great authorities on health care, Galen (see pp. 148–149) was a practicing doctor. He acted as a physician to emperors, and wrote about his experience of dealing with the Antonine Plague of 165–180. The astrologer and mathematician Ptolemy flourished in 2nd-century Egypt, his works remaining in use for centuries. Pedanius Dioscorides, meanwhile, served as a doctor with the Roman army and wrote books on herbal medicine.

If the Roman era lacked the great leaps forward in science that characterized ancient Greece, it did preserve and promulgate those earlier insights, while creating the conditions for later advances by the inquiring minds of other civilizations.

HYPATIA OF ALEXANDRIA, **SCHOLAR AND MARTYR**

Hypatia (right) was a brilliant philosopher, astronomer, and mathematician who lived in Alexandria, Egypt, in the turbulent decades around the turn of the 5th century. She was known as a popular teacher and an innovative thinker. Her scientific commentaries would later be widely copied and her insights were translated into Arabic in the Middle Ages. Although the Roman Empire had adopted Christianity as the state religion by the time Hypatia was active, she practiced—and taught—traditional beliefs to her students. This brought her into conflict with the authorities of Roman Egypt, and in 415 she was attacked and murdered by a mob on the streets of Alexandria. In later times, especially the Enlightenment of the 18th century, Hypatia was held up (not without contention) as a champion of science and a victim of dogmatic religious intolerance.

▽ **Page from *De materia medica (On Medical Material)***
This 6th-century CE Greek copy of a 1st-century CE Latin work by the Roman army physician Pedanius Dioscorides preserves a lavishly illustrated text used by doctors in the ancient world.

Later notes by readers have been added in Arabic

This illustration shows how to use dragon arum, or *dracunculus vulgaris*, a supposed aphrodisiac

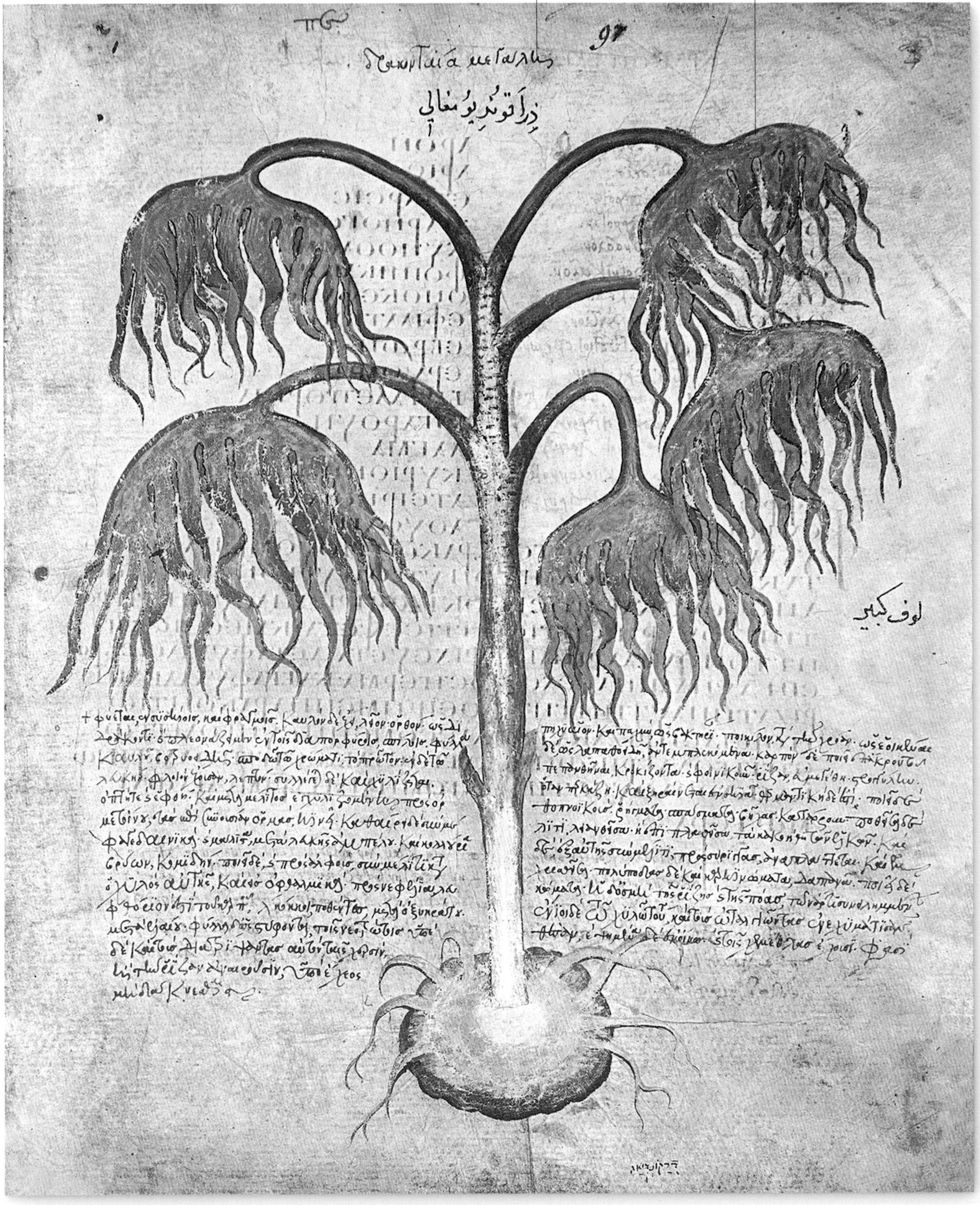

A golden halo reinforces Justinian's divine authority

MAXIM

The emperor carries a bowl with bread for the Eucharist

Purple robe detail identifies the two figures on the left as imperial officials

Bishop Maximianus, who built the Basilica of San Vitale in Ravenna

▷ **Roman lawgiver**
Justinian, portrayed in this c. 547 mosaic from the Basilica of San Vitale in Ravenna, did more than any other emperor to compile the Roman legal code with his *Body of Civil Law*; one of its parts was called the *Codex Justinianus*, or the *Code of Justinian*.

Law and Justice

Setting a legal standard for the empire

The Romans believed that their advanced legal system was better than anyone else's—including that of the Greeks, on which it was partly based. Roman law remains the basis of many legislative codes around the world today.

Roman law in the Republic was founded on an ancient code known as the Twelve Tables (see pp. 50–51). New laws were added over time, often to do with individual liberties, and covered, for example, adoption, divorce, murder, and theft. Since laws were mostly drawn up by the wealthy, their main concern was the protection of property. After the Republic, emperors delegated the task of issuing new laws to skilled lawyers called jurists, many of whom, such as Ulpian and Julianus, wrote influential legal books.

Legal theory and practice

In theory, Romans were equal before the law. Legal cases were presided over by magistrates and, later, provincial governors, prefects, and even the emperor. Law bureaus were set up to respond to legal petitions from across the empire, and the decisions they made could be used as precedents for future cases. An appeals system allowed Romans who felt let down by the legal process to seek remediation—although the costs involved were high and the system was corrupt. Women had limited rights: they could own property, divorce, and speak in court. However, they were also subjected to legal restrictions, such as not being able to act as advocates for others.

◁ **Coin showing Iustitia**
From the time of Augustus onward, the Romans often represented the concept of Justice, *Iustitia*, as a personified deity seated on a throne, as shown on this coin.

Many people were excluded from the justice system, notably foreigners and enslaved people. This is one reason why many non-Romans joined the army as auxiliaries, as they were awarded citizenship at the end of their service and benefited from all that this entailed—including the protection of Roman law. The same applied to enslaved people who bought or were given their freedom.

Abiding influence

By the 5th century Roman law was so complex it was decided to issue the first official, simplified, legal code. It took more than a century to complete, but the emperor Justinian's *Corpus Iuris Civilis* (*Body of Civil Law*) of 533–534 collected all the major points of Roman law in one multivolume work.

It fell out of use with the end of the Roman Empire, but was rediscovered in the Middle Ages and became the basis for much medieval law, and from there served as the framework for early modern European law systems, which were then exported around the world.

Today, civil law structures directly descended from Roman law are used in more than 100 countries around the world, including most of Europe.

▽ **Salvius Julianus**
Julianus (c. 110–c. 170 CE) was one of the most respected Roman jurists, serving under several emperors from Hadrian onward. His statue stands outside Italy's Supreme Court in Rome.

◁ **Art imitating life**
Courtroom scenes were sometimes depicted in Roman art, as in this depiction from a fresco found in Ostia, near Rome, of a magistrate overseeing a dispute.

Rome's Lost Architecture

New worlds repurposing the old

Even after the mighty Roman Empire finally fell, the city of Rome remained continuously inhabited, with new generations of Romans building their lives in and around the architectural splendor of their past.

△ **Casa dei Crescenzi** The remnants of earlier Roman and Byzantine buildings have been incorporated into the walls of this imposing 11th-century residence.

Following the collapse of the Western Empire in 476 CE, Rome did not disappear from the map, although it did shrink dramatically. At its height, the city was a vast cosmopolis and supported over a million people; by the 6th century, its population had declined to about 50,000.

Medieval Romans thus found themselves living in a city that had been designed for a populace more than 20 times their number. No longer the beneficiary of the empire's huge networks of trade and taxation, Rome became reliant on the Roman Catholic Church, particularly the powerful popes, for income. To accommodate their dramatically changed circumstances, the people of Rome were forced to turn for resources to the only major local source available—the monuments of the imperial past.

Adaptation and renewal

By Late Antiquity (4th–6th centuries), the Romans had become accustomed to reusing parts of earlier buildings in new projects, particularly Christian churches. The earliest churches in Rome had been built on the outskirts of the city; now, construction within the walls often meant demolishing pagan sites, which would then have elements reused in the new building. The early 5th-century Basilica of St Sabina, for example, incorporated magnificent columns from a Temple of Juno that had stood near the site. Materials reused from earlier buildings were known as *spolia* (see below).

In the later part of the first millennium, much of Rome fell into decay and neglect. The forums of Augustus and Trajan, for example, were reduced to overgrown gardens, while bath houses and public halls were converted into cemeteries, which under the Roman Empire were always situated outside the walls. When the need to build newer and more manageable dwellings arose, later generations of Romans turned to the crumbling remnants of antiquity. Sturdy surviving walls and foundations were used as the basis for new medieval houses; marbles and fine decorations were stripped from disused ruins and either brought to newer churches or sold abroad.

> "[Charlemagne] had **marble columns** brought from Rome ... he **could not find** others suitable"
>
> EINHARD, *THE LIFE OF CHARLEMAGNE*

THE ARCH OF **CONSTANTINE**

The use of *spolia* was not limited to the post-Roman era. A famous example of the Late Roman reappropriation of the past is the Arch of Constantine, dedicated in 315 CE. The arch is heavily decorated with images and reliefs taken from earlier structures celebrating achievements of 2nd-century emperors (such as the *tondo*, or circular relief, below). While historians used to point to this as a sign of the decline in Roman art in this period, modern scholars view it as a symptom of a rushed construction process—cutting corners to complete the arch quickly.

As the city's fortunes improved later in the Middle Ages, wealthy Italian aristocrats began to appropriate surviving structures, turning half-crumbled theaters and tombs into fortresses and palaces. Even natural disasters that caused irreparable damage created new supplies of stone for reuse—for example, when an earthquake in 1349 brought down an outer wall of the Colosseum, its stones were used in churches such as the papal Basilica of St John Lateran.

Spectacular coexistence

Countless buildings in modern-day Rome tell the story of 2,000 years of history, with Renaissance palaces set into the walls of Late Antiquity or restored medieval churches built on top of ancient temple stones. Some commentators have seen this as a wholly negative process of cultural vandalism, not least because few of the spoliated structures of medieval and Renaissance Rome have the same capacity to inspire awe as even the remnants of the great edifices of the Roman Forum. It is also true that some of Rome's authorities, especially during the Renaissance, engaged in wanton destruction in the service of self-aggrandizing monuments to their own glory.

However, Rome has always been a living city, and many of its leaders doubtless saw their duty to provide for present-day subjects as more pressing than the need to preserve the past. Many ancient monuments, such as the Baths of Diocletian and the Pantheon (see pp. 202–203), may not have been preserved at all had they not been reused in later projects, especially Christian churches. Rome's legacy thereby lives on as much in these reappropriated buildings as in structures that appear more superficially untouched.

◁ **Castel Sant'Angelo**
This impressive structure was constructed in Rome in 139 CE as a tomb for the emperor Hadrian, but was later converted into a fortress by medieval popes.

▽ **Theater of Marcellus**
Once the largest public theater in Ancient Rome (completed 13 BCE), this structure was turned into a fortress for aristocratic Romans in the Middle Ages. It is a striking example of how later Rome was built into the ruins of antiquity.

The 16th-century top layer is currently occupied by modern apartments

The oldest layer was completed under Augustus in 13 BCE

Much of the theater was recovered by 20th-century excavations

The Western Empire Ends

The gradual decline of Rome's Western Empire

The Roman Empire in the western Mediterranean had effectively ceased to exist in all but name long before its final emperor, Romulus Augustus, was at last deposed in 476 CE.

The slow unraveling of the Western Roman Empire during the 5th century was not halted by the death of its great enemy Attila (see pp. 290–291). Although spared immediate destruction by the Huns, the Western Empire was already in a parlous state, with imperial control mostly confined to Italy and its closest neighbors. Attila's death was itself followed by the assassination of Rome's last truly effective leader, a general named Aetius who had successfully organized resistance to the warlord's attacks. Aetius was killed on the orders of the Western emperor, who had tired of the general's influence on Roman politics.

◁ **Mausoleum of Theodoric**
Theodoric is buried in this tomb in Ravenna. The king of the Ostrogoths, he overthrew the warlord Odoacer on the orders of Zeno, the Eastern emperor.

In the absence of strong leadership, the Western Empire continued to drift slowly apart. Without its wealthiest provinces in North Africa, which had been conquered by the Vandals, it could not afford the upkeep of a significant army, while its greatest cities in Gaul and Italy had been devastated by the wars of the preceding years. Rome itself would be captured a second time in 455 by a Vandal raiding party. While less historically momentous than the Visigothic sack under Alaric, this attack was even more brutal, carrying away more of the old capital's wealth and enslaving many inhabitants. The Roman government was by this point unable to protect even its most privileged elites, let alone its ordinary citizens.

Throughout, the Eastern Roman Empire did not stand quietly by. Eastern emperors attempted to salvage their fellow Romans, including twice in the 5th century dispatching a new emperor to Italy with soldiers and money to try to stabilize the situation. On the second occasion, in 468, they even planned to cooperate with the newly installed Western emperor Anthemius in a large military expedition to reclaim North Africa from the Vandals, which could have lifted the Western Empire out of its seemingly permanent economic crisis. The campaign collapsed, however, due to poor leadership and bad weather, and Anthemius was murdered soon afterward. Following this debacle, no more help came from Constantinople.

▽ **Rule from Ravenna**
In its final century, the Western Empire was ruled not from Rome but rather from secure Ravenna, whose port of Classe is depicted in a mosaic here.

Last Western emperors

The story of Rome's final decades was one of withering central power, where ineffectual emperors became ever more removed from the lives and experiences of the people who theoretically remained their subjects. For many ordinary people, life went on as it always had, if somewhat less securely. Some still paid taxes to the emperor, while others now sent their surplus earnings to new rulers from farther abroad. In Ravenna, the final seat of power, the last emperors were mostly puppet figureheads dominated by a series of military strongmen, building on a trend established

by figures like Stilicho at the start of the century. In 476 one such figurehead was a boy of about ten, named Romulus Augustus after the founder of Rome, but better known as "Augustulus," a dismissive diminutive which translates to "Little Augustus." He was an undistinguished figure, elevated as the son of an influential magnate named Orestes in a coup against the previous ruler.

Only a year after his accession, the Germanic warlord Odoacer deposed the young sovereign. He was so insignificant that Odoacer did not even bother to kill him when he dispatched the diadem and the purple robe of the emperor to the Eastern court in Constantinople, explaining that they were no longer necessary. At the time, the event was barely noticed in either Italy or the Eastern Empire. With this final anticlimactic gesture, the Roman Empire founded by Augustus five centuries earlier ended in the west.

△ **Destruction of Rome**
From the 5th century until the present day, the fall of Rome has become a powerful metaphor for civilizational collapse. Here, its brutal destruction is famously imagined in a 19th-century painting by Thomas Cole, part of a series entitled *The Course of Empires*.

ODOACER, KING OF ITALY

Roman imperial rule in the west was finally ended by a Germanic warlord who rose to power in the 470s. Despite the infamous role that he has often assumed in historical accounts, Odoacer (right, on a coin c. 477) was only the latest in a series of non-Roman generals to dominate the now largely ceremonial office of emperor. Predecessors, such as the part-Gothic Ricimer, had been content to leave puppet rulers in place, removing them only if they sought to increase their authority beyond the nominal. Odoacer ended this charade to rule openly as king of Italy, though continuing to pay lip service to the Eastern emperor. He would be deposed in 493 by an Ostrogothic army led by their king, Theodoric, with the backing of Constantinople.

The Byzantine Empire

The Eastern Roman Empire that endured

While the Roman Empire fell in the west in the 5th century CE, the empire would endure in the east as the major power in Europe for a full millennium before its final demise in 1453.

△ **St Catherine's Monastery**
Many beautiful works of Byzantine iconography and art were preserved in sites such as this monastery at Mount Sinai in Egypt, which has remained continuously in use since the 6th century.

The people of what we today call the Byzantine Empire never regarded themselves as "Byzantine," but rather as Romans and the continuation of the Roman Empire in the east. They adhered to Roman law, built Roman buildings, and were ruled by Roman emperors into the Middle Ages. Yet they also spoke Greek, practiced a distinctive form of Christianity, and were ruled from the New Rome of Constantinople rather than the old. Later historians named them "the Byzantines" after *Byzantion* (Byzantium), the name of Constantinople before it was renamed in 330, to distinguish them from the subjects of the fallen Western Empire.

Increasing isolation

The early Byzantines resembled the classical Romans of the ancient world. They remained dominant in the Mediterranean, even reconquering much of the west under the emperor Justinian I, and issuing new sets of Roman law. However, in the 7th century the rise of the new Islamic faith in the Near East and the emergence of the Arabs as a major power led to a series of wars in which the Byzantines lost the majority of their empire, including their wealthiest provinces in North Africa and Egypt. After this, they became an insular, embattled civilization, centered ever more tightly on Constantinople.

In the Middle Ages, the Byzantine Empire became increasingly alienated from Western Europe, losing its remaining foothold in Italy and confronting an ideological challenge in the form of the new Holy Roman Empire, which claimed to be the true heir of Rome. Byzantine Christianity became consumed with a great struggle over the proper treatment of religious images, called icons, with some believing that these had to be destroyed in order to win back God's favor

◁ **Ivory casket**
The Byzantines produced many ivory and bone objects, like this example (10th to 11th centuries) adorned with scenes of hunters and warriors.

▷ **The empire under Justinian, 555**
The Byzantine Empire reached its greatest extent under the emperor Justinian I, following his reconquest of much of the Western Empire.

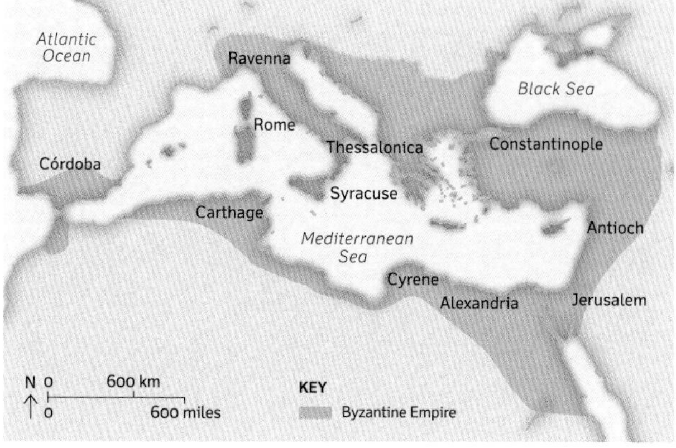

and reverse Byzantine defeats in war. The "iconoclasm" movement was ultimately unsuccessful, but further cut off the empire from the rest of Christianity, which had avoided such struggles. Tension between the emperor in Constantinople and the pope in Rome led to the "Great Schism" of Christianity into Latin Catholic and Greek Orthodox blocs in 1054, a split that endures today.

Byzantine civilization would change dramatically from its Roman inheritance, in ways both positive and negative. Due to a mix of structural factors and changing Christian attitudes, slavery declined precipitously, although it was never abolished. The Byzantines also occasionally accepted women reigning independently, as the Romans never had; the first of these was the empress Irene at the end of the 8th century. Yet the rights of ordinary women contracted in some areas, including tighter restrictions on the circumstances in which they could request a divorce.

Ultimately, the Byzantine Empire was caught between eastern and western rivals. A Byzantine appeal for help against the Turks in Asia Minor inadvertently resulted in a series of Christian crusades from the west, aimed at conquering the Near East. However, the Crusaders regarded the "foreign" Byzantines with almost as much hostility as they did the Muslim world. In 1204, one group of Crusaders sacked Constantinople for the first time in its nine-century history. The last "Roman" emperor died when the Ottomans took the city in 1453, a final end to the empire founded by Augustus almost 1,500 years earlier.

▽ **The Monomachus Crown**
This elaborate 11th-century crown from Constantinople depicts the Byzantine emperor Constantine IX Monomachus and his family.

EMPEROR **JUSTINIAN I**

Reigning from 527 to 565, Justinian presided over a dramatic expansion of Byzantine territory (led by his general, Belisarius), reconquering North Africa and Italy and bringing Rome back into the empire. Alongside his wife Theodora (see pp. 286–287) he was also active domestically, issuing a vast amount of Roman law and constructing many beautiful buildings. However, he also persecuted religious opponents and, in 532, massacred thousands of his citizens to suppress a popular revolt against his rule.

Roman and World History

A timeline of dynasties, empires, and global events

During 1,200 years of Roman history, other great civilizations rose and fell. New religions and political systems were born, nations were formed, and empires collapsed, and there were huge advances in culture and technology that shaped the world and left lasting legacies.

- **753 BCE** Rome is founded and Romulus becomes the city's first king
- **c. 545 BCE** Lucius Junius Brutus, founder of the Roman Republic, is born
- **509 BCE** Lucius Tarquinius Superbus is deposed and the city declared a republic
- **343 BCE** The Samnite Wars begin; they end in 290 BCE with victory for Rome
- **246 BCE** The Punic Wars start; they end in 146 BCE with defeat for Carthage

ANCIENT ROME

- **753–509 BCE** **The Roman Kingdom**
- **509–27 BCE** **The Roman Republic**

800 BCE | **690 BCE** | **580 BCE** | **470 BCE** | **360 BCE** | **250 BCE**

WORLD EMPIRES AND KINGDOMS

- **Ancient Greece**
- **Hellenistic kingdoms**
- **Ancient Egypt**
- **Later Vedic civilization**
- **Indian kingdoms**
- **Chinese civilization**
- **Achaemenid Persian Empire**
- **Napatan Kushite Kingdom, Nubia**
- **Ancient Andean civilization**

- **776 BCE** First Olympic Games are held at Olympia, in southern Greece
- **650 BCE** The earliest known coins are minted in Ephesus
- **600 BCE** The poems of *Shi Jing*, China's earliest work of literature, are compiled
- **600 BCE** Coins used in Phoenicia
- **c. 515 BCE** The Chinese become the first people to cast iron
- **507 BCE** Democracy is established in Athens
- **c. 496 BCE** Birth of the dramatist Sophocles
- **480 BCE** Persian ruler Xerxes I leads an unsuccessful campaign against the Greek city states
- **c. 427 BCE** Athenian philosopher Plato is born
- **c. 424 BCE** Buddha attains enlightenment
- **399 BCE** Socrates is sentenced to death
- **334 BCE** Alexander the Great begins his conquest of the Persian Empire
- **323 BCE** Alexander the Great dies
- **c. 272 BCE** Asoka, a follower of Buddhism, wins the Mauryan throne and establishes India's first empire

- **91 BCE** The Social War begins; it ends in 87 BCE
- **70 BCE** Virgil, Rome's greatest poet, is born
- **44 BCE** Julius Caesar is assassinated
- **27 BCE** Octavian becomes Augustus, Rome's first emperor
- **14 CE** Augustus dies and the imperial system begins
- **64 CE** The Great Fire of Rome destroys up to two-thirds of the city
- **64 CE** St Peter is executed in Rome
- **79 CE** Mount Vesuvius erupts, destroying Pompeii, Herculaneum, and several other settlements
- **80 CE** The Colosseum opens in Rome
- **193 CE** Septimius Severus becomes Rome's first African emperor
- **286 CE** Diocletian divides the empire into western and eastern halves; in 293 CE he will establish the Tetrarchy
- **312 CE** Constantine I defeats Maxentius in the Battle of the Milvian Bridge
- **380 CE** Theodosius makes Christianity the official religion of the Roman Empire
- **402 CE** Honorius moves the capital of the Western Empire from Milan to Ravenna
- **410 CE** Rome is sacked on August 24 by an army of Visigoths under Alaric I
- **453 CE** Attila the Hun, one of the Roman Empire's great foes, dies at his own wedding feast
- **476 CE** The Western Roman Empire comes to an end

27 BCE–476 CE
The Roman Empire

30 BCE | **80 CE** | **190 CE** | **300 CE** | **410 CE** | **520 CE**

Byzantine Empire

- **c. 69 BCE** Cleopatra VII is born; she takes her own life in 30 BCE
- **c. 50 BCE** The Maya introduce a calendar which has a cycle of 52 years, known as the Calendar Round
- **c. 33 CE** Jesus Christ is crucified
- **70 CE** Jerusalem is destroyed by the armies of Titus
- **c. 200 CE** The Pyramid of the Sun is built in Mexico
- **220 CE** Three Kingdoms period begins in China after the fall of the Han Dynasty
- **224 CE** The Parthian Empire falls and the Sasanian Empire rises
- **c. 321 CE** Chandra Gupta I conquers the Ganges Valley; lays foundation of the Gupta Empire

◁ **Entrance hall mosaic** This fragment of a limestone mosaic from a villa in Daphne (in modern Türkiye) dates from c. 325–330 CE. It depicts the god of wine, Bacchus, who was worshipped from as early as the 5th century BCE in Rome.

Directory

Rulers, Deities, and Sites

Rulers

The Kings of Rome (8TH–6TH CENTURIES BCE)

While there is no evidence that Rome's seven kings existed as actual figures, their legends were widely accepted. The stories of their reigns provide useful clues to Rome's foundation and history, and act as cautionary tales of the benefits and dangers of placing too much power in the hands of one man.

Romulus

r. 753–715 BCE

If Romulus and Remus, the legendary founders of Rome, existed at all, it's possible they were rival warlords leading clans of settlers on the site that became the city of Rome. There is evidence that the first humans arrived in the area and erected huts and other buildings around 1000 BCE. By the 4th century BCE, an origin story had developed around a pair of twin brothers, out of whose power struggle a great empire would emerge.

In this version of events, the brothers were direct descendants of both the Trojan hero Aeneas (via their mother, Rhea Silvia) and Mars, the god of war (their father). Abandoned at birth on the banks of the Tiber River, the brothers were saved by a wolf, which nursed them until a shepherd discovered and raised the boys. They learned of their history as adults and decided to establish a great city where the wolf had found them. Following a disagreement about where its center should be, Romulus murdered Remus and selected a hill known as the Palatine, naming the settlement after himself—"Rome."

After 37 years on the throne (including five years as joint ruler with the Sabine king Titus Tatius), Romulus was called home by the gods, ascending to heaven during a violent thunderstorm. In another, more cautionary, version of Romulus's death, Rome's senators murdered him, envious of their king's power. This theme of a powerful ruler at odds with the Senate is one that would run throughout Roman history.

Numa Pompilius

r. 715–672 BCE

Rome's second king was of Sabine origin. Numa Pompilius's wife, Tatia, was the daughter of Titus Tatius, the former Sabine king and short-lived joint Roman ruler. In contrast to the warlike Romulus, Numa was a peaceful and practical monarch. He was also a reluctant sovereign, and it took much persuading for him to become Rome's leader. During his 43-year reign, he established many of Rome's key institutions, including the cults of Romulus, Vesta, Jupiter, and Mars, as well as the office of *pontifex maximus* (high priest). He also inaugurated the Roman calendar.

Tullus Hostilius

r. 672–640 BCE

Believing Numa Pompilius's peaceful reign had weakened Rome, his successor Tullus Hostilius adopted a more aggressive policy, conquering the nearby cities of Veii, Fidenae, and, most significantly, Alba Longa—Rome's fiercest rival at that time. His long reign of 32 years came to an end when plague struck the city of Rome in 640 BCE. In the more prosaic version of his death, Tullus simply succumbed to the illness in the same way as many of his compatriots; in the more dramatic telling, he failed to make the correct religious offerings to the gods to end the plague and was obliterated by one of Jupiter's thunderbolts. Among his other legacies, Tullus reputedly built Rome's first senate house, the Curia Hostilia.

◁ Marble bust of Claudius wearing an honorary oak wreath from c. 50 CE

△ Mosaic depicting the foundlings Romulus and Remus being suckled by a she-wolf

Ancus Marcius

r. 640–616 BCE

Directly elected by a people's assembly, Ancus Marcius blended the warlike tendencies of Romulus and Tullus with the civic-minded, religious qualities of his grandfather, Numa Pompilius. He extended Rome's territory to the sea, establishing the port city of Ostia 20 miles (32 km) away, and built the first bridge over the Tiber River, the Pons Sublicius. He encouraged the first settlers to populate the Aventine and Janiculum Hills, many of them relocated from territories Ancus had conquered during his war with the Latins of central Italy. His surname, "Ancus," is Latin for "bent" and probably refers to the king's damaged or withered arm. This established a tradition whereby prominent Romans would often be given surnames that described their physical attributes, for example, "Scaurus" meaning "swollen ankle."

Lucius Tarquinius Priscus

r. 616–578 BCE

Originally named Lucomo, Lucius Tarquinius Priscus was the son of a nobleman from the Greek city of Corinth who settled in the Etrurian city of Tarquinii after fleeing persecution in his home country. Lucius changed his name after moving to Rome on the advice of his wife, Tanaquil, an Etrurian priestess, who foresaw he would become a great man if he left Tarquinii. Lucius duly became a key advisor to Rome's king, Ancus Marcius, and was named as the guardian to Ancus's young sons in his will. When Ancus died, Lucius persuaded the Senate that the monarch's sons were too young to succeed him and was elected king himself.

As Rome's new ruler, Lucius conquered the Sabine, Latin, and Etruscan kingdoms. He used the spoils of war to celebrate a Triumph (see pp. 264–265); erect new stone walls; commission the Temple of Jupiter Optimus Maximus; and build Rome's great sewer, the Cloaca Maxima, parts of which are still in use today. He is also credited with constructing the Circus Maximus, Rome's great chariot-racing stadium. After 38 years in power, Lucius was assassinated by the sons of Ancus Marcius, who hoped to finally seize power. Lucius's widow, Tanaquil, thwarted their attempt by taking advantage of the sons' temporary absence from Rome to persuade the Senate to choose her favorite, Servius Tullius, as king instead.

△ Painting showing Lucius Tarquinius Priscus (right) debating with a Roman priest by Sebastiano Ricci, c. 1690

Servius Tullius

r.578–534 BCE

Lucius Tarquinius Priscus adopted Servius Tullius after his wife Tanaquil had a vision that the boy, born to an enslaved mother, was destined to be king. As Rome's ruler, Servius expanded the city's boundaries to include the Quirinal, Viminal, and Esquiline hills, and built several religious temples. He reorganized Rome's army into its famous centurion-based system and defeated the powerful city of Veii in war, as well as the Etruscans. He also built the Servian Wall around Rome, instituted the first census, and was said to have introduced the city's first coinage. Most significantly, he allowed the city's plebeian class to take part in political life for the first time through the Comitia Centuriata voting assembly. His reforms during his 44-year reign led to Servius being called Rome's second founder, after Romulus.

However, in 534 BCE Servius was assassinated by his own daughter, Tullia, and her husband Lucius Tarquinius—the son of Lucius Tarquinius Priscus—who wanted to restore the undisputed power of the patricians and the monarch against the rising influence of the plebeians.

Lucius Tarquinius Superbus

r.534–509 BCE

Lucius Tarquinius Superbus began his reign by refusing to bury his father-in-law, Servius Tullius, whom he had killed. For this, and for his tyrannical rule, Lucius was given the mocking nickname "Superbus" (meaning "the proud" or "arrogant"). One of Lucius's first acts as king was to execute a number of senators he suspected of loyalty to the slain Servius. He did not replace the murdered senators, and instead ruled without senatorial advice or help, becoming an authoritarian ruler for the rest of his 25-year reign. Lucius continued the expansion of Roman territory across Italy that had begun under his predecessors and completed the construction of the Temple of Jupiter Optimus Maximus, initiated by his father.

Lucius's unpopular rule was ended after his son, Sextus Tarquinius, raped Lucretia, a famously virtuous Roman noblewoman, who took her own life after her assault. Her husband, Lucius Tarquinius Collatinus, and his friend Lucius Junius Brutus, led a group of outraged Roman noblemen who forced the despotic king into exile in 509 BCE and declared Rome a republic. Until his death in exile in 495 BCE, Lucius Tarquinius Superbus made several unsuccessful attempts to regain the Roman crown.

△ Fresco depicting an episode of the legend of Servius Tullius, in which he frees his friend Caelius Vibenna

The Roman Republic (6TH–1ST CENTURIES BCE)

The replacement of a single king by two consuls, both elected annually, changed Rome from a kingdom into a democratic republic that lasted for 500 years. Consuls took on many of the duties of the king, and could even nominate dictators. This section covers some of the most notable rulers of the Republic.

Lucius Junius Brutus

Consul: 509 BCE

Like Rome's seven kings, Lucius Junius Brutus, the "cofounder" of the Republic and the first co-consul, was probably more of a legendary than real character—the embodiment, perhaps, of the social and political issues affecting the city as it transitioned from one form of government to another.

For Romans, Brutus represented republican virtue. Not only did he help to end the tyranny of Rome's last king, Lucius Tarquinius Superbus, but he died defending the Republic he created at the Battle of Silva Arsia months later. In his time in power, Brutus became the model of an impartial ruler: he made his co-consul and friend Lucius Tarquinius Collatinus step down because he was a kinsman of the former king. Brutus realized that the people would reject any ruler with the hated Tarquinii name. When a plot to restore Lucius Tarquinius Superbus to the throne was uncovered, Brutus executed its ringleaders, including two of his own sons. In a neat piece of historical symmetry, the man who ended Rome's monarchy was also the ancestor of Marcus Junius Brutus, one of the assassins of Rome's would-be king Julius Caesar 450 years later.

▷ Bust of Lucius Junius Brutus (Ludovico Lombardo, c. 1550)

Agrippa Menenius Lanatus

Consul: 503 BCE

Elected consul in 503 BCE, Menenius won a great victory over the Sabines (see pp.26–27) that year and was awarded one of Rome's earliest Triumphs. Possibly of plebeian origin himself, he was chosen by the Senate to arbitrate in the Secession of the Plebs crisis of 495–493 BCE. In this dispute, Rome's plebeians, or plebs, argued that their interests were not being represented in Rome's government and left the city in protest, setting up camp on the nearby Mons Sacer (Sacred Mountain). Menenius regained the plebs' support by telling them a parable explaining how a body cannot live unless all its organs work together. When the secessionists came back to the city, they returned under the protection of the Tribune of the Plebs, a newly created civic position of 10 elected officers that safeguarded plebeian interests within Rome's power framework.

Titus Larcius

Consul: 501, 498 BCE
Dictator: 501 BCE

Consul in 501 BCE and 498 BCE, Titus Larcius is best remembered as Rome's first dictator. He was appointed as the city's sole ruler during his first consulate, when Rome's enemies among the Sabines, the Latins, and the exiled Tarquinius family were threatening war and invasion. The Senate originally appointed Larcius to *praetor maximus* (supreme magistrate) or *magister equitum* (master of the horse), but he quickly became dictator. The word did not carry the connotations then that it does today. In Roman terms, the dictatorship was a temporary position to be used in emergency situations only. An advocate of plebeian rights, Larcius was one of the delegates who negotiated with Rome's lower classes during the Secession of Plebs crisis.

Appius Claudius Sabinus Regillensis

Consul: 495 BCE

An unashamed and hard-line aristocrat, Appius Claudius Sabinus Regillensis devoted his time as consul in 495 BCE, and his political career in general, to maintaining the patricians' hold on power. Originally from the Sabine town of Regillum, Claudius defected to Rome when the two states were at war c. 505 BCE, earning him power, privilege, and a seat in the Senate.

Rome's plebeians had been expecting more from the end of the monarchy in 509 BCE; by the time of Claudius's consulate they were arguing that the republican revolution had simply replaced the self-interested rule of the king with the equally self-interested rule of the patrician class. The situation got worse when Claudius reneged on a promise to offer debt relief to any plebeians who fought in

Rome's conflict with a tribe known as the Volsci. The result was the Secession of the Plebs (see left), which Claudius suggested ending by sending in the troops. Although he was overruled, Claudius remained an implacable enemy of Rome's non-aristocratic citizens, and was later a supporter of the Roman general and demagogue Coriolanus, who unsuccessfully campaigned to abolish the plebs' hard-won voting rights.

Claudius also opposed reforms to Rome's farming industry that would have meant cheaper bread for the city's citizens—and lower profits for the state's wealthy landowners. As the founder of the Claudian dynasty, his descendants included the emperors Tiberius, Caligula, and Claudius.

Spurius Cassius Vecellinus

Consul: 503, 493, 486 BCE

In the decades after Rome's final king was banished, the city was plagued by tensions between the rich and the poor, patricians and plebeians, city-dwellers and country folk, and many other groups. The career of Spurius Cassius Vecellinus illustrates how volatile those conflicts could be.

A successful general, Cassius was elected consul in 502 BCE and led Rome to a resounding military victory over the Sabines, earning him a Triumph. During his second consulship in 493 BCE Cassius signed a peace treaty with the Latins, guaranteeing Rome's safety against another major regional rival.

Cassius's third and final consulship came in 486 BCE, during which he negotiated another important peace treaty, this time with the nearby Hernici tribe to the east of Rome. Cassius celebrated a second Triumph for his diplomacy.

Despite being one of Rome's most lauded leaders, Cassius died within a year, executed by his fellow countrymen. The cause, as ever, was the simmering class conflict between the patricians and the plebeians. When Cassius supported a bill proposing the redistribution of some of Rome's agricultural land among the lower classes and Latin allies, his aristocratic enemies accused the former consul of trying to make himself king. Following a speedy and secretive trial, Cassius was convicted of treason and sentenced to death. In the 2nd century BCE, the Gracchi brothers would also meet a similar fate when they attempted to distribute land to the Roman poor.

△ Fresco showing Spurius Cassius Vecellinus beheaded by his enemies (Domenico Beccafumi, c. 1532)

Gaius Julius Iullus

Consul: 482 BCE

Alongside Quintus Fabius Vibulanus, Gaius Julius Iullus won the consulship in 482 BCE in a bad-tempered election where both men were compromise candidates against the autocratic Appius Claudius. Three decades later, Julius was selected (as was Appius Claudius) as one of ten *decemvirs* charged with drawing up Rome's code of laws. After a year in office, the *decemvirs* stepped down—all except Appius Claudius, who assembled a more authoritarian group of *decemvirs*. They enacted a set of stringent laws that led to Rome's plebeians once more leaving the city as they had during the Secession of the Plebs crisis (see p. 312), but Julius persuaded them to return to Rome. As his name suggests, Julius was also an ancestor of Julius Caesar.

Appius Claudius Crassus Inregillensis Sabinus

Consul: 471 BCE

Denied the consulship in 482 BCE by Gaius Julius Iullus, Appius Claudius finally won Rome's highest office in 471 BCE.

In popular legend, he was the son of Appius Claudius Sabinus Regillensis. Like his conservative father, he was an opponent of land reform, voting reform, or any other measure that altered the balance of power in Rome in favor of the plebeians against the patricians. His controversial consulship began badly with a failed attempt to block a law that prevented the patrician-dominated Senate from controlling the elections of the Tribunes of the Plebs. Later that year, he was equally unsuccessful in leading an army to fight the Volsci tribe when his plebeian troops openly ignored his orders. Appius Claudius responded by subjecting his army to decimation—the first known use of this punishment of executing one man in every ten.

In later life, Appius Claudius's role as one of the ten *decemvirs* provoked a crisis that exposed dangerous fault lines in Roman society (see left). Once the crisis ended, the Senate had Appius Claudius and his *decemvir* allies arrested for their alleged crimes against the state. Appius Claudius died in prison before he could be tried, either by suicide or murder, depending on which account of his life you read.

△ *Cincinnatus Abandons the Plow to Dictate Laws to Rome* (c. 1806) by Juan Antonio Ribera y Fernández

Lucius Quinctius Cincinnatus

Consul: 460 BCE
Dictator: 458, 439 BCE

More legend than man, Lucius Quinctius Cincinnatus stood for centuries as one of the paragons of republican honor, second only to the Roman Republic's founder, Lucius Junius Brutus, as the ultimate model citizen.

Cincinnatus's reputation was based on his desire not to hold political power. Elected as a suffect consul (a replacement leader drafted in to replace a consul who had died in office or been removed) in 460 BCE, Cincinnatus gave up public life at the end of his term to tend to his farm in the country. Two years later, he returned to Rome to lead its army against Aequi and Sabine forces threatening the city. The Senate appointed the reluctant statesman as dictator; he defeated Rome's enemies in just 16 days, at which point he resigned from his office and returned to his farm. In 439 BCE, the Senate made Cincinnatus dictator again and asked him to suppress an alleged plebeian plot to seize control of the Roman state. Twenty-one days later, he was back behind his plow, having once again "saved" Rome and turned down the job offer of dictator. He died c. 430 BCE, aged 89.

△ Fresco of Marcus Furius Camillus (right) from the Palazzo Vecchio, Florence (Domenico Ghirlandaio, c. 1482)

Aulus Cornelius Cossus

Consul: 428 BCE

Rome's consul for 428 BCE is best known for his military prowess: Aulus Cornelius Cossus was one of three men awarded Rome's highest military honor, the *spolia opima* (rich spoils). This was the right of a Roman commander to dedicate the arms of an enemy commander at the Temple of Jupiter Feretrius, after personally killing him on the battlefield. Cornelius Cossus earned this right at the Battle of Fidenae in 437 BCE, when he vanquished and decapitated Lars Tolumnius, the king of Veii. During his year as consul, drought and plague ravaged Rome. Two years later, in 426 BCE, Cornelius Cossus once more took part in a successful military campaign against Veii.

Marcus Furius Camillus

Consular tribune: 401, 398, 394, 386, 384, 381 BCE
Dictator: 396, 390–389, 368–367 BCE

After a successful military career, Marcus Furius Camillus became consular tribune (an official with the power of a consul) in 401 BCE, and then censor. The Senate made him dictator in 396 BCE to end a decade-long conflict with the Etruscan city of Veii. He captured the city, slaughtering its adult male population, and selling its women and children into slavery. Controversy followed when he failed to honor a promise to share some of the treasures he had plundered on his military campaigns, forcing him into exile.

When the Gauls attacked and occupied Rome in 390 BCE, Camillus returned from exile and was reappointed dictator. He annihilated the invading army, earning himself the title of "the Second Romulus," as his fellow citizens began to rebuild their ruined city. Thereafter, each attempt Camillus made to retire was foiled by some new military or social crisis afflicting Rome. In total, he was a consular tribune six times, dictator five times, and won four Triumphs.

Despite being a conservative patrician, Camillus commissioned the Temple of Concord in the Forum after the passing of the *Lex Licinia Sextia* c. 367 BCE. This was the law that opened the consulship to the plebs. He also introduced salaries for Rome's legionnaires.

Gaius Licinius Stolo and Lucius Sextius Sextinus Lateranus

Consul: 366 BCE

From the time that Rome became a republic in 509 BCE, the patrician class controlled the city's power through the Senate. As a result of the Secession of the Plebs in 495–493 BCE, Rome's ordinary citizens earned voting rights for the first time and, with the creation of the Tribune of the Plebs, representation in government. However, in the 370s BCE, ongoing tensions between Rome's rich and poor were heightened with the continued reelection of Gaius Licinius Stolo and Lucius Sextius Sextinus Lateranus as Tribunes of the Plebs, every year between 376 and 367 BCE. Both men called for radical reform of the political process, and their popularity among the people was such that, in 367 BCE, the senate finally bowed to public pressure and authorized the *Lex Licinia Sextia*. This was a set of legal provisions, which included the concession that one of Rome's two annually elected consuls had to be plebeian. Lucius Sextius became the first plebeian consul the following year.

Titus Manlius Imperiosus Torquatus

Consul: 347, 344, 340 BCE
Dictator: 353, 349, 320 BCE

Titus Manlius Imperiosus Torquatus won renown for defeating a Gallic warrior in single combat, winning the epithet "Torquatus" in honor of the torc, or neck ring, he took from his opponent's body. He earned the consulship three times and was dictator on three separate occasions. Famously principled, Titus Manlius executed his own son for defying military orders, instantly earning himself a place in the pantheon of great heroes and giving birth to the phrase "Manlian discipline." This was used by Rome's soldiers for centuries to come to describe their army's ruthless code of behavior.

Marcus Valerius Corvus

Consul: 348, 346, 343, 335, 300–299 BCE
Dictator: 342, 302, 301 BCE

Like Titus Manlius, Marcus Valerius proved himself in battle by personally killing one of the champions of a Gallic army attacking Rome. Legend has it that a raven distracted Marcus Valerius's enemy by landing on his helmet. This earned Marcus Valerius the surname Corvus (meaning "raven").

His fame assured, Marcus Valerius won the consulship in 348 BCE at the very young age of 23. It was an office he would occupy five more times—in addition to the three occasions he was appointed dictator.

In between his multiple consulates and dictatorships, Marcus Valerius won glory several times on the battlefield, especially in the First and Second Samnite Wars (see pp. 56–57), and was awarded four Triumphs. When he died around 270 BCE, Marcus Valerius was supposedly 100 years old. His passing was mourned by all Romans, especially the plebs, whose rights he had championed throughout his career.

Appius Claudius Caecus

Consul: 307, 296 BCE
Dictator: 285 BCE

Appius Claudius Caecus is the first prominent Roman for whom there is verifiable historical information. He oversaw the construction of Rome's first aqueduct and Rome's first paved road, the Appian Way, which bears his name.

Having been censor for five years from 312 BCE, he won the consulship in 307 BCE. His

△ Painting of the blind statesman Appius Claudius Caecus entering the Roman Senate (Cesare Maccari, c. 1882)

political career was not without controversy: he alienated many of his fellow patricians by introducing laws to extend the political rights of the plebs, including the right to become senators. As a result of reforms, he became involved in a dispute with the powerful Fabii family. The historian Fabius Pictor wrote a contemporary account of Appius Claudius's life and career that is a valuable historical record, but it is perhaps not entirely reliable, as the author was a sworn enemy of his subject.

Later in life, having been consul twice and dictator once, Appius Claudius lost his sight, hence the name Caecus, which is Latin for "blind."

△ *The Battle of Zama* showing Scipio Africanus on horseback engaging Hannibal, riding a war elephant (Cornelis Cort, c. 1550)

Scipio Africanus

Publius Cornelius Scipio Africanus

Consul: 205, 194 BCE

Publius Cornelius Scipio was born into one of Rome's most respected families; his father, grandfather, and great-grandfather had all been consuls. Scipio himself achieved that office in 205 BCE, having distinguished himself on the battlefield in Rome's conflict with Carthage in the Second Punic War from 218–201 BCE (see pp. 82–83).

Three years after leaving office, Scipio embarked on the military campaign that would see his name immortalized in history, even earning him a mention in Italy's national anthem as an exemplar of martial glory. He invaded the Carthaginian homeland in North Africa and at the Battle of Zama, in modern-day Tunisia, the Roman general's legions defeated the seemingly invincible forces of the Carthaginian leader, Hannibal. The victory was one of Rome's greatest-ever, but the outcome for Scipio was mixed. In the short term, it saw him lionized by Rome's populace, celebrate a Triumph, and be awarded the honorific "Africanus." In the longer term, Scipio's success and popularity earned him many powerful enemies and, in 187 BCE, he and his brother Lucius were implicated in a fabricated bribery scandal that resulted in Rome's "savior" retiring from public life. He died four years later in southern Italy, an embittered and angry man.

Cato the Censor

Marcus Porcius Cato

Consul: 195 BCE

The highly conservative writer, orator, and statesman Cato the Censor won the consulship in 195 BCE. His career was marked by his implacable opposition to three great enemies: Carthage, the Scipio family, and the Hellenistic republics of Ancient Greece. For Cato, this unholy trio represented the degrading influences threatening to turn his beloved strong and virtuous Rome into a decadent and weak state, comparable to the Greek and Eastern civilizations. He famously ended every public speech he made with the words "*Delenda est Carthago*" ("Carthage must be destroyed") and never forgave Scipio Africanus in particular for sparing the life of the Carthaginian leader, Hannibal, after the Battle of Zama (see left). In time, Cato's unrelenting puritanism began to wear on his compatriots and his final years were largely spent out of the public eye as a successful farmer and moneylender.

△ Portrait painting of Gaius Marius in exile from Rome (John Vanderlyn, 1832)

Gaius Marius

Consul: 107, 104–100, 86 BCE

The soldier-politician Gaius Marius was consul seven times. As an administrator, he reformed and rearmed the army. As a general, he ended the Jugurthine War in 106 BCE, and defeated Teuton and Cimbric invasion forces in 102 and 101 BCE. For his military achievements, he was awarded two Triumphs. During the Social War of 91–87 BCE, he became a bitter enemy of his former underling and ex-comrade-in-arms Sulla, who took most of the glory for Rome's victory. This dispute developed into a civil war, during which first Sulla then Marius occupied Rome and butchered their enemies. Marius died on January 13, 86 BCE, aged 70 or 71.

Sulla

Lucius Cornelius Sulla

Consul: 88, 80 BCE
Dictator: 82–79 BCE

Consul in 88 and 80 BCE, Lucius Cornelius Sulla (see pp. 108–109) distinguished himself in the Jugurthine, Cimbrian, and Social Wars as a general, winning Rome's highest military honor, the Grass Crown. Politically, he supported the conservative faction in the Senate, rather than the plebeian-focused populist movement led by Gaius Marius.

Sulla achieved notoriety in 87 BCE, when disputes between the two opposing factions in the military leadership impelled him to march to Rome and seize the city by force, becoming the first citizen to do so. In the civil war that followed, Sulla crushed the populist movement at the Battle of the Colline Gate in 82 BCE, after which he appointed himself dictator and purged Rome of his opponents, real and perceived.

In his three years as dictator Sulla established the supremacy of the conservative faction, and limited the power of the Tribunes of the Plebs. He stood down in 79 BCE and died the following year. The precedent he set of overriding Rome's political leadership by military force would be used by others in the Republic's declining years.

Pompey

Gnaeus Pompeius Magnus

Consul: 70, 55, 52 BCE

In his early twenties, Pompey (see pp. 126–127) served under Sulla in the Civil War of 83–82 BCE. His youthful fame allowed him to gain the consulship in his mid-30s without having held any other major public office. This showed that, in times of crisis, the Senate was willing to disregard the conservative hierarchies promoted by Sulla to advance the careers of the strongest, most charismatic, or militarily successful statesmen. In total, Pompey would be consul three times and celebrate three military Triumphs.

To his supporters, he was "Pompey the Great," a new Alexander and Rome's savior; to his opponents, Pompey was Sulla's baby-faced assassin, *adulescentulus carnifex* (the teenage butcher). As Rome's politics dissolved into vicious factionalism, the conservatives bitterly opposed Pompey's uneasy alliance with both the wealthy businessman Marcus Licinius Crassus and the populist figurehead Julius Caesar in the so-called First Triumvirate of 60 BCE (see p. 113). Ultimately, this alliance of convenience descended into civil war. In the hope of winning favor with Caesar, the Egyptian pharaoh Ptolemy XIII had Pompey assassinated in 48 BCE. His murder was in some respects the symbolic death of the Roman Republic, too.

Cicero

Marcus Tullius Cicero

Consul: 63 BCE

The famous orator and writer Marcus Tullius Cicero (see pp. 118–119) was a central player in the last days of the Roman Republic. As consul in 63 BCE, Cicero attempted to unite the interests of the people and the Senate under his leadership, crushing the so-called Catilinarian Conspiracy—a shadowy plot among Rome's aristocracy to exploit popular grievances to their own ends. His mistrust of such politicians colored his view of the rise of Julius Caesar.

When the fragile alliance between Caesar and Pompey collapsed, Cicero naturally sided with Pompey. After Pompey's death, Cicero reconciled with Rome's new dictator-for-life, Caesar, hoping perhaps to rein in his authoritarianism. With Caesar's assassination in 44 BCE, Cicero became Rome's leading politician—alongside Caesar's chief lieutenant, Mark Antony. The two men were enemies, and the usually sure-footed Cicero made a fatal error by cultivating Caesar's teenage nephew and heir, Octavian, as a rival to Antony. When Octavian asked for Antony's support in bringing to justice Caesar's assassins, Antony's price for agreeing was the death of Cicero. Antony's forces murdered Cicero as he tried to flee to Macedonia in 43 BCE.

▷ Bust of Julius Caesar (Andrea di Pietro di Marco Ferrucci, c. 1512–1514)

Julius Caesar

Gaius Julius Caesar

Consul: 59, 48, 46–45, 44 BCE
Dictator: 49–44 BCE

Julius Caesar is something of an enigma: a patrician, he was also a champion of the plebs; ruthless in war, he was magnanimous in victory; a defender of the Republic, he would eventually become king.

Julius Caesar rose to prominence during a turbulent period, with slave revolts, provincial unrest, and political infighting weakening Rome, which allowed ambitious young generals like himself to make their mark.

From his many military successes in Gaul (see pp. 112–113) and genius for self-promotion, Caesar earned popularity with the masses. He first seized and shared power in Rome with Pompey and Marcus Licinius Crassus in 60 BCE, and then, in early 44 BCE, made himself Rome's dictator-for-life. In March that year, a group of conservative senators assassinated Caesar, vainly hoping to save the dying Republic (see pp. 128–129).

◁ Marble statue of Augustus, with head from 30–20 BCE and body from the 2nd century CE

The Roman Empire

The end of the Republic was both a new beginning and a return to the past. It initiated a new form of government and an age of imperial expansion, but it also marked a return to one-man rule, albeit in a form that pretended power was shared between the emperor and his Senate.

1ST CENTURY CE

The empire's first 100 years saw two great dynasties dominate: the Julio-Claudians, from Augustus to Nero; and the Flavians, comprising Vespasian, Titus, and Domitian. The remaining four emperors ruled for fewer than four years between them.

Augustus

Caesar Augustus

r. 27 BCE–14 CE

Gaius Octavius, or Octavian, as Augustus was originally named, was Julius Caesar's great-nephew and adopted heir. He became emperor in 27 BCE, and named himself "Augustus" (meaning "the venerable"). He held absolute power for the next 41 years, until his death. Augustus allowed institutions such as the Senate and the Tribunes of the Plebs to remain in operation, but took away most of their power to leave them as largely ceremonial offices.

Austere, moral, and actually quite a dull character, Augustus restored order after decades of conflict (see pp. 138–139), initiated new building projects to beautify the city, and made Rome a safer and considerably more pleasurable place to live.

Tiberius

Tiberius Caesar Augustus

r. 14–37 CE

A stern character, Tiberius was Augustus's stepson via his mother Livia's marriage to the emperor. Tiberius's long wait to become emperor ended in 14 CE, by which time the 54-year-old's best years as a successful military officer and diligent administrator were well behind him. Never comfortable as emperor, in 27 CE Tiberius moved his court behind closed doors on the island of Capri, where rumors of the debauched life he led there abounded. Rome, meanwhile, was controlled by the Praetorian prefect Sejanus. When Sejanus became too powerful, Tiberius had him executed in 31 CE. Tiberius died in 37 CE, unloved by his subjects.

Caligula

Gaius Caesar Germanicus

r. 37–41 CE

The nickname Caligula, meaning "little boots," derived from the tiny marching shoes he wore as an infant while on a campaign with his father, the general Germanicus. Defects in Caligula's character were well known before Tiberius named his

△ Painting depicting Nero (left) playing a type of harp called a lyre (Eugene Appert, 1839)

great-nephew as his successor—the emperor once stated that he was "nursing a viper in Rome's bosom." Stories abound of Caligula's deranged behavior, from incest with three of his sisters and arbitrary murders to an attempt to make his horse a consul. These tales should be taken with a pinch of salt, as most were circulated long after Caligula's death. Contemporary chroniclers such as Seneca and Philo, while criticizing his odd and erratic actions, make no mention of his wilder excesses. Modern historians attribute his eccentric and arbitrary behavior to attempts to compensate for his lack of personal achievements worthy of his status. His four-year reign ended on January 24, 41 CE, when the Praetorian Guard killed the 28-year-old emperor. He had recently talked of moving the imperial capital from Rome to Alexandria, in Egypt, which may have incited his murder.

Claudius

Tiberius Claudius Caesar Augustus Germanicus

r. 41–54 CE

Despite being a nephew to Tiberius and an uncle to Caligula, Claudius never expected to be emperor as he suffered from a range of physical ailments. Shunned by his family, Claudius immersed himself in study, writing dozens of volumes on Carthaginian history, the Etruscans, and other topics. As the last surviving adult of his family—following Caligula's murder—he became emperor by default. A good administrator, he built many aqueducts and new roads. He also expanded Rome's territory, by beginning the invasion of Britannia in 43 CE. According to legend, his wife Agrippina (see pp. 178–179) poisoned him, impatient for her son Nero to become emperor.

Nero

Nero Claudius Caesar Augustus Germanicus

r. 54–68 CE

Just 16 when he succeeded Claudius, Nero (see pp. 184–185) spent his first years as emperor under the influence of his mother Agrippina, the philosopher Seneca, and Burrus—the commander of the Praetorian Guard. Nero outlawed capital punishment, gave Rome's enslaved people legal rights, and lowered taxes. An actor and musician himself, he was also a generous patron of the arts.

Nero soon tired of his advisors' interference. In 59 CE, he sidelined Seneca and Burrus, and had his mother murdered. He divorced then executed his wife, Octavia, and married his lover, Poppaea. In 64 CE, Nero took advantage of a devastating fire in Rome to build himself a lavish palace (see pp. 186–187) and embarked on a life of self-destructive pleasure-seeking and arbitrary cruelty. To deflect allegations he started the fire, Nero blamed and persecuted Rome's small sect of Christians. A failed plot to remove Nero in 65 CE was followed by a military rebellion in 68 CE that ended with the emperor dying by suicide.

△ *Vitellius Dragged Through the Streets of Rome* (1883) by Georges Rochegrosse

Galba

Servius Sulpicius Galba

r. 68–69 CE

Aged 65, the Roman general Galba seized power after Nero's suicide. Austere and unwavering, he struggled to win the full support of the Senate and Rome's legions, as well as the people. In January 69 CE, his former ally and fellow general Otho bribed the Praetorian Guard to murder Galba by beheading him in the Forum, just eight months into his reign.

Otho

Marcus Salvius Otho

r. 69 CE

Otho was the former husband of Nero's second wife, Poppaea. Having succeeded Galba in January 69 CE, Otho faced opposition to his rule from the governor of Germania, Aulus Vitellius. Their two armies fought each other at the Battle of Bedriacum in April 69 CE. When Vitellius emerged triumphant, Otho died by suicide.

Vitellius

Aulus Vitellius

r. 69 CE

After Otho's death, only Vitellius's German legions were loyal to the new emperor. He found himself isolated when the troops of another imperial claimant, Vespasian, marched on Rome. Vitellius prepared to abdicate following defeat in battle, but Vespasian's men captured and executed him when they entered the city in December 69 CE.

Vespasian

Titus Flavius Vespasianus

r. 69–79 CE

A warrior of humble origins, Vespasian pointedly dated the beginning of his reign from the moment his legions had acclaimed him emperor, rather than when the Senate approved him. This was a signal that the army was the empire's dominant force now.

Vespasian set about stabilizing the empire's borders and replenishing Rome's depleted treasury by increasing taxes and reclaiming public land across Italy that had been occupied by squatters. With the money he raised, Vespasian began work on the Colosseum; built a new Forum (see p. 213); and repaired the Temple of Jupiter Optimus Maximus, which had been destroyed during the "Year of Four Emperors" in 69 CE.

Vespasian reformed the army, too, and extended Rome's holdings in Britannia. According to the historian Tacitus, Vespasian was "the only emperor who had changed for the better" during his rule. In June 79 CE, at the end of his 10-year reign, the dying emperor remarked, "Alas! I think I'm becoming a god," a sarcastic comment on the Romans' custom of deifying their dead emperors.

Titus

Titus Caesar Vespasianus

r. 79–81 CE

Titus saw military service in Britannia and Germania before his father Vespasian became emperor. In 70 CE, he conquered and sacked Jerusalem

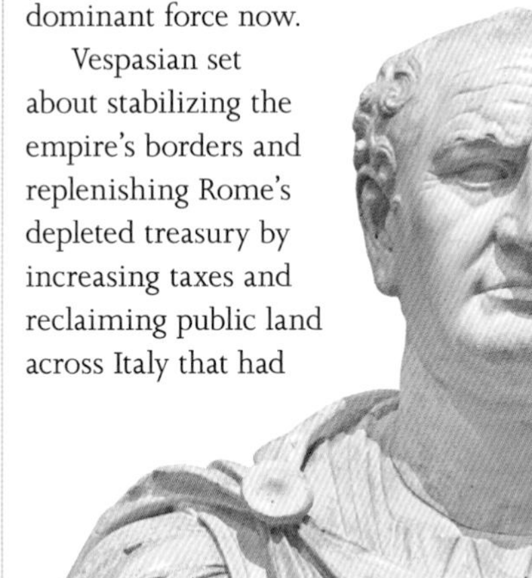

◁ Marble bust of Vespasian from the 1st century CE

△ The Arch of Titus in the Roman Forum, carved with scenes showing the conquest of Jerusalem

during the Jewish War (see pp. 188–189), the spoils of which helped pay for the Colosseum and the monumental Arch of Titus in the Forum. He gained notoriety in Rome, however, for his affair with the Judean princess Berenice, whom the public viewed as another Cleopatra.

Despite this, Titus was a popular emperor, especially after the 100 days of free games he held to celebrate the opening of the Colosseum (originally called the Flavian Amphitheater) in 80 CE. He died unexpectedly at the age of 41 in 81 CE—it's possible that his brother and successor, Domitian, poisoned him.

Domitian

Titus Flavius Domitianus

r. 81–96 CE

Unlike his brother Titus, Domitian was never a wholly popular emperor. The aristocracy hated him and resented the fact that Domitian ran his administration as a meritocracy, employing non-nobles and even freedmen in positions that the nobles had come to regard as theirs by birthright.

Domitian also had a cruel streak. He fostered an atmosphere in which people tried to guarantee their own safety and progression in his court by accusing others of treason. In 96 CE, a group of palace officials; Praetorian prefects; and the emperor's own wife, Domitia Longina, arranged his assassination after finding their names on his kill list.

Nerva

Marcus Cocceius Nerva

r. 96–98 CE

It's not clear if Nerva was involved in the plot to murder Domitian, but his unexpected elevation to the imperial throne on the same day that Domitian died made many Romans think that he was. In 97 CE, Nerva faced a mutiny from the army, who mourned Domitian and demanded the punishment of his killers. Nerva eventually gave in, allowing two of the main conspirators—the Praetorian prefect Titus Petronius Secundus and the palace chamberlain Parthenius—to be executed. Nerva's authority was further weakened by his lack of an heir. During a financial crisis, army leaders forced a reluctant Nerva to adopt the popular general Trajan as his successor. Nerva died in January 98 CE aged 67, after just two years in power.

2ND CENTURY

According to the historian Edward Gibbon, the empire's second century was one of the happiest periods in history, especially the so-called Age of the Antonines that encompassed the reigns of rulers from Trajan through to Marcus Aurelius. However, there were bad times—and bad emperors—too, and a worrying trend toward the militarization of politics and imperial rule.

△ Trajan's Column, a Roman triumphal column, and the Baroque church of Santissimo Nome di Maria in Rome

Trajan

Marcus Ulpius Traianus

r. 98–117 CE

Trajan was born in the Roman province of Baetica, in modern-day Spain. A good military leader whose career blossomed under Vespasian (see p. 322), he rose to become governor of, successively, Syria and Asia. Trajan was appointed governor of Germania Superior (Upper Germany) by Nerva, who adopted him his as heir when a financial crisis weakened the emperor's position and forced him to turn to the army for help—on condition he choose one of their own to succeed him.

When he became emperor in 98 CE, Trajan earned the approval of both the army and the Senate in a rare show of unity. Trajan repaid their trust by being an innovative and popular emperor. He gave out money and free grain to Rome's poor. He lowered taxes and appointed efficient administrators to run the empire, including his friend the writer Pliny the Younger. Trajan also ordered the construction of many roads, aqueducts, bridges, and public buildings, including a new Forum in Rome, in which stood Trajan's Column (see pp. 214–215), a tall carved sculpture that celebrates the emperor's victories in Dacia, in present-day Romania. He also campaigned successfully in Parthia (modern-day Iran). Trajan died in 117, having named his cousin Hadrian as his heir.

Hadrian

Publius Aelius Hadrianus

r. 117–138

Hadrian was 40 years old when he became emperor. Where Trajan had expanded the empire's boundaries, Hadrian adopted a policy of consolidation, holding onto what Rome already had. He understood that Rome needed to ensure its borders were safe before it could consider new conquests. A lasting symbol of his policy is the defensive structure in northern England known as Hadrian's Wall (see pp. 204–205), a 73-mile (117.5-km) barrier marking the farthest extent of the Roman Empire in Britain.

Hadrian spent much of his reign touring his empire, and his time in power was remarkably peaceful, with the exception of the Bar Kokhba uprising in Judea in the 130s. This erupted when the emperor announced his intention to build a Roman colony on the site of Jerusalem, which had been largely destroyed under Vespasian and Titus. With an interest in architecture, Hadrian rebuilt the Pantheon (pp. 204–205), which had burned down in 80 CE, and constructed the beautiful villa and grounds that bear his name at Tivoli, close to Rome.

Hadrian's love for the Greek youth Antinous raised some eyebrows among his peers, but the emperor ignored any scandal and created a cult around the boy after he drowned in 130, aged around 19. Hadrian died eight years later, aged 62.

Antoninus Pius

Titus Aurelius Fulvius Boionius Arrius Antoninus

r. 138–161

Hadrian adopted the 52-year-old Antoninus, an accomplished administrator and trusted advisor, shortly before his death in 138. No doubt to the delight of Rome's citizens, Antoninus Pius's almost 23-year reign was remarkably peaceful, with no military revolts, provincial troubles, or large-scale social unrest. The senate gave Antoninus the name "Pius," supposedly because of his devotion to Hadrian's memory.

A bureaucrat by nature, Antoninus Pius made the empire a leaner, more efficient entity. He provided free drinking water throughout the empire, for example, and gave formerly enslaved people the right to vote in elections. He also refilled Rome's treasury, which had been almost emptied by the near-constant military campaigns and building campaigns of his predecessors. Faithfully carrying out Hadrian's dying wishes, Antoninus Pius nominated Marcus Aurelius and Lucius Verus to succeed him as joint emperors.

Marcus Aurelius

Marcus Aurelius Antoninus

r. 161–180

When Antoninus Pius died in 161, the senate was inclined to approve only one of his two named successors as emperor. But Marcus Aurelius (see pp. 222–223) was famously honest and moral, and insisted that Antoninus Pius's instructions be carried out in full. So it was that Marcus Aurelius and Lucius Verus became joint emperors, until the latter's early death in 169.

Marcus Aurelius was the last of the so-called five "good emperors" of the Age of the Antonines who ruled Rome in succession and presided over more than 80 years of relative peace and prosperity. His time on the imperial throne, however, was marked by a devastating plague and increasing unrest in the empire. He led Roman forces into major conflicts with the Parthians of modern-day Iran and, more extensively, against Germanic tribes on the empire's northern border in the Marcomannic Wars.

While on campaign, Marcus Aurelius wrote his *Meditations*, a still-influential work of Stoic philosophy that outlined his self-sacrificing and virtuous approach to life and leadership. He died in 180, aged 58.

△ A 2nd-century CE relief probably showing Marcus Aurelius victorious in battle against a Sarmatian or Germanic tribe

△ *The Death of Emperor Commodus* (1879) by Fernand Pelez

Lucius Verus

Lucius Aurelius Verus

r. 161–169

Lucius Verus was Rome's first co-emperor, the junior partner to Marcus Aurelius (see p. 325). The emperor Antoninus Pius adopted Lucius Verus in 138 CE and groomed him for a leadership role in the empire—he became consul, for example, in 154 when he was just 24. He died on military campaign against the Germans in 169, of either smallpox or the plague.

Commodus

Lucius Aelius Aurelius Commodus

r. 176–192

Marcus Aurelius made his son Commodus co-emperor in 176, when he was 15. He became sole emperor in 180, ruling until his murder in 192.

Although peaceful militarily, Commodus's reign was politically tumultuous. With each passing year Commodus became more erratic, fighting as a gladiator in the Colosseum, for example, and initiating a personality cult around himself. In 192, his mistress Marcia discovered that Commodus was planning her execution. Striking first, she conspired with the Praetorian prefect Laetus and the emperor's chamberlain Eclectus to have him murdered.

Pertinax

Publius Helvius Pertinax

r. 193

A distinguished military man, Pertinax was serving as Rome's urban prefect (a kind of police chief) when Commodus was

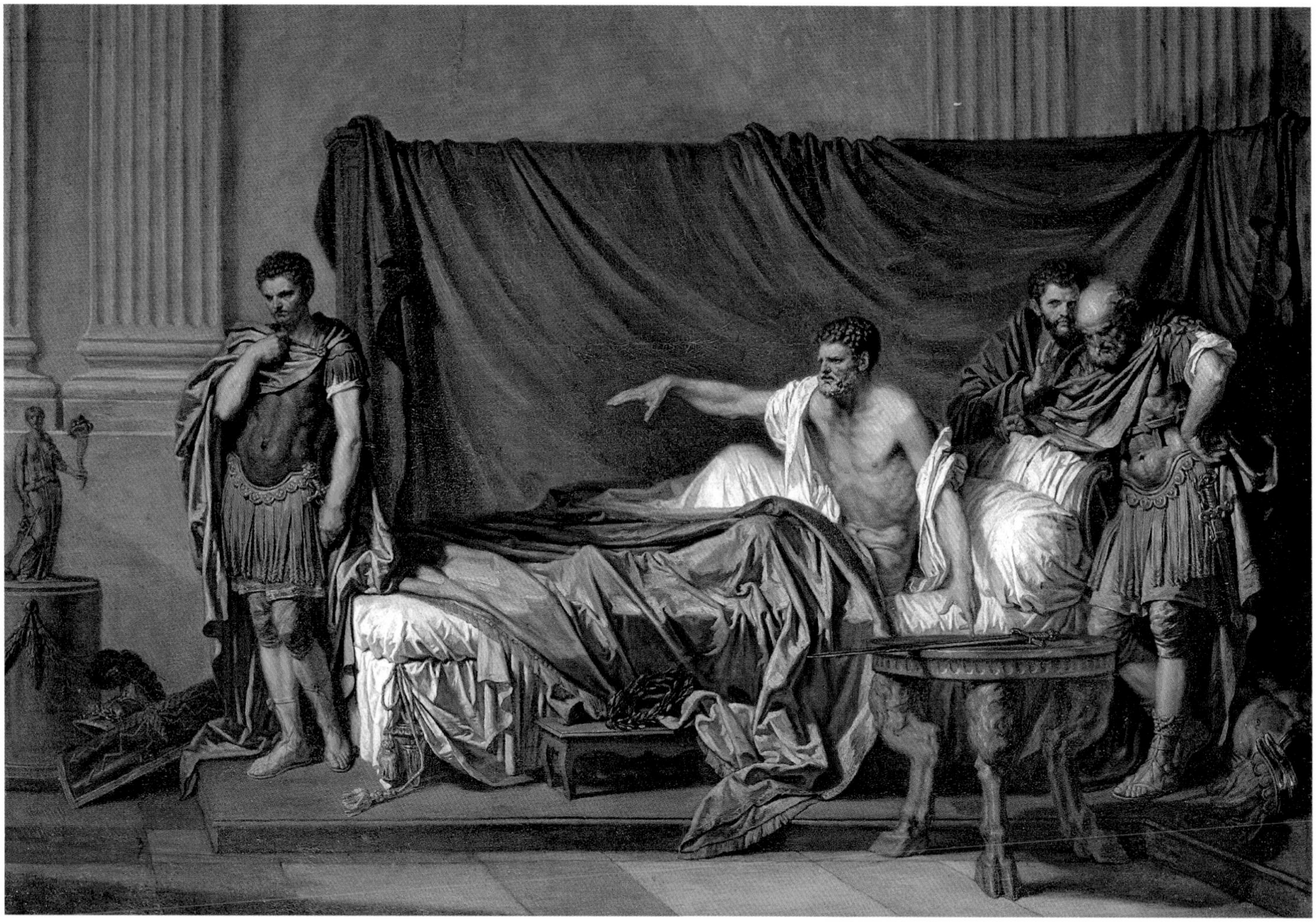

△ *The Emperor Severus Rebuking his Son, Caracalla, for Wanting to Assassinate Him* (1769) by Jean-Baptiste Greuze

assassinated on the last day of December 192. He was swiftly declared emperor, but failed to secure the support of the Praetorian guard and, just 87 days into his reign, Pertinax was murdered by a disaffected group of soldiers from that regiment.

Didius Julianus

Marcus Didius Severus Julianus

r. 193

Having killed Pertinax, the Praetorian Guard auctioned off the imperial throne to the highest bidder. The former consul and provincial governor Didius Julianus won the bidding war, but his elevation to Rome's highest office immediately sparked a civil war. Unable to win support to defeat the opposing armies, Julianus was killed by one of his own palace guards nine weeks after becoming emperor.

Septimius Severus

Lucius Septimius Severus

r. 193–211

The year 193 is known as "Year of Five Emperors," in which five men claimed the title of emperor. Septimius Severus ultimately won control of the city after this brief period of disruptive conflict. Born in the city of Lepcis Magna, in present-day Libya, Septimius was the first Roman emperor of truly "foreign" origin. Both of his parents had Punic ancestors, and Septimius considered himself at least part-Carthaginian. Having served as a Roman senator and tribune of the plebs, Septimius enjoyed a military career, and served as the governor of Pannonia Major, in modern-day Austria. When Pertinax died, Septimius's legions in Pannonia acclaimed him emperor. He was able to take Rome virtually unopposed, as Pertinax's successor Didius Julianus had been assassinated by the time Septimius reached the city.

Septimius was popular with the people but not with the Senate, which decried the fact that yet another military leader had seized power. Septimius returned the Senate's scorn, regularly murdering and replacing its members. Rather than accept senatorial advice, Septimius ruled with an inner circle that included his second wife, Julia Domna.

Septimius conducted several military campaigns, notably in Parthia, in present-day Iran, where he successfully expanded the empire's borders as far as the Tigris River. He died of an infectious disease in 211 at Eboracum (modern-day York) while campaigning in Britain.

3RD CENTURY

A time of crisis and conflict, the 3rd century saw emperors come and go with alarming regularity as the army and the Praetorian Guard installed new rulers at will. This period also included one of the "invincible" Roman army's worst-ever defeats.

Caracalla

Marcus Aurelius Antoninus

r. 198–217

The eldest son of Septimius Severus was 10 years old when he became co-emperor with his father. Born Lucius Septimius Bassianus and renamed Marcus Aurelius Antoninus, he was known by the nickname "Caracalla," referring to the Gallic cloak that he habitually wore.

In 202, the 14-year-old co-emperor married Fulvia Plautilla, the daughter of the Praetorian prefect Plautianus. By 205 Caracalla had had Plautianus executed for treason and Fulvia exiled (and, later, quietly killed).

Caracalla and his brother Geta became joint emperors in 211, on Septimius Severus's death. Caracalla soon had his younger sibling removed (see next entry), and from 212 ruled as sole emperor. The following year, Caracalla left Rome forever to campaign in Germania. He was stabbed to death in Türkiye in 217 by a disaffected soldier he had passed over for promotion.

Despite several lasting achievements, such as the great baths in Rome that bear his name (see pp. 236–237), or his granting of Roman citizenship to all free men of the empire, Caracalla is remembered as a cruel and ruthless ruler.

Geta

Publius Septimius Geta

r. 209–211

Geta shared rule with his father Septimius Severus and brother Caracalla from 209. After their father's death in 211, the siblings began to argue. Later that year, Geta met with Caracalla at their mother Julia Domna's house in Rome to discuss their problems, which Caracalla resolved by having centurions murder his sibling.

Macrinus

Marcus Opellius Macrinus

r. 217–218

The Praetorian prefect Macrinus briefly succeeded Caracalla, whose murder he may have engineered, and was the first man of non-senatorial rank to become emperor. He was overthrown and later killed following his loss to an army of rebellious legions at the Battle of Antioch in June 218.

◁ Bust of Caracalla (Bartolomeo Cavaceppi, c. 1750–1770)

Elagabalus

Varius Avitus Bassianus

r. 218–222

An aunt of Caracalla, Julia Maesa, instigated the opposition to Macrinus's reign—she wished to see her grandson, Elagabalus, become Rome's next emperor. Varius Avitus Bassianus became known as Elagabalus due to his devotion to the Syrian sun god El-Gabal (his Syrian mother came from a family of high priests dedicated to the god).

Elagabalus was 14 when he became emperor. His four-year reign was characterized by a court rife with allegations of sexual depravity and arbitrary cruelty. He particularly offended old Roman morality by marrying the Vestal Virgin Aquilia Severa, claiming their union would produce divine offspring. Allowing his mother and grandmother to sit in the Senate also alienated Rome's traditional elites, as did his construction of the Elagabalium, a gaudy temple in which he forced senators to watch him perform ritual dances around an altar.

By 222, the Praetorian Guard had had enough and murdered Elagabalus. His successor, Severus Alexander, issued a *damnatio memoriae*, which removed all trace of his rule from Rome's buildings and official records.

Severus Alexander

Marcus Aurelius Severus Alexander

r. 222–235

Alexander was only 13 when his grandmother Julia Maesa conspired to have him replace his cousin Elagabalus. He became the last emperor of the Severan line. His use of diplomacy to deal with the troublesome Germans on the empire's northern borders angered the army, which favored a more confrontational approach. His own troops killed him in 235, an event that initiated the so-called Third Century Crisis—50 years of instability that almost saw the empire collapse (see pp. 248–249).

Maximinus Thrax

Gaius Julius Verus Maximinus

r. 235–238

Hailing from the province of Thracia (Thrace, southeastern Balkans) Maximinus adopted the name "Thrax" to denote his origins. He was one of the so-called "barracks emperors"—the generals throughout the 3rd century who seized power

△ Painting of Elagabalus (wearing a golden robe) hosting an extravagant banquet (Sir Lawrence Alma-Tadema, 1888)

courtesy of their control of the army. By 238, three years into his reign, Maximinus faced a number of other army generals who challenged his position. Before he could confront his enemies in battle, his own troops assassinated him at Aquileia, in central Italy.

Gordian I

Marcus Antonius Gordianus Sempronianus Romanus

r.238

Little is known of this soldier-emperor's origins, though his name suggests he was of Phrygian (Turkish) origin. His rule lasted only 22 days. He died by suicide when his son Gordian II was defeated in battle.

Gordian II

Marcus Antonius Gordianus Sempronianus Romanus Africanus

r.238

The son of Gordian I, Gordian II shared power with his father during their short regime. Gordian II commanded an army of untrained soldiers at the Battle of Carthage in April 238 and was killed during the encounter by forces loyal to Maximinus Thrax.

Pupienus

Marcus Clodius Pupienus Maximus

r.238

The Senate appointed Pupienus emperor, along with Balbinus (see next entry), after Gordian II was killed in battle and his father, Gordian I, took his own life. He and Balbinus were murdered after just 99 days in power by Praetorian Guards who objected to serving under Senate-appointed emperors.

Balbinus

Decimus Caelius Calvinus Balbinus

r.238

Balbinus and Pupienus did not get along. The co-emperors each suspected the other of plotting his murder, and the two men lived in separate parts of Rome's imperial palace, both in a state of permanent paranoia. On one of the rare days they were in the same room together, in July 238, army assassins burst in and took the emperors back to the barracks, before torturing and killing them both.

Gordian III

Marcus Antonius Gordianus

r.238–244

Gordian III was the grandson and nephew respectively of Gordian I and Gordian II. The Senate selected him aged 13 to succeed Pupienus and Balbinus in 238 because Rome's leading patrician families hoped to control him. Instead, he fell under the influence of his father-in-law, the Praetorian prefect Timesitheus. Not yet 20, Gordian III died in 244 in mysterious circumstances, possibly in battle or at the hands of his successor, Philip.

Philip

Marcus Julius Philippus Arabs

r.244–249

The empire enjoyed a period of calm during the five-year rule of Philip "the Arab." He was born in present-day Syria and was Praetorian prefect when he came to power. One of his first acts as emperor was to pay a large indemnity to the Sasanian Empire (in present-day Iran) to end the war between the two states. Rome celebrated its millennium in 247 under Philip. He died in 249 at the Battle of Verona, during an army revolt.

Decius

Gaius Messius Quintus Traianus Decius

r.249–251

Decius led the rebellion that overthrew Philip. Unlike most of his immediate predecessors, Decius was well-qualified to administer the empire, having served as a senator, consul, governor, and urban prefect. He built the Decian Baths and restored the Colosseum, which had been damaged by fire.

Decius was devoted to Roman religion, and he embarked on a major suppression of the empire's Christians, whose influence was growing at that time. His persecutions only strengthened the faith of believers, especially when an outbreak of plague in Rome was interpreted by Christian leaders as divine intervention. Decius died fighting against the Goths in June 251.

Hostilian

Gaius Valens Hostilianus Messius Quintus

r.251

Hostilian was briefly co-emperor in 251 with Gallus (see next entry). The son of Decius, Hostilian offered continuity for Gallus's regime in its early days. Hostilian died just months after taking office: of plague, according to some sources, or murdered by Gallus, according to others.

△ Saint Reparata refuses to make sacrifices to the Roman traditional gods before Decius (Bernardo Daddi, c.1338–40)

Gallus

Gaius Vibius Trebonianus Gallus

r.251–253

As Rome's new ruler, the aristocrat and general Gallus made peace with the Gothic tribes that had killed Decius so that he could consolidate his position in Rome. On Hostilian's death, he made his 20-year-old son Volusianus co-emperor. His short reign was marked by colonial rebellions and military uprisings, and it was while attempting to put down one of these, led by the Roman general Aemilian, that Gallus and Volusianus were murdered by their own troops.

Aemilian

Marcus Aemilius Aemilianus

r.253

Aemilian was proclaimed emperor by his own troops in June 253. Those same men killed him three months later when the powerful general Valerian declared himself Rome's new ruler.

Valerian

Publius Licinius Valerianus

r.253–260

A former consul and well-connected aristocrat, Valerian was more than acceptable to Rome's Senate when he succeeded Aemilian in 253. He installed his son Gallienus as

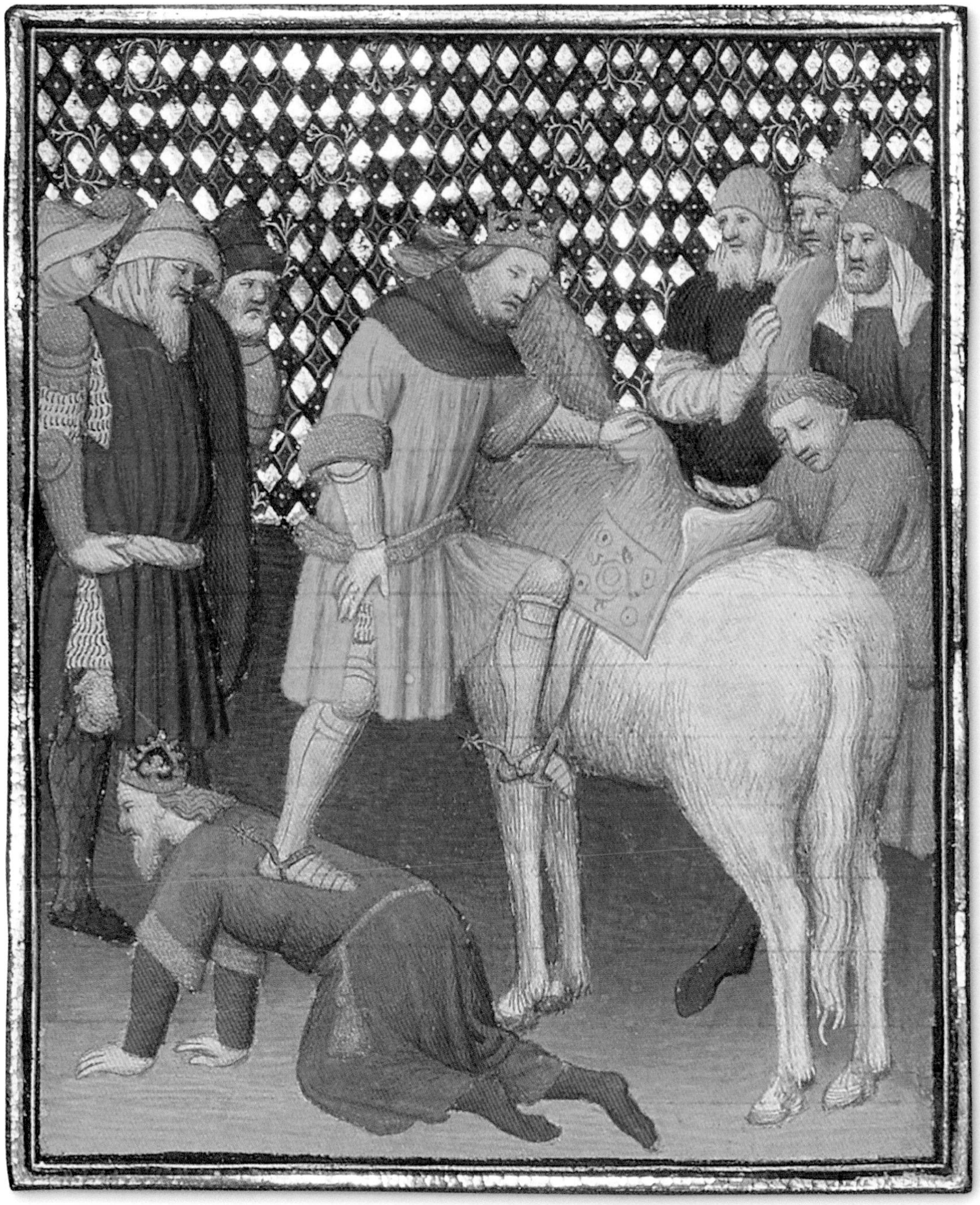

△ Scene from an illuminated manuscript showing Shapur I, King of Persia, using Valerian as a stool to mount his horse

co-emperor (see next entry), and they divided the empire into eastern and western regions in order to tackle the ongoing rebellions and wars across their territories. Valerian took the eastern half and had to face a Gothic army that had invaded Asia Minor (in modern Türkiye), as well as deal with threats from the Persian Sasanian Empire. Then, an outbreak of plague weakened his army and led the Sassanids to besiege Valerian at his stronghold of Edessa in 260. Valerian was defeated in the resulting battle, becoming the prisoner of the Sasanian ruler, Shapur I. It's not known exactly when or how Valerian died, but stories of his mistreatment at the hands of Shapur I circulated widely. The most infamous are that the Sasanian king used Valerian as a footstool whenever he mounted his horse, and that he finally executed the emperor by pouring molten gold down his throat, or by having him skinned alive.

Gallienus

Publius Licinius Egnatius Gallienus

r.253–268

Gallienus's rule from 253 to 260 as co-emperor and from 260 to 268 as sole emperor was the longest in Rome for 50 years. He successfully dealt with Germanic tribes in the western half of the empire, but Valerian's fall in 260 weakened his position, and he was unable to prevent the ambitious General Postumus setting up a breakaway Gallic empire in 260. In 268, while fighting a rival who had sided with Postumus, Gallienus was killed by one of his own men.

Claudius II Gothicus

Marcus Aurelius Claudius

r.268–270

Claudius was a physically imposing general from the Balkans, whose popularity during his two-year reign as emperor came from his successes on the battlefield. By the time Claudius seized power, the empire was in disarray. The rebel general Postumus had set up his own kingdom in the west, known as the Gallic Empire, while the Middle East had broken from Rome to form the Palmyrene Empire. Claudius was determined to restore order, and scored an early victory when he defeated a huge Gothic army at the Battle of Naissus—which earned him the surname "Gothicus." He then overcame the Germanic Alemanni confederation army at the Battle of Lake Benacus, and led some successful campaigns against the Gallic Empire. The soldier-emperor's run of success ended when he succumbed to a plague in 270.

△ Painting of Aurelian celebrating his victory over the Palmyrenes led by Queen Zenobia (Giovanni Battista Tiepolo, 1718)

Quintillus

Marcus Aurelius Claudius Quintillus

r. 270

The brother of Claudius Gothicus, Quintillus briefly took power in 270. Little else is known about him. His reign lasted for some time between 17 and 77 days (the sources disagree) and the circumstances of his demise in office are shrouded in mystery. It is generally agreed that his death was not by natural causes, but came either by suicide or murder.

Aurelian

Lucius Domitius Aurelianus

r. 270–275

Aurelian was a brilliant military leader (see pp. 248–249). He overcame the Goths, Alemanni, Vandals, Sarmatians, Palmyrenes, Carpi, and the Gallic Empire, for which a grateful Senate rewarded him with the title *Restitutor Orbis* (Restorer of the World). He also drove through several important domestic reforms, including the improvement of Rome's free food program for the poor.

In 275, a corrupt official fearing exposure and the emperor's punishment tricked the Praetorian Guard into thinking Aurelian planned to kill them. He was subsequently assassinated while on campaign in Thracia.

Tacitus

Marcus Claudius Tacitus

r. 275–276

A former consul, Tacitus ruled for just six months before dying of fever (or assassination) in the summer of 276.

Florian

Marcus Annius Florianus

r. 276

The half-brother of Tacitus, Florian proclaimed himself emperor on the death of his sibling, but was immediately challenged by the General Probus, who used skillful guerrilla tactics in combat to wear down the resolve of Florian's men. This worked, and the emperor's demoralized soldiers duly rose up and killed their commander after just 88 days in power.

Probus

Marcus Aurelius Probus

r.276–282

Most Roman emperors of the 3rd century spent much of their reigns fighting fires on many fronts, and Probus was no exception. A more competent military leader and administrator than the majority of his predecessors, he was an effective politician, too, and was careful to maintain the fiction established by Augustus that the emperor was merely a servant of the Senate. He put down several rebellions and defeated the Germanic tribes during his six years in power. A popular leader, he was nevertheless murdered by his own legionnaires during a mutiny in 282.

Carus

Marcus Aurelius Carus

r.282–283

Probably of Gallic descent, Marcus Aurelius Carus died less than a year into his reign after reportedly being struck by lightning while on military campaign in Persia (modern Iran).

Numerian

Marcus Aurelius Numerius Numerianus

r.283–284

Picked along with his older brother Carinus (see next entry) to succeed their father Carus, Numerian died of possible heatstroke, or according to some sources murder, while returning to Rome from a campaign in Persia. The commander of his cavalry, Diocletian, was chosen by the army to succeed the brothers.

Carinus

Marcus Aurelius Carinus

r.283–285

Rome's historians portrayed Carinus as an unpleasant and debauched character, who was little missed after he was defeated, and possibly killed, in battle against the usurper Diocletian in 285.

Diocletian

Gaius Aurelius Valerius Diocletianus

r.284–305 (East)

One of Rome's most significant leaders, Diocletian completely changed the way the empire was ruled (see pp. 254–255). He was a native of Salona, in modern-day Croatia, and his abilities as a soldier allowed him to rise through the ranks and become the cavalry commander of the Roman army. Two years after becoming emperor, he appointed General Maximian (see next entry) as his coruler and split the empire into western and eastern halves. Diocletian assigned Maximian the western half and kept the eastern half. Diocletian further divided the empire by selecting two junior emperors, the soldiers Galerius and Constantius. This arrangement was known as the Tetrarchy, or "rule of four."

As a military campaigner, Diocletian decisively beat the Sasanians in battle, capturing their capital, Ctesiphon, in modern-day Iraq. A born bureaucrat, he established new administrative centers across the empire in a process of decentralization that lessened the importance of Rome and made regional cities closer to the frontiers, such as Nicomedia, Mediolanum, and Sirmium, much more powerful.

His persecution of Christians was widespread and large-scale, but failed to halt the religion's unstoppable growth. In 305, the aging and ill Diocletian stepped down and retired to a purpose-built palace in modern-day Split, Croatia. He died in 312, aged 68.

△ Roman gold *aureus* coin showing the famously brawny Maximian as emperor

Maximian

Marcus Aurelius Valerius Maximianus

r. 286–305 (West)

Hailing from the city of Sirmium, in modern-day Serbia, Maximian provided the military strength to complement Diocletian's political wisdom. Maximian took control of the western half of the empire, basing himself at Trier, in modern Germany, and spent most of his rule on campaign. When Diocletian issued a decree naming himself and Maximian living gods, he called himself "Iovus," after Jupiter, the king of the gods, while Maximian was named "Herculius," after Hercules, the demigod who only became a full god after completing a set of 12 tasks, or labors.

△ Marble portrait of Marcus Aurelius Probus from the 3rd century

When Diocletian abdicated in 305, Maximian stepped down, too. He retired to the countryside but soon returned, at first supporting, then later opposing, his son Maxentius's claim on the imperial throne (see p. 334). In the power struggle that followed, where four separate candidates all claimed to be the legitimate emperor, Maximian ultimately sided with Constantine the Great (see p. 334). He tried to seize power for himself while Constantine was away on campaign against the Franks in Gaul (modern-day France) in 310, but his attempted coup failed, and he was arrested by Constantine's soldiers. Stripped of all his titles and honors by Constantine, Maximian died by suicide that same year.

4TH CENTURY

The dominant story of this century is the unstoppable rise of Christianity as the most powerful force in the empire, but traditional religion did not give up without a fight. In the meantime, Rome's borders came under threat for the first time.

Constantius I

Flavius Valerius Constantius

r. 305–306 (West)

One of the four Tetrarchs (see pp. 254–255), Constantius replaced Maximian as Western emperor in 305 CE. His time as emperor was spent mostly on campaign in Britannia, attempting to suppress the Picts of modern-day Scotland with the help of his son, the future emperor Constantine the Great. At the beginning of 306, as winter set in, Constantius withdrew to Eboracum (York) to wait for the spring campaign season to begin. He contracted an illness while there and died, after recommending his son to the army as his successor.

Galerius

Gaius Galerius Valerius Maximianus

r. 305–311 (East)

Galerius replaced Diocletian as the emperor in the east in 305, alongside Constantius in the west. Galerius was a shepherd in the Serbian region of Thracia, before joining the army and rising through the ranks. As senior co-emperor, he appointed two of his supporters—Severus and Maximinus Daza—to be junior co-emperors. After the death of Constantius, Galerius gave one of the positions to his co-emperor's son, Constantine, and promoted Maximinus Daza to Western emperor. A rebellion in Italy led by Maxentius, son of Maximian, confused matters further, as did the death of Severus in 307 while trying to put down Maxentius's revolt. With his hopes for total control of the empire in ruins, Galerius quietly ran the Eastern Empire until his death in 311.

Severus

Flavius Valerius Severus

r. 306–307 (West)

Galerius appointed the little-known army officer Severus as co-emperor after the unexpected death of Constantius as Western emperor in 306. This was complicated by Constantius's army declaring his son Constantine as the true heir to the Western throne. After some negotiation, Severus kept his role as Western emperor, and an unhappy Constantine became his deputy. Severus was captured and killed in battle against Maxentius in 307.

Maxentius

Marcus Aurelius Valerius Maxentius

r. 306–312 (West)

The son of Maximian (see p. 333), Maxentius expected to be given an imperial position when his father and Diocletian resigned as co-emperors in 305. When no role materialized, with Galerius, Constantius, Severus, and Maximinus Daza installed as the empire's four new Tetrarchs, Maxentius responded by seizing power in Rome. In the chaotic years of shifting alliances that followed, Maxentius found himself competing against Constantine for control of the empire, a struggle he lost at the Battle of the Milvian Bridge in 312.

Constantine the Great

Flavius Valerius Constantinus

r. 306–337

Constantine the Great's long road to assuming complete control of the empire began in 306, with the death of his father, the Western emperor Constantius. Although Constantine (see pp. 260–261) was proclaimed emperor by his father's troops, it took a long civil war before he was fully able to take up that position in 324, having on the way defeated his rivals Maxentius and Licinius (see left and right).

Constantine was a reforming emperor: he streamlined Rome's army and its political institutions, and replaced the existing currency with the *solidus* (which would last for a millennium as the empire's legal tender). He is best remembered, however, for two acts that would transform the empire. Constantine's conversion to Christianity brought to an end 1,000 years of traditional worship, imposing a whole new belief system and moral code on his citizens. He also founded the new city—and imperial capital—Constantinople (present-day Istanbul) in 330, completing the process begun by Diocletian of moving political power in the empire away from Rome and toward its eastern periphery.

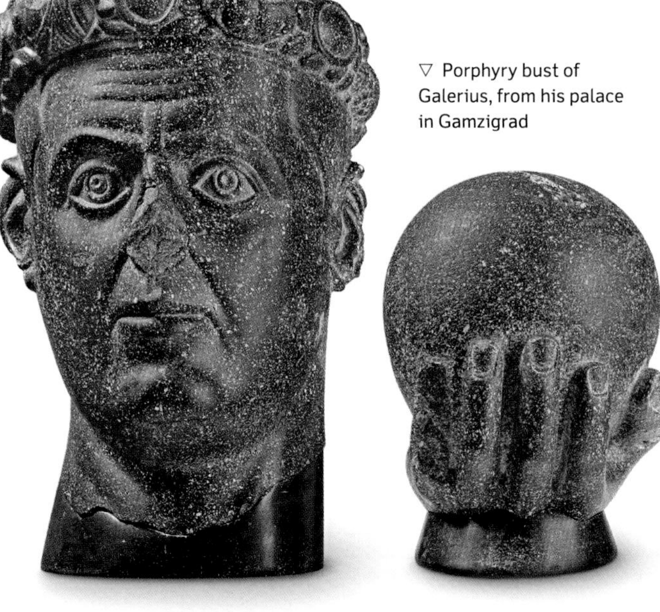

▽ Porphyry bust of Galerius, from his palace in Gamzigrad

Maximinus Daza

Galerius Valerius Maximinus

r. 310–313 (East)

The nephew of Galerius, Maximinus Daza (or Daia) became junior co-emperor of the east in 305. By 310 he was calling himself a senior emperor, a position he officially obtained the next year with the death of Galerius. In the civil wars that followed, he allied with Maxentius against Licinius (see right) and Constantine the Great. In April 313 he was defeated by Licinius at the Battle of Tzirallum, in the Turkish region of Thracia, and died later that year.

△ Fresco of Constantine's victory over Maxentius at the Battle of the Milvian Bridge in 312 (Giulio Romano, 1520–1524)

Licinius

Valerius Licinianus Licinius

r. 308–324 (East)

Galerius appointed his childhood friend Licinius emperor of the west in 308. When Galerius died in 311, Licinius acquired control of part of the Eastern Empire, too, and formed an alliance with Constantine the Great to prevent Maxentius and Maximinus Daza from seizing power. Once they had defeated their rivals, Licinius and Constantine became joint emperors, ruling in a state of wary coexistence that continually threatened to break down at any moment. Despite this, in 313, the two emperors together issued the Edict of Milan, a decree that granted religious tolerance to the empire's Christians.

In 323, the political tension between the joint emperors escalated into a series of conflicts that resulted in Licinius's execution, following his defeat at the Battle of Chrysopolis, in modern Türkiye, in 324.

Constantine II

Flavius Claudius Constantinus

r. 337–340 (West)

The second son of Constantine the Great, Constantine II was the first emperor to be born and raised a Christian. He was just a year old when he was made a junior emperor, 7 when he went on campaign with his father, and 10 when he was named commander of Gaul. Following Constantine the Great's death in 337, his sons split responsibility for the empire between themselves, with Constantine II receiving Gaul, Britannia, and Hispania.

It was not long, however, before Constantine II began to fall out with his siblings, first in a religious dispute with Constantius II, and then more seriously with his youngest brother, Constans, whose realm he invaded. The brothers' armies met at Aquileia in Italy in 340, where Constantine II was ambushed and killed by Constans's troops.

Constantius II

Flavius Julius Constantius

r. 337–361

Of all Constantine the Great's sons, Constantius II lived the longest. When his father died in 337, Constantius II ordered the massacre of several of his family members, which left himself and his brothers Constantine II and Constans (see right) in control of the empire. Constantius II took over the Eastern Empire, staying out of the conflicts between his two brothers in the west. By 353, he was the empire's sole ruler, and had won several wars against the Germans. He died of fever in 361 while campaigning in Persia (modern-day Iran).

Constans I

Flavius Julius Constans

r. 337–350

Constantine the Great's youngest son was in his late teens when he became the Western emperor, with responsibility for Italy, Illyricum (a Roman province in the Balkans), and North Africa. The early years of his rule were scarred by a dispute over the control of North Africa with one of his brothers, Constantine II, that led to a civil war. After defeating his older sibling in 340, Constans and his remaining brother, Constantius II (see left), controlled the Western and Eastern Empire respectively, if not always harmoniously. One source of tension between them was religion. Constans was tolerant of Judaism, whereas Constantius II was not, and while both men were Christians, Constans followed the orthodox Nicene creed, which deemed his brother's version of Christianity, Arianism, as heretical.

According to later biographers, Constans became cruel and unpredictable in the last years of his reign, surrounding himself with a clique of favorites and neglecting the needs of his people and, more importantly, the army. In 350, a general named Maxentius declared himself emperor and Constans' entire army transferred its support to the usurper. Constans attempted to flee to Hispania (Spain), but was intercepted and killed while trying to cross the Pyrenees mountains from Gaul.

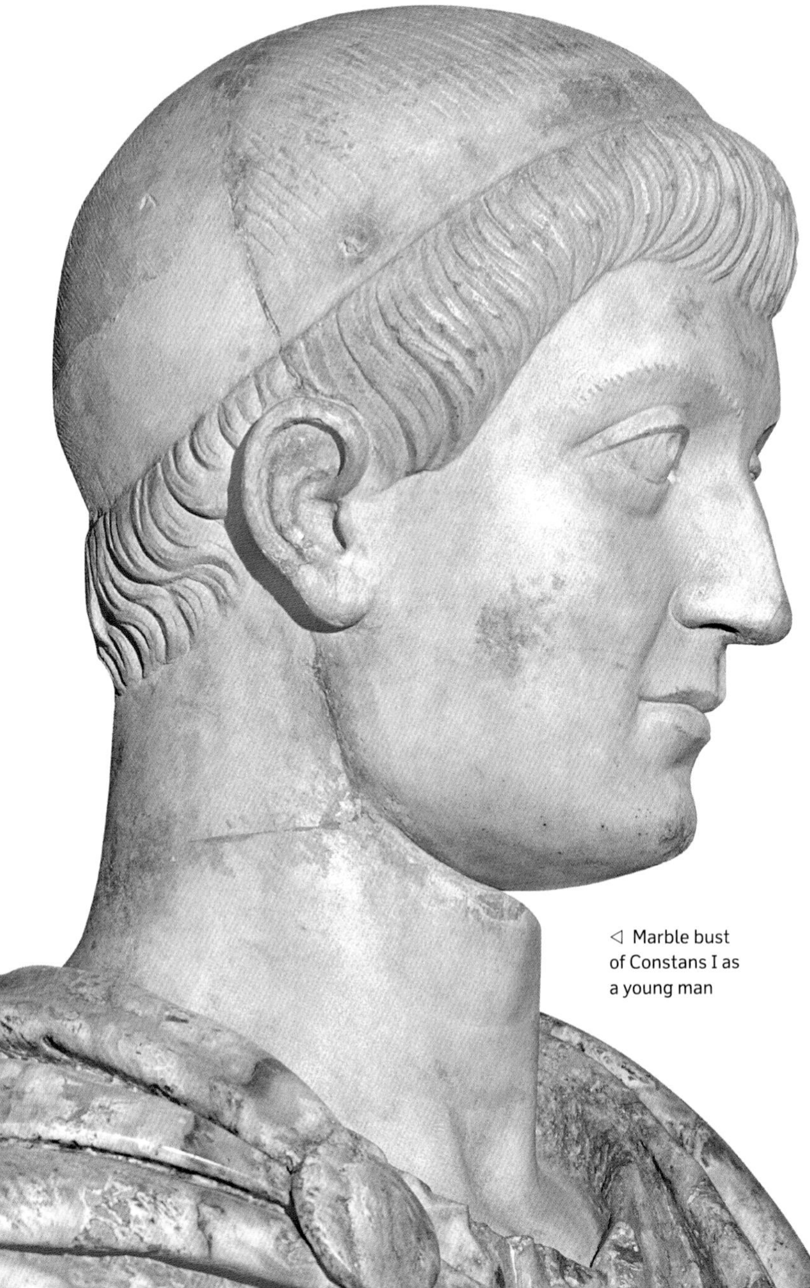

◁ Marble bust of Constans I as a young man

Constantius Gallus

Flavius Claudius Constantius Gallus

r. 351–354

Constantius II's junior emperor in the east was his cousin and brother-in-law Constantius Gallus. His power base was the city of Antioch (in modern Türkiye), and it was from there that he suppressed a Jewish revolt in 351–352. He struggled to win Constantius II's trust, however, and in 354 Gallus was replaced by his half-brother Julian and executed.

Julian

Flavius Claudius Julianus

r. 361–363

Remembered by history as "the Apostate," Julian was committed to the traditional gods and an enemy of Christianity. He worshipped Sol Invictus, the imperial god of conquest, and was an excellent military leader, as well as a thinker and writer who idealized Marcus Aurelius.

In 363, Julian led a difficult campaign into the Sasanian Empire in Persia (modern Iran), which faced extreme heat, supply issues, and dissent from within his own ranks, not least from the disaffected Christians. In June, he was fatally wounded by a spear thrown during his army's retreat from the capital, Ctesiphon.

Jovian

Flavius Iovianus

r. 363–364

The army proclaimed the general Jovian as emperor after Julian's death. He quickly ended Rome's unpopular war in Persia, albeit with a very unfavorable peace treaty, ceding key border provinces to the Sasanians. He died just months into his reign, but during that time he restored Christianity as the official religion of the empire.

Valentinian I

Flavius Valentinianus

r. 364–375 (West)

Jovian was succeeded nine days after his death by one of his officers, Valentinian, who then named his brother Valens (see right) as co-emperor. As the Western emperor, much of

△ The late-4th-century Aqueduct of Valens, in Istanbul

Valentinian's 11-year rule was occupied fighting the Germanic Quadi and Alemanni tribes, the latter of which he defeated at the bloody Battle of Solicinium in 368.

Valentinian constantly moved around his empire to fend off threats to its borders and he stayed for seven years in Trier (present-day Germany) to oversee the construction of fortifications. He was blessed with capable generals, not least Count Theodosius (father of the later emperor of the same name) and Jovinus, who both strengthened Rome's western borders and defeated major incursions by Saxons, Picts, and Scots into Britannia.

Continuing the reversal of Julian the Apostate's anti-Christian policies begun by Jovian, Valentinian promoted religious toleration and was generally seen as a capable and fair ruler. He had an unusual death in 375, when he launched into a furious tirade upon hearing of a Germanic invasion of his territory and promptly died of a stroke.

Valens

Flavius Valens

r. 364–378 (East)

Valentinian appointed his brother Valens coruler, despite his lack of military or leadership experience. Valens had a difficult time as the Eastern emperor. His reign was challenged after a year by a usurper, Procopius, who declared himself emperor in Constantinople. Following the guidance of his officials, Valens's forces captured and executed his rival in 366.

The rest of Valens's time in power was occupied in battle with Germanic tribes, as well as with Rome's Persian enemies, the Sasanian Empire. The powerful Visigoths, however, posed the main threat to the Roman Empire's eastern borders. These Germanic peoples were impinging on the Roman frontier, having been forced to migrate by Huns pushing in from the east. Valens had some initial successes against the Visigoths, but the pressure they exerted was such that he was ultimately forced to allow them to settle inside Roman imperial territory. Roman-Visigothic tensions eventually spilled over into war, and Valens was slain and his army defeated at the Battle of Adrianople in 378, one of the worst military defeats in Roman history. His death in battle was a symbolic moment that marked the beginning of the end of Roman hegemony in Europe and introduced an age of invasions that ultimately led to the fall of Rome itself (see pp. 282–283).

△ *St. Ambrose denies Theodosius entry to his Church* (c. 1673) by Juan de Valdés Leal

Gratian

Flavius Gratianus Augustus

r. 367–383 (West)

Gratian succeeded his father Valentinian I as Western emperor when he was 18 years old. Most of his reign was spent fighting in Gaul, repelling German tribes trying to enter the empire across the Rhine River.

As a devout Christian, Gratian removed the office of *pontifex maximus* (traditional high priest) from his list of titles and ordered the removal of an altar dedicated to the goddess Victory from inside the Roman Senate. He was killed in Lugdunum (present-day Lyon) during an army rebellion.

Valentinian II

Flavius Valentinianus

r. 375–392 (West)

The son of Valentinian I, Valentinian II became junior emperor of Italy, North Africa, and Illyricum (a province in the Balkans) at the age of four, after his father's death. When his rule was challenged by the rebel general Maximus in 387, he fled to the capital of the Eastern Empire, Constantinople. The Eastern emperor Theodosius (see right) overthrew Maximus the following year and restored the 17-year-old Valentinian II to power in Vienna (present-day Vienne, in France). He served as a figurehead (or puppet) emperor under the control of Theodosius's general, Arbogast.

Valentinian II was found hanged in his bedroom in 392. It is possible he died by suicide, but it is more likely he was murdered by Arbogast when Theodosius wanted to remove him from power.

Theodosius I
Flavius Theodosius

r. 379–392 (East)
r. 392–395 (East and West)

The general Theodosius was living quietly in his native Hispania (Spain) when the Western emperor Gratian appointed him as co-emperor in 379. As ruler in the east, Theodosius improved army discipline and allowed non-Romans to serve in his legions. He also signed peace treaties with the Visigoths and oversaw building projects in Constantinople.

In 380, Theodosius I issued a controversial religious edict declaring that only followers of the Nicene creed could legitimately call themselves Christians. This immediately alienated the followers of a rival interpretation of Christianity known as Arianism, and sparked a wave of persecutions.

After Valentinian II's death in 392, Theodosius took control of the whole empire, ignoring the claims of Eugenius, a usurper supported by Theodosius's general, Arbogast, that he was the Western emperor's chosen successor. Theodosius decisively settled the dispute in September 394, when he defeated the army of Eugenius and Arbogast in battle.

△ Roman gold aureus showing the emperor Arcadius with pearl-lined diadem

Arcadius
Flavius Arcadius

r. 383–408 (East)

Unlike his father Theodosius I, Arcadius was a weak and inefficient ruler. As emperor of the east, he was dominated by his wife, Eudoxia, and by his feuding ministers Rufinus and Eutropius.

When Eudoxia died in 403, Arcadius fell under the influence of his Praetorian prefect, Anthemius, who became the de facto ruler until the emperor's death in 408.

Magnus Maximus
Magnus Maximus

r. 383–388 (West)

An "unofficial" emperor of the west, the Spaniard Magnus Maximus was commanding Rome's forces in Britannia when his legions declared him emperor in 383. Crossing the Channel into Europe, Magnus Maximus overthrew the Western emperor Gratian and established a court at Trier, in modern Germany. In 387, Magnus Maximus invaded Italy, but was defeated in battle and killed the following year by the Eastern emperor Theodosius I.

Honorius
Flavius Honorius

r. 393–423 (West)

Honorius was the younger son of Theodosius I and was not quite 10 years old when he became the Western emperor. For the first half of Honorius's troubled reign, power was exercised by his regent, the general Stilicho, who campaigned virtually nonstop to put down the wars, rebellions, and invasions that plagued the Western Empire. To protect his position in the court, Stilicho arranged the marriage of his daughter Maria to the emperor in 389. When Maria died in 407, Honorius married Stilicho's other daughter, Thermantia.

Although Stilicho undoubtedly kept the weak and ineffective Honorius in power, his influence in the court ensured he had many enemies, and in 408 he was arrested on probably trumped-up charges of treason and executed. This could not have come at a worse time for Honorius. Incursions from Germanic tribes into Italy had already forced him to move his court from Milan to the more defensible city of Ravenna, but in 410 the unthinkable happened: an army of Visigoths under their king Alaric occupied and sacked Rome itself.

From that point on, Honorius only clung onto the throne through the efforts of his general, Constantius, who kept the emperor's enemies at bay until his death in 421; Honorius died of illness two years later.

△ The boy emperor Honorius, as imagined by French artist Jean Paul Laurens, 1880

5TH CENTURY

The empire's final century is the story of the decline of the once-great city of Rome and the rise of its eastern counterpart, Constantinople, as tribal invaders, migrating peoples, and incompetent emperors destroyed more than 1,000 years of history.

Theodosius II

Flavius Theodosius

r.408–450 (East)

A gentle, easily influenced soul, Theodosius II rarely exercised any power during his 42-year rule. Instead, his sister, wife, and court officials in Constantinople administered the Eastern Empire in his name.

He was seven years old when he became emperor, and for several years his territories were controlled by Anthemius, the Praetorian prefect of the east. Around 414, Anthemius gave way to Theodosius's older sister, Pulcheria, who became her brother's regent. His wars against the Sasanians (in 422 and 447) and the Vandals in North Africa (in 429) produced mixed results, and his policy of appeasement toward Attila the Hun (see pp. 290–291) in the 440s was an abject failure. More positively, he strengthened the walls of Constantinople in 413, and commissioned the Theodosian Code of 438, which listed the empire's laws.

Constantius III

Flavius Constantius

r.421 (West)

The general Constantius III was made co-emperor of the west by Honorius (see p. 339) in 421 for his help in suppressing revolts within his territory. He died after only seven months in power.

Valentinian III

Flavius Placidius Valentinianus

r.425–455 (West)

The son of Constantius III, Valentinian III became emperor at six years old, but his mother, Galla Placidia, oversaw state affairs as his regent until 437, when the statesman Flavius Aetius took over. In this period, Vandal tribes moved into North Africa, displacing the Romans in control there before crossing the Mediterranean Sea and seizing territory in Italy. That same year, Valentinian married and gave up all pretense of ruling his empire, surrendering himself to a life of hedonism instead. On the rare occasions he did try to intervene in public affairs, he only ended up weakening his own position, such as when he issued the Novel 17 notice of 444, which handed power over all of the empire's churches to the pope.

Valentinian's most infamous act came in September 454 when he murdered Flavius Aetius with his own hands, falsely believing his advisor had aims to seize power. A year later, two of Flavius Aetius's supporters killed Valentinian in revenge.

Marcian

Flavius Marcianus

r.450–457 (East)

Marcian was the last ruler of the Theodosian dynasty in the east. Later historians describe Marcian's seven-year reign in the east as an island of calm at a time when the Western Empire was rapidly falling apart. Despite Hunic invasions and palace intrigues

△ The remains of Theodosius II's walls surrounding Constantinople, with the Byzantine Palace of the Porphyrogenitus

raging across the empire, Marcian managed to refill the treasury, avoid entangling his state in any major conflicts, and establish the church's canonical doctrines at the Chalcedon Council of 451.

Petronius Maximus

r.455 (West)

Having encouraged the murders of both Flavius Aetius and the emperor Valentinian III, Petronius Maximus held imperial power for a few weeks before he was stoned to death by an angry mob in Rome.

Avitus

Flavius Maccilius Eparchius Avitus

r.455–456 (West)

Avitus was unusual in that, with the death of Petronius Maximus, he was proclaimed emperor by the Visigoths. Two Roman generals rejected his rule and defeated him in battle in northern Italy, forcing him to abdicate in 456.

Majorian

Julius Valerius Majorianus

r.457–461 (West)

Majorian was the last ruler to resist the Germanic invaders that were overtaking the empire. His territory consisted of little more than Italy and Dalmatia, but he fought bravely to preserve the crumbling Western Empire.

Majorian's efforts to reform the Roman administration, such as cracking down on taxation abuses, were his downfall as they upset powerful senators and noble families in Rome, who saw the last vestiges of power slipping away. In 461, the powerful General Ricimer executed him.

△ Painting of Marcian at the Ecumenical Council of Chalcedon (Vasily Surikov, 1876)

Libius Severus

Libius Severus Serpentius

r.461–465 (West)

Little is known about Libius Severus, except that he was first of the "shadow emperors" (or puppet emperors), under the control of General Ricimer.

Anthemius

Procopius Anthemius

r.467–472 (West)

Anthemius, an eastern noble from Constantinople and grandson of the Praetorian prefect Anthemius (see opposite), was viewed with suspicion by Romans. When he took power in 467, Rome was thoroughly Christianized and it was thought by some that Anthemius intended to reinstate the traditional gods. A disastrous campaign against the Vandals in 468 damaged his credibility and, in 472, General Ricimer deposed and executed his emperor.

Olybrius

Ancius Olybrius

r.472 (West)

The wealthy senator Olybrius was the last of Ricimer's puppet emperors. His only achievement lay in outliving the general by four months in 472.

Glycerius

473–474 (West)

Glycerius abdicated as Western emperor after one year, lacking support from the Eastern emperor.

Julius Nepos

r. 474–475 (West)

Having replaced Glycerius in 474, Julius Nepos was deposed a year later. He fled to Dalmatia (in modern-day Croatia), where he died in 480.

Romulus Augustus

Flavius Momyllus Romulus Augustus

r.475–476 (West)

Rome's last Western emperor was around 11 years old when the German general Odoacer led a mercenary army into the city. They were seeking payment for services they had rendered to Rome. When no money was forthcoming, they deposed Romulus and sacked the city.

Deities

Major Deities

For the Romans, the success of their state depended on winning and keeping the favor of the gods through rituals, sacrifices, and offerings. The number of gods they worshipped changed over time, but there was a constant core of 12 deities, most of them closely associated with Greek divinities.

Jupiter

Greek: Zeus

King of the Gods

In Roman mythology, Jupiter presided over an unruly pantheon of gods and goddesses. He was a member of the "Capitoline Triad," along with his wife Juno and daughter Minerva (see right). His role in Roman society dates to at least 509 BCE, when the Temple of Jupiter Optimus Maximus was built on the Capitoline Hill. Thereafter, Jupiter was always the patron deity of Rome, closely associated with a specific city in a way that his Greek counterpart Zeus never was.

From the Imperial Era, the veneration of Jupiter held its own alongside the growing cult worship of the emperor. He is an instantly recognizable figure in art and sculpture with his stern gaze, thunderbolt or scepter in hand, and sacred eagle by his side.

Juno

Greek: Hera

Queen of the Gods

The wife and sister of Jupiter and mother to Mars and Vulcan, among others, Juno was the goddess of love, marriage, and childbirth. On March 1 each year the *Matronalia* fertility festival was held in her name.

Closely associated with the Greek mother-queen goddess Hera, she also shared many qualities with the more warlike Athena, and was often portrayed carrying a spear and shield. Juno's role as protector of the Roman state goes back to at least 390 BCE, when, according to legend, the angry honking of sacred geese kept in her temple on the Capitoline Hill alerted the city's defenders to a surprise attack by Gallic invaders.

◁ Mosaic depicting Neptune in his chariot from the 2nd century

△ Antefix depicting the head of Uni, the Etruscan counterpart of Juno, from c. 500 BCE

Minerva

Greek: Athena

Wisdom, commerce, poetry, handicrafts, military strategy

Minerva's legend was aligned with that of her Greek counterpart, Athena. Both were goddesses of wisdom and warcraft, both had the owl as their sacred animal, and both were born from the heads of their fathers: Jupiter and Zeus, respectively. Romans believed that their city would endure so long as the Palladium, a statue of Minerva/Athena supposedly brought to the city by the Trojan hero Aeneas, remained safe in the Temple of Vesta.

Neptune

Greek: Poseidon

Fresh water, the sea

Neptune was originally a deity of fresh water. He also became the god of the sea around 400 BCE, as Rome's empire grew and its contacts with maritime civilizations such as Greece increased. The Romans did not forget Neptune's river-based origins and held a festival in his honor (the *Neptunalia*) in July, when water was scarcest, to prevent freshwater springs from drying up.

Venus

Greek: Aphrodite

Love, desire, beauty, sex, prosperity

Venus was originally an Italian deity responsible for cultivation, and this association with fertility may have led the Romans to adopt her as the goddess of love and sex. This allowed the Romans to identify Venus with the Greek goddess of love, Aphrodite, which strengthened the story that their city's first inhabitants were descended from Aphrodite's son, Aeneas.

Venus was the mother of several children by various fathers, including the fertility god Priapus with Bacchus, and Cupid with the god of war, Mars. She had no offspring with her husband, Vulcan.

△ Mosaic of Apollo (4th century) wearing a laurel wreath and holding his lyre, from the House of Aion, Cyprus

Mars

Greek: Ares

War

Mars probably originated as an agricultural divinity, but his supposed paternity of Romulus and Remus and the rise of Rome as a military power saw his role transformed. The month of March was named after Mars and was devoted to events honoring him. The outbreak of war was announced by one of Rome's consuls visiting the temple of Mars, offering their devotion, and commanding "*Mars, vigila*" ("Mars, wake up!"). Rome's armies would also assemble on the Campus Martius (Field of Mars), an area of land outside the city, before leaving on campaign. The god of war's importance was sealed in 2 BCE, when the emperor Augustus inaugurated the Mars Ultor (Mars the Avenger) temple, which commemorated his victory over the assassins of Julius Caesar at the Battle of Philippi in 42 BCE.

Apollo

Sun, music, archery, prophecy, healing

Rarely shown without either his curved bow or his lyre, Apollo was known to the Romans by his Greek name. Apollo had a mixed heritage, from Turkish, Cretan, Egyptian, Syrian, and even Indian culture, which perhaps explains why he was the god of many activities. His sexual interests were equally diverse, and Apollo's countless romantic partners included the nymph Daphne and the Spartan prince Hyacinthus. Hot-headed and impetuous, Apollo could be a solitary and often vengeful figure when dealing with his fellow divinities and with humans. For the Romans, Apollo's most admired gifts were for healing and, as the patron-god of the Oracle at Delphi, prophecy. Apollo was particularly dear to Augustus, who credited the god with his victory at Actium in 31 BCE and in thanks built a temple in his honor on the Palatine Hill.

Diana

Greek: Artemis

The hunt, wild animals, chastity, childbirth, enslaved people

The twin sister of Apollo, Diana was best known for her role as goddess of the hunt and wild animals. Romans also saw her as a protector of the lower classes and of enslaved people. Her festival day on August 13 was a holiday for enslaved people, who were given a rare day off.

Vulcan

Greek: Hephaestus

Fire, craftsmen

The god of fire and blacksmiths, Vulcan was the son of Jupiter and Juno, and the husband of Venus. Born lame and notoriously ugly, he was shunned by the other gods and devoted himself to his craft, creating—among many other important artifacts—Mercury's winged helmet and Jupiter's thunderbolts. On August 23 Rome held the annual *Volcanalia* festival in his honor.

Vesta

Greek: Hestia

Family, home, hearth

As the virgin goddess of the family, home, and hearth, Vesta's temple in the Forum was one of Rome's holiest sites. Its ever-burning flame symbolized Rome's eternal power; it was believed that if the flame were extinguished, Rome would fall. She was the only Roman deity to be served by priestesses rather than priests. Six priestesses, known as the Vestals, maintained her shrine. Selected for service between the ages of 6 and 10, the Vestals served for 30 years, during which time they could never marry and swore to remain virgins (see pp. 32–33). Vesta was so important to the Romans that her traditional cult was one of the last to be outlawed after Christianity became the empire's official religion. In 394, Theodosius I finally banned it.

Mercury

Greek: Hermes

Travelers and livestock; messenger of the gods

A versatile and somewhat ambiguous deity, Mercury was the messenger of the gods. Taking his name from the Latin *mecari*, meaning "to trade," Mercury was also the god of travelers, commerce, communication, thieves, and much more. In art and Roman poetry, he is usually portrayed wearing winged sandals or a winged helmet, and carrying a *caduceus*, a sacred staff circled by two entwined snakes that symbolized peace.

Ceres

Greek: Demeter

Agriculture and fertility

An important and beloved goddess, Ceres safeguarded grain crops and fertility. It is from her name that we derive the word "cereal." According to myth, Ceres taught humans how to sow and harvest grain. As protector of the plebeians, Ceres was popular among Rome's lower classes and her temple on the Aventine Hill, built around 500 BCE, was a focal point for plebeian religious and civil celebrations. It burned down in 31 BCE, but was rebuilt and remained in use until the later 300s CE.

◁ Relief from the 1st century depicting Vesta sitting with her head covered and four Vestals

Minor Deities

In their everyday lives, most Romans worshipped a number of minor deities, chiefly the household gods (see pp. 122–123). A blend of Greek, Middle Eastern, and ancient Italian forebears, the city's other minor gods helped Romans better understand the natural world and their fellow humans.

Aurora

Greek: Eos

Dawn

The goddess, in Homer's words, of "rosy-fingered dawn," Aurora appeared each morning to replace her sister Luna, the moon, and prepare the way for her brother Sol, the sun. She was also the mother of the wind and of the evening star, Hesperus. In art, she is often shown in a chariot being pulled across the sky by winged horses, or with wings of her own.

Bacchus

Greek: Dionysus

Wine, vines, fertility, festivity

The god of wine and festivity was unsurprisingly one of the most popular Roman deities. A fusion of the ancient Italian divinity Liber, or Liber Pater ("the free one" or "the free father"), and the Greek god of winemaking and religious ecstasy Dionysus, Bacchus was always shown as a beardless and often drunken youth, sometimes carrying an ivy-wrapped staff, or *thyrsus*, as well as a drinking goblet.

Along with Ceres and the goddess Libera, Bacchus was part of the Aventine Triad, whose temple on that hill was built around 493 BCE. So popular among the lower classes were the regular Bacchanalia drinking and fertility celebrations held in his name that these were outlawed by the Senate in 186 BCE, due to concerns by Rome's elites at their lack of control over these events. Nevertheless, festivities were allowed to continue from time to time, albeit on a smaller scale.

Caelus

Greek: Uranus

The first sky god

Despite being the first god and the father of Saturn, Caelus was not an important deity to the Romans. His Hellenic equivalent was Uranus and his name comes from the Latin *caelum*, meaning "the heavens," from where we derive the word "celestial."

△ Painting of a young Bacchus draped in a classical robe (Michelangelo Merisi da Caravaggio, c. 1595)

△ Mosaic detail of Faunus/Pan from the House of Dionysus, Cyprus

Cupid

Greek: Eros

Love, lust

The son of Venus and Mars, Cupid is a divine infant famous for firing arrows of love at his unsuspecting victims. In early Italian culture he was known as Amor, then Cupid, derived from the Latin *cupido*, meaning "desire."

In his Greek incarnation as Eros, Cupid was shown in art and sculpture as a slim and handsome winged youth; by the Roman era he had become a cherubic infant. In both traditions he was a mostly benevolent, if sometimes mischievous, minor god. His role increased in the imperial age after the poet Virgil used him as the means by which the Trojan hero Aeneas and the Carthaginian queen Dido fell in love in the *Aeneid*. In *The Golden Ass*, a novel of the 2nd century by Apuleius, Cupid's affair with the mortal princess Psyche became one of the most popular tales of the Roman Empire.

Faunus

Greek: Pan

Forests, fields

Faunus's lineage goes far back into Italy's prehistory. The horned, half-man, half-goat deity was not just the god of forests and fields but was also the father of Latinus, the king of the Latins. In Rome's origin myths, Latinus gives his daughter Lavinia in marriage to Aeneas, and it is from their union that the Roman people descend. (In another version of Rome's foundation story, Hercules is described as the father of Latinus.)

Flora

Greek: Chloris

Flowers, spring

According to the city's mythology, worship of the Roman goddess of flowers started as far back as the reign of Romulus. Flora's temple was close to the Circus Maximus and the festival in her honor was the *Floralia* from April 28 to May 3, a celebration of nature's renewal and the cycle of life.

Fortuna

Greek: Tyche

Fortune

Identifiable by her blindfolded or sightless eyes, Fortuna was the goddess of good or bad fortune. She had an important role in Romans' lives, as they believed that a lucky person was also good and virtuous. In art, she often holds a horn of plenty, or cornucopia, and a wheel of fortune. The tradition of showing her with covered eyes carried over into later personifications of justice, the idea being that both the law and luck are blind.

△ Marble statue of Fortuna holding a cornucopia

The Furies

Greek: Erinyes

Vengeance

In Greek legend, the Furies were goddesses of vengeance, black-clad daughters of Gaia who sprang from the blood of Uranus after he had been castrated by his son, Cronos. Their Greek name, Erinyes, has a double meaning, translatable as "I persecute" and "I am angry." Roman writers such as Virgil, Propertius, and Seneca recounted with approval stories of their punitive version of justice—a trait that suited the Romans' unforgiving and rigid moral code.

Hercules

Greek: Heracles

Strength and heroes

The demigod Hercules was crucial to the Romans as both a role model for valor and as an exemplar of apotheosis—the transfiguration of a mortal human into a god. This was important in the Imperial era, helping to legitimize the deification of Rome's emperors upon their deaths.

He was celebrated in Rome as early as the 6th century, and the circular Temple of Hercules by the Tiber River is the oldest surviving marble building in the city. He was said to be the father of Latinus, the progenitor of the Latin peoples and, through his Twelve Labors, was an agent of civilization against the dark, primitive forces of nature.

Janus

Gates, doorways, time

Always shown facing forward and backward, Janus was the two-faced god of doors and gates, and of transitions between new and old, and birth and death. As the month of January marked the end of the old year and the start of the new, it is named after Janus. The doors of his temple in Rome were left open in times of war and only closed when there was peace across the empire, which was rarely the case.

△ Bust of Janus in profile depicted with his two faces, from the Vatican Museums in the Vatican City

▽ Illustration of the Furies (right) chasing the Greek mythical heroes Orestes and Pylades

Luna

Greek: Selene

The moon

Luna was the sister of the sun god Sol and Aurora, goddess of the dawn. The story of Luna's love for the shepherd Endymion was a popular subject for Roman art. Luna was also associated with Diana, who was originally a goddess of fertility, as the Romans recognized the link between fertility, pregnancy, and the phases of the moon.

Nemesis

Revenge

In Greek legend, Nemesis was the ancient winged deity who protected the honor of the gods by taking retribution on those who displayed *hubris*, or arrogance, toward them. Traditionally armed with a dagger or whip, her victims include the overly proud hunter Narcissus, whom she punished for his rejection of the nymph Echo by making him fall in love with his own reflection. Nemesis was also a tutelary deity—these were divinities who acted as protectors of places. In Nemesis's case, she was the guardian of the military parade ground, making her particularly important to Rome's rank-and-file soldiers.

Nox

Greek: Nyx

The primordial night

Nox was one of the most ancient divinities, and a mirror image of the Greek goddess Nyx. Born at the dawn of creation as the child of the primordial god Chaos, she was a powerful, shadowy figure who lived in the lowest depths of the underworld and emerged in the evening to bring darkness to the world. She was also mother to the three Fates, as well as the deities of Sleep, Death, Strife, and Pain.

Pax

Greek: Eirene

Peace

A minor goddess in the Roman Republic, Pax was elevated under the empire into an important symbol of the peace established by Augustus after the civil war that brought him to power (see pp. 138–139). Augustus built the Ara Pacis (Altar of Peace) in her honor in Rome in 9 BCE (see pp. 140–141). He also erected hundreds of cult statues of Pax as the embodiment of peace, with olive branch in hand, across his empire.

Pluto

Greek: Hades

The underworld

Pluto ruled the underworld in the same way that his brothers Jupiter and Poseidon presided over the sky and the sea. Although mainly represented as the deity of the dead, Pluto was also the keeper of the earth's ores and precious stones, as he was the most powerful subterranean god. It is this association with precious metals and jewels that separates the Roman Pluto from his Greek equivalent, Hades, who was a more forbidding and darker deity. This is because Pluto incorporates elements of both Hades and the folk-divinity Plouton, an ancient Italian god of wealth. In art and sculpture, Pluto is often shown carrying a cornucopia and accompanied by his three-headed dog, Cerberus.

▷ Statue of Pluto with Cerberus by the sculptor Jacopo Sansovino, c. 1588

Proserpina

Greek: Persephone

Wine, fertility, agriculture

Proserpina's story is an example of how ancient cultures used mythology to make sense of the natural world. Her myth, which first appeared in the so-called *Homeric Hymns*, a work of unknown date credited to the supposed author of the *Iliad* and the *Odyssey*, begins with Pluto abducting Proserpina and taking her to the underworld as his wife. Unable to secure her permanent release, Proserpina's mother Ceres turns to Jupiter for help. As Proserpina's father, Jupiter commands Pluto to free his and Ceres's child for nine months of each year.

As a goddess of agriculture, Proserpina spends this period of freedom from the underworld providing grain to the world. After her nine months in the land of the living, she is then forced to return to Pluto's domain in the land of the dead.

The Romans thought that Proserpina's subterranean imprisonment explained why the earth "died" for three months in winter, only to be reborn again each spring with the goddess's temporary release from captivity.

Salacia

Greek: Amphitrite

Salt water, seas

As the wife of Neptune, Salacia (whose name translates as "the salty one") was the goddess of the oceans and was thought to possess the ability to calm the winds and still the stormiest of seas. She is best known as the mother of Triton, the sea god who was half-man, half-fish. Salacia was also the eldest of the Nereides, the 50 daughters of Nereus, the legendary "Old Man of the Sea." The Nereides protected the animals, plants, and coral reefs of the oceans. They also watched over sailors and seafarers.

In art, Salacia is shown as a beautiful nymph wearing a crown of seaweed. She is also often depicted in white robes and standing on a pearl-shell chariot pulled by dolphins and seahorses.

Saturn

Greeks: Cronos

Time

In early Roman history, Saturn was the god of generation, plenty, wealth, agriculture, renewal, and much more.

△ Fresco of Saturn by the painter Baldassare Peruzzi from the Villa Farnesina, Italy, 1555

As other, "younger" deities were admitted into the Roman pantheon, he would cede most of these responsibilities to his offspring: Jupiter, Juno, Neptune, Pluto, Ceres, and Vesta.

Saturn was the youngest of the Titans (elder gods) and he overthrew his father Caelus by castrating him. Although this made him the king of the gods, Saturn became worried by a prophecy that he would one day be overthrown by one of his offspring. So, each time his wife Ops gave birth, Saturn would devour the child. This worked until Ops gave birth to Jupiter. She hid him away and gave Saturn a stone to swallow instead. As an adult, Jupiter overcame Saturn and sliced his stomach open to release his siblings from captivity. So Jupiter became the new king of the gods and Saturn was imprisoned in the underworld.

Saturn was more important to the Romans than his counterpart Cronos was to the Greeks. Even before the foundation of Rome, a myth existed of an ancient time when Saturn and Janus jointly ruled an area known as the Mons Saturnius. This was the location the Romans would later name the Capitoline Hill and it was where they built their Temple of Saturn in 498 BCE.

Between December 17 and 23 each year, Romans celebrated the *Saturnalia*. Intended as a celebration of the harvest, it was the city's most important festival. It originally lasted just 24 hours, but by around 130 BCE the festival had been expanded into an almost week-long event. Businesses and schools shut, enslaved people were given time off, and Romans decorated their homes with greenery, feasted, celebrated, and gave each other gifts.

△ Mosaic of Terra reclining (right) with the god of cyclical time, Aion (inside a zodiac circle), and personifications of the four seasons

Somnus

Greek: Hypnos

Sleep

After the excesses of the *Saturnalia*, the god Somnus would have been called upon by many weary Romans. The son of the night goddess Nox and Scotus, the god of darkness, Somnus was also the twin brother of Mors, the Roman god of death. In mythological tales, the god of sleep lived in a cave so dark and deep that no light could reach inside. The cave's waters supposedly came from the Lethe, the so-called "river of forgetfulness." Somnus's wife was Pasithea, the goddess of relaxation, and together they had a thousand sons, known as the "somnia." These would appear to people while they slept, and this was perhaps the Greeks' and the Romans' way of explaining what dreams were.

Terra

Greek: Gaia

The Earth

For the Greeks, Gaia was one of the earliest so-called primordial gods from whom all other deities and forms of life were descended. Her Roman equivalent, Terra, was not as fundamental in Latin culture but was still an important figure. She was known as Tellus Mater, or Terra Mater, meaning "mother earth," and she was celebrated as a protector of agriculture and fertility. A temple was built in her honor in the 3rd century BCE on the Oppian Hill in Rome, but she had no priests specifically devoted to her. As with other Roman fertility deities, she is usually shown holding a cornucopia and surrounded by animals and children. She was honored in several farming-based events throughout the year.

Tiberinus

The Tiber River

Tiberinus was almost certainly a legendary figure, a local king or chieftain who drowned while swimming across the Albula River, which was thereafter renamed the Tiber. As the god of Rome's river, he watched over those who sailed its waters. In the city's foundation myths, he both helped the Trojan hero Aeneas navigate the Tiber River's waters and rescued the abandoned twins Romulus and Remus, giving them to the she-wolf Lupa to suckle. He also married their mother, Rhea Silvia. A shrine was erected to Tiberinus on Tiber Island, in the middle of the river, from which offerings to the god were placed in the river in May and December each year. On June 7, Rome's fishermen held contests in his honor, known as the *Ludi Piscatorii*, meaning "the fisherman games."

Veritas

Greek: Aletheia

Truth

Veritas's name means "truth." Like many Roman and Greek deities, there are contradictory versions of her origins and attributes. In some accounts, she is Jupiter's daughter; in others, Saturn's. In appearance, Veritas is described as either dressed in flowing, pure white robes—representing modesty—or in no clothes at all, symbolizing the naked truth. She is also often depicted holding a hand mirror.

As the personification of honesty, Veritas was central to the Romans' view of themselves as virtuous people—a quality embodied in her son, Virtus. According to the ancient Greek philosopher Democritus, Veritas was said to have lived at the bottom of a well, indicating that, like the truth itself, she was hard to find.

Adopted Deities

The Romans thought nothing of adding new divinities into their belief system when it suited their needs. This often resulted in older, more established Roman deities falling from prominence. But, ultimately, the traditional gods were swept away by the rise of Christianity.

Mithras

Indo-Persian: Mithra

Warfare, the sun

In the 1st century CE, Roman armies reached the territory of modern-day Iran and encountered the worship of Indo-Persian god Mithra, whose name meant "friend." He was the god of the sun, mutual obligations, justice, and war. A powerful, masculine, militaristic god, Mithra was immediately adopted by the rank and file of Rome's legions.

The veneration of Mithra in Asia went back many centuries. When Rome's legions brought Mithraism home to their capital city it spread rapidly—but not among women, as Mithraism was an all-male cult. The most famous ceremony held in his honor was the ritual sacrifice of a bull. His religious rites were held in a cave known as a Mithraeum, and acceptance into a Mithraic circle required seven stages of initiation. While not all aspects of the Mithraic system are known, it may have contained elements of death and resurrection beliefs, which undoubtedly added to its popularity. By excluding women, however, Mithraism possibly drove many people toward a rival death-and-resurrection cult that worshipped a Jewish holy man known as Jesus. By the 4th century, Mithraism had disappeared, swept away by Christianity and the decline of the Roman army, within which the god had found large numbers of his followers.

△ Relief of Mithras slaying the bull, from underneath the church of Santo Stefano Rotondo in Rome, 3rd century

Isis

Egyptian: Aset

Healing

To the ancient Egyptians, Isis was known as Aset rather than the Greco-Roman version of her name. She is most commonly shown wearing a headdress mounted with horns and a solar disc. The ancient Egyptians worshipped her for reanimating her brother-husband Osiris after he was murdered by his brother, Set, and for conceiving Horus, who would avenge his father. She was believed to be the ideal wife and mother.

Following the Roman conquest of Egypt in the 1st century BCE, she became a popular goddess throughout the empire, her cult reaching as far afield as the city of Londinium (London) in Britannia. As her influence spread, so did her responsibilities. In time, the Romanized version of Isis became a goddess of healing, magic, agriculture, good fortune, travel, and the sea.

▽ The *Triumph of Cybele* by the Italian artist Pinturicchio, c. 1509

Magna Mater

Anatolian: Cybele

Mother of the Gods

In 216 BCE, during the Second Punic War (see pp. 82–85), Rome suffered its greatest military disaster to date when the great Carthaginian general Hannibal defeated their huge army at the Battle of Cannae.

Over the next decade, Rome slowly regrouped and began to turn the conflict in its favor. As part of this process, Rome's leaders consulted an oracle, who told them they would be successful if they sought a new ally in the war in the form of a new goddess to add to their pantheon. They settled on the Anatolian nature goddess, Cybele. After a long and arduous journey, her cult icon—a huge black rock—was brought to Rome and she was renamed Magna Mater, or "Great Mother." In her new incarnation Magna Mater was described as a Trojan goddess, so that her legend would tie in with the story of Aeneas, the supposed ancestor of the Roman people.

When Rome finally defeated Carthage in 201 BCE, its people enthusiastically embraced the newly minted Magna Mater. The state built a temple for her on the Palatine Hill, established annual festivals, and erected statues of the matronly, nurturing mother-goddess in the city and across the empire.

Sol Invictus

Greek: Helios

The sun

In Rome's earliest days, Sol Indiges was a simple sun god, and the counterpart to his sisters Luna (the moon) and Aurora (dawn). But as Rome's empire grew and increased contact with other civilizations, he was combined with the powerful Syrian sun god El-Gabal. He was renamed Sol Invictus, "the Unconquered Sun"—a phrase that reflected the city's view of itself as a great imperial force. The emperor Aurelian, whose mother was a sun priestess, officially created a cult to Sol Invictus around 274 CE. His "birthday," which coincided with the winter solstice, was December 25. The *ludi Solis* ("sun games") were staged on this day, culminating in a chariot-racing tournament at the Circus Maximus, which was also the site of his temple.

Sites

Italy

Unsurprisingly, most Roman remains and sites are to be found in Italy—not just in Rome, but across the peninsula. And not all of the ancient structures are Roman. Some predate Roman civilization and show the influence of Greek, Etruscan, and other cultures on Roman architecture.

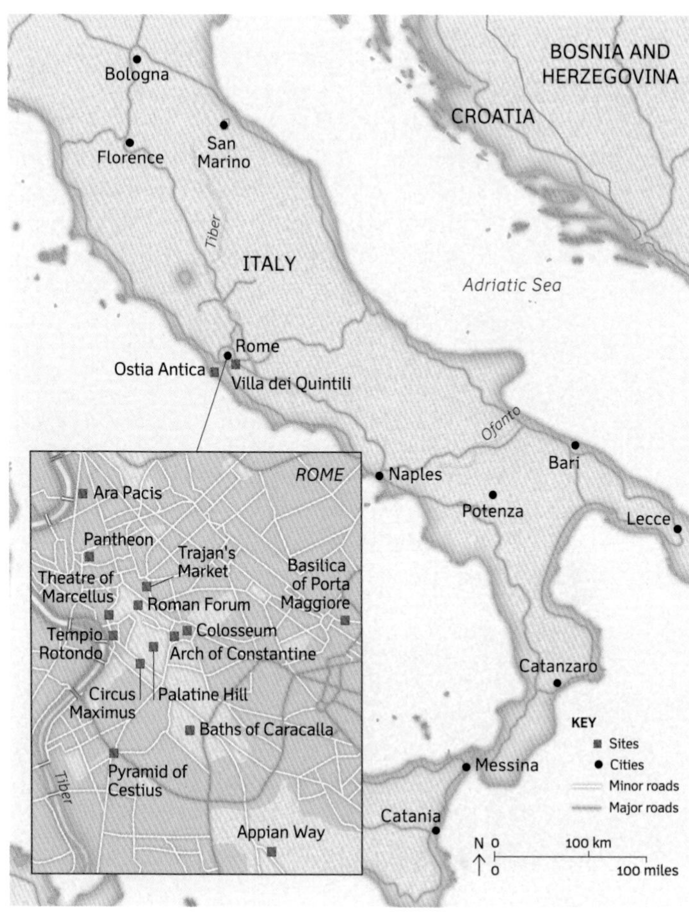

Ara Pacis

Rome

The emperor Augustus erected the Ara Pacis (Altar of Peace) between 13 and 9 BCE to celebrate his successful military campaigns in Hispania and Gaul (present-day Spain and France). It is decorated with symbolic carvings linking the foundation stories of Rome with depictions of Augustus, his family, and various Roman dignitaries (see pp. 140–141).

The central altar is surrounded by an outer precinct, all made of Carrara marble. Once a year, priests sacrificed a ram and two oxen on the altar to honor the Roman goddess of peace, Pax.

Originally built on a flood plain just outside Rome's city limits, the Ara Pacis was buried in mud and silt for centuries. It was unearthed in 1938 and relocated to its current site in central Rome, by the Tiber River.

Pantheon

Rome

The Pantheon (see pp. 202–203) is one of the largest and best-preserved Roman monuments. Its name comes from the Greek *pantheion*, meaning "of all the gods," although not all historians agree that the building was created as a site of worship for Rome's deities.

The general and son-in-law of Augustus, Marcus Vipsanius Agrippa, built the Pantheon on the site of a late-1st-century BCE temple. The emperor Hadrian restored the structure around 126 CE, keeping many elements of Agrippa's old structure.

The Pantheon's design is a showcase of Roman engineering. The entrance is a triangular portico supported by Corinthian columns. This is attached to a drum-shaped body, or rotunda, crowned with a coffered dome, which is still the largest unreinforced concrete dome in existence. The dome has an oculus, or opening, of 27 ft (9 m) that allows light (and rain) to flood in. The height from the floor to the oculus is the same as the diameter of the rotunda: 142 ft (43 m). In 609, Pope Boniface IV consecrated the Pantheon as a Basilica to the Virgin Mary and the Martyrs.

◁ The interior of the Pantheon in Rome, with light entering through the oculus

Trajan's Market

Rome

Space was always at a premium in ancient Rome. By the time Trajan became emperor in 98 CE the city was full and an area east of the Forum was cleared to make way for an expanded public space, called Trajan's Forum, and the associated buildings now known as Trajan's Market (see pp. 176–177). As the new forum and buildings were built against the Quirinal Hill, part of the slope was excavated to make room for the curving complex of offices and commercial outlets that has been described as the world's first shopping mall.

The project was probably overseen by Apollodorus of Damascus, the emperor's personal architect, who also designed Trajan's Column (see pp. 214–215), several triumphal arches, bridges across the Danube and Tagus rivers, and more. Its buildings are made of concrete and brick, cover an area roughly 361 by 492 ft (110 by 150 m), and originally rose to a height of 115 ft (35 m). After the end of the Roman Empire, the complex was converted into apartments; a defensive military tower was erected; and, in the 1500s, a convent was added.

Today, the remains of Trajan's Market house the Museo dei Fori Imperiali, a museum preserving artifacts from the city's various imperial forums.

Theater of Marcellus

Rome

With a capacity of up to 20,000, the Theater of Marcellus was the largest and grandest theater in Rome. It was an open-air semicircular theater, similar in appearance to Greek theaters. Unlike Greek designs, it was not built into a hill but freestanding.

Work began on the building under Julius Caesar and it was opened in 12 BCE by Augustus, who named the theater after his deceased nephew, Marcus Claudius Marcellus.

The structure is made from tufa (limestone) and concrete, faced in carved stone, and is still in use today. Shows are periodically performed in its grounds and, remarkably, wealthy Roman families live in the city-center apartments built into its upper few stories.

Roman Forum

Rome

In Rome's prehistory, the land at the base of the Palatine Hill was a marshy swamp. As the city grew, the marsh was drained, paved, and became the Forum Romanum (Roman Forum), a market, meeting place, and the center of Roman public life (see pp. 64–67). On any given day it was a bustling place, where Rome's plebeians and patricians rubbed shoulders.

Today, the Forum's ruins reflect Rome's many layers of history. The Forum's earliest buildings include the Regia (the 8th-century BCE palace of Rome's first kings) and the Temple of Vesta from a century later, where a sacred flame burned that was said to protect the city. As the centuries passed, new buildings and roads were added, including the Via Sacra, Rome's main street. It was the route of religious and triumphal processions, and passed the Senate House, the Temple of Vulcan, the Basilica Julia, and the Tribune Benches, where the tribunes of the plebs sat during the day. The Forum was also home to the Rostra, the platform from which official announcements and public speeches were made. In the Imperial age, emperors built new forums around the original site (see pp. 212–213), but the Forum Romanum remained the heart of the city.

Basilica of Porta Maggiore

Rome

Probably the world's oldest basilica, Porta Maggiore was used by a obscure Roman sect known as the Neo-Pythagoreans, but its purpose is unknown. It was

△ The columns of the Temple of Saturn, overlooking the ruins of the Roman Forum in Rome

only rediscovered in 1917, when construction work at Rome's Termini train station uncovered the temple buried $42^1/_2$ ft (13 m) underground. It was built in the 1st century BCE, probably by Titus Statilius Taurus, a senator who died by suicide in 53 CE following accusations that he was a devotee of "magical superstitions."

Colosseum

Rome

The Flavian Amphitheater opened in 80 CE on the site of Nero's Domus Aurea (Golden House), the vast pleasure palace torn down after the emperor's death in 68 CE. The location of the new arena was where a huge bronze statue called the Colossus of Nero had once stood, giving the new 50,000-seat arena the nickname by which it is remembered: the Colosseum (see pp. 194–197).

Work began under the emperor Vespasian and was completed under his sons, Titus and Domitian. The Colosseum was built with innovative engineering techniques to ensure its vast bulk remained upright. These included using heavy travertine stone for load-bearing walls and lighter tufa (a pumice-like volcanic rock) elsewhere, all held together with concealed metal clamps. The seating was hierarchical, with the emperor, senators, and VIPs occupying the lower levels, then, in ascending order, citizens, freedmen and enslaved men, and finally women at the top. They came to watch gladiatorial contests, animal fights, and public executions.

The Colosseum fell into disrepair as the Western Roman Empire declined, due to plunder, fires, and also earthquakes. The ruin today stands as a symbol of Rome's unique history.

△ The Tempio Rotondo, located in the ancient Forum Boarium, near Tiber Island in Rome

Arch of Constantine

Rome

The Senate dedicated this arch to the emperor Constantine in 315 CE, celebrating his victory over Maxentius at the Battle of Milvian Bridge in 312.

The arch stands next to the Colosseum, at the beginning of the Via Sacra, the road of the triumphal processions. It is a brick-and-concrete edifice, faced in marble, and is the last-built and largest of Rome's triumphal arches. An example of Roman recycling, it features marble panels, reliefs, and statues taken from earlier monuments to Trajan, Hadrian, and Marcus Aurelius. There is some debate, in fact, whether the arch preexisted Constantine and was simply redecorated to commemorate his victory. He spent little time in Rome; after defeating Maxentius at Milvian Bridge on Rome's outskirts, he did not return to the city until 326.

Tempio Rotondo

Rome

The Tempio Rotondo is Rome's oldest marble building. It is tucked away close to Tiber Island, in the ancient city's meat market, known as the Forum Boarium. Tempio Rotondo means "round temple." It was built in the 2nd century BCE and its circular, colonnaded design was heavily influenced by Greek architecture. It was thought to have been the Temple of Vesta for centuries after the fall of Rome, but this has long since been disproved. Today, the site is known as the Temple of Hercules Victor, as inscriptions dedicated to the god have been found near the site. However, no theory has confirmed which god this temple was dedicated to.

Palatine Hill

Rome

The Palatine (see pp. 146–147) is the most central of Rome's seven hills. According to legend, it was where Romulus and Remus settled when they founded Rome in 753 BCE, and where the she-wolf Lupa suckled the twins when she found them abandoned in a cave on the hill, known as the Lupercal. In the Republican era, Rome's rich and powerful lived in luxury villas on its steep slopes, which led down to the Forum on one side. It was also where Augustus built his residence when he established the empire. "Palatine" became synonymous with regal splendor, and the word "palace" derives from it.

Successive emperors made the Palatine their home, including Tiberius, Nero, and Domitian, whose palace looms large over the hill today even as a ruin. As well as Augustus's palace, in 2006 archaeologists believed they had also found the place where he was born: the so-called Palatine House. The following year, researchers claimed they had located the Lupercal cave on the hill, though this is disputed.

△ Brick walls from the ruins of the Baths of Caracalla in Rome

Circus Maximus

Rome

Nothing remains of the Circus Maximus except the elongated depression where it once stood in Rome's southwestern corner, in the valley between the Aventine and Palatine hills. Rome's chariot-racing and public games stadium was an imposing structure; its track was 2,037 ft (621 m) long, surrounded by banks of seating that held 250,000 spectators.

In local tradition, the Circus Maximus first appeared in the late 500s BCE, as a wooden structure. Over the centuries it was rebuilt in stone and expanded after being damaged in several fires. Its last use was some time in the mid-500s CE, after which its stones were removed and used to make new houses, palaces, and churches. Two obelisks in the stadium's central island, or *spina*, that helped the charioteers spot the turning point both survived. One now graces the center of one of Rome's main squares, Piazza del Popolo, while the other stands outside the Basilica of Saint John Lateran.

Baths of Caracalla

Rome

The Baths of Caracalla (see pp. 236–237) were Rome's largest baths, or *thermae*, when they opened in 216 CE and they remained in operation for more than 300 years. The baths are located in south-central Rome, close to the Circus Maximus, where the impressive remains represent just a fraction of the large complex of buildings and open spaces, including the hot-, tepid-, and cold-water bathing halls (the *caldarium*, *tepidarium*, and *frigidarium* respectively), a swimming pool (*natatio*), a gymnasium (*palaestra*), and changing rooms (*apodyterium*).

Large fires heated the water for the baths in a huge network of underground chambers known as the hypocaust. Most Roman houses and apartment buildings had no bathing facilities, so communal baths were vital—and free—centers for public health and cleanliness. They also served as informal places to meet with associates and to conduct business.

Pyramid of Cestius

Rome

Built c. 18–12 BCE, this pyramid is a tomb made for Gaius Cestius, a Roman former praetor, Tribune of the Plebs, and priestly official. The design may indicate that Cestius served in a Roman legion in Egypt or Nubia.

The Pyramid measures 97 ft (29.6 m) square at its base and stands 121 ft (37m) high. It is built from brick and faced in marble, and it sits on a travertine limestone base. Inside is a decorated barrel vault that once held Cestius's sarcophagus. In the 3rd century CE, it was incorporated into the city's new Aurelian Walls, which in part explains its good condition today.

Appian Way

Outside Rome

The Appian Way, or Via Appia, is Rome's best-known road and one of its oldest. The censor Appius Claudius Caecus commissioned its construction in 312 BCE to allow legions to move more easily around Rome's Italian territories. It is one of the most impressive civil engineering projects ever undertaken—one 39-mile (62-km) section remains the longest stretch of straight road in Europe. The structure was slightly curved, so that water on the surface would run off into side channels.

The Appian Way originally ran to Capua, 132 miles (212 km) south of Rome, but by 244 BCE it had been extended another

230 miles (370 km) to the port city of Brundisium (modern Brindisi) in the heel of Italy. Sections of the Appian Way (mainly close to Rome) are still intact, lined with monuments such as the Porta San Sebastiano, the Tomb of Priscilla, several Christian and Jewish catacombs, and the Circus of Maxentius.

Villa dei Quintili

Outside Rome

So extensive are the remains of the Villa dei Quintili on the Appian Way that the site was called *Roma vecchia* ("old Rome") when excavations began in the late 1700s, as archaeologists thought they had found a small town. In fact, the buildings were created for just two people: Sextus Quintilius Valerius Maximus and his brother Sextus Quintilius Condianus, Rome's consuls for 151 CE. It was not clear at first who the villa belonged to, until diggers found lengths of lead water piping inscribed with the brothers' names.

The villa was the largest, most luxurious private residence of its day, featuring baths, a hippodrome (a horse-racing track), and an ornate nymphaeum (a shrine to the gods of nature). In 182 the emperor Commodus executed the Quintili brothers and confiscated the estate for himself.

Ostia Antica

Ostia

Ostia, Rome's port, was located 15 miles (24 km) southwest of the city, at the mouth of the Tiber River. The word "Ostia" derives from the Latin *os*, meaning "mouth." The river's old course has silted up over the past 2,000 years and the archaeological site of Ostia Antica now lies 2 miles (3 km) inland.

Ostia Antica's Roman remains include an amphitheater, well-preserved apartment blocks, and baths. It is best known for its mosaics, which are found all over the city. In particular, the Baths of Neptune boast a fine depiction of the Roman sea god riding a chariot drawn by mythological seahorses, surrounded by sea nymphs, mermen, and dolphins.

As the size and importance of Rome grew, so, too, did the status of Ostia. Eventually, the harbor at the mouth of the relatively small and slow-moving Tiber River became too small to cope with the increase in traffic. In 42 CE, the emperor Claudius commissioned a new artificial harbor, known as Portus (see pp. 216–217), a few miles north along the coast. The emperor Trajan expanded the new port further by building a vast hexagonal basin with wharfs and warehouses, all of which have now been lost.

△ Floor mosaics and walls at the Baths of Neptune in Ostia Antica

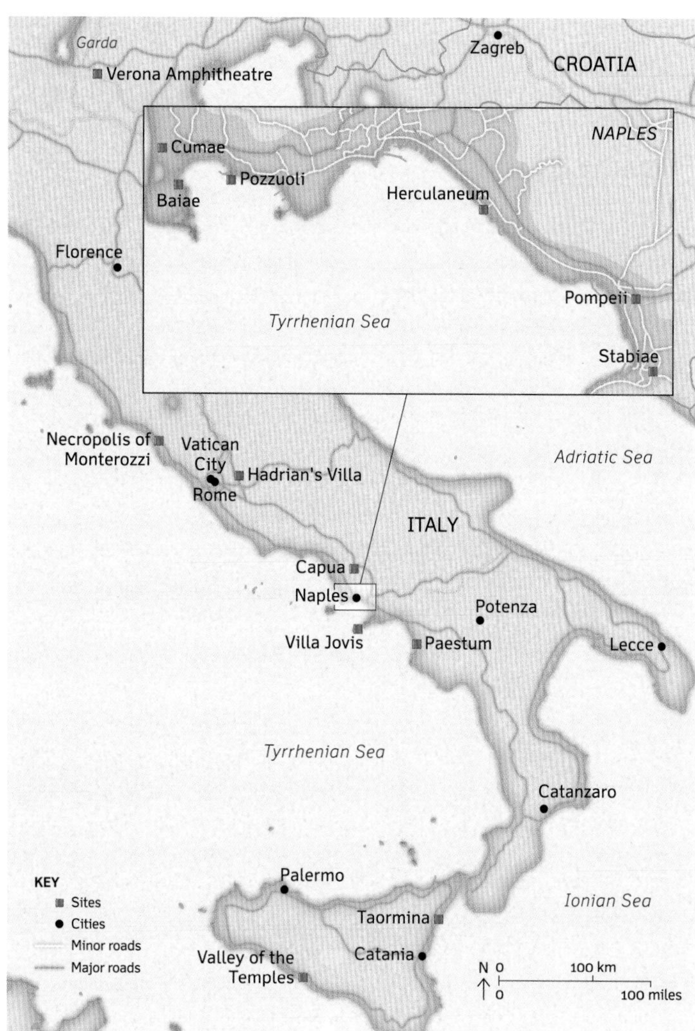

Verona Amphitheater

Verona

Older than the Colosseum in Rome by around 50 years, the Verona Amphitheater is still in use today as a venue for musical concerts and operas.

When it opened in 30 CE, the arena's capacity was 30,000. Spectators came to watch gladiatorial fights, beast hunts, and other *ludi* (games and spectacles). Situated just outside the ancient city's walls, the oval building comprised an inner, middle, and outer ring, threaded with covered walkways and stone staircases. The pink-and-white limestone outer ring was almost completely destroyed by an earthquake in 1117 and was never rebuilt, leaving only a small section standing, which is known today as the Wing. When all three rings were intact, the arena's perimeter was 1,427 ft (435 m), and its edifice was 102 ft (31 m) high.

The seating inside the arena was made from local Veronese marble and, as in the Colosseum, was arranged in strict hierarchy. The local nobles and wealthy took the lower levels, closest to the action taking place on the arena floor, while citizens, freedmen, enslaved men, and women (in that order) sat higher.

Necropolis of Monterozzi

Tarquinia, Lazio

The Etruscan city of Tarquinia lay 56 miles (90 km) northwest of Rome and, for several centuries, the two settlements were occasional allies and, more frequently, enemies.

The Necropolis of Monterozzi was Tarquinia's cemetery. The earliest of its 6,000 graves dates from the 7th century BCE. Its best-preserved grave chambers are those of Tarquinia's nobility, dating from around 470–450 BCE, including the Tomb of the Leopards (see pp. 18–19) and the Tomb of the Triclinium, whose beautiful and colorful frescoes have helped earn the site UNESCO World Heritage status.

Hadrian's Villa

Tivoli, Lazio

Hadrian's Villa and its grounds cover some 200 acres (80 hectares) of countryside at Tivoli, 18 miles (29 km) east of Rome in the Sabine Hills.

It was completed in the 120s CE as a retreat for the emperor Hadrian, who disliked the imperial palace on the Palatine Hill in Rome. In the final years of his reign, Hadrian moved into the villa full time.

The site was a complex of buildings, gardens, pools, and walkways, many of which were designed to reflect Hadrian's travels around his empire and, in particular, his love of Greek and Egyptian culture.

One of the villa's most celebrated areas is the Canopus, a large reflecting pool measuring 398 by 59 ft (121.4 by 18 m). It is designed to represent the Nile River and is set in an artificial valley. The pool's sides were once surrounded by a colonnade of Corinthian columns on one side and caryatids (columns carved into statues) on the other. At one end of the pool a shell-shaped grotto known as the Serapeum played host to the summer parties and nocturnal gatherings for which Hadrian was known.

Capua

Capua, Campania

The name Capua comes from the Etruscan *capeva*, or "city of marshes," reflecting the fact that the settlement was established by the Etruscans as far back as 600 BCE. When the Romans seized control of the Campanian city 300 years later, it became a strategically important outpost as the Roman Empire expanded southward. In 312 BCE the Appian Way was built to connect Rome and Capua, allowing troops to move more quickly between the two cities.

Capua's Etruscan heritage is also evidenced in the relics found there, such as the *Tabula Capuana*, a clay tablet from c. 500 BCE which, with 390 legible words, is the second-longest Etruscan text in existence. Roman-era artifacts include public baths, a Temple of Jupiter, and a Mithraeum, a subterranean temple to the eastern god Mithras who was popular among the Roman army's legions (see pp. 52–53). The jewel in the crown of Capua's archaeological treasures is its Augustan-era amphitheater, which was the second-largest in the empire after the Colosseum. Little remains of its exterior, but the inside is well preserved, as is its warren of underground chambers and tunnels.

Cumae

Outside Naples

Cumae, lying just to the north of Baiae (see below), predates the city of Rome itself. It was founded in the 8th century BCE by settlers from Euboea, the island off the Greek mainland to the east of Athens, and was the first Greek colony on the Italian peninsula. The islanders introduced the so-called "Euboean alphabet" to the Italian mainland, which quickly spread and became the basis for the Latin alphabet that began to develop a century later (see pp. 34–35).

In the 6th century BCE the Cumaeans founded Neapolis ("new city") nearby—the city we today call Naples. In 421 BCE a coalition of local Italian tribes defeated Cumae in battle, driving its Greek rulers to take refuge in Neapolis. By 338 BCE Cumae was under Roman control and, like other settlements in and around the Bay of Naples, it became a fashionable resort town, especially from the rule of Augustus onward. Among its archaeological sites are the city's public baths, its temples of Apollo and Jupiter, and, most important of all, the Cave of the Sibyl. In Roman legend, it was from here that the city's sibyl, or prophetess, predicted the Trojan hero Aeneas's role in the foundation of Rome.

Baiae

Bay of Naples

Around 15½ miles (25 km) west of modern-day Naples, Baiae was the stylish beach resort where Rome's wealthiest citizens came to have fun. Its heyday was from the Late Republican era until the 4th century CE. The generals Marius, Pompey, and Julius Caesar all had vacation villas there, and Augustus and Caligula were early imperial visitors, followed later by Hadrian and Septimius Severus. Its reputation as a place where anything went scandalized some, including the philosopher and politician Seneca, who called it a "harbor of vice."

Invaders sacked Baiae at the end of the Roman Empire, and, following earthquake activity in the 8th century, most of the lower town was flooded by the sea. Today, marine archaeologists are still recovering Classical-era statues, mosaics, and artifacts from the submerged ruins. On dry land, Roman remains in the upper town include the area known as the Sector of Sosandra—a spa and hotel complex—and the Temple of Mercury, which was actually a public bath that featured the world's largest concrete dome before the construction of the Pantheon.

Pozzuoli

Outside Naples

The modern site of Pozzuoli was known to the Romans as Puteoli. It was close to the resort towns of Baiae and Cumae but was in contrast a busy working port. Founded by Greek settlers in the early 500s BCE, it was taken over by the Romans around 341 BCE. The Carthaginian general Hannibal failed to take the city in 215 BCE, and it became Rome's main trading center for centuries afterward. Pozzuoli contains many Roman remains, such as the Flavian Amphitheater, the Macellum (or marketplace), the Temple of Neptune, Roman baths, and the Necropolis of Via Celle.

△ Passageway leading to the Cave of the Sibyl in Cumae

△ Water fountain on a stone-paved street in Pompeii

Pompeii

Bay of Naples

Pompeii was a busy commercial town of 12,000 people when it was covered by 16 ft (5 m) of ash and pumice by the eruption of Vesuvius in 79 CE. Archaeological digging began in 1861, and the many buildings, frescoes, and artifacts revealed since then have provided unparalleled insights into daily life in the Roman Empire of the 1st century CE. To date, two-thirds of the 163-acre (66-hectare) site has been excavated. Notable finds include the House of Sallust, the Temple of Apollo, the House of the Faun, and the Villa of Mysteries. The famous casts of some of Pompeii's victims were made in the mid 1800s by pouring liquid plaster into hollow spaces in the hardened volcanic ash, where the bodies of humans and animals had decomposed over the centuries.

Herculaneum

Bay of Naples

Like its nearby and larger counterpart Pompeii, the town of Herculaneum lay undiscovered for almost 2,000 years after it was buried under 66 ft (20 m) of volcanic ash by the eruption of the volcano Vesuvius in 79 CE. The small, wealthy town of around 4,000 inhabitants was rediscovered in 1709, when a local well-digger found Herculaneum's theater. Ongoing archaeology has since revealed a 49½-acre (20-hectare) site with well-preserved two- and three-story villas, stores, and public buildings. Especially poignant are the "boat houses," a series of vaults by what was then Herculaneum's quayside, where the skeletal remains of more than 300 people were found. It is believed they fled there in the hope of being evacuated by sea during the eruption.

Stabiae

Castellammare di Stabia, Campania

Of all the affluent communities fringing the Bay of Naples, Stabiae was the most exclusive. Like Pompeii and Herculaneum, it was completely buried following the eruption of Vesuvius in 79 CE. Despite partial attempts to excavate the site in the 1700s, it was not until the 1950s that extensive archaeological investigations began in earnest. What they found were some of the finest and most luxurious Roman villas ever discovered, such as the vast Villa San Marco, covering a floor area of some 118,403 sq ft (11,000 sq m), and richly decorated with stucco work and mosaics. Also revealed was the Villa Arianna, famed for its extensive and beautiful frescoes showing scenes from Roman and Greek mythology. These include the painting of Ariadne being abandoned by Theseus that decorates the *triclinium*, the villa's formal dining and entertaining room, which would have been furnished with couches for guests to recline on in comfort.

Villa Jovis

Capri

The island of Capri is today where Italy's most influential and powerful go to play—just as they did 2,000 years ago. In 27 CE the emperor Tiberius took up residence in the large palace complex he built atop the second-highest peak on the island. Perched 1,096 ft (334 m) above the sea and covering 75,347 sq ft (7,000 sq m) across eight terraces, Villa Jovis was where Tiberius spent his final ten years in power.

The villa is accessible only by foot, following a steep and dangerous climb. Tiberius sequestered himself inside the heavily guarded Villa Jovis because he famously disliked Rome and was paranoid that enemies in the capital were planning to have him assassinated. Tiberius's island retreat was as much a vacation home as it was a fortress. According to the (admittedly unreliable) ancient sources, as Tiberius grew older he abandoned himself to a life of increasingly depraved pleasure at the villa. The site today is extensive, but its ruins offer only faint glimpses of the villa's former splendor.

Paestum

Salerno, Campania

Greek settlers established Paestum, originally known as Poseidonia, between 550 and 450 BCE. At that time, Greeks were setting up city-states across southern Italy and Sicily in an area known as Magna Graecia (Greater Greece).

The Romans took over the city in the Gulf of Salerno in 273 BCE and renamed it Paestum. What they found in their new colony 166 miles (268 km) south of Rome was a treasure trove of Greek art and pottery, as well as some impressive buildings, including two temples dedicated to the Greek goddess Hera (from around 550 BCE and 450 BCE respectively) and one dedicated to Athena (from c. 500 BCE). In their size and architectural style, the three temples resemble slightly smaller versions of the Parthenon in Athens. This is especially true of the second Temple of Hera, which is an almost exact contemporary of its Athenian counterpart.

As well as the temples, Paestum's ancient defensive walls are mostly intact, and there is a half-destroyed Roman amphitheater in the city. In the nearby necropolis, the well-preserved burial chambers include the famous and much-reproduced Greek-era fresco, *Tomb of the Diver*.

Taormina

Sicily

Greek settlers founded the city of Tauromenium, known today as Taormina, in 392 BCE. The site was chosen because it occupied a strategically important position that overlooked a scenic spot on Sicily's east coast. More than a century later, in 212 BCE, the city submitted to Roman control in order to protect itself from the Carthaginian invaders who were attempting to seize control of Sicily. Augustus selected Taormina to be a Roman colony in 21 BCE, and in the process forcibly deported many of the Greek-descended inhabitants, replacing them with Roman families.

Of the ancient sites around the city, the best known is the 3rd-century BCE Greco-Roman theater, and the later, and wholly Roman, Odeon ("small theater") which had a seating capacity of just 200 and was discovered by accident in 1892.

Valley of the Temples

Agrigento, Sicily

One of the great sites of Magna Graecia (see left), the Valley of the Temples lies just outside modern-day Agrigento in Sicily. It was known as Akragas in the Classical era and today comprises an impressive collection of seven Greek temples. The best-preserved remains are those of the Temple of Concordia, from the 5th century BCE, while the earliest building is probably the Temple of Heracles, which is thought to have been built in the 6th century BCE.

There are also a few Roman remains on site, notably the Tomb of Theron, a brick-built funeral tower supposedly built to commemorate Roman soldiers killed in the Second Punic War of 218–201 BCE.

△ The Greek-influenced Temple of Concordia in the Valley of the Temples, Sicily

Northern and Eastern Europe

The Roman Empire's northern and eastern frontiers were often troubled places, as is indicated by the forts, walls, and gateways the Italian invaders left behind. But there are many examples of more settled times in these imperial outposts, too: in the villas, baths, arenas, and theaters that still stand.

Hadrian's Wall

England

One of the longest Roman remains in existence, Hadrian's Wall (see pp. 204–205) runs for 73 miles (117 km) from Bowness-on-Solway in the west to Wallsend on the Tyne River in the east. It was built to protect the Roman province of Britannia (England and Wales) from the peoples of modern-day Scotland.

Work began on the wall in 122 CE; the emperor Hadrian may have helped design the structure. It took 15,000 laborers, from three Roman legions stationed in Britannia, six years to build.

As well as the 17 forts along the wall, there were smaller castles at every mile, offering shelter in hot or cold weather. On the southern side, a road ran alongside the wall, allowing men and materials to move quickly along its length. Earthworks and ditches lined the other side, to slow down enemy attacks. The remains of the wall today represent just 10 percent of the original structure.

△ Hadrian's Wall near Caw Gap, Northumberland, England

Vindolanda Fort

Bardon Mill, England

Before Hadrian's Wall, the large fort complex Vindolanda (see pp. 258–259) guarded Roman Britannia's northern border and the east-to-west Stanegate Roman road nearby. In c. 85 CE, Roman legionnaires constructed the fort, which housed up to 1,000 Roman auxiliaries and cavalrymen, as well as their families.

Much of the fort was wooden, but stone remains include the commanding officer's house, barrack buildings, and a granary. There is also a settlement outside the fort walls, with vestiges of stores, houses, a tavern, and baths.

The fort is best known for the Vindolanda Tablets, a series of postcard-size wooden tablets containing what were, at the time of their discovery in 1973, the oldest handwritten documents in Britain. Mostly notes by Flavius Cerealis, the fort's 1st-century commander, his wife Sulpicia Lepidina, and their friends, the tablets describe everyday events in the camp, giving an insight into life in Roman Britain.

Arbeia Fort

South Shields, England

Constructed at the mouth of the Tyne River, Arbeia acted as the "gateway" to Hadrian's Wall (see left), the protective barrier between Roman-occupied Britannia and the unconquered Caledonia (Scotland) beyond. Supplies and new soldiers were shipped in to Arbeia, and then distributed along the 17 smaller forts along the wall's length.

It was built around 160 CE, and up to 600 Roman legionnaires were based there. Archaeological finds have shown these men came from as far afield as Iraq and Syria (Arbeia means "the fort of the Arab troops").

As well as its ongoing excavations, the Arbeia site also includes a recreation of the fort's twin-towered gateway.

Chedworth Villa

Chedworth, England

When Chedworth Villa was discovered in 1864, it revealed a complex of buildings arranged

△ The Roman Baths at Bath, England, sit within buildings of the Classically influenced style from the 18th century

around a central, luxurious house built in about 120 CE for someone of wealth and power.

One of the largest Roman-era houses in the British Isles, it features extensive floor mosaics, especially in the *triclinium* (dining room), with its portrayal of the god Bacchus hosting a lavish party. There are few physical remains of the villa, but a reconstructed outline of the building shows a vast complex that once contained baths, a nymphaeum (a shrine to the nymphs), and temples.

Roman Baths

Bath, England

To the Romans the town was Aquae Sulis ("the waters of Sulis"), but to modern Britons it is simply known as Bath—a rather more prosaic name that reflects its historic function.

The first settlers in Bath were Iron Age people known as the Dobunni, who were drawn to the site by the hot springs that bubbled up from underground aquifers. The Dobunni built a shrine on the site to their goddess, Sulis, who they believed had healing powers. The Romans wasted little time in creating something similar, if more elaborate, when they invaded Britain in 43 CE; the first imperial remains at Bath date from around 75 CE.

The springs were enclosed in a wooden, barrel-vaulted building, which included the hot-, tepid-, and cold-water pools that were standard for Roman baths. The Romans also converted the old shrine to Sulis into a temple to the hybrid goddess Sulis Minerva.

After the Romans withdrew from Britain in the 5th century the site fell into disrepair and became flooded. The thermal springs can be visited today but are housed in buildings from the Georgian era (albeit influenced by Classical architecture). The Roman remains, including some of the old pools and the temple to Sulis Minerva, can be seen in the underground chambers.

Fishbourne Roman Palace

Chichester, England

The West Sussex village of Fishbourne is the site of the largest Roman residence north of the Alps, covering an area greater than that of Buckingham Palace. It was built c. 75 CE, just 30 years after the Roman invasion of Britain. Although the palace burned down sometime in the 3rd century, the floor mosaics of the complex's 100 or so rooms were found to be in excellent condition when they were excavated in the 1960s. These included the now-famous *Cupid on a Dolphin* and *Medusa* mosaics.

Caerleon Fortress

Newport, Wales

On a rectangular site measuring 1,607 by 1,371 ft (490 by 418 m) and covering 50 acres (20.5 hectares), this large fortress guarded the Romans' western border in Britannia (England and Wales). It is in Caerleon, just outside Newport in Wales, and was known to the Romans as Isca Augusta (*isca* means "water" and refers to the nearby Usk River).

The fortress was built in the early 70s CE, and was home to the Second Augustan Legion until the site was abandoned in the 4th century. The ruins include a barracks, a granary, workshops, officers' quarters, baths, and an open-air swimming pool, or *natatio*. The fort could hold up to 5,000 men—as could the wooden amphitheater just outside Isca Augusta's walls, the remains of which draw most visitors to the site today, along with the only surviving legionary barracks building in Europe.

◁ Replica of a Jupiter column, dedicated to the Romans' chief deity, from the Saalburg Fort in Germany

Saalburg Fort

Saalburg, Germany

The *Limes Germanicus* was the chain of northern forts that the Romans constructed along the empire's frontier with Germany. Saalburg occupied a strategically important position by a mountain pass. Its fort was built around 90 CE, first of wood and earth, and later of stone. The Romans abandoned Saalburg in about 250, as continuous tribal attacks and political instability in Rome made its occupation untenable.

Today, however, Saalburg is in use as an almost completely reconstructed Roman fort. Its walls, monumental gateways, grain stores, barracks, and command center have all been re-created as they were in around 200, to give visitors a glimpse of life in an imperial military camp.

Varusschlacht Park and Museum

Kalkriese, Germany

The Battle of Teutoburg Forest in 9 CE was one of the worst defeats ever experienced by the Roman army, and one of the events that helped to foster an idea of "Germanness" among the peoples living north of the Rhine River (see pp. 154–155). Leading an army of Germanic Cherusci tribesmen, the German-born Roman citizen Arminius organized a series of ambushes on three veteran legions under the command of the Roman general Publius Quinctilius Varus, massacring almost every last man.

The exact site of the battle was a matter of speculation for centuries, but in 1987 British Army major and amateur archaeologist Tony Clunn uncovered Roman coins and weapons at Kalkriese Hill, close to the city of Osnabrück in northwest Germany. The long sought-for location of the Battle of Teutoburg Forest had at last been found.

The Museum of the Battle of Teutoburg Forest, also known as the Varusschlacht ("Varus Battle") Park and Museum opened in 2002, and contains 6,000 artifacts recovered from the battlefield, including armor, weapons, and human remains. There is also a 131-ft (40-m) observation tower, from which visitors can get an overview of the site.

Porta Nigra

Trier, Germany

The Porta Nigra (Black Gate) only acquired its evocative name in the Middle Ages, after centuries of fires, dirt, and grime had darkened its originally gray sandstone brickwork. It is not known what, if anything, the Romans called the northern entrance into their German stronghold of Trier, then known as Augusta Treverorum.

Built some time after 170 CE, the Porta Nigra (see pp. 154–155) is the largest Roman gateway north of the Alps. It consisted of two four-story towers and two outer gates, a courtyard, and two inner gates. Despite its vast bulk, the Porta Nigra was never completed—archaeologists do not know if its gate opened or closed, or whether it even had a gate installed in the first place. The stones used to build the Porta Nigra, the largest weighing up to 6½ tons (6 metric tons), were laid on top of each other without mortar and were affixed with iron clamps, a similar technique to that used to construct the Colosseum in Rome.

The Romans left Augusta Treverorum around 400 CE, and all four of the city's gates then remained in use until the 11th century, when all but the Porta Nigra were demolished.

Imperial Baths

Trier, Germany

Trier has more Roman buildings than any other German city, and among the finest—and certainly the biggest—are the Imperial Baths. Known locally as the Kaiserthermen (Emperor's Baths), their footprint covers an area of 564 by 787 ft (172 by 240 m). The barrel-shaped walls still standing rise to 62 ft (19 m), a reminder of how the Kaiserthermen were one of the empire's largest baths when they were built in the early 4th century CE by the Western emperor Constantius I, the father of Constantine the Great.

The Imperial Baths were so ambitious in design that they were never completed. Factional in-fighting among Rome's rulers and troubles with local Germanic tribes, who sacked the city in 360, made Augusta Treverorum (Trier) politically unstable. When the Romans regained control of the city, they converted the Imperial Baths into barracks. It would later be used as a castle, as part of new city walls, and as a monastery. Visitors today can explore the underground tunnels where fires were lit to heat water for the *caldarium*, or hot-water bath.

△ The well-preserved interior of the Porta Nigra in Trier, Germany

Pula Arena

Pula, Croatia

Of all the remaining Roman amphitheaters, Pula, in Croatia, is the only one that has all four of its entrance towers (north, south, east, and west) preserved. It is one of the largest surviving arenas, with a capacity of 23,000 spectators. Like the Colosseum in Rome, Pula had underground tunnels and passageways that opened onto the arena floor—the remains of which are still accessible today. Also like the Colosseum, a sail-like cover could be affixed across the open roof to protect spectators from the sun. Built during the reign of Augustus, it was first a small arena made of wood. By the time of Claudius the timber had been replaced by stone, and over the next few decades the arena was gradually expanded. It reached its final size during the reign of Vespasian, around 79 CE.

From the 5th century, Pula's locals began to plunder the arena for its stone, recycling the blocks to erect new houses, churches, and other buildings. Despite this, much of the amphitheater remains intact today.

Palace of Diocletian

Split, Croatia

When the emperor Diocletian retired in 305 CE due to ill health, he retreated to his native Illyria (modern Croatia) to live out his days in a purpose-built palace in present-day Split.

Covering a site of 7½ acres (3 hectares), the rectangular complex was built in the style of a military encampment, with 66-ft (20-m) walls and four fortified gates—two of which still survive. Inside the walls, Diocletian's Palace included extensive and luxurious apartments for the emperor, at least three temples, a mausoleum, and the peristyle—a large colonnaded courtyard that served as a kind of mini forum. The main building materials used were limestone and marble.

Most of the palace's buildings are now gone, but parts of the walls remain, as does much of the peristyle, which is perhaps the best-known part of the palace today. Adjacent to the peristyle is the Mausoleum of Diocletian, which was designed to be emperor's last resting place. Octagonal on the outside and

△ Aerial shot of the Roman amphitheater known as the Pula Arena in the city of Pula, Croatia

circular within, it is now the Cathedral of St Domnius, although Diocletian's sarcophagus has long since been lost. After the Pantheon in Rome, the cathedral has possibly the best-preserved Roman interior in existence, including a fine dome measuring 44 ft (13.25 m) across. The barrel-vaulted coffered ceiling in what was probably a Temple of Jupiter is also regarded as a masterpiece of Roman design. The rest of the surviving Roman-era buildings, which grew up around the palace, have now been absorbed into the city of Split.

Roman Theater of Philippopolis

Plovdiv, Bulgaria

The Roman Theater of Philippopolis, in the center of modern-day Plovdiv, Bulgaria, is so well preserved that it is still in use almost two millennia after its construction in the 1st century CE.

The seating area, or *cavea*, was built into a small hill, in order to make construction easier and more secure. It features 28 rows of marble seats, arranged in a semicircle, and could seat up to 6,000 spectators. As well as plays and recitals, the Roman Theater of Philippopolis also hosted gladiatorial contests and wild beast hunts.

△ The Butrint Theater in Albania shown with groundwater flooding and a temporary stage

Butrint Theater

Butrint, Albania

Like many Classical-era open-air theaters, the Butrint Theater in southern Albania was constructed in the excavated hollow of a hillside. Greek settlers built it in the 3rd century BCE as they moved up from the peninsula's western Ionian coastline toward the Adriatic Sea. It is designed in the classic semicircle style of Greek and Roman theaters, bordered on one side by a covered and colonnaded walkway, or *stoa*, and on the other by a shrine to the Greek god of medicine, Asclepius. Both of these structures have been lost to history.

The theater itself may not have survived the centuries had it not been buried for 2,000 years under landslide debris from the hill above it. Following slow and painstaking clearance work, archaeologists excavated the theater between 1928 and 1932, and found it to be remarkably intact underneath the many thousands of tons of rubble.

When the Romans arrived in the 1st century BCE, renaming the Greek city of Bouthroton as Buthrotum, the settlement doubled in size. Julius Caesar and Augustus both settled veteran soldiers in the colony and ordered the construction of baths, an aqueduct, and many other new buildings. The majority of these were lost following a devastating earthquake in the 3rd century CE. Today, the whole of Butrint has been designated a UNESCO World Heritage Site.

Southern Europe

France, Spain, and Portugal contain some of the finest examples of Roman building achievements anywhere. Engineers and architects are still discovering how this ancient civilization created the aqueducts, amphitheaters, walled cities, and theaters found in this part of the world.

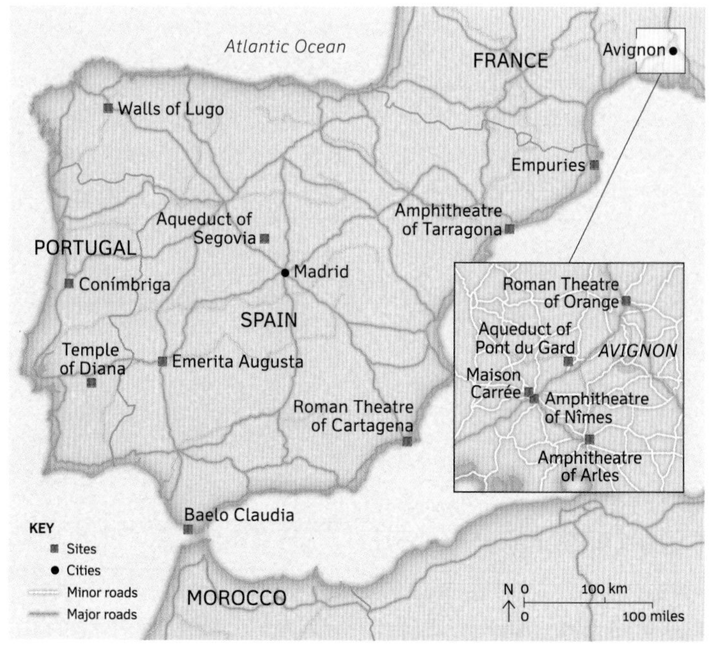

Roman Theater of Orange

Orange, France

The 1st-century CE Roman Theater of Orange is almost unique in that its stage and the wall behind it (known as the *scaenae frons*), are largely intact. This gives a good impression of the size and scope of an ancient Roman theater: the stage and wall is 200 ft (61 m) long and 121 ft (37 m) high.

The *scaenae frons* today looks quite different from how it would have looked to audiences 2,000 years ago. All of the marble that once decorated the wall has been stripped away, exposing the brick structure beneath. Its niches, windows, columns, and doors are all still visible, however, and it is not difficult to imagine how it would have originally resembled the facade of a Classical temple or palace.

After centuries of neglect, restoration work began in 1825, and in 1869 it hosted its first theatrical performance for hundreds of years. The theater is still used to host plays and concerts today, with audiences of up to 7,300 people.

Aqueduct of Pont du Gard

Pont du Gard, France

Pont du Gard is the tallest surviving aqueduct from the Roman world. It was built across the Gardon River in the 1st century CE to supply the city of Nemausus (present-day Nîmes) with water from natural springs near the town of Uzès, 31 miles (50 km) away. A masterpiece of Roman engineering, the aqueduct slopes down a constant gradient of ⅓ in (1 cm) for each 598 ft (182.4 m) of its length. It is made from a fossil-heavy material called shelly

△ The Pont du Gard aqueduct over the Gardon river in the Languedoc-Roussillon region of France

limestone, which has proven highly durable, and may be the best-preserved Roman aqueduct. Where it crosses the Gardon River, it stands 161 ft (49 m) high and features three tiers of arches: 6 on the bottom, 11 in the middle, and 35 at the top. It is 896 ft (273 m) long, but was originally 1,181 ft (360 m) and included an extra 12 arches along the top. It weighs 55,000 tons (50,000 metric tons) and took five years to build.

The aqueduct's water supply became silted up in the Dark Ages, and the aqueduct became a toll road in the medieval period, then a traffic bridge in the 20th century. Vehicles were banned in 2000, and today Pont du Gard is a pedestrianized and popular national monument.

△ The fully restored Maison Carrée in the city of Nîmes, France

Maison Carrée

Nîmes, France

The Maison Carrée (Square House) is so well preserved that it is often mistaken for a modern building created in the Classical style. It stands in the center of Nîmes, in southern France, and was finished between 4 and 7 CE.

Apart from its excellent condition, the Maison Carrée is recognized as being one of the best expressions of the principles laid down by the 1st-century CE Roman architect and engineer Vitruvius: that all buildings should express strength, utility, and beauty. The Maison Carrée achieves this through harmony and proportion, being almost twice as long as it is wide, at 86¾ by 44½ ft (26.4 by 13.5 m).

The pitched roof and pediments at the front and rear are supported by ornate Corinthian columns: 6 each at the front and back, and 11 on each side. The building's original purpose as a temple can be seen in its interior, which is a single, windowless room, or *cella* ("cult room"), containing the shrine to the unknown deity that was once worshipped there.

Amphitheater of Nîmes

Nîmes, France

The gladiatorial arena at Nîmes is one of the best-preserved Roman amphitheaters in existence. It was built in the 1st century CE, around the same time as its larger cousin in Rome, the Colosseum.

Designed in the standard elliptical shape, the arena stands 69 ft (29 m) high and is 436 ft (133 m) long and 331 ft (101 m) wide on the outside; the arena floor is 223 by 128 ft (68 by 39 m). The activities that took place there included gladiatorial contests, beast fights and hunts, and public executions. It held 24,000 people accommodated in 34 tiers. As in most Roman amphitheaters, there was a strict seating hierarchy, with four separate zones, or *maeniana*, for spectators. Public officials and the city's leaders sat in the seats closest to the front, while women and enslaved people sat at the top.

In the 4th century CE, as the Roman Empire was declining, the archways on the lower of the arena's two levels were bricked up and the amphitheater was turned into a fortress, or *castrum*. The Romans built emergency shelter inside for the locals and dug a moat around the perimeter.

In the 1780s, the temporary houses were cleared away and, gradually, the arena was refurbished and restored to its previous use as a place of spectacle—namely bullfights, which are still held there today.

Amphitheater of Arles

Arles, France

Built around 90 CE, the Amphitheater of Arles in southern France held gladiatorial contests and beast hunts for around 400 years. The amphitheater is a two-story structure, with seating for 20,000 spectators, and features 60 arcaded walkways and more than 100 Doric and Corinthian columns. After the fall of Rome, it was converted into a fortress, containing up to 200 small houses as well as two chapels. There was even space for a small public square in the arena's floor.

Today, the refurbished Amphitheater of Arles is a UNESCO World Heritage Site and hosts bullfighting tournaments, as well as plays, concerts, and other entertainment events.

△ Aerial view of the Roman remains in Empúries, Spain, of which only one-fifth has been excavated

Walls of Lugo

Lugo, Spain

Known as Lucus in ancient times, Lugo was one of the Roman Empire's most westerly outposts, in far-flung Galicia in northwestern Spain. By the late 2nd century CE, local peoples and Germanic invaders threatened the Romans' control of the area. In response, they erected walls that were 39 ft (12 m) high and 14 ft (4.2 m) thick around the city for protection. With a slate and granite exterior, these extended for more than 1¼ miles (2 km). The walls were so well built and densely compacted that they are still largely intact today, and they feature battlements, towers, and a moat. Access in and out of the city was controlled through five gates, two of which remain in use.

UNESCO added these city walls to its World Heritage List in 2000, in which they were described as "the finest example of Roman fortification in Western Europe."

Empúries

Alt Empordà, Spain

Greek settlers founded the city of Empúries on modern Spain's eastern coast in 575 BCE. The Romans occupied it after the Second Punic War of 218–201 BCE.

Archaeological digs began in the early 20th century, initially working on the Greek remains. To date, just 20 percent of the Roman buildings have been revealed: these include several large houses featuring frescoes and floor mosaics; a temple dedicated to Jupiter, Juno, and Minerva; a basilica; and a Senate House.

Amphitheater of Tarragona

Tarragona, Spain

Fifteen thousand people could fit into the Roman amphitheater at Tarraco (present-day Tarragona) when it first opened toward the end of the 1st century BCE. Its current state of repair is not as impressive as many other Roman amphitheaters still in existence, and this is largely due to its association with the Christian persecutions that were carried out inside it in the 3rd century CE. In 259, the governor of Tarraco, Aemilianus, sentenced the city's bishop, Fructuosus, and two of his deacons to be burned at the stake in the middle of the arena. When the Roman Empire became Christianized around a century later, parts of the amphitheater were dismantled and the stones were reused to build a church honoring the three martyrs who died so unpleasantly there.

Aqueduct of Segovia

Segovia, Spain

Thought to have been built between the reigns of Domitian (81–96 CE) and Trajan (98–117 CE), the Aqueduct of Segovia served the city of that name, north of Madrid, in central Spain.

It is an imposing structure, at 93½ ft (28.5 m) high and 2,388 ft (728 m) long, consisting of 165 arches over its two levels. The building material was 24,000 large granite blocks, put in place without the use of mortar. So well-engineered was the aqueduct that it continued to supply the city of Segovia with water until the mid-19th century.

Emerita Augusta

Mérida, Spain

The emperor Augustus founded this city in 25 BCE specifically to resettle veterans of Rome's campaigns in Hispania (modern Spain and Portugal). Located in the southwest of Hispania in the Roman province of Lusitania, Emerita Augusta was a large settlement with two separate forums and three aqueducts. At its height, Emerita Augusta had a population of 30,000.

The city was a *colonia iuris Italici* (a provincial colony with the same rights as a colony founded within Italy) and became the capital of Lusitania. The settlement grew and prospered over the centuries, but its position in a quiet corner of the empire meant that little happened there that would be noticed by Rome. After the fall of Rome, Emerita Augusta became an important pilgrimage site based around the cult of the Christian martyr Eulalia of Mérida.

Today, Emerita Augusta is one of the most extensive Classical-era sites in Spain and is part of a wider heritage area known as the Archaeological Ensemble of Mérida, a UNESCO World Heritage Site since 1993. The highlights of Emerita Augusta's Roman remains include its 6,000-seat theater, 15,000-seat amphitheater, 30,000-seat chariot-racing circus, 2,598-ft (792-m) bridge, aqueducts, Temple of Diana, triumphal Arch of Trajan, and scores of other buildings.

Roman Theater of Cartagena

Cartagena, Spain

Built into the highest hill overlooking the seafront at Cartagena in southeastern Spain, the city's Roman Theater was completed between 5 and 1 BCE and could accommodate more than 6,000 spectators. It was dedicated to Gaius and Lucius Caesar, the grandsons and named successors of Augustus (although both men ultimately died before the emperor himself did).

Despite its elevated position, the theater was lost for almost two millennia: locals built over it in the 3rd century CE, and the Vandals burned the site down in 425. Builders rediscovered the theater in 1988, while laying the foundations for a new cultural center in Cartagena. They came across some of the pink marble columns supporting the stage wall, or *scaenae frons*, which stood 52 ft (16 m) high. The remains are now the centerpiece of the Museum of the Roman Theater of Cartagena, which opened in 2008.

△ The Aqueduct of Segovia in Spain, shown running through the old city

Baelo Claudia

Bolonia, Spain

Lying close to the Straits of Gibraltar in southern Spain, Baelo Claudia was once a fishing village that grew, from the 2nd century BCE, into a sizable Roman settlement that traded with the cities of North Africa. It became wealthy through tuna fishing and the production of garum (the fish sauce that Romans ate with almost every meal).

Baelo Claudia went into decline following a major earthquake in the 2nd century CE, but its abandonment meant that archaeologists have been able to uncover many well-preserved remains. These structures include the Forum, the Curia (Senate building), the courthouse, the baths, several temples, a *macellum* ("meat market"), and many houses and shops.

Conímbriga

Coimbra, Portugal

Conímbriga was a settlement that dated back to around the 9th century BCE. When the Romans arrived at the site in 140 BCE, they turned it into a town of more than 10,000 people, with temples, walls, an amphitheater, and a forum. The Germanic Sueves invaded and destroyed Conímbriga in the mid-4th century CE. Archaeological digs on the site began in 1930, and conservation projects have continued to this day. Thus far, many houses, mosaics, thermal baths, part of the town's aqueduct, and much else from both the Late Republican and the Imperial eras of Conímbriga have been recovered.

Temple of Diana

Évora, Portugal

Despite being named the Temple of Diana, this Roman ruin in Évora, 84 miles (135 km) east of the Portuguese capital of Lisbon, was more likely a celebratory monument built in honor of Emperor Augustus. It is located in the city's forum, then known as Liberalitas Iulia, and stood for around 300 years until Germanic invaders destroyed it in the 5th century CE. Archaeologists have uncovered a watchtower, a slaughterhouse, and a butcher's premises built inside its remains.

In design, it was similar in style to the Maison Carrée (see p. 371), although much less of the Temple of Diana remains today—only 14 of its original Corinthian columns, some of the lintels, and the platform upon which the temple sat survive.

△ A geometric-pattern floor mosaic from Conímbriga, Spain

Greece, Türkiye, and Cyprus

While Roman architecture shows undeniable Etruscan and Italic influences, it is from the Greeks that the Romans learned—and copied—the most. The Classical remains of this region are a testament to the Greeks' genius and the Romans' ability to adopt and adapt their cultural achievements.

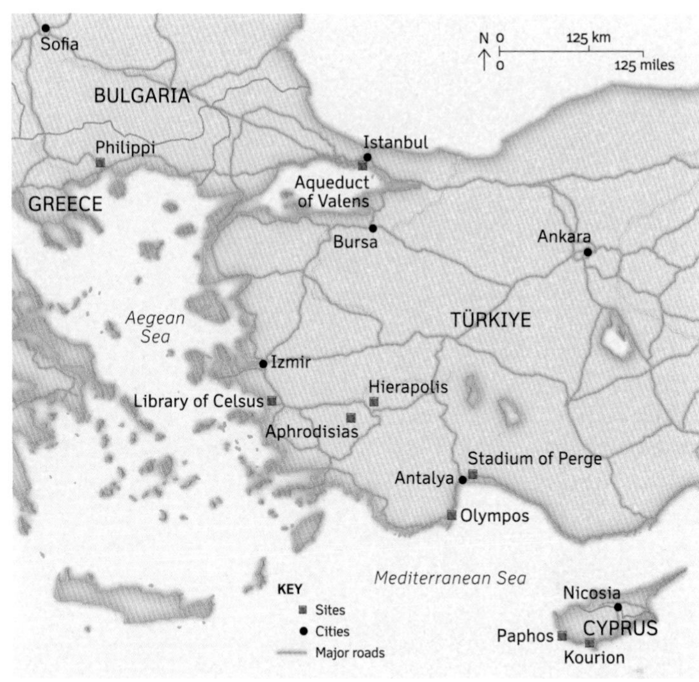

Philippi

Philippi, Greece

Philippi is an ancient city in northeastern Greece, founded around 360 BCE. Originally called Krenides, it was captured and renamed by King Philip II of Macedonia in 356 BCE. The town gained everlasting fame in 42 BCE when it became the site of the battle between the forces of Mark Antony and Octavian against those of Marcus Junius Brutus and Gaius Cassius Longinus, the assassins of Julius Caesar. Following Mark Antony and Octavian's victory, Philippi was resettled with Roman army veterans.

Archaeological excavations have revealed both Greek and Roman remains of a forum, an amphitheater, baths, a basilica, a necropolis, and several houses.

Aqueduct of Valens

Istanbul, Türkiye

In a city of many landmarks, Istanbul's Aqueduct of Valens is one of the oldest and most noticeable. Work began under the emperor Constantius II and was completed under Valens in 368 CE. A masterpiece of Roman engineering, the aqueduct was still in use at least 13 centuries later. The entire system was initially 167 miles (268 km) long, but in the 5th century an extra 280 miles (451 km) were added.

The remains of the large aqueduct in Istanbul (formerly Constantinople) today are from this later addition and are 3,022 ft (921 m) long. They cross Istanbul's main thoroughfare, Atatürk Boulevard, like a giant two-tiered bridge. In Turkish, the famous waterway is known as the "Aqueduct of the Gray Falcon."

Library of Celsus

Ephesus, Türkiye

After Alexandria and Pergamum, Celsus was the third-most important library in the empire. The Romans built it in the ancient city of Ephesus, in present-day Türkiye, around 110 CE. The consul Gaius Julius Aquila commissioned it as a funerary monument to honor his father, Tiberius Julius Celsus Polemaeanus. Celsus was buried in a crypt beneath the building, while some 12,000 scrolls were kept in the reading room above, which measured 55¾ by 36 ft (17 by 11 m).

The architect Vitruoya applied Greek principles of architecture when designing the library: its two-story facade is supported by Corinthian and Ionic columns, and contains niches that hold statues representing wisdom, knowledge, intelligence, and virtue.

The building's interior was destroyed in 262, either by fire or an earthquake, and the facade was further damaged by another earthquake in the 10th or 11th century. Restoration work carried out between 1970 and 1978 repaired much of the damage to the facade, leaving behind the stately ruin that attracts many visitors to Ephesus today.

◁ The restored frontage of the Library of Celsus, with its derelict interior visible between the doors

△ The well-preserved theater at Hierapolis, Türkiye

Hierapolis

Pamukkale, Türkiye

Hierapolis, in southwestern Türkiye, had existed since at least the 7th century BCE. It was built over hot springs, and when the Romans took over Hierapolis and the surrounding area in 133 BCE, it became a fashionable, affluent spa town with a population of up to 100,000. Much of Hierapolis had to be rebuilt following major earthquakes in 17 and 60 CE; today, the remains of the city date from this period and include a gymnasium, hot spring baths, the colonnaded main street, temples, and several fountains.

Aphrodisias

Geyre, Türkiye

A city-state founded in the 2nd century BCE by Greek settlers in present-day southwest Türkiye, Aphrodisias would become the sculptural "workshop" of the Roman Empire. The quarry nearby provided high-quality white and gray marble and the city's craftsmen and sculptors were regarded as among the finest in the known world.

Among the Roman remains in Aphrodisias today, the Sebasteion is one of the best maintained. This temple was dedicated to Augustus and the emperors from the Julio-Claudian family who succeeded him.

Stadium of Perge

Perge, Türkiye

While not the best preserved of the ancient world's sporting venues, the Stadium at Perge, in southern Türkiye, is one of the longest. It is 768 ft (234 m) long

△ Section of the archaeological site of Kourion, overlooking the Mediterranean Sea

and 177 ft (54 m) wide, and held up to 20,000 spectators who came to watch athletics events, wrestling matches, and boxing bouts. There were 17 rows of tiered seats, under which were arcades of stores.

Perge went into decline from the 2nd century CE, when the river on which it was built began to silt up. In the meantime, the city had become an important center of early Christianity: Saint Paul and his companion Saint Barnabas visited it at least twice.

Olympos

Olympus, Türkiye

Olympos, or Olympus, was a small but prosperous town dating back to around the 4th century BCE, long before the Romans arrived in southern Türkiye. However, by the 2nd century CE it had become part of the Lycian League, a Roman-controlled association of local city-states.

One of the reasons why Olympos is famous is that it was here, in 78 BCE, that a young military officer named Julius Caesar helped his commander, Publius Servilius Isauricus, recapture the town for Rome after a rebel pirate leader named Zekenites tried to break away from the empire. When Hadrian visited Olympos in the early 100s CE, the town was renamed Hadrianopolis in his honor (but only temporarily).

The Greek and Roman ruins of Olympos today sit among picturesque woodland, not quite forgotten but not as "managed" as more famous remains from the Classical era nearby. The site includes the partial remains of a Roman theater, the gate of a destroyed temple (dedicated to the emperor Marcus Aurelius), and an unusual sarcophagus belonging to a little-known Greek sailor called Captain Eudemos.

Paphos

Paphos, Cyprus

People have lived in and around the Cypriot city of Paphos since 10,000 BCE. The Tomb of the Kings was a necropolis built around 300 BCE when Paphos was under Greek control. It was a place reserved for the city's rulers, and there are Roman tombs dating from after they arrived in the 1st century CE.

The famous Temple of Aphrodite, built by the Greeks possibly as far back as 1500 BCE, was destroyed in an earthquake around 77 CE. It had to be rebuilt by the city's Roman occupiers, and these are the remains that are visible today. In general, Paphos is an interesting blend of Greek and Roman architecture.

Kourion

Kourion, Cyprus

The ancient Kingdom of Kourion flourished around the 10th century BCE, after which Assyrians, Egyptians, and Persians successively took possession of Cyprus. Rome annexed the island in 58 BCE and Kourion became an important administrative center. Most of the Classical remains discovered so far are from the era of Roman occupation. Notable examples include a Greco-Roman theater, aqueducts, the forum, baths, a nymphaeum (a shrine to the nymphs), and the so-called House of the Gladiators and the House of Achilles, both known for their fine floor mosaics.

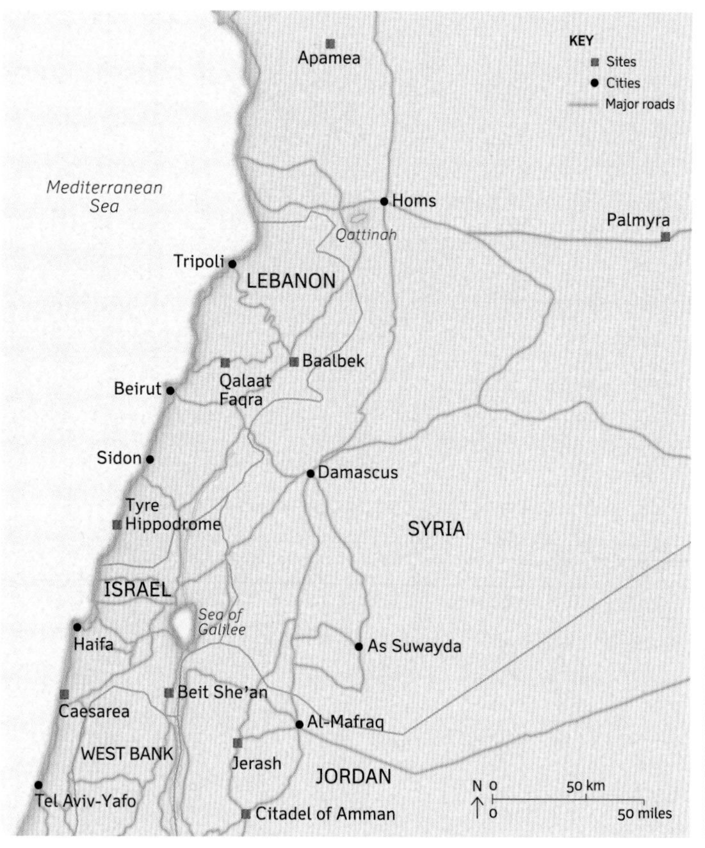

The Middle East

When the Romans conquered the eastern Mediterranean they literally found themselves building on civilizations thousands of years older than their own. This is reflected in the structures they made, which, while recognizably "Roman," show local religious, social, and cultural influences.

Qalaat Faqra

Lebanon

Perched 4,921 ft (1,500 m) up Mount Lebanon, Qalaat Faqra was a sacred Classical site that today is dominated by the remains of a mysterious tower. A two-story structure from the 1st century CE, 49 ft (15 m) square, it originally had a third floor and was topped by a pyramid-shaped roof. Its function is unknown, though it could have been a tomb, an altar, or even a lookout post.

More easily identifiable are the site's sanctuary to Zeus Beelgalasos (a Greco-Roman version of the local father-god Baal), the Temple of Atargatis, (dedicated to a local fertility mother-goddess adopted by Roman settlers), two sacrificial altars, and the remains of a later Byzantine church and baptistery.

Baalbek

Baalbek, Lebanon

Situated 42 miles (67 km) north of the Lebanese capital, Beirut, Baalbek was known as Heliopolis (Sun City) in Greek and Roman times. Among its treasures are two important Roman buildings: the Temple of Jupiter and the Temple of Bacchus, from the 1st and 2nd centuries CE respectively. The first of these was the largest temple in the Roman world, measuring 290 ft (88 m) in length and 144 ft (44 m) in height. Its pillars were 65 ft (19.9 m) high and 8 ft (2.5 m) in diameter. Six of its Corinthian columns remain, along with their entablature (the lintel running across the top of the column). The smaller Temple of Bacchus is in better condition. Most of its columns remain, as do several reliefs and sculptures.

Tyre Hippodrome

Tyre, Lebanon

This chariot-racing track in the southern Lebanese city of Tyre dates from the 2nd century CE. It was one of the Roman world's finest sporting arenas and could seat 20,000 spectators.

The median strip (*spina*) that ran down the center of the track is still intact, along with its large decorative obelisk and the turning posts (*metae*) at each end of the stadium.

Apamea

Apamea, Syria

At 1¼ miles (2 km) long, the Great Colonnade in Apamea was the city's main north–south avenue, the *Cardo Maximus*, and was one of the longest streets in the Roman world. It is just one of the well-preserved Roman ruins in the Syrian city, which included a 25,000-seat theater, one of the largest in the empire.

Like many other ancient sites in Syria, Apamea was badly damaged and its treasures looted when ISIS forces seized it during the country's civil war that began in 2011.

△ Only partial remains of the stands at Tyre Hippodrome are still in existence today, but they give an idea of the stadium's grandeur

Palmyra

Palmyra, Syria

The Syrian city of Palmyra is at least 4,000 years old and was a wealthy mercantile center at the western end of the ancient Silk Road when Rome annexed it in the 1st century CE. Its surviving architecture reflects the many cultures that mixed there. The Temple of Bel, for example, was a Roman-style temple built for the worship of the Mesopotamian father-god Bel, or Baal.

Other Roman-era ruins at Palmyra include the Great Colonnade, the ¾-mile (1.1-km) main street, the Baths of Diocletian, the Senate House, and the so-called "Funerary Temple no. 86," which dates from the 3rd century—around the time the city attempted to break away from the Roman Empire under its rebel queen, Zenobia (see pp. 244–245).

ISIS forces occupied Palmyra between 2015 and 2017. They inflicted major damage on the Temple of Bel in particular, and on other valuable antiquities.

◁ Ruins of Palmyra's main street, the Cardo Maximus, with triumphal arch, before its destruction by militants from ISIS

△ Mosaic from the hippodrome (1st century BCE) in Caesarea, Israel

Caesarea

Caesarea, Israel

A coastal town and port, Caesarea was the provincial capital of Roman Judea. It was established in the 1st century BCE, during the reign of Herod the Great. This is the same Herod who, according to the Gospel of Mark, ordered the execution of all male babies under the age of two when he heard of the birth of Jesus.

A small settlement known as Stratonos Pyrgos (Straton's Tower) existed there before the Romans assumed control of the region in 63 BCE. Under Herod, what was essentially a small fishing village was renamed and greatly enlarged into a major port, with an associated harbor known as Sebastos, with docks, public buildings, temples, and a large royal palace that overlooked the sea. According to the historian Flavius Josephus (see pp. 240–241), its size rivaled that of another major port, Piraeus in Athens.

Unfortunately, Caesarea and in particular Sebastos, were built over a geological fault line; in the 1st or possibly 2nd century CE an earthquake followed by a tsunami either completely destroyed the port or damaged it beyond any hope of repair or future use. Caesarea Maritima remained an important city, however, and a succession of Roman governors and procurators were based there.

Archaeological work since the 1950s has revealed many Roman treasures, such as a hippodrome; theater; a temple to the goddess Roma; and, significantly, the "Pilate Stone." Discovered in 1961, this is an inscribed marble block that is the only instance in all of the Roman Empire's records where Pontius Pilate is mentioned by name—providing historical evidence of his existence to support the accounts that mention him in the Bible.

Beit She'an

Beit She'an, Israel

Neolithic nomads, Bronze Age Canaanites, ancient Egyptians, Iron Age Israelites, and Macedonian Greeks had all left their mark on the ancient settlement of Beit She'an in the province of Galilee, in modern-day northern Israel, before the Romans arrived in the 1st century BCE. The city lies in the Beit She'an Valley about 394 ft (120 m) below sea level. In the Old Testament, Beit She'an is named as the place where the bodies of King Saul and his sons were hung after their defeat at the Battle of Gilboa by the Philistines.

Most of Beit She'an's Roman remains have yet to be uncovered by archaeologists, although a very well-preserved theater, a hippodrome, a main road (or *cardo*), a bathing complex, and several tombs have been revealed and can be visited. There are also very rare floor mosaics from a 5th–7th-century CE synagogue showing, among other items, the seven-branched candelabrum known as a menorah.

Galilee was a troubled region during the Roman occupation. One of the defining events of the period was the Jewish Uprising of 66 CE, and Beit She'an is thought to have sided with Rome during that conflict.

Jerash

Jerash, Jordan

The earliest human remains around Jerash date back to c. 7500 BCE. The city itself was said to have been founded by Alexander the Great and his general Perdiccas in 331 BCE while the Macedonians were campaigning in what is today Jordan—Jerash is just less than 30 miles (50 km) north of the capital city of Amman.

The Romans arrived in 63 BCE, and the city and its surrounding regions were relatively peaceful under imperial control. Trade and commerce helped make Jerash prosperous, and it was adorned with several impressive buildings, which the Romans' Byzantine and Muslim successors as conquerors of the city left intact. Unfortunately, though, an earthquake badly damaged Jerash in 749 CE, burying many of its buildings under rubble.

The site was not rediscovered until 1925; since then, the ongoing excavations and the well-preserved remains they have uncovered have led to Jerash being called "the Pompeii of the East." Roman-era buildings at Jerash include a triumphal arch dedicated to Emperor Hadrian, a 15,000-seat hippodrome, a colonnaded street, several temples, a monumental gateway (or *propylaeum*), and a theater.

Citadel of Amman

Amman, Jordan

Many civilizations passed through Amman. The Neo-Assyrians of the 8th century BCE were followed 200 years later by the Neo-Babylonians, then the Ptolemies, the Seleucids, and the Romans—who in turn were succeeded by the Byzantines, then the Umayyad Caliphate of the 7th century CE.

Like Rome, the capital of Jordan is built on seven hills; the Citadel of Amman sits atop the highest of these, Jebel Al Qala'a.

△ Corinthian columns preserved in the Citadel of Amman

The citadel contains the remains of buildings from several ancient cultures dating from the 1st to the 7th centuries. Chief among these buildings is the Roman-era Temple of Hercules from the 2nd century. Its design was slightly unusual, in that its colonnaded portico at the front was thought to extend beyond its side walls, making a T-shape. Little of the temple building exists today, and even less of the 39-ft (12-m) statue of Hercules that it once contained: only three fingers and an elbow survive.

△ The nymphaeum's fountain, behind a screen of Corinthian columns, in Jerash

North Africa

Two words that sum up Rome's relationship with North Africa are conflict and commerce, and the buildings left there display this to often stunning effect. The Romans completely destroyed and rebuilt some enemy cities, while other, more friendly settlements were beautified and enhanced.

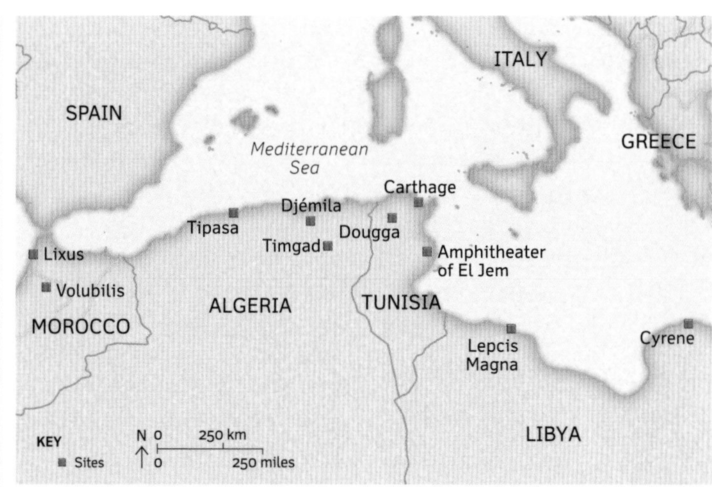

Lixus

Larache, Morocco

Phoenician settlers from the eastern Mediterranean founded the city of Lixus around the 8th or 7th century BCE. It is on Morocco's Atlantic coast, close to the Strait of Gibraltar and mainland Europe, and was an important port in antiquity. Because of its strategically valuable position next to the "gateway" of the Mediterranean, Lixus has been fought over by Carthaginians, Romans, Berbers, and Arabs.

Evidence of the city's history of occupation is found in the remains that exist there today, with a series of archaeological layers representing each era of its rule. The city's "Temple Quarter" is extensively excavated, with Roman finds dating from 40 BCE to the 5th century CE. These include baths, a covered walkway (or *cryptoporticus*), an amphitheater, a forum, a temple, and villas.

Volubilis

Meknes, Morocco

Originally a Berber and then a Carthaginian settlement, Volubilis was controlled by Rome for less than two centuries. The Romans took over what would be one of their most southwesterly outposts in the 1st century CE. It was part of the Kingdom of Mauretania, in present-day Morocco, which was in essence a Roman vassal state, and was a prosperous, well-appointed city encircled by 1½ miles (2.6 km) of walls.

Volubilis's wealth came from olives, which were grown, pressed, and shipped around the empire. This allowed some of its inhabitants to build large villas filled with fine objects, sculptures, and mosaics, several

△ The remains of the basilica at Volubilis, Morocco, which would have once looked out over the city's forum

of which have been revealed in archaeological digs, such as the so-called House of Orpheus, with its Orpheus-themed floor decorations. There is also a triumphal arch dedicated to Caracalla, the Capitoline Temple, and a basilica. Ancient olive presses have also been found at the site. Rome lost control of the city in 285 and, due to its remote location, never retook it.

Tipasa

Tipaza, Algeria

Now known as Tipaza, the city of Tipasa became a military colony under the emperor Claudius after the Romans took over the old Carthaginian trading port on this stretch of Algerian coastline.

With a population of up to 20,000, Tipasa became an early center of Christianity: the first Christian inscription in the city dates from 238 CE, long before it became the official religion of Rome. Tipasa city went into decline in the 6th century, and it was not until a village was reestablished on its site in 1857 that interest in its Roman remains was revived.

Tipasa's Christian heritage is reflected in the three Roman- and Byzantine-era basilicas that have been discovered there, along with more traditional Roman structures such as a forum, a Senate House, thermal baths, and a cemetery.

Djémila

Djémila, Algeria

The Romans knew Djémila as Cuicul, which they established in the 1st century CE as a garrison town in present-day Algeria. It is almost unique in Roman urban development, in that Cuicul was built at 3,000 ft (900 m) amid the rocks and crags of a high pass between two mountain streams.

Despite these topographical constraints, the Romans showed typical endeavor by imposing a grid-like formation of streets and buildings over the steep and rocky terrain. The result was a beautiful city in a spectacular location, whose remains are among the most impressive in the Roman world. These include a Temple of Venus Genetrix, an Arch of Caracalla, the Temple of Gens Septimia (dedicated to Septimius Severus), a 3,000-seat theater, a forum, baths, cult buildings, and several private dwellings with mosaic floors.

△ View of the furnaces that heated the water of the Great Baths at Djémila, Algeria

Timgad

Batna, Algeria

The emperor Trajan founded the town of Timgad in 100 CE, at the height of Rome's imperial expansion. Its official name was Colonia Marciana Ulpia Traiana Thamugadi, the second and third words in its title referring to Trajan's mother, Marcia, and his sister, Ulpia. "Thamugadi" was the local Berber name for the place where the city was built in Algeria's Aurès Mountains.

Timgad was established as a city for Roman army veterans, and this is reflected in its rigid, grid-like design. Straight streets and neat intersections were common features of Roman new towns in this period, and Timgad is one of the finest examples of imperial town planning in the world. It enjoyed a fairly peaceful existence until the final years of the Roman Empire, and became a well-known center of Christian worship. However, Arabs invaded it in the 7th century and by the 8th century Timgad was completely deserted.

Archaeological investigations were carried out at Timgad between 1881 and 1960, and today most of the city has been uncovered, with a triumphal arch dedicated to Hadrian at the end of the partially restored colonnaded main street among the highlights. There are also temple remains, a theater, and many fine statues and carvings.

△ View of the Capitol building in Dougga, Tunisia, with its intact columns and pediment

Carthage

Carthage, Tunisia

Founded in the 9th century BCE on the northern coast of present-day Tunisia by Phoenician merchants from Tyre, Carthage was Rome's main rival for control of the Mediterranean.

Rome ultimately won the power struggle between the two states in the Punic Wars, which lasted on and off from 264 to 146 BCE. Victorious, Rome razed the city of Carthage to the ground, completely destroying much of its rich material culture so that few Carthaginian buildings or artifacts exist today.

Visitors to Carthage, whose ruins are around 9 miles (15 km) east of the Tunisian capital Tunis, will find mostly Roman remains. These include the Baths of Antoninus from the 2nd century CE, behind which is the Archaeological Park, where the old grid of pre-Roman streets is still visible—this area also contains some early Carthaginian graves and tombs. There is also a theater, an amphitheater that once seated 50,000 spectators, and several villas that survived the city's near-total destruction by Arab invaders in 692.

Dougga

Dougga, Tunisia

According to UNESCO, Dougga, or Thugga, is "the best-preserved Roman small town in North Africa." Its remote location, in the north Tunisian countryside some distance from the coast, means it was never an important target for invaders. Consequently, a good proportion of its Berber, Carthaginian, Roman, and Byzantine buildings are in reasonable condition. Its 2nd-century Roman theater, for example, is among the best preserved from the Imperial era, as is its Capitoline temple from the same period. The site is also rich in floor mosaics and statuary.

Amphitheater of El Jem

El Jem, Tunisia

El Jem, in eastern Tunisia, was known to the Romans as Thysdrus. Its amphitheater is exceptionally well preserved: its arena floor, underground passages, seating area, and most of its three-story surrounding walls are very well maintained and can all still be visited. It was built around 238 CE, supposedly by the local proconsul (governor) and future emperor Gordian III.

Lepcis Magna

Khoms, Libya

With a history stretching back to the 7th century BCE, Lepcis Magna, on the northwestern coast of present-day Libya, is almost as old as Rome itself. It was first a Phoenician settlement, and was later incorporated into the Carthaginian Empire. After Rome defeated Carthage in the Punic Wars, Lepcis Magna (sometimes known as Leptis Magna) became part of the empire.

The main source of the city's wealth was olive oil, which it exported across the empire. Scores of ancient olive oil presses have been unearthed in and around the Roman settlement. The city is probably most famous as the birthplace of the emperor Septimius Severus, who greatly expanded Lepcis Magna and beautified it with many new and monumental buildings, including a forum and refurbished docks. A tsunami in 365 CE destroyed large areas of Lepcis Magna, while the decline of the Roman Empire's power in the next century allowed Vandal invaders and local Berbers to raid the city with impunity.

Today, Lepcis Magna is one of the best-preserved Roman sites in North Africa. Whole swathes of the city have been uncovered, revealing extensive mosaics, a marketplace, a virtually intact theater, an impressive amphitheater, the distinctive triumphal Arch of Septimius Severus, and much more.

△ Statues of Demeter and Persephone that once decorated a temple building in Cyrene, Libya

Cyrene

Shahhat, Libya

Founded in 631 BCE, Cyrene became an important Greek colony close to North Africa's Mediterranean coast, in modern-day Libya.

The city was very prosperous under the Greeks; its wealth was based on silphium, a local, unidentified plant used in Classical times for medicine, perfume-making, and as a cooking herb. Today, many botanists believe that silphium was so widely used, it ultimately became extinct.

In 96 BCE the last Greek king of Cyrene, Ptolemy Apion, left the city to Rome in his will. It became a full Roman province in 74 BCE. Ever eager to leave their mark on newly acquired territories, the Romans erected their own buildings and temples among those the Greeks had already created. Cyrene today has many Greek, Roman, and hybrid ruins; for example, the Temple of Zeus was built by the Greeks in the 6th century BCE and partially reconstructed by the Romans in the 2nd century CE.

Glossary

A

aedile An elected office of the Roman Republic. Based in Rome, aediles were responsible for maintaining public buildings and infrastructure, as well as public order—for instance, the regulation of public festivals.
ager publicus Fertile land in Italy confiscated by the Roman state, divided into smallholdings and farmed by Roman citizens.
Altar of Victory A monumental altar to Peace, decreed by the Roman Senate in 13 BCE to commemorate the emperor Augustus's safe return from campaigns in Gaul and Spain.
apotheosis The elevation of a person, usually a Roman emperor following their death, to divine status.
aquila The Latin term for an eagle, Jupiter's bird. Displayed on the legionary standards carried by Roman soldiers, they symbolized Rome's divinely ordained imperial might.
atrium The central hall of a Roman household.
augur A Roman statesman appointed for life to ensure that political decisions follow the will of the gods (achieved through studying the flight of birds).
***augustus* (pl. *augusti*)** Meaning "great," this title was assumed by the first emperor, Octavian, and adopted as an honorific for the emperors who followed. Also used during the Tetrarchy to denote senior emperors.
auxiliaries Non-citizen soldiers fighting in the Roman army. A full period of service was rewarded with a grant of citizenship.

B

Britannia The southern two-thirds of Britain, which became a Roman province after the conquest of 43 CE.

C

caesar An imperial title derived from the name Julius Caesar. During the Tetrarchy, it indicated an emperor of secondary status to the *augusti*.
caldarium A "hot room" heated by a hypocaust in a Roman bathhouse; it contained a heated plunge pool.
cataphracts The heavily armored cavalry that were used by the Parthian and Sasanian Empires in their wars against the Roman Empire.
censor One of two magistrates who were responsible for maintaining the census, supervising public morality, and allocating public contracts and tax-collecting rights. The censor's decisions could not be overturned.
census The recording of all Roman citizens, their wealth, and their tax obligations, carried out by the censor.
Chi Rho A symbol formed by the combination of the Greek letter *Chi* (X) and the Greek letter *Rho* (P), the first two letters of Christos, the Greek name for Christ.
Comitium Rome's earliest open-air public meeting space. It had great religious significance and was where the Roman people convened to fulfill various civic functions.
columbarium A building, either public or private, containing multiple niches for storing funerary urns.
consul The highest elected annual office in the Roman Republic. Two consuls served at the same time, for a period of one year.
cursus honorum The "course of honors" was a ladder of public offices or magistracies that needed to be climbed in hierarchical order. Positions were elected and held for the duration of one year.

D

dictator A magistrate with supreme authority appointed at a time of military or political emergency. The dictator traditionally resigned the office when the crisis passed, but this tradition eroded under Julius Caesar.

E

Eastern Roman Empire The Eastern part of the Roman Empire, which split in the 3rd century CE. The Eastern Empire was ruled from Nicomedia at first and later from Constantinople. It survived for 1,000 years after the fall of the Western Roman Empire and also became known as the Byzantine Empire.
equestrian Citizens placed by the censors in the highest wealth category, but not participating in political life as members of the Senate. Despite this, they were part of the Roman elite and were influential in politics.
Etruscans Members of the ancient people of Etruria, whose civilization reached its height in the 6th century BCE. The Romans, who later dominated the region, adopted many Etruscan practices.

F

familia The Roman "family" included the enslaved members of a household as well as family members.
fasces A bundle of rods surrounding an ax, carried by a lictor before magistrates in ancient Rome. The bundled sticks stood for unity through strength, while the ax symbolized the magistrate's power (*imperium*) and his authority to punish those who disobeyed.
Field of Mars Known to the Romans as the Campus Martius, this flat area of land beyond the city walls was where the Roman army mustered, and was where elections took place.
***flamen* (pl. *flamines*)** Priest devoted to specific gods. For instance, there were *flamines* of Jupiter and Mars. A *flamen* was married to a *flaminica*.
***flaminica* (pl. *flaminicae*)** Priestess devoted to specific gods.
Flavian Relating to the ruling dynasty founded by the emperor Vespasian.
Floralia A Roman festival celebrated on April 27 or 28 and dedicated to the deity Flora, goddess of spring and flowering plants.
frigidarium One of the three main bath chambers of a *thermae*, or Roman bathhouse, this cold room contained an unheated bath or swimming pool.

G

Gaul A region of Western Europe encompassing modern-day France and neighboring areas on all sides. It comprised four Roman provinces, and was inhabited by predominantly, but not exclusively, Celtic peoples, to whom the Romans gave the blanket name "Gauls."
Germanic Pertaining to the historical groups of people who lived in Central Europe and Scandinavia from antiquity until the early Middle Ages.
Greek-speaking world Rome's early history ran parallel with Greek colonization in the Mediterranean. Spoken on the Greek mainland and around the Aegean, Greek was also the common language of western Türkiye, southern Italy, the Black Sea, and Cyprus, as well as parts of North Africa, France, and Spain. The conquests of Alexander the Great and his successors consolidated the use of Greek in the eastern Mediterranean, which was the official language of the Eastern Roman Empire until the fall of Constantinople.

H

haruspex (pl. haruspices) An Etruscan soothsayer often employed by the Senate to interpret the will of the gods by inspecting animal entrails.
Hellenistic The historical period beginning in 323 BCE with Alexander the Great's death and ending in 31 BCE with Rome's conquest of the last Hellenistic kingdom, the Ptolemaic dynasty of Egypt, which was ruled by Greek monarchs. Also: relating to Greek history or culture.
Hispania The Roman name for the Iberian Peninsula and its provinces.
hypocaust A system of central heating, which produces and circulates hot air below the floor of a room, and may also warm the walls with a series of pipes or *tubuli* through which the hot air passes.

I

Ides In the Roman calendar, this denotes either the 13th or 15th day of every month.
imperium The right to command troops and exercise jurisdiction, assigned for a fixed period to senior magistrates.
***insula* (pl. *insulae*)** Multistory apartment blocks in urban areas.

J

Julio-Claudian Relating to the ruling dynasty established by Octavian (Augustus) and Livia.

K

king of sacrifices A lifetime appointment of a priesthood in Rome in which the priest performed sacrifices on behalf of the state, alongside his wife, queen of sacrifices.

L

***lararium* (pl. *lararia*)** A shrine for the *Lares* within a Roman household, where sacrifices to household gods were conducted.
Lares familiares The protective spirits of the family.
latifundia Large agricultural estates, often comprising smallholdings consolidated into one farm.
Latium The region in central Italy that contained Rome and was the home of the Latin language; it was bounded by the Tiber River to the north, the Apennines to the east, and Monti Lepini to the south.
legatus An official assigned to carry out a particular task using authority delegated from a senior magistrate.
legion The main operational unit of the Roman army, made up of around 5,000 citizen soldiers. Their combat and noncombat activities were supported by a similar number of non-citizen auxiliaries.
Liberalia A Roman festival celebrated on March 17 every year. During the festival, boys marked their transition to manhood by adopting the toga.
lictor Originally an attendant who carried the *fasces* of a magistrate with *imperium*. Their chief role was to part crowds to allow the magistrate passage. As the magistrate's retinue grew more complex, they increasingly took on the role of bodyguard.
ludi saeculares The "secular games" were theatrical games and sacrifices held over three days in the Campus Martius in Rome, to mark the end of the old age or *saeculum* (a cycle of 100 or 110 years) and the start of the new.
Lupercalia A Roman festival celebrated on February 15 to promote health and fertility. Celebrated by an association of young men called the *luperci* ("brothers of the wolf") who ran through Rome in loincloths striking bystanders (often female) with goatskin whips.

M

magistrate A person meeting the criteria for election (male, of suitable age and wealth, free-born) and elected by the Roman people in a formal assembly to carry out certain tasks. These ranged from lower-level responsibilities, such as acting as a judge in a property dispute, to the highest, for instance being a provincial governor or commanding an army.
matrona The idealized Roman wife and mother.

N

Nones In the Roman calendar, these denoted either the 5th or 7th day of every month.

O

optimates An ideological term applied to a senior group of senators in the Late Republic who directed policy by power and influence. They are typically seen as being in opposition to the *populares*, and consistently opposed the rise of Julius Caesar.

P

Parilia A Roman festival celebrated on April 21, dedicated to the deity Pales, protector of flocks and herds.
Parthia A historical region located in northeastern Iran, and the political and cultural base of the rulers of the Parthian Empire (247 BCE–224 CE).
paterfamilias The "father of the family" was the eldest male and head of the Roman household.
patrician In the Early Republic patricians were the elite families who monopolized public office. Over time they lost the exclusive right to rule, and by the Late Republic held little or no collective influence.
Pax Romana The "Roman peace" was a period lasting about 200 years (27 BCE to 180 CE), seen as a golden age when the empire was relatively peaceful, prosperous, and stable.
Penates Household gods, protectors of the storeroom.
peristyle In Roman architecture, a continuous porch formed by a row of columns surrounding the perimeter of a building or an open courtyard.
plebeian Roman citizens who did not belong to the small number of elite patrician families who monopolized political power in the Early Republic. They fought for their rights in the Struggle of the Orders (494–287 BCE), and by the Late Republic plebeian families were predominant at every level of Roman society.
***pontifex* (pl. *pontifices*)** A priesthood held by a major statesman. The *pontifex* oversaw religious life within the city of Rome; subordinate to the *pontifex maximus*.
pontifex maximus The chief high priest of the College of Pontiffs and holder of the highest religious office of Rome. Under Augustus, the role became part of the position of emperor.
populares A term applied to politicians in the Late Republic who circumvented the Senate and worked directly through the people's assemblies and Tribunes of the Plebs to ensure that non-elite Roman citizens received their share of the profits of empire.
praetor The most senior magistrates after the consuls. This was primarily a judicial magistracy, concerned with running the public courts.
Praetorian Guard The Roman army unit that served as the emperor's personal bodyguard.
principate The office of the emperor.
proconsul A former consul, who then became governor of a province or a military commander.
province Roman administrative area controlled by a governor (either a proconsul or a legate).

Q

quaestor The most junior of the major magistracies and primarily concerned with financial matters. Election to the quaestorship in the Late Republic brought with it membership of the Senate.
queen of sacrifices *See* king of sacrifices.

R

***rex* (pl. *reges*)** A term for the Roman leader during the Regal period, usually translated as "king."
Robigalia A Roman festival celebrated on April 25 to honor Robigus, god of rust, by sacrificing a dog to protect the grain fields from disease.

S

Saturnalia The festival of Saturnus, an ancient national god of Latium, was held at the end of December when all classes of Romans feasted and exchanged gifts.
Senate The most senior political body in Rome, made up of the city's ex-magistrates. The Senate's function was to advise each year's magistrates. In the Republic it had a special concern for foreign policy.
stele A block of stone or wood set up for a monumental purpose in the ancient world, usually inscribed or carved.
Suovetaurilia The sacrifice of a pig (*sus*), sheep (*ovis*), and bull (*taurus*) to the god Mars. The word is an amalgam of the three animals sacrificed.

T

tablinum A room or alcove where family records were stored on tablets; it was situated between the atrium and the peristyle of a Roman house.
tepidarium A warm room in a Roman bathhouse.
Tetrarchy "Rule of Four," the name given to Diocletian's division of the empire into four units during the 3rd century CE, ruled by two senior *augusti* and two junior *caesares*.
thermae The large public baths used throughout the empire. There were also smaller bath buildings, called *balneae*.
toga The traditional civic dress of a male Roman citizen.
Tribune of the Plebs Rome's plebeians annually elected 10 tribunes whose role was to safeguard their interests.
triclinium A formal dining room in a Roman building, named for the three couches typically present.
Triumph A great procession in Rome to celebrate a significant military victory. The victorious general rode a chariot through Rome accompanied by his troops, plunder, and captives.

V

Vestal Virgins Six priestesses devoted to the goddess Vesta, who entered into service as children and were charged with keeping the eternal flame of Rome burning in the Temple of Vesta in the center of the Forum. After 30 years Vestals could leave, but during their service were required to remain chaste or risk being buried alive. The cult possibly dates to the 7th century BCE and lasted until 394 CE, when it was banned.

W

Western Roman Empire The western part of the Roman Empire, which split in the 3rd century CE. It fell in 476, but the Eastern Roman Empire survived for another 1,000 years, based in its capital city of Constantinople.

Index

Page numbers in **bold** refer to the main pages for the topic.

D

U

V

W

Y, Z

Acknowledgments

DK London would like to thank the following for their help with this book:
Professor Matthew Nicholls and Peter Bull Art studio for CGI artworks of The Roman Forum, Atrium Villa, The Palatine Hill and Circus Maximus, A Grand New City, The Colosseum, Baths of Caracalla, and Vindolanda Fort; Moataz Samir and Frosso Tsapanidou at University of Reading for their assistance with access to materials for the CGIs; Daksheeta Pattni for secondary artworks; Jo Walton, Roland Smithies, and Sarah Hopper for picture research assistance; Diana Loxley, Bonnie Macleod, Abigail Mitchell for editorial support; Helen Peters for the index; Diana Vowles for proofreading; Tom Morse for creative technical support; Simon Mumford for cartographic advice.

DK Delhi would like to thank the following:
Nandini D. Tripathy and Ankita Gupta for editorial assistance; Tanvi Sahu, Devika Awasthi, and Ragini Rawat for design assistance; Senior DTP designer Neeraj Bhatia; DTP designers Pawan Kumar and Ashok Kumar.

The publisher would like to thank the following for their kind permission to reproduce their photographs and artworks:
The following CGI artworks and line drawings were based on artworks originally created by Professor Matthew Nicholls: **64-67** The Roman Forum, **146-147** The Palatine Hill and Circus Maximus, **162-165** A Grand New City (Images from Virtual Rome by Prof Matthew Nicholls © 2021 University of Reading), **166** The Ulpian Library, **213** The Imperial Forums and **236-237** Baths of Caracalla.

(Key: a-above; b-below/bottom; c-centre; f-far; l-left; r-right; t-top)

1 © The Trustees of the British Museum. All rights reserved. **2 Dreamstime.com:** Scaliger. **4 Getty Images:** Marco Cantile. **5 The Art Institute of Chicago:** Katherine K. Adler Memorial Fund / Public Domain (cla). **The Cleveland Museum Of Art:** Gift of Mrs. Ernest Brummer 1986.185 / Open Acces (ca). **The Metropolitan Museum of Art:** (cra). **6 © KHM-Museumsverband:** (tc). **The Metropolitan Museum of Art:** (tr); Fletcher Fund, 1926 (tl). **7 Getty Images:** Marco Cantile. **8 The Metropolitan Museum of Art**. **9 Alamy Stock Photo:** Panther Media GmbH (br). **10 Science Photo Library:** Marco Ansaloni (br). **11 Alamy Stock Photo:** Artepics. **12-13 The Art Institute of Chicago:** Katherine K. Adler Memorial Fund / Public Domain. **14 Alamy Stock Photo:** IanDagnall Computing. **15 Getty Images:** DEA / G. Carfagna (c). **Shutterstock.com:** 190291154 (t); ste77 (b). **16 Getty Images:** Heritage Images (l); Leemage (b). **17 The Metropolitan Museum of Art:** (b). **Shutterstock.com:** Gianni Dagli Orti (t). **18-19 Getty Images:** DEA / G. Dagli Orti. **20 Getty Images:** DEA / G. Nimatallah. **21 © The Trustees of the British Museum. All rights reserved:** (tr). **The Metropolitan Museum of Art:** Rogers Fund, 1903 (b). **22 Bridgeman Images:** © Museumslandschaft Hessen Kassel / Ute Brunze (b). **© The Trustees of the British Museum. All rights reserved:** (tl). **Getty Images:** Photo Josse / Leemage (tr). **23 Bridgeman Images:** Luisa Ricciarini. **24 AF Fotografie:** (c, r). **Alamy Stock Photo:** Interfoto (l). **25 AF Fotografie:** (c, l, r). **26 The Metropolitan Museum of Art:** (t). **Photo Scala, Florence:** Courtesy of the Ministero Beni e Att. Culturali e del Turismo (b). **27 akg-images:** Pirozzi. **28-29 Alamy Stock Photo:** Wieslaw Jarek (t). **28 AWL Images:** ImageBROKER (bc). **© The Trustees of the British Museum. All rights reserved:** (clb). **29 Ancestry Images:** (br). **30-31 © The Trustees of the British Museum. All rights reserved:** (bc). **30 © The Trustees of the British Museum. All rights reserved:** (ca). **Getty Images:** Sepia Times (bc). **The Metropolitan Museum of Art:** (tr, cla, fbl). **31 © The Trustees of the British Museum. All rights reserved:** (bc, br). **The Metropolitan Museum of Art:** (tr, crb); Gift of Mr. and Mrs. Klaus G. Perls, 1997 (tl); Purchase, 1915 (cla); Rogers Fund, 1916 (bl). **32 akg-images:** Nimatallah. **33 Getty Images:** DEA / V. Pirozzi (l); Julian Elliott Photography (r). **34 © The Trustees of the British Museum. All rights reserved:** (bl). **The Metropolitan Museum of Art:** (c). **35 Photo Scala, Florence:** bpk, Bildagentur fuer Kunst, Kultur und Geschichte, Berlin (b). **University of Oxford:** Egypt Exploration Society (t). **36 © The Trustees of the British Museum. All rights reserved:** (ca). **Carole Raddato:** (bl). **37 Alamy Stock Photo:** Album. **38-39 The Cleveland Museum Of Art:** Gift of Mrs. Ernest Brummer 1986.185 / Open Acces. **41 Alamy Stock Photo:** Eddy Galeotti (r); **40 Getty Images:** P. Eoche (c). **The Metropolitan Museum of Art**; imageBROKER (l). **42 © The Trustees of the British Museum. All rights reserved:** (bc). **Getty Images:** DEA / G. Dagli Orti (t). **43 Alamy Stock Photo:** Adam Eastland (t); The Picture Art Collection (br). **44 Alamy Stock Photo:** Peter Eastland. **45 Alamy Stock Photo:** Ionut David (cr); Marek Stepan (br). **Los Angeles County Museum of Art:** (c). **46 Alamy Stock Photo:** The Print Collector (c); Visual Arts Resource (l). **Bridgeman Images:** Raffaello Bencini (r). **47 Alamy Stock Photo:** imageBROKER (l). **Bridgeman Images:** © Patrice Cartier. All rights reserved 2022 (c). **Getty Images:** DEA / G. Dagli Orti (r). **48 Alamy Stock Photo:** BYphoto (bl). **Bridgeman Images:** © Museum of Fine Arts, Boston (c). **The Metropolitan Museum of Art:** Gift of Christos G. Bastis, in honor of Philippe de Montebello, 1995 (br); Rogers Fund, 1906 (bc); Rogers Fund, 1919 (cr). **48-49 The Metropolitan Museum of Art:** (c). **49 akg-images:** Landesmuseum Württemberg / Peter Frankenstein und Hendrik Zwietasch (clb). **Alamy Stock Photo:** Fabrizio Troiani (crb). **Getty Images:** VCG Wilson / Corbis (tr). **The Metropolitan Museum of Art:** Gift of Mrs. Frederick F. Thompson, 1903 (ca); Gift of Henry G. Marquand, 1897 (br). **Photo Scala, Florence:** Image Copyright Museo Nacional del Prado © Photo MN (tl). **50 Getty Images:** Werner Forman / Universal Images (cr). **Musei Capitolini, Roma:** (b). **Wikipedia:** Jastrow (cla). **51 Shutterstock.com:** Gianni Dagli Orti. **52 Alamy Stock Photo:** Prisma Archivo (c). **Getty Images:** DEA Picture Library (l). **© Marie-Lan Nguyen/Wikimedia Commons:** (r). **53 Alamy Stock Photo:** adam eastland (c). **American Numismatic Society:** (tr). **Getty Images:** Crisfotolux (r); Martin Child (l). **54 Photo Scala, Florence:** Courtesy of the Ministero Beni e Att. Culturali e del Turismo. **55 Getty Images:** Print Collector (br). **The Metropolitan Museum of Art:** Purchase by subscription, 1896 (l). **Photo Scala, Florence:** Courtesy of the Ministero Beni e Att. Culturali e del Turismo (tr). **56 Getty Images:** DEA / A. Dagli Orti (t). **Photo Scala, Florence:** bpk, Bildagentur fuer Kunst, Kultur und Geschichte, Berli (bl). **57 Digital image courtesy of the Getty's Open Content Program:** The J. Paul Getty Museum, Villa Collection, Malibu, California, Gift of Barbara and Lawrence Fleischman, 96.AC.232 (b). **Getty Images:** Heritage Images (t). **58 © The Trustees of the British Museum. All rights reserved:** (l). **Getty Images:** DEA / G. Nimatallah (r). **59 Alamy Stock Photo:** Wiliam Perry (b). **Justus Liebig University Giessen:** (t). **60 Getty Images:** DEA / M. Carrieri (b). **Wellcome Images http://creativecommons.org/licenses/by/4.0/:** Science Museum, London (cl). **60-61 Photo Scala, Florence:** RMN-Grand Palais / Herve Lewandowski. **61 Getty Images:** Werner Forman (b). **62 Alamy Stock Photo:** Universal Art Archive (l). **Bridgeman Images:** Electa (r). **Getty Images:** (c). **63 Alamy Stock Photo:** Universal Art Archive (bc). **Bridgeman Images:** Museum of Fine Arts, Houston / museum purchase funded by the estate of Mary Alice Wilson and the Director's Accessions fund (br). **© The Trustees of the British Museum. All rights reserved:** (tr). **Photo Scala, Florence:** Christie's Images, London (bl). **65 Alamy Stock Photo:** Vito Arcomano (r); eye35.pix (l). **66 Alamy Stock Photo:** Vito Arcomano (cb); Chris Hooton (bl). **67 Alamy Stock Photo:** Adam Eastland (ca); Fabrizio Troiani (cra); Peter Horree (br). **68 Alamy Stock Photo:** Adam Eastland (br). **American Numismatic Society:** (cl). **69 Getty Images:** Ashmolean Museum / Heritage Images (l). **The Metropolitan Museum of Art:** Rogers Fund, 1903 (br). **70 akg-images:** MPortfolio / Electa (bl). **© The Trustees of the British Museum. All rights reserved:** (br). **Wellcome Images http://creativecommons.org/licenses/by/4.0/:** (ca). **71 Getty Images:** DeAgostini (c). **72-73 Getty Images:** font83. **74 akg-images:** Erich Lessing (ca). **Alamy Stock Photo:** Stefano Ravera (cla). **Getty Images:** Print Collector (b). **75 akg-images:** Eric Vandeville (cr). **Getty Images:** DEA / G. Nimatallah (l). **76 Alamy Stock Photo:** Erin Babnik (b). **© The Trustees of the British Museum. All rights reserved:** (t). **77 Getty Images:** DeAgostini (b). **The Metropolitan Museum of Art:** Gift of Darius O. Mills, 1906 (t). **78 Getty Images:** Giorgio Cosulich (b). **79 Alamy Stock Photo:** WHPics (b). **80 akg-images:** Interfoto / Hermann Historica Gmbh (bc). **Alamy Stock Photo. Bridgeman Images:** Musee du Bardo, Tunis, Tunisia (c). **The Metropolitan Museum of Art:** (tr, br). **Museo Nazionale Romano:** (cla). **81 akg-images:** Museum Kalkriese (ca). **Alamy Stock Photo:** Artokoloro (cb); dpa picture alliance (tc); Royal Armouries Museum (tr). **Bridgeman Images:** Israel Museum, Jerusalem / Gift of Professor W. Weinberg (bc). **Wikipedia:** Jebulon / Public Domain (br). **Yale University Art Gallery:** (l). **82 Alamy Stock Photo:** Peter Horree (b). **Bridgeman Images:** Christie's Images (t). **83 Alamy Stock Photo:** Peter Horree (b). **84 Bridgeman Images**. **85 Alamy Stock Photo:** agefotostock (cr); Panther Media GmbH (bl). **Bridgeman Images:** NPL - DeA Picture Library (t). **86 akg-images:** Erich Lessing. **87 MAK Center for Art and Architecture:** (ca). **rowanwindwhistler:** (br). **88 akg-images:** De Agostini Picture Lib. / W. Buss (bl). **Alamy Stock Photo:** Art Collection 2 (cr). **Photo Scala, Florence:** (cl). **89 Bridgeman Images:** NPL - DeA Picture Library. **90 Alamy Stock Photo:** Peter Eastland (bc). **The Metropolitan Museum of Art:** (cr).

91 Alamy Stock Photo: Zev Radovan (b). **Getty Images:** estivillml (t). **92 Shutterstock.com:** Francesco De Marco (ca). **93 Alamy Stock Photo:** Adam Eastland (t). **Shutterstock.com:** Tatsuo Nakamura (bc). **94 Alamy Stock Photo:** Abaca Press (br). **Amgueddfa Cymru – National Museum Wales:** (bl). **Shutterstock.com:** Gianni Dagli Orti (ca). **95 Getty Images:** DEA / L. Pedicini. **96 © The Trustees of the British Museum. All rights reserved:** (cl). **97 © KHM-Museumsverband:** (t). **Photo Scala, Florence:** Image Copyright Museo Nacional del Prado © Photo MNP (br). **98 Getty Images:** Jumping Rocks (b). **Photo Scala, Florence:** Luciano Romano (ca). **99 Getty Images:** Nando Pizzini Photography (t). **Photo Scala, Florence:** Luciano Romano (br). **100-101 The Metropolitan Museum of Art**. **102 Alamy Stock Photo:** Heritage Image Partnership Ltd (b). **103 Alamy Stock Photo:** Album (c); Tuul and Bruno Morandi (l); Hercules Milas (r). **104 Photo Scala, Florence:** RMN-Grand Palais / Herve Lewandowski (br). **105 Getty Images:** DEA / A. Dagli Orti (b); DeAgostini (t). **106 Photo Scala, Florence:** bpk, Bildagentur fuer Kunst, Kultur und Geschichte, Berlin (br). **107 Getty Images:** DEA Picture Library (r). **108 Alamy Stock Photo:** Erin Babnik. **109 Getty Images:** DeAgostini (b). **Photo Scala, Florence:** RMN-Grand Palais (t). **110 Emma Taricco:** (bl). **Winchester Museum Service:** (cra). **111 akg-images:** Hervé Champollion (br). **Getty Images:** PHAS (t). **112 Getty Images:** Photo Josse / Leemage (t). **Musée d'Aquitaine:** (bl). **113 Alamy Stock Photo:** Adam Eastland (br). **Lyon MBA:** Alain Basset (crb). **114 Alamy Stock Photo:** Greg Balfour Evans (tl). **The Metropolitan Museum of Art:** Rogers Fund, 1918 (tr). **Photo Scala, Florence:** Fotografica Foglia - courtesy of the Ministero Beni e Att. Culturali e del Turismo (b). **115 Getty Images:** DEA / A. Dagli Orti. **116 Alamy Stock Photo:** Album. **117 Alamy Stock Photo:** Domenico Tondini (br). **Gareth Harney:** (t). **118 Bridgeman Images:** Luisa Ricciarini. **119 American Numismatic Society:** (t). **Bridgeman Images:** Fine Art Images (b). **120-121 akg-images:** Album. **121 The Metropolitan Museum of Art:** Fletcher Fund, 1926 (t). **Wikipedia:** Jean-Pol Grandmont (br). **122 Bridgeman Images:** Ashmolean Museum (bl). **© The Trustees of the British Museum. All rights reserved:** (tl). **123 Bridgeman Images**. **124 Getty Images:** DEA / V. Pirozzi (br); Mondadori Portfolio (bl). **The Metropolitan Museum of Art:** Edith Perry Chapman Fund, 1952 (tr); Gift of J. Pierpont Morgan, 1917 (tl); Rogers Fund, 1912 (cb). **125 © The Trustees of the British Museum. All rights reserved:** (tr). **Ludwig Maximilians Universität:** (br). **The Metropolitan Museum of Art:** Bequest of Walter C. Baker, 1971 (c); Gift of J. Pierpont Morgan, 1917 (tl); Fletcher Fund, 1926 (tc); Rogers Fund, 1906 (cl); Purchase, Lila Acheson Wallace, Howard S. and Nancy Marks, Mr. and Mrs. Ronald S. Lauder, The Jaharis Family Foundation Inc., Philodoroi, Leon Levy Foundation, Renée E. and Robert A. Belfer, Mr. and Mrs. John A. Moran, Mr. and Mrs. Mark Fisch, Annette de la Renta, Beatrice Stern, Frederick J. Iseman, The Abner Rosen Foundation Inc., Mr. and Mrs. Richard L. Chilton Jr., Martha Stewart Living Omnimedia, Barbara G. Fleischman, in memory of Lawrence A. Fleischman, and Malcolm Hewitt Wiener Foundation Gifts; and The Bothmer Purchase and Diane Carol Brandt Funds, 2019 (cr); Gift of Philip Hofer, 1938 (bl). **126 Alamy Stock Photo:** Prisma Archivo. **127 Alamy Stock Photo:** Universal Art Archive (cra). **Getty Images:** Art Images (l). **128 © The Trustees of the British Museum. All rights reserved:** (ca). **128-129 Alamy Stock Photo:** REDA &CO srl (bc). **129 Getty Images:** Leemage. **130 The Art Institute of Chicago:** (fbl). **© The Trustees of the British Museum. All rights reserved:** (ftr, tr, fcla, ca, fcra, c, fcrb, fclb, fbr). **131 The Art Institute of Chicago:** (c, clb). **© The Trustees of the British Museum. All rights reserved:** (tl, tc, tr, ftr, ca, fcra, fbl, bc). **The Metropolitan Museum of Art:** (fbr). **132 © The Trustees of the British Museum. All rights reserved:** (bl). **Dreamstime.com:** Fotocvet (br). **History of Science Museum, University of Oxford:** (ca). **133 Alamy Stock Photo:** Lanmas. **134-135 James Glazier:** (bc). **134 Alamy Stock Photo:** Peter Horree (bc). **© The Trustees of the British Museum. All rights reserved:** (cla). **135 akg-images:** Hervé Champollion (tc). **136 Bridgeman Images:** Fitzwilliam Museum, University of Cambridge, UK (br). **Getty Images:** DeAgostini (t). **The Metropolitan Museum of Art:** Gift of J. Pierpont Morgan, 1917 (bl). **137 Alamy Stock Photo:** Giorgio Morara (t). **Science Photo Library:** Pasquale Sorrentino (b). **138 Alamy Stock Photo:** Michal Sikorski (bl). **© The Trustees of the British Museum. All rights reserved:** (ca). **139 Alamy Stock Photo:** Erin Babnik (l). **Jamie Mubler:** (tr). **140 Photo Scala, Florence:** DeAgostini Picture Library (t). **141 ALTAIR 4 MULTIMEDIA Srl**. **142 A.G.F. Agenzia Giornalistica Fotografica S.r.l**. **143 Alamy Stock Photo:** Heritage Image Partnership Ltd (br). **Bridgeman Images:** Photograph © 2022 Museum of Fine Arts, Boston. All rights reserved. / Henry Lillie Pierce Fun (c). **Getty Images:** DEA Picture Library (tr). **144 Alamy Stock Photo:** Vintage Archives (c). **Photo Scala, Florence:** Luciano Romano (bl). **145 Getty Images:** DEA / G. Roli. **146 Alamy Stock Photo:** Krisztian Juhasz (bl). **148 Getty Images:** DEA / A. De Gregorio (tr); DEA / A. Dagli Orti (bl). **Science & Society Picture Library:** Science Museum (br). **149 Getty Images:** Leemage. **150 Alamy Stock Photo:** Realy Easy Star. **151 Alamy Stock Photo:** Adam Eastland (br). **Getty Images:** DEA Picture Library (bl). **Photo Scala, Florence:** (tr). **152 © The Trustees of the British Museum. All rights reserved:** (l, br).

153 © The Trustees of the British Museum. All rights reserved: (t). **154 Germanisches Nationalmuseum,:** (br). **The Metropolitan Museum of Art:** Edward C. Moore Collection, Bequest of Edward C. Moore, 189 (ca). **155 Alamy Stock Photo:** Niday Picture Library (br). **Getty Images:** Rainer Herzog (t). **156-157 The Metropolitan Museum of Art:** Fletcher Fund, 1926. **158 The Metropolitan Museum of Art:** Gift of Henry G. Marquand, 1881. **159 Alamy Stock Photo:** Lukasz Janyst (l). **Shutterstock.com:** Nejdet Duzen (c). **160 Alamy Stock Photo:** Damir Vujnovac (t); Viliam.M (b). **161 Alamy Stock Photo:** David Keith Jones (t). **© The Trustees of the British Museum. All rights reserved:** (b). **162 © The Trustees of the British Museum. All rights reserved:** (cla). **Getty Images:** DEA Picture Library (bc); Maremagnum (tr). **166 Davide Monaco:** (bc). **Shutterstock.com:** Naaman Abreu (cra). **167 Biblioteca Apostolica Vaticana**. **168 Alamy Stock Photo:** agefotostock (bl). **© The Trustees of the British Museum. All rights reserved:** (cra). **169 Getty Images:** Geoff Caddick (b); Mondadori Portfolio (t). **171 Photo Scala, Florence:** RMN-Grand Palais / Herve Lewandowski (tc, bc). **172 Alamy Stock Photo:** Adam Eastland. **173 Alamy Stock Photo:** Vito Arcomano (br); Masterpics (cr). **The Metropolitan Museum of Art:** Gift of Joseph H. Durkee, 1899 (ca). **174 Bignor Roman Villa:** (t). **175 Alamy Stock Photo:** Heritage Image Partnership Ltd (ca). **© The Trustees of the British Museum. All rights reserved:** (tr). **© Museum of London:** Museum of London Archaeology (b). **176 Getty Images:** Anshar73 (b); fbxx (t). **177 Alamy Stock Photo:** Romas_ph. **178 Getty Images:** Heritage Images. **179 Alamy Stock Photo:** Interfoto (tl). **Courtesy of the RISD Museum, Providence, RI.:** (r). **180 Alamy Stock Photo:** CPA Media Pte Ltd. **181 Alamy Stock Photo:** Album. **182 Alamy Stock Photo:** Album (cla); Adam Eastland (bc). **Bridgeman Images:** Photograph © 2022 Museum of Fine Arts, Boston. All rights reserved. / Gift in memory of R. E. and Julia K. Hecht (ca). **183 Carole Raddato**. **184 Getty Images:** DEA / G. Dagli Orti. **185 Getty Images:** Pictures from History (br); Universal History Archive (tr). **© Marie-Lan Nguyen/Wikimedia Commons:** (ca). **186 Science Photo Library:** Marco Ansaloni (l). **187 Getty Images:** Luso (b). **188 123RF.com:** graceenee (t). **Getty Images:** Heritage Images (b). **189 Bridgeman Images:** Israel Museum, Jerusalem / Israel Antiquities Authority (br). **Getty Images:** svarshik (bl). **Shutterstock.com:** Mikhail Semenov (tr). **190 © The Trustees of the British Museum. All rights reserved:** (cla). **Shutterstock.com:** Balate Dorin (b). **191 © The Trustees of the British Museum. All rights reserved:** Archivi. Il Parco Archeologico di Pompei (tr). **Dreamstime.com:** Bographics (br). **Getty Images:** DEA / G. Dagli Orti (tl). **192 Alamy Stock Photo:** Adam Eastland (bl); Sites & Photos / Shmuel Magal (cra). **193 Getty Images:** DEA / G. Nimatallah. **194 Alamy Stock Photo:** The Picture Art Collection (cl). **Getty Images:** Michael Nicholson. **196 Alamy Stock Photo:** Adam Eastland (c). **197 Alamy Stock Photo:** EmmePi Images (r). **198 © The Trustees of the British Museum. All rights reserved:** (cla). **Rheinisches Landesmuseum Trier:** GDKE / Th. Zühme (bl). **198-199 Bridgeman Images:** Alinari (br). **199 © The Trustees of the British Museum. All rights reserved:** (tr). **200 Getty Images:** DEA / G. Nimatallah. **201 Alamy Stock Photo:** agefotostock (tr); Universal Art Archive (b). **Getty Images:** DEA / G. Dagli Orti (ca). **202 Alamy Stock Photo:** Sergey Borisov (t). **203 akg-images:** Peter Connolly (b). **AWL Images:** (t). **204 © The Trustees of the British Museum. All rights reserved:** (ca). **The Vindolanda Trust:** (cl). **205 Bridgeman Images:** Arbeia Roman Fort & Museum, Tyne & Wear Archives & Museums (bc). **Getty Images / iStock:** StockSolutions (t). **206 Alamy Stock Photo:** Prisma Archivo (bc). **Digital image courtesy of the Getty's Open Content Program:** (br). **Shutterstock.com:** Lev Levin (bl). **207 Alamy Stock Photo:** Julian Money-Kyrle (bl). **Getty Images:** DEA / A. Dagli Orti (br); Heritage Images (tr). **Courtesy Israel Antiquities Authority:** (bc). **208-209 Phoenix Ancient Art**. **210 AWL Images:** Jordan Banks (ca). **Photo Scala, Florence:** bpk, Bildagentur fuer Kunst, Kultur und Geschichte, Berlin (bl). **210-211 © The Trustees of the British Museum. All rights reserved:** (bc). **211 © The Trustees of the British Museum. All rights reserved:** (l). **The Metropolitan Museum of Art:** Gift of C. and E. Canessa, 191 (crb). **212 Alamy Stock Photo:** Nikreates (t). **Getty Images:** DEA Picture Library (b). **213 AWL Images:** Ian Trower. **214 Alamy Stock Photo:** Frank Bach (r). **Getty Images:** Independent Picture Service (l). **216 akg-images:** Eric Vandeville (b). **© The Trustees of the British Museum. All rights reserved:** (tl). **216-217 ALTAIR 4 MULTIMEDIA Srl:** (c). **Poly Haven:** Rob Tuytel (texture, texture2). **217 Getty Images / iStock:** LuckyTD (r). **Photo Scala, Florence:** (t). **218 Digital image courtesy of the Getty's Open Content Program:** The J. Paul Getty Museum, Villa Collection, Malibu, California, 83.AM.227.2 (crb). **The Metropolitan Museum of Art:** Gift of Helen Miller Gould, 1910 (cl/Earring); Rogers Fund, 1921 (cl/Necklace); The Cesnola Collection, Purchased by subscription, 1874–76 (bc); Gift of Mrs. Wallace Phillips, 1957 (br); Rogers Fund, 1922 (c); Purchase, 1896 (cra). **The Walters Art Museum, Baltimore:** Gift of Mr. Furman Hebb, 1990 (tr). **219 © The Trustees of the British Museum. All rights reserved:** (tr, clb, br). **Digital image courtesy of the Getty's Open Content Program:** The J. Paul Getty Museum, Villa Collection, Malibu, California, Gift of Barbara and Lawrence Fleischman, 96.AM.256 (tl);

The J. Paul Getty Museum, Villa Collection, Malibu, California, 83.AM.227.3 (ca). **The Metropolitan Museum of Art:** Fletcher Fund, 1925 (bc); Purchase, Deanna Anderson Gift and funds from various donors, 2002 (tc); Gift of Christos G. Bastis, in honor of Philippe de Montebello, 1995 (cl); The Cesnola Collection, Purchased by subscription, 1874–76 (bl). **220 Alamy Stock Photo:** imageBROKER (tr). **Getty Images:** DEA / A. Dagli Orti (l); DEA / G. Dagli Orti (b). **221 Getty Images:** Carlo A. **222 Alamy Stock Photo:** Adam Eastland Art + Architecture (br). **© The Trustees of the British Museum. All rights reserved:** (tl). **223 Alamy Stock Photo:** Peter Eastland (l); The Picture Art Collection (tr). **224-225 © KHM-Museumsverband**. **226 The Metropolitan Museum of Art:** Rogers Fund, 1918. **227 Alamy Stock Photo:** John Zada (r); Michael Wheatley (l); Kenio (c). **228 Alamy Stock Photo:** history_docu_photo (br); Universal Art Archive (ca). **Photo Scala, Florence:** bpk, Bildagentur fuer Kunst, Kultur und Geschichte, Berlin (bl). **229 Science Photo Library:** David Parker. **230 Carole Raddato**. **232 Alamy Stock Photo:** John Astor (br). **Getty Images:** Mondadori Portfolio (bc). **The Metropolitan Museum of Art:** Purchase, Joseph Pulitzer Bequest, 1955 (bl). **233 Alamy Stock Photo:** Vito Arcomano (bc); Universal Art Archive (tr); Dmitriy Moroz (br). **Digital image courtesy of the Getty's Open Content Program:** (bl). **234 Bridgeman Images:** Luisa Ricciarini (ca). **Getty Images:** DeAgostini (t). **235 © The Trustees of the British Museum. All rights reserved**. **236 Shutterstock.com:** Angelo Carconi / EPA-EFE (bl). **237 Alamy Stock Photo:** Adam Eastland (tl). **238 Photo Scala, Florence:** bpk, Bildagentur fuer Kunst, Kultur und Geschichte, Berlin (cla). **238-239 Photo Scala, Florence:** RMN-Grand Palais / Maurice et Pierre Chuzeville. **239 Alamy Stock Photo:** Ken Welsh (tr). **240 Alamy Stock Photo:** Jozef Sedmak (br); Universal Art Archive (bl); Shotshop GmbH (bc). **241 Dreamstime.com:** Bernhard Richter (bc). **Getty Images:** Helmut Meyer zur Capellen (br). **Wikipedia:** Wolfgang Sauber / CC BY-SA 3.0 (bl). **242 Alamy Stock Photo:** Hemis (cr). **Getty Images:** Bashar Shglila (l). **243 Alamy Stock Photo:** 360b (br); Arterra Picture Library (t). **244 Photo Scala, Florence:** RMN-Grand Palais / Herve Lewandowski. **245 Getty Images:** Richard Hutchings (t); Sepia Times (b). **246 Alamy Stock Photo:** Science History Images (bc). **© The Trustees of the British Museum. All rights reserved:** (cl). **247 Alamy Stock Photo. Getty Images:** DEA / G. Dagli Orti (t). **248 Getty Images:** DEA / G. Dagli Orti. **249 © The Trustees of the British Museum. All rights reserved:** (bl). **Dreamstime.com:** Giuseppe Di Paolo (tl). **250-251 The Metropolitan Museum of Art:** Rogers Fund, 1903. **252 Alamy Stock Photo:** Prisma Archivo (bl). **The Metropolitan Museum of Art:** Fletcher Fund, 1934 (ca). **253 Alamy Stock Photo:** Universal Art Archive (br); Ivan Vdovin (t). **254 Alamy Stock Photo:** Uber Bilder (cla). **© The Trustees of the British Museum. All rights reserved:** (cra). **255 Alamy Stock Photo:** Stefano Politi Markovina (bl). **© The Trustees of the British Museum. All rights reserved:** (br). **256-257 Alamy Stock Photo:** Norman Barrett (b). **256 Alamy Stock Photo:** Norman Barrett (tr). **257 Alamy Stock Photo:** Norman Barrett (t). **258 The Vindolanda Trust:** (bc). **258-259 Poly Haven:** Rob Tuytel (texture). **259 Alamy Stock Photo:** Jaime Pharr (tr). **260 Alamy Stock Photo:** agefotostock (bl). **© The Trustees of the British Museum. All rights reserved:** (ca). **261 Alamy Stock Photo:** CPA Media Pte Ltd. **262 Bridgeman Images:** Philadelphia Museum of Art, Pennsylvania, PA, USA / John G. Johnson Collection, 191 (t). **© The Trustees of the British Museum. All rights reserved:** (bl). **263 akg-images:** Gilles Mermet (tr). **Alamy Stock Photo:** Vito Arcoman (cb); The Picture Art Collection (br). **264 Alamy Stock Photo:** shapencolour (bl). **© The Trustees of the British Museum. All rights reserved:** (tr). **264-265 AWL Images:** (b). **266 Digital image courtesy of the Getty's Open Content Program:** (ca, bc). **The Metropolitan Museum of Art:** Fletcher Fund, 1959 (cl); Fletcher Fund, 1926 (bl); Theodore M. Davis Collection, Bequest of Theodore M. Davis, 191 (br). **The Walters Art Museum, Baltimore:** (cra). **267 Bridgeman Images:** AISA (cr). **© The Trustees of the British Museum. All rights reserved:** (l). **Digital image courtesy of the Getty's Open Content Program:** (ftr, tr). **Getty Images:** DEA Picture Library (c). **The Metropolitan Museum of Art:** Gift of Renée E. and Robert A. Belfer, 2012 (cb); Gift of Henry G. Marquand, 1881 (bc). **268 Alamy Stock Photo:** Norman Barrett (ca); Universal Art Archive (bl); Granger - Historical Picture Archive (br). **269 Alamy Stock Photo:** Universal Art Archive. **270 © The Trustees of the British Museum. All rights reserved:** (ca). **270-271 © The Trustees of the British Museum. All rights reserved:** (bc). **271 © The Trustees of the British Museum. All rights reserved:** (br). **272 Alamy Stock Photo:** Science History Images (bl). **The Metropolitan Museum of Art:** Rogers Fund, 1911 (cra). **273 Getty Images:** DEA / A. De Gregorio (bl). **Photo Scala, Florence:** RMN-Grand Palais / Thierry Ollivier (r). **274-275 The Metropolitan Museum of Art**. **276 Getty Images:** DEA Picture Library. **277 Alamy Stock Photo:** F1online digitale Bildagentur GmbH (c). **Getty Images:** ermess (l). **278 AWL Images:** Michele Falzone (t). **279 Getty Images:** Emad Aljumah (t); Salvator Barki (bl). **The Metropolitan Museum of Art:** (br). **280 The Metropolitan Museum of Art:** Rogers Fund, 1988 (cla). **281 akg-images:** Mainz, Römisch-German. Zentralmuseum. **282 Getty Images:** Universal Images Group (b). **Musée des Beaux-Arts et d'Archéologie de Troyes:** Carole Bell, Ville de Troye (ca). **283 Alamy Stock Photo:** Lanmas (br). **The Walters Art Museum, Baltimore:** (l). **284 Alamy Stock Photo:** WHPics (cl). **Bibliothèque nationale de France, Paris:** (bl, br). **© The Trustees of the British Museum. All rights reserved:** (tr, fcl, clb). **285 Bibliothèque nationale de France, Paris:** (ftr, fcla, cla). **© The Trustees of the British Museum. All rights reserved:** (cb, br). **Magyar Nemzeti Muzeum:** (tr). **The Metropolitan Museum of Art:** (cr); Gift of Malcolm Wiener, on the occasion of the reinstallation of the Greek and Roman galleries, 200 (bl). **286 Alamy Stock Photo:** Adam Eastland Art + Architecture (bl). **Getty Images:** Fine Art Images / Heritage Images (bc); Heritage Images (br). **287 Getty Images:** Art Images (br); DEA / G. Dagli Orti (bc). **Photo Scala, Florence:** (bl). **288-289 AWL Images:** Catherina Unger. **290 Museum of Fine Arts - Hungarian National Gallery**. **291 Alamy Stock Photo:** Interfoto (tr). **© The Trustees of the British Museum. All rights reserved**. **Photo Scala, Florence:** (ca, br). **292 Alamy Stock Photo:** Keith Corrigan (bl). **Getty Images:** Ashmolean Museum / Heritage Images (br). **293 Alamy Stock Photo:** Askanioff (tl). **© The Trustees of the British Museum. All rights reserved:** (br). **294 Alamy Stock Photo:** The Picture Art Collection (bc). **AWL Images:** Hemis (cra). **Getty Images:** DEA / A. Dagli Orti (l). **295 Alamy Stock Photo:** Austrian National Library / Interfoto. **296 Getty Images:** DeAgostini. **297 © The Trustees of the British Museum. All rights reserved:** (ca). **Photo Scala, Florence:** Courtesy of the Ministero Beni e Att. Culturali e del Turismo (bl). **298 Alamy Stock Photo:** Adam Eastland (r). **Dreamstime.com:** David Sanchez Paniagua Carvajal (l). **299 Alamy Stock Photo:** Classic Image (b). **AWL Images:** (t). **300 Alamy Stock Photo:** Pavel Dudek (ca). **Photo Scala, Florence:** A. Dagli Orti (bl). **301 © The Trustees of the British Museum. All rights reserved:** (br). **Getty Images:** The New York Historical Society (tc). **302 Alamy Stock Photo:** Imagebroker (cla). **The Metropolitan Museum of Art:** Gift of J. Pierpont Morgan, 1917 (bl). **302-303 Magyar Nemzeti Muzeum:** (bc). **303 Alamy Stock Photo:** Science History Images (br). **306-307 Courtesy of the RISD Museum, Providence, RI.**. **308 Alamy Stock Photo:** Lanmas. **309 Getty Images:** Stuart Paton. **310 Getty Images:** Sepia Times. **311 Getty Images:** DEA PICTURE LIBRARY. **312 Alamy Stock Photo:** Jonathan ORourke. **313 Photo Scala, Florence**. **314 Alamy Stock Photo:** Artmedia. **315 Photo Scala, Florence:** Courtesy of Musei Civici Fiorentini. **316 Photo Scala, Florence**. **317 Getty Images:** Heritage Images. **318 Getty Images:** Fine Art Images / Heritage Images. **319 The Metropolitan Museum of Art:** Bequest of Benjamin Altman, 1913. **320 Alamy Stock Photo:** FOST. **321 Alamy Stock Photo:** Peter Horree. **322 Dreamstime.com:** Ruslan Gilmanshin (br). **Musées de Sens:** (tl). **323 Shutterstock.com:** wiesdie. **324 Alamy Stock Photo:** pytyczech. **325 Getty Images:** DEA / G. DAGLI ORTI. **326 Getty Images:** Fine Art Images / Heritage Images. **327 Getty Images:** Josse / Leemage. **328 Getty Images:** Sepia Times. **329 Getty Images:** Fine Art Images / Heritage Images. **330 The Metropolitan Museum of Art**. **331 Digital image courtesy of the Getty's Open Content Program**. **332 Alamy Stock Photo:** Peter Horree. **333 Getty Images:** DeAgostini (b, t). **334 Bridgeman Images:** Andrea Jemolo. **335 Getty Images:** Godong. **336 Getty Images:** CM Dixon / Print Collector. **337 Alamy Stock Photo:** Roy Conchie. **338 Getty Images:** Pictures from History. **339 Getty Images:** Hoberman Collection / Universal Images Group (bl); Leemage / Corbis (br). **340 Alamy Stock Photo:** Chris Hellier. **341 Alamy Stock Photo:** Artefact. **342 Alamy Stock Photo:** Ancient Art and Architecture. **343 Alamy Stock Photo:** Peter Horree. **344 Dreamstime.com:** Anthony Baggett. **345 Getty Images:** DeAgostini. **346 Getty Images:** Leemage. **347 Alamy Stock Photo:** Adam Eastland. **Bridgeman Images:** Prismatic Pictures (tl). **348 Alamy Stock Photo:** Chronicle (b). **© Marie-Lan Nguyen/Wikimedia Commons:** (tr). **349 The Metropolitan Museum of Art:** Gift of George Blumenthal, 1941. **350 akg-images:** Eric Vandeville. **351 Shutterstock.com:** Sahara Prince. **352 akg-images:** Rabatti & Domingie. **353 Getty Images:** Heritage Images. **354 Alamy Stock Photo:** Hercules Milas. **356 Getty Images:** Joe Daniel Price. **357 Alamy Stock Photo:** Bailey-Cooper Photography.
358 Dreamstime.com: Antonios Karvelas. **359 Shutterstock.com:** Bill Perry. **361 Dreamstime.com:** Leonardoboss. **362 Alamy Stock Photo:** EyeEm. **363 Getty Images:** Robert Mulder. **364 Shutterstock.com:** Dave Head. **365 Alamy Stock Photo:** Anthony Brown. **366 Alamy Stock Photo:** Stuart Forster. **367 Alamy Stock Photo:** Frank Bach. **368 Getty Images:** Ratnakorn Piyasirisorost. **369 Alamy Stock Photo:** agefotostock. **370 Alamy Stock Photo:** Michel & Gabrielle Therin-Weise. **371 Alamy Stock Photo:** RossHelen editorial. **372 Alamy Stock Photo:** Sergi Reboredo. **373 Getty Images:** Miroslav Petrasko. **374 Alamy Stock Photo:** Vítor Ribeiro. **375 Dreamstime.com:** Alexander Khripunov. **376 Alamy Stock Photo:** Michele Falzone. **377 Dreamstime.com:** Luckyphotographer. **378-379 Getty Images:** Alison Wright (b). **379 Alamy Stock Photo:** Leonid Andronov (tr). **380 Alamy Stock Photo:** Hemis. **381 Dreamstime.com:** Gualtiero Boffi (tr); Ledokol (bc). **382 Alamy Stock Photo:** Allen Brown. **383 Alamy Stock Photo:** Prisma by Dukas Presseagentur GmbH. **384 Alamy Stock Photo:** Sklifas Steven. **385 Getty Images:** Moment / Bashar Shglil

All other images © Dorling Kindersley
For further information see www.dkimages.com